Merry Merry
Christmas
Debbie

from Theresa
Dec 25/81

CHATELAINE'S
ADVENTURES IN COOKING

CHATELAINE'S

ADVENTURES IN COOKING

By the Editors of Chatelaine

Drawings by Preston Fetty

MACLEAN-HUNTER, LTD.

Toronto

Library of Congress Catalog Card No. 73-81765
13-128157-7
1 2 3 4 5 73 72 71 70 69
PRINTED IN CANADA

❦ INTRODUCTION ❦

We at *Chatelaine* feel this is a new kind of cookbook—and a very necessary one. It truly is all things to all cooks—the new bride who is wondering how to plan a meal and cook a hamburger and the experienced cook who would like to experiment with classic dishes of the world's exotic cuisines.

It is many cookbooks under one cover—and a lifetime cooking course as well. Each recipe explains not just *what* to do but *why,* as well as how to use the same techniques in other dishes. Make the Creamed Chicken in Patty Shells in *Chapter One,* for instance, and, as the note explains, you have mastered a simple white sauce. Other ways of making white sauce are discussed too. And you not only have a delicious dish, you are a wiser cook than when you began.

To get full value from this book we suggest browsing through it on occasion instead of just pulling it off the shelf to find a certain recipe. There's a world of helps that most cookbooks never mention. For instance, almost every chapter includes a host of menus built around the dishes in that chapter, with the dishes for which specific preparation instructions are included in the book set off in *italics*—a wonderful boost for days when you just can't dream up something different to entice family or guests.

How to describe all the wonders of *Adventures in Cooking?* The best way is to give a peep into each chapter.

Chapter One, The Art of Good Cooking, is an excellent introduction—a treasure trove of good advice on how to plan meals nutritionally, how to shop ahead, how long various foods keep, how to divide a recipe or substitute ingredients, how to watch calories—even how to pack a lunchbox. Be sure to notice the menus—two solid weeks each of family meals with year-round and hot-weather menus.

Chapter Two, Hearty Main Dishes, includes all the meat, fish, poultry and casserole entrees you'll ever need, plus tips on how to plan a meal for appetite appeal, how to carve, buy and cook meat and which herbs, seasonings and garnishes are soulmates with which main dishes. There's even a section of main dishes and menus *just for two.*

Fruits and Vegetables are the subject of *Chapter Three,* but you'll also find advice on herbs, dessert sauces, pickling, home freezing, home canning and lots of menus. *Chapter Four, Creative Baking,* will turn any bride into a prize-winning baker. Festive breads from around the world, cake decorating, pastries plain and fancy, even what to do if you don't have the right cake pan—it's all here.

Chapter Five, An Introduction to Gourmet Cookery, is a special bonus—a tour of the world's cuisines. What could be timelier in these days when everyone is travelling abroad? Don't worry if you don't know a Bordeaux from a Brie. After reading the sections on great wines and cheeses of the world and how to serve them, you will never be guilty of a *faux pas.* The special equipment used for gourmet cookery is explained. There is a complete guide to seasoning with herbs, spices and seeds. Best of all are the recipes and explanations of French gourmet cooking, exotic dishes from Spain, lively Italian cuisine, famous dishes from Central Europe, translations from the Scandinavian, dishes from the land of pilaff and kebab, curries of India, foods from the Far Pacific, Oriental meals, Mexico's spicy theme, regional cooking in the United States, Canada's rich bounty of varied traditions and, of course, international gourmet menus.

We are especially proud of the last two chapters, geared for today's young, adventurous, active housewives. *Chapter Six* is called *Parties Large and Small.* It's not just party recipes, but hints on everything from the guest list to decorations. There are menus and preparation plans for dozens of parties: informal or formal, buffets, barbecues, teas, cocktail parties, dessert-and-coffee parties, teen-age parties, holiday entertaining and lots more.

Chapter Seven, The Bridal Corner, is just for the bride. At *Chatelaine* the new bride is a Very Important Person, so we've included this section to take her through the first days of entertaining, meals for unexpected guests, and all the special parties that cluster around a wedding, from announcement parties to showers to the Golden Anniversary.

Don't overlook the *Appendix* at the back that will help you plan a convenient kitchen—choose the right cooking utensils and get the best results from your major equipment. Here you will also find the glossary of cooking terms.

All this is addition to countless recipes, 32 beautiful color pages and hundreds of black-and-white illustrations!

Now you know why we call this the cookbook that has everything for everyone. Browse through it, try the recipes—you'll find it a lifetime adventure in good cooking and good eating.

The Editors of Chatelaine

❦ CONTENTS ❦

Introduction v

CHATELAINE'S
ADVENTURES IN COOKING

CHAPTER ONE 🌸

The Art of Good Cooking

🌸

Before you embark on the road to good cooking take a few minutes now to understand why meals will be healthier and taste and look better if your menus include nutritious foods, prepared perfectly and served attractively.

THE BASIC FOODS

Every successful pattern of 3 meals a day should begin with an understanding of the 5 essential food groups. If your daily meals include foods recommended in "Canada's Food Guide," you can be sure that your family is receiving all the nutrients necessary for a complete and well-balanced diet.

CANADA'S FOOD GUIDE

These foods are good to eat. Eat them every day for health. Have three meals a day.

Milk: Children (up to about 11 years), 2 1/2 cups; adolescents, 4 cups; adults, 1 1/2 cups; expectant and nursing mothers, 4 cups.

Fruit: Two servings of fruit or juice, including a source of vitamin C (ascorbic acid) such as oranges, tomatoes, vitaminized apple juice.

Vegetables: One serving of potatoes; two servings of other vegetables, preferably yellow or green and often raw.

Bread and Cereals: Bread (with butter or fortified margarine), one serving of whole-grain cereal.

Meat and Fish: One serving of meat, fish or poultry, liver occasionally. Eggs, cheese, dried beans or peas may be used in place of meat. In addition, eggs and cheese each at least three times a week.

Vitamin D: 400 International Units for all growing persons and expectant and nursing mothers.

Approved by the Canadian Council on Nutrition, 1961.

1. Milk

Milk is our best source of calcium and is necessary for strong bones and teeth. It also supplies proteins for body building and repair. The daily milk quota may be fulfilled in many ways—as a beverage, in soups, sauces, puddings, custard and ice cream, or on cereals and puddings.

2. Fruits

These provide essential vitamins and minerals. Citrus fruits and vitaminized juices are the best sources followed by other fresh fruits such as berries, melons, apricots, peaches, bananas, apples, pears and the canned and dried varieties. Fruits on the menu may be in fruit cups, salads and desserts.

3. Vegetables

Potatoes are a good source of vitamins A and C. Serve them baked, often, to protect their vitamin C content. Include potatoes on the dinner menu or in soups, salads, stews and casseroles. Dark green and deep yellow vegetables such as cabbage, broccoli, spinach, carrots, squash and turnip are good sources of vitamin A. Plan on serving a green salad such as cabbage and carrot often. When cooking vegetables, cook quickly in a minimum of water.

4. Breads and Cereals

Include 4 or more servings wholegrain or enriched breads and cereals. Cereals provide protein, iron, B vitamins and energy. The quality of vegetable protein in cereals is improved by serving them with animal protein as in milk. This group includes wholegrain or enriched breads, cooked and ready-to-eat cereals, crackers, cornmeal, spaghetti and macaroni, noodles, rice, quick breads and other baked goods made with wholegrain or enriched flour.

In addition to being served plain, toasted and in sandwiches, bread may be introduced in stuffings, meat loaves, toppings for casseroles, puddings and fine crumbs for frying or baking.

Cereals may be in hot cooked or ready-to-eat form for breakfast or the major ingredient in griddle cakes, waffles, hot breads and muffins.

5. Meat, Fish, Poultry, Eggs and Cheese

One serving of meat, fish or poultry should be 4 ounces raw, boneless or 3 ounces when cooked. Serve some other protein food that same day: an egg, cheese, peanut butter, cooked beans or peas. Protein foods may be prepared in salads, casseroles or sandwiches. Variety meats such as liver, heart, kidney and sweetbreads are especially high in vitamin B and iron and should be served occasionally.

Additional Foods

Include fats and sugars, plus more servings from each of the first 5 food groups to meet energy needs and round out meals.

PLANNING AHEAD

It's easy to plan meals for your family a week in advance by making a chart—with days across the top as in a calendar. You can list 3 menus under each day. You may wish to start with Sunday's meals, but, if you do your marketing on Thursday or Friday, it may be better to start with the day following the shopping routine. You can avoid monotony in your meal pattern by serving different foods on the same days of the week. Plan your meals so that the family does not know in advance it will be "Sunday—roast beef, Monday—stew."

Plan your menus so that leftovers may be prepared and served in attractive ways when they reappear at the table—preferably 1 or 2 days later, rather than at the very next meal.

When you have planned your menus for the week, check each day, keeping an eye on "Canada's Food Guide." Have you included foods from each group? You may need to make some changes in your original plan to be sure that you are following the guide. If your budget must be kept to a minimum, savings can be made by selecting the least expensive foods in each category.

Stocking Your Kitchen

Buy perishable foods only for your immediate use, and restock as needed. Many other supplies, however, keep well for weeks, months—even years, in the case of canned goods—and there is no risk of overstocking if you have plenty of kitchen space.

Your Shopping Plan: Prepare in Advance

Make out your list before you leave home. Check the forthcoming week's menu needs, supplies on hand, the state of your budget and your family's preferences ahead of time.

An Organized Expedition. If you have the time, it is to your advantage to shop in person rather than by telephone. Telephone ordering and delivery service usually cost more, and you cannot select foods personally and choose the best buys. You can save time by shopping at an hour when the stores are least busy.

If you shop in a supermarket it would be useful to organize your list according to groups of foods: all the refrigerated foods like milk, cream, cheese, butter and margarine together; meats, poultry and fish together, frozen foods together, and so on down the list. After you have come to know your supermarket, try to keep these groups in the order in which foods are displayed in the store, which will save tiresome backtracking, so that 1 trip through each aisle will be sufficient.

If you have outlined your menu plan, ensuring that it is nutritionally right by checking it with "Canada's Food Guide," you can readily make a list for your marketing. A planned shopping list prevents overlooking needed supplies and eliminates unnecessary items. A good shopping plan includes special and seasonal buys as announced in newspaper advertisements or on radio and television. Besides your list of needs for each meal, be sure to include staples. It is a good idea to keep a checklist handy in the kitchen and to jot down items as they are used up. Remember to check your refrigerator supplies too, so that items can be added to your list as necessary.

STORAGE UP TO 1 YEAR

Canned fruits, vegetables, juices, meats, fish, milk
Freeze-dried foods
Packaged desserts, gelatine
Macaroni, spaghetti, noodles
Rice, tapioca, barley
Dried peas, beans
Sugars, syrups
Flour, cornstarch
Hard cheeses

STORAGE UP TO 6 MONTHS

Frozen fruits, vegetables, juices, roasts, poultry (at 0° F.)
Shortening, salad oil (in refrigerator)

Packaged cereals
Crackers
Nuts (in refrigerator or freezer)
Dried fruits (in covered container)
Spices, condiments
Baking powder, soda

STORAGE UP TO 3 MONTHS

Butter, margarine (in refrigerator)

STORAGE UP TO 1 MONTH

Ice cream
Cookies
Potatoes, onions, carrots

STORAGE UP TO 1 WEEK

Fresh milk, cream
Cottage cheese
Eggs
Breads, cakes

USE AS SOON AS POSSIBLE

Ground meat, fresh poultry, fish, chops, variety meats
Fresh fruits, vegetables

Whether you wish to shop only once a week or at more frequent intervals is a point to be taken into account when planning your list. Your food budget and your family's preferences will also affect your shopping. Remember also that it is unwise to buy more food than you can store properly. Try not to overstock perishables. Cross items off your list as they go into your basket, in order to avoid overlooking any item.

How Much To Buy. Your shopping list of course should indicate the required amounts of each item, according to the number and ages of family members. Following is a guide to show you how much raw or packaged foodstuff in various categories is generally found adequate for 1 serving per person. Allow 1/3 less per serving for young children or elderly people. For special recipes be guided by amounts called for.

AMOUNT TO BUY PER SERVING

Steaks, 3/4 pound
Meat with fat and bone, 1/2 pound
Lean meat with some bone, 1/3 pound
Broiling or frying chicken, 1/2–3/4 pound
Roasting chicken and turkey, 1/2–1 pound
Geese and ducks, 1 pound
Whole fish, 1/2 pound
Fish fillets, 1/3 pound
Shrimp, 1/3–1/2 pound (6–8)
Whole lobster, 1–1 1/4 pounds
Oysters (shucked), 1/3 pint
Cooked and canned meat and fish, 2–3 ounces

Shopping for Value

If you plan your shopping, you can save money and time and make your meals more interesting and better balanced. Haphazard shopping is expensive so check the food supplies you have on hand, and then plan your shopping list to cover next week's meals, taking advantage of the specials.

Compare prices at your local stores, and shop where you get the best value for your money. Try not to buy unnecessary items. For family meals "convenience foods" can save time but often cost more.

Read labels on containers, and compare costs per edible portion before you buy. This comparison should be made both between brands and between package sizes of the same brand. Sometimes large sizes are less economical than are medium sizes. Premiums you do not need can upset your food budget.

Ways To Save. Choose the grade or quality of canned goods that best suits your purpose. Fancy whole tomatoes are not necessary for a mixed dish. Less expensive "choice" will do just as well.

Skim milk or skim-milk powder is as rich in minerals as is whole milk and much less expensive for both cooking and drinking. Whole milk is cheaper in 1/2 gallons and costs even less if bought at the store rather than delivered to your door. Ice cream costs less when you buy it in large quantities if you have freezer storage facilities and if you know it will be eaten before it develops an off-flavor associated with prolonged storage. The best money values in cheese are Cheddar and cottage varieties, and process cheeses are a great convenience.

How Much Waste? Compare prices of fresh, frozen and canned vegetables; buy the best value available. Potatoes are an inexpensive mainstay; good menu planning makes use of them often, along with a dark-green or deep-yellow vegetable at least every other day. Use the coarse outer leaves of green vegetables to flavor salads. Some fresh vegetables, such as peas in the pod, have a good deal of waste, but there is no waste when you buy the canned or frozen packs. Use liquids from canned or cooked vegetables for soup, sauces, gravy. The good cook will find interesting uses for many of these by-products. Juice from canned beets, for example, can be used in making Harvard sauce or soup.

Buying Fruits

Economical frozen or canned fruit juices are a year-round source of vitamin C. When you buy fresh oranges or grapefruit for eating, shop for the thin-skinned heavy ones, which give you more for your money. Of course, some varieties naturally have thicker skins than do others. Other kinds of fruit should be eaten regularly—buy them when they are in season. Fresh apples and bananas are inexpensive during most of the year. Supplement them with frozen, canned and dried fruits.

Study Egg Sizes

The size of eggs is only important from the standpoint of quantity, not quality. The 4 common divisions are based on the weight of a dozen uniform-size eggs: extra large, 27 ounces or more; large, 24–27 ounces; medium, 21–24 ounces; small, 18–21 ounces. For your best egg buys, choose medium when they cost 1/8 less than large, or small when they cost 1/4 less than large. The color of the shell—white, brown or speckled—has no bearing on the quality, nor does it mean a stronger or milder flavor. It merely indicates the breed of hen.

Meats, Fish and Poultry

Buy only required amounts of meats, fish or poultry. Estimate amounts of edible meat in various cuts to make sure you are getting the best value. For economy, buy meats that are lower in price and those featured as weekend specials. Steaks, chops and oven roasts add up to an expensive meal pattern. Meats for stewing and braising cost less, yet they are just as nutritious as the expensive cuts, and with proper cooking they lack nothing in appetite appeal. Large chickens and turkeys are more economical than are small ones, and what is left from 1 meal can be used up later.

Inexpensive chicken wings and backs from cut-up poultry displays make flavorful casseroles and soups. Fish is as nourishing as is red meat and has the additional value of vitamin A. Dark-fleshed fish also gives vitamin D. Serve fish at least once a week for both economy and menu variety.

Meatless Main-dish Foods

Eggs and cheese are inexpensive sources of high-quality protein, and dried beans and peas, nuts and peanut butter can be used occasionally for economical protein. Home-style baked beans and

split-pea soup are steady favorites. Peanuts and peanut butter offer both food and money value and are almost essential in a household with children.

Breads and Cereals

Serve products of the grain family at every meal. There is a wide variety of breads, crackers and baked goods to choose from. Cereals you cook are less expensive than the ready-to-eat kind. Use noodles, macaroni, rice, rolled oats to stretch leftover meats in interesting dishes. Breads, too, have versatility in stuffings and toppings.

Save on Beverages

If you wish, have coffee beans ground at the store, or use instant coffee. Both types are less expensive than is the ground coffee in the can, and there is no waste with the instant type. For family use loose tea is less expensive than are tea bags and instant tea. When shopping assess the advantages of large sizes versus those of small sizes for your particular household.

Fats and Flavorings

Fats provide calories and some vitamin A. Butter and margarine are comparable in food value; both have vitamin A, but margarine is less expensive. Shortening, oils, lard and salt pork help to make meals enjoyable. Save meat drippings for cooking.

Condiments, flavorings, herbs and spices add appetite appeal. It is best to buy spices in small quantities because they lose strength after they are opened.

WHAT TO LOOK FOR

Your family enjoys better meals, and your food dollar goes further when you do your shopping with a keen eye for food-grading marks that guide you to quality with economy.

There are many considerations in selecting the food for your family's meals, and of course you want to be assured that your selections are right —that you have chosen wholesome foods of good

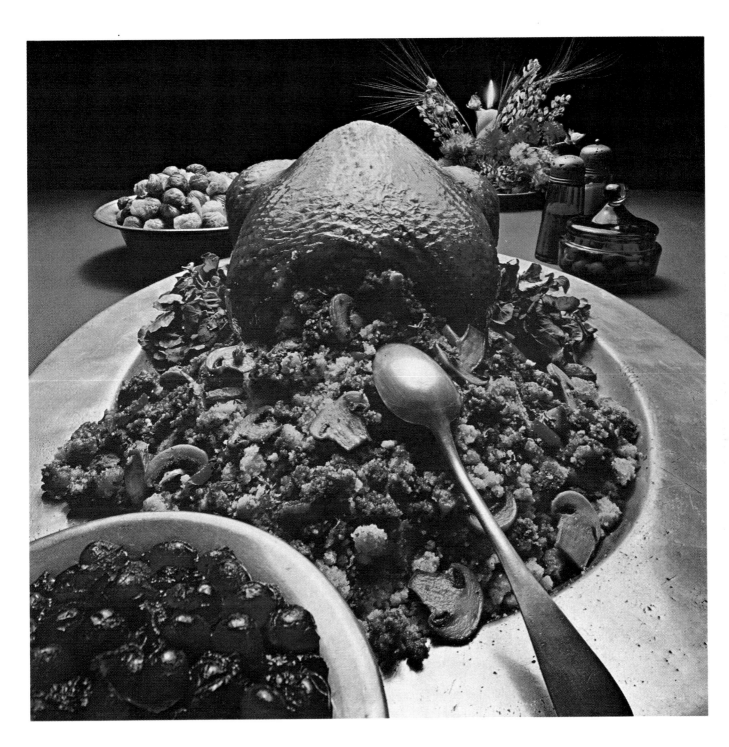

Roast Turkey (pp. 68-69) with Mushroom Stuffing (pp. 307-308).
CREDIT: *Bernard Gray.*

Tomato juice, but with a difference—buttered, spiced and served hot (p. 19).
CREDIT: *Bernard Gray.*

Cheese Bread (p. 167).
CREDIT: *Bernard Gray.*

Crème Caramel (pp. 211-212).
CREDIT: *Richard Litwin.*

Fruit and cheese tray.
CREDIT: *Bernard Gray.*

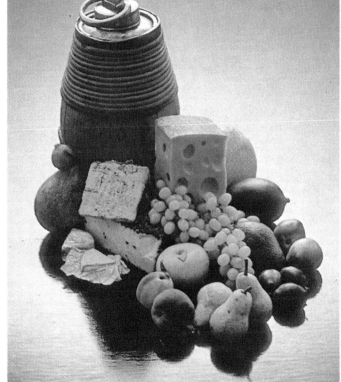

6-Layer Mocha Cake (p. 319).
CREDIT: *Bernard Gray.*

Crêpes Gismonda (p. 161).
CREDIT: *Bernard Gray*.

quality and have obtained good value for your money. With some foods there are very definite points to look for when you shop.

Buying Meat

At the moment, beef is the only meat in Canada regularly government-graded and stamped to ensure proper quality levels. A ribbon-like mark down the length of a side of beef indicates in color:

* A—choice (red-brand beef), denoting finest quality, with maximum proportion of meat to bone, best fat marbling and cover.

* B—good (blue-brand beef), also of fine quality, but with somewhat less lean meat to bone and a little less fat.

* C—commercial, a brown ribbon indicating a standard type of beef not eligible for the former grades.

* D—known in the meat-packing business as utility, and used mostly by manufacturers of processed products.

Select beef according to grade, keeping in mind money invested and results desired. Rump roasts, for example, from red- or blue-brand beef respond excellently to dry oven heat, but the same cut from brown-brand will require pot roasting.

As trimming may remove the colored ribbon stamp, you should learn to recognize good meat of each type when you see it. Here are the signs for beef:

* Lean—uniform, bright-red color; firm and smooth but moist; high proportion of meat to bone; good marbling, which means small flecks of fat are well distributed throughout the lean.

* Fat—moderately thick outer covering of firm, creamy-white, flaky fat.

* Bone—cut surfaces of bones that are porous and reddish-pink.

Good young pork should be grayish-pink in color; pork from older animals is a delicate rose color.

Good lamb is pinkish-red; mutton, coming from an older animal, is a deeper red.

Good veal is pale pink, almost gray, in color. Veal is never marbled with fat because the animal is very young when slaughtered.

Always choose the right cut for the right dish. The quick-cooking cuts—steaks and chops—are most expensive, but they are no more nutritious than are the less expensive cuts. The latter take a little more time and skill to prepare. They are excellent for casseroles, stews, pot roasts and braised dishes.

Poultry

Look for the government grade mark on fowl, chickens, turkeys, geese and ducks. This mark is either printed on the bag or appears on a tag attached to the breast of the bird.

* Grade A—well-fattened and well-fleshed birds, normally shaped.

* Grade B—not so well fattened or well fleshed as Grade A; slightly crooked bones that do not affect the meat arrangement permitted; slight tears and pinfeathers that do not detract from the appearance of the bird also allowed.

You should also buy the poultry that is best suited for your purposes. Capons are large, de-sexed male birds, raised for their tender flesh and flavor. A capon has a high proportion of white meat and is splendid for roasting. Broiler-fryers may be prepared with any dry-heat method. Roasting chickens are perfect for stuffing and baking. For a meaty bird, choose one with a wide body, a broad full-fleshed breast, and thick, short legs. A long, thin, poorly fleshed bird offers more bone and less meat. Stewing fowl should be stewed or braised.

Today most poultry is sold "ready to cook." It has had the head, feet and feathers removed; the giblets and neck have been removed and wrapped separately. The bird has been thoroughly cleaned and is all ready to cook.

Chickens and turkeys are available whole or cut up, as well as in selected parts.

Fresh Fish and Seafood

There are many varieties and forms of fish from which to make your selection. Be sure to buy fish that is really fresh. Fresh fish has little or no odor: Do not buy fish if it has a strong odor. In a whole fresh fish, the flesh should be firm and elastic and should show no signs of separation from the bone. The eyes should be clear and bright and the gills red. Fish steaks are slices cut crosswise. Fish fillets are boneless, lengthwise slices. If you buy oysters or clams in shells, see that the shells are tightly closed. Fresh crabs and lobsters should be alive and moving.

Fruits and Vegetables

Fresh vegetables and fruits are graded for the wholesale trade, but the grade is not necessarily indicated in the retail market. For some products, there are more grades than for others. As the grades are often not available to you, select fresh produce by the following standards.

Vegetables should appear garden fresh, with no soft, discolored spots or blemishes; leafy vegetables should not look wilted, and the outer leaves should not be discolored. Vegetables are best when they are not too mature. Undersized vegetables may lack flavor, and oversized ones may be tough and fibrous. Green and wax beans should be fresh and should snap crisply. Potatoes and onions should be firm. Also note the care that your dealer gives to fresh vegetables. They are best kept covered with chipped ice or kept moist with frequent ice-water sprays. They should be protected from dust and flies and should not be handled unnecessarily.

In choosing fresh fruit, judge color and firmness, degree of ripeness and absence of decay. The larger fruit may not have so much flavor and juice as the smaller fruit. The use for which it is intended will also affect your choice. Oranges to be used for juice need not be large; on the other hand, if they are to be served whole or in salads, large ones are a better choice. Bargains in overripe fruit are not always economical, as they may be partly decayed.

Oranges, tangerines, grapefruit, lemons and limes should be well shaped. The heavier ones are your best choice, as they have less pulp and more juice. A thin, fine-grained skin is also an indication of juicy citrus fruit. Florida oranges usually have more juice. California oranges are better for sections or for peeling and eating. Navel oranges have a sweeter flavor and are seedless. Oranges need not be bright in color to be good (indeed, juice oranges are frequently color-sprayed for eye appeal). Grapefruit should be springy to the touch. Do not choose those with very coarse skins or soft decayed areas. Limes should be green; yellow ones do not have such pungent flavor.

Bananas are ripe when they are all yellow or mottled with brown spots. Green-tipped bananas ripen at home in a few days. Pineapples should be heavy and without soft areas at the bases. They are perfectly ripe when the flesh yields *slightly* to pressure. The freshest grapes are those that are still well attached to the stem. Ripe cantaloupes, honeydew melons and muskmelons have characteristic aromas. Watermelon is best when it is firm, with a fresh, good color and slightly yellow or whitish skin on the lower side. Berries of all kinds should be solid, clean and bright in color. Strawberries should have hulls still attached and be bright, solid red. When the caps cling tightly to the berries, the berries are underripe. Avoid buying overripe berries, which are dull in color and soft. Rhubarb should not have a musty odor.

Canned Fruits and Vegetables

Read the labels on cans to learn the weight and contents and to compare prices. A dented can is not a sign of spoilage unless the dent has caused a leak. A bulging can may denote spoilage.

Once opened, canned fruits and juices should be covered and stored in the refrigerator. They may safely be left in their original containers, but high-acid juices, like those of tomatoes, pineapples and so forth keep their flavor better and develop no metallic taste if they are poured into clean glass jars or plastic containers before refrigerator storage.

Frozen Fruits and Vegetables

The weight and contents of frozen fruits and vegetables must be shown on the main part of the label.

Butter

Butter is sold salted or sweet. Both kinds are made from cream, but sweet butter has no salt added. The grade mark must be shown on the main panel of the carton or wrapper in which the butter is sold.

Eggs

Eggs are sold by grade and size. Grade A-1 and grade A eggs are clean, with unbroken shells, and are practically perfect in shape. The whites are thick and firm, and the yolks are well centered. These eggs are especially suitable for cooking in the shells, for poaching and for frying. Grade B eggs may show definite ridges or some roughness. Their whites are less firm and the yolks less well centered than those of grade A eggs. These eggs may be used for scrambling, baking and other cooking purposes. Eggs are also sold with definite size markings: Extra Large, Large, Medium and Small. When selecting eggs, it is advisable to look at the bottom of the carton for stain or soil, which usually denotes that there may be some breakage in that carton. Cracked or broken eggs will not keep fresh as long as those with unbroken shells. These eggs are also difficult to remove, as they may stick to the carton and be a complete loss to you, a waste of money.

Bread and Bakery Products

The best method for storing bread is in your home freezer: Keep fresh bread in its original wrapper, and immediately place in the freezer. The next-best method for home storage is to keep bread in its original wrapper in a ventilated container at room temperature. The least desirable method of storing bread is to keep it in the refrigerator. Refrigerator storage hastens rather than retards staling. Bread properly wrapped and stored in the refrigerator, however, is less subject to mold than is bread kept at room temperature. Refrigerator storage is only recommended when freezing facilities are not available and your bread use is so limited that mold growth becomes a problem.

All cakes should be covered to keep them fresh. Most plain cakes keep well in a ventilated cake tin or breadbox for several days. Unfrosted or butter-frosted cakes may be wrapped in moisture-vapor proof paper and frozen. If icing is soft, it is a good idea to freeze cake for a few minutes; then as soon as top is firm, wrap cake for freezer storage. Large cakes should be cut before wrapping and freezing, to reduce thawing time.

Cakes or puff pastries containing whipped cream and cream fillings should be refrigerated until served; plan to use them quickly. Fruitcakes should be left in their original wrappings until served.

Crisp cookies should be stored in a container with a loose-fitting cover that permits some circulation of air. Soft, chewy cookies should be stored in an airtight container. Filled cookies should be stored in a cool place and used within a reasonable time.

Cream should be refrigerated until used. But, even when refrigerated, cream pies should not be kept more than 1 day before using.

Staples

Packaged foods, canned foods, dried foods and freeze-dried foods can be stored on kitchen shelves or in any cool, dry place. Flour and cereal products should be stored in tightly covered containers in a dry place; treat granulated sugar in the same way. Brown sugar should be stored in a tightly covered container in a cool place.

Herbs and spices will keep their full flavors longer if they are tightly covered and stored in a cool dry place.

Coffee

Ground coffee should be stored in a tightly covered container in as cool a place as possible. If you have space in your refrigerator, it is the best storage place, and there will be less loss of flavor and aroma.

Shortening and Oils

Shortening and oils keep best when tightly covered in a cool place. Some oils may cloud and solidify in the refrigerator, but such changes are not harmful. If returned to room temperature, they will become clear and liquid again. It is helpful to keep some shortening at room temperature for ease in creaming when making cakes and cookies.

Salad Dressing

Commercially-made salad dressing does not need refrigeration to keep it fresh, but it is an advantage to chill it before using it in salads. Once it has been opened, it should be refrigerated.

Dried Fruits

Keep dried fruits in tightly closed containers. They may be stored at room temperature, except in warm humid weather, when they should be refrigerated.

Nonfat Dry Milk

Dry milk should be stored in a tightly closed container and will keep for several months on the kitchen shelf. When it has been reconstituted, it should be stored in the same way as is fresh fluid milk—covered and in the refrigerator.

Evaporated and Condensed Milk

These items may be stored at room temperature on the cupboard shelf until opened. Then cover and refrigerate.

MEASURES FOR SUCCESS

Read the recipe carefully! Assemble all the ingredients; measure the quantities accurately.

When following a tested recipe, it is important to measure the ingredients as accurately as they were measured when the recipe was developed and tested. Otherwise the recipe may be thrown out of balance and may yield disappointing results. In all reliable test kitchens, the same methods are used, and certain basic rules are maintained. So if you follow the following suggestions you are assured of success.

Always use standard measuring cups and spoons.

Use 8-ounce glass measuring cups for liquids. The glass permits you to see the level of the liquid being measured. The cup for liquids should have additional space above the 1-cup line, so that a full cup can be accurately measured without spilling. Stand cup on level surface, and fill to amount indicated. Check the measurement at eye level.

When measuring thick liquids like honey and syrup, do not let them overflow the measuring cup or spoon. Be careful to scrape out the cup or spoon thoroughly. A light greasing of the cup or spoon helps in measuring sticky ingredients.

To measure dry ingredients, use standard individual cups (as in a nested set), in 1/4-, 1/2-, 1/3- and 1-cup sizes. Lightly spoon dry ingredients into appropriate cup, heap up and level off with edge of spatula by cutting across the top. Use measuring spoons in this way, too, for dry ingredients. Flour need not be sifted before measuring unless recipe specifies. Sifting flour onto a sheet of waxed paper instead of into a bowl cuts down on dishwashing. Measure brown sugar by packing firmly or lightly into a measuring cup, depending on the recipe.

Shortening, lard and butter can be measured accurately by using the same fractional measuring cups used for dry ingredients. Fats are more easily measured if they are soft and measured at room temperature.

How To Use Half a Recipe

Do you want to make only 1/2 the amount? Some recipes may be successfully "halved."

Measuring-spoon sets do not include 1/2-tablespoon measures. When you want to measure 1/2 tablespoon of a dry ingredient or fat, fill 1 tablespoon, level off with a flat knife or spatula and cut in half from tip to handle. Flick off 1/2 the ingredients in the spoon, and you will have accurately measured 1/2 tablespoon. Or you can measure out 1 1/2 teaspoons, which equals 1/2 tablespoon. For measuring 1/2 tablespoon of liquid, use 1 teaspoon and 1/2 teaspoon.

When a recipe calls for 1/3 cup of an ingredient and you wish to use 1/2 this amount, remember that 1/3 cup is 5 1/3 tablespoons or 5 tablespoons plus 1 teaspoon. Half this amount can be easily and accurately measured by using 2 1/2 tablespoons plus 1/2 teaspoon or 2 tablespoons and 2 teaspoons.

If you are using a cake mix and a whole cake is more than you require at one time, remember that a mix that yields a cake to fill an 8-inch square pan will make 2 thinner 8-inch layers. Cut one layer in half horizontally, spread filling over one half, place other half on top and frost. This method will give you 1/2 a fresh layer cake for immediate use. The other layer can be tightly wrapped and frozen for future serving. Or, instead of two 8-inch layers, you might prefer to make 1 layer and bake the remaining batter as cupcakes.

In dividing a recipe, the time for cooking may need adjustment—although not necessarily by an exact 1/2 of the normal period. For instance, a casserole that requires 45 minutes baking time will cook nicely in 30-35 minutes when you are preparing 1/2 the recipe.

In making 1/2 the regular recipe for meat loaf or salmon loaf, you might like to vary the usual plan by baking the mixture in individual custard cups or muffin pans. In this case, you will find that cooking can be completed in a little less than 1/2 the usual time. A family-size meat loaf to serve 6 people will bake in a loaf pan at 350°F. 1 1/4 hours. By dividing all ingredients in half and baking mixture in 1/2 dozen custard cups, the oven time can be cut to 30 minutes at 350°F. When you double a recipe, it is important to remember that, besides doubling ingredients, you must allow longer cooking time, depending on the depth of pan.

MEASURES
(All measurements are level)

1 cup (8 fluid ounces) = 16 tablespoons
3/4 cup (6 fluid ounces) = 12 tablespoons
2/3 cup (5 1/3 fluid ounces) = 10 tablespoons plus 2 teaspoons
1/2 cup (4 fluid ounces) = 8 tablespoons
1/3 cup (2 2/3 fluid ounces) = 5 tablespoons plus 1 teaspoon
1/4 cup (2 fluid ounces) = 4 tablespoons
1/8 cup (1 fluid ounce) = 2 tablespoons
1 tablespoon (1/2 fluid ounce) = 3 teaspoons

TABLE OF EQUIVALENTS

1 gallon (160 fluid ounces) = 4 quarts
1 quart (40 fluid ounces) = 5 cups
1 pint (20 fluid ounces) = 2 1/2 cups

If you have to convert weights to measures in a recipe, this table will help you.

FOOD	WEIGHT OF 1 CUP	MEASURE IN OUNCES
Butter	8 oz.	1 oz. = 2 tbsps.
Cocoa	4 1/2 oz.	1 oz. = 3 1/2 tbsps.
Cornstarch		1 oz. = 3 1/2 tbsps.
Gelatine		1 oz. = 3 tbsps.

FOOD	WEIGHT OF 1 CUP	MEASURE IN OUNCES
Flour (all-purpose, sifted)	4 1/2 oz.	8 oz. = 1 7/8 cups
Macaroni	4 oz.	8 oz. = 2 cups
Rice	6 1/2 oz.	8 oz. = 1 1/6 cups
Rolled oats	2 3/4 oz.	8 oz. = 3 cups
Sugar (brown, packed)	7 oz.	8 oz. = 1 1/8 cups
Sugar (granulated)	7 oz.	8 oz. = 1 1/8 cups
Sugar (icing, sifted)	4 1/2 oz.	8 oz. = 2 cups
Shortening	7 oz.	8 oz. = 1 1/8 cups

If a recipe calls for an ingredient like 4 1/2 cups cooked macaroni, you have to know the amount of raw macaroni to be cooked. Here is a guide.

ESTIMATING RAW INGREDIENTS

Macaroni	1 cup uncooked = 3 cups cooked
Rice	1 cup uncooked = 3 cups cooked
	1 cup precooked = 2 cups cooked
Icing sugar	1 pound = 3–4 cups sifted
Brown sugar	1 pound = 2 1/4 cups packed
Granulated sugar	1 pound = 2 1/4 cups
Heavy cream	1 cup = 2 cups, whipped
Cheese	1 pound = 4 cups grated
Egg whites	1 cup = 8 egg whites

Occasionally, you may find that you do not have the exact ingredient called for in the recipe. The following list will help in easy adjustment of recipes with replacements.

SUBSTITUTION CHART

1 ounce chocolate	= 3 tablespoons cocoa plus 1 tablespoon fat
1 tablespoon flour (for thickening)	= 1/2 tablespoon cornstarch or 1 egg or 2 teaspoons quick-cooking tapioca
1 egg (in custards)	= 2 egg yolks
1 egg (in batter)	= 1/2 teaspoon baking powder
1 cup whole milk	= 1/2 cup evaporated milk plus 1/2 cup water or 1 cup reconstituted nonfat dry milk plus 2 1/2 teaspoons fat
1 cup sour milk	= 1 tablespoon vinegar with sweet milk to make total of 1 cup (let stand 5 minutes to sour) or 1 cup buttermilk
1 cup instant flour	= 1 cup sifted all-purpose flour
1 cup cake flour	= 7/8 cup all-purpose flour
1 cup butter or margarine	= 7/8 cup shortening plus 1/2 teaspoon salt
1 cup light cream	= 3 tablespoons butter, plus 7/8 cup milk
1 cup granulated sugar	= 1 cup brown sugar, packed, or 1 cup honey or corn syrup* (reduce other liquids in recipe by 1/4 cup)
1 teaspoon baking powder	= 1/4 teaspoon baking soda plus 5/8 teaspoon cream of tartar

*Never replace more than 1/2 the prescribed sugar with syrup.

BEST COOKING METHODS

Knowing the best ways of cooking means good eating and good economy. Here are some tips on preparing and cooking various kinds of food.

Meat

Washing meat destroys some of its soluble nutrients and diminishes its flavor. Wipe it on all sides with clean, damp cloth or damp paper towel.

During cooking, do not pierce meat with fork, thus allowing juices to escape; to turn meat, use kitchen tongs, spatula or 2 spoons.

For less shrinkage, roast meat in slow-to-moderate oven, and do not overcook. A meat thermometer is the best way to determine when roast is done.

Use meat juices from pan in gravies, sauces, stews or casseroles.

The roast should stand in a warm place for a short time before carving, to let meat absorb juices and make carving easier.

When you cook meat bones for soup or stock, start cooking in cold water. This method ensures extraction of more food value and flavor from the bones into the liquid; the bones are to be discarded.

Poultry

Follow the same hints when you cook poultry. Most poultry on the market today has been thoroughly cleaned but, for safety's sake, still must be washed. Wash bird in water, and dry it well inside and out with paper towels.

Fish and Seafood

Unlike meat, fin fish, which has very little connective tissue, should be cooked quickly at high temperatures to retain its flavor and keep it moist and juicy. The thickness of fish determines cooking time. In general, fin fish needs only 10 minutes cooking time for each inch of thickness.

Whereas fin fish may fall apart if overcooked, shellfish will become tough, so particular care not to overcook is required with lobster, crab, shrimp, oysters and clams.

Milk

When heating milk, use low heat, or cook it in top of double boiler. When scalding milk, do not discard the skin that forms on top; it contains milk solids and valuable nutrients.

Vegetables

In preparing any vegetable—fresh, canned, or frozen—be careful not to overcook. Overcooking

destroys color, flavor and palatability and results in greater loss of nutrients. Vegetables that are reheated also lose many of their nutrients. Cook only enough vegetables for 1 meal at a time, and serve as soon as cooking is done. And remember that, for variety of flavor and texture, raw vegetables should be served often.

Some minerals and vitamins in vegetables may be destroyed by dissolving them in water or by exposing them to heat and air during cooking. Mineral content will also be lost if too thick a layer of skin is removed, as most iron in root vegetables is right under the skin.

So remember:

1. Bake vegetables in their skins whenever possible, in order to retain nutrients. Pressure-cooking is next best. Waterless cooking, in special heavy pots for the purpose, is very satisfactory and steaming is another good method.

2. In peeling, remove as thin a layer of skin as possible. Scraping is better than peeling. Cooking in the skin, after thorough scrubbing, retains even more food values.
3. Do not soak vegetables in water before cooking. If you find it necessary to prepare veg-

etables in advance, put them in a covered container or storage bag in the refrigerator until time to cook them.

4. Do not cut vegetables into small pieces for cooking. There will be less nutrient loss if they are left in larger pieces. Mashing after cooking causes still more nutrient loss.

5. Cook mild-flavored vegetables in as little water as possible, and cover tightly. Cook leafy greens in water that clings to leaves after washing and in tightly covered saucepan; they require only a few minutes boiling. For strong-flavored vegetables such as cabbage and cauliflower, use a little more water 1/2—1 inch in depth. *Never add baking soda*—it destroys some vitamins.

6. To shorten cooking time, which means less loss of vitamins and minerals, bring water to boiling point *before* vegetables are added.
7. Do not pour away liquid in which mild-flavored vegetables have been cooked. Use it for gravies, sauces and stews.
8. Serve vegetables as soon as they are cooked; much of their food value is lost if they are kept waiting, and flavor is lost too.

Canned Vegetables

When heating canned vegetables, do not discard liquid in can. Drain it into a saucepan, and boil until reduced by 1/2; add vegetable and heat through as quickly as possible. Save vegetable juice for use in gravies or soups.

Frozen Vegetables

All frozen vegetables (except corn on the cob) should be cooked without thawing. Use only a small amount of boiling water, and cover tightly. Cook only for time given in package directions. Do not overcook. These vegetables need much less time than do fresh vegetables. Serve at once.

MENUS AND RECIPES

Here is a special portfolio of well-balanced family meals with recipes planned for consecutive days over 2 weeks, menus for year-round use and for hot weather, including uses for leftovers.

Good meals don't simply "happen." They are the result of planning. The care you take in shopping, storing, refrigerating and all other preliminary activities helps you to give your family satisfactory year-round menus.

Plan your timing well in advance: Chill dessert; wash salad stuffs, and keep in plastic bags; open new bottles; make dressing; measure flour for thickening; seperate eggs for last minute use if necessary. Start longest-cooking item (roast, stew or the like) a little ahead of required cooking time. Get out all tools necessary—beater, shredder and so forth—to save endless opening of drawers and cupboards. Set the table. Start vegetables cooking at desired time. Warm plates and platters. Measure coffee and water into pot. Organize dessert service on a side table or in the kitchen. Complete the table with bread, water and so forth. Start coffee, and serve the first course.

In this section of consecutive days' menus with recipes, note how planning from many angles is demonstrated. Although breakfast may be a standard meal, its components of vitamins, proteins and other food elements have a bearing on the evening dinner plan.

Contrast in food colors, textures and flavors is considered in every menu. Planned leftovers become tempting in fresh guises. Planning covers cooking methods too; while the oven is hot it can be utilized for more than 1 dish. Seasonal variety in menus is always worth forethought, and the hot-weather menus make full use of summer's bounty.

Recipes are given for items printed *in italics*. *Italics* are used too when the recipe will be found by reference to other chapters of the book.

Year-round Menus

SUNDAY

BREAKFAST	LUNCHEON	DINNER
Citrus-fruit cup	*Puree Mongole*	*Roast Capon*
Eggs in Cream	*with*	with
with Bacon	*Croutons*	*Savory Bread*
Curls	Grilled-cheese	*Stuffing*
Pecan rolls	sandwiches	*Baked Cottage*
Coffee Milk	Pears	*Potatoes*
	Tea Milk	*Baked Crumbed*
		Tomatoes
		Tossed green
		salad
		Peach pie
		Coffee Tea Milk

Eggs in Cream with Bacon Curls

> 6 eggs
> 1 tablespoon butter or margarine
> 1/2 cup heavy cream
>   Salt and pepper to taste
> 1 recipe *Fried Bacon Curls*

Butter shallow baking dish generously. Break eggs into dish, dot with butter, pour cream over eggs and bake at 350°F. until eggs are barely set, about 15 minutes. Garnish with crisply fried bacon curls. Serves 6.

Fried Bacon Curls

> 12 bacon slices

Place bacon in cold skillet. Cook slowly over low heat, turning occasionally, until evenly crisp but not brittle. Pour off excess fat. Remove from pan, and curl with fork. Drain on paper towels. Serves 6.

Puree Mongole with Croutons

> 1 (10-ounce) can tomato soup
> 1 (10-ounce) can green-pea soup
> 2 cups milk or 1 cup milk and 1 cup cream
>   Croutons

Combine and stir 2 cans soup. Add milk, stirring to smooth out any lumps. Heat thoroughly. Serve soup sprinkled with croutons. Serves 4–5.

Roast Capon

> 1 (5-pound) drawn capon, completely thawed
> 1/4 teaspoon salt
> 1 recipe *Savory Bread Stuffing*
> 1/4 cup soft butter or margarine
> 1/2 cup melted fat
>   Salt to taste

Remove any pinfeathers from bird. Wash bird under cold water tap, inside as thoroughly as outside, and make sure all traces of red, spongy lungs near ribs are removed. Pat as dry as possible, using clean cloth or paper towels. Sprinkle inside with a little salt.

Stuff with dressing, placing a little against upper breast meat under neck skin and filling body cavity from rear vent. Do not pack dressing, as it swells during cooking. Using small poultry skewers, pin vent closed, and hold together with twine laced round, or sew up with heavy thread and darning needle. Truss bird for roasting by tucking wing tips under back and pressing legs close to body. Loop middle of yard-long piece of twine over tail; bring ends up tightly to loop legs and hold them securely against the body; then carry each length along side to wing and up over wing joint; tie together over neck skin at back. This method avoids marks across breast.

Rub softened butter or margarine over entire bird. Place breast up on rack in open roasting pan. Use no water in pan; do not cover and do not sear. Place in oven pre-heated to 325°F. Dip small square of clean, dry cheesecloth in melted fat and place over bird for self-basting.

Cook at low-to-medium temperature, allowing 35 minutes to the pound—or about 3—3 1/2 hours for 5-pound capon. Salt bird midway in the cooking.

Remove basting cloth about 45 minutes before end of cooking time, for nice browning of skin. When bird is done, allow it to stand in warm place for 5 minutes before serving. This period allows for absorption of juices and easier carving. Serves 4—6.

Note: Allow ample time for frozen bird to thaw completely before beginning preparation.

Savory Bread Stuffing

    1/3 cup butter or margarine
    1/4 cup chopped onion
    1/4 cup chopped celery
    5 cups soft bread crumbs
    2 teaspoons poultry seasoning
    1/2 teaspoon salt
    Pinch pepper

Melt butter or margarine, add onion and celery and cook gently over low heat until vegetables are tender but not brown. Mix in crumbs and seasonings. Cool completely before inserting in bird. Do not pack stuffing in tightly, because bread must have room to swell during cooking. Also it will cook more thoroughly—and not be too damp—if it is loosely packed. Makes enough stuffing for 5-pound bird.

Note: Discard brown crusts of bread before preparing crumbs.

Baked Cottage Potatoes

    6 medium potatoes
    4 tablespoons hot milk
    6 tablespoons cottage cheese
    Salt, pepper and onion juice

Scrub potatoes. Prick skin all over with fork. Bake in oven last 1 1/2 hours with capon. Just before serving, slash top of each and split open; remove potato pulp, and mash. Mix in milk and cottage cheese. Season with salt, pepper and onion juice. Divide mixture evenly into empty potato shells. Return to oven for 10 minutes to reheat. For a crisper skin, brush each potato with fat before putting it in oven. Serves 6.

Note: Usually, potatoes are baked about 1 hour at 450°F. As oven is set for 325°F. for capon, allow longer, slower cooking time.

Baked Crumbed Tomatoes

    6 medium tomatoes
    Salt to taste
    Pinch ground cloves
    4 salt-flavored crackers, crushed
    2 tablespoons melted butter or margarine
    1/4 teaspoon savory
    1/4 teaspoon oregano
    Dash of Worcestershire sauce
    1/2 cup water

Wash tomatoes, and cut out stem ends. Place in baking dish, cavity side up, and sprinkle with salt and cloves. Combine salt-flavored crackers with butter or margarine, savory, oregano and Worcestershire sauce. Spoon some of this mixture into each cavity. Pour water around tomatoes, and bake at 350°F. about 30 minutes. Serves 6.

MONDAY

BREAKFAST	LUNCHEON	DINNER
Orange sections	*Cheese Puff*	*Swiss Steak*
Cornflakes	Celery hearts	Mashed potatoes
Cinnamon	Fresh apple	Green beans
Toast	Cookies	with pimento
Coffee Milk	Tea Milk	Chocolate
		pudding
		Coffee Tea Milk

Cinnamon Toast

    6 slices white, whole wheat or raisin toast
    2 tablespoons butter or margarine
    3 tablespoons icing sugar
    1 teaspoon cinnamon

Butter toast lightly. Trim crusts if desired. Blend sugar and cinnamon; sprinkle over toast.

Place on rack in shallow baking pan. Toast in moderate oven (350°F.) or under broiler until sugar melts. Cut in triangles or strips. Serves 6.

Cheese Puff

        8 slices day-old bread
    1/2 pound Cheddar cheese, grated
        3 eggs
        2 cups milk
        1 teaspoon finely chopped onion
        1 teaspoon prepared mustard
    1/2 teaspoon salt
        Pepper to taste

Remove crusts from bread. Arrange 4 slices in greased shallow baking dish. Add cheese; cover with remaining bread. Beat eggs; add milk, onion and seasonings. Pour into dish, and refrigerate about 1/2 hour. Bake at 325°F. about 45 minutes or until puffed and golden brown on top. Serve immediately. Serves 4.

Swiss Steak

    1 1/2 pounds round or rump beef, 1 1/2 inches thick
        2 tablespoons flour
        1 teaspoon salt
    1/8 teaspoon pepper
        2 tablespoons salad oil or melted fat
    1 1/2 cups canned tomatoes
        3 large onions, peeled and thinly sliced
        1 stalk celery, diced
        1 clove garlic, crushed
        1 tablespoon thick meat sauce

Trim excess fat from meat. Combine flour, salt and pepper. Lay beef on chopping board; sprinkle with 1/2 flour mixture; with rim of saucer pound flour into meat. Turn meat over, and pound remaining flour into other side. Cut into serving pieces if desired. Heat salad oil in heavy skillet or Dutch oven. Brown meat well on 1 side over medium heat. Turn and brown other side. Add remaining ingredients. Stir well, cover and simmer 1 3/4–2 hours or until meat is tender. Skim off fat if necessary. Serves 4–5.

TUESDAY

BREAKFAST	LUNCHEON	DINNER
Prunes with cream	Consommé	Roast Pork Loin
Soft-cooked Eggs	Cabbage Salad with Fruit and Cream Cheese Balls	Baked Sweet Potatoes
Toasted English muffins	Melba toast	Broccoli with lemon butter
Coffee Milk	Tea Milk	Baked Apples
		Coffee Tea Milk

Soft-cooked Eggs

        6 eggs
        Cold or lukewarm water

Cover tops of eggs with water by at least 1/4 inch. Cover pan. Heat rapidly until water boils; turn off heat, and, if necessary, set pan aside to prevent further boiling. Let stand, covered, for following time periods:

* For very soft-cooked eggs, about 2 minutes

* For medium soft-cooked eggs, 3–3 1/2 minutes

* For firmer soft-cooked eggs, about 4 minutes

Serves 6.

Note: If eggs are extra large or very cold, you may have to increase cooking time 2–4 minutes. If 4 or more eggs are being cooked, lower heat to keep water hot but not simmering, and cook 4–6 minutes.

Cabbage Salad with Fruit and Cream Cheese Balls

        10 dates, pitted
        1/4 cup seedless raisins
        3 cups shredded raw cabbage
        1 teaspoon cream
        1/2 cup mayonnaise
        6 large lettuce leaves
    6–12 small cream cheese balls

Cut dates into small pieces. Add dates and raisins to cabbage. Add cream to mayonnaise and use to moisten cabbage thoroughly. Serve in lettuce cups, and garnish each with 1 or 2 little balls of cream cheese. Serves 6.

VARIATIONS:

* Add 1 cup diced, cored, unpared red apples; increase amount of dressing if necessary.

* Sprinkle coarsely chopped nuts over each salad mound after arranging.

* Omit cream cheese balls, and crumble blue cheese over each salad.

Roast Pork Loin

        1 (5 1/2–6-pound) pork loin roast
        Salt and pepper to taste

Take pork loin from refrigerator at least 1/2 hour before placing in oven. Wipe with damp cloth or damp paper towels. Place on rack in uncovered roasting pan, fat side up, and roast at 350°F., allowing 35 minutes per pound. If meat thermometer is used, it will register 185°F. when meat is done. Season about 40 minutes before cooking is completed. Do not baste or turn roast during cooking. Serves 6.

Note: The first rule for pork is that it must be thoroughly cooked. Underdone pork should never be eaten.

Baked Sweet Potatoes

    6 medium sweet potatoes
    2 tablespoons salad oil
    2 tablespoons butter or margarine

Scrub potatoes well, and dry with paper towels. Rub each with a little salad oil, and arrange on small baking sheet. Cooking time will be approximately 1 hour at 350°F., so put potatoes in 1 hour before pork roast is done. Test potatoes with fork for tenderness. When baked soft, remove from oven, and prick with fork to let steam out. Cut 1 1/2-inch cross in top of each potato. While holding with clean towel, press each potato from bottom until it partially bursts through cross. Top with butter or margarine. Serves 6.

Note: Select firm smooth-skinned sweet potatoes of bright appearance.

Baked Apples

    6 firm medium-size baking apples
    3/4 cup granulated sugar
    1 cup water

Wash apples; then with knife or corer remove cores and seeds as neatly as possible. To help prevent skin from bursting during cooking, pare each apple about 1/3 the way down from stem end. Arrange in shallow baking pan, allowing apples to touch one another. Make syrup by boiling

sugar and water 10 minutes. Some red parings may be added to syrup for extra color. Remove parings before pouring syrup over apples. Put apples into a moderate oven 350°F. Baste with syrup from time to time. Apples are done when they can be pierced easily with fork. Serve apples warm or chilled, with plain or whipped cream. Serves 6.

Note: For an extra touch, try sprinkling 1 teaspoon sugar on each cooked apple and broiling under low heat a few minutes.

VARIATIONS:

* To vary baked apples by filling centers, leave base intact when removing cores. Set in baking dish, fill each center with mincemeat, dot with bit of red currant jelly, add sugar-syrup and bake and baste. Serve warm.

* Fill centers of tart apples with liquid honey, and add a little grated lemon rind, cinnamon and nutmeg. Bake without extra liquid in covered dish until fruit is almost tender; remove cover to finish cooking. Serve warm or chilled.

WEDNESDAY

BREAKFAST	LUNCHEON	DINNER
Grapefruit juice	*Frankfurters and*	*Creamed*
Hot cereal	*Sauerkraut*	*Chicken in*
Toast Jelly	Rolls	*Patty Shells*
Coffee Milk	Apple	Hot potato
	Tea Milk	chips
		Peas with mint
		Tossed salad
		Pineapple
		Brownies
		Coffee Tea Milk

Frankfurters and Sauerkraut

    8 frankfurters
      Boiling water
    1 (28-ounce) can sauerkraut

Place frankfurters in pan of boiling water, cover, remove from heat and allow to stand 7—8 minutes. Remove from water with tongs or spoon, to prevent pricking skins. Simmer sauerkraut in its own juice 15—20 minutes; drain before serving. If less pronounced flavor is desired, juice may be poured off first and sauerkraut barely covered with boiling water, and simmered 20 minutes. Serves 4.

Note: As frankfurters are completely cooked when you buy them, they have only to be heated through. For serving with sauerkraut, they are best heated in boiling water.

Sauerkraut may be bought in cans or in bulk.

Creamed Chicken in Patty Shells

        3 tablespoons butter or margarine
        3 tablespoons flour
    1 3/4 cups milk
      1/2 teaspoon salt
          Pepper to taste
          Paprika to taste
        3 cups diced cooked chicken
        6 heated patty shells
          Chopped parsley

Melt butter or margarine in saucepan over low heat. Remove from heat, and stir in flour; blend until smooth. Add milk gradually, stirring to blend. Return saucepan to heat, add seasonings and stir and cook until sauce is smooth and thickened and there is no taste of raw starch. Add chicken. Keep hot until time to turn into heated patty shells. Sprinkle with chopped parsley before serving. Serves 6.

Note: This recipe starts with a dependable basic procedure for that most versatile menu item, *white sauce*. If you prefer a thicker sauce, use 1 tablespoon *more* of both butter and flour. A good white sauce can also be made by scalding milk, then adding paste made by blending together softened butter or margarine and flour in correct proportions and stirring constantly until mixture thickens and bubbles and there is no taste of uncooked starch. Season to taste. When making white sauce to serve over hot vegetables, use vegetable water as part of liquid for extra flavor. Add shredded cheese to make cheese sauce.

Brownies

 3/4 cup unsifted all-purpose flour
 1/4 teaspoon baking powder
 1/4 teaspoon salt
 1/3 cup soft butter or margarine
  1 cup brown sugar, firmly packed
  2 eggs, beaten
  2 (1-ounce) squares unsweetened chocolate, melted
 3/4 cup chopped pecans or walnuts
  Powdered sugar

Sift together first 3 ingredients. Work shortening with spoon until fluffy and creamy; add sugar slowly, continuing to work until mixture is light. Add eggs and chocolate. Stir in flour mixture with nuts. Turn into a well-greased pan 8″x8″x2″ and bake at 350°F. 30—35 minutes or until done. Immediately cut into 2-inch squares with knife; sprinkle with powdered sugar. Cool; remove from pan with broad spatula. Makes 16.

THURSDAY

BREAKFAST	LUNCHEON	DINNER
Tomato juice	Chicken with	*Braised Veal*
with lemon	rice soup	*with*
wedges	Egg sandwich	*Vegetables*
French Toast	Carrot sticks	Noodles
with syrup	Tea Milk	*Apricot Ice*
Coffee Milk		Cookies
		Coffee Tea Milk

French Toast

   3 eggs
  1/4 teaspoon salt
1/3–1/2 cup milk
   3 tablespoons butter or margarine
   8 slices stale bread
   Cinnamon to taste

Beat eggs until mixed; add salt and milk. Heat butter or margarine in frying pan. Using fork,

dip each bread slice into egg mixture for thorough moistening. Fry until golden brown, turn-

ing once. Dust with cinnamon, and serve with syrup, jam, butter or margarine. Serves 4.

Braised Veal with Vegetables

   1 pound stewing veal
 1 1/2 tablespoons flour
   3 tablespoons salad oil
  1/2 cup sliced onions
   1 cup stock or 1 cup water and 1 beef-bouillon cube
   1 teaspoon salt
  1/4 cup diced celery
  1/2 cup diced carrots
   2 tablespoons chopped green pepper
  1/2 cup green peas
   8 ounces noodles, boiled
   Parsley sprigs

Cut veal into 1-inch cubes. Dredge with flour. Heat oil in large skillet. Add veal, and cook until light brown, turning several times. Add onions, and cook until golden, stirring once or twice. Add stock and salt to veal mixture. Cover pan tightly, and cook over low heat 1 hour, adding vegetables for last 30 minutes. Arrange cooked noodles on platter with veal and vegetables in center, and garnish with parsley. Serves 4—6.

Apricot Ice

1 egg white
2/3 cup fine white sugar
3/4 cup pulp of *Stewed Apricots*
1/2 cup orange juice
2 tablespoons lemon juice
2 teaspoons grated orange or lemon rind
1 cup ice-cold evaporated milk or heavy cream

Beat egg white until fluffy but not dry. Gradually fold in sugar, then apricot pulp, juices and rind. Beat milk in chilled bowl to form softly rounded peaks. Fold in apricot mixture. Put into refrigerator tray, and freeze to mushy consistency. Remove to chilled bowl, and beat quickly with rotary beater until smooth. Return to tray and refreeze. Serves 4.

FRIDAY

BREAKFAST	LUNCHEON	DINNER
Stewed Apricots	*Welsh Rarebit*	Vegetable juice
Hot oatmeal	*on Toast*	*Tuna Fish—*
Bacon Muffins	Chilled cherries	*Mushroom*
Coffee Milk	Cookies	*Casserole*
	Tea Milk	Buttered spinach
		Gingerbread
		Lemon Sauce
		Coffee Tea Milk

Stewed Apricots

1 pound dried apricots
Cold water
1/2–3/4 cup sugar

Put apricots in saucepan with enough cold water to cover completely. Cover and simmer 30 minutes. Add sugar to taste. Stir to dissolve. Makes 4 cups.

Note: For apricot pulp, force cooked fruit through sieve. If thicker syrup is desired for plain stewed apricots, remove fruit when tender, and simmer juice until reduced by 1/2. Pour over fruit and chill.

Welsh Rarebit on Toast

2 tablespoons butter or margarine
2 tablespoons flour
1 teaspoon dry mustard
1/4 teaspoon salt
1 cup milk
1 teaspoon Worcestershire sauce
Cayenne pepper
1/2 pound Cheddar cheese, diced
3 tablespoons beer or ginger ale
9–12 toast points

Melt butter or margarine in top of double boiler. Add flour, mustard and salt; then stir in milk gradually. Cook over direct heat until mixture thickens. Place over gently simmering water. Add Worcestershire sauce and cayenne; stir in cheese, and continue to stir until cheese is melted. Just before serving, stir in beer. Serve over toast points. Serves 3—4.

Tuna Fish—Mushroom Casserole

2 (7-ounce) cans (2 cups) coarsely flaked tuna
2 tablespoons flour
2 teaspoons Worcestershire sauce
1/2 teaspoon salt
Pinch pepper
2 cups milk
3/4 cup sautéed sliced fresh mushrooms (1/2 pound raw)
1 cup (approximately 2 1/2 ounces) potato chips, broken up

Measure 2 tablespoons oil from canned tuna into double boiler. Gradually stir in flour, Worcestershire sauce, salt, pepper and milk. Cook over boiling water until smooth and thickened, stirring constantly. Add mushrooms. Cover bottom of greased 1 1/2-quart casserole with 1/4 cup potato chips. Top with 1/3 the tuna, then 1/3 the sauce. Repeat, making 3 layers of each, and top with remaining potato chips. Bake, covered, at 375°F. 20 minutes. Uncover, and bake 5 minutes or until brown. Serves 4.

Gingerbread

1/2 cup soft shortening
2 tablespoons sugar
1 egg
1 cup fancy molasses
1 cup boiling water
2 1/4 cups sifted all-purpose flour
1 teaspoon baking soda
1/2 teaspoon salt
2 teaspoons ginger
1 teaspoon cinnamon

Blend together thoroughly shortening, sugar and egg. Mix molasses and boiling water together, and add to first mixture. Sift together remaining ingredients, and stir in, beating until smooth. Pour into well-greased and floured 9-inch square pan, and bake at 325°F. 45—50 minutes. Cut into 3-inch squares in pan, and serve warm. Serves 9.

Lemon Sauce

1 tablespoon cornstarch or 2 tablespoons flour
1/3 cup sugar
Grated rind of 1 lemon
1 cup cold water
1 1/2 tablespoons butter or margarine
Juice of 1 lemon, strained

Mix cornstarch, sugar and lemon rind. Slowly add water, keeping mixture smooth. Cook, stirring until sauce is thick and clear. Serve hot, adding butter or margarine and lemon juice just before pouring over gingerbread. Makes 1 1/4 cups sauce.

SATURDAY

BREAKFAST	LUNCHEON	DINNER
Grapefruit halves	Split-pea soup	Chicken soup
Cold cereal	Watercress sandwiches	*Pork Chop Suey*
Poached eggs	Carrot sticks	*Fluffy Rice*
Toast	*Spiced Fruit Compote*	Sliced tomatoes
Coffee Milk	Tea Milk	Chocolate refrigerator dessert
		Coffee Tea Milk

Spiced Fruit Compote

  1 (15-ounce) can sliced peaches
  1 (15-ounce) can green gage plums
  6 whole cloves
  1 stick cinnamon, broken
  2 thin slices lemon
  2 ripe pears
  2 bananas

Drain juice from canned fruit into a saucepan, and add spices and lemon slices. Simmer, uncovered, for 10 minutes. Strain the juice. Peel and thinly slice pears into a serving bowl. Add drained peaches and plums. Cover with hot spiced juices, and chill in refrigerator. Just before serving, add peeled sliced bananas. Serves 5—6.

Pork Chop Suey

  2 tablespoons salad oil
1/2 cup chopped green pepper
1/2 cup chopped onion
  2 cups cooked pork, cut in strips
  1 cup chopped celery with leaves
  1 cup canned bean sprouts
  1 cup chicken bouillon
  1 tablespoon cornstarch
  1 tablespoon soy sauce
1/2 cup sautéed or canned mushrooms
1/2 cup blanched, shredded and toasted almonds

Heat oil in large skillet. Add green pepper and onion; sauté 3 minutes. Add pork, and cook 3 minutes. Add celery, bean sprouts and 1/4 cup chicken bouillon. Make paste of remaining bouillon and cornstarch. Add paste to pork mixture and cook, stirring until thickened. Add soy sauce and mushrooms. Heat thoroughly, turn out on platter and scatter almonds over top. Serves 4—6.

Fluffy Rice

  1 cup raw white rice
2 1/2 cups cold water
  1 teaspoon salt

Combine rice, water, and salt in a deep saucepan with tight-fitting lid. Bring to full boil, uncovered, and stir once or twice as water starts rolling. Lower heat to simmer, place lid on pan and cook about 14 minutes without stirring or uncovering. If after you have tested a grain or 2, rice seems not quite tender, replace lid, and continue to simmer 3—4 minutes longer. Fluff rice lightly with fork, stirring a few times from bottom of pan to make sure no moisture remains there. All water should be absorbed by this amount of rice, so that there is no need to drain it. If serving is delayed, let rice stand in covered pan to steam-dry and keep hot. Serves 4.

SUNDAY

BREAKFAST	LUNCHEON	DINNER
Blended fruit juice	*French Onion Soup*	*Roast Beef*
Puffed wheat	Carrot and celery sticks	Horseradish gravy
Scrambled Eggs with chives	*Applesauce*	*Yorkshire Pudding*
Toast	Cookies	*Oven-browned Potatoes*
Marmalade	Coffee Milk	Scalloped tomatoes
Coffee Milk		*Peaches Melba*
		Coffee Tea Milk

Scrambled Eggs

  6 eggs
1/3 cup milk
1/2 teaspoon salt
1/8 teaspoon pepper
  2 tablespoons butter or margarine

Beat eggs, milk and seasonings together lightly in a bowl. Melt butter or margarine in skillet over low-to-medium heat, tipping pan so that sides too are greased. Pour in egg mixture, and cook over low heat. As mixture begins to thicken, gently scrape with spoon from bottom and sides of pan. Continue cooking until mixture is uniformly set but still moist. Serve at once. Serves 4.

Note: If you prefer, eggs may be cooked in top of double boiler; melt butter or margarine first, and scrape and lift mixture as in skillet. Water in lower section should be boiling, but should not touch upper container. This method takes a little longer.

VARIATION:

* Add a few sautéed chopped mushrooms, 1 tablespoon grated cheese, 1 tablespoon chopped cooked ham or 1 tablespoon chopped chives.

French Onion Soup

4—5 medium-size onions
1/4 cup butter or margarine
  2 (10-ounce) cans bouillon
  2 soup cans water
  2 tablespoons cognac
    Salt and pepper to taste
  6 (1/2-inch) slices French bread
1/2 cup grated Parmesan cheese

Peel onions, and slice thinly, keeping in rings. Heat butter or margarine in pot. Add onions; cover and cook slowly until soft. Uncover, increase heat and allow onions to brown. Remove

from heat, and add bouillon, water and cognac. Return to heat, and simmer 1/2 hour, adding salt and pepper. Toast French bread. Just before serving time, turn on broiler; ladle soup into fireproof bowls, float toast slice on top of each, sprinkle with cheese and place under broiler until topping is melted. Serves 5–6.

This recipe is a simple, easily made version of *soupe à l'oignon*.

Applesauce

          6 large tart apples
          Cold water
          Granulated sugar

Wash apples, quarter, remove stems and blossom ends but leave cores and seeds. Do not peel. Put into saucepan. Add enough water to come not quite to top of the apples, cover and cook over low-to-medium heat 20–30 minutes or until tender. Add sugar to give desired degree sweetness, which will depend on personal taste and tartness of apples. Put through strainer, and cool. Serves 6–8.

Note: In late winter or spring, as apples become older, it may be desirable to add an extra flavor touch, like nutmeg, cloves or lemon juice.

Roast Beef

          1 (4-pound) standing rib roast of beef

Place roast, fat side up, on rack in shallow pan. If meat thermometer is used, insert so that tip reaches center without touching fat or bone. Place, uncovered, in 325°F. oven. Do not add water to pan. For rare beef, allow 18–20 minutes per pound; for medium, 22–25 minutes; for well done, 27–30 minutes. Meat thermometer will read 140°F., 160°F., or 170°F. respectively. Remove from oven when thermometer registers 5° less than the internal temperature you prefer. Let

finished roast stand in warm place a few minutes while gravy is being made. Serves 6.

Roast Beef with Roast Vegetables: Scrape large carrots and cut in half vertically. Peel small to medium white onions. Remove roast from the oven 1 1/4–1 1/2 hours before roasting is completed. Arrange carrot halves and onions around the roast, and turn over and baste with meat drippings. Sprinkle lightly with salt, and continue roasting. After 30 minutes turn vegetables again; then roast until tender. Roasting time for vegetables will depend on their size and maturity.

Note: For roast beef at its best, select your cut with care. A standing rib roast is one of the finest cuts for roasting; if you prefer it without bone, buy rolled rib piece. Round-steak roast and rump may also be used for same type of dry-heat roasting in open pan. If possible, allow meat to come to room temperature before putting it in oven; a roast directly from refrigerator requires longer cooking time per pound. For less shrinkage, better flavor and juiciness, do not sear in hot oven, and withhold salt and other seasoning until last 1/2 hour of cooking time.

Yorkshire Pudding

          1 cup sifted all-purpose flour
          1 teaspoon salt
          2 eggs, well beaten
          1 cup milk
          1/4 cup drippings from hot roast beef

Sift flour and salt together; combine eggs and milk, gradually stir into flour and beat until smooth. Let stand until roast is done. Remove roast from oven and increase heat to 450°F. Pour hot drippings into preheated 9-inch square pan. Pour batter into pan, and bake 15–20 minutes while you make gravy and carve the roast. Cut into squares, and serve at once with roast beef. Individual greased muffin tins may be used instead. Divide batter into equal parts. Serves 6.

Oven-browned Potatoes

          6 medium potatoes, peeled

About 1 1/4 hours before roast is done, parboil 6 potatoes for 10 minutes. Drain, and arrange around roast in roasting pan. Bake 40–60 minutes or until tender, turning occasionally. Baste with fat in pan. Serves 6.

Peaches Melba

          6 canned peach halves
          Vanilla ice cream
          1 package or pint sweetened mashed raspberries
            (fresh or frozen)

Hot, Spiced Tomato Juice

        5 cups tomato juice
        2 tablespoons butter or margarine
        2 tablespoons lemon juice
        1 tablespoon Worcestershire sauce
        1 teaspoon basil
    1/4 teaspoon pepper
    1/8 teaspoon mace
        6 lemon slices (optional)

In a large saucepan, heat tomato juice, butter or margarine, lemon juice, Worcestershire sauce, basil, pepper and mace. Cook gently for 2 minutes. Serve in 8-ounce mugs, cups or glasses. Garnish each with a lemon slice. Makes 6 (6-ounce) servings.

Place one peach half, cut side up, in each of 6 sherbet dishes. Top with ice cream, and add chilled raspberries. Serves 6.

MONDAY

BREAKFAST	LUNCHEON	DINNER
Grapefruit	*Creamed*	*Hot, Spiced*
Hot oatmeal	*Salmon*	*Tomato Juice*
Bacon	Toast points	*Vegetables with*
Muffins	Celery and	*Liver*
Tea Milk	carrot sticks	*Fluffy Rice*
	Prune Whip	Tossed green
	Tea Milk	salad
		Banana Sponge
		Coffee Tea Milk

Creamed Salmon

    1 (8-ounce) can salmon
    1 cup hot medium white sauce made with cream and
        liquid from fish
    2 teaspoons grated onion
        Dash mace
    2 teaspoons finely chopped parsley
        Toast points

Drain salmon, reserving liquid. Discard dark skin. Flake salmon, mash bones and add to hot white sauce with onion and mace. Heat thoroughly, and serve, sprinkled with parsley, on toast points. Serves 2—3.

Prune Whip

    2 egg whites
    1/3 cup granulated sugar
    1 (4 3/4-ounce) jar strained prunes
    2 teaspoons lemon juice

Beat egg whites until stiff peaks form. Gradually add sugar, beating continuously, until mixture forms stiff, dry peaks. Combine prunes and lemon juice, fold into egg whites and chill. As this dessert does not "stand up" well, it should be used within 1/2 hour of preparation. The mixture may be baked in the oven if preferred, at 350°F. about 20 minutes or until lightly browned. Serves 4.

Note: Unused egg yolks can be used in a custard sauce to serve with this prune whip, or they can be used in tomorrow's breakfast omelet.

Vegetables with Liver

        2 pounds beef or pork liver, sliced
            Seasoned flour
        3 tablespoons hot fat
        2 medium onions, chopped
    6—8 whole carrots, sliced
    2—3 stalks celery, sliced
            Salt and pepper to taste
    1/2 cup hot water

Remove skin from liver by inserting sharp knife under it and pulling or scraping it away from the meat; snip edges, and slice separately. Carefully cut out tubes with sharp-pointed scissors. Roll each slice separately in seasoned flour, and brown in hot fat, together with onions, carrots and celery. Season. Place in greased casserole, add water, cover, and bake at 350°F. for 45–60 minutes or until vegetables are tender. Serves 6.

Banana Sponge

        1 envelope plain gelatine
        2 tablespoons cold water
    1/2 cup boiling water
    1/2 cup sugar
        3 bananas, mashed
        2 teaspoons lemon juice
    1/4 teaspoon salt
        3 egg whites
    1/2 teaspoon sugar
    1/2 cup heavy cream, whipped

Mix gelatine with cold water; set aside 5 minutes. Dissolve in boiling water. Stir 1/2 cup sugar into gelatine mixture until dissolved. Cool. Add bananas and lemon juice. Chill until mixture begins to set. Add salt to egg whites; beat until they form softly rounded peaks. Beat gelatine mixture until frothy, and fold in egg whites. Pour into chilled serving dishes. Add 1/2 teaspoon sugar to whipped cream, and mound on top of banana mixture. Serves 5–6.

TUESDAY

BREAKFAST	LUNCHEON	DINNER
Orange juice	Bacon-tomato	Casserole of
Dry cereal	sandwiches	Lamb with
Omelets	Chilled canned	Vegetables
Toast	plums	Pickled beets
Marmalade	Tea Milk	Tossed green
Coffee Milk		salad
		Cottage Pudding
		Caramel Sauce
		Coffee Tea Milk

Casserole of Lamb with Vegetables

    1 1/2 pounds lean uncooked lamb
    1 1/2 teaspoons salt
        1/8 teaspoon pepper
        2 tablespoons flour
        2 tablespoons shortening
    1/4 cup chopped onion
        Boiling water or broth
        3 medium potatoes, diced
        3 carrots, diced
        1 small white turnip, diced
        2 tablespoons chopped parsley

Cut lamb in 1-inch cubes. Combine seasonings and flour. Toss well with lamb cubes. Heat shortening in frying pan. Add lamb, and cook until light brown, stirring 2 or 3 times. Add onion, and

cook until golden, stirring occasionally. Turn into 2-quart casserole, and add enough boiling water to cover lamb. Cover, and bake at 350°F. 70 minutes. Add potatoes, carrots and turnip, and cook 30 minutes longer or until vegetables are tender. Garnish with parsley. Serves 4.

Cottage Pudding

    1/2 cup soft shortening
        1 teaspoon vanilla
    1 1/4 cups sugar
        1 egg
    1/2 teaspoon salt
        3 teaspoons baking powder
    2 1/4 cups sifted all-purpose flour
        1 cup milk

Grease the bottom of a 9-inch square pan, and line with greased waxed paper. Beat shortening, vanilla and sugar together until light. Add the egg, and beat until fluffy. Sift dry ingredients together, and add alternately with the milk to the shortening mixture. Scrape into prepared pan, and bake at 350°F. about 45 minutes. Cool 5 minutes, and invert pan. Peel off paper; cut into squares. Serve hot with *Caramel Sauce*. Serves 9.

Note: Frost cold leftover pudding with your favorite icing, and serve as cake another day.

Caramel Sauce

    2/3 cup brown sugar, firmly packed
        1 cup boiling water
        1 tablespoon cornstarch
        1 tablespoon cold water
        Few grains salt
        1 tablespoon butter or margarine
    1/2 teaspoon vanilla

Melt sugar in small, heavy saucepan over medium heat. When it has colored to a rich brown, add boiling water very carefully, a little at a time, stirring. Dissolve cornstarch in cold water; then stir in a little of the hot mixture, and blend well. Stir cornstarch mixture into sugar mixture, and cook until smooth and thick; simmer a few minutes. Add salt, butter or margarine and vanilla. Serve hot over pudding. Makes approximately 1 cup of sauce. Double the recipe for 9 servings of pudding.

WEDNESDAY

BREAKFAST	LUNCHEON	DINNER
Blended juice	Pizza	Pork Chops with
Oatmeal	Fresh fruit	Apple Rings
Toast Jelly	Tea Milk	Mashed potatoes
Coffee Milk		Corn-stuffed
		Tomatoes
		Tapioca Parfait
		Coffee Tea Milk

Fine pickles.
CREDIT: *Murray Dutchak.*

A fall table, featuring baked ham and Acorn Squash with Mushrooms and Lime (p. 112).
CREDIT: *Ben Somoroff.*

Pork Chops with Apple Rings

    1 tablespoon shortening
    6 lean pork chops
    2 tablespoons flour
    1 cup hot water
    1 tablespoon vinegar
    1 teaspoon salt
  1/2 teaspoon sage
  1/8 teaspoon pepper
    3 tart apples, cored and cut into rings
  1/4 cup brown sugar, firmly packed

Heat shortening in frying pan. Add chops, and cook until lightly browned, turning once. Remove chops to baking dish. Pour off drippings; return 1 1/2 tablespoons drippings to frying pan, and place over low heat. Add flour to drippings, stirring until smooth. Add water and vinegar slowly, and continue stirring. Add seasonings, and continue to cook until bubbling. Pour gravy over chops, and bake, covered, 25—30 minutes at 350°F. Place apple rings on chops, and sprinkle with brown sugar. Bake 20 minutes longer or until tender. Serves 6.

Corn-stuffed Tomatoes

    6 large firm tomatoes
  1/2 teaspoon salt
    1 (12-ounce) package frozen whole-kernel corn,
        thawed
    2 tablespoons chopped green pepper
    2 tablespoons chopped celery
    2 tablespoons chopped onion
  1/2 cup bread crumbs
    2 tablespoons corn liquid or cream
    1 tablespoon melted butter or margarine
      Water
    2 tablespoons grated cheese

Scoop out pulp from tomatoes, and salt them inside; then turn upside down to drain a few minutes. Combine other ingredients, except water and grated cheese, and fill tomato shells with mixture. Set in baking dish with very small amount of water to prevent burning. Sprinkle with grated cheese. Bake 20—30 minutes at 350°F. Serves 6.

Tapioca Parfait

  1 1/2 cups milk
    1/8 teaspoon salt
      3 tablespoons quick-cooking tapioca
    1/4 sup sugar
      2 eggs, separated
    1/2 teaspoon vanilla extract
        Jam

Combine milk, salt, tapioca and 3 tablespoons sugar in top of double boiler. Cook over boiling water, stirring occasionally, until tapioca becomes transparent and mixture thickens, about 20 minutes. Meanwhile, beat egg whites until stiff but not dry; beat in remaining sugar. Beat egg yolks; add some of cooked tapioca, and quickly add egg-yolk mixture and vanilla to double boiler over heat. Stir until mixture thickens, about 3 minutes. Remove from heat, and cool slightly. Fold in beaten egg whites. Allow to chill thoroughly. To serve, place small teaspoons of jam against side of sherbet or parfait glasses alternately with large tablespoons of pudding. Serves 4—5.

THURSDAY

BREAKFAST	LUNCHEON	DINNER
Vegetable juice	Cream of	*Crisp Roast Beef*
Poached eggs	tomato soup	*Hash*
Toast	*Mexican Salad*	Buttered turnips
Coffee Milk	Rolls	Green peas
	Angel Food	*Lemon*
	Cake	*Meringue Pie*
	Tea Milk	Coffee Tea Milk

Mexican Salad

      1 (12-ounce) package frozen green lima beans, cooked
          and drained
    1/4 cup *French Dressing*
    1/2 green pepper, cut in strips
    1/4 cup sliced green onion
    2–3 fresh tomatoes, diced
    1/2 cup sliced celery
        Mayonnaise
        Lettuce
    1/4 cup sliced olives or 2 sliced hard-cooked eggs

Marinate lima beans in dressing about 1 hour. Combine with next 4 ingredients, adding just enough mayonnaise to moisten. Pile into a lettuce-lined bowl, and garnish with olives or sliced eggs. Serves 6.

Crisp Roast Beef Hash

      3 cups diced cooked roast beef
      3 cups diced cold, cooked potatoes
    1/2 cup chopped onion
    1/4 cup chopped green pepper
        Salt and pepper to taste
        Milk or leftover gravy

Combine beef, potatoes, onion, green pepper, salt and pepper. Moisten with milk, and spread evenly in lightly greased hot skillet. Brown thoroughly on 1 side over low heat. Fold over as with an omelet. Turn onto hot platter, and serve. Serves 6.

Note: Leftover meat should be diced small but not ground. The cooked potatoes should be diced about the same size as the meat cubes.

FRIDAY

BREAKFAST	LUNCHEON	DINNER
Orange juice	*Macaroni and*	*Baked Stuffed*
Cornflakes	*Cheese*	*Fish*
Broiled sausages	Crisp relishes	*Cucumber Sauce*
Coffee Milk	*Prune Compote*	Macédoine of
	Tea Milk	vegetables
		Baked potatoes
		Grapefruit
		halves
		Coffee Tea Milk

Macaroni and Cheese

          1 (8-ounce) package elbow macaroni
          3 tablespoons butter or margarine
          3 tablespoons flour
          2 cups milk
      1/4 teaspoon salt
      1/8 teaspoon pepper
          2 cups grated cheese
      1/2 cup dry bread crumbs
          1 tablespoon butter or margarine

Boil macaroni until tender, following directions on package. Rinse and drain in sieve. Pre-

pare medium white sauce of 3 tablespoons butter or margarine, flour, milk and seasonings; add 2/3 cup cheese, and stir until melted. Add macaroni, and spread in 1 1/2–2-quart baking dish. Sprinkle

remaining cheese over macaroni, and add crumbs and 1 tablespoon butter or margarine. Bake at 350°F. 20–30 minutes. Serves 5–6.

Prune Compote

      1/2 pound packaged tenderized prunes
  2 1/2 cups hot water
      1/4 cup sugar
          1 tablespoon lemon juice

Put prunes in saucepan with hot water, and simmer until tender (10–15 minutes). Remove from heat; stir in sugar and lemon juice. Chill. Serves 4.

Note: Packaged tenderized prunes need no soaking. Orange sections or slices may be added when serving.

Baked Stuffed Fish

          6 medium fresh or frozen haddock fillets
  1 1/2 tablespoons chopped onion
      1/4 cup chopped celery
          3 tablespoons butter or margarine
          2 cups soft bread crumbs
      1/2 teaspoon salt
          Few grains pepper
          1 teaspoon thyme (or sage or savory)
          Milk
          Lemon juice
          Salt and pepper to taste

If using frozen fish, thaw. For stuffing, brown onion and celery in butter or margarine. Add bread crumbs, salt, few grains pepper and thyme, and moisten with a little milk. Place heaping spoonful of stuffing on each fillet; roll fillet and secure with skewer. Brush with lemon juice, and sprinkle with salt and pepper to taste. Bake in greased shallow pan, uncovered, at 375°F. 30–40 minutes or until tender. Serves 6.

Cucumber Sauce

          1 cup sour cream
      1/4 cup unpared, chopped cucumber
          4 radishes, thinly sliced, or 1 teaspoon chopped
              pimento
          2 teaspoons prepared horseradish
          1 teaspoon lemon juice
      1/4 teaspoon salt
          Dash cayenne
          Dash tarragon vinegar

Combine ingredients, and chill 1–2 hours before serving. Makes about 1 1/3 cups.

SATURDAY

BREAKFAST	LUNCHEON	DINNER
Tomato juice	Beef bouillon	*Meat-stuffed*
Pancakes and	Cabbage,	*Squash*
syrup	orange and	Parsley potatoes
Coffee Milk	date salad	Creamed celery
	Cookies	*Cinnamon-*
	Tea Milk	*Apple Crisp*
		Coffee Tea Milk

Meat-stuffed Squash

    1/2 small Hubbard squash
         Boiling salted water
         Soft butter or margarine
         Salt to taste
      2 slices bacon, diced
    1/4 cup diced onion
    1/4 cup chopped green pepper or drained pickle relish
    1/3 cup tomato juice or tomato soup
      1 cup soft stale bread crumbs
      1 egg
    1/4 pound sausage meat or minced pork
    3/4 pound minced veal, lamb or beef
      1 teaspoon salt
      1 tablespoon prepared mustard
         Mace and sage to taste

Discard seeds and any stringy pulp from squash. Cut off small slice of underside so that it will rest flat. Parboil 10 minutes in boiling salted water. Drain, and dry with absorbent paper. Brush inside with soft butter or margarine, and sprinkle with salt. Sauté bacon until clear, and remove from heat. Combine with all remaining ingredients. Pile mixture into squash cavity, and set in baking dish containing 1/2 inch boiling water. Bake at 350°F. 1 1/4—1 1/2 hours or until squash is tender when tested with fork. To serve, cut in wedges to make equal portions. Serves 6.

Cinnamon-Apple Crisp

      4 cups sliced peeled apples
      1 teaspoon cinnamon
    1/4 teaspoon salt
    1/4 cup cold water
    1/2 cup sifted all-purpose flour
      1 cup sugar
    1/3 cup butter or margarine

Place apples in buttered baking dish, preferably the shallow, oblong type. Sprinkle with cinnamon, salt and water. Combine flour and sugar, and rub in butter or margarine to make crumbly mixture. Scatter lightly over apples, and bake at 350°F. 40 minutes. Serve warm with cream. Serves 6.

Hot-weather Menus

SUNDAY

BREAKFAST	LUNCHEON	DINNER
Fresh berries	Make-your-own	Broiled minute
Cold cereal	sandwiches	steaks
Toast Jam	Watermelon	Broiled tomato
Coffee Milk	wedges	halves
	Milkshakes	*Mashed Potatoes*
		Tossed salad
		Glazed Straw-
		berry Cream
		Pie
		Coffee Tea Milk

Simplify for Summer Sundays. Here's a Sunday meal pattern that will appeal to everybody,

including the cook. A picnic lunch with milkshakes, an easy hot dinner, a summer pie, quick to make.

Milkshakes

With chilled milk, a large carton of ice cream and an assortment of flavorings, sauces or crushed fruit, everybody can make his or her favorite shake. For mixing, use a bowl and rotary beater or a portable electric mixer, electric blender, plastic juice shaker or screw-top sealer.

* *Mocha Shake*: 2—3 tablespoons chocolate sauce, 1 teaspoon instant coffee, 1 cup cold milk, 1 scoop vanilla ice cream.

* *Cherry Shake*: 2 tablespoons cherry jam or sauce, dash almond extract, 1 cup cold milk, 1 scoop vanilla ice cream.

* *Banana Shake*: 1/2 banana, crushed; 1—2 tablespoons sugar, 1 cup cold milk, 1 scoop vanilla ice cream.

Glazed Strawberry Cream Pie

    1 1/2 cups milk
        2 tablespoons cornstarch
      1/4 cup sugar
      1/8 teaspoon salt
        1 egg, slightly beaten
        1 teaspoon vanilla extract
        1 (9-inch) chilled graham-cracker crust
        3 cups fresh strawberries
      1/2 cup sugar
        4 teaspoons cornstarch
        1 tablespoon lemon juice
           Drop red vegetable coloring

Heat 1 cup milk in top of double boiler. Combine remaining 1/2 cup milk with 2 tablespoons cornstarch, 1/4 cup sugar and salt. When mixture is smooth, pour into hot milk, and cook over direct heat until thickened and no starch flavor remains. Stir a little hot mixture into egg; then blend egg into mixture. Cook over hot not boiling water, stirring, about 3 minutes. Remove from heat, and add vanilla extract. Cool; then pour into prepared crust and chill.

Wash and hull berries. Drain, and dry on absorbent paper. Slice 1/2 the berries, and arrange over custard filling. Crush remaining berries, stir in 1/2 cup sugar and 4 teaspoons cornstarch and cook, stirring constantly, until mixture is thick and clear. Add lemon juice and vegetable coloring. Spread mixture over fresh berries, and chill thoroughly before serving, with whipped cream if desired. Serves 6–8.

Note: To make graham-cracker crust, follow directions in Chapter 4, omitting cinnamon if you prefer. Chill crust thoroughly without cooking; early preparation of this kind of shell means that it will have time to set.

MONDAY

BREAKFAST	LUNCHEON	DINNER
Grapefruit juice	Vegetable soup	*Summer Sausage*
Bacon Toast	Crusty rolls	*Casserole*
Coffee Milk	Celery sticks	Whole new car-
	and radishes	rots
	Raspberry whip	Lettuce wedges
	Cookies	*Thousand Island*
	Tea Milk	*Dressing*
		Fresh Peach
		Crumble with
		cream
		Coffee Tea Milk

Summer Sausage Casserole

       1 pound sausages
       2 slices bacon, cut in small pieces
       1 small onion, chopped
       2 tomatoes, peeled and diced
    1/4 cup chopped green pepper
       1 teaspoon salt
    1/2 teaspoon dry mustard
          Pinch cayenne pepper or 2 drops hot pepper sauce
       2 teaspoons Worcestershire sauce
       1 (15-ounce) can kidney beans
       1 cup soft bread crumbs
    1/2 cup grated Cheddar cheese

Prick sausages, and partly fry over medium heat about 10 minutes; lift out, and drain on paper towels. Add bacon to pan, and fry until transparent. Pour off and reserve all but 1 tablespoon fat. Add onion, tomatoes, green pepper, salt, mustard, cayenne and Worcestershire sauce. Fry 5 minutes over low heat. Add beans with juice, and remove from heat. Mix bread crumbs with cheese and 2 tablespoons reserved fat. Spread 1/2 the crumb mixture in bottom of greased 9″ x 5″ x 4″ baking dish. Cover with bean mixture, and spread with remaining crumbs. Arrange partially cooked sausages on top, and bake 30 minutes at 350°F. or until brown and bubbly on top. Serves 4–6.

Mayonnaise

       2 egg yolks or 1 egg
       1 cup salad oil
       1 teaspoon sugar (optional)
       1 teaspoon dry mustard
       1 teaspoon salt
       2 tablespoons vinegar or lemon juice
       1 tablespoon hot water

Beat egg yolks until thick, and add salad oil, very gradually, 1 teaspoon at a time. Continue beating until mixture is thick. Add remaining ingredients, and beat until blended. Keep in covered jar in refrigerator. Makes about 1 1/4 cups.

Note: All ingredients *must be* at room temperature. Beat very hard. If mixture "curdles," reconstitute by placing an additional egg yolk in a bowl. Stir it constantly, and slowly add "curdled" dressing. Increase the flow as mixture thickens.

VARIATIONS:

* *Tartar Sauce*: Combine 1/2 cup mayonnaise with 2 tablespoons chopped dill pickle, 2 teaspoons chopped pimento, 1 teaspoon each chopped onion and parsley and 1 teaspoon lemon juice.

* *Cucumber Mayonnaise*: Combine 1/2 cup each mayonnaise and diced peeled cucumber; add sprinkle of chopped chives, with extra salt to taste. Prepare only just before serving as cucumber makes mayonnaise watery.

* *Remoulade Mayonnaise*: Combine 1 cup mayonnaise with 1 teaspoon dry mustard and 1 tablespoon each chopped parsley, capers and chopped olives. Add tarragon or horseradish to taste.

* *Sour-cream Dressing*: Use 1/2 cup mayonnaise or "boiled" dressing, and add 1/4 cup sour cream, whipped or plain; 2 teaspoons chopped chives; and dash black pepper.

* *Curry Mayonnaise*: To 1/2 cup mayonnaise, add 1/4 teaspoon curry powder, for use with fish salads, or 1 teaspoon capers and 1/2 teaspoon tarragon vinegar.

* *Piquant Mayonnaise*: Rub bowl with 1/2 clove garlic; add 2 tablespoons each chopped green pepper and pimento, and 1/4 cup each chopped celery, dill pickle and chili sauce; add 1 cup mayonnaise, and combine gently. Serve with green salads.

* *Norwegian Sauce*: To 1 cup mayonnaise add 1 tablespoon prepared horseradish.

* *Mustard-Cream Dressing*: Add 1/4 cup prepared mustard to 1 cup mayonnaise; fold into 1/2 cup heavy cream, whipped. Serve with meat and vegetable salads.

* *Pimento-Cheese Dressing*: Add 1/4 cup pimento-cheese spread, dash of salt and 1 hard-cooked egg, finely chopped, to 1 cup mayonnaise. Serve with vegetable salads.

* *Russian Dressing*: Add 2 teaspoons each chopped green pepper, pimento and chives; 1/2 teaspoon paprika; 3 tablespoons chili sauce; and yolk of hard-cooked egg, sieved, to 1 cup mayonnaise.

* *Quick Russian Dressing*: Combine 1/2 cup mayonnaise with 2 tablespoons chili sauce, 1 teaspoon lemon juice and few drops of hot pepper sauce.

* *Thousand Island Dressing*: Combine 1/2 cup mayonnaise with 1/4 cup chili sauce, 2 tablespoons each chopped onion, green pepper, celery and sweet pickle and 1 chopped, hard-cooked egg.

* *Honey-Cream Dressing*: Blend 1/4 teaspoon dry mustard with 1 tablespoon honey and 1/2 teaspoon lemon juice. Add to 1 cup mayonnaise; season to taste with salt, then fold in 1/2 cup heavy cream, whipped. Serve with fruit-salad plates.

Fresh Peach Crumble

    3 cups peeled sliced fresh peaches
    1/4 cup water
    2 teaspoons lemon juice
    3/4 cup all-purpose flour
    1/8 teaspoon salt
    1 cup brown sugar, firmly packed
    2 tablespoons butter or margarine

Place peaches in greased baking dish, and sprinkle with water and lemon juice. Combine remaining ingredients until mixture resembles cornmeal. Sprinkle over peaches, and bake in moderate oven 350°F. 40 minutes. Serves 4–6.

TUESDAY

BREAKFAST	LUNCHEON	DINNER
Orange sections	Chicken noodle	*Ground-beef*
Bran flakes	soup	*Patties*
Scrambled Eggs	Cucumber and	Parsley new
with chives	cream cheese	potatoes
Toast	sandwiches	*Mixed Green*
Coffee Milk	Fruit cup	*Salad*
	Iced tea Milk	*French Dressing*
		with Blue
		Cheese
		Butterscotch
		pudding
		Coffee Tea Milk

Ground-beef Patties

    1/4 cup dry bread crumbs
    1/2 cup evaporated milk or tomato juice
    1 1/2 pounds hamburger
    1 1/2 teaspoons salt
    1/4 teaspoon pepper
    1 egg, slightly beaten
    1/4 cup finely chopped onion
    1 teaspoon prepared mustard

Soak bread crumbs in milk. Mix all ingredients together lightly; dampen the hands, and shape into 10–12 patties, about 1/2 inch thick. For tender patties, avoid pressing or packing meat too firmly. Fry about 3 minutes on each side. For broiling, brush patties with oil and broil about 3 inches from heat; then turn and continue broiling, 3–5 minutes on each side. Serves 6.

Note: Chopped parsley, Worcestershire sauce and your favorite herbs may be added for flavor variations. Chili sauce makes a good accompaniment.

Mixed Green Salad

    1 medium head lettuce
      Few leaves escarole or romaine
    1 bunch watercress
    1 clove garlic, cut
    2 tomatoes, quartered
    2 green onions, chopped
    1/4 cup *French Dressing with Blue Cheese*

Discard any wilted lettuce leaves. Wash greens well, drain and chill 1/2 hour. Dry by wrapping in towel. Tear into pieces. Rub salad bowl with cut clove of garlic, letting tiny shreds remain in bowl. Add greens and other vegetables, and toss lightly with dressing, using fork in each hand. Dressing should be added to salad just before serving. Serves 6.

French Dressing

        1 cup salad oil
        1/4 cup vinegar
        1 1/2 teaspoons salt
        1/4 teaspoon pepper
        1/2 teaspoon dry mustard

Measure ingredients into covered jar, and shake well before using.

Note: Add 1 teaspoon sugar for a sweeter dressing.

VARIATIONS:

* *French Dressing with Blue Cheese*: Combine 2 tablespoons crumbled blue cheese with 1/2 cup French dressing, stir and shake well before using.

* *Italian Dressing*: Use olive oil in place of salad oil, and add 1/4 teaspoon oregano or sweet basil and 1/2 clove garlic. Let dressing chill several hours, and remove garlic before serving.

* *Piquant Dressing*: Add 1 clove garlic, cut crosswise; let stand in dressing 1 hour. Remove; add 1 tablespoon sugar and 1 teaspoon each celery seed and grated onion.

* *Roquefort Dressing*: Mash 1/4 cup Roquefort with dash of Worcestershire sauce, and blend into 1/2 cup dressing: cheese may be quickly crumbled in before serving.

* *Lorenzo Dressing*: Add 1 tablespoon chili sauce to 1/2 cup dressing.

Note: There are many possible variations of basic *French Dressing*. For a flavor change, try wine vinegar or tarragon vinegar. Add a pinch of celery seed, a drop of hot pepper sauce or the merest pinch of cayenne pepper for sharpness.

WEDNESDAY

BREAKFAST	LUNCHEON	DINNER
Chilled melon wedges	Fresh asparagus on toast with pimento strips	*Baked Orange-glazed Ham*
Cereal	Cucumber sticks	*Scalloped Potatoes with Cheese*
Toast Honey	Sherbet	
Coffee Milk	Cookies	*Spiced Peaches*
	Tea Milk	Swiss chard
		Angel Food Cake
		Coffee Tea Milk

Baked Orange-glazed Ham

        1 boned ready-to-eat ham, 6–8 pounds
        1 teaspoon dry mustard
        3 tablespoons grated orange rind
        2 (6-ounce) cans frozen orange juice concentrate
        1/2 cup icing sugar

Place ham, fat side up, in roasting pan. Mix mustard with 1 tablespoon orange rind, and rub over ham. Spoon 1 can orange juice concentrate over top of ham. Bake in slow oven, 300°F. 25 minutes per pound. If dripping should brown, add small amount water. During last 1/2 hour of baking, baste with remaining can of orange juice and pan drippings. Sprinkle with remaining orange rind, and, just before removing from oven, sprinkle on icing sugar. Turn oven heat to 475° F., and glaze top of ham about 20 minutes. Serves 8—10 with some left over.

Scalloped Potatoes with Cheese

        6 medium potatoes
        1 onion, thinly sliced
        1 teaspoon salt
        1/8 teaspoon pepper
        2 tablespoons flour
        3 tablespoons butter or margarine
    1 1/2–2 cups hot milk
        1/4 cup grated cheese

Wash, peel and thinly slice potatoes. Butter 1 1/2-quart casserole or baking dish. Place layer of onion slices and layer of sliced potatoes in dish, using about 1/3 of each. Sprinkle with salt, pepper and flour. Dot with butter or margarine. Repeat layers, finishing with potatoes. Pour on hot milk. Sprinkle top with grated cheese. Bake, uncovered, at 375°F. 1 hour or until potatoes are tender and top is lightly browned. Serves 6.

Spiced Peaches

        1 cup water
        3/4 cup sugar
        1/4 cup vinegar
        1 broken stick cinnamon
    3 or 4 freestone peaches
    18 or 24 whole cloves

Simmer water, sugar, vinegar and cinnamon in 8-inch skillet 5 minutes. Peel peaches, and halve, removing stones. Press 3 whole cloves into rounded side of each half, and drop into simmering syrup. Cover pan, turn heat low and gently cook 3—4 minutes. Turn peach halves over, and continue cooking until just tender, about 2 minutes longer. Cool in syrup, drain and serve. Keep leftover syrup in covered jar to use again. Serves 6.

THURSDAY

BREAKFAST	LUNCHEON	DINNER
Sliced peaches	Grilled tomato-cheese sandwiches	Cold-meat platter
Cold cereal		*Potato Salad*
Toast Jam	Raw celery hearts	*Marinated Green Beans*
Tea Milk	Chilled melon	Carrot sticks
	Tea Milk	*Grape Sherbet*
		Coffee Tea Milk

Potato Salad

2 cups diced, cooked potatoes
1/4 cup chopped green pepper
2 green onions, sliced
1 hard-cooked egg, diced
1/2 teaspoon salt
Few celery seeds
1/2—1/3 cup *Mayonnaise* or *Cooked Salad Dressing*
Salad greens
2 tablespoons pimento

Combine potatoes, onion, hard-cooked egg, seasonings and mayonnaise, tossing lightly. Chill. Arrange salad on greens; garnish with pimento. Serves 4—5.

Cooked Salad Dressing

3 tablespoons flour
1 1/2 teaspoons salt
5 tablespoons sugar
2 tablespoons dry mustard
Pinch cayenne pepper
1 1/4 cups milk
2 egg yolks or 1 egg, slightly beaten
1/2 cup vinegar
2 tablespoons butter or margarine
Milk or sweet or sour cream

Combine first 5 ingredients in top of double boiler with 1 1/4 cups milk. Cook over direct heat, stirring, until mixture is thick and smooth. Place over hot water. Beat in egg yolks. Add vinegar and continue cooking 2—3 minutes longer. Remove from heat, and stir in butter or margarine. Taste for seasoning, and add more salt or sugar if necessary. Pour into covered jar, and keep in refrigerator. Beat before using, and dilute with milk to desired consistency. Makes approximately 2 cups.

Note: You may want to add 1/3 cup salad oil for a semi-oil-type dressing when mixture has cooled.

VARIATION:

* *Honey Fruit-salad Dressing*: Blend 2 tablespoons honey into 1/2 cup cooked dressing; then fold in 1/2 cup whipped cream.

Marinated Green Beans

2 tablespoons oil
2 tablespoons vinegar
Salt and pepper to taste
1 pound cooked, chilled, fresh green beans

Combine oil and vinegar, season with salt and pepper and pour over beans. Cover, and chill 1—2 hours to absorb flavors. Oil and vinegar can be poured off and used again to dress a salad. Serves 4—5.

Note: Use 2 (10-ounce) packages frozen green beans, cooked, in place of fresh beans.

Grape Sherbet

1 envelope plain gelatine
1 cup water
1/2 cup sugar
1 1/2 cups unsweetened grape juice
3 tablespoons lemon juice
1 egg white, stiffly beaten

Heat gelatine, water and sugar in small saucepan. Stir until sugar melts. Cool, and add grape and lemon juices. Pour into freezing trays, and freeze until mushy, stirring occasionally after first 15 minutes. Turn into cold bowl, break up with fork and beat until light. Fold in stiffly beaten egg white, and return mixture to freezing tray. Freeze until firm, stirring occasionally. Serves 6.

FRIDAY

BREAKFAST	LUNCHEON	DINNER
Vegetable juice	*Fresh Fruit—*	Fried fish fillets
Puffed wheat	*Cheese*	*Tartar Sauce*
Toasted fruit	*Salad*	New potatoes
bread	Butter tarts	Pickled beets
Coffee Milk	Tea Milk	*Spinach or Beet*
		Greens
		Lemon Snow
		and *Custard*
		Sauce
		Coffee Tea Milk

Fresh Fruit—Cheese Salad

Crisp lettuce
1 small melon, peeled
1/2 pint cottage cheese
1 cup fresh berries
Fine white sugar
2 or 3 oranges, peeled
2 fresh pears or peaches, sliced
1 banana, sliced
Lemon juice
Honey Fruit-salad Dressing

Arrange crisp lettuce on 4 serving plates. Cut melon in half, and scoop out seeds. Slice each 1/2 into 4 wedges. Arrange 2 wedges overlapping in center of each lettuce-lined plate, and fill with scoop of cheese. Dip fresh berries in sugar; surround melon with berries and orange slices. Dip pear and banana slices in lemon juice to prevent discoloring, and add to salad. Pour on dressing. Serves 4.

Spinach or Beet Greens

1 1/2 pounds raw spinach or beet greens
Butter or margarine
Salt and pepper to taste

Discard coarse stems, roots and wilted or discolored leaves. Wash in warm water, then in 2 rinses of cold water. Put greens loosely into saucepan without adding water, cover tightly, bring to quick boil and cook 3—4 minutes, turning greens just once. Drain thoroughly; add butter or margarine, salt and pepper. Serves 6.

Note: Spinach, beet greens and Swiss chard are at their best when crisply fresh and quickly cooked.

Lemon Snow

       3 tablespoons cornstarch
     3/4 cup sugar
   1 1/4 cups boiling water
         Grated rind of 1 lemon
     1/2 cup lemon juice
       2 egg whites

Mix cornstarch and 1/2 cup sugar together in small saucepan, and stir in boiling water and lemon rind. Place over medium heat, and cook, stirring until thick and clear. Add lemon juice, and bring to boil. Remove from heat. Cool. Beat egg whites until soft peaks form; then add remaining sugar, and beat until stiff. Fold in cooled lemon mixture. Pour into serving dish, and chill thoroughly. Serve with *Custard Sauce*. Makes 5–6 servings.

Custard Sauce

       1 cup milk
       2 egg yolks
       2 tablespoons sugar
         Pinch of salt
     1/4 teaspoon vanilla extract

Heat milk in top of double boiler until small bubbles form around edge. Beat egg yolks, sugar and salt together, and add to the hot milk. Turn heat low, so that water in bottom stays hot but not rapidly boiling. Cook mixture, stirring, until it coats a metal spoon. Remove from heat, and add vanilla. If custard curdles, beat with rotary beater until smooth. Cover, and chill thoroughly. Makes approximately 1 cup sauce.

SATURDAY

BREAKFAST	LUNCHEON	DINNER
		(Outdoor barbecue)
Sliced bananas	Peanut butter–	*Lamb Shish*
Shredded wheat	crumbled	*Kebab*
Soft-cooked	bacon	Potato chips
eggs	sandwiches	Mixed green
Toast	*Rhubarb-*	salad
Coffee Milk	*Strawberry*	Watermelon
	Compote	*Brownies*
	Tea Milk	Coffee Tea Milk

Rhubarb-Strawberry Compote

       1 pound rhubarb
       3 tablespoons cold water
     3/4 cup granulated sugar
       1 pint strawberries

Wash rhubarb, cut in pieces and place in a saucepan with water over low heat. Cover and, when fruit has started to soften, add sugar, stirring to dissolve. Cook until tender. Meanwhile wash and hull berries, and cut in half. Remove rhubarb from heat, and immediately add berries. Chill. Serves 6.

Note: Choose crisp stalks of rhubarb. They should break easily, and the rosier the skin the better.

Lamb Shish Kebab

1 1/2–2	pounds lean lamb leg
1/4	cup *French Dressing*
6	strips bacon
12	cherry tomatoes
18	whole mushroom caps
12	small onions
1	green pepper, cut in 1-inch squares
	Salt and pepper to taste

Have 6 metal skewers ready. Cut meat into 1– 1 1/2-inch cubes, and marinate in dressing 1–2 hours; then divide into 6 parts. Cut each strip of bacon into 1 1/2-inch pieces. Thread lamb, bacon, tomatoes, mushrooms, onions, and green pep-

per on each skewer. Salt and pepper lightly, and place over hot coals of barbecue grill or under broiler to brown on all sides. After 5 minutes, brush with marinade, and broil for 5–10 minutes longer. Turn several times. Serves 6.

Note: Bacon may be left in strips and threaded between ingredients as above.

VARIATIONS:

* *Chicken Liver Kebabs*: Substitute 1 pound fresh chicken livers cut in uniform pieces for lamb, but do not marinate before cooking.

Brush livers with seasoned melted butter or margarine when turning from time to time during grilling.

* *Scallop Kebabs*: Pick over and wash 1 1/2 pounds fresh raw scallops. Pat dry with paper towels. Dip in melted butter or margarine, then in finely crushed cracker crumbs to which salt and pepper have been added to taste. Thread long slice of bacon on each skewer; add scallop; weave bacon back and forth continuously between another 4 or 5 scallops. Lay prepared skewers on grill (or under range broiler). Turn frequently until evenly browned. Garnish with chopped parsley, and serve with sprinkle of lemon juice.

* *Meatball Kebabs*: To 1 pound hamburger or ground round steak, add 1/2 cup fine dry bread crumbs, 2 tablespoons grated onion, 2/3 cup milk or evaporated milk. Salt and pepper to taste. Form into small balls, and spear alternately with onion and tomato pieces.

* *Pork and Pineapple Kebabs*: Thread alternate pieces of lean pork, marinated in soy sauce, and pineapple cubes. Green-pepper pieces also go well with this combination.

SUNDAY

BREAKFAST	LUNCHEON	DINNER
Fresh blueberries	Cream of pea soup	*Stuffed Chicken Breasts*
Corned Beef Hash	Crisp raw vegetables	*Mushroom Sauce*
Whole wheat toast	Cheese	Buttered zucchini
Coffee Milk	Melba toast	Sliced tomatoes
	Tea Milk	*French Paddle Ice Cream* sundaes
		Sugar cookies
		Coffee Tea Milk

Corned Beef Hash

      2 tablespoons bacon drippings or oil
  1/2 cup chopped onion
2–2 1/2 cups cooked potatoes, diced
      1 teaspoon dry mustard
      1 teaspoon Worcestershire sauce
      1 (12-ounce) can corned beef, diced
          Salt and pepper to taste

Heat bacon drippings or oil in large, heavy frying pan or skillet, and add onion. Fry slowly until onion begins to color. Add potatoes, mustard, Worcestershire sauce and corned beef. Season with salt and pepper. Cover pan 1–2 minutes or until fat in corned beef begins to melt. Uncover, and scrape mixture up from bottom of pan with spatula. Press down evenly in pan, and increase heat to medium. When the hash begins to brown on bottom, scrape up again with spatula, and

turn mixture over. Press down, and continue browning until crusty. Serves 4–5.

Stuffed Chicken Breasts

      2 tablespoons butter or margarine
  1/2 cup chopped onion
  2/3 cup dry bread crumbs
  1/2 teaspoon marjoram
  1/2 teaspoon mace
  1/4 teaspoon salt
  1/3 cup milk
      1 egg, slightly beaten
      8 small single chicken breasts or 4 double breasts
      2 tablespoons flour
  1/2 teaspoon salt
          Salad oil

Melt butter or margarine in small frying pan, and add onion. Fry slowly until onion begins to color. Remove from heat, and add bread crumbs, marjoram, mace and 1/4 teaspoon salt. Combine milk with beaten egg, and stir in. Wipe chicken breasts with damp cloth. Cover rib sides of 4 of

breasts with dressing, and place remaining breasts on top, rib side down. Tie breasts together with string; mix flour and 1/2 teaspoon salt, and sprinkle both sides of breasts. Heat salad oil about 1/4 inch deep in skillet, and brown chicken breasts on both sides. Reduce heat to medium

low, and cover pan. Continue cooking 45 minutes or until tender, turning breasts halfway through cooking. Drain on absorbent paper, and serve with hot mushroom gravy. Serves 4 generously.

Note: If double breasts are used, stuff the cavity; then secure top and bottom edges with toothpicks.

These can be "oven-fried" by baking at 375°F. for 45 minutes. Brush with salad oil occasionally.

Mushroom Sauce

    1/4 pound mushrooms, chopped
      2 tablespoons butter or margarine
         Salt and pepper to taste
      2 tablespoons flour
1 1/4 cups chicken stock or broth

Sauté mushrooms in butter or margarine. Season with salt and pepper, and blend in flour. Gradually add stock, and cook until thickened. Pour fat out of the pan in which chicken was cooked. Add mushroom sauce to the pan, and stir and heat with remaining brown bits from the chicken.

Note: Make quick mushroom sauce by heating 1 can mushroom soup and 1/4 cup milk in pan in which chicken was cooked.

French Paddle Ice Cream

       4 egg yolks
    1/2 cup fine white sugar
1 1/2 cups light cream
    1/4 teaspoon salt
       1 teaspoon vanilla extract
    1/2 pint heavy cream

Beat egg yolks until thick and lemon-colored; add sugar gradually, and continue beating. Stir in light cream and salt, and cook in top of double boiler over hot water until custard thickens. Add vanilla; chill. Whip heavy cream until stiff, and fold in cold custard. Pour into center cylinder of 2-quart hand freezer. Cylinder should be only 3/4 full, to allow for expansion. Cover. Pack rock salt and crushed ice around outside, and put top in place. Crank handle until it becomes difficult to turn. Open freezer and remove paddles. Cover again, repack outer sections with ice and salt. Leave to ripen about 1/2 hour or until serving time. Makes 1—1 1/2 quarts.

Note: This recipe makes a rich, very smooth ice cream. It can also be made in a refrigerator freezing compartment.

MONDAY

BREAKFAST	LUNCHEON	DINNER
Tomato juice with lemon wedges	Frankfurters *Corn on the Cob*	Grapefruit halves *Pot Roast of Beef with Vegetables*
Cornflakes	Bran muffins	
Toast	Celery sticks	
Conserves	Watermelon	Sponge cake with *Fresh Lime Filling*
Coffee Milk	Tea Milk	Coffee Tea Milk

Corn on the Cob

       Water
    6 cobs fresh corn
       Butter or margarine
       Salt and pepper to taste

Half fill large saucepan with water, and bring to boil. Add corn. Cover, and bring again to boil. From this point, count cooking time, allowing 5—8 minutes, depending on size of cobs and age of corn. Uncover, and lift out corn with tongs. Serve at once with butter or margarine, salt and pepper. Serves 6.

Note: Flavor of older corn can be improved by adding 1—2 teaspoons sugar to the cooking water.

Pot Roast of Beef with Vegetables

       4 pounds beef chuck or round
       3 tablespoons flour
1 1/2 teaspoons salt
    1/4 teaspoon pepper
    1/8 teaspoon marjoram
    1/8 teaspoon summer savory
2—3 tablespoons shortening
1/2—3/4 cup water
    6—8 small onions
    6—8 small potatoes, peeled
      12 carrots, scraped
    2—3 celery stalks
         Cooking liquid from roast
       2 tablespoons flour
    1/4 cup cold water

Wipe beef with clean damp cloth or paper towel. Mix 3 tablespoons flour and seasonings together, and rub into beef. Heat shortening in heavy pan, and add beef. Cook slowly until meat is brown on all sides, about 20 minutes. Add 1/2—3/4 cup water, cover and cook slowly 3 hours or until tender. Add vegetables for last hour of cooking. Remove from heat. Arrange meat and vegetables on heated platter, and keep warm. Skim excess fat from top of liquid with spoon. Mix 2 tablespoons flour with 1/4 cup cold water until smooth. Or measure water into small screw-top jar, add flour and cover tightly; shake well. Pour flour mixture into hot liquid, and return pan to heat. Cook, stirring, until thickened. Taste, and add more seasonings if you wish. Pour into gravy boat to serve with meat and vegetables. Serves 6.

Fresh Lime Filling

       3 eggs plus 1 egg yolk
       1 cup sugar
    1/2 cup butter or margarine, cut in pieces
         Juice of 3 fresh limes, strained

In top of double boiler, beat eggs and egg yolk slightly; add sugar, butter or margarine and lime juice. Cook over simmering water, stirring frequently, 20—25 minutes until thick and smooth. Chill thoroughly. Use as filling for 2 cake layers or as topping on individual sponge rounds. Makes 6 servings.

TUESDAY

BREAKFAST	LUNCHEON	DINNER
Fresh cherries	Sliced tomatoes	*Sautéed Liver*
Poached Eggs	with fresh	*Fried Green*
Toast	basil	*Tomatoes*
Tea Milk	Peanut butter	*Succotash with*
	sandwiches	*Pimento*
	Green	Crisp raw
	applesauce	relishes
	Iced coffee	Quick-set
	Milk	gelatine
		Coffee Tea Milk

Poached Eggs

       Water
1/2 teaspoon salt
   6 eggs
   6 slices toast

Half fill skillet with cold water and bring to boil. Add salt. Break eggs 1 at a time into saucer, and slip each carefully into boiling water. When all are added, cover pan, and remove from heat. Let stand until eggs are set to soft or medium stage, about 3 minutes. Lift eggs out, 1 at a time, with slotted spoon or lifter, and set on toast slices. If solid spoon is used, tip edge on absorbent paper for a moment to drain before slipping eggs onto toast slices. If pan does not have cover, turn heat to low and baste eggs with surrounding hot water until yolks are filmed and white is set. Serves 6.

Sautéed Liver

1 1/2 pounds baby beef or calf liver, sliced
2—3 tablespoons flour
1/2 teaspoon salt
1/8 teaspoon pepper
   3 tablespoons shortening

Remove skin, veins and membrane from liver, and wipe with damp cloth. Mix flour and seasonings together. Dip liver into flour mixture, coating each piece. Heat shortening in frying pan, and add liver slices. Cook until golden brown or until each piece is tender, turning once. Be careful not to overcook. Drain liver on absorbent paper. It may be served with broiled bacon or fried onions. Serves 4—5.

Note: If skin is difficult to remove, gash edges of liver slices in several places to prevent curling when frying.

Fried Green Tomatoes

   4 firm green tomatoes
    Salt and pepper to taste

Wash tomatoes; remove stem ends but do not peel. Cut into 1/2-inch slices, allowing several slices per serving. After removing sautéed liver from pan, put in tomato slices, adding a little more fat if necessary. Turn once. When tender but still shapely, remove, season well with salt and pepper and serve. Serves 4—5.

Succotash with Pimento

   1 tablespoon butter or margarine
   1 (14-ounce) can whole-kernel corn, drained
   1 (15-ounce) can green lima beans, drained
    Light cream or milk
    Salt and pepper
    Pimento, finely chopped

Melt butter or margarine; add vegetables, a little light cream or milk, and salt and pepper. Heat thoroughly. When serving, sprinkle with finely chopped pimento. Serves 5.

WEDNESDAY

BREAKFAST	LUNCHEON	DINNER
Green	Jellied	*Deluxe Ham*
applesauce	consommé	*Loaf with*
French toast	*Hero Sandwich*	*Spiced Cherry*
and jelly	Cookies	*Sauce*
Coffee Milk	*Milkshakes*	*Corn on the Cob*
		Relishes
		Macaroons
		Coffee Tea Milk

Hero Sandwich

   1 long loaf Italian bread
    Butter or margarine
    Mayonnaise
1/2 head curly leaf lettuce
   2 large tomatoes, sliced
   2 cucumbers, sliced
    Mustard
1/2 pound cheese slices
   1 Spanish onion, sliced thin
   3 dill pickles, sliced thin
1/2 pound corned beef, sliced

Slice bread in 3 lengthwise slices. Butter bottom slice, and spread with mayonnaise. Cover with lettuce, over which arrange alternate slices of tomatoes and cucumbers. Top with buttered center slice, and spread with mustard. Cover with cheese slices, onion, and dill pickle. Add corned beef, and top with buttered crust. To serve, cut through from top to bottom in 1-inch slices, and secure with toothpicks. Serves 5—6.

Note: For small hero sandwich, use 1/2 loaf French bread; use large, crusty rolls for individual hero sandwiches, sometimes called "torpedoes."

Deluxe Ham Loaf

    1 pound ground ham
    1 pound ground fresh pork
    2 eggs, slightly beaten
1 1/2 cups milk
    2 teaspoons prepared mustard
1 1/4 teaspoons salt
    2 cups dry bread crumbs
  1/2 teaspoon summer savory
  1/4 teaspoon sage
  1/4 teaspoon dry mustard
    Black pepper to taste

Mix ingredients in order given, and pack into deep 9″ x 5″ x 3″ greased loaf pan. Cover with foil, and bake at 350°F. 1 hour. Uncover, and bake 20 minutes longer. Remove any fat around loaf with baster, and invert on heated platter. Slice. Serves 6—8.

Note: If soft bread crumbs are used, reduce milk to 1 cup.

Spiced Cherry Sauce

    1 (15-ounce) can sweetened pitted red cherries
  1/3 cup water
    Juice of 1/2 orange
    2 tablespoons white vinegar
    1 stick cinnamon, broken
    6 whole cloves
    2 tablespoons cornstarch
    3 tablespoons cold water

Drain cherries, reserving juice. Mix next 5 ingredients with cherry juice, and simmer, covered, 20 minutes. Remove spices. Combine cornstarch with water, and add to juice. Cook, stirring, until thickened and clear. Add drained cherries. Serve hot over ham loaf. Serves 6—8.

Macaroons

  1/8 teaspoon salt
    2 egg whites
  3/4 cup sugar
  1/2 teaspoon vanilla extract
    1 cup cornflakes
    2 cups shredded coconut

Beat salt and egg whites together until shiny peaks form; then beat in sugar gradually, and beat until very stiff. Add vanilla, and fold in cornflakes and coconut with a fork. Drop by heaping teaspoons onto well-greased cookie

sheets, and form into mounds. Bake at 300°F. 20 minutes. Remove at once from pan, using spatula. If macaroons stick to pan, return to oven to reheat, or place sheet on wet cloth. Makes 2 1/2 dozen.

THURSDAY

BREAKFAST	LUNCHEON	DINNER
Fresh fruit	*Combination*	*Savory Beef-*
Cold cereal	*Salad Plate*	*Vegetable*
Toasted waffles	Hard-cooked	*Casserole*
with syrup	eggs	Broccoli
Coffee Milk	Sherbet	Crisp relishes
	Cookies	*Chilled Baked*
	Tea Milk	*Pears*
		Coffee Tea Milk

Combination Salad Plate

  1/2 cup grated carrot
  1/2 cup diced celery
1 1/2 cups shredded cabbage
    Drained cooked leftover vegetables (peas, beans, asparagus)
    1 tablespoon chopped chives or onion
    Mayonnaise
    4 lettuce cups
    Cucumber slices
    Radishes or cherry tomatoes
    Hard-cooked egg slices
    Cheese strips

Combine first 6 ingredients, and arrange in mounds in centers of lettuce cups. Add a few overlapping cucumber slices to each plate, and garnish with radishes or tomatoes, egg slices and strips of cheese. Serves 4.

Savory Beef-Vegetable Casserole

    2 onions, sliced
    2 tablespoons bacon drippings
  3—4 fresh, peeled tomatoes, diced
    2 stalks celery, sliced
  3—4 new carrots, scraped and quartered
    1 teaspoon monosodium glutamate (optional)
  1/2 teaspoon salt
    2 tablespoons ketchup
    1 bay leaf
1 1/2—2 cups diced leftover pot roast
  1/2 cup or more leftover gravy
  2—3 cups cooked, seasoned, diced potatoes
  1/2 cup grated Cheddar cheese

Sauté onions in drippings 2—3 minutes. Add tomatoes, celery and carrots. Turn heat low, and cover. Let mixture simmer about 5 minutes. Stir in next 6 ingredients, and heat thoroughly. If necessary, pour in a little water; amount will depend on thickness of gravy, but avoid making mixture too liquid. Taste for seasoning, and remove bay leaf. Scrape mixture into greased 1 1/2-quart casserole or deep oblong baking dish. Spread potatoes over top, and press down lightly. Sprinkle with cheese, and bake at 350°F. 35—

40 minutes or until potatoes brown and meat mixture is bubbly. Serves 6.

Note: Condensed canned mushroom, chicken, vegetable or meat soup may be used instead of gravy.

Chilled Baked Pears

    6 large firm pears
    12 whole cloves
    1/4 cup maple syrup
    1/4 cup orange juice

Halve pears lengthwise; peel, core and discard stem and blossom ends. Pierce each half with 2 cloves. Place, rounded sides up, in baking dish. Mix maple syrup and orange juice, and pour over fruit. Cover, and bake in oven at 350°F. about 30 minutes or until fruit is tender when tested with fork. Chill before serving. Serves 6.

VARIATION:

* *Baked Pears with Honey*: Substitute 1/4 cup each honey and water for maple syrup and orange juice.

FRIDAY

BREAKFAST	LUNCHEON	DINNER
Fresh grapes	*Barbecued*	*French Onion*
Toasted English	*Hot Dogs*	*Soup*
muffins	*Fresh Fruit*	*Paisley Rice*
Bacon Jelly	*Compote*	Carrot curls
Coffee Milk	Tea Milk	*Ginger-*
		Pineapple
		Sherbet
		Coffee Milk Tea

Barbecued Hot Dogs

    1/2 cup ketchup or chili sauce
    1 cup tomato juice
    2 tablespoons vinegar
    2 tablespoons brown sugar
    1 tablespoon prepared mustard
    1/2 cup chopped onion
    1/4 cup chopped celery
    1/4 cup chopped green pepper
    1 pound frankfurters
    10 hot finger rolls

Combine the first 8 ingredients in skillet or saucepan, and bring to a boil. Cover, and simmer 2—3 minutes. Add frankfurters, and cover again. Cook until frankfurters are thoroughly heated and glazed, about 3 minutes. Lift each frankfurter into heated roll, using tongs or fork, and spoon sauce over each. Serve at once. Makes 10 hot dogs.

Fresh Fruit Compote

    3 firm ripe pears
    1 large peach
    6 fresh apricots
    1 cup sugar
    3/4—1 cup water
    1 tablespoon or more lemon juice

Thinly peel pears and peach, halve and core. Wash apricots, but do not peel. Halve, and remove pits. Combine sugar and water in saucepan, and heat to boiling. Put in pears, and cover. Let simmer gently 2—3 minutes. Add peach and apricot halves, and simmer 4—5 minutes more. With slotted spoon, remove cooked fruit to serving bowl. Boil syrup a few minutes until it thickens slightly. Remove from heat, and add lemon juice, judging amount according to sweetness of fruit syrup. Pour over fruit. Chill thoroughly before serving. Serves 6.

Note: Various other fruits may be used in this simple compote. Washed cherries (do not pit) should be simmered 6—7 minutes. With plums, prick skins before adding, and cook until just tender. Strawberries, raspberries and blackberries should not be cooked on stove. After washing, place in bowl with cooked fruits to mellow in hot syrup.

Paisley Rice

    2 1/2 cups water
    1 chicken-bouillon cube
    1/2 clove garlic, stuck on toothpick
    1/2 bay leaf
    1 cup long-grain rice
    1 tablespoon grated onion
    1/4 cup *French Dressing*
    1—2 teaspoons soy sauce
    1/4 pound fresh mushrooms, sliced
    1/4 cup diced pimento
    1/4 cup slivered black olives
    1/2 cup toasted almonds
    1 cup diced chicken
    1 cup cooked shrimp
    Salt and pepper to taste
    Curly endive

Bring first 4 ingredients to boil, and stir in rice. Cover, and turn heat low. Allow to simmer until rice is tender, about 20 minutes (the water will be completely absorbed) . Stir rice, and make sure bottom of pan is quite dry. Lift out garlic and bay leaf, and stir in onion and dressing. Add next 7 ingredients, and heat thoroughly, but do not cook any further. Season with salt and black pepper. Turn out on serving platter, and garnish with curly endive. Pass mayonnaise or a bowl of sour cream with chopped chives. Serves 6.

Ginger-Pineapple Sherbet

    1 envelope plain gelatine
    1/4 cup cold water
    1 cup boiling water
    1 cup sugar
    1/4 cup lemon juice
    3 cups ginger ale
    1 cup pineapple juice

Soften gelatine in cold water. Combine boiling water and sugar in small saucepan, and heat until sugar is melted. Add gelatine, and stir until dissolved. Cool, and add lemon juice, ginger ale and pineapple juice. Pour into freezer trays. Place in refrigerator until mixture is thoroughly chilled. Set in freezer, and freeze until mushy, stirring occasionally. Turn into bowl, and beat until light. Return to freezer trays, and freeze until firm. Serves 6—8.

SATURDAY

BREAKFAST	LUNCHEON	DINNER
Bing cherries	*Fluffy Omelets*	Tomato juice
Oatmeal	Crisp relishes	*Jellied Salmon*
Toast	Fresh fruit	*Loaf*
Marmalade	Cookies	Potato chips
Coffee Milk	Tea Milk	*Paprika*
		Cucumber
		Orange Tapioca
		with
		Strawberries
		Coffee Tea Milk

Fluffy Omelet

       3 tablespoons butter or margarine
     1/2 teaspoon salt
       4 eggs, separated
       2 tablespoons milk
         Pepper to taste

Heat butter or margarine in large skillet over low heat. Add salt to egg whites, and beat to form stiffly pointed peaks. Beat egg yolks (with same beater) until thick. Add milk and pepper to egg yolks, stirring until blended. Fold egg yolks gently into whites. Pour egg mixture into skillet. Cook 5 minutes on top of range, moving skillet gently several times. Put under broiler until omelet is light brown. When set, crease through center, fold 1/2 over with spatula and roll omelet from skillet to heated platter. Serves 2.

Note: Allow 2 eggs for each serving, and never try to make an omelet using more than 4 eggs.

Jellied Salmon Loaf

       1 envelope plain gelatine
     1/2 cup cold water
     3/4 cup Italian-style salad dressing
       2 tablespoons lemon juice
       1 cup chopped celery
     1/2 cup stuffed olives, sliced
       1 tablespoon chopped parsley
       1 teaspoon salt
         Dash pepper
       1 (1-pound) can salmon
         Lettuce
         Olive slices

Soften gelatine in water 5 minutes; then heat in double boiler over hot water until dissolved. Stir in salad dressing, lemon juice, celery, stuffed olives, chopped parsley and seasonings. Discard skin from salmon. Mash salmon bones, salmon and juice together, and add to vegetable mixture.

Chill, stirring occasionally, until mixture thickens; then scrape into oiled 7″ x 4″ loaf pan. Chill until set. Unmold on lettuce, and garnish with olive slices. Serves 4.

Paprika Cucumber

       1 cucumber
         Wine vinegar
         Paprika

Peel cucumber, and slice very thin. Cover with wine vinegar and generous sprinkling of paprika. Chill a few minutes before serving. Serves 2.

Orange Tapioca with Strawberries

     1 1/3 cups skim milk
       1/3 cup quick-cooking tapioca
       1/2 cup sugar
       1/4 teaspoon salt
     1 1/2 teaspoons grated orange rind
         1 teaspoon vanilla extract
       2/3 cup chilled evaporated milk
         2 tablespoons lemon juice
       1—2 cups fresh hulled strawberries, sliced and lightly
             sweetened

Heat skim milk, and stir in tapioca. Cook 5 minutes, stirring. Remove from heat, and add sugar, salt, orange rind and vanilla. Chill mixture. Beat evaporated milk until fluffy. Add lemon juice, and beat until stiff. Fold tapioca mixture into whipped milk. Chill thoroughly. To serve, spoon strawberries into 6 fruit bowls, and spoon tapioca cream over top. Serves 6.

POINTERS ON SOME FAVORITE BEVERAGES

For good coffee, start with clean pot and grind suitable to method used. Measure both coffee and water accurately; for medium strength, 2 tablespoons coffee to 6 ounces water. If your method involves cloth filters, keep them in clean cold water when not in use; replace with new ones every 2 weeks. Avoid buying large quantities of ground coffee or leaf tea; flavor is fresher when supply is regularly renewed and kept closely covered. Don't boil reheated coffee—it will have a bitter taste. For good tea, start with fresh water, never water left in kettle.

Percolator Coffee

Measure cold water into percolator. Measure medium-grind coffee into basket; set basket in water. Cover, and place percolator over medium heat. When coffee begins to "perk," reduce heat, and percolate slowly 7—8 minutes. Remove basket and serve.

Drip Coffee

Hot water is allowed to seep through fine-grained coffee while pot stands in warm place but not over direct heat. Heat lower container first by scalding with boiling water. Set coffee holder in place, and measure coffee into it. Set top compartment in place, and slowly pour in freshly boiling water. Cover, and let stand until all liquid has dripped through.

Vacuum Coffee

Measure cold water into lower bowl of coffee maker. Place filter in upper bowl. Measure correct amount of fine-grind coffee into it; set upper bowl in place over lower bowl, and twist to make airtight seal. Turn heat to medium. When nearly all water has risen, turn off. Stir, to mix coffee and water. Cover, and let stand while brew filters through. Remove upper bowl.

Hot Tea

Allow 2 teaspoons leaf tea or 1 tea bag for each 1 1/2 cups boiling water. When water in kettle gets hot, pour a little into teapot; allow pot to heat thoroughly; then empty it. Measure tea into pot and add required amount of fresh boiling water. Brew tea 3—5 minutes, letting pot stand in warm place. Remove tea bags.

Iced Tea

Because ice dilutes the brew, it is necessary to make tea extra strong. Use 4 teaspoons tea leaves for 2 measuring cups boiling water. Make tea in regular pot, and allow to stand in warm place 5 minutes. Pour into tall glasses filled with chipped ice. Serve with lemon wedges, orange slices or sprigs of mint and sugar.

Instant Coffee and Tea

Find brands that suit your taste, and follow directions on labels. Instant powders are particularly useful for making iced coffee and tea in a hurry.

Cocoa

For 6 servings, mix 5 tablespoons cocoa, 5 tablespoons sugar, and a dash of salt in saucepan. Add 1 cup cold water, and mix together; cook, stirring, over medium heat until thickened and bubbling. Stir in 3 1/2 cups milk; keep stirring and heat just to boiling point. Remove pan from heat, and pour into serving cups or mugs. A drop or 2 of vanilla extract may be added.

Before attempting to reduce your weight, consult your physician. He will advise you on the basis of your age, frame, activities and "ideal" body weight. He will also suggest how much you should limit your calorie intake and give you a diet plan to follow.

In order to lose 1 pound of fat, you must take in about 3,500 calories per week fewer than you need to maintain your weight, which means that if you want to lose 2 pounds a week, you must reduce your caloric intake 1,000 calories a day below your maintenance needs.

Faster weight loss is not usually recommended, for it doesn't give you a chance to re-educate your eating habits so that you won't gain the lost pounds right back.

Do Not Skip Essentials

The basic foods that you are careful to include in the family menus each day should continue to be part of any reducing diet. There should be plenty of lean meat, fish, eggs, milk and milk products; fruits and vegetables in variety, including a little plain baked or boiled potato; whole wheat or enriched cereals and bread; and even a small amount of fat for certain food elements and flavor. Stunt diets, fad foods and pills have no place in sensible weight control.

Enjoy Your Family Meals, but

Omit some of the high-calorie items. Eat your roast beef without gravy, your salad without mayonnaise, your breakfast cereal without sugar. A rich sauce on cooked vegetables can play havoc with your calorie counting; reserve your own portion without sauce before sending the vegetable dish to the table. Have an egg soft-cooked or poached, not fried. Use skim milk, lemon juice for vegetables, commercial low-calorie salad dressings, water-packed tuna, artificially sweetened fruits and beverages.

Keep Servings Small

Avoid large portions generally. Get used to small servings, and eat slowly—and your appetite will be satisfied. Banish second helpings entirely, and don't eat tidbits of this or that in the kitchen as you put leftovers away. This little routine, perfectly natural though it is, has added unwieldy pounds to generations of homemakers.

Between-meal Nibbles

These snacks can help you stay with a reducing plan, as long as you count the calories and include the extras in the total day's intake. You will be less ravenous for lunch if you have a cup of coffee or an apple in mid-morning. A celery stick or a glass of skim milk or tea with lemon may be just what you need at 4 p.m. But sweet soft drinks or doughnuts should be banned. Be discriminating about your "nibbles."

Avoid These Temptations

Cut out entirely those rich concoctions that are high in starch, fat and sugar content. Cakes and pastry, whipped-cream desserts, candies, jams and deep-fried foods should not be permitted on your dieting program. Artificial sweeteners used in beverages and gelatine desserts or fresh fruit will satisfy your sweet tooth, yet keep your calories within bounds. Avoid alcoholic or malt beverages; they can defeat a reducing plan.

How Is Your Daily Score?

It will help a great deal if you keep a daily score card showing how many calories you are eating each day. At the end of each week weigh yourself, and check your weight against your calorie consumption. Persevere until you have said good-bye to excess pounds. And then determine that you can and will continue to control the kinds and quantities of food you eat.

Menus and Recipes for Calorie Counters

Good basic eating habits will keep you fit while you slim. The measure of a successful reducing diet is whether or not you also learn precisely how much you can eat without gaining weight.

A good breakfast is particularly important for the weight watcher. Take your serving of unsweetened juice or fruit without sugar. Have a small helping of unsweetened cereal with milk. Or, instead of cereal, have a soft-cooked or poached egg. A thin slice of toast lightly buttered may be included, but skip jams and jellies, except the dietetic kind. Coffee or tea adds no calories; use milk instead of cream, artificial sweeteners instead of sugar.

Using this basic breakfast and menus like the following ones for a week's lunches and dinners, you can keep your caloric intake at 1,200—1,500 calories daily, depending on sizes of servings.

* Recipes are given for items printed in *italics*.

* Use low-calorie salad dressings.

* Use unsweetened or artificially sweetened fruits.

* Add a glass of skim milk at lunch or dinner.

SUNDAY

DINNER

Roast turkey, 2 ounces	190
Mashed yams, 4 ounces	114
Lettuce wedge, 1/4 head	13
Rye roll and 1 pat butter	115
Lemon ice, 1/2 cup	72
	504

SUPPER

Salami, 1 slice on hard roll	120
Sliced beets (1/3 cup), sliced egg (1/3 cup)	80
Apple Cloud, 1 serving	63
	263

MONDAY

LUNCH

Consommé, 1 cup	26
Hamburger (2 ounces) on roll	251
Coleslaw, 1/2 cup	24
Small banana	85
	386

DINNER

Broiled salmon (7 ounces) with lemon	250
Small baked potato with yogurt	100
Green Beans Italian, 1/2 cup	27
Dietetic butterscotch pudding, 1/2 cup	60
	437

TUESDAY

LUNCH

Vegetable juice, 1 cup	40
Open-faced grilled cheese sandwich (1 slice cheese)	187
Dill pickle, 1 large	11
Plums, 2 red	50
	288

DINNER

Pan-broiled liver and onions	597
Paprika cauliflower, 1 cup	22
Tossed green salad, 1 cup	15
Apricot Bavarian, 1/2 cup	59
	693

WEDNESDAY

LUNCH

Chicken broth, 1 cup	18
Cottage cheese, 1/2 cup	97
Canned fruit, 1/2 cup	31
Whole wheat roll	85
Small pat of butter	35
Dietetic cherry gelatine, 1/2 cup	59
	325

DINNER

Veal chop, 3 1/2 ounces	220
Peas with mushrooms, 2/3 cup	70
Cucumber salad	18
Cinnamon Baked Apple, 1 medium	58
Skim milk, 8 ounces	82
	448

THURSDAY

LUNCH
Vegetable beef soup, 1 cup	65
Egg salad (2 eggs)	160
Pumpernickel, 1 slice	62
Celery hearts, 2	17
Low-calorie dressing, 1 tablespoon	24
Cantaloupe, 1/2	90
	–––
	418

DINNER
Curried Crab	144
Rice, 2/3 cup	109
Chopped green pepper, chopped tomato chutney, pineapple chunks, 1 cup	40
Lime sherbet, 1/2 cup	120
	–––
	413

FRIDAY

LUNCH
Clear tomato soup, 1 cup	80
Crackers, 2	34
Tuna salad, 1/2 cup	145
Lettuce	9
Grapes, 2/3 cup	67
	–––
	335

DINNER
Spicy Herb-baked Chicken, 6 ounces	190
Carrots, 2/3 cup	31
Lettuce, 2 leaves	9
Tomato, 1 small	22
Angel Food Cake, 2-inch slice	108
Skim milk, 8 ounces	88
	–––
	448

SATURDAY

LUNCH
Vegetable soup, 1 cup	64
Frankfurter	153
Roll	118
Mustard	7
Sauerkraut, 1/4 cup	8
Fresh pear, medium	63
	–––
	413

DINNER
Poached Halibut with Horseradish Sauce, 6 ounces	225
Boiled potato, medium	76
Broccoli, 2/3 cup	26
Strawberry-pineapple cup, 2/3 cup	45
Skim milk, 8 ounces	88
	–––
	460

Apple Cloud

        1 envelope plain gelatine
    1 3/4 cups apple juice
        1/2 teaspoon non-caloric liquid sweetener
        1 egg white, stiffly beaten

Soften gelatine in 1/2 cup apple juice. Heat over boiling water until dissolved, and add re-

maining juice and sweetener. Chill until syrupy, and fold into egg white. Pile into sherbet glasses. Serves 4–6.

Green Beans Italian

        1 (15-ounce) can green beans
    1/4 cup low-calorie Italian dressing
        2 tablespoons chopped onion
    1/4 teaspoon prepared horseradish
    1/2 teaspoon dry mustard
    1/4 teaspoon lemon juice
            Dash pepper
            Lettuce

Drain green beans; put in bowl. Make mixture of dressing, onions, horseradish, mustard, lemon juice and pepper, and pour over beans. Mix well. Cover, and marinate in refrigerator 30 minutes. Drain, and serve beans in lettuce cups. Serves 4.

Apricot Bavarian

        3 (8-ounce) cans dietetic apricots
        5 teaspoons plain gelatine
            Non-caloric liquid sweetener
    3/4 cup skim milk powder
    1/2 cup icy cold water
        2 teaspoons lemon juice

Drain 1/2 cup apricot juice from the apricots into a glass measuring cup, and add the gelatine. Stand the cup in a pan of boiling water, and stir until melted. Puree apricots and remaining juice in blender, or press through a sieve. Stir in dissolved gelatine and enough liquid sweetener to suit your taste. Chill until thickened. Beat skim milk powder and water together until thick. Add lemon juice, and beat until stiff. Fold in apricot mixture, and spoon into comports. Chill. Makes 8 servings.

Cinnamon Baked Apples

        4 medium apples
        1 teaspoon non-caloric liquid sweetener
        1 teaspoon cinnamon

Set oven at 400°F. Core apples, and pare 1/2 inch down from tops. Sprinkle each apple with 1/4 teaspoon liquid sweetener and 1/4 teaspoon cinnamon. Wrap each apple in aluminum foil, and bake in shallow baking dish at 400°F. 25 minutes or until tender. Serves 4.

Curried Crab

    1/4 cup chopped onion
        1 tablespoon butter or margarine
        3 tablespoons flour
    3/4 teaspoon salt
    1/8 teaspoon pepper
        1 teaspoon curry powder
    1 1/2 cups skim milk
        2 (6-ounce) cans crabmeat, drained and flaked

Sauté onion in butter or margarine until transparent. Remove pan from heat; add flour, salt, pepper and curry powder. Mix well. Add skim milk; blend well; stir and cook until mixture thickens. Add crabmeat; heat 5 minutes. Serves 4.

Spicy Herb-baked Chicken

    1 (2 1/2-pound) broiling chicken
    2 tablespoons low-calorie French dressing
    1/2 teaspoon onion powder
    1/2 teaspoon ginger
    1/2 teaspoon mixed herbs
    3/4 cup boiling water
    1 chicken-bouillon cube

Have chicken cut in quarters. Discard fat and heavy skin. Brush chicken with a mixture of the next 4 ingredients. Place in a covered baking dish, skin side down, and pour in a mixture of water and crumbled bouillon cube. Bake, covered, at 350°F. 30 minutes. Turn chicken, and bake, uncovered, 30 minutes longer. Serves 4.

Poached Halibut with Horseradish Sauce

    2 cups water
    4 onion slices
    1 tablespoon chopped parsley
    1 bay leaf
    1 teaspoon salt
    4 (1 3/4 pounds) halibut steaks
    1 tablespoon butter or margarine
    1 tablespoon flour
    2 teaspoons prepared drained horseradish

Put water, onion, parsley, bay leaf and salt in a large skillet. Simmer 10 minutes. Put in halibut steaks, and simmer 10–12 minutes or until fish flakes. Remove steaks from skillet; save 1 1/2 cups liquid. Keep fish hot. In a small saucepan melt butter or margarine. Add flour, and stir until smooth. Gradually add 1 1/2 cups liquid saved from poaching, stirring constantly. Still stirring, simmer 10 minutes. Remove from heat; add horseradish, and mix well. Serve sauce over halibut steaks. Serves 4.

PACKING AN APPETIZING LUNCHBOX

What's in a lunchbox? Good food, attractively packed, and perhaps a surprise.

The best sandwiches are those that have generous and substantial fillings between not-too-thick slices of bread that are spread right to the edges with butter or margarine. The spread adds nourishment and also helps to keep the filling from soaking into the bread and making it soggy.

Vary the bread from day to day—whole or cracked wheat, enriched white, dark or light rye, fruit bread, rolls, hot dog or hamburger buns.

Pack fillings with proteins—meat, fish, eggs, cheese, nut butters—and season to taste. Here are some suggestions:

Meat

Use several thin layers of cooked meat rather than 1 thick slice; they make a more generous filling and are easier to eat.

Add a little chili sauce, chopped parsley, grated onion or horseradish to butter for meat-filled sandwiches.

Put raw vegetables (carrots, celery, cucumber, onion or crisp spinach leaves) through food chopper with cooked meat.

Fish

Flake or mash drained canned salmon; include crushed bones for extra food value. Add sliced green pepper, olive, celery or parsley; sprinkle with lemon juice.

Use canned tuna with the same additions.

Leftover fish can be flaked and made into delicious mixtures; moisten with salad dressing or tomato juice.

Eggs

Chopped hard-cooked eggs, seasoned and moistened with cream or salad dressing, are always a favorite. Occasionally add a little grated onion, chopped chives or green onion, chopped crisp bacon, flaked sardine or sliced stuffed olives.

Cheese

There is a wide range of cheese products, and there are many ready-to-use cheese spreads. You can make your own spreads, using either cream cheese or grated Cheddar as bases. Season to taste, and blend to desired consistency with a little milk or cream. Store, covered, in refrigerator—ready for quick spreading with or without additional fillings.

Try cream cheese spread with ground ham, or chopped, dried fruit and nuts.

Use Cheddar spread with hard-cooked eggs or chopped, crisp bacon.

Some Sandwich Combinations

COLD

Salami, Swiss cheese and sliced green pepper on Italian bread
Smoked salmon and sliced onion on pumpernickel
Chopped chicken livers, bacon and tomato on rye
Corned beef or pastrami and mustard on rye or pumpernickel

Herring salad on dark bread of any kind
Liverwurst and relish on whole wheat toast
Cold roast pork with horseradish on rye
Cream cheese on date-nut bread
Sliced chicken and Russian dressing on whole wheat bread
Tuna fish salad and sliced egg on roll
Muenster cheese and sliced tomato, sprinkled with oregano, on roll
Sliced frankfurter and beans on rye
Cream cheese and walnuts on raisin bread
Deviled ham, relish and mayonnaise on white bread
Pork roll and mustard on rye bread

HOT

Meatballs in small amount of spaghetti sauce, Italian bread
Sautéed sweet sausage and peppers, Italian bread
Frankfurters wrapped in fried bacon, rolls
Brown-and-serve sausage patties, rolls
Chili, buns
Barbecued beef in barbecue sauce, buns

To make a hot sandwich possible in a lunchbox, package filling in a wide-mouthed vacuum container. Wrap bread separately.

For variety, pack salad-type fillings such as chopped meat, flaked fish or hard-cooked eggs in small jars with screw tops or in individual plastic containers. Accompany with buttered buns or sliced bread.

A small container will also carry salads of vegetables or fruits. Lettuce will wilt if it is combined in a salad or sandwich, but a crisp wedge wrapped separately keeps well in the lunchbox. Shredded cabbage with green pepper, pimento, diced apple, well-drained crushed pineapple and a small amount of dressing make a not-too-perishable salad. Grated raw carrot with raisins or chopped dates, moistened with dressing, makes another easily transportable salad.

A cooked chicken leg, cold cooked spareribs, a round of liverwurst, slices of cold meat rolled up and fastened with toothpicks, a deviled egg or a wedge of cheese will carry well when wrapped in aluminum foil or plastic wrap.

Fresh fruit can be included as well as containers of fruit salad, stewed or canned fruit or berries. Raw carrots, turnip strips, radishes, small whole tomatoes, Swiss cheese and celery, stuffed with cheese or plain, can also be included.

Pies, if they have double crusts and are not too juicy, can be carried in individual portions. Use pie-shaped plastic containers, or make triangular "plates" for pie. Cut thick cardboard slightly larger than pie wedge, and cover with aluminum foil. Place piece of pie on it; then cover all with aluminum foil or plastic wrap.

Tarts, turnovers, cakes with firm icing, doughnuts, cupcakes and cookies are always welcome.

The beverage, if it is milk, should be chilled and carried in a vacuum bottle, which is equally useful for hot liquids.

If you prepare lunches the night before, be sure to keep perishables in the refrigerator until final packing. Never combine protein foods with salad dressing, but you can put dressing in a small plastic container to be added at lunchtime.

Frozen Sandwiches. If you have a home freezer you can prepare sandwiches weeks ahead. Many kinds freeze perfectly. Taken from the freezer in the morning, they are just right for eating at noon and will be colder and fresher than otherwise. Spread with butter or margarine, then meat, fish or cheese fillings, etc. Do not freeze lettuce, tomato, cucumber or celery; and remember that cheese and cooked egg white get tough in the freezer.

CHAPTER TWO

Hearty Main Dishes

🌺

Dinner is usually the family's big meal of the day. It is a time to be together and a meal to enjoy unhurriedly. A good dinner menu needs planning.

When you start to plan a meal, think first of the members of your family—the foods they like and the amounts they need. Keep in mind which foods are in season and the best buys at that particular time of year. For your sake, as well as theirs, it's wise to plan for wide variety.

The main dish should be decided first and then the accompanying appetizer, vegetables, salad, bread and dessert.

A good starting point when you are choosing the main dish is "Canada's Food Guide," which advises daily servings of meat, fish, poultry, eggs, cheese or dried beans, peas or nuts. You'll be sure then that your family is receiving an adequate supply of essential proteins.

But good, nutritious foods in themselves don't always provide the necessary appetite appeal. So remember that your menu must have color harmony. Visualize the servings together on a plate. You can then foresee that the rich, dark color of beets will lose much of its attraction next to the bright red of tomatoes. And you will realize the need for something brighter than boiled parsnips to offset pale mounds of mashed potatoes.

Flavors, too, should harmonize and complement one another. Avoid 2 strong-flavored foods, like onions and turnips, at the same meal, although each combines well with mild-flavored food.

Keep the meal interesting by avoiding repetition. Shrimp cocktail may be delectable, but it takes a little of the zest out of a main fish dish. The textures of your foods are important too. Two mashed vegetables should not be served together. Instead, replace one with something that contributes shape and texture. When your main course is a creamed dish or other soft food,

offer crisp, raw vegetables in a salad or on a relish tray. Another way to ensure variety is to vary temperatures thoughout the meal. Hot soup can be a tempting introduction to a cold main dish, and a chilled dessert is often a delightful climax to a substantial hot meal.

Maintain appetite appeal by serving new and different main courses. And always plan your main dish with thought for the preparation time it requires. Avoid steak or chops, which require watchful last-minute cooking, when you are having a large group for dinner. Instead, choose a roast or a big casserole, which can be started well ahead and allowed to cook slowly. Then, before dinner, you'll be free to enjoy your guests. Casseroles or other specialties that can be prepared at your leisure and stored in the refrigerator or freezer are wise choices for busy days.

Be sure that the main dish fits the type of service you plan. For a casual buffet meal, fork foods, like croquettes, hash or creamed dishes, are much easier to serve and eat than is a roast or thick steak.

Whatever you plan for your main course, there is one important rule to follow to ensure that the dish will be at its best: *Always serve hot foods piping hot and cold foods icy cold.* The plates for hot foods should be warm. If you have no warming oven, heat plates by placing them in your oven, turned low, 5 minutes just before serving. Plates for cold foods can be chilled in the refrigerator ahead of time.

POINTS TO KNOW ABOUT CARVING

Good carving depends chiefly on good tools, kept in good condition. A good knife, properly cared for, will last a lifetime, so it's worth investing in quality. The basic carving set consists of a knife with a 9-inch blade, a fork with long tines and a guard to protect the carver's hand and a steel for honing the knife edge.

As well as the standard "carving knife," there are others—the meat slicer, for example, which has a slender flexible blade and is useful for carving poultry and ham, in which there is a lot of bone. Choose your basic "wardrobe" of cutting tools; learn how to use them and how to care for them.

Learn this honing technique: Hold steel in left hand, with thumb *over* handle and steel pointing upward and away from the body. Hold knife in right hand, and place heel of knife blade (the end near the handle) against the far tip of the underside of the steel. Draw knife edge *down and diagonally across* steel, ending stroke with knife point at handle of steel. Repeat motion with *other* side of knife edge against *other* side of steel.

A few such quick strokes before each use of the knife (the way your butcher does it) will keep your knife sharp. Professional sharpening is also necessary occasionally.

Carving Tips

A large roast can be carved more easily when it has stood for a few minutes after cooking. Use a heated platter large enough to leave room for the carved slices, or have another heated platter ready. Heat all plates because meat cools quickly. Cut across the grain—long meat fibers are tough and stringy. Plan servings before you begin so that choicest portions can be divided equally among all. Don't cut second helpings before they are wanted; that way meat will stay hot and juicy. Lay slices with newly cut surfaces up, to save juices, which escape more freely when meat is first cut. Carving is usually easier when the carver is standing up.

BUYING AND COOKING MEAT

Meat is one of the most expensive items in the family food budget. An average family of 4 will eat more than 700 pounds of meat in a year. It is thus to your advantage to know the various kinds and cuts of meat and how best to prepare them to get the most value. To stretch your meat budget, the trick is to balance your purchases of such tender, expensive cuts as porterhouse steaks with some of the cheaper cuts. The latter have the same food values, but may require more time and attention to prepare.

How Much To Buy

Your family's ages and tastes will to some extent affect the amount of meat required in your household. But, when you are estimating how much meat to buy, keep in mind also the amount of bone, fat and gristle in each particular cut. They may account for 10—15 percent of the total weight. Shrinkage in cooking can double even this percentage of waste. Here is a guide to the approximate weights of meat to buy for 1 average serving.

Roasts, boneless, 1/4—1/3 pound
Roasts, bone in, 1/3—1/2 pound
Steaks, 1/3—1/2 pound
Chops, 1/3—1/2 pound
Stewing meat, boneless, 1/4 pound
Stewing meat, bone in, 1/2 pound
Ground meat, 1/4 pound
Liver, 1/4 pound
Kidneys, 1/4 pound
Heart, 1/4 pound

Safeguards in Selection

Meats with the Federal inspection stamp have been inspected for your protection (see Chapter 1). The dye in the stamp is quite harmless, by the way.

Hanging and aging of meat vary with each type. All beef should be properly aged for flavor and tenderness—1—2 weeks or perhaps longer before cutting. Top-quality lamb is sometimes aged a few days only. Pork and veal do not require aging but are merely chilled before cutting.

When buying frozen meats, be sure that they are thoroughly frozen. Check that the wrappings are not broken. Frozen meats that have "freezer burn"—patches that appear white and dry—have received poor storage handling; they will lack flavor and texture.

Success with Seasoning

All fresh meats need some salt to bring out their full flavor. As salt tends to draw out juices, it is best to add it after meat has been cooked,

when roasting, broiling or pan-broiling. For braising or stewing, in which the rich flavored sauce is a main feature, the seasoning can be added to the dredging flour before initial browning of the meat.

Other seasonings, from bottled sauces to herbs, add zest to meat dishes. Experiment, and become familiar with the spices best suited to the meat types and your own taste. Freshly ground pepper and monosodium glutamate (a prepared chemical salt) enhance the flavor of any meat.

Methods of Cooking Meat

Good meats deserve careful cooking. Be sure to use the best method for each particular cut. An expensive oven roast should not be braised in moist heat, whereas a pot roast cut, costing perhaps 1/3 less, should.

Do not pierce meat with fork during cooking, for piercing releases natural juices that are so desirable for the final result. Use tongs and lifter for turning.

You can save juices and pan fat for gravy and sauces. If much fat accumulates in pan, pour it off from time to time.

When braising or stewing, keep liquid at a slow simmer. Boiling toughens meat fibers.

To Roast. Roasting is a dry-heat method for cooking large, tender cuts of meat. For a succulent result, use low-to-moderate temperatures. Do not sear, as it causes dryness and shrinkage.

The size, shape, fat covering and initial temperature of the meat all influence the length of the cooking period. A meat thermometer is the only dependable way to test the doneness of your roast.

1. Wipe meat with damp cloth or paper towel.
2. Place meat, fat side up, on rack in open pan in slow oven (325°F.).
3. Do not add water; do not cover pan.
4. Insert meat thermometer in thickest part of meat; be sure tip is not touching bone or fat.
5. Roast meat until thermometer registers desired internal temperature; internal temperature will rise about 10°F. after roast is removed from oven, so be sure to allow for it in determining when to remove roast.
6. Let roast stand at least 10 minutes in warm place before carving, to make carving easier.
7. Use drippings in pan to make gravy.

Frozen roasts cook more evenly if they are first thawed. Leave meat in wrapping while thawing. Allow 2 hours per pound when thawing at room temperature. Allow 24–36 hours to thaw a 4-pound roast in the refrigerator.

Cook immediately after thawing, following same procedure as for fresh meat. Once thawed, meat should not be refrozen.

Frozen meats may be cooked without thawing, but an additional 10–20 minutes per pound should be allowed. To ensure proper doneness, insert meat thermometer midway through estimated cooking period.

To Broil. Broiling is a dry-heat method of cooking small, tender cuts like steaks and chops. The kind of meat, thickness and desired degree of doneness all affect broiling time. Broiled meats will retain less fat than will fried meats, as it drips away during cooking. Manufacturer's directions for using broilers in gas and electric ranges vary. Follow the instructions supplied with your range for preheating broiler, positioning broiler door and so forth.

1. Snip fat around edge of meat with shears or knife to help prevent curling.
2. Place meat on rack of broiler pan at recommended distance from heat.
3. When meat is brown on 1 side, turn with tongs, and broil to desired doneness on other side.
4. Season, and serve.

To Pan-broil. Pan-broiling is a quick, top-of-the-stove method for cooking small, tender cuts of meat. Use heavy frying pan for even distribution of heat.

1. Heat pan, and grease it lightly with piece of fat cut from meat.
2. Snip fat edge of meat with shears or knife to prevent curling.
3. Brown meat on both sides, using tongs to turn; do not prick meat with fork while cooking.
4. Do not add extra fat.
5. Reduce heat, and complete cooking; do not cover pan except for meats like pork chops, which must always be thoroughly cooked.
6. Season, and serve.

To Braise. Braising is a moist-heat method for cooking less tender cuts of meat. They may be large pieces such as pot roast or small cuts such as shoulder chops. Use a heavy skillet or Dutch oven.

1. Coat meat in seasoned flour. Such boneless pieces as round or flank steak may be pounded to tenderize.
2. Brown meat well on all sides in hot fat.
3. Add small amount of liquid and any additional seasonings desired.
4. Cover kettle tightly to keep steam in during cooking; add more liquid, if needed while cooking.
5. Cook slowly until very tender over low heat on top of stove or in slow oven, 325°F. (if using oven, be sure that kettle and lid have heat-proof handles).
6. Uncover oven-cooked pot roasts for last 1/2 hour of cooking time for better color.

To Stew. Stewing is similar to braising, except that more liquid is generally used in order to provide ample, thick sauce with meat and vegetables. Less costly cuts of lamb, veal and beef are ideal for stewing.

1. Cut meat into small pieces, and dredge in flour according to recipe.
2. Brown in melted fat.
3. Cover with liquid—tomato juice, water, vegetable stock or wine.

4. Cover tightly and simmer until tender (if vegetables are to be cooked with meat, add to simmering stew at proper time, according to their cooking requirements).
5. Thicken stew with smooth paste made from equal parts flour and cold water; allow 2 tablespoons flour for each cup gravy.
6. Season to taste, and serve piping hot.

To Pressure-cook. Pressure-cooking is a fast, moist-heat method for cooking less tender cuts of meat. Follow the manufacturer's directions for each type of pressure saucepan. In general, the following steps apply.

1. Brown meat well on all sides, if directed.
2. Add small amount of liquid; vegetables may also be added at this time.
3. Cover, and cook for specified time.
4. Allow pressure saucepan to cool slowly to prevent juices from being drawn out of meat; but if vegetables were added with liquid, cool quickly.
5. If desired, vegetables may be added part way through the cooking time.

Barbecue and Rotisserie. In general, any meat that can be roasted or broiled can be successfully barbecued. Food may be barbecued on a flat grill over hot coals, on a turning spit close to heat source or under regular broiler of your range. Because of the closeness and intensity of the heat, it is important to coat and baste meat with rich, well-seasoned sauce to prevent drying out.

If less tender cuts of meat are to be used, an enclosed, moist-heat method is recommended. Wrap meat, with sauce, fat or such other accompaniments as vegetables in aluminum foil. Allow to cook until tender.

If you are using an oven rotisserie, study and follow directions for your specific equipment. It is particularly important to know maximum weights that your rotisserie motor can handle. Meat must be centered correctly on skewer to ensure even rotation. Always set a pan containing a little water under meat to catch drippings. When you are basting with sauce or liquid seasoning, a more desirable color can be obtained if you wait until the last hour of cooking. When very lean meat is to be cooked on rotisserie, tie a layer of suet or other firm fat around piece before cooking.

BEEF

Whether it is served as a choice roast for special company dinner or in an everyday stew for hearty family appetites, beef can fill the bill.

Beef in its great variety of cuts is one of the favorite meats. The rich, red color and firm, fine-grained texture of good beef are a constant challenge to the homemaker who enjoys mastering many different methods of preparation. And beef's tempting aroma and hearty flavor can be highlighted by many variations. Among the herbs, basil, thyme, marjoram and rosemary make good beef seasonings.

Beef is available in specific grades, each a different quality.

Know the Cuts

The tenderest cuts in a beef carcass come from the center back, chiefly the loin and ribs. From this area—the least exercised and therefore having the most delicate fiber—the highest-priced roasts and steaks are cut.

As you move towards the more exercised portions of the animal—the rump, shoulders, and shanks—the meat becomes leaner, coarser and less tender. And the cuts become cheaper. The nutritional value of these less tender cuts is as high as that of the tender cuts, but cooking methods must be varied accordingly.

Tender cuts of beef are at their best cooked with dry heat, as in roasting, broiling or pan-broiling. Less tender cuts develop full flavor and succulence when cooked with added moisture for sufficient time at low temperatures, as in braising, stewing, or pot-roasting. Other methods of tenderizing these cheaper cuts are grinding, waffling (minute steaks) and applying commercial tenderizer.

Keep in mind that one cut of beef may be purchased in several different ways: as a roast, boned and rolled or with the bone in or sliced as steak, for example. "Bone-in" roasts usually cost less per pound, but a rolled boneless piece has no bone, and the carving will be easier.

Your choice depends on your own personal taste, as cost works out about the same.

Tender Beef Steaks

The tender cuts are spoiled by overcooking, and some cooks like to marinate medium-tender cuts before broiling them.

These choice cuts from the least exercised portion of the carcass should be carefully cooked with a dry heat to retain their delicate texture and flavor. No liquid is added during the cooking period, and they are best cooked uncovered.

There is no hard-and-fast rule for cooking the moderately tender cuts of beef. They are the cuts (e.g. the rump) that fall between the 2 extremes of tender and least tender. The cooking methods therefore vary with the *grade* of beef from which the cuts come.

The higher-grade, moderately tender cuts may be cooked in the same way as tender cuts, by a dry-heat method. The same cuts from a lower-grade carcass should be cooked with moist heat, at low temperatures and for longer periods.

Quick Tips on Steak

Steaks for broiling to medium or rare must be at least 1 inch thick. Broiling heat will quickly penetrate a thinner steak and cook it well done without browning its surface. Allow about 5 minutes per side or 10 minutes total broiling time for a rare 1-inch steak, 12 minutes total time for medium. For well-done steak, place pan farther from heat, and allow 14—16 minutes total broiling time.

Fry thinner steaks if you like them medium or rare—a hot, lightly greased cast-iron frying pan or an electric pan at "steak" setting will give good results.

Roast Fillet of Beef (Beef Tenderloin)

1/3—1/2 pound beef fillet per serving
Fat bacon or salt pork
Mushroom caps, sautéed

Fillet is the most delicately tender beef and the most costly, in this case bought in a solid piece for oven roasting. Have the butcher lard the meat, or lay strips of fat bacon or salt pork over the top. Place in shallow pan, uncovered, and roast at 450°F. Allow about 30 minutes for rare, 40 for medium rare, 50 for well done. Serve on hot platter, garnished with sautéed mushroom caps.

Note: To be sure of the doneness you prefer, use a meat thermometer.

London Broil

1/2 cup orange marmalade
1/4 cup soy sauce
1/4 cup lemon juice
1 (2—2 1/2-pound) flank steak, about 3/4—1 inch thick

In large shallow dish, combine orange marmalade, soy sauce and lemon juice. Marinate steak at least 30 minutes, turning frequently. May be marinated, covered, up to 12 hours, with less frequent turning in refrigerator. Remove steak from marinade, and drain. Broil 3—4 inches from heat in preheated broiler, allowing 4 minutes per side for medium. Brush with remaining marinade while broiling if steak was marinated only briefly. Heat remaining marinade, and serve with steak. Serves 4—6.

Roast Beef Steak

1 teaspoon coarsely crushed pepper
1 (4-pound) sirloin tip steak, about 3 inches thick
4 cloves garlic, crushed
2 teaspoons salt
2 tablespoons butter or margarine
2 tablespoons olive oil

Press pepper into both sides of steak. Mix garlic with salt to make a paste. Spread on both sides of meat. Melt butter or margarine in large skillet; add olive oil. Fry meat on medium heat 5 minutes per side. Bake in 350° oven 35—45 minutes. Serves 6—8.

Boeuf en Gelée

2 (10-ounce) cans consommé
1/2 cup sherry
2 envelopes plain gelatine
1 clove garlic
1 bay leaf
1 cup thinly sliced carrots
1 cup thinly sliced onion rings
1/2 teaspoon salt
1 pound cooked, sliced roast beef
2 tablespoons chopped parsley

To consommé and sherry add enough water to measure 4 cups. In large bowl, blend unflavored gelatine with 1 cup of this beef liquid. Let soften 5 minutes. Add garlic and bay leaf. Dissolve by blending in remaining 3 cups boiling beef liquid. Set aside to cool. Discard garlic clove and bay leaf. Meanwhile, in small saucepan, cook carrots and onion rings with salt and 1 cup water. Simmer until just tender. Drain and cool. To assemble: Rinse a 1 1/2-quart mold with cold water. Drain, but do not dry. Pour in 1/2 cup beef liquid. Refrigerate 15 minutes or until set (or put in freezer 10 minutes). Arrange roast beef slices, rolled-up jelly roll fashion, cooked carrots and chopped parsley in layers over set aspic until you have used 1 pound beef slices, 1 cup cooked carrots, 1 cup cooked onions and 2 tablespoons chopped parsley. Fill to top of mold with remaining beef liquid. Refrigerate 2 hours or 30 minutes in freezer until firmly set. Unmold on a platter. Serves 6.

Note: To serve *en terrine* as in France, cook onions and carrots separately as above. Drain, and set aside. Cook about 1 cup green peas or baby lima beans until tender. Drain and set aside. Spread cooked onions in 1 1/2-quart serving dish, and sprinkle with parsley. Pour about 1 cup cool, but liquid, aspic over the onions, and chill until almost set. Arrange rolls of roast beef slices over the aspic in 1 layer, keeping the rolls towards the center. Spoon cooked carrots on either side of the rolls, and spoon peas at either ends. Carefully pour remaining aspic over the arrangement, and chill until set. At serving time, cut into chunks, slices, or wedges.

Spicy Rump Roast

       4-pound rump roast
    1 teaspoon salt
    1 cup vinegar
    1 teaspoon cinnamon
    1/2 teaspoon pepper
    1/2 teaspoon cloves
    1/2 teaspoon allspice
    1/4 teaspoon nutmeg

Wipe roast with clean, damp cloth. Blend all other ingredients into paste-like marinade. Place roast in dish that holds it snugly, and pour marinade over. Cover dish, and set in cool place 5–6 hours or longer, basting and turning meat occasionally. Preheat oven to 325°F. Place roast, fat side up, on rack in open pan. For medium rare, allow about 35 minutes per pound; for well done, 40 minutes. Serves 8.

Steak au Poivre

       1 tablespoon coarsely cracked pepper
    2–2 1/2 pounds porterhouse or sirloin steak, 1 inch thick
    2 tablespoons butter or margarine
    2 tablespoons chopped green onions
    1/2 cup beef stock or canned beef bouillon
    1/3 cup cognac
       Watercress

Wipe steak with damp paper towels. Press pepper well into each side of steak. Cover with waxed paper, and let stand at least 1/2 hour to let flavor of pepper penetrate meat. Pan-broil steak in lightly greased skillet, and cook to desired doneness. Remove to hot platter, and keep steaks warm. Pour off excess fat in skillet. Add 1 tablespoon butter or margarine and onions. Cook slowly 1 minute, but do not brown. Pour in stock, and cook briskly until liquid is reduced by 1/2. Add cognac, and boil rapidly to evaporate alcohol. Remove from heat, and gradually add remaining butter or margarine, cut in small pieces. Pour over steak on hot platter, and garnish with watercress. Serves 5–7.

Steak Sauce

    1/4 cup finely chopped onion
    2 tablespoons steak drippings or butter or margarine
    1/2 cup boiling water
    1 teaspoon Worcestershire sauce
    1/2 teaspoon dry mustard
    1/2 teaspoon salt
    1/8 teaspoon pepper
    1 egg, beaten

Sauté onion in drippings 5 minutes. Add remaining ingredients, except egg. Cover pan, and simmer 10 minutes. Just before serving steak, strain sauce, and pour slowly over beaten egg, beating constantly. Cook sauce, stirring 1 minute over low heat.

Note: Prepare this sauce while steak is being broiled.

Broiled Porterhouse Steak

    1 porterhouse steak, 1–1 1/2 inches thick
    1 clove garlic, cut
    2 tablespoons salad oil
    2 tablespoons red wine
    1/2 teaspoon Worcestershire sauce
    2 thickly sliced boiled potatoes
    1 large tomato, halved
    1 tablespoon butter or margarine, melted
       Salt and pepper to taste

Trim excess fat from steak, and gash remaining fat edge to prevent curling. Skewer tail close to steak. Rub each side with garlic. Combine salad oil, wine and Worcestershire sauce, and brush over steak. Leave at room temperature 20 minutes. Preheat broiler 10 minutes, and set broiling rack in place. Center steak on rack. Broil 5–6 minutes about 2 inches from heat. Turn steak with tongs to avoid piercing meat and losing juice. Add potatoes and tomato halves, brush with melted butter or margarine, season and continue broiling 3 minutes. Turn potatoes, brush again with butter, and broil 2–3 minutes longer. Remove steak to heated platter, and season. Garnish with vegetables. Serves 2.

Note: Carve steak in 1/2-inch strips, starting at bone and slicing toward you. Serve a slice of tenderloin and less tender portion to each person.

Fried Steaks (Argentine Style)

       4 egg yolks
    1 1/2 cups sifted flour
    1/2 cup milk
    1 clove garlic, chopped
    1 1/2 teaspoons salt
    1/2 teaspoon pepper
    1/2 teaspoon marjoram
    4 egg whites, stiffly beaten
    6 fillets of beef or 6 individual boneless sirloin steaks
    1 cup cooking oil

Beat egg yolks in bowl, and add half the flour and the milk, beating until smooth. Add remaining flour, garlic and seasonings, and beat again until smooth. Fold in egg whites carefully. Dip steaks in batter, coating well. Heat oil in skillet, and fry steaks 2 minutes on each side. Serves 6.

Less-tender Beef Cuts

There's a special way of cooking less tender cuts to bring out all their flavor and make them fork-tender. A tenderizing method is necessary. There are several. First, the cooking method must be different. Because these less tender cuts come from more used muscular parts of the animal, the fibers are tougher and there is more connective tissue. It takes long cooking in moisture to soften this meat and make it tender. This long, slow cooking, incidentally, adds considerably to the flavor of the meat, especially when subtle herbs and spices are used.

Another way to prepare such meats is with one of the commercial tenderizers, which are made from protein-digesting enzymes and are most effective on steaks and other thin cuts. They should not be used on roasts. Several kinds are available, plain and seasoned. Some methods of moist-heat cooking use marinades that add piquant flavor to meats and sauces to be served with them.

A good basic marinade is standard *French Dressing*, which is of course simply oil and vinegar. You can add soy sauce, a little dry mustard and 1 tablespoon sherry. Let meat stand in this marinade, turning it often, for anything from 1/2 hour to several days, as with *Sauerbraten*. Meat should be refrigerated, covered, for the marinating period.

Every nation has its characteristic ways of using these less tender cuts. What we call "stew" is closely related to what the Hungarians call "goulash" and the French call "ragoût." The differences are in the seasonings; the method remains the same. You will enjoy trying new recipes that provide variety and save you money.

Braised Stuffed Flank Steak

```
    2 cups Savory Bread Stuffing
    1 flank steak
    2 tablespoons fat
1–1 1/2 cups hot water
  1/2 teaspoon peppercorns
  1 1/2 teaspoons cider vinegar
      Pinch garlic salt
    1 beef-bouillon cube
    2 tablespoons flour
    2 tablespoons cold water
```

Pack dressing over unscored side of steak. Roll up as for long jelly roll; secure with skewers or string. Melt fat in heavy skillet or electric frying pan, and brown steak roll thoroughly over high heat. Reduce heat to simmer, adding 1 cup hot water and peppercorns and sprinkling meat with vinegar and garlic salt. Cover tightly, and simmer until tender—1 1/2–2 hours. Place steak on warm platter, and remove skewers or string. To liquid in pan add bouillon cube; boil until the latter dissolves. Make smooth paste of flour and 2 tablespoons cold water, and use to thicken liquid. Cook 5 minutes. Dilute with boiling water if necessary, and strain. Serve gravy in separate dish. Serves 4–5.

Note: Have butcher score flank steak on 1 side to improve tenderizing during cooking. Various seasonings may be used, according to your taste. Leftover stewed tomatoes can replace some of the liquid. Bottled meat sauces, a spoonful of chili powder or a pinch or two of powdered herbs make an interesting variation.

Oven-barbecued Round Steak

```
1 1/2 pounds round steak, 1 inch thick
    2 tablespoons salad oil
  1/2 cup ketchup
    1 clove garlic
  1/4 cup vinegar
    2 tablespoons Worcestershire sauce
    1 tablespoon sugar
    1 teaspoon paprika
    1 teaspoon salt
    1 teaspoon dry mustard
  1/8 teaspoon pepper
```

Cut beef into strips or squares. Heat oil in skillet, and brown meat on all sides. Remove to casserole. Pour off excess fat from pan, and make sauce by simmering all remaining ingredients a few minutes. Pour over meat pieces, cover and bake in 325°F. oven about 1 hour or until meat is completely tender to the fork, basting occasionally. Remove garlic before serving. Serves 4.

Pressure-braised Short Ribs or Oxtails

```
    1 tablespoon flour
    2 teaspoons salt
  1/8 teaspoon pepper
    3 pounds short ribs or oxtails, cut in 2-inch pieces
    3 tablespoons fat
    1 cup tomato juice
  1/2 cup chopped onion
```

Combine flour, salt and pepper, and dredge meat in flour mixture. Heat fat in uncovered pressure cooker, and add meat. Brown on all sides thoroughly over moderate heat. Add tomato juice and onion. Follow manufacturer's directions for using your pressure-cooker. At 15-pound pressure, short ribs should be nicely done in 25 minutes, oxtails in 30 minutes. Allow pressure cooker to cool slowly before removing lid. Serves 5–6.

Tomato Swiss Steak

```
1 1/2–2 pounds round steak, 3/4 inch thick
    2 tablespoons flour
    1 teaspoon salt
  1/8 teaspoon pepper
      Suet, drippings or cooking oil
    1 small onion, sliced
1 1/2–2 cups tomato juice
    1 tablespoon chopped celery
    1 tablespoon chopped green pepper
    1 teaspoon Worcestershire sauce
```

Snip fat edge of steak to prevent curling. Mix flour, salt and pepper, and, using edge of plate, pound mixture into both sides of meat. Heat small amount of fat in heavy frying pan. Brown steak thoroughly on both sides over high heat. Add onion slices, and cook until brown and softened. Reduce heat, and add remaining ingredients. Cover tightly, and cook slowly about 1 1/2 hours, turning meat once and adding a little more tomato juice or hot water if necessary. Serves 5–6.

Note: Swiss steak may be baked at 325°F. after top-of-the-stove browning.

Northern Stew

1/4 cup flour
1/2 teaspoon salt
   Pepper to taste
2 pounds shank beef, cut in 2-inch pieces
2 tablespoons melted fat
   Boiling water
1/2 teaspoon marjoram
1/2 teaspoon thyme
1/4 teaspoon celery salt
6—7 small onions, peeled
6 medium potatoes, peeled
4 scraped carrots, quartered
2 tablespoons flour
2 tablespoons cold water

Mix 1/4 cup flour, salt and pepper, and coat beef pieces thoroughly. Heat fat in good-sized heavy skillet, and brown meat over high heat, browning on all sides. Reduce heat, add boiling water just to cover and add marjoram, thyme and celery salt. Cover tightly, and simmer over low heat about 2 1/2 hours, keeping water level adjusted. Add vegetables, and continue to cook until tender—30—40 minutes. Blend 2 tablespoons flour with cold water, thicken gravy and cook 5 minutes longer. Serves 6—8.

Note: Stew may be cooked in oven at 300°F. after top-of-the-stove browning, in which case vegetables should be allowed at least 1 hour's cooking.

Beef Brisket with Lima Beans

1 (12-ounce) package dry lima beans
4 cups water or vegetable juice
1 pound lean beef brisket
1—2 tablespoons hot drippings
2 onions, sliced
1—2 tablespoons molasses
1 bay leaf, broken
1 teaspoon salt
2—3 sliced carrots
   Salt and pepper to taste

Soak beans overnight in water. Brown brisket slowly in drippings until well cooked. Pour off and save fat. Add onions, molasses, bay leaf, salt and water drained from beans. Cover, and simmer 15 minutes. Add beans, and cook until meat and beans are tender, about 1 hour. Add carrots, and cook 15 minutes longer. Season with salt and pepper to taste. More water may be added during cooking if necessary. Serves 5—6.

Glazed Corned Beef

4 pounds rolled corned beef brisket
   Cold water
2 bay leaves
6 whole allspice berries
1 onion, peeled and sliced
1/3 cup chili sauce
1/3 cup brown sugar, firmly packed
3 tablespoons lemon juice
1 1/2 teaspoons dry mustard
   Whole cloves

Wash meat; place in saucepan, and cover with cold water. Add bay leaves, allspice and onion. Cover and bring slowly to simmering point. After about 1 hour, skim, and continue to cook at low temperature until meat is tender—about 2 hours longer. Remove bay leaves. Meanwhile make glaze by mixing other ingredients except cloves. Preheat oven to 350°F. Lift meat from its liquid, drain thoroughly and place in shallow roasting pan. Stick whole cloves here and there over surface. Pour glazing mixture over meat, and bake about 1/2 hour, basting with sauce from time to time. Serves 6—8.

Spicy Pot Roast

2 tablespoons fat
4 1/2—5 pounds chuck or rump
1/2 teaspoon salt
   Pepper to taste
1 cup hot water
1 onion, sliced
3 bay leaves
3/4 teaspoon thyme
1/4 teaspoon powdered ginger
8 small potatoes, peeled
12 carrots, halved
1 tablespoon flour
2 tablespoons cold water

Use a Dutch oven, deep-well cooker, roasting pan or any large, heavy, covered kettle. Melt fat and brown roast thoroughly on all sides. Turn with spatula, rather than fork, which would pierce meat and allow juices to escape. Sprinkle with salt and pepper. Add hot water, onion and spices. Cover and simmer about 3 hours. Add potatoes and carrots. Cover, and cook another 45 minutes or until vegetables are tender. Remove pot roast to platter, and surround with potatoes and carrots. Keep warm; blend flour and cold water, and thicken liquid. Serve gravy separately. Serves 8.

Note: This recipe can be used with any suitable "less tender" cut of beef—chuck, fresh brisket, rump or heel of round. A roast of this size makes a dozen or more generous servings. Leftovers can be used in any way suitable for roast beef: sliced for sandwiches, reheated in gravy, cut up and added with canned-soup sauce to lightly cooked vegetables for a quick casserole dish, used in hash with chopped cooked potatoes and raw onions or ground up for *Shepherd's Pie*.

Hungarian Goulash

2 pounds stewing beef
1 tablespoon bacon drippings or fat
5 tablespoons flour
1 small onion, peeled and sliced
1 tablespoon Worcestershire sauce
2 teaspoons salt
1 teaspoon paprika
1 teaspoon caraway seeds (optional)
1/8 teaspoon pepper
3 1/2 cups hot water
1/2 cup sour cream

Cut meat into neat 1-inch cubes. Melt fat in heavy skillet. Brown meat cubes on all sides; sprinkle with flour, and stir again to brown further. Add onion, Worcestershire sauce and dry seasonings. Add hot water, and continue stirring. Reduce heat, cover tightly and simmer until meat is very tender—about 2 hours. Stir in sour cream just before serving. Drained boiled noodles are a traditional accompaniment with the spicy goulash. Serves 4—6.

Beef Strips with Raisins

      1/2 cup seedless raisins
      1/2 cup red wine
        1 pound minute steaks
    1 1/2 tablespoons flour
          Salt and pepper to taste
    1 1/2 tablespoons salad oil
          Boiling water
          Bay leaf
          Pinch thyme
          Fluffy Rice

Pick over, wash and drain raisins. Put to soak in wine. Prepare steaks by cutting into strips about 1/2″ x 2″. Combine flour, salt and pepper and coat strips. Heat oil in frying pan until it begins to sputter. Put in flour-coated meat, and brown thoroughly. Reduce heat to simmer; add wine with raisins and only enough boiling water to barely cover. Add bay leaf and thyme. Cover tightly, and simmer 1 hour or less or until meat is very tender. Remove bay leaf before serving over *Fluffy Rice*. Serves 2.

Ground Beef

Ground beef may either be ground round steak, ground chuck or beef trimmings ground with some of the less tender cuts such as flank, shank or neck. "Ground round" and "ground chuck" are always labeled as such and cost more than the other, which is known variously as "hamburger" or "ground beef." Hamburger contains more fat, and therefore loses more weight during cooking.

Ground beef is one of the most versatile meat purchases. It may be pan-broiled, broiled, braised or baked. It is economical, particularly as it lends well to "stretching" with various other ingredients to make interesting main courses. Ground beef is ideal for use in a hearty sauce for spaghetti or rice; in baked pies with pastry, biscuit or potato toppings; teamed with kidney beans in chili con carne; or as stuffing with such baked vegetables as peppers and squash.

Do not overcook ground beef. High temperatures cause meat to harden and lose flavor.

Warning: Ground beef is very perishable. It should be refrigerated and used within 1—2 days. For a longer period, it should be wrapped in freezer paper and frozen.

If you are freezing a quantity of ground meat to be used later in patties, shape patties before freezing. Separate with layers of waxed paper; then wrap for the freezer.

Deluxe Hamburgers

        2 pounds ground round steak
      1/4 cup melted butter or margarine
      1/4 cup milk or tomato juice
        2 tablespoons ketchup
        2 tablespoons cracker crumbs
        1 tablespoon chopped onion
    1 1/2 teaspoons salt
        1 teaspoon Worcestershire sauce
          Pinch oregano or chervil

Mix all ingredients together thoroughly, and with wet hands shape into 10 or 12 large, flat, round patties. In lightly greased skillet, pan-broil quickly until medium-well done, 1 1/2—2 minutes per side. Centers should still be quite pink; overcooking makes hamburgers dry and shriveled. Serve on toasted hamburger rolls with Spanish onion and tomato slices lightly sprinkled with salt. Serves 6.

Note: Omit melted butter in mixture if less expensive hamburger or ground beef (containing more fat) is used in place of ground steak.

Beef Patties in Sherry Sauce

        2 pounds ground round steak
        2 tablespoons butter or margarine
        2 medium onions, chopped
      1/4 pound mushrooms, chopped
      1/2 teaspoon salt
      1/4 teaspoon thyme
      1/4 teaspoon coarse black pepper
          Pinch rosemary
      1/2 cup sherry
      1/2 cup water

With wet hands shape meat into patties, and broil or fry until thoroughly brown on each side. Hamburgers should be slightly pinkish inside for tenderness. While they are cooking, melt butter or margarine in small pan, and add onions, mushrooms and seasonings. Cook gently until golden brown; add sherry and water, bring to boiling point and simmer 2—3 minutes longer. Serve sauce over hamburger patties. Serves 6.

Beef-Rice Balls in Sour Cream Sauce

        1 pound hamburger
      1/2 cup milk
      1/2 cup quick-cooking rice
        2 tablespoons chopped onion
        1 teaspoon salt
      1/2 teaspoon mixed Italian herbs or 1/8 teaspoon nutmeg and 1/8 teaspoon allspice
      1/8 teaspoon pepper
      1/3 cup flour or dry bread crumbs
      1/4 cup bacon drippings
    1 1/2 cups rich beef stock or 1 (10-ounce) can bouillon diluted with 1/4 cup water
      1/4 cup red wine
        2 tablespoons tomato paste
        1 (5-ounce) can mushrooms, drained
  1/4-1/2 cup sour cream
          Salt and pepper to taste
          Plain buttered or margarined noodles

Mix the first 7 ingredients together, and form into 40 small balls. Roll in 1/3 cup flour or bread crumbs, and fry slowly in drippings until lightly browned. Lift out meat, and stir in 2 tablespoons flour. Add stock slowly, and cook until smoothly thickened. Mix in wine and tomato paste, and add mushrooms and meatballs. Season. Cover, and simmer slowly about 20 minutes. Stir in sour cream and salt and pepper to taste, and reheat without boiling. Serve over plain buttered noodles; accompany with tossed salad. Serves 4.

Swedish Meatballs

    1 1/2 pounds ground round steak or 1 pound beef and
            1/2 pound ground veal
      1 large onion, diced (1 cup)
    1/4 cup cracker crumbs or fine bread crumbs
      2 eggs, beaten
    1/2 teaspoon ground allspice or mace
        Salt and pepper to taste
      2 tablespoons butter or margarine
    1/2 cup red wine
    1/2 cup water
      3 tablespoons sour cream or 1 teaspoon flour and 1
            tablespoon water

Mix together meat, onions, crumbs, eggs and seasonings. Shape into small balls, about the size of a walnut. Cook gently in butter or margarine in frying pan, turning as they brown until uniformly colored. Pour in wine and water, and cover. Simmer 20 minutes. A little more water may be added if the sauce boils away. Just before serving, stir in sour cream. Serve with hot buttered or margarined noodles, baked potatoes or fluffy rice. Serves 4—5.

Quick Tips—Hamburger.

Hamburger lends itself to easy and economical cooking in many different ways: Patties may be pan-broiled in a little fat over medium heat (for thick patties, allow 4—8 minutes on each side; for thin patties, 2—6 minutes on each side, or cook until done). Or they may be broiled, grilled or barbecued—about 4—6 minutes on each side, about 3 inches from heat (brush with fat or barbecue sauce if desired).

Or hamburger may be browned in skillet in very little fat, then braised with small amount of water, consommé or tomato juice and seasonings to taste (use covered skillet or casserole, and cook slowly 20—30 minutes).

Stuffed Green Peppers

      6 green peppers
        Boiling salted water
      2 small onions, chopped (1/2 cup)
      1 clove garlic
      1 tablespoon olive oil, butter or margarine
      1 pound ground round steak
      1 (10-ounce) can tomato soup
      1 teaspoon salt
    1/4 teaspoon pepper
        Pinch rosemary
        Pinch cayenne
      1 tablespoon chopped parsley or 1/4 teaspoon dried
            parsley

Cut off stem ends of peppers, and scoop out seeds and membrane. Parboil peppers 5 minutes in boiling salted water to cover. Reserve liquid. Fry onions and garlic in olive oil until golden brown. Add meat, and fry, stirring constantly, until thoroughly browned. Add 1/2 can of soup with seasonings to mixture, and blend well; pile mixture loosely into pepper cups. Set in shallow baking dish. Dilute remaining soup with a little less than 1 soup can of water in which peppers were parboiled, and pour around stuffed peppers in dish. Bake at 375°F. 30—40 minutes. Sprinkle tops of peppers with chopped parsley. Serves 6.

Sweet-Sour Meatballs

      1 pound ground round steak
    1/2 pound pork-sausage meat
    3/4   cup fine dry bread crumbs
    3/4 cup milk
    1/4 cup finely chopped onion
      1 egg, slightly beaten
    3/4 teaspoon salt
        Pinch pepper
      2 tablespoons salad oil
      2 tablespoons chopped green pepper
      1 clove garlic, peeled
    1/2 cup pineapple juice
    1/2 cup wine vinegar
    1/4 cup sugar
      3 tablespoons brown sugar
      1 teaspoon soy sauce
    3/4 teaspoon cornstarch
      1 teaspoon cold water

Combine meat, crumbs, milk, onion, egg, salt and pepper. Shape into firm, small balls, using rounded teaspoonful of mixture for each. Heat oil in frying pan, and brown a few balls at a time, turning frequently for even coloring. Transfer to shallow casserole. To remaining fat in frying pan (add more if necessary to make 2 tablespoons) add green pepper and garlic. Cook, stirring, 5 minutes; discard garlic. Add pineapple juice, vinegar, sugar, and soy sauce. Blend cornstarch and cold water. When juice mixture reaches boiling point, stir in cornstarch; cook and stir until smooth. Pour sauce over meatballs. Set covered casserole in 325°F. oven, and cook about 30 minutes. Serve with *Fluffy Rice.* Serves 6—8.

Ground-beef Casserole

      1 pound ground beef
      1 large onion, diced
      2 tablespoons shortening, melted
    2—3 potatoes, sliced
      1 cup chopped celery
    1/2 cup chopped green pepper
    1 1/2 cups canned tomatoes
        Salt and pepper to taste
        Pinch cayenne
    1/4 teaspoon garlic salt

Sauté ground beef and onion in shortening until onion is soft and all trace of pinkness disappears from meat. Cover bottom of 2-quart casserole with meat and onions; add layer of potatoes, celery and green pepper. Repeat layers, add seasonings and pour canned tomatoes over. Cook, covered, 45–60 minutes or until potatoes are done. Serves 4.

Gold-topped Beef Loaf

    1/2 cup dry bread crumbs
      1 cup evaporated milk
      1 pound hamburger
    1/2 pound sausage meat
      2 grated raw potatoes
      1 small onion, diced
      1 tablespoon dark steak sauce
      1 teaspoon salt
      1 teaspoon meat extract
      1 teaspoon monosodium glutamate
    1/2 teaspoon dry mustard
      1 recipe *Corn Bread Topping*

Soak crumbs in milk, and blend in remaining ingredients, except topping, thoroughly. Spread 1/2 topping mixture in bottom of greased loaf pan. Evenly cover with meat, and top with remaining corn bread. Bake at 350°F. 1–1 1/2 hours. Cool slightly, and invert on breadboard; then turn right side up onto heated platter. Serves 8.

Corn Bread Topping

      1 cup unsifted all-purpose flour
    3/4 cup cornmeal
    2 1/2 teaspoons baking powder
      1 teaspoon sugar
    1/2 teaspoon salt
      1 cup milk
      2 eggs, beaten
    1/4 cup salad oil

Combine flour, cornmeal, baking powder, sugar and salt. Blend together milk, eggs and salad oil. Stir into dry ingredients to make smooth batter.

Cabbage Rolls

      1 medium-size green cabbage
      1 pound minced pork, veal or beef
      3 smoked sausages, minced
    1/2 onion, chopped fine
      1 clove garlic, crushed
      1 egg, beaten
    1 1/4 teaspoons salt
    1/3 cup long-cooking rice
        Tomato juice or sour cream
    2 1/2 cups stewed tomatoes

Cut the core out of the cabbage. Cover cabbage with boiling water, and let stand 10 minutes. Drain; then separate the leaves. Shave off the thick spine of each with a knife to make rolling easier. Combine the next 7 ingredients. Moisten with about 1/4 cup tomato juice. Spoon about 3 tablespoons of the mixture on each of the larger leaves. Overlap outside edges, and roll up loosely. Cover bottom of a baking dish with a few small leaves. Cover with cabbage rolls, then any remaining small leaves. Pour tomatoes over the top. Cover, and bake 2 hours at 325°F. Serves 6–8.

Scotch Beef Loaf

      2 pounds hamburger
    2/3 cup rolled oats
      1 cup milk
      2 eggs, well beaten
      3 tablespoons finely chopped onion
      3 tablespoons finely chopped celery
      2 tablespoons Worcestershire sauce
    1 1/2 teaspoons salt
    1/2 teaspoon summer savory
    1/8 teaspoon pepper

Blend meat and oats together thoroughly. Mix milk and eggs, and add to meat. Add remaining ingredients, mixing thoroughly. Turn into lightly greased 9″ x 5″ x 3″ loaf pan large enough to leave about 1/2-inch space at top. Bake about 1 1/2 hours at 350°F. Let loaf stand in pan a few minutes before turning out on serving platter. Serves 6–8.

Note: For an interesting change in flavor, try beef broth or tomato juice in place of milk. Or spread top of loaf with chili sauce or ketchup before putting in oven.

Chili in Potato Shell

      1 egg, slightly beaten
      4 cups seasoned mashed potatoes, fresh, not instant
    1/4 cup crushed cornflakes
      2 onions, chopped
    1–2 cloves garlic, chopped (optional)
      2 tablespoons fat
      1 pound hamburger
      1 cup canned tomatoes or 1/2 cup tomato juice
      1 tablespoon flour
      1 tablespoon chili powder
      1 (15-ounce) can red kidney beans
        Dash salt, sugar, Worcestershire sauce, herbs or cayenne

Stir about 1/2 the egg into potatoes, and mold mixture into nest shape in greased deep pie dish (for free-standing nest, use greased removable bottom of round cake tin). Brush surface with remaining egg, and sprinkle with flakes. Bake 15–20 minutes at 375°F. Meanwhile sauté onions and garlic in fat until tender. Add hamburger and fry, stirring, until meat is brown all through. Stir in tomatoes, flour and chili powder. Boil 5 minutes. Add beans, stir and continue cooking 5 minutes longer. Taste, and flavor. Pour chili into hot potato shell, and keep hot until serving. Cut in wedges. Serves 6.

Spaghetti with Romano Sauce

    1 pound hamburger
    1/2 pound spicy smoked Italian sausage, sliced
    1 large onion, chopped
    2 tablespoons chopped parsley
    1–2 cloves garlic, crushed
    1 (6-ounce) can tomato paste
    3 cups water
    2–3 fresh tomatoes, peeled and sliced, or 1 cup canned
        tomatoes
    1–2 crushed chili peppers
    1 teaspoon chopped mint or 1/4 teaspoon dried
        mint
    1/2 bay leaf
    1/4 teaspoon oregano
    1/4 teaspoon salt
    1 pound spaghetti, cooked and drained
        Parmesan cheese

Sauté hamburger and sausage together until thoroughly cooked. Pour off fat, and add onion, parsley and garlic. Sauté 5 minutes; add remaining ingredients except spaghetti and cheese. Cook slowly until thickened; taste for seasoning. Remove bay leaf before serving. Serve over hot cooked spaghetti, and pass bowl of Parmesan cheese. Serves 6.

MILD-FLAVORED VEAL

Because of its subtle, delicate flavor, veal needs gentle, slow cooking, with plenty of help from seasonings, sauces and stuffings.

Veal is the delicately flavored meat of beef cattle 4–14 weeks old. Beef from animals 14 weeks to 1 year old is called "calf," but for practical purposes the term "veal" covers this meat also. As it comes from young animals, veal has little exterior fat and no marbling. Although the muscle fibers are tender, veal does contain considerable connective tissue and thus is at its best cooked slowly to well done. The best cooking methods for veal are roasting, frying, braising and stewing. Because meat contains little fat (some cuts have no fat covering at all), most veal dishes are improved by the addition of butter, margarine or cooking oil. And because its natural flavor is bland, veal becomes more interesting when combined with condiments, tomatoes or other vegetable or soup mixtures. Sage, tarragon, summer savory, rosemary, thyme and basil add a lively tang to a veal dish.

What To Look for

Good veal is pinkish-grey and moist in appearance. There is considerably less fat in veal than in other meats; what there is may be white, creamy-white or tinged with pink.

Veal is most plentiful in the spring and early summer months, but there is generally a supply on the market the year round.

To Cook Veal Roasts and Chops

Many veal cuts can be temptingly prepared by roasting, braising or stewing. All veal should be well cooked, so that meat is pale gray throughout, with no trace of pink. Extra fat should be added at start of cooking; seasonings should be added at halfway point.

To Braise. Brown chops, steaks or cutlets in 2—4 tablespoons fat over moderate heat; allow several minutes on each side. Add seasonings and 1/2 cup liquid. Cover and cook slowly until tender—for 1-inch thickness, 30 minutes on each side; for 1/2-inch thickness, about 20 minutes on each side.

To Bake (Breaded). Dip chops, steaks or cutlets in seasoned flour, then in slightly beaten egg mixture (2 tablespoons water to 1 egg). Roll in fine bread crumbs. Brown in 2—4 tablespoons fat over moderate heat, allowing 3—4 minutes on each side. Use extra fat after turning. Place, uncovered, in oven preheated to 325°F. Bake 1-inch thickness about 40 minutes, turning meat once during cooking.

TIMETABLE FOR ROASTING VEAL*

TYPE OF ROAST	WEIGHT IN POUNDS	MINUTES PER POUND**
Leg, bone in	3—8	30—40
Rump	4—6	40—50
Loin or rib	4—6	35—40
Rolled, boned shoulder	3—5	40—45

*Oven temperature is 325° F.; meat thermometer reading is 180° F.

**Times given are for roasts taken directly from the refrigerator (40° F.). For unthawed roasts extend cooking period by 1/2 the total time required for same size and cut of fresh veal. The shorter times apply to roasts of heavier weights specified; for smaller cuts, allow longer times listed.

Roast Veal with Pennsylvania Stuffing

    4–6-pound boned shoulder or boned leg of veal
    2–3 skinless fresh sausages
        Boiling water
    1 recipe *Bread Dressing*
    1/2 cup chopped celery
    1/2 cup peeled chopped apple
        Cream
    4 slices fat bacon or salt pork
        Salt to taste
        Pepper to taste
        Thyme to taste (optional)

Wipe meat, both outside and in the cavity, with clean damp cloth or paper towels. Put sausages in saucepan with boiling water to cover; simmer 10 minutes. Lift out, break up sausage meat, and add to dressing, along with celery and apple. Bind dressing with a little cream. Stuff meat cavity, and skewer or sew opening to hold dressing firmly. If veal is very lean, lay bacon strips over top. Preheat oven to 325°F. Roast, uncovered, on rack in shallow pan, allowing 45—50 minutes per pound if meat is chilled at start of cooking time, slightly less if at room temperature (meat thermometer should indicate an internal temperature of 180°F. for well-cooked roast). After first hour or so of roasting, sprinkle veal with salt, pepper and a little thyme. For even browning, remove bacon strips during last hour of roasting time. Serves 7—10.

Marinated Veal Roast

        4-pound sirloin roast of veal
    1/2 cup chopped onion
    1/3 cup salad oil
    1/4 cup lemon juice
      2 tablespoons thick meat sauce
      2 teaspoons salt
      2 teaspoons monosodium glutamate (optional)
      1 clove garlic, halved
    1/2 teaspoon marjoram
    1/8 teaspoon basil
      1 cup water

Wipe meat with clean damp cloth. Make marinade of remaining ingredients, except water (for easy removal of garlic later, spike each piece with toothpick). Put meat in container, pour marinade over, cover and let stand in refrigerator or other cool place 7—8 hours. Turn occasionally. Heat oven to 325°F.; place meat on rack in roasting pan equipped with cover. Blend water with marinade, and pour over roast. Cover tightly, and cook about 2 1/2 hours, basting occasionally. Remove cover, and continue cooking another 1/2 hour. Serves 8.

Note: The marinade plus meat juices make a delicious gravy, thickened with a smooth paste of equal parts flour and cold water and allowed to simmer at least 5 minutes.

Curried Veal

    1 1/2 pounds veal cutlet
           Flour
    1/4 cup butter or margarine
    3/4 cup chopped onion
    3/4 cup chopped tart apple
    2—3 teaspoons curry powder
    1/2 teaspoon salt
    1/2 teaspoon grated lemon rind
         Speck cayenne
      1 (10-ounce) can bouillon
    1/2 cup water
      1 tablespoon lemon juice
      2 cups cooked rice
      1 banana
    1/4 cup shredded coconut

Cut meat into 1-inch pieces, and flour lightly. Melt butter or margarine in heavy skillet, and gently fry meat, turning till all sides are golden. Push meat to one side, and add onion and apple. Continue cooking over low heat a few minutes, stirring and turning. Add curry powder, salt, lemon rind and cayenne. Add bouillon, water and lemon juice, continuing to stir until mixture reaches simmering point. Cover, and simmer about 45 minutes or until meat is tender. Serve over hot fluffy rice, scattering banana slices and shredded coconut on top of curry. Serves 5—6.

Note: The same amount of lamb or beef may be used instead of veal. Simmer 1 1/2 hours.

Veal Wellington

      1 cup coarsely grated or chopped raw carrots
    1/2 cup finely chopped celery
      2 tablespoons butter or margarine
      1 (5-ounce) can drained, sliced mushrooms
      1 egg
         Heavy cream
      2 teaspoons salt
    1/2 teaspoon thyme
    1/2 teaspoon pepper
      2 pounds minced veal
      1 package refrigerated, ready-to-bake crescent rolls
      1 egg
      1 tablespoon cold water

Turn on oven to 400°F. Sauté carrots and celery in butter or margarine until tender (about 15 minutes). With a slotted spoon remove them from skillet and place in large bowl. Add mushrooms and one egg beaten with enough heavy cream to make 1/2 cup liquid. Stir in salt, thyme and pepper. Using spatula and a light touch, fold in veal. Turn out onto wooden board, and shape with fingers into a loaf about 12 inches long, 4 inches wide and 3 inches high.

For crust, use ready-to-bake crescent rolls. They come 8 to the package. Open out 7, and wrap around and under the loaf. Brush whole loaf with an egg wash made by beating 1 egg with 1 tablespoon cold water. From the eighth roll, cut small shapes, brush them with egg wash and use for decoration. (Decorations optional.) Bake loaf for 15 minutes at 400°F. Cover with aluminum foil. Bake 30 minutes longer at 350°F. Lift onto serving platter. Garnish with watercress. Serves 6.

Jellied Veal

      2 pounds veal shank or neck
      1 veal knuckle
    6—8 cups cold water
      1 large onion, sliced
      1 slice lemon
    2—3 celery stalks with leaves, coarsely cut
      1 small bunch parsley
      2 teaspoons salt
      4 peppercorns
      1 bay leaf
    1—2 envelopes plain gelatine, softened in 1/2 cup cold water
    1/4 cup chopped gherkins
    1/4 cup chopped pimento
    1/4 cup chopped green pepper

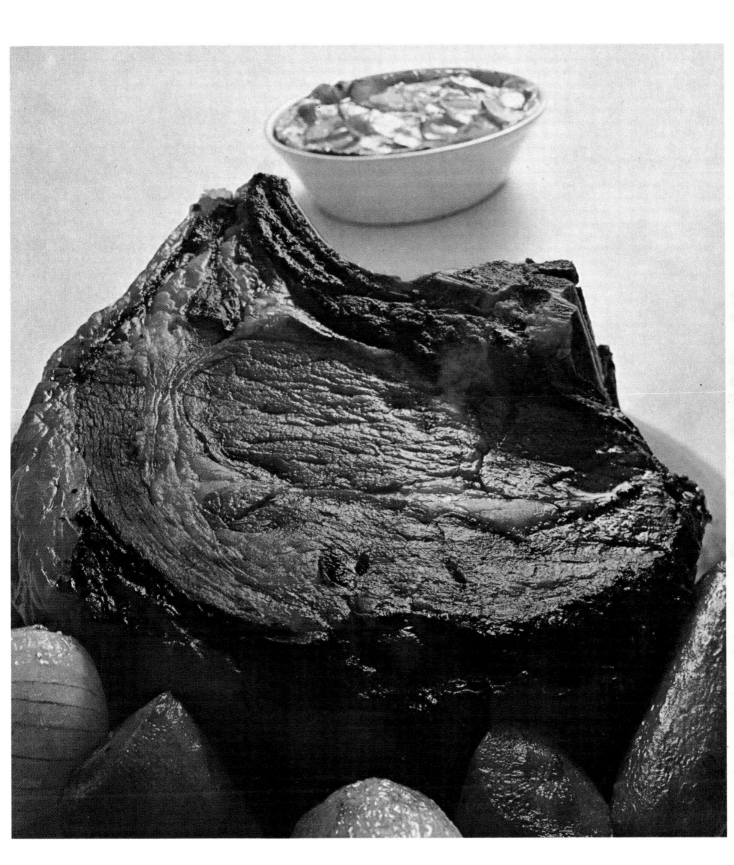

Roast Beef with Roast Vegetables (p. 18).
CREDIT: *Bernard Gray.*

Cold Apricot Glazed Ham (pp. 62-63).
CREDIT: *Bernard Gray.*

Put meat, with all skin and bone, in big sauce-pan. Cover with water. The amount of water will depend on the diameter of pan and size of meat chunks. Bring to a boil. Skim scum off the top. Add the next 7 ingredients. Cover. Reduce heat, and simmer until meat is very tender, about 2–3 hours. Drain, and reserve the broth. Remove meat from the bones, and chop finely; then re-frigerate. Discard fat and seasonings. Return bones to the broth, and simmer until broth is reduced to 3 cups. Strain into a bowl, and refrig-erate. Discard bones. Chill broth overnight. Next morning scrape off the fat and cut into the jellied broth. If quite soft use 2 envelopes of gelatine; if firm, 1 envelope. Add softened gelatine to the broth and heat. Stir until gelatine dissolves. Add the meat, and remove from heat. Taste, and add more seasoning if necessary. Stir in gherkins, pi-mento and green pepper. Pour into loaf mold or individual molds. Chill until completely firm; turn out on platter for serving. Serves 8–10.

Spanish Veal Casserole

     1 1/2 pounds thin veal cutlets
         2 tablespoons flour
     1/4 cup butter or margarine
         1 onion, thinly sliced
         1 (10-ounce) can tomato soup
         1 cup canned mixed vegetable juice
     1/2 cup sliced stuffed olives
         1 teaspoon salt
     1/4 teaspoon pepper
     1/4 teaspoon ground cloves
         1 (10-ounce) package frozen lima beans, thawed
             Parmesan cheese, grated

Preheat oven to 375°F. (moderately hot). Coat veal lightly with flour. Brown richly in heated butter or margarine. Place in broad, shallow bak-ing dish. Fry onion until tender, but not browned, in same pan. Stir in soup, juice, sliced stuffed olives, salt, pepper and cloves. Mix in lima beans. Pour over veal; cover baking dish with foil. Bake in preheated oven until veal is tender—about 1 hour. Remove foil and sprinkle meat with grated cheese. Place under broiler a few minutes until cheese is melted and bubbly. Serves 6.

Veal Viennese

     1/4 cup bacon drippings or fat
         2 pounds lean stewing veal
         2 bouillon cubes
         1 cup boiling water
     1/4 cup finely chopped onion
         1 teaspoon salt
     1/8 teaspoon pepper
         1 cup sour cream
         4 thin slices lemon, unpeeled
         2 tablespoons flour
         2 tablespoons cold water
             Parsley, finely chopped

Melt fat in heavy saucepan, and brown meat thoroughly. Dissolve bouillon cube in boiling water, and pour over meat. Add onion, salt and pepper. Stir in sour cream and lemon slices; cov-er, and simmer until meat is tender, about 1 hour, stirring occasionally and adding more boiling water if necessary. To thicken gravy, make smooth paste of flour and cold water; stir in and cook 5 minutes longer. Garnish with finely chopped parsley. Serves 8.

Breaded Veal Chops

     1/3 cup flour
         1 teaspoon salt
     1/2 teaspoon dry mustard
     1/4 teaspoon pepper
             Pinch garlic salt
         6 thin loin veal chops
         3 tablespoons milk
     1 1/2 teaspoons salad oil
         1 egg, slightly beaten
             Fine dry bread crumbs
     2–3 tablespoons fat
         2 tablespoons hot water

Mix together flour, salt, dry mustard, pepper and garlic salt. Coat chops lightly with this mix-ture. Combine milk and oil with beaten egg and dip each chop in this mixture; then roll in bread crumbs, coating completely. If there is time, chill chops in refrigerator for 1/2 hour to set coating. Melt fat in heavy skillet over moderate heat. Fry chops slowly turning to brown well on both sides —about 15 minutes. Add hot water, cover pan and cook slowly another 15 minutes or until perfectly tender. Serves 6.

Note: Veal steaks or cutlets may be cooked in same way.

Savory Veal Loaf

         2 pounds lean ground veal
         1 cup rolled oats
     1/2 cup finely chopped onion
         2 tablespoons chopped parsley
         2 teaspoons salt
     1/2 teaspoon pepper
         6 slices bacon
         2 eggs, slightly beaten
         1 cup tomato juice
         1 tablespoon bottled thick meat sauce
         2 teaspoons prepared mustard
             Parsley sprigs
             Lemon wedges or slices

Put veal and next 5 ingredients in mixing bowl. Fry bacon until crisp; drain, crumble and add to mixture. Mix lightly together. Combine eggs, to-mato juice, meat sauce and mustard; add to meat mixture, and pack into lightly greased 9″ x 5″ x 3″ loaf pan. Bake at 350°F. about 1 1/2 hours. Stand pan on wire rack in warm place 10 min-utes; turn meat loaf out on warm serving platter, and garnish with parsley and lemon. Serves 8.

Veal Birds with Prunes

    1 1/2-pound veal steak, 1/2 inch thick
    4–5 pitted prunes, uncooked
      1 small cube salt pork
      1 cup soft bread crumbs
    1/4 teaspoon salt
        Dash pepper
      1 egg yolk
      1 tablespoon lemon juice
        Meat stock
        Salt and pepper to taste
    1/2 cup flour
    1/4 cup butter or margarine
      1 cup light cream

Remove bone from steak, trim off skin and fat, reserving trimmings, and wipe meat with damp cloth. Pound meat with mallet until very thin (or have butcher do it at time of purchase). Cut meat into 12 individual serving pieces. Prepare stuffing by putting through grinder prunes, veal trimmings and salt pork or chop very fine. Mix with crumbs, 1/4 teaspoon salt and dash pepper. Moisten all with egg yolk, lemon juice and a little meat stock (or hot water). Spread stuffing over each portion of veal to within about 1/4 inch of edge; roll, and fasten with twine or toothpicks. Sprinkle with salt and pepper to taste, roll in flour and sauté in butter or margarine, turning so that all sides brown. Reduce heat, add cream and simmer, covered, until meat is completely tender—about 30 minutes, depending on the thickness. Lift out meat, and carefully remove twine or toothpicks. Pour sauce around birds arranged on a platter. Serves 6.

Note: Meat rolls, after initial browning, may be baked at 325° F. 45–50 minutes or until tender.

VARIATIONS:

* Instead of prunes use 1/4 cup drained pineapples or same amount seedless raisins.

* A regular bread stuffing or bread-and-apple mixture makes an excellent center for veal birds.

Mexican Veal with Macaroni Shells

      2 onions, chopped (1 cup)
      2 tablespoons bacon drippings
    1–2 stalks celery, sliced
      1 (20-ounce) can tomatoes, drained
        Diced leftover veal, pork or lamb
    1/2 cup or more gravy
      1 (15-ounce) can kidney beans
    1–3 teaspoons chili powder
    5–6 cups hot cooked macaroni shells
        Grated Cheddar cheese

Sauté onions in bacon drippings until tender. Add celery, tomatoes, meat and gravy. Cover, and simmer 20 minutes. Uncover, and add kidney beans and chili powder to taste. Season with Worcestershire sauce and garlic to suit your taste. Serve on macaroni shells and sprinkle with cheese. Serves 6–8.

Note: One bouillon cube or 1 teaspoon beef extract dissolved in 1/2 cup boiling water may be used instead of gravy.

FINE-FLAVORED LAMB

When it's time for a special Sunday dinner or when you want a hearty, flavorful casserole, it's time to use a lamb recipe.

Lamb is good all year round, but in the spring it is most plentiful and reasonably priced.

The term "lamb" covers meat from animals up to around 14 months of age. After that, lamb becomes "mutton." Most mutton is used in commercially prepared soups and processed meats; it is not often seen on the retail market. "Spring lamb"—a tender, juicy meat—comes from lambs 3–5 months old.

Look for velvet-smooth, fine-grained, pink-to-dark-pink meat and small bones tinged with red. Young lamb bones can be quite easily cut. As the animal matures, the bones grow larger, whiter and harder to cut and the meat becomes redder.

The thin, paper-like covering on lamb is called the "fell." It is usually left on lamb roasts but is generally removed from chops. Mutton "fell" should always be removed before cooking.

Most lamb cuts are sufficiently tender to be cooked with dry heat—roasted, broiled or pan-broiled. The fresh, distinctive flavor of lamb is best when it is served hot or cold, never lukewarm. Lamb is usually cooked to medium or well done, although some people prefer lamb chops and roasts cooked rare.

Two of the finest lamb roasts are the leg and the circular crown roast formed by the tender chops. Both are ideally suited to dry-heat (oven-roasting) preparation. The less expensive cuts are useful in any recipe using the moist-heat (braising) method of cooking. The inexpensive cuts include neck, flank, breast and shank.

Broil or pan-broil lamb chops to desired doneness, which depends on whether you like them medium or well done. Test by slitting next to bone to check color. The lower-price shoulder chops are an excellent value for braising with vegetables in casseroles. Marinating adds flavor when lamb is to be cooked by such dry-heat methods as roasting, broiling and barbecuing. Oil and vinegar or soy sauce contribute flavor, and honey-garlic glaze is especially good on a leg of lamb for roasting or barbecuing.

If you want to vary the traditional mint seasoning with lamb, try a little thyme, marjoram, ginger, basil or rosemary. Or rub dry mustard or chili powder over cut surface of lamb roast before you put it in the oven. Another way to season a roast is to make several slits on top before cooking; fill openings with slivers of garlic, mint leaves or parsley.

When you serve your lamb dish at the dinner table, be adventurous with accompaniments. Try your favorite barbecue sauce, whipped grape or currant jelly or a firm mold of green mint jelly. And for a final dash of color and flavor, garnish with broiled tomatoes, mushrooms, peach halves, pear halves, orange or pineapple slices or watercress.

To Cook Lamb Roasts and Chops

Lamb cuts should be roasted uncovered until meat is medium or well done. Mint or currant jelly may be basted over roast toward end of cooking period.

To Pan-broil Chops. Snip fat edges of chops. Rub hot pan with a little lamb fat. Brown meat over high heat 1 minute on each side. Reduce heat, and cook to desired doneness. Test color by slitting along bone.

To Broil. Place chops on cold rack under preheated broiler, with top about 3 inches from heat. Broil 6–8 minutes on each side for 1-inch chops, 9–11 minutes for 1 1/2-inch chops.

To Bake. After browning chops over high heat, place pan in 325°F. oven. For 1-inch chops bake 12–18 minutes, turning once, depending on desired doneness.

Unthawed frozen lamb chops should be allowed to cook twice as long as fresh ones.

TIMETABLE FOR ROASTING LAMB*

TYPE OF ROAST	WEIGHT IN POUNDS	MINUTES PER POUND**
Leg	5–8	25–30
Loin	2–3	50–55
Rack	4–5	40–45
Rolled shoulder	3–5	40–50
Cushion shoulder	3–5	30–35

*Oven temperature is 325°F.; meat thermometer reading is 180°F. for well done, 175°F. for medium

**For meat taken from refrigerator (40°F.); for unthawed frozen roasts, extend cooking period by 1/2 the total time required for same size and cut of fresh lamb. The shorter times apply to roasts of heavier weights specified; for smaller cuts allow longer times listed.

Roast Leg of Lamb

```
    6-pound leg of lamb
1/4 cup French Dressing
  1 teaspoon salt
1/2 teaspoon rosemary
1/2 teaspoon thyme
1/2 teaspoon sweet basil
  2 cups boiling water
4–5 tablespoons flour
1/2 cup cold water
    Salt and pepper to taste
```

Have meat at room temperature. Place in shallow pan lined with greased heavy-duty aluminum foil. Score fat; mix dressing, 1 teaspoon salt and herbs, and brush all surfaces of meat. Pour remaining herb mixture over top. Roast at 325°F. allowing 30 minutes per pound, or until meat thermometer registers 180°F. for well done. Remove meat to hot platter, and keep warm. Skim most of fat from drippings, and add boiling water. Stir to dissolve brown bits, lift out foil and pour drippings into saucepan. Combine flour with cold water and thicken gravy to smooth consistency. Taste, and season. Serves 6–8.

Crown Roast of Lamb

```
    Ground lamb
    4-pound crown roast (7 ribs) of lamb
1/2 pound ground ham or beef
1/2 cup tomato juice
1/4 cup finely chopped onion
1/2 teaspoon salt
1/4 teaspoon thyme
1/4 teaspoon rosemary
1/4 teaspoon sweet basil
1/2 cup soft bread crumbs
  1 egg
    Garlic slivers
  1 teaspoon dry mustard
  1 teaspoon salt
1/2 teaspoon rosemary
  7 cubes salt pork
```

Remove ground lamb packed in center of roast, and mix it with ham, tomato juice, onion, 1/2 teaspoon salt, thyme, 1/4 teaspoon rosemary, and basil. Stir in soft bread crumbs and egg. If beef is used in place of ham, add more salt. Refill crown, and insert garlic in meat near base. Make a mixture of dry mustard, 1 teaspoon salt and 1/2 teaspoon rosemary and rub all surfaces of meat. Cover each projecting rib end with cube of salt pork (to prevent charring) or small squares of aluminum foil, and set in open roasting pan. Roast slowly at 325°F. about 3 hours. Lift to hot platter, and remove salt-pork cubes or aluminum foil. Garnish bone ends with preserved kumquats, and spoon hot baby green lima beans or peas into the center over the ground lamb filling. Surround with buttered small white onions. Keep roast warm while making gravy. Serves 5–6.

Note: A crown roast is a special-event cut. Your butcher will usually prepare this roast for you if you order ahead of time. Be sure backbone is removed to make carving easier.

Roast Lamb with Herbs

    3–4-pound rack or shoulder lamb
    1 teaspoon salt
    1/2 teaspoon thyme
    1/2 teaspoon rosemary
    1/2 teaspoon sweet basil
    3/4 cup water (can be water in which vegetables have
        been cooked)

Cut 1/2-inch gashes in fat of lamb roast. Mix salt, thyme, rosemary and basil and rub into meat. Roast uncovered at 400°F. for 45 minutes. Pour off excess fat; lower heat to 325°F. Add water, cover and continue roasting slowly 2 1/2–3 hours. Baste now and then with pan juices. Lift lamb to hot platter, and make gravy.

Grilled Lamb Chop à l'Anglaise

    1 double loin lamb chop with pocket
      Vegetable oil
      Bread crumbs
    2 strips partly cooked bacon
    2 tablespoons finely chopped ham
    1 teaspoon dry mustard

Brush chop with vegetable oil, and dip in bread crumbs. Combine chopped ham and mustard. Fill pocket with mixture. Encircle with bacon, and secure with toothpicks. Broil 10–15 minutes, turning 3 or 4 times. Season, and remove to hot platter. Serves 1.

Casserole Dinner of Lamb Chops

    2 tablespoons fat
    4 lamb-shoulder chops
    4 medium potatoes, halved
    8 small onions, sliced
    8 medium or 4 large carrots, sliced lengthwise
    2 tablespoons butter or margarine
    2 tablespoons flour
    1/4 cup milk
    1 cup sour cream
      Salt and pepper to taste
    1/4 teaspoon powdered ginger
      Paprika

Heat fat in skillet, and brown chops well. Put a layer of potatoes and onions in bottom of deep baking dish; add chops, then another layer of potatoes and onions and top with carrots. Melt butter or margarine, and stir in flour. Remove from heat, and slowly stir in milk, then sour cream. Add ginger, salt and pepper. Return to heat, and cook until smooth and thickened, stirring constantly. Pour over chops, sprinkle with paprika and bake, covered, at 325°F. about 1 1/2–2 hours. Serves 4.

Stewed Breast of Lamb

    1 1/2 pounds breast of lamb
    1/4 pound mushrooms
    1/2 cup chopped onion
    2 tablespoons fat
    1 (10-ounce) can celery soup
    1 cup light cream
    2 tablespoons flour
    1/4 cup cold water
    1 (12-ounce) package frozen green peas, just thawed

Wipe meat with damp cloth or paper towels, and cut into 1-inch cubes. Wash mushrooms, quarter and sauté slowly with onion in fat. Add lamb, soup and cream. Cover, and simmer about 1 1/2 hours or until meat is tender, stirring occasionally. Blend flour and cold water smoothly, and stir into pan to thicken gravy. Simmer another 10 minutes, stirring constantly. Add green peas, and continue slow cooking until just tender. Serves 4–5.

Note: This stew is pale, as meat is stewed without initial browning.

Lamb Stew with Mint Dumplings

    2 pounds trimmed stewing lamb (breast or neck)
    2 tablespoons fat
    2 cups water
    1 (10-ounce) can consommé
    1 tablespoon lemon juice
    1/2 teaspoon salt
      Pinch rosemary
    6 (or more) peeled small potatoes
    6 small onions, peeled
    1/2 cup sliced celery
    1 (11-ounce) package frozen peas and carrots
    2–3 tablespoons flour
    1 recipe *Mint Dumplings*

Cut lamb in pieces; dredge meat with flour. Brown slowly in fat about 15 minutes, turning now and then to color all sides. Add next 5 ingredients. Cover, and simmer 40 minutes. Add potatoes, onions and celery, and continue simmering 15 minutes. Shake in frozen vegetables. Mix 2–3 tablespoons flour with water into smooth paste. When lamb mixture comes to boil, thicken with flour paste. Drop in small mint dumplings, and cover pan tightly. Steam without lifting lid 10 minutes. Serves 6.

Note: For additional flavor, add any or all of the following: pinch sweet basil, Worcestershire sauce, onion flakes, whole clove.

Mint Dumplings

    2 slices white bread
    2/3 cup milk
    1 tablespoon chopped fresh mint
      Dry biscuit mix

Cut crusts off bread; crumble bread into bowl, and add milk and mint. Stir in enough biscuit mix (as it comes from package) to make soft drop dough. Shape lightly into small balls. Makes about 12.

Lamb and Eggplant Ragoût

1 1/2 pounds stewing lamb
1/4 cup flour
1 teaspoon salt
1 teaspoon pepper
2 tablespoons fat
1 (28-ounce) can tomatoes, undrained
5 onions, quartered
3/4 cup sliced celery
3/4 cup diced carrot
1/2 teaspoon salt
1/2 teaspoon sugar
1 eggplant
3 tablespoons flour
1/4 cup water

Cut meat into cubes. Combine 1/4 cup flour, 1 teaspoon salt and pepper; then roll meat cubes in seasoned flour. Heat 2 tablespoons fat in skillet, and brown meat; drain off excess fat, add tomatoes, vegetables (except eggplant), 1/2 teaspoon salt and sugar. Cover and simmer 3/4 hour. Peel eggplant, cut into 1-inch cubes and add to ragoût. Cover, and simmer 1/2 hour longer. Make smooth paste of 3 tablespoons flour and 1/4 cup water and thicken gravy. Cook 10 minutes longer. Taste, and add extra seasoning if required. Serves 4–5.

Lamb and Kidney Pie

3/4 pound ground stewing lamb
2 tablespoons milk
1 teaspoon salt
1/2 teaspoon rosemary
1/8 teaspoon basil
1/8 teaspoon dried mint
2 tablespoons flour
2 tablespoons bacon drippings
1/2 pound lamb kidneys, diced
1 large onion, chopped (1 cup)
1/2 cup sliced celery
1 sliced carrot
1 (10-ounce) can thick soup (Scotch broth, minestrone or chicken gumbo), diluted according to label directions
1 chicken- or beef-bouillon cube
1 tablespoon flour
1 tablespoon cold water
1 deep 9- or 10-inch unbaked pastry shell
1 1/2 cups shredded or riced cooked potatoes or 9- or 10-inch pastry top crust
Fresh mint or parsley sprigs

Mix lamb, milk and seasonings together. Roll into walnut-size balls. Dust with 2 tablespoons flour and brown slowly in drippings. Push to one side of pan, and sauté diced kidneys. Add next 5 ingredients, and cover. Simmer 15 minutes. Combine flour and cold water. Stir in soup and flour-water mixture. Taste, and correct seasonings. Pour into pastry shell. Arrange cooked potatoes around top, or cover with pastry circle. Bake at 400°F. 40–45 minutes. Garnish top with fresh mint sprigs. Serves 5–6.

Curried Lamb with Rice

2 tablespoons flour
1 teaspoon paprika
1/2 teaspoon salt
1/4 teaspoon black pepper
2 pounds stewing lamb
1/2 cup chopped onion
2 tablespoons bacon drippings
2 1/2 cups chicken broth
2 tablespoons vinegar
1 tablespoon curry powder
3 cups hot cooked rice

Mix flour, paprika, salt and pepper. Cut lamb into cubes, and dredge in flour mixture. Brown onion in hot bacon drippings. Add meat, and brown slightly. Add chicken broth, vinegar and curry powder, cover pan and bake 1 1/2 hours at 350°F. (If gravy is too thin, stir in 1 tablespoon flour mixed to paste with 2 tablespoons cold water, and cook 10 minutes more.) Taste for seasoning. Serve around mound of rice. Serves 5–6.

Shish Kebab

1 pound lamb patties (about 2 cups ground lamb)
1/4 cup packaged seasoned bread crumbs
1 teaspoon salt
1/4 teaspoon pepper
1 egg
6 lamb kidneys
3 lemons
6 thick onion wedges
6 cherry tomatoes
Thin barbecue sauce

Lightly mix lamb patties with bread crumbs, salt, pepper, and egg. With wet hands, shape into 12 balls. Cook kidneys 5 minutes in 2 cups boiling water. Drain. Have ready lemons, quartered, and 6 thick wedges of onion. Assemble six skewers as follows: first a wedge of lemon, then a lamb meatball, a wedge of onion, a kidney, another lemon wedge, another meatball. To top it all, a cherry tomato. Place the skewers on a broiler pan. Brush with barbecue sauce. Broil 5 minutes; turn, and brush with sauce again. Broil 5 minutes longer. Serves 6.

BUYING AND COOKING PORK

Rich in distinctive flavor, pork in its almost endless range of cuts and forms—fresh, smoked, cured—is a most versatile meat and rivals beef in popularity. It is high in essential nutrients and always available.

Because it has very little connective tissue and is by nature tender, pork can be successfully cooked by dry-heat methods (as for tender beef parts) and in various other ways as well. But there is one hard-and-fast rule basic to all pork preparations: It must be *thoroughly* cooked, that is, there should be no pink color—the meat should be all grey, and internal temperature 185°F.

In selecting your cut, look for a good proportion of lean to fat. The lean should be firm and fine-grained—light greyish-pink, a deeper rose in older animals. Fat should be firm and white, and bones porous and slightly pink. In pork the proportion of bone to meat is small.

The choicest roasting cuts are the rib, loin, shoulder and leg (the last sometimes known as "fresh ham"). The all-meat tenderloin may be baked or fried. Pork chops and steaks are best braised. Broiling is not recommended because meat is likely to become hard and dry by the time it is well done. Half-inch chops may be pan-broiled successfully. "Pink pork" must never be eaten. Take care that you cook your fresh pork, whatever the cut, until it is greyish-white in color all through.

Pork in roasts, chops, sausages or braised dishes takes agreeably to a wide range of seasonings and accompaniments. When cooking a roast, drop cored apple halves or parboiled onions in pan for last 1/2 hour or so of cooking; or serve it with sauerkraut and caraway seeds. Sage, oregano, paprika and marjoram have an affinity for pork. Garlic, dry mustard or chili powder rubbed over the surface add zest. More than any other fresh meat, pork can support plenty of freshly-ground pepper, in addition to the salt used.

Most pork cuts, no matter what part of the carcass they come from, are tender and therefore suitable for roasting. But shoulder chops and steaks do take well to slower cooking methods, and they give a delicious flavor to vegetables cooked with them.

Because pork is a sweet meat, with a pronounced flavor of its own, it takes very well to a contrasting tart flavor, which is why we so frequently see it combined with applesauce or apple rings or served with sauerkraut. Peaches or pineapple slices make good accompaniments for fresh, smoked or cured pork cuts.

But, in addition to being a valuable standby for varying family menus, pork adds strength to other dishes as a flavor ingredient in a good many recipes in which savory accents provide special touches.

Skewered Pork Cubes

      1/2 cup chopped onion
      1/4 cup lemon juice
      1/4 cup apple juice
        2 tablespoons brown sugar
      1–2 cloves garlic, crushed
        2 tablespoons soy sauce
        1 tablespoon prepared mustard
        2 pounds lean pork
        6 preserved kumquats, crab apples or sweet pickles

Combine everything but pork and kumquats. Use blender if you have one, and let ingredients liquefy. Cut pork in 1-inch cubes, and thread on 6 skewers. Brush meat generously with sauce. Place skewered meat in greased baking pan, and refrigerate, covered, 1/2 hour. Put in 375°F. oven, and roast, 20 minutes. Turn skewers, and brush with remaining sauce; continue cooking until meat is tender, about 20 minutes more. Garnish ends of skewers with preserved kumquats, crab apples or sweet pickles. Serves 6.

Sausages with Apple Rings

      Pork sausages
      1 recipe *Sautéed Apple Rings*

Place sausages in cold frying pan, and cook slowly over moderate heat until browned on all sides and thoroughly cooked, depending on thickness. Average or medium sausages will take 20—25 minutes. Sausages in casings may first be simmered in a very little boiling water; do not prick casings. After 5—6 minutes, drain off water, and fry slowly. Serve with fried apple rings.

Sautéed Apple Rings

      2 large apples
      2 tablespoons sugar
      1 teaspoon cinnamon
      2 tablespoons butter or margarine

Peel and core apples, and cut each into 4 thick slices. Combine sugar and cinnamon. Dip slices into sugar mixture, and sauté gently in butter or margarine in heavy frying pan, browning rings on both sides. Makes 8 rings.

Sweet-and-Sour Pork Wheels

      3/4 cup diced apple
        1 tablespoon butter or margarine
      1/2 cup soft bread crumbs
      1/4 cup raisins
        2 tablespoons milk
          Salt and cinnamon to taste
    10–12 round slices (1/4 inch thick) canned luncheon pork
        1 recipe *Sweet-and-Sour Sauce*

Sauté the apple in melted butter or margarine until tender. Remove from heat, and add bread crumbs, raisins and enough milk or fruit juice to moisten. Season with salt and cinnamon, and spread on half the pork slices; top with remaining pork slices. Place in a greased baking pan, and pour sauce over and around. Bake at 350°F. 25 minutes. Serves 5—6.

Sweet-and-Sour Sauce

    1 small onion, chopped
    2 stalks celery, chopped
    1 (28-ounce) can tomatoes, undrained
    2 tablespoons ketchup or chili sauce
    1 tablespoon brown sugar
    1 tablespoon vinegar
      Salt and pepper to taste
    2 tablespoons flour

Simmer onion, celery and tomatoes with their juice, until tender (about 10 minutes). Add ketchup, brown sugar and vinegar. Season to taste, and thicken slightly with flour.

Layered Sausage Loaf

    1 pound pork-sausage meat
    2 cups soft bread crumbs
    2 cups peeled, diced raw apple
    2 small onions, peeled and chopped
    1/2 teaspoon sage
      Salt and pepper to taste

Divide sausage meat into 2 equal parts. Combine crumbs, apple, onions, sage, salt and pepper. Pat out 1/2 sausage meat in bottom of 9″ x 5″ x 3″ loaf pan. Spread dressing on top, and press down lightly. Cover with remaining meat in smooth layer. Bake at 350°F. about 45 minutes. Invert onto serving platter. Serves 6.

Pigs in Potatoes

    6 small link sausages
    1/4 cup water
    2 cups cold mashed potatoes
    1 egg yolk
    1 tablespoon finely chopped onion
    1 teaspoon finely chopped parsley
    1/4 cup fine dry bread crumbs
    1 egg, diluted with 1 tablespoon water or milk
    2 tablespoons hot fat

Place sausages in heavy skillet, add water, cover and steam 5 minutes. Drain off water, and continue cooking 20 minutes. Beat together potatoes, egg yolk, onion and parsley; then coat each cooked sausage with this mixture, roll in bread crumbs, then in diluted egg, then again in bread crumbs. Fry sausages in very hot fat until golden brown. Serves 3.

Hawaiian Pork

    3–4-pound loin of pork roast
      Salt and pepper to taste
    1/2 cup honey
    1/2 cup pineapple juice

Score fat surface of pork. Season with salt and pepper, and place on rack, fat side up, in roasting pan. Make glaze of honey and pineapple juice. Roast meat 3 hours at 350°F., basting at intervals with glaze. Add a little water to the pan during roasting to prevent glaze from burning. Serve with gravy made from pan juices. Serves 6.

Note: This dish is excellent served cold.

To Cook Pork Roasts and Chops

Any cut of fresh pork of suitable size and shape can be roasted. Use shallow pan, and do not cover; allow sufficient time for slow cooking to bring meat to completely well-done stage, when it will be fork-tender. Season halfway through cooking.

Pork chops and steaks from leg can be pan-broiled, baked or braised. Broiling may be used for loin or rib chops, but thorough cooking is essential. To check doneness, cut slit in meat near bone; if any pink shows, cooking is incomplete.

To Fry Chops. Remove excess fat from chops if desired; snip edges to prevent curling. Use a little fat to rub over hot pan. Brown meat, 3—4 minutes on each side. Reduce heat, cover and cook slowly according to thickness: for 1-inch chops 10 minutes each side, for 1/2-inch chops 4—5 minutes on each side. Pour off accumulation of fat during cooking.

To Bake. After browning each side, place chops uncovered in 325°F. oven, and allow to cook according to thickness: 1/2-inch chops, 8—10 minutes on each side; 1-inch steaks, 18—20 minutes on each side. Turn as required, and pour off excess fat as it accumulates.

In cooking unthawed frozen chops or steaks, extend cooking period by 1/2 the total amount required for a fresh cut of similar thickness.

If rind is left on roast, it should be scored with very sharp knife before cooking begins. This rind makes crisp "crackling," which some people enjoy very much with pork.

TIMETABLE FOR ROASTING PORK*

TYPE OF ROAST	WEIGHT IN POUNDS	MINUTES PER POUND**
Leg, whole, boned	10–14	25–30
Leg, half, bone in	4–6	35–40
Loin, center	3–5	30–35
Picnic shoulder, rolled	3–5	35–40

*Oven temperature 325°F.; meat thermometer reading 185°F.

**For meat taken from refrigerator (40°F.); for unthawed frozen roasts, extend cooking period by 1/2 total time required for same size and cut of fresh pork. Shorter times apply to roasts of heavier weights specified, for smaller cuts allow longer time listed.

One-dish Creole Chop Dinner

    1/2 pound fresh mushrooms, sliced, 2 cups
      1 medium onion, sliced
    1/2 green pepper, sliced
      3 tablespoons butter or margarine
      4 shoulder pork chops
      2 tablespoons flour
      1 teaspoon dry mustard
         Dash sage
      1 (15-ounce) can lima beans
      1 (7 1/2-ounce) can tomato sauce
      2 tablespoons brown sugar
      1 tablespoon molasses

Sauté green pepper, onion and mushrooms in butter or margarine until just tender but not brown; put in 8″ x 10″ baking dish, reserving fat in pan. Combine flour, mustard and sage and sprinkle mixture on chops. Brown chops lightly in fat left in pan; remove. Rinse pan with 1/4 cup juice from lima beans, and pour contents of pan over fried vegetables. Add drained lima beans, tomato sauce, brown sugar and molasses, and stir until well mixed. Set chops on top of mixture, and cover dish with lid or foil. Bake 25 minutes at 350°F. Uncover, and bake 20 minutes longer or until meat is very tender. Serves 4.

Pork Chops with Rice

      4 pork-shoulder chops, 1 inch thick
      4 slices onion, 1/4 inch thick
      4 rings green pepper
    1/4 cup uncooked rice (not quick-cooking)
      3 cups canned tomatoes
      1 cup diced celery

Cut off and fry some pork fat in pan. In this fat, brown chops well on both sides—about 15 minutes total. Place slice of onion on each pork chop and ring of green pepper on top onion, and 1 tablespoon uncooked rice in each ring. Pour tomatoes over meat, and add celery. Cover pan, and simmer 1 hour, or transfer to covered baking dish, and bake at 350°F. 1 hour. Serves 4.

Stuffed Pork Chops

      6 rib pork chops, 3/4 inch or more thick
      1 cup soft bread crumbs
    1/4 cup celery
    1/4 cup chopped onion
      2 tablespoons chopped parsley
         Milk to moisten
    1/4 teaspoon salt
    1/8 teaspoon paprika
    1/4 cup milk or sour cream

Wipe chops with damp cloth, remove bones and trim off excess fat. Prepare dressing by combining remaining ingredients except 1/4 cup milk. Cut large gash or pocket in side of each chop, and fill with dressing. Sew chops up with coarse needle and thread. Sear in hot skillet; transfer to baking pan. Cover bottom of pan with 1/4 cup milk. Cover pan, and bake chops at 350°F. until tender—about 1 hour. Serves 4—6.

Stuffed Roast Pork

    4–5-pound pork butt or leg, boned
      1 recipe *Apricot Dressing*
      3 tablespoons flour
         Chicken broth or vegetable stock

The roast should be taken out of refrigerator at least 1/2 hour before cooking. Stuff cavity with apricot dressing. Fasten securely with string to hold shape. If rind is still on, score it with sharp knife to facilitate carving. Place meat on rack in roasting pan, and cook, uncovered, until well done—about 3 1/2 hours at 325°F. Let roast stand in warm place 10 minutes while making gravy, to make carving easier. Skim fat from pan juices. Stir flour into pan juices to thicken, adding enough chicken broth to achieve correct consistency. Taste for seasoning. Remove string from roast before bringing to table. Serves 6—8.

Note: Have your butcher remove bone from roast when you buy it; ask him to leave rind on if you prefer crisp, crunchy top.

Apricot Dressing

    1/3 cup soft dried apricots
    1/2 cup cold water
      2 cups soft, stale bread crumbs, packed
    1/2 cup chopped celery
      3 tablespoons melted butter or margarine
    1/2 teaspoon salt
    1/2 teaspoon rosemary
      2 teaspoons sugar

Combine apricots and water in saucepan, and bring to boil. Simmer 5 minutes; then drain, reserving liquid, and cut into strips. Mix strips with remaining ingredients, and moisten slightly with water from apricots, if necessary.

Baked Pork Tenderloin

      2 whole pork tenderloins (1/2–3/4 pound each)
         Bread (or apple) stuffing
    4–6 bacon strips

Split tenderloins lengthwise. Cover 2 pieces with stuffing. Top each with remaining pieces; fasten together with skewers or string. Place bacon over top. Roast on rack in shallow pan in center of moderate oven, 325°F., 1 1/4—1 1/2 hours. Serves 4—6.

Mock Geese

     12 thin slices lean pork tenderloin
         Salt and pepper to taste
      2 apples, each cut into 6 vertical sections
      6 prunes, halved
    1/4 cup grated onion
      2 eggs, beaten
    1/2 cup fine dry bread crumbs
      2 tablespoons butter or margarine
    3/4 cup (approximately) stock, water or sweet cider

Pound meat, and rub with salt and pepper. Lay apple section and 1/2 prune on each pork slice. Top each with 1 teaspoon grated onion; roll up, and tie with string. Dip in beaten egg, then in crumbs; brown rolls in butter or margarine in heavy frying pan; add stock to depth of 1/4 inch. Cover, and braise about 1 hour or until meat is tender. Turn rolls once, and baste a few times while cooking, adding more liquid if necessary. Remove string, place rolls on platter and pour a little gravy from pan over them. Serves 4—6.

Baked Spareribs

    2 pieces side spareribs (1 1/2 pounds each)
    Bread (or apple) stuffing
    Salad oil
    Salt and pepper

Cut ribs into serving-size pieces, 5—6 ribs each. Spread well-seasoned stuffing over each piece; roll up, and tie with string. Brush with oil, and sprinkle with salt and pepper. Bake in shallow roasting pan at 325°F. 1 1/2—2 hours. Serves 4—6.

Note: Spareribs may be cooked for carving at the table. Place 1 long piece hollow side up, and spread with stuffing. Cover with second piece, hollow side down, and skewer or tie ribs together.

Pork Hocks with Sauerkraut

    3 pounds fresh pork hocks
    6–8 cups hot water
    3/4 cup chopped onion
    1 tablespoon salt
    1 tablespoon mixed pickling spice
    1 (28-ounce) can sauerkraut, drained, or 1 small
        cabbage, cut in wedges

Scrub pork hocks thoroughly. Cover with water; add onion, salt and spices. Cover tightly and simmer 1 1/2—1 3/4 hours. Skim off fat. Strain cooking liquid. Return 1 cup liquid to saucepan. Arrange sauerkraut or cabbage around hocks. Simmer 10—12 minutes or until cabbage is tender. Drain, and serve hocks surrounded by vegetable on hot platter. Serves 6.

Stuffed Pork Steaks

    2 pounds pork-shoulder steaks
    2 teaspoons lemon juice
    1/2 teaspoon salt
    1/4 teaspoon pepper
    2 cups dry bread crumbs
    3/4 cup cream
    1/2 cup raisins, chopped
    1 teaspoon salt
    2 tablespoons flour
    2 tablespoons fat
    2 bouillon cubes
    1 cup boiling water

Pound steaks to 1/4-inch thickness; cut into 6 oblong serving pieces. Make a mixture of lemon juice, 1/2 teaspoon salt and pepper and rub into meat. Combine next 4 ingredients, and spread over pork slices. Roll slices, and secure with toothpicks or twine. Dredge with flour, and

brown well in hot fat. Dissolve bouillon cubes in boiling water, and add to rolls. Cover pan, and simmer 30—40 minutes. Serves 6.

CURED OR SMOKED HAM

Bacon and ham products are available in a wide variety of forms; there are also many ways to serve them.

Hams—the cured, smoked legs of pork—are available in almost bewildering variety today; uncooked, partially cooked or completely cooked; boneless or bone in; whole or in various small sections; canned or in dry wrap. The price rises according to the amount of pre-preparation. Most packers identify each type of ham and suggest home procedures on wrapper or tag. Always follow these directions for best results.

Nowadays hams are very mildly cured, compared with earlier times, when cold storage was inadequate and strong brines had to be used as preservatives. Today's hams should be stored in the same way as fresh pork—refrigerated until just before cooking.

Bacon comes sliced or in slabs. It has a high proportion of fat to lean—the former white and firm, the latter deep pink to reddish-brown. Canadian-style bacon comes from the loin and is leaner and more expensive. It's sold sliced or by the piece.

All bacon is best started in a cold pan, cooked over low to moderate heat and turned frequently. High heat toughens and hardens meat.

Bacon or ham can be useful as a flavor emphasis in other cooked dishes, or can perk up otherwise bland dishes. They combine well with many other ingredients—fish, cheese, eggs, vegetables, dried beans and other meats.

Here are a few suggestions. Fry bacon until crisp, and crumble into cream soups. Cut slices into 1-inch pieces and scatter over tops of such casserole dishes as macaroni and soufflés. Add small bacon pieces to any savory crumb topping. Strips of bacon or ham about 1/2 inch wide, fried until crisp and drained of any fat, can be scattered over the top of cooked green peas or beans at the last minute, in which case 1 teaspoon or so of chopped onion may be fried with bacon.

Bacon can add flavor to soups, stews, and casseroles. When you make a meat loaf, place strips of bacon across top of loaf before putting it in oven.

Ham and bacon also can lend variety to salads. Add crumbled bacon or cubes or strips of cooked ham to potato salad. Crumbled bacon adds a novel touch to any green salad, and cubes of ham and cheese add protein to make it a main-dish attraction. Then, of course, there are many uses for these meats in snacks and sandwiches.

To Cook Cured and Smoked Pork

Many of the cured, smoked pork cuts on to-day's market are packaged with full instructions for home preparation, according to the degree of tenderizing or cooking that has already been done by the processor. These directions should be followed for best results.

In general, hams should be baked, uncovered, in a moderately slow oven. Casing should be left on until cooking is completed, then removed before glazing or other finishing. The casing on a boned, rolled ham is easier to remove before cooking.

Cooking in Water. Cottage rolls and uncooked picnic shoulders may be cooked in simmering water on top of the stove. Add water to cover meat; add spices and raw vegetables for flavor; cover kettle, and cook until tender. Allow about 40 minutes per pound for cottage rolls; 30—35 minutes for 5—7-pound picnic shoulder; 35—40 minutes for boneless picnic shoulder.

To Cook Ham Steaks. Ham steaks may be baked in preheated 325°F. oven, allowing 50—55 minutes for 1-inch thickness and 1—1 1/4 hours for 1 1/2-inch thickness; pour 1/2 cup milk or fruit juice over them during cooking.

To Pan-broil. Brown over high heat for a few minutes on each side; cover, and cook slowly, allowing 8—10 minutes on each side for 1-inch steak, 6—8 minutes on each side of a thinner slice.

To Broil. Place on cold rack under preheated broiler, with meat 3 inches from heat. Broil 9—10 minutes on each side for 1-inch steak, 4—5 minutes on each side for 1/2-inch slice.

To Bake Bacon. If you have to cook a large amount of bacon at one time, use oven instead of frying pan. Place slices, with fat edge of each overlapping lean edge of next slice, on rack in shallow pan or broiler pan. Bake in oven pre-heated to 400°F., allowing 12—15 minutes or until bacon is crisp. There is no need to turn or drain.

To Broil Bacon. Place slices of bacon on rack of preheated broiler about 3 inches from heat. They take only 1—2 minutes on each side and should be turned once. Watch carefully, as they cook very rapidly.

Note: To seperate bacon with speed, put whole layer of sliced bacon in pan without sepa-rating slices; as bacon heats, slices can be easily separated.

TIMETABLE FOR BAKING HAM*

TYPE OF HAM	WEIGHT IN POUNDS	MINUTES PER POUND**
Whole ham	10—14	18—20
Ham (boneless)	7—10	22—25
Half ham	5—7	22—25
Picnic shoulder	5—8	35
Picnic shoulder (boneless)	3—5	45

*Oven temperature is 325°F.; meat thermometer reading is 170°F.

**Times are for hams taken directly from refrigerator (40°F.). Shorter times apply to roasts of heavier weights specified; for smaller cuts allow times listed.

Glazed Baked Whole Ham

The mildly cured, high-grade hams of today usually come in packers' wraps with complete cooking instructions for each specific product. For best results it is wise to follow the method and timing suggested. As a general rule, a fine whole raw ham needs no presimmering; it is baked, uncovered, on rack in roasting pan, with-out added moisture, in moderately slow oven (325°F.). Minutes per pound depend on total weight and initial temperature of meat. If taken from refrigerator just before cooking, allow 20 minutes per pound for large, heavy ham; 25 min-utes for 10—12 pounds. If a meat thermometer is used, internal temperature should register 170°F. to indicate doneness. At the end of cooking period take ham from oven, and remove rind by loosen-ing with sharp knife and lifting off gently, leaving smooth white fat. Cut gashes 1/4 inch deep in long diagonal lines to form diamonds. Stick clove in center of each diamond. Spread with 1 of the following glazes, covering all fat. Return meat to oven, with heat increased to 425°F., and allow glaze to brown, about 15 minutes. Baste once or twice.

GLAZES:

* *Sugar Glaze*: Mix 1 1/2 cups firmly packed brown sugar, 2 teaspoons dry mustard, 3 table-spoons flour; blend in 1/4 cup cider vinegar.

* *Marmalade Glaze*: Mix 1/2 cup orange mar-malade, 3/4 cup brown sugar, 1 tablespoon flour, 2 teaspoons dry mustard and sufficient orange juice to make thick paste.

* *Pineapple Glaze*: Mix 1 1/2 cups brown sugar and 3/4 cups crushed pineapple that has been thoroughly drained of its juice and 2 teaspoons dry mustard.

Note: A simple finish can be given by basting with maple syrup, liquid honey or beaten apple jelly.

Cold Apricot Glazed Ham

Buy a fully cooked or ready-to-serve whole ham. With a sharp knife trim fat to an even thickness.

Gash 2 or 3 large concentric circles in the top of the remaining fat towards the shank end. Place ham in a shallow roast pan, and rub top and sides with a mixture of flour and dry mustard. If the flour-mustard mixture is rubbed in well the glaze will cling more evenly. Combine 2 cups apricot jam or marmalade, 1–2 tablespoons prepared mustard, 1/4 cup corn syrup and 1/4 cup brown sugar in a saucepan. Heat and stir until bubbly. Cool slightly, and spoon and spread over top and sides of the ham. Bake at 400°F. 15 minutes. Spoon more glaze over the ham to cover any bare areas, and bake 10–15 minutes longer. Remove from oven, and brush any remaining glaze over ham where needed. Chill. Lift to a platter. Garnish with branches of mint and cheese flowers, cut out with small aspic cutters. Secure branches and flowers with toothpicks, and add bits of red glacé cherries for flower centers.

Ham Rolls

    1 1/2 cups cooked rice
    1/4 cup toasted almonds
      2 tablespoons chopped parsley
      2 tablespoons butter or margarine, melted
      8 thin slices cooked ham
      1 (10-ounce) can cream of chicken soup
    1/2 soup can water

Mix first 4 ingredients, and place rounded tablespoon of mixture on each ham slice. Roll, fasten with toothpicks and place in baking dish. Mix soup and water, and pour over ham rolls. Bake at 350°F. 20 minutes. Serves 4–6.

Ham-Noodle Scallop

    1/2 package (4 ounces) broad noodles
    1/4 pound mushrooms (1 cup)
      2 tablespoons butter or margarine
      2 cups diced cooked ham
      2 teaspoons prepared mustard
      2 cups medium white sauce
      2 tablespoons finely grated cheese
      2 tablespoons fine dry bread crumbs

Cook noodles as directed on package; drain, and rinse with cold water. Chop mushrooms, and sauté in butter or margarine. Combine noodles, mushrooms, ham and mustard with white sauce in greased casserole. Mix bread crumbs and cheese, and use resulting "cheese crumbs" to top casserole. Serves 5–6.

Cauliflower-Ham Scallop

      1 medium head cauliflower, cooked
      3 cups medium white sauce
      2 cups diced cooked ham
    1/4 cup almonds, blanched
      2 tablespoons butter or margarine
      1 cup cracker crumbs

Cauliflower may be left whole or broken apart. Arrange it in baking dish. Combine white sauce, ham and almonds, and pour over cauliflower. Melt butter or margarine, stir in crumbs and use to top cauliflower mixture. Bake at 350°F. until crumbs brown and dish is heated through—about 30 minutes. Serves 6–7.

Roast Ham

    2–3-pound cooked picnic ham
    1/2 cup apple juice or cider

Set ham on heavy-duty foil in roasting pan, folding up sides and ends of foil to make narrow container to fit ham with just 1 inch to spare. Pour apple juice over the meat, and bake at 375°F. at least 45 minutes (meat thermometer should register 145°F.).

Note: The secret of success here is to have the pan fit the meat, so that the apple juice gently flavors the meat and you don't have to baste it.

Broiled Ham Steaks

Preheat broiler 5 minutes. Snip fat edges of raw ham steaks, and place on cold rack of broiler pan so that meat is 3 inches from heating unit. For 1-inch steaks, broil 9–10 minutes on each side, for 1/2-inch steaks, 4–5 minutes on each side. After turning, glaze with your favorite ham glaze, or baste several times during cooking, using maple syrup, honey, apple jelly or fruit juice.

Ham with Cranberries

      2 cups cranberries
      2 slices raw smoked center-cut ham, 1 inch thick
      1 cup brown sugar, firmly packed
        Whole cloves

Wash and chop cranberries. Place 1 slice ham in baking dish, and cover with 1/2 the berries and 1/2 the sugar. Place other ham slice on top, and cover with remaining berries and sugar. Stud fatty edges of ham with whole cloves, and bake 1 hour at 300°–350°F., basting occasionally with liquid in pan. Serves 4–5.

Baked Ham with Potatoes and Onions

      2-pound slice raw smoked ham, 1/2 inch thick
      6 medium potatoes, peeled and sliced
    1/4 cup flour
      2 onions, peeled and sliced
      1 cup milk (approximately)

Place ham in casserole, and cover with layer of potato slices. Sprinkle with flour, and add layer of onion. Repeat layers, ending with potatoes. Pour in milk until it is halfway up the dish. Cover, and bake at 350°F. 1 hour. Uncover during last few minutes to brown. Serves 4–6.

Paprika Ham

2 tablespoons butter or margarine
1 small onion, sliced
2 cups cooked ham, cubed
1 (7 1/2-ounce) can tomato sauce
2 tablespoons prepared mustard
1 teaspoon paprika
1 cup sour cream

Melt butter or margarine, and sauté onion until transparent. Add ham. Mix together tomato sauce, mustard and paprika. Stir into ham, and simmer 30 minutes. Just before serving, stir in sour cream; heat, but do not boil. Serve with rice. Serves 4.

Ham with Tarragon Sauce

6 scallions or 1 small onion, chopped
1 teaspoon dried tarragon
1/2 cup wine vinegar
2/3 cup heavy cream
1/3 cup chicken bouillon
2 egg yolks
2 tablespoons butter or margarine
Salt and pepper to taste
4 slices baked or boiled ham

Simmer onions with tarragon and vinegar until reduced by 1/2. Place in top of double boiler over hot water, and add cream, bouillon and egg yolks. Cook, stirring, until mixture thickens, taking care not to boil. Stir in butter or margarine and salt and pepper. Pour over baked or boiled ham. Serves 4.

VARIETY MEATS

"Variety meats" are the edible parts of an animal that are not classified as flesh: liver, kidney, tongue, heart, sweetbreads, brains, tripe, oxtail. Most are rich in minerals and vitamins and inexpensively add variety to your menus. They must be handled with care and speed, for they spoil very quickly. Be sure they are fresh when you buy them, and use them within 1 day of purchase; or freeze in proper wrapping, and use within 3—4 months.

Liver

Calf or veal liver is the choicest and costliest kind. It has the lightest reddish-brown coloring; it is mild-flavored, tender and very suitable for sautéing or broiling. Beef and pork liver are stronger in flavor and less tender. Braising makes them more tender and the liquid added may provide tempting flavor.

Thin, even slices of liver are desirable for uniform cooking. Allow about 1/4 pound for each serving. Cook calf liver only to desired doneness; overcooking toughens it.

Kidney

Allow about 1/4 pound of fresh kidneys per serving. This meat requires careful preparation to ensure good flavor and tenderness. Cut away membrane, fat and tubes, and slice meat in neat pieces. The strong flavor of beef and pork kidneys can be diminished by soaking uncooked meat in salted cold water (1 teaspoon salt to 1 cup water) in refrigerator for 1 hour or so.

Heart

All heart meat is close-textured and muscular and must therefore have long cooking at low temperatures. Choose hearts that are smooth, shiny and well rounded. One beef heart will serve 8—10; one veal or pork heart makes 2—3 servings; small lamb hearts yield 1 serving each. Before cooking, wash heart thoroughly, and trim away any fat, tubes or coarse fibers.

Tongue

Tongue is not so tender as are most of the other variety meats and requires long, slow cooking in moist heat.

Calf and veal tongues are usually sold fresh. Lamb and beef tongues are available either fresh or pickled. Pork tongues usually come in cans or jars as "lunch tongue." The cooking method is the same for fresh and pickled types, but pickled tongue should be soaked for a minimum of 2 hours beforehand in cold water.

Allow about 1 pound for 4 servings.

Sweetbreads

Sweetbreads are the pinkish-white thymus glands of young calves and lambs. They are delicate in flavor and generally considered gourmet food. Allow 1/4 pound of sweetbreads for each serving.

Nowadays sweetbreads are usually sold frozen because of their high perishability. After thawing, sweetbreads should be precooked. To achieve firmer texture, parboil in water with a little vinegar or lemon juice and salt, drain quickly, chill in fresh water and slip off membrane with fingers. The sweetbreads may then be heated in a cream sauce, fried, broiled or braised.

Brains

Another tender and delicate-flavored specialty, brains should be parboiled and recooked in the same way as sweetbreads. Allow 1/4 pound per serving.

Tripe

Tripe comes from the muscular inner lining of the stomach of cattle, is creamy-yellow in color and is either smooth or honeycombed. All tripe is cleaned and partially cooked before it is sold; nevertheless additional cooking is required to tenderize. Cover, and simmer until tender, about 1 1/2 hours.

Much of the tripe on the market is used commercially in canned meat products, soups and so forth.

Liver-Onion Hot Pot

    1/2 pound beef liver
    1/4 cup seasoned flour
    1/2 pound sausages
    1–2 tablespoons bacon drippings
  1 1/2 cups consommé or tomato juice
      1 bay leaf
    3–4 medium potatoes, peeled and sliced
      2 sliced onions
    1/4 cup flour
         Salt and pepper to taste
    1/4 teaspoon Worcestershire sauce
      2 tablespoons bread crumbs, buttered

Dip liver in seasoned flour. Fry liver and sausages together in bacon drippings until lightly cooked; remove from pan. Put consommé and bay leaf in pan; stir to dissolve brown bits. Cut liver and sausage into 1-inch pieces. Grease 1-quart baking dish, and add alternate layers of potatoes, onions, liver and sausage, ending with potatoes. Between layers, sprinkle 1/4 cup flour, salt, pepper and Worcestershire sauce. Pour in consommé, and sprinkle top with buttered crumbs. Cover, and bake at 350°F. 30 minutes. Uncover, and continue baking 30–40 minutes. Serves 3–4.

Note: This dish is just as tasty made with leftover liver and sausage.

Liver-Bacon Croquettes

    3/4 pound pork liver
         Salted water
    1/2 small onion
    3/4 cup canned tomatoes or tomato juice
    1/2 cup dry bread crumbs
      2 teaspoons prepared mustard
         Salt and pepper to taste
    1/4 cup dry bread crumbs or flour
    5–6 slices bacon
      1 tablespoon melted drippings

Cover and cook liver in salted water about 10 minutes. Drain and cool. Mince liver and onion together; add tomatoes, 1/2 cup crumbs, mustard and seasonings. Form into 5 or 6 cylindrical croquettes. Roll each in crumbs or flour, and encircle with bacon. Secure with toothpicks, brush with melted drippings and bake at 400°F. about 20 minutes or until bacon is crisp. Serves 5–6.

Fried Liver

Coat liver slices with seasoned flour, melt small amount of fat in pan (if serving liver with bacon, fry bacon first, and cook liver in hot bacon fat). Turn heat to high. Cook just 1 minute to brown on both sides; reduce heat to medium, and cook 2–3 minutes longer, turning once or twice. Partial covering of pan at this stage will keep liver tender and juicy.

VARIATION:

* *Fried Kidney*: Use sliced or halved kidneys, but cook over medium heat a few minutes longer or until all red color at center of meat has disappeared. Avoid overcooking.

Kidney Stew

  1 1/2 pounds beef kidneys
      1 quart cold salted water
    1/4 cup seasoned flour
    1/2 cup chopped onion
      2 tablespoons hot fat
      1 (10-ounce) can consommé
      1 cup water
         Salt and pepper
    1–2 tablespoons vinegar

Split kidneys, and remove all fatty tissue. Cut into 1-inch pieces, and soak 1/2 hour in cold salted water. Drain; dry on paper towels. Roll kidneys in seasoned flour, and brown with onion in fat. Add consommé and water, and simmer, covered, about 1 1/2 hours. If necessary, thicken with 1 tablespoon flour mixed with 2 tablespoons water. Season with salt and pepper; add vinegar last. Serves 6.

Oxtail-Kidney Ragoût

      1 oxtail, cut in pieces
    1/2 pound beef kidney, diced
    1/4 cup flour
      2 tablespoons fat
      2 tablespoons Worcestershire sauce
      1 teaspoon salt
      1 beef-bouillon cube
      1 (28-ounce) can tomatoes
      2 bay leaves
      4 small onions, peeled
    1/2 cup sliced celery
    1/2 cup diced turnip
      3 tablespoons flour
      3 tablespoons water

Dredge oxtail and kidney in flour, and brown slowly in fat until all sides are colored. Add Worcestershire sauce, salt, bouillon cube, tomatoes and bay leaves. Cover, and simmer 45 minutes; then add onions, celery and turnip. Cook 30 minutes longer or until meat and vegetables are tender. Remove bay leaves. Make smooth paste of flour and 3 tablespoons water; use to thicken cooking liquid. Serves 4.

Braised Chicken Livers

    1 pound chicken livers
    1/4 cup flour
    3/4 teaspoon salt
        Pinch pepper
    3 tablespoons fat
    2 tablespoons chopped onion
    2 tablespoons chopped green pepper
    2 cups chicken broth
    1/2 teaspoon Worcestershire sauce

Cut away any stringy portions from livers. Wash meat in cold water, and dry with paper towels. Mix flour and seasonings (varying latter if desired); put in paper bag, add livers and shake to coat all surfaces. Melt fat in frying pan. Brown meat in fat, add onion and green pepper and cook 1 minute. Add chicken broth and Worcestershire sauce. Simmer, covered, about 10 minutes or until livers readily break apart with fork. Serves 4–5.

VARIATION:

* *Braised Chicken Giblets*: Substitute 1 pound mixed giblets—hearts, gizzards, livers—for chicken livers. Before cooking, cut away membranes, fat and so forth, and slice gizzards. Simmer, covered, until tender. Serve over boiled noodles or fluffy rice.

Liver Loaf

    1 1/2 pounds beef or other liver
    1 1/2 cups boiling water
    1/4 pound salt pork
    3/4 cup rolled oats
    1 medium onion
    2 eggs
    1/2 cup tomato juice
    1/2 teaspoon thyme
        Salt and pepper to taste
    6 bacon strips
    6 tomato slices

Cover liver with boiling water, and let stand 10 minutes. Drain off liquid, and grind liver with salt pork, oats and onion. Add eggs, tomato juice and seasonings, mix well and pack mixture into greased casserole. Garnish with bacon strips and tomato slices, and bake 1 hour at 350°F. Serves 6.

Chicken Livers Supreme

    1 pound chicken livers
    2 tablespoons butter or margarine, melted
    1 tablespoon flour
    1 (10-ounce) can mushroom gravy
    1 tablespoon chopped onion
    1/2 teaspoon salt
        Dash hot pepper sauce
    3 tablespoons sherry
    24 melba toast points

Halve chicken livers, and sauté slowly in butter or margarine until lightly browned. Stir in flour, mushroom gravy, onion, salt and pepper sauce. Cover, and cook until livers are tender,

about 10 minutes. Remove from heat, and add sherry. Pour into serving dish, and keep hot. Serve over points of melba toast. Serves 6.

Savory Hearts

    2 veal or lamb hearts
    1 tablespoon flour
    2 tablespoons hot shortening
    1 small onion, sliced
    2 bouillon cubes
    2 cups boiling water
    1/4 cup vinegar
    2 tablespoons sugar
    1/2 teaspoon salt
    1/2 teaspoon mixed herbs, crushed
    1/4 teaspoon pepper

Clean hearts, removing membranes and large veins. Cut into cubes, dredge with flour in paper bag and brown in hot fat over medium heat. Add onion. Crumble bouillon cubes in boiling water, and combine with remaining ingredients. Pour over meat in skillet. Cover, and simmer 1/2 hour or until tender. Serves 4.

Oven-braised Stuffed Heart

    1 tablespoon fat
    1 tablespoon chopped onion
    1 tablespoon chopped celery
    2 cups soft bread crumbs
    1 teaspoon sage
    1/2 teaspoon salt
    1/8 teaspoon pepper
    1 beef heart (about 3 pounds)
        Salt and pepper to taste
    1/4 cup seasoned flour
    1 tablespoon hot fat
    3/4 cup hot water or vegetable stock

Melt 1 tablespoon fat, and cook onion and celery until lightly colored. Add to bowl with next 4 ingredients, and mix well. Wash heart, dry, hollow out a cavity for stuffing and sprinkle with salt and pepper. Stuff heart, fasten with skewers and tie firmly in place with string. Roll heart in seasoned flour, and brown in 1 tablespoon hot fat, turning to color all surfaces. Place heart in oven pan or casserole that can be tightly covered. Rinse out searing pan with hot water, and pour over heart. Cover and cook in oven at 300°F. until tender—3–4 hours. Serves 4.

Herbed Tongue

    1 fresh beef tongue (3–4 pounds)
    2 stalks celery, sliced
    2 carrots, sliced
    1 medium onion, sliced
    3 bay leaves
    1 tablespoon mixed pickling spice
    1 clove garlic, cut
    1 tablespoon salt
    2 peppercorns
    10–12 cups hot water

Scrub tongue thoroughly. Put in pan with vegetables and seasonings; pour hot water over.

Cover tightly, and simmer slowly until tender, about 60 minutes per pound. Tongue is done when it can be readily pierced with fork and the skin comes off easily. Lift out tongue, and while still hot, remove skin and any ragged glands, gristle, fat and bones from root end. Serve hot with suitable sauce, or allow to cool thoroughly and serve sliced in sandwiches or accompanied by other cold meats and salad. Serves 4—6.

VARIATION:

* Substitute 1 pickled for fresh tongue, and soak in cold water at least 2 hours before cooking. Omit salt, and cook about 45 minutes per pound.

POULTRY

Poultry, always available, is a year-round favorite.

Because it is rich in protein, minerals and vitamins, poultry is an ideal alternate for animal meats and as a main course often costs considerably less. (See Chapter 1 for explanation of poultry grading.)

Turkey

Before buying, estimate your special requirements. For each serving of roast turkey, you will need 1/2 pound very large turkey, or 1 pound small turkey. When making stuffing, allow 3/4 cup for every pound of turkey's weight.

Estimate your oven capacity as well. A huge king-size bird that crowds an oven, blocking heat circulation, will require extra cooking time. Unless you are preparing for a big occasion with guests, you would be better advised to choose a smaller bird. The recently developed 6—8-pound turkey, plump and delicate in flavor, is ideal for average family use the year round, and there is no long-drawn-out leftover problem.

Turkey can be cooked by methods used for chicken: simmered or stewed, oven-broiled or fried in covered skillet on top of stove. Have turkey cut up—in most cases it is an advantage to cut it into serving-size pieces, which will reduce total cooking time necessary to bring meat to perfect tenderness.

Chicken

This familiar term now covers a sizable group of fowl, most bred and finished for special culinary use. Rock Cornish hens are tiny birds, averaging 1 pound and never more than 2 pounds. They may be roasted or broiled; a larger bird makes 2 servings. Broiler-fryer chickens, 1 1/2—3 1/2 pounds, are excellent for roasting, broiling or frying; allow 1/4—1/2 bird per serving. With roasters (more than 3 1/2 pounds) and capons—the plump, desexed males, weighing as much as 8 pounds—stuffing and roasting or oven-frying is the ideal treatment. Allow 3/4 pound per serving. Stewing fowl is the market name for laying hens; they must be cooked in moist heat as in stewing, to make them tender. The weight of stewing fowl varies from 2 1/2—6 pounds, 1/2—3/4 pound is about right for each serving.

Cut-up chicken is readily available and offers many advantages. You may purchase legs, breasts or wings separately, according to your family's tastes or your preferred method of preparation: frying, oven-frying, braising, fricasseeing and so on.

Ducks and Geese

These birds are quite different from chickens and turkeys. Their meat is dark, they have distinctive flavors not unlike those of wild game and they have high proportions of fat. Always look for a duck or a goose that is not too fat. Estimate at least 1 pound per serving.

Ducklings are young ducks, 8—12 weeks old, weighing up to 5 pounds. Geese vary from 6—14 pounds. As their meat is tender and delicate, these birds may be roasted or cut up and broiled.

Because ducks and geese contain so much fat themselves, fat is never applied to them when roasting. Boiling water is sometimes used to "baste" a fat bird, or fruit juices to counteract richness and add flavor. A well-seasoned bread stuffing may be used. Or stuff cavity with sliced apple, onion, celery bits and poultry seasoning. Discard apple stuffing before serving, as bird will have absorbed flavors during cooking.

It is unwise to keep fresh poultry, even under refrigeration, longer than 1—2 days before cooking. Loosen wrappings, and store in coldest part of refrigerator. If you do not plan to cook it within the next 2 days, freeze it. Giblets should be washed and cooked immediately or wrapped in a separate package and frozen.

To Freeze. Tie wings and legs close to body. Wrap airtight in freezer paper, aluminum foil or plastic wrap, pressing the wrapping material close to the bird to exclude as much air as possible.

Mark with weight and date. Stored at 0°F., turkey should be used within 6 months; whole chicken or stewing fowl within 12 months at the most.

Never freeze home-stuffed poultry, either before or after cooking, as it carries the risk of food poisoning. The heat to be applied later cannot penetrate quickly enough to the center of the chilled dressing to ensure that possibly harmful food organisms are destroyed. (Commercially stuffed and frozen raw birds are protected by "stabilizers" in their preparation. Simply follow instructions on the package.)

Home-prepared poultry should be stuffed just before cooking. If you prepare stuffing ahead, store it in shallow pan, covered, in refrigerator until ready to use.

Frozen poultry must be thawed before cooking. Do not remove freezer wrap. Allow 5 hours per pound when thawing in refrigerator. For speedier thawing, place wrapped bird under cold, running water. Room-temperature thawing requires about 1 1/2 hours per pound—less if cool air from electric fan is directed on bird while thawing.

Note: Certain frozen poultry purchased stuffed "ready for the oven" should be roasted *unthawed* as indicated on package.

Cleaning and Cooking

Most poultry on the market today is ready to cook, but if the bird has not been drawn (entrails removed), here is the procedure.

Place bird on its back. Make an incision through skin along line from end of keel to vent. Do not cut vent. Lift out intestines located at left side of bird, but do not detach. Place left forefinger under intestines close to vent. Make incision around vent so that entrails (intestines, gizzard, heart, lungs, liver, kidneys, crop and windpipe) may be removed intact. Grasp gizzard, located at right side and to rear of body cavity, and remove. All entrails must be completely removed, including red, spongy lung bits adhering to ribs. Detach giblets (heart, liver and gizzard) from entrails.

Remove any pinfeathers with tweezers. The oil sac (a small nodule under skin at back of bird, close to tail) should be cut out. It will produce a strong flavor if left in.

Ask your butcher to remove leg tendons on large birds like turkeys.

If necessary, singe off hairs by rotating bird over flame. Wash outside of bird thoroughly. Rinse body cavity with plenty of cold water. Drain well.

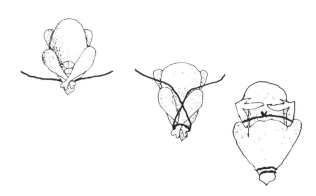

Dry with soft cloth. Sprinkle cavity with salt, and fill lightly with stuffing. Allow room for expansion during cooking; otherwise stuffing may become soggy. To close slit, use poultry pins, and lace with cord—or sew with darning needle and coarse white thread.

Because a cooked bird looks better and is moister if legs and wings are kept close to body, poultry should always be trussed after dressing.

Before putting bird in oven, insert meat thermometer into inside thigh muscle (thermometer must not touch bone). Cook until reading is 190° F. If thermometer is inserted through center of bird, having tip surrounded by stuffing, reading should be 165°F.

If you do not have a thermometer, make the drumstick test. If the bird is properly done, the leg will move freely at the hip socket, and the meat will feel soft.

Follow timetable for each kind of fowl for approximate cooking periods. Remember that size and shape of uncooked bird influences length of time necessary to roast it.

Keep cooked bird in warm place 10 minutes before carving to allow juices to be absorbed, so that meat will stay moist and carving will be easier.

Roast Turkey

Sprinkle body cavity with salt. Lightly fill both neck and body cavities with dressing; do not pack. Truss. Place bird on rack in shallow pan, breast side up. Dip double thickness of cheesecloth into pan of melted fat; place cloth on top of turkey. Or brush bird generously with fat, and cover loosely with aluminum foil, putting the shiny surface next to the skin to reflect the heat. Have extra melted fat ready for occasional remoistening of cloth or for basting. Always remember that tender, succulent roast turkey is the result of a steady, moderate temperature. If heat is too high, meat will dry out and skin will scorch and blister. If oven door is opened frequently, cooking temperature will drop and extra cooking time will be needed.

A buffet, including Seafood Cocktail and Boeuf en Gelée *en terrine* (p. 44).
CREDIT: *Bernard Gray.*

London Broil (p. 44).

CREDIT: *Bernard Gray.*

Poached Trout in White Wine Sauce (p. 75).
CREDIT: *Arthur Beck*.

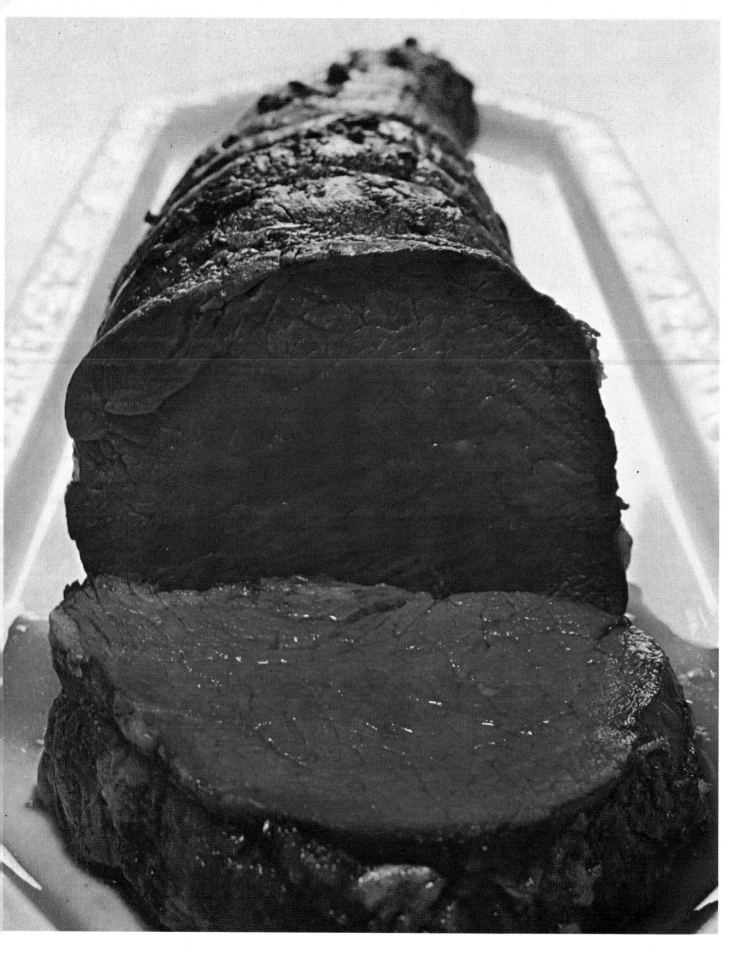

Roast Fillet of Beef (p. 44).
CREDIT: *Bernard Gray*.

Roasting in aluminum foil shortens total cooking time by about 1 hour for birds up to 12 pounds and by about 1 1/2 hours for larger turkeys. The prepared bird is laid on the *shiny* side of well-greased heavy-duty foil, which is then folded around bird, completely enclosing it. It is not sealed airtight. Oven temperature is 450°F.; allow about 12—15 minutes per pound. Foil should be opened for last 1/2 hour to brown bird.

TIMETABLE FOR ROASTING TURKEYS*

WEIGHT IN POUNDS**	APPROXIMATE TIMES†	
6—8	3 3/4—4	hours
8—12	4	hours
12—16	5—6	hours
16—20	6—7 1/2	hours
20—24	7 1/2—9	hours

*Oven temperature 325°F.
**For eviscerated, stuffed ready-to-cook birds.
†For unstuffed birds allow 5 minutes less per pound.

Roast Half-turkey

Tie leg to tail, and skewer wing flat against body. Place, skin side up, on rack in roasting pan. Completely cover with cheesecloth dipped in melted fat, or rub bird with fat and cover loosely with foil. Roast at 325°F., allowing 3 1/2—4 hours for 5—8 pounds. Dressing may be cooked under bird if foil is placed over rack; or bake it separately in greased casserole.

Broiled Half-turkey

Have a 4—6-pound turkey split in half by the butcher. Wipe clean. Skewer wing close to side. Rub skin with lemon, oil, salt, and melted fat. Place, skin side down, in pan without rack. Broil 8—10 inches from heat about 40 minutes or until nicely browned. Turn skin side up, and baste with pan drippings. Broil until brown and done, about 40 minutes longer.

Broiled Chicken Halves

Have the butcher split a 2 1/2-pound young chicken in half lengthwise. Fold wing tip back onto cut side, exposing thick breast area. Place in broiler pan without rack. Brush all chicken surfaces with melted fat, and season with salt and pepper. Arrange skin side down, place pan under broiler 6—8 inches directly below heat source. Let halves cook slowly; they should just begin to brown lightly after 10 minutes. Turn halves skin side up for even broiling; brush with fat several times. Test for doneness after 25 minutes or so. Drumstick should twist out of thigh joint readily when chicken is cooked. Serve pan drippings over chicken.

Fried Chicken

      1/2 cup flour
        2 teaspoons paprika
  1 1/2 teaspoons salt
      1/4 teaspoon pepper
        4 pounds chicken pieces (legs, wings, breasts and so forth)
          Fat

Mix flour with seasonings, and put in paper bag. Add chicken pieces, a few at a time, and shake to coat. Save remaining flour for gravy. Heat fat in heavy frying pan—enough for at least 1/4-inch depth. Fat is at right temperature when a drop of water sizzles in it. Put in thickest chicken pieces first, turning frequently until evenly and lightly browned; continue till all pieces are nicely browned—15—20 minutes. Cover pan tightly, and cook until meat is tender—20—25 minutes longer. For crispy coating, uncover pan for last 10 minutes, and turn pieces once. Serves 8.

Note: Other seasonings may be used as desired: thyme, oregano, garlic powder, rosemary, ginger or curry powder.

VARIATIONS:

* *Oven-fried Chicken*: After browning in frying pan, remove to shallow roasting pan. Melt 1/4 cup butter or margarine, and spoon over chicken. Bake uncovered at 350°F. 30—40 minutes, turning pieces once for even crisping.

* *Deep-fried Chicken*: Use deep fryer or pot, and heat 2—3 inches of fat to about 350°F. Place some of chicken in frying basket, leaving space between pieces. Immerse in fat and fry at about 325°F. until golden brown on all sides and tender—about 15 minutes. Lift out, and drain on crumpled paper towels in warm oven. Continue until all pieces are cooked; hold fat at steady temperature throughout.

* *Crumb-coated Fried Chicken*: For thicker, richer coating dip flour-coated chicken pieces in mixture of 2 teaspoons water to 1 beaten egg, and roll in fine bread or cornflake crumbs. Cover pieces completely, and allow to set a few minutes before frying by any of the methods outlined.

Chicken Fricassee

        1 (4-pound) stewing fowl, cut up
        2 teaspoons salt
        2 peppercorns
        1 stalk celery
        1 onion
        1 carrot
        1 bay leaf
          Boiling water
        3 tablespoons flour
      1/4 cup water

Wash chicken thoroughly inside and out. Place with spices and vegetables in deep kettle; barely cover with boiling water. Cover tightly, and simmer 2–3 hours or until meat is tender. Lift out chicken. Strain stock. Measure 3 cups for gravy, and set remainder aside to cool quickly (it makes an excellent soup for next day). Blend flour and 1/4 cup water to smooth paste. Thicken 3 cups stock with paste. Cook 5 minutes, adding extra seasoning to taste. If fowl is cooked whole, cut into serving pieces, arrange on platter, and pour gravy over. Serve with hot fluffy rice. Serves 4–5.

TIMETABLE FOR ROASTING CHICKEN*

WEIGHT IN POUNDS**	APPROXIMATE TIME†	
1 1/2–2 1/2	1 1/4–2	hours
2 1/2–3 1/2	2–3	hours
3 1/2–4 3/4	3–3 1/2	hours
4 3/4–6	3 1/2–4	hours

*Oven temperature 325°–350°F.
**For eviscerated, stuffed, ready-to-cook birds.
†For unstuffed birds allow about 5 minutes less per pound.

Roast Goose

Have your butcher draw the goose. Make sure oil sac at base of tail is removed. Pull out pinfeathers and singe to remove any down. Check body cavity for bits of lung and so forth. Wash very thoroughly inside and out under cold running water. Dry thoroughly. Rub body cavity with salt. Stuff bird with highly seasoned bread dressing, to which chopped raw apple may be added if desired. Skewer or sew up vent; truss. If goose is very fat, prick through skin into fat around legs and wings to encourage fat to drain off during cooking. Rub salt over skin. Place bird, breast side up, on rack in roaster. If using meat thermometer, insert in breast to rest in stuffing. Roast at 325°F. 2 hours. Pour all fat from pan, and continue roasting, uncovered, until done. A little apple juice makes a flavorful addition to pan juices for basting during last cooking period. An 8–10-pound goose (eviscerated weight) will take approximately 4–5 hours. The meat thermometer should register 165°F. when bird is done.

Roast Duckling

> 1 (4–5-pound) drawn duckling
> 1 small orange, quartered
> Juice of 1/2 lemon
> 1/2 teaspoon salt
> 1/2 cup ginger ale
> 1/4 cup sherry

Wipe duckling inside and out with damp cloth. Fill cavity with orange quarters. Roast, breast side up, uncovered, 1 hour at 350°F. Drain off all fat. Sprinkle with lemon juice and salt. Add ginger ale and sherry. Reduce heat to 325°F. Continue roasting 1 1/2 hours or until drumstick separates easily from thigh bone. Baste several times during roasting. Make gravy of pan drippings. Serves 4.

COOKING WILD GAME

Each type of game has its own characteristics and requires specific handling in the kitchen.

Venison

Venison is the flesh of deer. A young animal, which has not run too much, will be tender, with delicate, fine-grained meat. An older animal may be rather tough and should be cooked with moist heat.

Venison cuts are similar to those of mutton, and the fat is similar too. It must always be served piping hot. The leg, rump, saddle and loin are the best cuts for roasts, steaks and cutlets. The less tender flank, shank and neck portions should be stewed. Tender venison cuts suitable for broiling and roasting may be served rare . . . "the blood follows the knife," as the saying goes.

Marinating venison will make it moist and tasty but won't, as is sometimes thought, counteract the strong, gamey flavor. This taste comes from the fat; therefore as much fat as possible should be cut away before cooking.

During cooking period, replace natural fat with mild-flavored lard, shortening or bacon fat, so that meat will not dry out but will stay moist and juicy. Properly cooked venison has a good natural flavor that is adequately highlighted and complemented by salt, freshly ground pepper and monosodium glutamate.

Larding is a process for introducing fat directly into meat to increase tenderness and flavor. Cut meat with sharp knife or steel larding needle, making gashes deep enough to hold strips of bacon fat or fat pork. Close gashes by tying roast in several places with twine. When venison roast is larded, it is not necessary to add any other fat during cooking period.

Wild Fowl

Partridge are small, tender birds; they may be broiled or roasted and served with wild rice or mushrooms. One partridge may serve 2 people. Allow about 1 pound, drawn weight, for each serving. Partridge should be prepared in the same way as chicken (see poultry section in this chapter for directions on how to clean, draw and singe).

The delicious tender meat of edible wild ducks —canvasback, mallard, teal, redhead and black duck—may be roasted to your own taste, rare or well done. If you prefer it rare, use shorter cooking period; increase time if you prefer it well done.

Rabbit

Rabbits generally have tender meat that tastes best when broiled, fried, fricasseed or roasted. Before cooking, soak rabbit overnight or at least several hours in marinade or in salt water, vinegar and water. During cooking period, add fat for browning or basting, as very little natural fat remains after rabbit has been skinned.

Venison Loin Roast

    1 (3—4-pound) loin of deer
    1/4 pound fat, suet or pork fat
        Salt and pepper to taste
    1 cup red currant jelly
    1/2 cup water
    2 medium onions, quartered

Wipe roast with damp paper towel or clean damp cloth. Trim off all fat. Place on rack in shallow roasting pan, skin side up. Cut suet in pieces, and lay on top of roast. Roast in 325°F. oven 1/2 hour. Season with salt and pepper. Add other ingredients to pan. Continue roasting until done, about 1 hour longer. Baste every 15 minutes. Allow 20—25 minutes per pound roasting time. Do not overcook venison. Serves 6—8.

Roast Leg of Venison

    1 (4-pound) venison leg roast
    3 cups cold water
    1 cup tomato juice
    1 cup sliced celery
    1/2 cup wine vinegar or red wine
    1/4 cup sugar
    2 bay leaves
    2 cloves garlic, crushed
    1/4 lemon, sliced
    1/2 teaspoon salt

Wipe roast, and place in bowl. Make marinade of next 9 ingredients, and pour over. Marinade should come at least halfway up roast. Cover bowl, and place in refrigerator. Turn roast frequently. Allow roast to soak in marinade 1—2 days. Before roasting, drain and dry roast, put on rack in open pan; then proceed as for *Venison Loin Roast,* using marinade for basting.

Note: The leg roast is better if it is marinated before roasting; the marinade makes it moist and flavorful.

To broil venison steaks or to make stew with flank, neck or shank, follow any recipe for similar cooking methods with beef, remembering to trim away as much fat as possible before cooking and to replace natural fat with other milder fat for cooking.

Broiled Partridge

    1 (2 1/2-pound) partridge
    2 tablespoons soft butter or margarine
        Salt and pepper to taste

Singe, draw and clean partridge. Wash inside and out. Dry. Split, allowing 1/2 bird per serving. Rub outside well with soft butter or margarine. Place on broiler rack, skin side down, and broil 20—25 minutes, turning halfway through the cooking. Season with salt and pepper. Serves 2.

Roast Partridge

    1 (2 1/2-pound) partridge
    1 tablespoon lemon juice
    4 strips bacon

Singe, draw and clean partridge. Wash inside and out. Dry. Rub with lemon juice. Push legs toward breast, and secure with skewer pushed through middle of bird. Cover with strips of bacon. Roast, uncovered, at 350°F. 1 1/4—1 1/2 hours or until tender. Baste several times during roasting. Serve with red currant jelly. Serves 2.

Note: 2 tablespoons brandy, heated and set afire, may be poured over roast on platter at serving time, for distinctive flavor.

Roast Wild Duck

    1 wild duck
    1/4 cup olive oil
    1/2 teaspoon salt
    1/8 teaspoon pepper
    1 apple, peeled and sliced
    3 strips bacon

Singe, draw and clean; wash inside and outside thoroughly. Dry. Combine olive oil, salt and pepper, and brush bird all over with mixture. Insert apple in cavity, and place bird, breast side up, on rack in open shallow pan. Arrange bacon strips over breast, securing with toothpicks if necessary. Roast bird 25—35 minutes at 425°F., basting several times during cooking. Good accompaniments for wild duck are candied sweet potatoes and apple-celery salad with sliced-orange garnish.

Note: Allow 1 pound wild duck, drawn weight, per serving.

Fried Rabbit

    1 drawn rabbit
    1 1/2 cups cold water
    1/4 cup cider vinegar
    1 clove garlic, halved
    1 teaspoon salt
    1/8 teaspoon pepper
    1/3 cup flour
    1/2 teaspoon salt
    1/4 cup fat or bacon drippings
    2 tablespoons flour
    1 cup milk or light cream
    1 teaspoon grated onion
        Salt and pepper to taste

Wash rabbit thoroughly inside and out under cold water. Cut into serving pieces, and place in bowl. Make marinade by combining next 5 ingredients. Pour over rabbit, cover and soak several hours in refrigerator. Remove rabbit, drain and pat dry with paper towel. Combine 1/3 cup flour and 1/2 teaspoon salt; use to coat meat surfaces. Melt fat in heavy frying pan over moderate heat; add rabbit pieces, brown on all sides, cover and cook over slightly reduced heat. Turn occasionally, and cook until tender, about 1 1/4 hours. Remove meat to platter, and keep warm. Add 2 tablespoons flour to remaining fat in skillet; mix thoroughly. Then stir in milk to make smooth sauce; simmer 5 minutes. Add grated onion and extra seasoning to taste. Serve very hot with cooked rabbit. Serves 3–4.

USE FISH FOR VARIETY

Fish is a protein food, rich in important nutrients and an excellent alternative to meat.

Fat fish and fish livers provide abundant supplies of essential vitamins A and D. For nutrition, variety and economy, include fish often in your menus. Learn interesting new ways to use the various forms so readily available—fresh, frozen, dried, canned.

How To Select Fish

The flesh of fresh fish should always be firm and should adhere firmly to bone. The odor should be distinctly fresh and mild. Fresh fish is marketed in a number of ways. "Whole, round" means fish are exactly as they came from the water. The eyes should be clear, the gills bright red and the skin shiny with tightly clinging scales. Allow 1 pound per serving. "Dressed or pan-dressed fish" are fish with scales and entrails removed and usually also with head, tail and fins removed. Allow 1/2 pound per serving. "Drawn" is applied to whole fish with only entrails removed. "Steaks" are ready-to-cook cross-sectional slices of large fish, which may also be divided by cutting through backbone. Allow 1/3–1/2 pound per serving. "Fillets" are ready-to-cook sides of fish cut lengthwise from backbone. They are practically boneless. Allow 1/4–1/3 pound per serving.

Frozen fish should be solidly frozen with no discoloration in the flesh. Frozen fish is usually sold in fillets, in individually wrapped packages or 1-pound cartons. Frozen whole fish is seldom wrapped but is coated with a glaze that prevents discoloration.

Smoked and dried fish include cod, haddock, salmon, sturgeon, herring, eels and whitefish. Dried salt fish has a distinctive flavor; and, although the salting process delays spoiling for a time, it does not preserve fish indefinitely.

Many kinds of fish can be bought canned. Some may be bought in several qualities, each priced accordingly. For instance, the price of canned salmon is determined largely by its color. Red sockeye is the choicest and the highest-priced; the pinks, ranging from cohoe to the palest chum, cost less on a diminishing scale. Tuna is also sold in several varieties. "White tuna meat" costs more than the darker type. Tuna flakes are cheaper than are the solid-pack cans and are a sensible buy for sandwich spreads or casseroles.

Fresh fish is very perishable, and should be refrigerated or frozen as soon as possible after purchase. Wipe thoroughly with clean damp cloth. Wrap loosely in waxed paper, and place in tightly covered container to prevent odor from spreading; then refrigerate. If fish is whole, clean and scale it before storing.

Frozen fish should ideally be kept solidly frozen at a constant temperature of 0°F. This low temperature is difficult to maintain in home freezer units, and it is therefore wise to use frozen fish within a reasonably short period. Once fish thaws, it must be treated as fresh fish and cooked immediately. *Never refreeze fish.*

Smoked fish should be handled and stored in the same way as fresh fish, as the smoking process is not sufficient to preserve it.

Freshly caught fish may be stored whole, filleted or in steaks in the home freezer. Eviscerate and thoroughly wash fish as soon as possible after taking from the water. If unable to freeze immediately, pack carefully in ice, and refrigerate. Before freezing, rinse well in cold water. Then pat dry, and wrap airtight in heavy moisture-vapor proof wrap or aluminum foil, and place in freezer.

Fish has little connective tissue; it should be cooked quickly at moderate temperature, just until translucent flesh becomes opaque. Cooked fish should flake easily. If overcooked, it falls apart.

There are 4 basic methods for cooking fish—frying or broiling with a little added fat; baking; poaching in liquid (or steaming over water); and deep frying.

Basic Cooking Methods

To Fry. This method is particularly good for small whole fish, steaks, or fillets. Cut into serving pieces and coat with seasoned flour or bread crumbs. Heat fat in heavy pan. Fry fish quickly on 1 side; turn and fry on other. Fish should flake easily with fork.

Note: Defrost frozen fish partially before coating and frying to prevent the dredging mixture from separating from the fish during frying.

To Broil. Sprinkle with salt and pepper. Place on greased broiler rack 2—3 inches from heat, and brush with melted fat (place frozen fish farther from heat to prevent burning before it is cooked through). Broil 5—10 minutes, depending on thickness. Turn and broil until fish flakes easily with fork.

To Bake. Cut 2 pounds fish fillets into serving portions. Season on both sides or bread by dipping in 1/2 cup milk to which 1 teaspoon salt has been added, then rolling in fine bread crumbs. Place in greased baking dish, and dot with butter or margarine. Bake in a hot oven, 450°F. 12—15 minutes or until fish flakes easily with fork. Remove at once, and serve.

To bake whole fish, prepare fish as for fillets, and stuff loosely with dressing, using string to tie fish in shape. Place in greased pan and brush with fat or oil. Bake in a hot oven, 450°F. 10—15 minutes per inch or until fish flakes easily with fork. (Fish may also be baked in greased aluminum foil, which should •be folded tightly over it, so that steam cannot escape. Add 5 minutes to cooking time to allow heat to penetrate foil.)

To Poach. Poaching is a good method for whole fish or fillets to be used in salads, fish cakes, casseroles or creamed dishes. Place on greased, double-thickness, heavy aluminum foil; season with salt, pepper, chopped celery, chopped onion. Fold over, and secure open edges with double fold to make watertight. Place in rapidly boiling water. When water returns to boiling, cover pan, and cook 5—10 minutes or until fish flakes with fork. Also see court-bouillon method, pages 74—75.

Deep frying. This method requires a deep pan, allowing at least 3 inches between boiling fat and rim. Allow 1 quart salad oil for 3-quart kettle. Heat fat to 375°F. Always thaw frozen fish before deep frying. Cut fish into uniform serving pieces, season and dip in batter. Lower gently in frying basket, or carefully use egg lifter or kitchen tongs. Fry until golden brown. Drain on paper towel.

Deep-fried Fillets in Pancake Mix

Use your favorite packaged pancake mix, and make batter according to manufacturer's directions. Use slightly more liquid than specified and, if you like a very crisp coating, substitute water for milk. Frying kettle should be 1/2 full of fat heated to 375°F., at which point a small cube of bread will brown in 60 seconds. Cut fish fillets into uniform pieces no more than 1/2 inch thick, sprinkle with salt, coat in batter and lower carefully into hot fat to avoid dangerous splashing. A frying basket is useful, but do not crowd it. Fry until golden brown, 5—7 minutes. Drain on paper towels; keep warm while remaining fillets are cooking. Frying a few pieces at a time permits fat to retain its hot frying temperature.

Homemade Batter for Fried Fish

    1 1/2 cups all-purpose flour
        3 teaspoons baking powder
        1 teaspoon salt
        1 cup milk
        2 eggs, well beaten

Mix and sift dry ingredients. Add milk to eggs. Pour liquid into dry mixture, and beat until smooth. Dip fish pieces into this mixture, and fry in deep fat until golden brown.

Fried Smelts

        2 pounds smelts
        2 eggs, beaten
        2 tablespoons milk
        1 teaspoon salt
    1/2 cup flour
    1/2 cup fine cracker crumbs
          Hot fat

Cut off heads and tails of smelts; eviscerate fish, and wash thoroughly inside and out. Drain on paper towels, and pat as dry as possible. Combine egg, milk and salt. Mix flour and crumbs together. Dip fish in liquid, then in dry mixture. Have about 1/4-inch depth of hot fat in frying pan. Fry smelts quickly on 1 side; turn, and brown on other side. Serves 4–5.

Broiled Salmon Steaks

      2 pounds salmon steaks, 1 inch thick
   1/4 cup butter or margarine
   1/2 teaspoon salt
   1/8 teaspoon pepper

Wipe fish with clean, damp cloth. Pin flank ends together with toothpicks. Melt butter or margarine. Preheat broiler. Place steaks on greased broiler pan. Brush with melted butter or margarine, and position 2–4 inches from heat. When top side is browned, sprinkle with 1/4 teaspoon salt and dash pepper; turn with lifter, brush with melted butter and complete broiling and seasoning. Steaks should be done in about 10 minutes. Serves 4.

Note: Any fish fillet or steak may be prepared as above. A piece 3/4–1 inch thick is ideal for broiling, as it is sufficiently thick to retain moisture. Another easy way, especially when it comes to turning, is to use an old-fashioned wire toaster with handle. Lay it over broiler pan; when fish is browned on one side, turn toaster, protecting hand with oven mitt. In broiling unthawed frozen fish, it is best to place it farther from heat source and to double cooking time.

Baked Fillets in Lemon Butter

      2 pounds fish fillets, fresh or thawed
   1/4 cup melted butter or margarine
      2 tablespoons lemon juice
      2 tablespoons chopped parsley
   1/2 teaspoon salt
   1/8 teaspoon pepper

Grease shallow baking dish and arrange single layer of fillets in it. Combine remaining ingredients and pour over fish. Place in 450°F. oven, and allow 10 minutes cooking time per 1-inch thickness of fillets. You will know fish is done when it becomes opaque, flakes readily and can be easily pierced with a fork. Serves 6.

Baked Fillets with Cream

      2 pounds fish fillets
      2 tablespoons butter or margarine
   3/4 cup chopped onion
      1 tablespoon flour
      1 teaspoon salt
   1/8 teaspoon pepper
      1 cup light cream
         Paprika to taste
         Curls lemon rind

Cut fillets into uniform pieces suitable for serving. Arrange in greased baking dish. Melt butter or margarine in saucepan, and sauté onion gently until tender but not browned. Add flour, salt and pepper; blend. Then stir in cream slowly. Simmer sauce until smooth; pour over fish. Sprinkle top with paprika. Bake in 450°F. oven 15–20 minutes or until fish is cooked. Garnish with curls of lemon rind. Serves 6.

Note: Fillets and steaks and solid chunks may also be simmered or baked odorlessly in parchment or heavy aluminum foil, in which case seasonings are wrapped with fish. Sprinkle fish with salt and place on sheet of dampened parchment or greased foil. Estimate thickness of fish. Add a little chopped onion, parsley and celery. Wrap securely, preferably in pouch fashion and tie with string to make watertight. Place parcel in rapidly boiling water, and cover. Time cooking period after water returns to boiling point. Allow 10 minutes per inch thickness for fresh fish; double the amount for unthawed frozen fish. The parcels are ready to serve and there is no pan to clean.

Poached Fish

      2 pounds fillets or 1 solid piece fish (salmon, halibut
         or cod)
      5 cups boiling water
   1/2 cup vinegar
   1/4 cup sliced onion
      1 tablespoon salt
      1 stalk celery
      1 bay leaf
   2–3 peppercorns

Tie fillets in double thickness of clean cheese-cloth. Prepare court bouillon by boiling remaining ingredients 10 minutes. Drop in fish, cover and, when liquid bubbles again, reduce heat to simmer. Cook about 10 minutes per inch thickness. Test fish for doneness; when it flakes easily with toothpick, remove it at once. Double the time for unthawed frozen fish. Serves 6.

Poached Trout in White Wine Sauce

          3 (10-ounce) packages frozen rainbow trout
          1 teaspoon salt
      1/2 teaspoon pepper
  1 3/4 cups white wine
      1/2 cup thin onion rings
      1/4 cup parsley sprigs
          1 clove garlic, slivered
          2 bay leaves
          2 sticks celery, sliced
      1/8 teaspoon thyme
          2 tablespoons soft butter
          2 tablespoons flour
          2 egg yolks

Butter a large, shallow pan. Arrange frozen trout evenly in pan. Sprinkle with salt and pepper. Mix together white wine, onion rings, parsley, garlic, bay leaves, celery, and thyme. Pour mixture over fish.

Bake at 450°F. 15–18 minutes or until fish is tender when tested with fork. Spoon juices over fish 2 or 3 times during baking.

Lift fish with slotted spoon or spatula. Arrange on large warmed serving platter. Cover with foil. Keep warm.

Strain fish broth. Measure 1 1/2 cupfuls into medium saucepan. Add a smooth mixture of butter and flour. Bring to boil over medium heat, stirring constantly. Remove from heat. Beat 2 egg yolks. Add a little of the sauce to egg yolks and then stir mixture into the sauce and cook 3 minutes. Makes about 2 cups sauce. Serve sauce with fish. Serves 6.

Crunchy Baked Haddock

          1 pound fresh or defrosted haddock fillets
          1 egg, slightly beaten
          3 tablespoons Worcestershire sauce
          1 cup crushed cereal crumbs
          1 tablespoon butter or margarine, melted
          2 cups *Curried Cream Sauce*

Cut fish into 5 or 6 pieces. Combine egg and Worcestershire sauce, and dip fish in mixture. Coat with crumbs; then dip again in egg mixture and again in crumbs. Place in greased dish and drizzle with melted butter or margarine. Bake at 450°F. 15—20 minutes. Serve with *Curried Cream Sauce*, quickly cooked spinach garnished with hard-cooked egg slices and fluffy whipped potatoes. Serves 4.

Curried Cream Sauce

              Salt and pepper to taste
    1–2 teaspoons curry powder
          2 cups medium cream sauce

Add seasoning and curry powder to cream sauce.

Finnan Haddie Poached in Milk

          1 cup milk
          2 pounds smoked haddock fillets
          1 tablespoon butter or margarine
              Pepper to taste

Heat milk in a skillet, add fillets and cover. Simmer until fish flakes readily at touch of fork. Transfer fillets to serving platter, and dot with butter or margarine and pepper. Serves 6.

Note: Cooking milk can be thickened with flour and butter rubbed together and served as sauce.

Cod with Tomatoes

          2 tablespoons butter or margarine
          1 carrot, sliced
          1 stalk celery, thinly sliced
          1 small onion, thinly sliced
          1 (10-ounce) can tomato soup
          2 tablespoons water
          1 pound fresh or frozen cod fillets
      1/2 cup buttered bread crumbs
      1/2 cup grated cheese

Melt butter or margarine in small saucepan, and add carrot, celery and onion. Sauté 2 minutes; cover, and cook 3 minutes. Add soup and water. Arrange fillets in greased baking dish; cover with vegetable mixture. Sprinkle with bread crumbs and cheese. Bake in hot oven, 425° F., about 20 minutes for fresh fish and 30 minutes frozen. Serves 4.

Cod Soufflé

      1/2 pound salt cod
              Cold water
          4 slices bacon, diced
      2/3 cup chopped onion
      1/4 cup diced green pepper
      1/4 cup chopped celery
          1 tablespoon flour
  1 1/4 cups milk
      1/4 teaspoon thyme
      1/4 teaspoon pepper
          2 eggs, separated

The salt cod should first be freshened by soaking overnight in cold water to cover. Drain, and put in pan with fresh water to cover. Place over low heat, and bring to simmer. Drain. Fish should now be ready to use, but if still too salty, repeat simmering procedure, and drain. Flake fish. Fry bacon bits till crisp; lift out, and gently cook next 3 ingredients in bacon fat. Sprinkle flour over vegetables, and add 1 cup milk gradually, stirring and cooking until thickened. Add flaked fish, bacon and seasonings. Beat egg yolks and 1/4 cup milk; add carefully to mixture, and cook gently 2–3 minutes. Beat egg whites until stiff but not dry, and fold into hot mixture. Turn into greased baking dish, and bake at 350°F. about 30 minutes or until soufflé is high, firm and lightly browned. Serves 4–5.

Salmon Puff

        1 envelope (4-serving size) instant potatoes
    1/2 pound canned red salmon
      2 eggs, separated
      2 tablespoons mayonnaise
    1–2 tablespoons chopped parsley
    1/2 teaspoon salt
    1/2 teaspoon grated lemon rind
      1 (10-ounce) can tomato soup
    1/4 cup tomato juice
      2 tablespoons sherry

Prepare instant potatoes according to directions. Discard skin from salmon and add salmon and juice from can to potatoes. Mix egg yolks with mayonnaise, and stir into potatoes. Add parsley, salt and lemon rind. Stiffly beat egg whites, fold into potatoes and spread in greased baking dish. Bake in a pan of water at 375°F. 30 minutes or until set and puffed. Heat soup, tomato juice and sherry together; spoon over salmon puff. Serves 6.

Mushroom-Tuna Soufflé

      3 eggs, separated
      1 (7-ounce) can flaked tuna, drained
      1 tablespoon lemon juice
      1 (10-ounce) can mushroom soup

Beat egg yolks until thick, and stir in drained tuna, lemon juice and soup. Stiffly beat egg whites; fold into tuna mixture, and scrape into buttered 1 1/2-quart baking dish. Bake at 325°F. 35–45 minutes or until center is set. Serves 4–6.

Salmon Loaf

        1 (1-pound) can salmon
      3/4 cup (approximately) milk
    1 1/2 cups soft bread crumbs
      2 tablespoons chopped sweet pickle
      2 teaspoons lemon juice
      1 teaspoon salt
    1/4 teaspoon pepper
      1 egg, slightly beaten

Drain salmon, reserving liquid. Add sufficient milk to liquid to make 1 cup in all. Remove skin, and flake salmon, mashing bones. Combine all ingredients well, and turn mixture into small greased loaf pan. Bake at 375°F. 1/2 hour or until loaf is nicely browned with crust on top. Serve hot with suitable sauce—egg, parsley or cucumber, for example. Loaf is also delicious chilled, sliced and served with potato salad or in sandwiches. Serves 4–5.

Note: Finely chopped onion may be substituted for sweet pickle for a slightly different flavor.

30-Minute Baked Fish Dinner

    1 1/2–2 pounds frozen halibut steaks
        1/4 cup evaporated milk
          3 tablespoons bottled dark steak sauce
        3/4 cup crushed crackers
          6 small unpeeled potatoes, quartered
        1/4 cup salad oil
            Salt to taste
          2 (10-ounce) packages frozen mixed vegetables
        1/4 cup butter or margarine
    1 1/2 cups *Mustard Sauce*

Preheat oven to 425°F. Spread halibut in foil-lined pan, mix evaporated milk and steak sauce, and spread over fish. Sprinkle with crackers. Dry potato quarters, and dip in salad oil. Sprinkle generously with salt, and arrange in second baking dish. Unwrap frozen vegetables, and place on 2 squares of heavy-duty foil. Sprinkle with salt, and top each with 2 tablespoons butter or margarine. Wrap each block separately, to be airtight. Set potatoes and vegetables in oven, and bake 20 minutes. Turn vegetable packages over; put pan of fish in oven. Continue baking 25 minutes. Serve fish steaks, mixed vegetables and potatoes on individual plates, and pass *Mustard Sauce*. Serves 6.

Mustard Sauce

      1 cup tartar sauce
    1/2 cup diced cucumber
      2 tablespoons prepared mustard
      1 tablespoon lemon juice

Combine all chilled ingredients. Makes 1 1/2 cups.

SEAFOOD

The edible parts of the various molluscs (oysters, scallops, clams and mussels) and of the crustacean group (including lobster, crab and shrimp) have a delicacy of texture and special flavors that most gourmets enjoy. One reason is that these seafoods take so well to sauces, seasonings and complementary touches. And the fact that they do so makes them economical, for they can be "stretched" with such inexpensive items as rice, noodles, breadstuffs, vegetables, milk and eggs.

The flesh of shellfish becomes tough if cooked too long, so it is important to remember that only a few minutes cooking is necessary.

The cooked meat adds a great deal to salads.

Lobster

Live lobsters vary in size from 1 to 3 pounds. A healthy lobster is very active, with a color that is deep blue to shades of green and brown (the handsome red color comes during cooking). If you buy lobster cooked in the shell, you can check that it was alive and healthy when cooked by straightening the tail; it should spring back into curled position. A 1-pound lobster serves 1.

When you buy frozen cooked lobster meat, thaw in refrigerator overnight, or open container at room temperature (this way a 14-ounce can will thaw in about 6 hours). Before serving lobster, whether home-cooked or canned, check carefully through claw meat to remove any thin pieces of cartilage that might be present.

Shrimp

You can take your pick when buying shrimp, choosing either the very small variety or the good-sized meaty jumbo shrimp. Though they may be gray or green at this stage, all shrimp turn pink when cooked. One pound of raw or "green" shrimp will give you enough meat for about 3 servings in a main course.

Peel off shells; then with small, sharp knife cut along outside curvature and lift out dark vein running length of body. Rinse under cold water, and drain. Raw shrimp may be simmered in boiling, salted water (1 tablespoon salt per 1 quart water) or sautéed in fat, depending on the recipe. Frozen shrimp need not be thawed. When water has returned to boiling point, reduce heat, and simmer. Allow 2 minutes for small shrimp, 5 minutes for large jumbo shrimp. Drain and cool. Shrimp are ready for use in a variety of dishes.

Crab

Live crabs survive only a short time out of water and when purchased should be promptly cooked by being plunged, head first, into rapidly boiling salted water (1 tablespoon salt per 1 quart water). Cover and simmer 15-20 minutes. Cool quickly in cold water; shell, clean and refrigerate till serving time. Allow 2 crabs per serving.

In some localities you may buy cooked and frozen whole crabs in plastic bags; you can also buy cooked and shelled frozen crabmeat. Check carefully through canned crabmeat, and remove any small bits of cartilage and shell.

To shell and clean cooked crab, hold it with your left hand and pull off top shell from rear (discard shell, or use it as a serving plate, after scrubbing well to remove yellow fat that clings to it). Lift off gills on either side of back, and discard. Turn crab on its back. Break off mouth parts, and tailpiece apron. Turn crab over again. Scrape out center fat and entrails. Flush cavity thoroughly under cold running water. Hold crab with both hands, and crack body shell in half over edge of sink. Shake out body meat from each 1/2 shell by crushing shell and knocking it against edge of bowl. Hold legs curved side down, and hit sharply with loosely held mallet. Break off. Pull out movable pincer claws and sharp inside shell. Extract meat from shell. Rinse meat in salt water, and drain.

Clams

Live clams have tighly closed shells, which may be steamed opened or pried apart with a knife. Allow about 6 per serving. Raw clams are also available shucked by the pint or quart. Canned clams may be bought whole or minced.

Oysters

Oysters are available in the shell by the dozen. Use soft brush to clean oyster shells under cold, running water. Do not let oysters stand in water. Hold each scrubbed oyster with deep part of shell down, and insert a strong blunt oyster knife near hinge. Pry shells apart with twisting motion. To prevent knife from slipping, wear heavy glove, or hold oyster in folded cloth. Sever muscle that holds shell together and under-muscle holding oyster to shell. Take care to retain as much salty-flavored juice as possible.

If you do not intend to serve your oysters raw on the half-shell, drain them and strain juice to remove particles of shell. Store oysters with juice in tightly covered container, and refrigerate. Raw oysters are also available shucked, by the 1/2 pint, pint or quart. Use within 24 hours.

Scallops

Tender white scallops are packaged and sold by the pound, both fresh and frozen. They need no shelling as they are "shucked" as soon as they are harvested from the sea. Always wipe scallops with clean, damp cloth before using. Frozen scallops should be sufficiently thawed to separate before cooking. Allow 1/4–1/3 pound per serving.

Shellfish, which used to be special treats to be enjoyed near their coastal habitats, are now available almost everywhere, fresh, canned or frozen.

Experimenting with the various types is bound to be rewarding.

Fried Rice Ring with Shrimp

  2 cups boiling water
  1 (7-ounce) package frozen ready-to-cook shrimp
  1/4 cup butter or margarine
  1/2 cup chopped green pepper
  1/4 cup chopped onion
  1 1/3 cups quick-cooking rice
  1/4 teaspoon salt
  1 1/3 cups chicken bouillon
  1 (10-ounce) can frozen shrimp soup, undiluted
  2 teaspoons cornstarch
  1/2 cup milk
  1 (12-ounce) package frozen peas

Pour boiling water over shrimp to separate. Drain well. Cook shrimp lightly in butter or margarine; lift out, and cut into 1/2-inch pieces. Put green pepper and onion in frying pan, and cook until transparent. Add rice; stir and cook until lightly browned. Add salt, bouillon and shrimp. Bring to boil; pour into greased 5-cup ring mold. Cover and set in pan of boiling water 15 minutes. Heat soup in top of double boiler until defrosted. Mix cornstarch with milk, add to soup and cook until thick and smooth. Cook frozen peas according to directions on package. Unmold rice ring on hot platter. Fill center with hot cooked peas. Top with hot shrimp sauce. Serves 6.

French-fried Shrimp

  1 1/2 pounds large shrimp, fresh or frozen
  3/4 cup flour
  1 teaspoon baking powder
  1/2 teaspoon salt
  3/4 cup milk
  1 egg, beaten
  Salad oil

If using frozen shrimp, allow to thaw. Peel shrimp, and cut almost through lengthwise. Remove veins, wash and drain. Make batter by sifting dry ingredients together; combine milk with beaten egg, and add liquid to dry ingredients, stirring until smooth. Heat salad oil in skillet until very hot (375°F. if using thermometer.) Use enough oil to cover shrimp completely. Dip shrimp in batter and fry until golden brown—5—7 minutes. Drain on paper towels. Serve plain or with *Tartar Sauce*. Serves 5—6.

Lobster Newburg

  1/4 cup butter or margarine
  1/4 cup flour
  1/2 teaspoon salt
  1/8 teaspoon pepper
  1 1/2 cups milk
  2 cups cooked lobster meat or 2 (5-ounce) cans lobster cut into bite-size pieces
  2 tablespoons sherry or lemon juice
  6 toast slices or patty shells

Make a white sauce, using butter or margarine, flour, seasonings and milk. Add lobster meat, and heat thoroughly. Add wine just before serving. Serve on toast or in patty shells. Serves 6.

Lobster-Grapefruit Mold

  2 cups bite-size pieces cooked lobster meat or 2 (5-ounce) cans lobster, drained
  1 tablespoon lemon juice
  1 envelope plain gelatine
  2/3 cup canned grapefruit juice
  1 cup mayonnaise
  1 cup grapefruit sections, drained and diced
  1/2 teaspoon salt

Sprinkle lobster pieces with lemon juice. Soak gelatine in 1/3 cup grapefruit juice 5 minutes; then melt by setting container in hot water. Combine remaining grapefruit juice with mayonnaise; add dissolved gelatine, stirring thoroughly. Add grapefruit and salt. Fold in lobster, mix well and pour into 1-quart mold rinsed in cold water. Chill until firm, and unmold on bed of salad greens. Serves 6.

Note: Or use small individual molds instead of 1 large one.

Boiled Fresh Lobster

Fill deep kettle with sufficient water to cover lobsters, adding 2 tablespoons salt for each quart water. Bring water to fast boil; plunge each lobster in, grasping it by the back, behind head. Allow water to return to gentle boil, cover container and cook 18 minutes from the time lobsters were put in water. Lobsters weighing less than 1 pound will cook in 15 minutes. Lift out, and cool immediately by holding under running water; then drain.

Note: Turn lobster on its back, and split lengthwise down center, using sharp knife or kitchen scissors. Remove meat, and discard dark vein, small sac at back of head, and spongy green tissue on each side of back. Do not discard bright green liver or red roe (if present) as these are

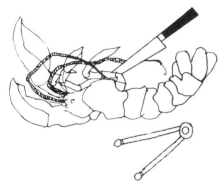

delicious tidbits. Crack large claws with nut-cracker. Repack body shell. If to be served hot, put lobster in very slow oven to heat through; serve with melted butter or margarine and lemon wedges. Or serve cold with lettuce garnish, mayonnaise and lemon slices.

Stuffed Broiled Lobster

```
    1 (2—3-pound) lobster
    2 tablespoons butter or margarine, melted
    5 tablespoons soft bread crumbs
    2 tablespoons chopped parsley
  1/4 teaspoon salt
      Dash pepper
```

Split lobster in 2, and lay open as far as possible. Discard vein and spongy green tissue on each side of back. Crack big claws. Place lobster, shell side up, on broiler rack 3 inches from heat. Broil 8 minutes under medium heat. Turn lobster. Combine remaining ingredients, and spread mixture in lobster cavity. Broil 4 minutes or until crumbs are golden brown. Serves 1—2.

Deep-fried Scallops

```
    1 pound scallops
      Salt to taste
  1/4 cup flour
    1 egg, beaten
  3/4 cup fine, dry bread crumbs
    1 cup salad oil or fat
```

Sprinkle scallops with salt. Roll each in flour, dip in egg and roll in bread crumbs. Heat fat over low heat until very hot (375°F. if using thermometer), using just enough to cover an uncrowded single layer of scallops in frying basket. Lower basket, and fry scallops until golden brown on all sides—3—4 minutes. Drain on paper towels, and serve with lemon wedges or *Tartar Sauce.* Serves 3.

Scallop Casserole

```
      1 pound scallops
      2 tablespoons butter or margarine
  1 1/2 cups chopped celery
      1 cup sliced mushrooms
      1 cup chopped green pepper
    1/2 cup chopped onion
    1/4 cup butter or margarine
    1/4 cup flour
      1 teaspoon salt
      2 cups milk
      2 tablespoons butter or margarine
      2 cups soft bread crumbs
    1/4 cup finely grated cheese
```

Melt butter or margarine in skillet, and gently fry scallops with vegetables until partially cooked, about 10 minutes. Make white sauce with 1/4 cup butter or margarine, flour, 1 teaspoon salt and milk; when thickened, add scallops and vegetables. Combine thoroughly, and taste for seasoning. Transfer to greased 1 1/2-quart casserole. Melt remaining 2 tablespoons butter and stir into bread crumbs. Scatter buttered crumbs over top of casserole; then sprinkle grated cheese over crumbs. Bake uncovered at 375°F. about 20 minutes or until sauce is bubbling and crumbs lightly browned. Serves 6.

Spicy Oyster Stew

```
  1/4 cup butter or margarine
    2 dozen raw oysters, with liquid
    1 tablespoon Worcestershire sauce
    1 teaspoon celery salt
  3/4 teaspoon salt
  1/4 teaspoon paprika
  1/8 teaspoon pepper
    1 quart milk
    4 small lumps butter or margarine
```

Heat 1/4 cup butter or margarine in skillet, but do not brown. Add oysters with liquid and next 5 ingredients. Heat only until edges of oysters curl slightly; then add milk. Heat quickly, but do not boil. Serve with additional dash of

paprika and lump of butter or margarine in each bowl. Serve with oyster crackers and small dish of sliced dill pickles. Serves 4.

Broiled Oysters

      1/2 pint oysters
           Salt to taste
        3 tablespoons melted butter or margarine
      1/2 cup dry bread crumbs

Drain oysters, and sprinkle lightly with salt. Dip in melted butter or margarine, and roll in bread crumbs. Place on greased rack about 4 inches from heat, and broil approximately 2 minutes on each side, turning once. Bread crumbs will be lightly browned. Serves 1—2.

Note: To bake, place breaded oysters in greased, shallow baking dish, and bake at 450°F. 8—10 minutes or until lightly browned.

Steamed Clams

Scrub clams well under running cold water to remove sand. Cover bottom of large skillet with 1/2 inch water; add clams, cover tightly and steam until shells start to open—about 10 minutes (or place clams in steamer). Top shells can be removed for serving if desired. Serve clams hot with side dishes of melted butter or margarine. If desired, liquid remaining in pan after cooking may be added to butter or margarine for dipping.

Manhattan-style Clam Chowder

        2 slices bacon, diced
        1 medium onion, thinly sliced
        1 cup diced raw potato
        1 small bay leaf
        1 (20-ounce) can tomatoes
        1 pint clams and liquid or approximately 20 ounces
           canned clams
        1 teaspoon salt
      1/8 teaspoon pepper
      1/8 teaspoon thyme

Fry bacon until crisp; add onion, and fry until tender, about 5 minutes. Add potato, bay leaf and undrained tomatoes. Simmer 10—15 minutes until potato is tender; then add remaining ingredients. Heat until piping hot, but do not allow to boil. Remove bay leaf before serving. Serves 6.

Fundy-style Clam Chowder

        2 tablespoons finely diced bacon
      1/2 cup chopped onion
        1 cup diced raw potato
        2 cups water
        1 pint clams and liquid or approximately 20 ounces
           canned clams
        1 (15-ounce) can evaporated milk
        3 tablespoons butter or margarine
        1 teaspoon salt
      1/4 teaspoon white pepper

Fry diced bacon until crisp; remove from pan, and save for garnish. Sauté chopped onions in bacon fat until tender but not brown. Combine potato and cooked onion in deep saucepan; add water, bring to simmering point and simmer until potato is cooked, about 15 minutes. Stir in clams, clam liquid, milk, butter or margarine and seasonings, and heat until piping hot. Do not boil. Garnish with crisp diced bacon. Serves 6.

Clam-Potato Cakes

        4 (3-ounce) cans minced clams, drained
        2 cups cooked mashed potatoes
        2 tablespoons butter or margarine
        1 tablespoon lemon juice
      1/2 teaspoon salt
      1/4 teaspoon nutmeg
        2 eggs, beaten

Combine drained, minced clams with remaining ingredients, and mix well. Shape into 12 patties, and fry in hot fat until lightly browned on both sides. Serves 6.

Crab Creole

2 tablespoons butter or margarine
1 cup diced celery
1/2 cup chopped onion
2 cloves garlic, finely chopped
1 (28-ounce) can tomatoes
1 1/2 teaspoons Worcestershire sauce
1 teaspoon salt
1/2 cup raw rice
2 cups fresh cooked crabmeat or 2 (6-ounce) cans crabmeat
1/4 cup chopped parsley

Melt butter or margarine in skillet, and gently fry celery, onion, and garlic until tender. Add tomatoes, Worcestershire sauce and salt; bring to boil. Add rice, mix well and cover skillet. Simmer 20 minutes or until rice is cooked, stirring occasionally. Add crabmeat and chopped parsley, and heat through. Serves 6.

Crabmeat Alaskan

3 cups cooked fresh, frozen or canned crabmeat
1 egg yolk, beaten
1/2 cup heavy cream
1/2 teaspoon salt
1/8 teaspoon pepper
6 slices bread
3 tablespoons melted butter or margarine
1/2 cup soft bread crumbs
1 tablespoon melted butter or margarine

Flake crabmeat, and combine with next 4 ingredients. Brush bread slices on 1 side with 3 tablespoons butter or margarine. Then fry on buttered side until golden brown. Heap crab mixture on unbuttered side; combine bread crumbs with 1 tablespoon butter or margarine, and sprinkle over crab. Bake at 400°F. 10 minutes. Garnish with parsley. Serves 6.

Deviled Shrimp

2 cups (1 pound frozen) cooked shrimp or 2 (5-ounce) cans shrimp
2 tablespoons chopped onion
1/4 cup melted butter or margarine
1/4 cup flour
1/2 teaspoon dry mustard
1/2 teaspoon Worcestershire sauce
2 cups milk
1 (12-ounce) package frozen peas, cooked
24 toast points
Paprika to taste

If using large shrimp, cut in half and set aside. Sauté onion in butter or margarine until tender, not brown. Blend in flour, seasonings and Worcestershire sauce. Gradually add milk, and cook over very low heat until thickened, stirring constantly. Add reserved shrimp and peas; heat through. Serve piping hot on toast points or unsweetened waffles; sprinkle with paprika. Serves 6.

Shrimp in Curry Mayonnaise

2 cups (1 pound frozen) cooked shrimp shrimp or 2 (5-ounce) cans shrimp
1/2 cup diced red-skinned apple
1/2 cup celery leaves, chopped
1/4 cup diced green pepper
1/2 teaspoon salt
1/2 teaspoon curry powder
1/4 cup mayonnaise
12 lettuce leaves

Combine shrimp with next 3 ingredients. Add salt and curry powder to mayonnaise, combine with salad mixture and toss lightly. Arrange in chilled lettuce cups. Serves 6.

Seafood Cocktail

1 pound cooked crabmeat or 3 (6-ounce) packages frozen crabmeat
1/2 pound cooked lobster, canned, fresh or frozen
3 avocados, peeled and cut up (brush with lemon juice)
Lettuce leaves
1 cup ripe olives
1 1/2 cups cocktail sauce (or 1 1/2 cups chili sauce plus 2 tablespoons horseradish and 4 drops hot-pepper sauce)

Arrange crabmeat, lobster and avocados, brushed with lemon juice, all cut up, on lettuce leaves along with olives. Chill well. Serve with cocktail sauce (or use combination of chili sauce, horseradish and hot-pepper sauce). Serve in individual shell plates. Serves 6.

ALTERNATIVES TO MEAT

It is a good idea to vary your menu with fish, eggs, cheese, lentils or other legumes and nuts.

Although every well-balanced meal should be built around a protein-rich main course, it does not always have to be meat, poultry or even fish. A number of other foods make a variety of attractive substitutes possible. These "meat alternates" are good as well as inexpensive.

Eggs

Eggs are the most versatile and nutritious of the alternatives to meat, providing quality protein, essential vitamins and iron. They are sold by grade: grade A-1, grade A, grade B.

Grade A is the top quality most commonly sold, and there are 5 classifications according to size and weight: extra large (27 ounces), large (24 ounces), medium (21 ounces), small (18 ounces) and peewee (15 ounces). The last class is not often found in stores.

Always store eggs, covered, in the refrigerator.

It is worthwhile to master a range of egg specialties, for the basic ingredient is always available and the results always popular. Eggs should never be cooked at high temperatures, as texture toughens and gives an unattractive appearance.

Cheeses

All cheese is rich in protein, calcium, riboflavin and vitamin A. In buying cheese you have a wide variety from which to choose, for most food markets stock many types at many prices.

One of the most economical buys is Cheddar—mild, sharp or very sharp. A constant supply of Cheddar is never wasted. Cottage cheese, too, is worth buying regularly—and using up quickly, as it is perishable. The various process cheeses and cheese spreads have an important place in every kitchen today; they are easy to use in toppings, sauces, grilled or plain sandwiches and so forth. Through cheese, the whole world is practically at your door—Gruyère and Swiss from Switzerland; Edam and Gouda from Holland; Brie, Camembert and Roquefort from France; Romano, Parmesan and Mozzarella from Italy and numerous others.

Keep cheese tightly wrapped, and store covered in refrigerator. To enjoy the full flavor, always serve cheese, except cottage cheese, at room temperature.

When cooking cheese, use low heat so that it will melt smoothly. Too long cooking or too high heat will make some cheese stringy and tough.

Dried Beans and Peas

Dried beans and peas make possible a considerable range of low-cost, high-protein dishes. However, some animal protein, like that in cheese and milk, should be included in the menu. When bought in ready-to-eat form like canned pork and beans, these legumes are a dependable convenience item.

To prepare dried beans and peas, use the following guide. One cup raw dried beans or peas will give you 2–3 cups cooked beans; 1 pound (2 1/4–2 1/2 cups) dried beans or peas after cooking gives 10–11 cups. Soak beans overnight; then add more water and seasonings, and cook.

If you are preparing beans for same-day use, here is a quick trick that shortens the preliminaries. Boil 2 cups beans in 6 cups water 2 minutes. Remove from heat, and soak 1 hour. Return to stove, and cook in same water until beans are just tender.

Generally in good supply on the market are lima beans, navy beans, lentils, kidney beans, pinto beans, soybeans, black-eyed peas and split peas.

Nuts for Protein

Nuts contain valuable proteins. Aside from their appeal as garnishes and between-meal nibbles, nuts in large amounts in salad can be a main dish for luncheon.

Peanuts are from the legume family but are treated as nuts. They are the most economical of "nuts" and have a variety of uses: in soups, sauces, sandwich fillings, salads, vegetable dishes, main-dish casseroles, cookies, cakes, pies and puddings.

A bowl of nuts brought to the table for dessert adds extra nutrients to meals.

Cheese Soufflé

    3 tablespoons butter or margarine
    3 tablespoons flour
    1 cup milk
    4 egg yolks
    1/4 teaspoon salt
      Dash cayenne
    5 egg whites
    3/4 cup grated sharp cheese

Melt butter or margarine in saucepan; add flour, and cook until mixture is bubbling. Remove from heat, and add milk all at once. Return to heat and cook, stirring constantly, until thick and smooth. Allow to cool slightly; then beat in egg yolks with seasonings. Beat egg whites until stiff but not dry; lightly fold 2 mixtures together with grated cheese. Pile lightly into buttered 1 1/2-quart soufflé dish, and bake at 350°F. about 45 minutes or until soufflé is well puffed and firm. Serve at once. Serves 4—5.

Cheese Mousse

    1 envelope plain gelatine
    3/4 cup cold water
    1 (10-ounce) can tomato soup
    2 (4-ounce) packages plain cream cheese
    1/2 cup finely chopped celery
    1/2 cup grated carrot
    1/2 cup shredded cabbage
    1/4 cup finely chopped green pepper or 1 green pickle,
      finely chopped
    1 tablespoon grated onion
    1/8 teaspoon mace
      Dash cloves
    1 cup mayonnaise

Soften gelatine in water. Heat soup in top of double boiler, and stir in gelatine to dissolve. Remove from heat, and add cheese. Beat with electric mixer or hand beater until smoothly blended. Cool, and, when mixture begins to thicken, add all remaining ingredients, except mayonnaise. Pour into oiled ring mold. Chill until firm. Unmold, and spread with mayonnaise. Serve in wedges. Serves 6—8.

Cheese-Celery Loaf

    1/2 cup chopped celery
      2 tablespoons chopped onion
      2 tablespoons butter or margarine
      3 cups cooked elbow macaroni
      1 (10-ounce) can celery soup
    1/2 cup skim milk
      1 egg, beaten
    1 1/2 cups grated cheese

Sauté celery and onion in butter or margarine until tender. Remove from heat, and stir in macaroni, soup, milk and egg. Alternate layers of macaroni mixture and cheese in greased 9″ x 5″ x 3″ loaf dish, ending with cheese. Cover with foil, and place in pan of hot water. Bake at 350°F. 1 hour or until center of loaf is set. Invert on heated platter. Serves 6—8.

Curried Eggs and Mushrooms

    1/2 pound sliced fresh mushrooms (2 cups)
      2 tablespoons butter or margarine
    1/2 teaspoon lemon juice
        Salt and pepper to taste
      2 cups milk
      1 chicken-bouillon cube, crumbled
    1/4 cup soft butter or margarine
    1/4 cup flour
      2 teaspoons curry powder
    1/4 cup mayonnaise
    1/4 teaspoon salt
    1/8 teaspoon pepper
        Dash cayenne
        Dash nutmeg
      2 egg yolks
      2 tablespoons sherry
      6 hard-cooked eggs, quartered
    1/4 cup chopped parsley
      6 slices hot toasted French bread, buttered
        Bacon curls

Sauté mushrooms in 2 tablespoons butter or margarine. Season lightly with lemon juice, salt and pepper. Set mushrooms aside, but keep them hot. Heat milk and bouillon cube in top of double boiler, but over direct heat. Make smooth mixture of flour and butter or margarine; add to milk. Whisk until smoothly thickened. Add mushrooms, curry powder and mayonnaise; season to taste with salt, pepper, cayenne and nutmeg. Mix together egg yolks and sherry, and stir in. Keep mixture hot over boiling water, or make it earlier in the day, refrigerate and re-heat. Just before serving, add hard-cooked eggs and parsley. Heat thoroughly and spoon over hot French bread. Garnish with bacon curls. Serves 6.

Baked Meringue Eggs

      6 slices buttered toast
      1 (10-ounce) can asparagus soup
      6 egg whites
        Pinch salt
      6 individual egg yolks
    1/4 cup grated cheese

Spread toast with undiluted soup. Place slices side by side on cookie sheet. Beat egg whites and salt together until stiff; then mound egg whites on toast, being careful to cover each slice completely. Make depression in center of each mound, and drop in 1 egg yolk. Sprinkle with grated cheese. Bake at 350°F. until egg whites are set and cheese melts, about 10 minutes. Serve with hot tomato sauce or additional asparagus soup diluted and heated with a few tablespoons cream. Serves 6.

Mushroom Soufflé in Green-pepper Cups

      4 large green peppers
      3 egg yolks
      1 (10-ounce) can mushroom soup
    1/2 cup grated sharp cheese
      3 egg whites
        Pinch salt

Slice tops off peppers and remove seeds and pith. Beat egg yolks, and blend well with soup and grated cheese. Beat egg whites until stiff but not dry, adding salt. Lightly fold soup mixture into egg whites. Place peppers close together for support in greased baking dish, and fill each with egg mixture. Bake at 350°F. about 30 minutes or until knife inserted in soufflé comes out clean. Serves 4.

Note: Large tomatoes may be used in place of green peppers. Cut tops off tomatoes, remove pulp and invert to drain.

Rice Ring with Creamed Vegetables

      2 cups water
    3/4 teaspoon salt
      1 cup rice (not quick-cooking type)
    1/4 teaspoon grated nutmeg
    3/4 cup blanched almonds, coarsely chopped
    1/4 cup butter or margarine
      2 cups creamed or buttered vegetables

Bring water to rolling boil; add salt, then rice. Cover, let come to high boil again, reduce heat and simmer 20—30 minutes, removing cover last 5 minutes and shaking pan to separate grains. Season with nutmeg. Grease a 7-inch ring mold generously, and sprinkle bottom with almonds. Press in the rice. Melt butter or margarine, and pour over mold. Set mold in pan of hot water, and bake 20 minutes at 350°F. Loosen edges, invert on platter and fill center with vegetables. Serves 6.

Macaroni and Cheese à la King

    4 cups cooked and drained elbow macaroni
    2 cups grated Cheddar cheese
    1 (10-ounce) can mushroom soup
    1 cup commercial sour cream
    1/2 green pepper, chopped
    1/4 cup diced pimento
    2 tablespoons pimento juice
    1 teaspoon salt
    1/2 teaspoon pepper
    1/2 teaspoon dry mustard
    3/4 cup crushed bacon-flavored crackers

Combine all ingredients except crackers, and spread mixture in a greased baking dish. Add about 1/2 cup milk if you want a moister consistency. Sprinkle with crackers, and bake at 350°F. 35—40 minutes. Serves 8.

Tomatoes and Macaroni with Cheese

    2 cups uncooked elbow macaroni
    4 quarts boiling salted water
    3 tablespoons butter or margarine
    1/2 cup chopped onion
    1 green pepper, cut in strips
    1 (28-ounce) can tomatoes
    1 cup grated cheese
    1 1/2 teaspoons salt
    1/8 teaspoon pepper
    1 egg, beaten
    Cheese-Crumb Topping

Cook macaroni in boiling water until tender. Drain; rinse in cold water. Melt butter or margarine in skillet, and sauté onion and green pepper until soft. Remove from pan, and combine with tomatoes, cheese and seasonings. Stir in egg. Pour over macaroni in greased casserole, and sprinkle with topping. Bake at 350°F. 30 minutes. Serves 6.

Cheese-Crumb Topping

    2 tablespoons butter or margarine
    1/4 cup dry bread crumbs
    1/4 cup grated cheese

Melt butter or margarine, and combine with bread crumbs and cheese.

Easy Cheese Bake

    3 cups uncooked elbow macaroni
    4 quarts boiling salted water
    2/3 cup milk
    2 (10-ounce) cans cream of chicken soup
    12 slices process cheese
    4 tomatoes, sliced

Cook macaroni in boiling water until tender; drain, and rinse. Stir milk into soup; heat, and combine with cooked macaroni. Place in buttered shallow baking dish. Top with alternate slices of cheese and tomatoes, ending with layer of cheese. Bake at 325°F. until cheese is melted and golden brown, about 25 minutes. Serves 8.

Luncheon Rarebit

    2 tablespoons butter or margarine
    2 tablespoons flour
    3/4 cup milk
    1/8 teaspoon baking soda
    1 1/2 cups canned tomatoes, drained
    1—1 1/2 cups shredded Cheddar cheese or 1/2 pound diced
        nippy process cheese
    1/2 teaspoon dry mustard
    1/4—1/2 teaspoon salt
    6 slices toasted French bread, buttered
    Bacon Curls

Melt butter or margarine, and stir in flour. Remove pan from heat, and gradually stir in milk. Return pan to heat, and whisk until thick and smooth. Mix soda with tomatoes, and add to white sauce. Stir in remaining ingredients, and heat until cheese melts. Spoon over French bread, and garnish with crisp bacon curls. Makes 6 servings.

Savory Luncheon Custard

    2 tablespoons butter or margarine
    2 cups thinly sliced onion
    6 eggs
    1 1/2 cups milk
    1 teaspoon salt
    Dash pepper

Melt butter or margarine in skillet, and sauté onions until tender. Beat eggs lightly, and add milk, salt and pepper. Place onion slices in greased casserole; pour egg mixture over. Set casserole in pan of warm water, and bake at 350°F. 50 minutes. Serves 4.

Baked Cheese Fondue

    2 cups whole wheat bread, cut in 1/2-inch cubes
    1 cup grated cheese
    2 cups milk
    2 eggs
    2 tablespoons butter or margarine, melted
    2 teaspoons salt
    Pinch pepper

Grease casserole. Arrange bread cubes in layers with grated cheese between, ending with bread on top. Beat milk, eggs, butter or margarine and seasonings together; pour mixture over bread. Let stand about 20 minutes. Set casserole in pan containing hot water to at least 1-inch depth. Bake in 350°F. oven 35—40 minutes. Serves 3—4.

Cheese Chiffon Pie

    1 1/3 cups unsifted all-purpose flour
    1/2 cup mayonnaise
    2 tablespoons water
    1 (8-ounce) package process cheese
    1/2 cup milk
    1/8 teaspoon cayenne
    3 egg yolks, well beaten
    3 egg whites

Crown Roast of Lamb (pp. 55-56).
CREDIT: *Elbert Budin*.

Roast Beef Steak (p. 44).
CREDIT: *Bernard Gray.*

Stir flour into mayonnaise and water to form firm dough. Knead slightly, and roll out to fit deep 9-inch pie plate. Bake at 425°F. 12 minutes. Meanwhile, melt cheese in milk in top of double boiler, and, when creamy-smooth, remove from heat. Stir in egg yolks and cayenne. Beat egg whites until stiff but not dry, and gently fold into cheese mixture. Scrape into pastry shell, and bake at 300°F. 30–35 minutes. Serve in wedges with fresh tomato slices. Serves 6–8.

Onion-Mushroom Bake

        8 medium onions, peeled
1 1/2 cups salted water
    1/2 pound mushrooms, sliced
    1/3 cup melted butter or margarine
    1/3 cup flour
    1/2 teaspoon salt
    1/2 teaspoon paprika
    1/4 teaspoon celery salt
        2 cups milk
        1 cup shredded Cheddar cheese
        3 tablespoons butter or margarine
        1 cup soft bread crumbs

Parboil onions in salted water 15 minutes. Drain well, and place in a shallow baking dish. In medium saucepan sauté mushrooms in 1/3 cup butter or margarine until tender. Blend in flour and seasonings. Stir in milk gradually, and cook until mixture thickens, stirring constantly. Remove from heat; stir in cheese, and pour sauce over onions. Melt 3 tablespoons butter or margarine, and combine with bread crumbs. Sprinkle over sauce, and bake at 350°F. 30–35 minutes. Serves 8.

Lima Beans in Sour Cream

        1 pound dried lima beans
        3 cups cold water
        3 teaspoons salt
    1/4 cup butter or margarine
    3/4 cup finely chopped onion
    1/2 pound mushrooms, sliced
            (approximately 2 cups)
        1 tablespoon flour
        1 tablespoon paprika
        2 cups commercial sour cream
        2 tablespoons chopped parsley

Cover beans in kettle with cold water; leave to soak overnight. Add 1 teaspoon salt and enough fresh water to barely cover beans. Bring to boiling point, reduce heat and simmer about 1 1/2 hours or until beans are tender, stirring several times during cooking. Drain well (save liquid for soup). Melt butter or margarine in large skillet, and sauté onion until just golden; add mushrooms, and cook 5 minutes. Stir in flour and paprika; cook until bubbling. Add drained beans, remaining salt and sour cream. Heat thoroughly, but do not boil. Garnish with parsley. Serves 6–8.

Mexican Kidney Beans

        1 pound dried kidney beans
        3 cups cold water
    1/4 pound salt pork, cut into bits
        3 cloves garlic, finely chopped
    1/2 cup chopped onion
        2 tablespoons chili powder
3 1/2 cups canned tomatoes
    1/4 cup tomato paste
1 1/2 teaspoons salt
    1/2 teaspoon oregano
        Pinch cumin
        Dash pepper

Put beans in deep kettle, and cover with cold water; leave overnight. Next day add enough fresh water to barely cover beans. Bring to boiling point; reduce heat to low, and simmer, covered, about 1 hour. Drain off any remaining liquid. In small saucepan sauté salt pork until quite crisp; add garlic and onion, and cook until just golden. Scrape contents of pan into beans; add all remaining ingredients, combining thoroughly. Let cook, covered, over very low heat about 1 1/2 hours or until beans are tender, stirring several times during cooking period. Serves 6–8.

Note: Second phase of preparation may be done in oven, using covered casserole.

Spiced Beans

        1 pound dried pinto beans
        3 cups cold water
    1/2 teaspoon whole cloves
        1 medium onion, sliced
    1/4 pound salt pork, cut into bits
        2 teaspoons salt
        1 (7 1/2-ounce) can tomato sauce
        2 tablespoons molasses
        1 tablespoon Worcestershire sauce

Put beans in deep kettle, and cover with 3 cups cold water; leave overnight. Next day add enough fresh water to barely cover beans. Tie cloves in small square of cheesecloth. Add cloves, onion, salt pork and salt to beans. Bring mixture to boiling point; reduce heat to low, cover and simmer about 2 hours or until beans are tender. Stir several times during cooking. Remove bag of cloves, and add tomato sauce, molasses and Worcestershire sauce, mixing thoroughly. Let simmer another 30 minutes. Serves 6–8.

Lima Bean Casserole Deluxe

        1 pound dried lima beans
        4 cups cold water
    1/4 cup salad oil
        1 small onion, chopped (1/4 cup)
    1/2 teaspoon salt
    1/4 cup green pepper, diced
        2 teaspoons sugar
        Pinch cayenne
        1 (28-ounce) can tomatoes, drained
        Salt and pepper to taste
        1 teaspoon sugar
    1/2 cup grated Parmesan cheese

Cover beans with cold water and soak overnight. Add 1 teaspoon salt. Simmer until tender and drain. Heat salad oil, and sauté onion until just golden. Put beans in shallow casserole, and add oil and onion, scraping pan thoroughly. Add green pepper, salt, 2 teaspoons sugar, and cayenne. Combine well, so that beans glisten with oil. Top mixture with chopped canned tomatoes, sprinkle lightly with sugar, salt, and pepper; finish with grated cheese. Bake uncovered in oven at 350°F. about 35 minutes. Serves 6—8.

Old-fashioned Baked Beans

       4 cups pea or navy beans
       3 cups cold water
   3/4 pound fat salt pork
          Strip of pork rind
   1/2 cup boiling water
       1 medium whole onion (optional)
       1 cup dark molasses
       3 tablespoons brown sugar
       2 teaspoons salt
   1/2 teaspoon dry mustard
       2 cups boiling water

Wash and pick over beans, and soak overnight in cold water to cover. Before cooking, add more water, if necessary, barely to cover beans. Heat slowly, keeping water under boiling point. Cook until beans skins begin to burst and peel back; test by removing a few beans on spoon tip and blowing on them. Drain beans and save liquid. Wash pork, scald in 1/2 cup boiling water and scrape if necessary. Put a thick slice of pork at the bottom of a bean pot. Turn beans into pot. For extra flavor, bury whole onion in center of mass. Make gashes in rind, and place piece, rind side up, on top of beans. Mix molasses, sugar, salt and mustard; dissolve in 1 cup reserved liquid, and pour over beans. Add more liquid and boiling water to cover contents of pot completely. Put on lid, and place in center of oven, at 250°F. Bake 6—8 hours. Check about every hour, and add more water as needed; liquid should be visible at least 4 hours of cooking period. Remove pot lid for last hour of baking to brown and crisp pork rind. Serves 7—8.

Note: If bacon or other smoked pork is used instead of salt pork, decrease amount of salt.

French Omelet

       2 eggs
       2 teaspoons water
          Pinch salt
          Dash pepper
       1 tablespoon butter or margarine

Break eggs into bowl. Add water and seasonings. Beat until frothy. Heat small omelet pan until drop of water dances when dropped in center of pan. Put butter or margarine in pan, and tilt so that all surfaces are coated. Pour in eggs, and stir with tines of fork until edges begin to set. Allow omelet to cook until surface is creamy; then fold in half or roll and slide onto warm plate. Serves 1.

VARIATIONS:

Fillings should be arranged over 1/2 the cooked omelet before folding it.

* *Bacon Omlet*: Crumble 6 slices crisp, cooked bacon.

* *Cheese Omelet*: Sprinkle 1/3 cup grated cheese over omelet as it cooks.

* *Chicken-Curry Omelet*: Melt 2 tablespoons butter or margarine, and sauté 1 tablespoon chopped onion. Add 1/2 cup diced cooked chicken, and heat through; add salt and curry powder to taste.

* *Herb Omelet*: Add 1/8 teaspoon each fresh chopped thyme or sage and marjoram or savory and 1 teaspoon minced parsley to egg mixture before cooking.

* *Mushroom Omelet*: Scatter 1/2 cup sautéed sliced mushrooms on omelet as it cooks.

* *Jelly Omelet*: Omit pepper from egg mixture; spread omelet with jelly before folding.

Hearty Main-dish Soups

Sometimes a favorite soup can be the *pièce de résistance*. Here are some you'll enjoy. If the menu is nicely balanced, a hearty soup, perfectly seasoned and served steaming hot, can be readily substituted for the more familiar type of main course.

A thick soup made with dried legumes—beans of various kinds, peas or lentils—is a good source of protein. The meal should also include some milk or cheese. For example, a crisp vegetable salad with cottage cheese.

Old-fashioned vegetable soup, slowly cooked with a beef bone; *Mulligatawny*, with its generous pieces of chicken and its whiff of curry; cream soups; potato or corn chowder and oyster stew can also be main attractions for luncheon, dinner or supper. Individual portions should be ample—served in chowder bowls or big soup plates—and you should be prepared to offer second helpings as well as crisp crackers, Melba toast, hot French bread, and hot rolls.

Follow a main-dish soup with a change of texture, taste and color—a crisp salad, raw relish platter or hot fresh asparagus. A dessert, of the type that is perhaps too heavy or rich for a meat-and-vegetable menu, is appropriate. Consider baked-apple dumplings, dessert pancakes, ice-cream waffles with sauce.

The many excellent commercial soups are ready for the table in minutes. They lend themselves to experimenting too—as in quick *Puree*

Mongole with Croutons, which blends cream of green pea with cream of tomato. To leftover creamed celery add cream of celery and so on to create many other combinations.

Canadian Pea Soup

    2 cups dried whole yellow peas
    8 cups water
    2 onions, chopped
    1 stalk celery, chopped
    1 cooked ham bone or 4 slices bacon, cut in pieces
    2 teaspoons salt
    1/2 teaspoon pepper
    1/8 teaspoon thyme (optional)

Pick over and wash peas. Soak overnight in water, using large cooking kettle. In morning, add onions, celery and ham bone. Put kettle on medium heat, bring to boil, reduce heat and simmer 3–4 hours. More water may be needed, but remember that the famous pea soup of French Canada should be quite thick. Taste soup, and season; salt needed will depend on ham bone's contribution. Serves 6–8.

Lentil Soup

    1 1/2 cups dried lentils
    2 quarts cold water
    1 smoked ham hock or bone left from baked ham
    1 large onion, chopped fine
    2 large stalks celery, chopped fine
    2 bay leaves
      Salt and pepper to taste
    1/4 cup sherry
    1/4 cup cream (optional)

Soak lentils in cold water at least 6 hours, preferably overnight. Add ham bone, onion, celery and bay leaves; bring to boil, and simmer, covered, 4 hours. Remove bone and bay leaves; skim fat. Cut meat off bone, chop into tiny pieces and return to soup. Stir well, taste and add salt unless ham has salted it enough; add pepper and sherry. If soup becomes too thick during simmering, more water may be added. A little cream may be stirred into soup just before serving. Serves 6.

Mulligatawny

    1/4 cup butter or margarine
    1 medium onion, sliced
    1 green pepper, diced
    1 stalk celery, diced
    1 carrot, diced
    1 tart apple, diced
    2 tablespoons flour
    2 cups boiling water
    1 1/2 cups canned tomatoes
    2 chicken-bouillon cubes
    1 teaspoon curry powder
    1 teaspoon salt
      Sprig parsley
    2 cloves
      Pinch mace
    3 cups milk
    1 cup cooked chicken

Melt butter or margarine in deep kettle, and sauté next 5 ingredients, stirring frequently, until onion is tender but not browned. Stir in flour, then remaining ingredients except milk and chicken. Cover, and simmer 1/2 hour. Just before serving, add milk and chicken, and heat through. Serves 4–6.

Borsch

    1 1/2 pounds beef, neck or shin, with bone
    2 1/2 quarts salted water
    1 large onion
    2 tablespoons butter or margarine
    1/3 cup tomato paste
    6 beets
    4 stalks celery
    1 small head of cabbage
    1 tablespoon sugar
    1 bay leaf
    1 tablespoon salt
    4 potatoes, peeled and diced
    1/2 cup sour cream

Put beef into salted water, boil 15 minutes and skim; simmer 2 hours longer. Drain, and reserve broth and meat from the bones. Cut onion into julienne strips; sauté in butter or margarine until tender but not brown. Add tomato paste, and mix into beef broth. Slice beets, celery and cabbage in fine strips, and add to soup, with sugar and seasonings. Allow soup to simmer 1 1/2 hours; 1/2 hour before serving, add potatoes, and cook until tender. Add meat, and reheat. Serve in deep soup plates, stirring into each 1 large tablespoon sour cream. Serves 6.

Note: Canned beef broth, diluted to 2 1/2 quarts liquid, can be substituted for beef cooked in water. Strained borsch may be served ice-cold in the same way.

Beef-Vegetable Soup

    1 pound shin beef with bone
    3 1/2 quarts water
    2 cups shredded cabbage
    1 cup cut-up green beans
    1 cup diced carrots
    1 (20-ounce) can tomatoes
    3/4 cup diced celery
    2/3 cup fresh peas
    1/2 cup chopped onion
    1 1/2 teaspoons salt
    1 clove garlic, chopped
    1/8 teaspoon pepper
      Chopped parsley

Place beef and bone in large kettle, cover with water and add salt. Cover kettle, bring to boil and skim. Simmer 4 hours; then remove bone, skin and fat. Chop meat, and reserve. Add remaining ingredients, except parsley, cover, and simmer 1/2 hour. Add meat, and reheat. Garnish with parsley. Serves 8–10.

Gazpacho

    1 small onion, chopped
    1 cup peeled and diced fresh tomatoes
 1/2 cup diced green pepper
 1/2 cup diced celery
 1/2 cup diced cucumber
 1/2 clove garlic
    3 cups tomato juice
 1/3 cup *French Dressing*
    1 tablespoon lemon juice
      Salt and cayenne to taste

Place all vegetables and garlic in blender with 1 cup tomato juice. Blend until mixture is smooth. Add *French Dressing*, lemon juice, salt and cayenne with remaining tomato juice. Chill thoroughly. Serve very cold with small bowls of cubed tomato, celery, green pepper and cucumber, to be sprinkled over soup. Serves 5—6.

Clam-Tomato Bisque

    1 (28-ounce) can tomatoes
 1/2 cup water
    1 onion, chopped
    2 stalks celery, chopped
 1/4 cup chopped green pepper
    1 bay leaf
    2 tablespoons chopped parsley
    1 teaspoon sugar
      Dash thyme
      Salt and pepper to taste
      Juice of 1/2 lemon
    1 (6-ounce) can clams
 1/2 cup whipped cream, slightly salted

Put tomatoes in heavy saucepan with water, onion, celery, pepper and bay leaf. Cover tightly, and simmer 20 minutes. Remove bay leaf. Add parsley, sugar, seasonings, lemon juice and clams. Serve topped with whipped cream. Serves 4—5.

Green-and-Gold Chowder

    4 slices salt pork, diced
1 1/2 cups water
    1 cup diced peeled potatoes
    2 chicken-bouillon cubes
    1 (15-ounce) can cream-style corn
    1 (14-ounce) can kernel corn
1/4–1/2 cup sliced green onions including some tops
    3 tablespoons flour
 1/2 cup cold water
      Dash cayenne
      Pinch mace
    1 pint hot milk

In deep saucepan fry salt pork slowly until crisp; don't allow it to burn. Add 1 1/2 cups water, potatoes and bouillon cubes. Simmer about 15 minutes; add both cans corn, and onions, Simmer 2 minutes. Make smooth mixture of flour and 1/2 cup water, and stir into corn. Add cayenne and mace. Bring to boil. Stir in milk and reheat thoroughly, but do not boil. Serves 5—6.

Chicken-Meringue Soup

    1 quart strong chicken broth
    1 carrot, grated
 1/4 cup onion, chopped
    2 tablespoons minute tapioca
    2 cups hot milk
    2 egg yolks, well beaten
 1/2 cup cream
 1/2 cup diced cooked chicken (optional)
    2 tablespoons chopped parsley
      Salt and pepper to taste
    2 egg whites
 1/2 teaspoon salt
 1/2 cup grated Parmesan cheese

Heat chicken broth with carrot and onion until vegetables are tender. Add tapioca, and simmer gently until tapioca is transparent. Add milk. Mix egg yolks with cream. Add cream-and-egg mixture to soup. Cook slowly until soup is slightly thickened; do not boil. Add salt, pepper, chicken and parsley. Beat egg whites with 1/2 teaspoon salt until stiff. Place soup in oven-proof casserole or individual pottery bowls. Cover top with beaten egg whites, sprinkle with cheese and brown quickly under hot broiler. Serve at once. Serves 6—8.

Minestrone

    1 slice day-old bread
 1/2 cup red wine or tomato juice
    1 pound fresh-ground meat
    1 egg, lightly beaten
    2 tablespoons chopped onion
    1 teaspoon salt
 1/4 teaspoon marjoram
 1/4 teaspoon sweet basil
 1/4 teaspoon garlic salt
    1 cup dried navy beans
    5 cups water
    1 teaspoon salt
 1/4 cup hot oil
 1/2 cup diced celery with leaves
 1/2 cup shredded cabbage
 1/2 cup diced turnip
    1 clove garlic, crushed
    2 cups beef broth or bouillon
    2 sliced onions
    1 (28-ounce) can tomatoes
      (strained if you wish)
    1 bay leaf
    1 clove
    1 cup tiny macaroni shells or elbow macaroni
    2 quarts boiling salted water
 1/4 cup grated Parmesan cheese

Crumble bread into wine; add next 7 ingredients. Form into small balls, the size of hazelnuts, and refrigerate until needed. Wash beans, and soak overnight in 5 cups water. Next morning add 1 teaspoon salt, and simmer 30 minutes. Sauté meat balls in oil; when richly browned, drain and set aside. Pour off 1/2 the fat, and add celery, cabbage, turnip and garlic to pan; fry, stirring, 5 minutes. Scrape into large saucepan, and add next 5 ingredients and undrained beans.

Cover, and simmer 1 hour or until beans are almost tender, stirring occasionally. Meanwhile, cook macaroni in boiling water until almost tender. Drain. Add macaroni and meat balls to soup. Cover, and simmer 20 minutes. Taste for seasoning. Serve in deep bowls, sprinkled with cheese. Serves 10.

Oxtail Soup

    1 1/2 pounds oxtail, cut in small pieces
        1 tablespoon melted butter or margarine
    1 1/2 quarts water
        4 teaspoons salt
      3/4 cup diced raw carrots
      1/2 cup diced onions
      1/2 cup diced raw celery
        2 tablespoons regular rice
    1 1/2 cups canned tomatoes

Brown oxtails in butter or margarine. Add water and salt; cover, and simmer 2 hours. Add carrots, onions, celery and rice, and simmer 1/2 hour longer. Skim fat off surface, add tomatoes and heat thoroughly. Serves 4.

Cold Cream of Asparagus Soup

      1/2 pound fresh asparagus
    1 1/2 cups water
        1 sliced onion
        2 chicken-bouillon cubes
        2 tablespoons quick-cooking tapioca
        1 (10-ounce) can cream of chicken soup
      1/2 cup light cream
           Salt and pepper to taste

Wash asparagus, and discard tough ends. Simmer in water with onion and bouillon cubes 10 minutes. Add tapioca, and simmer 5 minutes. Pour into blender, and blend 30 seconds. Add soup and cream, and blend 10 seconds. Season to taste, and chill well.

IDEAS FOR LEFTOVERS

Do plan to have leftovers so that you can put meals together quickly at times and extend the enjoyment of a fine roast or a whole fish over several meals, each individually distinctive and tempting.

Cooked roast beef, pot roast or steak can be ground or chopped and used in casseroles, expanded with macaroni and vegetables. Or substitute it for raw meat in spaghetti sauce. Mixed with thick cream sauce, it can become croquettes, fried delicately brown, with a little cooked rice; it can stuff cabbage rolls, peppers and tomatoes to be baked with sauces of canned soup, for example. Beef bones can form the basis of a good soup, with onions, carrots, and barley added.

Cooked lamb roast or chops can be used as the basis of lamb curry, in a meat and macaroni casserole or in a pot pie. Leftover lamb stew needs only a can of lima beans, a handful of frozen peas and some curry powder to become a version of curried lamb.

Cooked pork can be used in any of the same ways as beef and lamb, or as the basis for small or family-size pork pies. The meat is ground and mixed with onions and a little seasoning. Or cut it into thin strips and use it in Chinese fried rice, pork chop suey, and so forth.

Baked or boiled ham bones can go into lentil, lima bean or died-pea soup. Dice any remaining meat, and serve it with cream sauce or in ham omelet. Ground, it can be mixed with a little salad dressing for deviled-ham sandwiches. Mixed with diced onion and cooked rice, it can stuff peppers or tomatoes.

Roast, broiled or fried chicken can be used in Chinese fried rice or chop suey; it can also form the basis for a chicken casserole, made with cream of chicken soup, frozen peas and carrots and a biscuit crust. It is excellent of course, in chicken salad, chicken à la king or croquettes. Or try making toast cups: Trim crusts from fresh bread, press each slice into muffin cup and toast in oven. Fill with creamed chicken mixture to make a quick snack.

Even the smallest amounts of cooked vegetables can be used to advantage. Mashed potatoes go into sautéed fish cakes with an egg to bind the mixture. Leftover carrots, turnips or spinach, combined, pureed and added to thin white sauce, make a delicious cream of vegetable soup.

Chicken-Almond Casserole

        3 tablespoons fat or drippings
      2/3 cup chopped celery
      1/3 cup chopped onion
      1/4 cup chopped green pepper
        2 tablespoons flour
        1 cup canned tomatoes or chicken gravy
        2 chicken-bouillon cubes dissolved in 1 1/2 cups hot
           water or chicken stock
      1/2 teaspoon salt
      1/4 teaspoon dry mustard
    1 1/2 cups diced cooked chicken
      1/2 cup toasted almonds
 2 1/2–3 cups cooked noodles
      1/2 cup buttered bread crumbs

Melt fat in frying pan; add celery, onion and green pepper. Sauté until vegetables are lightly colored. Stir in flour. Add tomatoes, bouillon, salt and mustard, and cook until mixture thickens. Remove from heat, and add diced chicken, almonds and noodles. Pour into greased 2-quart casserole. Sprinkle with buttered crumbs, and bake at 350°F. 30–40 minutes. Serves 6.

Note: Any leftover poultry or cooked meat may be substituted, so don't be afraid to experiment. Most dishes specifying finely cut or chopped meat can be varied.

Casserole of Turkey Slices

      1/4 cup chopped onion
        1 tablespoon melted butter or margarine
        1 cup tomato ketchup
    1 1/2 teaspoons prepared mustard
      1/2 cup chopped celery
      1/4 cup water
      1/4 cup lemon juice
        1 tablespoon Worcestershire sauce
        2 tablespoons brown sugar
          Dash pepper
          Dash cayenne
        6 thick slices cooked turkey (2 pounds)

Sauté onion slowly in butter or margarine until golden; do not brown. Add remaining ingredients, except turkey, and simmer, covered, 15 minutes. Adjust seasoning to taste. Pour sauce over turkey slices in casserole; cover, and heat about 20 minutes at 350°F. Serves 6.

Jellied Turkey Salad

        1 (3-ounce) package lime- or lemon-flavored jelly
            powder
        1 cup boiling water
        1 cup less 2 tablespoons cold water
        1 tablespoon lemon juice
        1 cup diced cooked turkey
      1/2 cup finely chopped cabbage
      1/4 cup diced green pepper
        2 tablespoons chopped pimento or sliced radishes
        1 tablespoon chopped chives or green-onion tops
        1 tablespoon diced sweet pickle

Dissolve jelly powder in boiling water; add cold water and lemon juice. Chill in refrigerator until syrupy. Oil 6 1-cup individual molds (or 1 6-cup mold). Thoroughly combine remaining ingredients, and divide among molds. Pour chilled jelly over contents, and chill until set. Serves 5—6.

Mock Brunswick Stew

        3 cups diced leftover cooked meats (roast beef, pork
            or veal)
        1 (10-ounce) can consommé
        1 (28-ounce) can tomatoes
        3 tablespoons white wine
          Salt and pepper to taste
        1 (12-ounce) package frozen lima beans
      6–8 potatoes, peeled
        1 (14-ounce) can kernel corn, drained

Cut meat into bite-size pieces, and place in saucepan. Cover with consommé, and add tomatoes. Bring just to boil. Add wine and seasonings, and reduce heat to simmer. Meantime cook frozen lima beans separately, following package directions, and boil potatoes. When beans are almost tender, drain, and add to meat mixture. When potatoes are done, drain, cube and add to stew, together with corn. Heat thoroughly, and add further seasonings if necessary. Serves 6—8.

Fish in Aspic

        1 envelope plain gelatine
    1 3/4 cups cold fish stock or chicken broth
        2 tablespoons capers
        1 tablespoon caper juice
        1 tablespoon lemon juice
          Salt and pepper to taste
          Paprika
    2 1/2 cups cooked flaked fish
      3/4 cup mayonnaise
        2 tablespoons chopped chives
        2 tablespoons chopped parsley
        2 tablespoons diced cucumber

Soak gelatine in 3 tablespoons of the cold fish stock. Heat remaining stock, and dissolve gelatine in it. Add capers and caper juice. Season stock well with lemon juice, salt, pepper and paprika. Chill until mixture begins to thicken; pour a thin layer of aspic in 8-cup rinsed mold. Chill until almost set. Mix flaked fish with rest of aspic, and pour into mold. Chill until set, and unmold. Serve very cold with mayonnaise to which chopped chives, chopped parsley and diced cucumber have been added. Serves 4.

Scalloped Fish with Cheese

        3 tablespoons butter or margarine
        2 tablespoons chopped green pepper
        1 tablespoon chopped onion
        2 tablespoons flour
        1 cup milk
        1 teaspoon bottled thick meat sauce
    1 1/2 cups flaked cooked fish
  1/4-1/2 teaspoon salt
      1/3 cup grated Cheddar cheese
      1/2 cup soft bread crumbs

Melt butter or margarine in double boiler over direct heat. Add green pepper and onion, and cook until tender. Stir in flour, and slowly add milk and meat sauce. Cook over boiling water until smooth, stirring constantly. Add fish, and salt to taste. Scrape into buttered casserole or individual ramekins. Combine cheese and crumbs, and spread on top. Bake at 400°F. until brown. Serves 4.

Quick Vermicelli Supper

        8 ounces long vermicelli
        3 quarts boiling salted water
      1/4 cup fat
        4 medium onions, sliced
        2 green peppers, chopped
        2 cloves garlic, finely chopped
        2 tablespoons flour
        1 (20-ounce) can tomatoes
        2 cups diced leftover beef
    2 1/2 teaspoons salt
        1 teaspoon thyme
          Pinch ground cloves
      1/4 cup Parmesan cheese, grated

Boil vermicelli in salted water. While it cooks, melt fat in good-sized skillet. Add raw vegetables and garlic, and cook until tender. Push vegetables to one side. Add flour, and stir into fat thoroughly, letting bubble for 1–2 minutes. Gradually add tomatoes, stirring constantly until well mixed. Add meat and seasonings. Drain vermicelli, and arrange in deep serving dish. Pour sauce over, and sprinkle with cheese. Serves 4–6.

Shepherd's Pie

        3 cups ground cooked beef
    1/4 cup leftover gravy or bouillon
        1 tablespoon bottled thick meat sauce
    2 1/2 cups mashed potatoes
        2 tablespoons finely chopped onion
        1 egg, beaten
            Salt and pepper to taste
        2 tablespoons butter or margarine

Combine meat with enough leftover gravy and condiment sauce to moisten well and hold mixture together. Turn meat into baking dish; pat level. Combine mashed potatoes, onion, egg, salt and pepper. Cover meat with potato mixture, and smooth. Dot with butter or margarine, and bake at 375°F. 25–30 minutes or until potato topping is puffed and lightly browned. Serves 6.

Note: When preparing beef, remove hard bits and gristle, but put some of the fat through the grinder with the lean.

Speedy Chow Mein

    1/4 cup fat
        2 cups sliced celery
        2 cups sliced mushrooms
        2 cups sliced onion
    1/2 cup sliced green pepper
        2 cups cooked pork or beef cut in 1/4-inch strips
        1 cup chicken broth
        1 tablespoon cornstarch
        2 teaspoons Worcestershire sauce
        1 teaspoon salt
        1 (20-ounce) can bean sprouts
            drained and rinsed
        1 tablespoon soy sauce
        1 teaspoon preserved ginger, finely chopped
        1 package chow mein noodles, heated

Melt fat in skillet, and gently sauté celery, mushrooms and onion about 5 minutes. Add green pepper, and sauté 2–3 minutes longer. Then add meat. Mix chicken broth with cornstarch; add Worcestershire sauce and salt. Stir this mixture lightly into meat and vegetables. Bring to a boil. Add bean sprouts, and toss mixture lightly with fork. Cover pan, and heat 5 minutes. Add soy sauce, and scatter ginger over top; then sprinkle noodles over all. Accompany with hot rice. Serves 6.

Half-hour Veal Creole

        1 cup sliced onion
    1/4 cup salad oil
        2 cups cubed cooked veal
        1 (28-ounce) can tomatoes
        1 cup diced green pepper
        1 cup sliced mushrooms
        2 teaspoons salt
        2 teaspoons sugar
            Pinch cloves
        1 bay leaf
            Dash pepper
    1/4 cup flour
    1/3 cup water

Sauté onions in hot oil until just tender. Add all except last 2 ingredients. Cover, and simmer 25 minutes. Remove bay leaf. Make smooth paste of flour and water, and thicken veal mixture. Cook another 5 minutes, stirring constantly. Serves 5–6.

Ham-Bean Casserole

        1 (15-ounce) can lima beans
        1 (15-ounce) can red kidney beans
        1 cup diced cooked ham
        1 (10-ounce) can mushroom soup
        1 teaspoon Worcestershire sauce
        1 medium green pepper, thinly sliced
        1 small onion, thinly sliced

Drain both cans beans, reserving liquid from kidney beans. Combine beans and ham, and place in casserole. Blend soup with Worcestershire sauce and 1/4 cup kidney-bean liquid; pour over beans and ham. Arrange rings of pepper and onion over top, and bake at 350°F. 35 minutes or until bubbling hot. Serves 8.

Creamed Ham with Mushrooms

        3 tablespoons butter or margarine
    1/4 pound fresh mushrooms, sliced
    1/4 cup flour
    1 1/2 cups milk
    1/4 teaspoon salt
    1/8 teaspoon pepper
    1 1/4 cups diced cooked ham
    1/4 teaspoon bottled thick meat sauce

Melt buttter or margarine, and sauté mushrooms until tender. Stir in flour, add milk and seasonings, and cook until smooth and thickened, stirring constantly. Add ham and meat sauce. Heat 5 minutes longer. Serve over split and buttered corn bread, tea biscuits or toasted English muffins. Serves 4.

VARIATION:

* Diced cooked chicken may be used instead of ham, and paprika or curry powder added to taste. Serve over tea biscuits or toast or in toast cups.

Fish Timbale

        2 cups flaked cooked fish
    1/4 cup butter or margarine, melted
    3/4 cup bread crumbs
        3 egg yolks, lightly beaten
        3 egg whites
        2 teaspoons lemon juice
            Salt and pepper to taste

Combine first 4 ingredients. Beat egg whites until stiff, and fold into mixture. Add lemon juice and seasonings. Place in greased 4-cup mold, and steam 1 hour. Serve with cream sauce spiked with dash of Worcestershire sauce. Serves 6.

Jellied Deviled Tongue

        2 envelopes plain gelatine
    1/2 cup cold water
  1 3/4 cups boiling water
    1/4 cup mayonnaise
        2 tablespoons bottled horseradish
        1 tablespoon prepared mustard
        1 teaspoon salt
    1/4 teaspoon pepper
        2 cups chopped cooked tongue
        2 hard-cooked eggs, chopped
    1/4 cup chopped sour pickle

Soften gelatine in cold water 5 minutes. Add to boiling water, and stir until dissolved. Let stand until almost cool; then beat in next 5 ingredients. Chill until thick and syrupy. Add tongue, eggs and pickle. Rinse loaf pan with cold water, pour in mixture and chill until firm. Unmold, and slice. Serves 8.

Stuffed Baked Potatoes

        6 medium potatoes
            Drippings or butter
        1 cup chopped cooked meat
        1 tablespoon butter or margarine
        1 tablespoon cream
        1 tablespoon finely chopped onion
        1 tablespoon finely chopped parsley
    1/2–1 teaspoon salt
    1/4 cup stock or gravy
            Worcestershire sauce
    1/4 cup grated cheese

Choose well-shaped potatoes of even sizes. Scrub well, pat dry and grease lightly with drippings or butter. Bake at 350°F. about 1 hour or at 450°F. about 40 minutes. Larger potatoes require more time. When potatoes are done, cut thin slice off flat side of each, and remove as much potato as possible without breaking skin. Combine potato lightly (do not mash) with next 6 ingredients, using fork; then moisten with stock, and season with Worcestershire sauce. Fill potato skins with mixture, and heap tops. Sprinkle each with grated cheese, and brown in 400°F. oven or under broiler. Serves 6.

Note: Baked potatoes may be filled with leftover fish, vegetables and so forth in any palatable combination, in cream sauce or merely buttered. Interesting additions to leftover mixtures are chopped bacon, sautéed sliced mushrooms, chopped chives or browned, chopped onion.

Ham-Rice Pompoms

  1 1/2 cups cooked rice
  1 1/2 cups ground cooked ham
    1/2 cup chopped Brazil nuts
    1/4 cup chopped onion
        2 tablespoons butter or margarine, melted
        2 eggs, beaten
        1 tablespoon prepared mustard
        1 tablespoon flour
            Salt to taste
    1/2 cup fine dry bread crumbs
  1 1/2 cups pineapple juice

Combine first 9 ingredients, and form into 12 croquettes (the variation in salt depends on the mildness of ham). Roll in crumbs, and place in well-greased baking pan. Pour pineapple juice around croquettes. Bake uncovered at 350° F. 30 —40 minutes, basting now and then with juice. Serve with *Mushroom Sauce*.

Note: Any leftover cooked, smoked or pickled pork, free of fat and bone, may be substituted.

GOOD COMPANIONS

Main dishes have maximum appeal when accompaniments help to create balanced flavors, colors and textures.

In planning meals, the most important factor of course is your choice of meat or alternative. Accompaniments, though, should be thoughtfully chosen. There are many combinations that can add different looks and flavors to main courses.

Color, texture and flavor are the points that will decide what goes with what, which is why the blandness of veal, for instance, is offset by a spicy tomato sauce or a savory herb dressing.

There are certain accompaniments—spiced fruit with ham, the well-known stuffings and cranberry sauce with turkey, currant jelly or mint sauce with lamb, applesauce with pork, crisp relishes with almost any cooked meat, dumplings with beef stew—that add special notes to many a meal. And garnishes are not always strictly ornamental. The sprigs of parsley and lemon wedges you serve with fish add flavor, as well as color.

Sometimes an ordinary meal can win you extravagant compliments, and the difference may lie in a little added note, something you have done to point up the flavors or something you serve with your main dish to take it right into the class of very special cooking.

Never be afraid to be adventurous. Something that's completely new with you may in time become a tradition. Do look to other lands for examples: to the Chinese, with their sweet-and-pungent accents, or to the French, with their simple green salads and epicurean sliced tomatoes.

Affinities with Herbs

You can point up the natural flavor of your meat with herbs. For lamb use the time-honored touch of mint or rosemary, savory or dill. Beef takes well to basil, thyme, marjoram, savory or rosemary. Veal goes with sage, tarragon, summer savory, thyme or basil. Monosodium glutamate, a prepared chemical salt long known to the Chinese, enhances the flavor of meat. And if you have not yet tried freshly ground pepper, you'll find that it adds piquancy to any dish.

Gravies and Sauces

The most appetizing gravy takes only a few minutes to make, and, when you've mastered the basic method, you can apply your skill with virtually all meats.

You need a thickener (flour or cornstarch) and a separating ingredient (melted fat or cold water) to prevent lumping when boiling water or stock is added to the mixture. Flour will give you a more opaque gravy than will cornstarch, which produces a clear gravy. When you use cornstarch, remember that it has about double the thickening power of flour so that you need only 1/2 as much.

If the drippings in your roasting pan are not brown enough when the flour is blended with them, brown them further by cooking and stirring over medium heat. Remember, gravy will not brown any more after you have added water or stock. Gravy made from beef drippings seldom needs additional color or flavor, but you might like to add bouillon cubes or liquid bouillon when you make gravy from pork, lamb or veal drippings.

Vary the flavor of your gravies by experimenting with seasonings. Two teaspoons of chopped onion or a couple of tablespoons of sliced mushrooms can be added to brown gravy, or if you prefer the fresh sweet taste of celery use 2–3 teaspoons finely chopped fresh celery.

Some meat dishes and many types of fish dishes taste best when served in smooth, creamy white sauce. Like brown gravy, white sauce needs only the simplest ingredients—fat, flour, liquid. Butter or margarine is the best fat to use in white sauce; the liquid can be milk, light cream or a mixture containing the nutritious stock from mild-flavored vegetables.

If you use 1 tablespoon butter or margarine and 1 tablespoon flour to 1 cup liquid, you will have a thin sauce ideal for cream soups. Increasing the flour and butter to 2 tablespoons each for the same amount of liquid will make the sauce thicker and richer for your meat and fish dishes, poultry and vegetables. For croquettes and soufflés you will need an even thicker sauce; increase the but-

ter or margarine and flour measurements to 3 tablespoons of each, again keeping liquid constant. Season your white sauce with salt and freshly ground pepper. If cream sauce is not to be served immediately, it must be covered with a tightly fitting lid to prevent a skin from forming on top, and placed in refrigerator. Cream sauce taken off the heat and kept at room temperature 2 hours or longer is hazardous to use because of bacterial growth. Reheat refrigerated sauce slowly, until very hot, before serving.

Horseradish Sauce

> 1 tablespoon butter or margarine
> 1 tablespoon all-purpose flour
> 1/8 teaspoon salt
> 1 teaspoon sugar
> 1 tablespoon lemon juice
> 1/4 cup prepared horseradish
> 1 bouillon cube
> 1/4 cup boiling water
> 1/2 cup commercial sour cream

Melt butter or margarine. Blend in flour, salt, sugar, lemon juice and horseradish. Dissolve bouillon cube in boiling water, and add to sauce. Cook, stirring, over medium heat until thickened. Simmer 10 minutes. Remove from heat, and allow to cool 3 minutes. Stir in sour cream. Makes 1 cup.

Note: Serve with beef, tongue, steak, veal or meat loaf; it is a very smooth sauce but with a tang.

Chicken Gravy

> 3 tablespoons fat remaining from frying chicken
> 3 tablespoons flour
> 2 cups hot meat juices, stock, water or milk
> Salt and pepper to taste

Pour off fat and juices that remain after cooking chicken; leave all brown residue in pan. Measure fat back into pan, and stir in flour. Cook over low heat, stirring constantly, until mixture bubbles; continue cooking to brown flour-fat mixture as desired. Pour in hot liquid, and cook, stirring constantly, and scraping bottom and sides of the pan to blend brown particles into gravy. Simmer about 5 minutes till uniformly thickened; season, and serve very hot. Chopped, cooked giblets may be added to gravy. Makes 1 pint.

Mustard Sauce

> 2 tablespoons dry mustard
> 2 tablespoons flour
> 1 teaspoon sugar
> 1/4 teaspoon salt
> 3/4 cup boiling water
> 1 teaspoon meat extract
> 2 tablespoons vinegar
> 2 egg yolks, slightly beaten
> 1 teaspoon butter or margarine

Combine mustard, flour, sugar and salt in top of double boiler. Combine water and meat extract, and add to mustard mixture. Stir in vinegar. Add egg yolks and butter or margarine. Cook over hot water until thickened, stirring constantly. Serve hot or cold, with ham, tongue or corned beef. Makes 1 cup.

Garlic Cheese Sauce

>   1 tablespoon butter or margarine
>   1 clove garlic, halved
>   1 cup evaporated milk
>   1 cup grated Canadian Cheddar cheese
>   1/2 teaspoon salt
>   1/4 teaspoon pepper

Melt butter or margarine in top of double boiler. Add garlic; cook 5 minutes. Remove garlic; add milk, and heat. Stir in cheese until melted. Season with salt and pepper. This sauce is good with macaroni, vegetables (especially asparagus) or poached eggs on toast. Makes 1 3/4 cups.

Mint Sauce

>   1/4 cup hot water
>   1/4 cup vinegar
>   3 tablespoons sugar
>   1/4 cup finely chopped mint leaves

Combine water, vinegar and sugar. Stir until sugar is dissolved. Pour over mint leaves. Set in warm place 1/2 hour. Serve with lamb. Makes 1/2 cup sauce.

Raisin Sauce

>   1/2 cup brown sugar, firmly packed
>   2 teaspoons cornstarch
>   1/4 cup water
>   1/2 cup seedless raisins, washed and drained
> 1 1/2 tablespoons vinegar
>   1 tablespoon butter or margarine
>   Juice and grated rind of 1 orange
>   1/2 teaspoon salt

Combine sugar and cornstarch in saucepan. Stir in water. Cook, stirring, over medium heat 5 minutes. Add raisins. Cook, stirring, 5 minutes longer. Add next 4 ingredients. Serve with ham or pork. Makes approximately 1 cup sauce.

Cranberry Sauce

>   2 cups sugar
>   1/2 cup water
>   1 pound (about 4 cups) cranberries

Measure sugar into saucepan. Add water. Bring to boil, stirring constantly. Lower heat. Cook, stirring 5 minutes over low heat. Pick over and wash cranberries. Remove any tiny stems. Add cranberries to sauce, and cook over low heat until berries are tender, a few minutes only. This sauce is traditional with poultry. Makes 3 cups.

Cranberry Jelly

>   1 pound (about 4 cups) cranberries
>   1 cup water
>   2 cups sugar

Pick over and wash cranberries, removing any stems. Put cranberries in saucepan. Add water, and cover. Cook until cranberries stop popping and are very soft. Press through sieve. Add sugar, and stir until sugar in dissolved. Return to medium heat, and cook 5 minutes. Pour into 5 small jelly glasses, and chill. Serve with poultry.

Easy Hollandaise Sauce

>   3 egg yolks
>   1/4 teaspoon salt
>   2 tablespoons lemon juice or vinegar
>   1/3 cup butter or margarine, melted
>   1/4 cup boiling water

Beat egg yolks slightly; add salt and lemon juice. Stir in melted butter or margarine, and add boiling water. Place over hot but not boiling water. Cook, stirring, until thickened, about 5 minutes. Serve immediately, or set aside and reheat when needed. Makes 3/4 cup.

Tomato Sauce

>   2 tablespoons chopped onion
>   2 tablespoons butter or margarine
>   2 tablespoons flour
>   1 teaspoon sugar
>   1 teaspoon salt
>   1/8 teaspoon pepper
>   6 peppercorns
>   1 bay leaf
>   1 (20-ounce) can tomatoes

Cook onion in butter or margarine until tender. Stir in flour and cook until bubbly. Add sugar and seasonings. Slowly add tomatoes, and cook, stirring, until thickened. Simmer 5 minutes. Remove peppercorns and bay leaf before serving. Makes 2 cups.

Curry Sauce

>   2 tablespoons butter
>   1 small onion, chopped
> 1-1 1/2 teaspoons curry powder
>   1 (10-ounce) can crushed pineapple, undrained
>   4 teaspoons cornstarch
>   1/2 cup cold water
>   2 teaspoons lemon juice
>   Salt to taste

Melt butter in a medium-size saucepan, and add onion. Sauté slowly until tender. Stir in curry powder and undrained pineapple. Bring to a boil. Add cornstarch mixed smoothly with cold water. Cook and stir until thickened and clear. Add lemon juice and salt to taste. Serve hot with chicken, lamb or ham. Makes about 1 3/4 cups.

Note: Meat or vegetable stock can replace some or all of the water.

Barbecue Sauce

1/2 cup chopped onion
1/2 cup tomato ketchup
1/3 cup water
1/4 cup vinegar
2 tablespoons sugar
1/2 teaspoon chili powder
1/2 teaspoon salt
Few drops hot pepper sauce

Combine all ingredients in saucepan. Bring to boil; lower heat, and simmer 5 minutes. Serve with spareribs, lamb, meat patties, pork chops or wieners, or use to baste any barbecued meats. Makes about 1 1/4 cups.

Lemon Butter Sauce

1 cup butter or margarine
1/4 cup fresh lemon juice
1/4 teaspoon salt
1/4 teaspoon pepper

Mix all ingredients together, and heat. Serve over fish or seafood.

VARIATIONS:

* *Parsley Sauce*: Add 1 tablespoon finely chopped parsley.

* *Caper Sauce*: Add 2 tablespoons drained pickled capers.

Lemon Cream Sauce for Fish

1 1/4 cups milk
2 tablespoons soft butter
2 tablespoons flour
1/4 cup mayonnaise
1 tablespoon lemon juice
1/2–1 teaspoon grated lemon rind
1/4 teaspoon salt
2 tablespoons chopped parsley

Scald milk in the top of a double boiler. Stir in a smooth mixture of butter and flour. Cook and stir until smoothly thickened. Add the next 4 ingredients, and reheat thoroughly. Stir in parsley. Makes about 1 2/3 cups.

Seafood Cocktail Sauce

3 tablespoons ketchup
1 tablespoon mayonnaise
2 teaspoons lemon juice
1 teaspoon horseradish
1/4 teaspoon prepared mustard
1/4 teaspoon barbecue sauce
2 drops hot pepper sauce

Mix ingredients until well blended. Makes 1/4 cup.

Egg Sauce

1 cup white sauce
1 hard-cooked egg, coarsely chopped or sliced

To sauce add egg, and mix well. Makes 1 cup.

Parsley Butter or Maître d'Hôtel Sauce

1/4 cup soft butter or margarine
1 tablespoon chopped parsley
2 teaspoons lemon juice
1/2 teaspoon salt

Cream butter, and blend in other ingredients. Shape into tiny pats or balls, and chill. Dot over steak before serving.

Stuffings

Stuffing for meat, fish or poultry fills the cavity with an aromatic mixture of seasonings and at the same time absorbs some of the juices that would otherwise evaporate (and of course the juices absorbed in turn add flavor to the dressing).

For best results, bread should be a few days old, so that, having lost some of its own moisture, it will be more uniform in bulk and will absorb more flavor and juice. The bread may be treated in different ways: Some cooks prefer to soak stale bread in beaten egg and some liquid, then stir bread and add onions, herbs and other ingredients; you can stir chopped onions and bread cubes or crumbs into foaming butter in frying pan and sauté them lightly before adding other ingredients, or you can dry bread slowly in oven, which adds an almost nutlike flavor.

Stuffing should be packed into cavity very lightly. Remember, bread will swell during cooking, so leave plenty of room. Remember too that dressing absorbs some of the juices, so it should be fairly dry to start with. Allow about 3/4 cup stuffing for each pound of bird, drawn weight.

It isn't necessary to take the word "stuffing" too literally. Most people like it for its own texture and flavor, and it can be served apart from the roast or fowl: cooked in a baking dish, in aluminum foil, in individual muffin cups. It can be rolled lightly into balls about the size of a golf ball and baked in a separate pan. Such methods are best, though, with dressings that contain egg for binding ingredients together.

It it important that stuffing for poultry be completely cooled before inserting in bird.

Basic Bread Stuffing

1/4 cup chopped onion
2 tablespoons fat
2 cups soft stale bread crumbs
2 tablespoons chopped parsley
1/2 teaspoon salt
1/8 teaspoon pepper

Brown onion lightly in fat. Add bread crumbs and seasonings, and heat slightly. Makes about 2 cups.

Note: For use with beef, as in rolled flank steak, add 1/2 teaspoon savory or marjoram. For veal, spice should be thyme or savory. For pork, use sage or savory, plus 2–3 tablespoons chopped tart apple. For lamb, add 4 tablespoons chopped fresh mint or 1/2 teaspoon thyme.

Old-fashioned Poultry Stuffing

    8 cups fine fairly dry crumbs
    3/4 cup finely chopped onion
    1/2 cup melted butter or margarine
      2 tablespoons finely chopped celery leaves
    2–3 teaspoons poultry seasoning or combination of
           savory and sage
      1 teaspoon salt
    1/4 teaspoon pepper

Combine ingredients thoroughly. Taste, and adjust seasonings. Moisten, if necessary. Stuff lightly into neck and body cavities of turkey, and close openings. Increase or reduce recipe to suit size of bird to be stuffed. (Makes about 8 cups or enough for a 12–15-pound bird.)

Caribbean Rice Stuffing

      3 cups cooked rice
      1 (10-ounce) can crushed pineapple, drained
    1/3 cup melted butter or margarine
      1 teaspoon cinnamon
           Salt and pepper to taste

Combine crushed, drained pineapple, cooked rice, butter or margarine and seasonings. Mix well. Stuff body and neck cavity. Makes enough for 5-pound chicken. Delicious with pork, too.

Southern Stuffing

      2 cups soft stale bread crumbs
    1/3 cup butter or margarine, melted
    1/2 cup pecans
      2 tablespoons finely chopped onion
      2 tablespoons diced celery
    1/2 teaspoon salt
    1/2 teaspoon rosemary
    1/4 teaspoon ginger
    1/4 teaspoon savory

Mix ingredients, tossing lightly but thoroughly. Adjust seasonings to taste. Stuff lightly into neck and body cavities of bird. Makes about 2 1/2 cups or enough for a 4-pound bird.

Note: If baking chicken breasts, arrange stuffing in mounds on baking pan, cover with breasts, skin side up, and sprinkle with lemon juice, salt, pepper and melted butter or margarine; bake in moderately hot oven 350°F. 50–60 minutes. Cover chicken breasts with aluminum foil for first 35 minutes of cooking period.

Cranberry Stuffing

    1/4 cup butter or margarine, melted
      4 cups bread crumbs (3–4-day-old bread)
      1 cup canned whole-cranberry sauce
    1/4 cup raisins
      2 tablespoons sugar
      2 teaspoons grated lemon rind
      1 teaspoon salt
    1/4 teaspoon cinnamon

Blend butter or margarine and bread crumbs. Add cranberries and other ingredients. Toss lightly until well mixed. Moisten if necessary. Stuff bird.

Note: 1 cup fresh cranberries, chopped, and 2 additional tablespoons sugar may be substituted for canned cranberry sauce.

Potato Stuffing

      6 cups fluffy mashed potatoes
    1 1/2 cups soft bread crumbs
    1/4 cup finely chopped onion
    1/4 cup butter or margarine, melted
      3 tablespoons cream or top milk
      2 egg yolks
    1–2 teaspoons poultry seasoning
      1 teaspoon salt
    1/4 teaspoon pepper

Combine potatoes, butter or margarine, onion, egg yolks, crumbs and cream. Add seasonings, a little at a time, to taste. Pile stuffing lightly into neck and body cavities of chicken. Do not pack. The amount is approximately enough to fill a 6–8-pound turkey, allowing some extra to be baked separately during final hour of roasting.

Rice-Raisin Stuffing

      1 cup regular rice
      1 (10-ounce) can boiling bouillon, diluted, or 2 1/2
           cups boiling stock
      2 tablespoons butter or margarine
      1 cup finely chopped celery
    1/4 cup chopped onion
      1 cup seedless raisins
      2 tablespoons chopped parsley
      1 teaspoon poultry seasoning
    1/4 teaspoon nutmeg or cinnamon (optional)
           Salt and pepper to taste

Add rice to boiling bouillon, and cook, covered, until rice is tender and stock absorbed, about 20 minutes. Melt butter or margarine, and sauté celery and onion. Add with remaining ingredients to cooked rice. Mix lightly, and use to stuff 2 small roasting chickens or a small turkey. Makes approximately 5 cups.

Lemon-Rice Stuffing

    1/3 cup butter or margarine, melted
      1 cup chopped celery
    1/3 cup chopped onion
    1 1/2 cups water
      3 tablespoons lemon juice
      2 teaspoons grated lemon rind
      1 teaspoon salt
    1/4 teaspoon thyme
    1/8 teaspoon pepper
    1 3/4 cups quick-cooking rice

To butter or margarine, add celery and onion, and cook until tender, about 5 minutes. Add remaining ingredients, except rice, and bring to boil. Add rice, and mix just to moisten. Cover, and remove from heat. Let stand 10–15 minutes. Makes 4 cups—enough for 3–4-pound dressed fish.

Whole Wheat–Pecan Stuffing

    2 cups fine soft whole wheat bread crumbs
    1/4 cup chopped pecans
    1/4 cup butter or margarine, melted
    2 tablespoons chopped onion
    2 tablespoons chopped celery
    1–3 teaspoons poultry seasoning
    1/2 teaspoon salt

Combine all ingredients. Adjust seasonings to taste. Yields enough stuffing for a 4-pound chicken (makes approximately 2 1/2 cups).

Almond Stuffing

    1/3 cup butter or margarine
    1/2 cup chopped almonds
    1/2 cup chopped celery
    1/4 cup chopped onion
    3 cups coarse soft bread crumbs
    3/4 teaspoon salt
    1/8 teaspoon pepper
    1 egg, slightly beaten

In large pan, melt butter or margarine. Fry almonds until golden. Stir in celery and onion, and cook until almost tender. Add bread crumbs, and sprinkle with salt and pepper. Stir in egg. Use to stuff 3–4-pound dressed fish for baking. Makes about 4 cups.

Rice-Gherkin Stuffing

    1/4 cup butter or margarine
    3/4 cup diced celery
    3/4 cup chopped onion
    1 1/2 cups cooked rice
    3/4 cup chopped gherkins
    1/4 teaspoon salt
    1/4 teaspoon pepper
    1/4 teaspoon dill seed
    1/4 teaspoon dried thyme

To melted butter or margarine, add celery and onion, and cook until tender. Add remaining ingredients. Use to stuff 4–5-pound dressed fish. Makes about 3 cups.

Fruits as Accompaniments

Fruits balance the dryness of meats, as you know from using applesauce with pork, cranberry sauce with turkey. But there are so many more combinations—oranges, sliced in their skins and served with roast or fried chicken; spiced cherries with ham; red currant jelly with lamb—all worth adding to your repertoire.

* *Cinnamon Apples*: Core and peel small firm sour apples. Cook, covered, till tender in syrup made with 1 cup sugar and 1 cup water, flavored with about 1/4 cup tiny red cinnamon candies. Serve hot or cold with pork or ham.

* *Cinnamon Apple Rings*: Cook gently in syrup as for cinnamon apples; slice apples thickly.

* *Spiced Peaches*: Make syrup by boiling liquid from 1 can peaches and adding 3 tablespoons brown sugar, 1 tablespoon wine vinegar (or vinegar from jar of sweet pickles of any kind), 4 or 5 cloves, 1/2 teaspoon cinnamon and 1/4 teaspoon ginger or few slices of preserved ginger. Simmer mixture until it is reduced and slightly thickened; then add peach halves, and heat gently. Serve over broiled ham steaks.

* *Spiced Pears*: Follow procedure for *Spiced Peaches*. Spiced crabapples, spiced plums and spiced pineapple rings are made in the same way.

Garnishes for the Main Dish

A garnish is primarily a means of making a dish look appealing, so it's wise to keep it simple. The herbs, fruits or vegetables that you use should be fresh, perfect in shape, eye-catching—and usually edible. The paper frills used to cover the unattractive exposed bones of Frenched lamb chops or crown roasts after cooking are an exception.

Do make the most of color, texture, flavor and attractive arrangement.

13 GARNISH SUGGESTIONS:

* Peel oranges, slice thinly, stick clove in center of each; serve with ham, duck, pork.

* Use pineapple slices, and attach maraschino cherry to center of each; serve with ham, pork, veal.

* Serve lemon boats or baskets with fish, veal cutlets.

* Peach or pear halves can be filled with mint jelly, red currant jelly, cranberry sauce; serve with roast lamb, grilled or baked ham.

* Very thin slices of white turnip can be rolled into cones to represent calla lilies, with julienne carrot sticks as stamens, and secured with toothpicks.

* Radish roses, celery fringed or stuffed with cheese, and olives are good garnishes.

* Cucumber slices are excellent with fish.

* Tomatoes, cut into 8 wedges each with a sprig of parsley in each wedge, accompany steak, veal cutlets, pork chops.

* Make flowers of hard-cooked eggs, halved; then cut into wedges. The whites make petals, the crumbled yolks flower centers.

* Use candied or maraschino cherries, cut in sections, to form petals, with blanched almonds as centers.

* Or use blanched almonds as petals, and maraschino cherry halves as centers.

* Spanish-onion slices, crossed with strips of pimento, are good with beef.

* Alternate onion and green-pepper rings with beef.

MAIN DISHES FOR 2

Everything has to be scaled down when you are cooking for 2, but that's no reason why meals can't be prepared efficiently and well.

You don't always have to divide recipes in half. You can save work by preparing enough stew and spaghetti sauce or similar foods for 2 meals; such dishes even improve in flavor with refrigeration and reheating.

Make the most of compact, canned and packaged staples—soups, dehydrated milk, canned or instant potato—and keep ample supplies of condiments and flavorings for finishing touches. Have a good-size Sunday roast—an excellent starting point for casserole, croquettes and hash later in the week.

6 MENUS FOR 2*

Seafood Newburg	*Barbecued Spareribs*	Chilled tomato-clam juice with lemon
Rice	Spinach	
Tossed green salad	Baked potatoes	*Curried Eggs and Mushrooms*
Toasted French bread	Grapefruit salad	
	Jelly roll	
Chilled fruit cup		Lima beans
Ginger wafers		Hot corn muffins
		Apple Crisp
Cream of corn soup	*Skillet Meat Loaf* with *Creole Lima Beans*	*Chicken with Almond-Cream Sauce*
Baked Trout Normande		Noodles
Sautéed cucumbers	Endive and baby-beet salad	Asparagus with lemon butter
Boiled new potatoes	Biscuits	Baked peaches with pureed raspberries
Fresh fruit and cheese	Lemon pie	

*Recipes are given for items printed in *italics*.

French Toast Ham Sandwich with Rarebit Sauce

    3/4 cup chopped canned ham
        Mayonnaise or salad dressing
      1 teaspoon pickle relish, drained (optional)
      4 slices French bread, buttered
      1 egg, slightly beaten
    1/4 cup mlik
        Dash barbecue sauce
      2 tablespoons butter or margarine, melted
        Rarebit Sauce

Mix meat with enough mayonnaise to moisten, and add relish. Makes 2 generously filled sandwiches of bread and meat mixture. Mix egg, milk and barbecue sauce. Dip sandwich quickly in mixture. Fry in melted butter on both sides until golden. Cut diagonally, and serve covered with *Rarebit Sauce*. Serves 2.

Rarebit Sauce

      1 tablespoon butter or margarine
      1 tablespoon flour
    1/2 cup milk
    1/4 pound process cheese, diced, or 1/2 cup grated cheese
    2–3 tablespoons beer or ale
        Salt and pepper to taste

Melt butter or margarine in small saucepan, and add flour and milk. Cook until smoothly thickened; then stir in cheese. Heat until cheese melts, and stir in beer. Season to taste. Makes approximately 1 cup sauce.

Seafood Newburg

      1 (10-ounce) can shrimp or oyster soup
      2 tablespoons flour
      2 tablespoons soft butter or margarine
    1/4 cup dry sherry
      1 egg yolk, slightly beaten
    1/2 cup light cream
      1 teaspoon onion juice
      1 (6-ounce) can crabmeat plus juice or 1 (5-ounce) can lobster, plus juice
        Salt and black pepper to taste
        Chopped parsley (optional)
    1/2 (10-ounce) package frozen asparagus tips
    1/2 teaspoon salt
      1 package frozen waffles, toasted and buttered
      1 tablespoon chopped parsley

Melt soup in top of double boiler over boiling water. Make smooth mixture of flour and butter, and stir into hot soup. Combine next 4 ingredients; add to soup, and cook until smoothly thickened. Fold in crabmeat and juice, with salt and pepper. Drop frozen asparagus tips into bottom part of double boiler, and add 1/2 teaspoon salt. Set top part of pan in place, and cook until asparagus is tender. Spoon seafood mixture over toasted waffles. Sprinkle with parsley, and serve with drained asparagus. Serves 2.

New England Boiled Dinner (Pressure-cooker Method)

      2 pounds packaged corned beef brisket or pickled pork
      3 cups water
      1 bay leaf
    1/2 clove garlic
      4 small potatoes, peeled
      4 medium-size onions, peeled
      4 medium-size carrots, scraped
        Mustard Cream Sauce

Remove the bag from the corned beef, and place on a rack in a *small* pressure cooker. Add water, bay leaf and garlic. Cover, and pressure-cook about 35 minutes. Cool, and remove cover. Add the whole vegetables, and replace the cover. Continue cooking 6–8 minutes. Lift beef to a hot platter, and surround with vegetables. Serve with *Mustard Cream Sauce*. Serves 2 with left-overs.

Note: If corned beef is not the mildly salted packaged variety, pre-soak the brisket before cooking by covering the meat with cold water. Place in the refrigerator overnight; then drain, and proceed.

Mustard Cream Sauce

Prepare about 1 cup of medium-thick cream or white sauce, and stir in 2–3 teaspoons each prepared mustard and chopped parsley.

Barbecued Spareribs

    1 1/2 pounds spareribs, cut in pieces
    1/2 cup commercial barbecue sauce
      1 tablespoon brown sugar or molasses
    1/4 cup water or tomato juice
    1/4 teaspoon onion salt
      2 teaspoons Worcestershire sauce
         Few dashes garlic powder

Spread spareribs in a lightly greased, 8-inch square, shallow pan. Bake at 400°F. 15 minutes. Combine remaining ingredients, and spoon and spread over spareribs. Reduce heat to 350°F., and bake about 1 hour, turning 2 or 3 times. Add a few tablespoons hot water during baking if the pan seems dry. Serves 2.

Baked Trout Normande

      1 (10-ounce) package frozen rainbow trout or 2 fresh
            brook trout
         Salt and black pepper to taste
    1/4 cup butter or margarine
    2–3 tablespoons white wine
      2 teaspoons chopped parsley
      2 teaspoons chopped onion
         Generous pinch chervil
         Generous pinch tarragon
      2 tablespoons heavy cream
      2 tablespoons buttered crumbs

Remove heads and tails from trout, and wipe inside and out. Sprinkle with salt and pepper. Place each trout in center of 8″ x 6″ oblong of heavy-duty foil, and cup foil edge. Heat butter, wine, parsley, onion, chervil and tarragon together, and spoon over each trout. Cover with ob-longs of foil, crimping upper and lower edges together to seal. Bake on cookie sheet at 425°F. 12–15 minutes. If fish is frozen, allow 5–10 minutes longer. Slit top of each package, and pull edges back from fish. Spread fish with cream, and sprinkle with crumbs. Broil 1–2 minutes. Serve in foil.

Chicken with Almond-Cream Sauce

      3 tablespoons fat
      2 servings chicken pieces
    1/2 lemon
      1 tablespoon flour
    1/2 teaspoon salt
         Dash black pepper
    1/4 cup slivered almonds
      2 tablespoons flour
    3/4 cup chicken broth
    1/2 cup light cream or 1/4 cup milk and 1/4 cup
            evaporated milk
      1 teaspoon sherry
      1 tablespoon chopped parsley
         Salt and pepper to taste

Melt fat in skillet. Rub chicken all over with lemon; sprinkle with 1 tablespoon flour, 1/2 teaspoon salt and dash pepper. Brown chicken pieces on both sides about 10 minutes. Remove chicken, and brown almonds lightly in same pan. Stir in 2 tablespoons flour, then broth and cream. Cook until thick and smooth. Add chicken, and turn in sauce. Cover pan, and lower heat. Simmer 20 minutes. Lift chicken to heated platter, and add chopped parsley and sherry to sauce. Whisk until smooth; then season to taste. Pour over chicken. Serve with potato puffs and glazed carrots. Serves 2.

Skillet Meat Loaf with Creole Lima Beans

    1/2 cup soft bread crumbs
    1/2 can or 2/3 cup onion soup
    1/2 can luncheon meat, finely chopped
    1/2 pound hamburger or ground fresh pork
    1/4 cup dry bread crumbs
      1 egg
    1/2 teaspoon salt
         Pinch sage
         Pinch thyme
      2 tablespoons salad oil
      3 slices bacon
      1 (15-ounce) can lima beans in tomato sauce
    1/4 cup diced green pepper

Soak crumbs in onion soup a few minutes; then mix in next 7 ingredients. Shape meat into small loaf, and roll in crumbs. Heat salad oil in covered skillet over low heat. Place strips of bacon close together in pan. Set meat loaf on bacon, which will add flavor and prevent bottom of loaf from cooking too quickly. Cover, and cook slowly, about 10 minutes. Turn meat loaf, and add lima beans and green pepper. Cover, and continue cooking 10–15 minutes.

Chipped Beef Scramble

  3 tablespoons butter or margarine
  3 or 4 fresh mushrooms, sliced, or 1 peeled diced tomato
 1–2 green onions, sliced
  4 eggs, slightly beaten
1/3–1/2 cup shredded chipped beef
 1/4 cup sweet or sour cream
  2 slices buttered toast
  1 teaspoon grated Parmesan cheese

Heat butter or margarine in chafing dish or frying pan, and add mushrooms and onion. Fry slowly, stirring, until onion is tender. Mix next 3 ingredients, and pour into pan. Scramble softly, using metal spoon. Serve on toast. Sprinkle with Parmesan cheese.

Pick Your Utensils

Make do with 1 saucepan for your dinner vegetables. There's no danger of mingled flavors if you wrap one seasoned vegetable in airtight foil and drop it into boiling water containing potatoes. Use both sections of your double boiler at once: hard-cooked eggs below, and sauce above.

Try making up standard-lot sauces, salad dressings and so forth once a week. Store each, covered in refrigerator, ready for use. Use your freezing compartment for shaped meat patties that are ideal for a quick dinner, for sliced turkey left over from company occasions, the second 1/2 of layer cake recipe and so forth. Make use of leftovers, and remember that even 1/2 cup of cooked vegetables will provide the character ingredient for 2 servings of cream soup the next night.

When you divide a cake recipe or mix that normally required 1 egg, simply use the whole egg in 1/2 the amount; you will not endanger the result. Here is a meal that you can cook all at once in 8 large muffin cups. Oil 6 cups, and leave 2 unoiled.

Meal in a Muffin Tin

 1/2 pound ground lamb
  2 tablespoons dry bread crumbs
  1 tablespoon ketchup
  1 teaspoon chopped fresh mint or 1/2 teaspoon dried mint
 1/2 teaspoon salt
   Pinch crumbled rosemary
  1 large potato, cut in half
  4 tablespoons canned fruit cocktail or 2 canned peach halves or 4 canned apricot halves
  2 teaspoons brown sugar
  2 teaspoons lemon juice
 1/3 cup biscuit mix
  2 teaspoons sugar
  1 teaspoon soft butter or margarine
  3 tablespoons milk or cream
   Dash vanilla or almond extract
  1 cup frozen peas
  2 teaspoons butter or margarine
  2 teaspoons water
 1/8 teaspoon salt

* *Minted Lamb Cups*: Combine lamb with first 5 ingredients, and spoon into 2 oiled muffin cups.

* *Baked Potato*: Prick potato halves, and place, cut side down, in 2 oiled cups.

* *Fruited Upside-down Cake*: Place spoonful of fruit cocktail, peach half or 2 apricot halves in 2 oiled muffin cups. Sprinkle brown sugar and lemon juice over. Spoon biscuit mix into a 1-cup measuring cup, and add sugar, 1 teaspoon butter, 3 tablespoons milk and vanilla. Stir quickly until quite smooth, and spoon over fruit. Bake all together at 350°F. 35 minutes.

* *Buttered Peas*: Cup 2 squares of foil, and sprinkle 1/2 cup peas in each. Add butter, water and salt. Wrap like a grab bag by twisting tops, and place in unoiled cups for last 20 minutes of baking time.

MENUS FEATURING DISHES FROM CHAPTER 2

Good menu planning involves using several kinds of meat (beef, pork, lamb, veal), as well as the variety meats, fish, cheese, eggs and legumes. You'll thus be able to vary your main dishes with different kinds of protein.

BEEF

Braised Stuffed Flank Steak
Potatoes
Baked whole carrots
Coleslaw
Rice-raisin pudding

Deluxe Hamburgers
Spanish onions and tomato slices
Hot buttered rolls
Fresh fruit bowl
Cheese tray

Stuffed Cabbage Rolls
Kernel corn with green pepper
Toasted French bread
Zabaglione

Broiled Porterhouse Steak
Horseradish Sauce
Lyonnaise potatoes
Peas
Fresh fruit
Custard Sauce

Scotch Beef Loaf
Browned potatoes
String beans
Pickled beets
Butterscotch meringue pie

VEAL

Veal Viennese
Boiled noodles
Red cabbage
Lemon Snow with *Custard Sauce*

Roast Veal with Pennsylvania Stuffing
Baked potatoes
Tossed green salad
Raspberry whip
Ladyfingers

Breaded Veal Chops
Whipped potatoes
Green limas
Celery stuffed with cheese
Half grapefruit

Jellied Veal
Potato Salad
Tossed greens
Chilled stewed rhubarb
Cheese-cracker tray

Curried Veal
Rice
Garnishes
Cooked vegetable salad
Mayonnaise
Doughnuts
Coffee

LAMB

Roast Leg of Lamb
Mint jelly
Mashed Potatoes
Vegetables Macedoine
Relish platter
Fresh pumpkin pie

Casserole Dinner of Lamb Chops
Green peas
Celery hearts
Individual tea-biscuit shortcakes with strawberries

Curried Lamb with Rice
Pineapple rings
Tossed salad with orange sections
Maple-nut sundae

Grilled Lamb Chop à l'Anglaise
Broiled tomato halves and mushrooms
Boiled potatoes
Mint sprinkle
Trifle with orange garnish

Barbecued Lamb
Rice
Tossed green salad
French Dressing
Cottage cheese
Cherry upside-down cake

PORK

Layered Sausage Loaf
Baked sweet potatoes
Zucchini
Lemon jelly
Icebox cookies

Barbecued Spareribs
Scalloped Potatoes
Broccoli
Mélange of fruits in meringue pie shell

Skewered Pork Cubes
Baked Eggplant with Rice Stuffing
Sliced tomatoes
Herb dressing
Devil's food cake
Marshmallow sauce

Golden Ham Roast
Scalloped sweet potatoes
Creamed onions
Celery sticks
Cucumber fingers
Apple Crisp
Caramel Sauce

Broiled Ham Steak
Sautéed Apple Rings
Succotash
Mixed salad in lettuce cups
Coconut cream pie

POULTRY

Roast Turkey
Cranberry Sauce
Whipped potatoes
Broccoli
Celery
Olives
Steamed fruit pudding

Cream of green pea soup
Turkey, celery and nut salad
Jelly roll and cranberry filling

Oven-fried Chicken
Shoestring potatoes
Baked stuffed tomatoes
Chocolate blanc mange

Chicken Fricassee
Fluffy rice
Grapefruit, orange and prune salad
Cheese wedges

Roast Duckling
Boiled wild rice
Harvard beets
Jellied raw vegetable salad
Blueberry tarts

FISH AND SEAFOOD

Vegetable juice cocktail
Deep-fried Fillets in Pancake Mix
Mashed potatoes
Scalloped tomatoes
Vanilla pudding

Spicy Oyster Stew
Heated crackers
Cabbage, onion and apple salad
Gingerbread with hot lemon sauce

Mushroom Soufflé
Asparagus with cream sauce
Carrot sticks
Celery curls
Lemon chiffon pie

Corn chowder
Lobster-Grapefruit Mold on salad greens
Peach shortcake
Whipped cream

Tomato juice cocktail
Finnan Haddie Poached in Milk
Baked potatoes
Spinach
Fresh apple pie
Cheese

VARIETY MEATS

Liver-Onion Hot Pot
Baby beets
Beet greens
Orange sherbet
Chocolate-chip cookies

Braised Chicken Giblets
Fluffy Rice
Mixed garden vegetables
Ice cream with caramel sauce
Cupcakes

Herbed Tongue
Baked potatoes
Baked squash
Jellied tomato salad
Angel food cake

Braised Chicken Livers
Boiled noodles
Minted green peas
Fresh fruit cup
Cheese tray

Oven-braised Stuffed Heart
Whipped potatoes
Brussels sprouts
Poached pears

ALTERNATES

Mexican Kidney Beans
Apple, celery and nut salad
Chilled baked custard

Hot consommé
Crackers
Cheese Mousse
Lettuce wedges
French Dressing
Applesauce
Cookies

Luncheon Rarebit
Toasted French bread
Celery curls
Gherkins
Jellied fruits
Nuts

Tomato juice cocktail
Mushroom Soufflé in Green-pepper Cups
Potato chips
Parsleyed carrots
Raisin pie

Cream of potato soup
Baked Meringue Eggs
Buttered broccoli
Stuffed Baked Apples

❧ CHAPTER THREE ❧

The Wonder World of Fruits and Vegetables

❧

It is important to note all the forms in which fruits and vegetables are available, to consider food value in relation to price and to learn the methods for storing, cooking and serving. Impulse buying can be costly.

Prepare your shopping lists from definite menus drawn up for the next few days. Keep in mind substitutions that can be made when price makes substitution profitable. For example, canned tomato juice may replace orange juice for breakfast—but double the amount; lettuce greens with dressing may replace fresh asparagus for dinner.

If adequate home storage is available, take advantage of specials on canned and frozen items by purchasing in larger quantities.

When comparing costs of fresh fruits and vegetables with those of frozen or canned fruits and vegetables, consider amount of waste from fresh items. Remember also that out-of-season and long-stored raw products may not be as high in food values as those that were processed and packed where they were grown.

Buy fresh fruits and green vegetables in amounts to be used within a few days. Patronize a dealer who has quick turnover and proper facilities for keeping his produce in good condition in order to ensure more food value. Oranges, for instance, that have been kept on display for weeks in a sunny store window offer less than constantly replenished supplies.

Discard any spoiled or inedible portions immediately after purchasing; store according to kind—in your refrigerator, or, with roots and apples, in a cool, dark place.

Know the various grades on the market—government grades, Federal inspection stamps, manufacturers' or retailers' brands—check weights, and in buying fresh produce, purchase by weight whenever possible; usually the heavier a fruit or vegetable for its size, the more value you receive.

Always wash fresh fruits and vegetables thoroughly before using, even if you intend to peel them.

Vegetables provide almost endless food value.

The *carbohydrate* (sugar and starch) content in vegetables varies, depending on water content and variety of vegetable. The actively growing parts (leaves, stems, flowers, fruits) contain high amounts of water and are therefore lower in carbohydrates.

Parts of the plant used for storage (roots, tubers, pods and seeds) contain less water and more carbohydrates. Dried vegetables such as dried beans and peas do not have all their water restored, even in soaking and cooking, so they remain higher in carbohydrates than do fresh vegetables.

Most vegetables have more starch and less sugar than fruits have. As vegetables ripen, sugar decreases, and starch increases, which accounts for the greater sweetness of young green peas and new potatoes.

Because of their carbohydrate contents, tubers and some roots are valuable sources of energy.

The amount of *protein* in vegetables also varies, and in most cases it is not of top nutritional quality. The only vegetables considered really valuable sources of protein are the legumes (dried beans, peas and lentils), especially soybeans. The protein in potatoes is good in quality, even though the amount is low.

Vegetables are relatively free of *fat* and are therefore valuable in low-fat diets. They also can provide a large part of the day's *mineral* requirements.

The green leafy vegetables are valuable, among other things, for their *calcium* content, particularly broccoli, chard, collards, kale, mustard greens and turnip tops. Another good source of calcium is dried beans. Spinach, although it tests high in calcium, contains oxalic acid, which changes calcium in the body so that it cannot be assimilated.

Green leafy vegetables have high *iron* content, especially asparagus, beet greens, broccoli and chard. In general, the greener the leaf, the higher the iron content. Also valuable for iron are dried beans, mushrooms and potatoes.

Vegetables grown near the coast absorb *iodine* from the soil, though more dependable sources of iodine are seafoods and iodized salt. And soils rich in *fluorine* and *manganese* transfer these minerals to their vegetable crops.

A knowledge of *vitamin* values helps to explain the importance of daily consumption of green and yellow vegetables, tomatoes and potatoes.

Yellow and green vegetables, in general, are high in *vitamin A*. Among yellow vegetables, the deeper the color, the higher in vitamin A; white potatoes are very low, and sweet potatoes very high. Carrots, the yellow varieties of squash and tomatoes are high. And green varieties of cabbage, lettuce and the like are much higher than are the white varieties.

Although whole grains are the most dependable sources of *vitamin B1* (thiamine) in the diet, vegetables provide a useful supplementary supply, especially fresh asparagus, corn, lima beans, dried navy beans, raw mushrooms, peas (fresh or dried) and potatoes.

Leafy greens score high among vegetable sources of *vitamin B2* (riboflavin). Fresh asparagus, broccoli, Brussels sprouts, dandelion greens and spinach are especially good. Legumes (beans, peas and lentils), mushrooms and winter squash also contribute.

Tomatoes are the best vegetable source of *vitamin C*. Also valuable are greens, broccoli, Brussels sprouts, cabbage (especially raw), cauliflower, chard, green peppers, spinach, turnips and turnip greens. Potatoes are a good regular source, though the amounts are not high. Cooking and exposure to air decrease the quantity of vitamin C, and the fresher the vegetable, the higher its vitamin C content.

Meats, fish and other high-protein foods are the most dependable source of *niacin,* but dried beans, peas and other legumes provide supplementary amounts.

One of the most important contributions of vegetables is *bulk* or *roughage* (cellulose), which has a regulating effect on the digestive system. Cellulose, however, can upset digestive systems that are unable to stand irritation—those of ulcer patients, and others on bland diets.

Certain vegetables must be cooked before serving to render them digestible; others are simply more appealing if cooked before serving hot or cold. Make full use of the many cooking methods to ensure variety.

To retain maximum nutrients, any cooking method that permits leaving the vegetable whole in its skin is best. If paring is to be done, remove a minimum of skin. A vegetable's minerals and vitamins can be drawn out by lengthy immersion in water or by cooking in too much water. So avoid peeling ahead of time and holding raw vegetables in cold water, and cook them in as little water as possible. Nutrients will also be lost if vegetables are cut finely or chopped before cooking. Whole vegetables or large pieces are best for boiling; carrots should be cut lengthwise to preserve more nutrients.

Besides retaining food values, correct cooking procedures will ensure maximum appeal. Methods that develop and retain flavor, attractive color and good texture are desirable, even if a little food value is sacrificed. For example, a family that refuses to eat turnips with the strong flavor brought about by cooking them in a waterless cooker may readily accept the same vegetable boiled in water to cover, with the resulting milder taste.

COOKING FRESH VEGETABLES

First, 2 groups are frequently referred to—mild-flavored, which includes asparagus, beans (all types, fresh or dried), beets and beet greens, carrots, celery, chard, corn, cucumber, young dandelion greens, eggplant, lettuce, mushrooms, okra, peas, potatoes, squash and tomatoes, and strong-flavored, which includes broccoli, Brussels sprouts, cabbage, cauliflower, kale, onions, rutabagas, spinach and turnips.

To Bake

Baking is the best method for retaining food values, especially if vegetable is baked whole in its skin.

Suitable for uncovered baking are potatoes (sweet or white), squash (all varieties), onions, peppers (generally stuffed) and tomatoes. Place on rack or in open pan. Squash should be halved or cut in pieces, and the seeds removed.

Many vegetables can be baked covered, although such baking is not generally recommended for strong-flavored vegetables and greens. Vegetables may be left whole in their skins (beets, for example) or peeled and cut in pieces. Use covered casserole, add a little water or brush with oil, season and bake covered until tender.

Bake all vegetables at 350°–400°F. or according to recipe directions.

To Boil

Boiling is the most common and convenient method and one suited to all vegetables. Correct procedure keeps loss of food values to a minimum.

Bring water to rapid boil before adding raw vegetables; return quickly to boiling point, reduce heat and allow vegetables to simmer gently until just tender. Drain immediately, and serve. Salt should be added at beginning of cooking period or halfway through. More important is the *amount of water* used and the care taken to avoid overcooking. Mild-flavored vegetables should be boiled, covered, in very little water, just enough to prevent burning. Strong-flavored vegetables will also retain their maximum food value when cooked in minimum amounts of water, but their flavors may be unpleasantly strong.

To retain good color in green vegetables, cook uncovered. *Do not add baking soda* for it destroys vitamin values. To leave mild green vegetables uncovered during cooking is best for preservation of color, but there will be a slight decrease in vitamin C. A compromise for both green and strong-flavored vegetables is to let them remain uncovered until they boil, and then to cover them and reduce heat.

To Braise

Braising is best for celery, cucumbers, summer squash and the like. Melt 2 tablespoons oil or fat in frying pan; add 2 cups prepared raw vegetables plus 2 tablespoons water or consommé. Cover, and cook slowly until just tender, seasoning at midway point. Flavor and food values are retained in braising, but color may fade.

To Broil

Broiling is handy for eggplant slices, mushrooms, summer squash, halved tomatoes, parboiled carrots or potatoes when broiler is being used for other foods. Brush with oil, melted fat or French dressing. Broil 3–5 inches from heat, and turn once during cooking, or put canned or cooked vegetables in tray under rack while broiling meat; they will heat through nicely and will absorb meat juices.

To Fry

Diced or thinly sliced young vegetables such as vegetable marrow, summer squash and green tomatoes may be fried. Melt fat in frying pan, and, when hot, add vegetable. Cover tightly, and cook at moderate heat, turning as necessary and seasoning to taste.

To Deep-fry

Deep-frying is not a method that retains full food values, but potatoes, vegetable croquettes and vegetables like onion rings in batter taste good deep-fried.

Use at least 1 1/2 inches of fat in pan. Prepare vegetables as required; for instance, potatoes in fingers or julienned should be soaked 10 minutes in ice water, then dried on towel. Fry small amounts at a time. Drain on absorbent paper, and serve very hot. A deep-fat thermometer ensures correct temperature and is especially useful

in cooking potatoes by the blanch-and-brown method, which involves prefrying potatoes at 365°F. until they are soft but not brown. They are then removed from fat, set aside and drained. Just before serving time, quickly brown at 390°F. In place of thermometer, the crumb test may be used: Drop 1-inch cube of day-old bread into fat; it should brown in 1 minute at first temperature. A similar bread cube should brown in 20 seconds at second temperature. When deep-frying potatoes in one operation, have fat at 385°F., hot enough to brown a cube of bread in 40 seconds.

Onion rings and other batter-fried foods are best cooked at 365°F.

To Parboil

Parboiling is a first step toward further cooking; boil only until half-tender.

To Pressure-cook

Food values are well preserved by pressure cooking, as only a small amount of water is used and the cooking is done very quickly. Pressure-cooking results in a steamed flavor, and strong vegetables retain their full characteristic taste. It is most important to follow the manufacturer's directions exactly and to avoid overcooking. Pressure-cooked green vegetables have a tendency to change color. Leafy greens develop a mushy consistency, and an ordinary saucepan is generally preferable for them.

To Steam

Steaming is appropriate for almost all vegetables; it is slow, but results in high food values. Use a 2-section steamer, placing vegetables in perforated upper pan, or place vegetables on rack over boiling water in saucepan. Cover tightly, and make sure water does not boil away.

To Roast

Roasting is a variation of baking. Suitable vegetables like carrots, parsnips and potatoes—either raw or parboiled—are placed around meat and roasted in fat and juice until tender. They should be turned several times and seasoned to taste.

Waterless Cooking

This method requires no special equipment. After thorough washing, thin leafy greens such as spinach can be cooked in water that adheres to leaves. Cover pot, and gently boil greens, turning once; drain well, and serve.

To Barbecue

For barbecuing, put small whole raw vegetables, pieces or combinations of both (Frenched green beans, tomato wedges and onion slices, for example) on a square of heavy aluminum foil, dot with butter or margarine, add salt and pepper, wrap foil into airtight parcel and cook over gray-hot coals about 40 minutes. Several parcels of individual servings are handy; plates will not be needed.

To Scallop

To scallop cooked or partially thawed frozen vegetables, place in greased casserole, and pour over them 1 cup medium white sauce. Sprinkle bread crumbs, croutons or coarsely crushed potato chips on top, dot with butter or margarine and bake at 350°F. about 20 minutes.

POTATOES

Actually, although it contains energy-giving material in the form of starch, an average potato supplies only 100 calories, which is about equal to 1 serving of cooked cereal, a fair-size apple or 1/2 pint skim milk. It's the butter or gravy that should be watched by calorie counters.

Potatoes keep best in a cool, dark place with rather high humidity, the same conditions that existed in the old-time root cellars. After storage at 40°F., quality is improved by bringing potatoes into warm room for a few days before using.

Note that warm *dry* air causes potatoes to shrivel in storage whereas warm *moist* air may cause sprouting. Exposure to light causes greenish patches, which give a bitter flavor. Apartment dwellers should buy supplies sufficient only for a week or so, and they may find it best to store potatoes in the refrigerator.

Baked Potatoes

6 medium or large potatoes
2 tablespoons butter or margarine or drippings or salad oil

Scrub potatoes thoroughly, using cool water and vegetable brush. Rinse well. If soft skin is preferred, rub potatoes all over with butter, margarine, bacon drippings or salad oil. Otherwise skin will bake crisp, which many people prefer. Place in a shallow pan in preheated oven. For light, mealy potatoes, use oven temperature of 425°–450°F., but for convenience when baking complete oven dinner, temperatures as low as 350°–375°F. may be used. Allow about 1 hour for medium potatoes. At very high heat they will be ready sooner, of course. When potatoes are baked, prick tops or cut a cross on each. Squeeze potatoes to allow steam to escape, making potatoes fluffier. Serve with butter or margarine and sprinkle of paprika, with commercial sour cream mixed with chopped chives or with butter mixed with crumbled blue cheese.

Note: Select sound potatoes of even sizes. Medium or large potatoes bake better than do small ones. New potatoes do not bake well. To retain maximum vitamin C, it is best that potatoes *not* be pricked with a fork before baking. Pricking before baking does, however, prevent potatoes from bursting in oven, and it may result in drier baked potatoes. If desired, potatoes may be wrapped in aluminum foil for baking; potatoes are then actually oven-steamed, which keeps skins soft.

Broiled Potatoes

>   6 potatoes
>   Boiling water
>   Salt to taste

Scrub potatoes thoroughly, and remove any blemishes. Do not peel. Drop potatoes into smallest amount of rapidly boiling water that can do the job, possibly only 1-inch depth. Add salt, return rapidly to boil, cover and reduce heat to a gentle simmer. Cook until potatoes are just tender, about 25 minutes. Drain at once; then shake pan, uncovered over low heat to evaporate moisture. Serve in skins or peel quickly before serving. Serves 6.

Note: Select potatoes of even size.

Whipped Potatoes

>   6 medium potatoes
>   2 tablespoons butter or margarine
>   Salt and pepper to taste
>   1/4–1/3 cup hot milk
>   1 tablespoon butter or margarine
>   Paprika

Boil potatoes, peel quickly, and return to saucepan. Place over low heat. Mash quickly until free of lumps. Add 2 tablespoons butter and seasonings. Gradually stir and beat in milk. Whip until fluffy. Serve in heated dish. Dot with 1 tablespoon butter or margarine and sprinkle with paprika. Serves 6.

Note: If potatoes are very dry or if they are to stand briefly before using, add extra milk. New potatoes are not satisfactory for whipping. More nourishment is retained when potatoes are boiled in their skins, but peeling before cooking makes whipped or mashed potatoes whiter. Serves 6.

Oven-roasted Potatoes

The familiar method is to place peeled potatoes in drippings about 1 1/2–2 hours before meat is to finish cooking. But potatoes need *high* temperatures for best results, whereas beef and other roasts develop juicy tenderness in a fairly *slow* oven. The compromise is to give potatoes a fast parboiling before placing in oven. About 45 minutes before meat is to finish cooking, boil required number of peeled medium potatoes 10–

15 minutes. Drain. Remove rack from under the meat if a rack was used. Arrange in fat and juices around meat. Roll potatoes in the drippings for better color. Continue cooking at correct temperature for roast. Turn potatoes once or twice to brown all sides. Sprinkle lightly with salt just before serving.

Fried Raw Potatoes

>   4–5 medium potatoes
>   2 onions
>   4 tablespoons fat (butter, margarine or salad oil or 2 tablespoons fat plus 2 tablespoons bacon drippings)
>   1 teaspoon salt
>   1/8 teaspoon pepper

Peel potatoes and onions; slice fairly thin. Melt fat in large frying pan over medium heat. Put in about 1/2 the potatoes, next the onions, then remaining potatoes; sprinkle with seasonings. Cover pan, and cook about 10 minutes, at which time bottom layer will be lightly browned and potatoes almost tender. Turn potatoes, using wide spatula. Let cook uncovered another 15–20 minutes, turning once or twice for even browning. Serves 4.

VARIATIONS:

Both baked and boiled potatoes may be used in following recipes. Estimate 1 medium cooked potato per serving. For fat, use butter or margarine, bacon or beef drippings or salad oil. Allow about 2 tablespoons fat for 3 cups prepared potato.

* *Hash-browned Potatoes*: Melt fat, add finely-chopped potatoes and sprinkle lightly with salt and pepper; add a little chopped onion (optional). Using spatula, press down potatoes until they are a compact mass. If very dry, add a little top milk. Let cook, uncovered, over low heat about 20 minutes or until brown crust is formed on bottom. Do not stir during cooking. Fold as with omelet; lift out to hot platter.

* *Potatoes O'Brien*: To diced or chopped potatoes add chopped onion, green pepper and pimento, allowing about 1 tablespoon each for 3 cups potatoes. Cook in melted fat over low-to-medium heat, stirring occasionally, until mixture is piping hot and potatoes delicately browned. Season to taste.

* *Potato Cakes*: Use leftover mashed potatoes. For extra richness, add a lightly beaten egg yolk to potatoes. Dip hands in flour, and shape mixture into little flat cakes about 2 inches across. Brown on both sides in hot fat in frying pan. Serve very hot.

Broiler Fried Potatoes

    4 medium potatoes
      Cold water, lightly salted
    1/4 cup salad oil
      Salt to taste

Scrub potatoes; peel, and slice about 3/4 inch thick and then into lengthwise strips. Soak in cold water, about 30 minutes. While broiler is preheating, drain potatoes, and dry between paper towels. Spread potatoes in a shallow pan; add salad oil, and stir to coat all potatoes. Broil 3 inches below heat 15—20 minutes, stirring frequently. When potatoes are golden brown on all sides, sprinkle with salt, and serve. Serves 4.

New Potatoes with Peas

    8 small new potatoes
    1 cup freshly cooked peas, drained
    1/2 cup hot thin cream, seasoned with salt and pepper
      Chopped parsley or chives

Scrub potatoes, leave unpeeled and boil. When just tender, drain; skins may be quickly peeled off or left on. Place in heated vegetable dish, and add peas. Pour seasoned cream over all. Sprinkle with chopped parsley or chives. Serves 4.

Herbed New Potatoes

    8 small new potatoes
    1/4 cup soft butter or margarine
    3 tablespoons chopped parsley
    3 tablespoons chopped chives
    1 teaspoon chopped fresh dill
      Pinch thyme
      Pinch salt

Boil potatoes without peeling. Drain; if desired, remove skins. Combine butter or margarine, parsley, chives, dill, thyme and salt; add to potatoes. Set pan over very low heat 5—10 minutes; stir potatoes carefully to coat with melted herb butter. Serves 4.

Spanish Scallop

    4 medium potatoes, sliced
    1 teaspoon salt
    2 tablespoons flour
    1/2 green pepper, diced
    1 onion, sliced
    1 1/2 cups tomato juice
    3 tablespoons butter or margarine

Place layer of potatoes in bottom of greased 1-quart casserole. Sprinkle with a little of the salt and flour. Cover with layer of green pepper and onion slices. Repeat layers until all vegetables, seasonings and flour are used, ending with remaining potatoes. Pour tomato juice over, and dot with butter or margarine. Bake at 375°F. until potatoes are quite tender and top is nicely browned. Serves 4.

Sour Cream Mashed Potatoes

    1 cup water
    1/4 teaspoon salt
    2 tablespoons butter or margarine
    1 cup instant mashed potato flakes
    1/4–1/3 cup commercial sour cream
      Chopped chives or bacon bits or chopped parsley
        or chopped green onion

Bring water, salt and butter or margarine to boil. Stir in mashed potato flakes as directed on package. Beat in sour cream to moisten, and taste for seasoning. Top with chives. Serves 2—3.

Potato Pancakes

    6 medium potatoes
    1 small onion
    2–3 tablespoons flour
    1 egg
    1/2 teaspoon salt
      Cooking oil

Peel potatoes, and grate on medium grater. Drain well. Peel onion, and chop very fine. Add onion to potatoes, and quickly add flour, egg and salt, mixing well. Pour into heavy frying pan enough cooking oil or fat to cover the bottom to depth of about 1/4 inch, and heat to frying temperature. Spoon potato mixture into hot pan, spreading each cake with tip of spoon so that it will be as thin as possible, not heaped up. Cook cakes until golden brown on one side; then turn with spatula, and brown on other side. Remove cakes from pan, and drain on absorbent kitchen paper to eliminate greasiness. Serve as soon as possible, or pancakes will become soggy. Serve with applesauce or sour cream. Serves 6.

Consommé Scalloped Potatoes

    6 medium potatoes
    1 (10-ounce) can consommé
    3/4 cup water
    2 tablespoons flour
      Salt and pepper

Peel potatoes, slice, and parboil 5 minutes in the consommé and water. (This lets the consommé flavor get into the potatoes more than if they are baked without parboiling.) Drain, and save the liquid. Place potatoes in a buttered casserole in layers, sprinkling flour, salt and freshly ground black pepper on each layer. Pour the consommé back over the potatoes, and dot with butter. Bake at 375°F. 45 minutes. Serves 6.

Top-of-the-stove Potatoes au Gratin

    1/2 cup boiling water
    1 teaspoon salt
    4 cups diced raw potatoes
    1/2 cup chopped onions
    1/2 cup milk
    1/2 cup grated Cheddar cheese
      Pepper to taste
      Few sprigs parsley

To boiling water and salt in saucepan add potatoes and onion; cover, and boil 10 minutes.

Remove lid, and, stirring several times, let mixture simmer until water is almost evaporated. Add milk, cheese, pepper and extra salt, if needed. Heat thoroughly. Turn into warm dish, and garnish with parsley. Serves 4—5.

Potato Puffs

    2 cups cold mashed potatoes
    2 tablespoons butter or margarine
1/2 cup grated cheese
1/2 teaspoon salt
      Few grains cayenne
    2 tablespoons cream
    1 egg, beaten
      Hot fat

Mix first 7 ingredients, and beat well until light. Shape into balls, and chill well. Fry in deep hot fat until golden brown. Serve at once. Serves 4—6.

Packaged Potatoes

Potatoes ready to cook, to heat or to use are available in various forms and can be a boon when you are busy. The forms include instant mashed potatoes, instant sliced potatoes for scalloped mixtures, frozen small whole potatoes for cooking, frozen French fries and canned cooked **white and** sweet potatoes and yams. The nutritional level may vary with the type of preparation (as in home cooking of raw potatoes), but fast factory processing and laboratory controls have tended to safeguard most of the potato's food values in these packaged forms. Cost per serving compared with home-prepared potatoes is high.

Quick Potato Soup

    1 beef-bouillon cube
1 1/4 cups boiling water
2 1/2 cups milk
   3/4 teaspoon salt
      Few grains pepper
    1 tablespoon chopped onion
1/2 cup mashed potato flakes
1/2 cup grated Cheddar cheese
    2 tablespoons chopped parsley
    1 tablespoon butter or margarine

Crumble bouillon cube into boiling water. Add milk, salt, pepper and onion. Heat to boiling. Remove from heat. Mix in instant potato, cheese, parsley and butter or margarine. Cook, stirring, over low heat until cheese is melted. Seves 6.

Curried Chicken Pie with Potato Topping

    2 tablespoons butter or margarine
    1 tablespoon flour
    1 teaspoon curry powder
    1 (10-ounce) can chicken gravy
1/2 cup sliced canned mushrooms, drained
1/2 cup cooked peas
1 1/2 cups diced cooked chicken
1/4 teaspoon salt
1/8 teaspoon black pepper
    2 tablespoons sherry
      Enough potato flakes to make 4 servings

Heat oven to 350°F. Melt butter or margarine, and stir in flour and curry powder. Gradually add chicken gravy. Cook, stirring constantly, until mixture thickens. Stir in mushrooms, peas, chicken, seasonings and sherry. Pour into casserole. Prepare instant mashed potato flakes according to package directions. Press through pastry tube to form decorative potato border, or drop in rough mounds over chicken mixture. Bake 15—20 minutes or until potatoes are delicately browned. Serves 4—6.

SWEET POTATOES OR YAMS

Sweet potatoes and yams are interchangeable in menus and recipes. They are generally cooked by baking or boiling, as with white potatoes, but will be finished in about 3/4 the time. Peel after cooking. One medium-to-large potato is allowed per serving. In various recipes calling for parboiled sweet potatoes or yams, the canned product can be substituted conveniently.

Sweet Potatoes with Apples

    4 boiled sweet potatoes
    1 cup sliced tart apples
1/4 cup brown sugar, firmly packed
    3 tablespoons butter or margarine
    1 teaspoon salt

Peel and slice boiled potatoes. Place layer in greased baking dish; cover with 1/2 the other ingredients. Continue layers, and finish with potato slices and few dots butter or margarine. Bake, covered, in 375°F. oven 30 minutes; uncover, and continue cooking until apples are perfectly tender and top potatoes nicely browned. Serves 4.

Note: With apples that have little juice, it may be advisable to add 2 tablespoons water before baking.

VARIATIONS:

* *Sweet Potatoes with Pineapple*: Instead of apples use drained canned pineapple tidbits plus 2 tablespoons pineapple juice, and reduce brown sugar to 2 tablespoons.

* *Sweet Potatoes with Tangerines or Oranges*: Make syrup by simmering together 1/4 cup each butter or margarine and orange juice and 1/2 cup corn syrup. Pour over potatoes as substitute for other ingredients. Bake, covered, in medium oven 30 minutes. Remove cover. Arrange on top thin slices from 2 tangerines, peeled, or from 1 large navel orange, leaving rind on 2 or 3 slices for extra flavor. Baste fruit with hot syrup, and slide dish under broiler 4—5 minutes to glaze and heat.

Yam and Ham Dinner for 2

    2 medium yams
    1 tenderized ham steak (not more than 1/2 inch
        thick)
    3 tablespoons butter or margarine
    4 canned pear halves
    1 (10-ounce) package frozen asparagus spears
      Salt to taste
  1/4 cup honey or corn syrup
    3 tablespoons pear juice
    3 slices process cheese, cut in strips

Parboil yams 25 minutes. Peel, and slice thickly lengthwise. Gash fat edge of ham in several places. Melt butter or margarine in large covered skillet or electric frying pan. Add ham slice and potatoes; sauté 3—5 minutes over low heat; turn contents over. Arrange pear halves on top of ham slice, and between them neatly pile asparagus. Lightly salt vegetables, and brush potatoes with honey. Pour pear juice around them. Cover pan, keep heat low and cook 10—15 minutes or until asparagus is tender. Top asparagus with cheese strips and keep covered 1 minute until cheese melts. Serves 2.

Sweet-potato Puffs

    2 sweet potatoes
  1/4 teaspoon salt
  1/8 teaspoon pepper
    1 tablespoon butter or margarine
    2 eggs
    2 tablespoons warm milk

Boil, peel and mash potatoes. Add salt, pepper and butter or margarine. Add eggs, and beat vigorously until potatoes are perfectly smooth and fluffy. Add milk, and continue to beat. Mixture should be quite moist. Turn into buttered casserole, and bake at 450°F. about 15 minutes or until rough crest of potatoes shows brown points. Serves 2.

VEGETABLES IN MENUS

A wide choice is always available—fresh, canned, frozen, dried or pickled. Vary your cooking methods, and add sauces and last minute touches.

Use fresh chives (easily grown in pot on kitchen windowsill) and parsley. Add just a dash of 1 other zesty herb—dill, fresh or dried, marjoram, thyme, rosemary, oregano, mint or nutmeg.

Experiment with a sprinkle of celery seed, mustard seed or curry powder over hot vegetables or coleslaw. Keep garlic and other seasoned salts handy. Try horseradish over hot buttered beets,

a dusting of ground ginger on carrots. To enhance the flavor of winter root vegetables, add 1 teaspoon sugar towards the end of cooking time or while mashing.

Other possibilities range from lemon or lime touches, plain, or herbed vinegars, grated cheese and diced firm jelly to swirls of thick sour cream and toasted nuts. Scatter fried bacon bits over chopped cooked spinach. Sprinkle hot croutons over buttered vegetables. Strew a few seedless raisins over creamed cabbage or Brussels sprouts.

The popular white or cream sauce is best when it emphasizes the character of the vegetable that it accompanies; substitute vegetable water for some of the milk, unless it has too strong a flavor for your taste. For 2 cups drained cooked vegetables you will need 1 cup medium white sauce. If you use condensed canned soup (celery, mushroom, asparagus) for sauce, mix 1/2 can with 1/3 cup milk. Blend and heat thoroughly before pouring over 2 cups of hot vegetables.

Melted butter or margarine brings out flavor of hot cooked vegetables. Add a few drops of lemon juice occasionally. For mashed squash, use orange juice plus a sprinkle of brown sugar and nutmeg.

In choosing vegetables, aim for harmony of color, texture and flavor in total meal. Beef is compatible with almost any vegetable, with the possible exception of cucumber. Pork takes to beets, carrots, cauliflower, red cabbage, greens, squash, leeks and onions. Ham teams well with sweet potatoes or yams, peas, corn, beans of all kinds, asparagus, broccoli, Brussels sprouts and zucchini. With lamb serve beets, carrots, peas, cauliflower, yellow turnips, winter squash, sweet green or red peppers and tomatoes. Veal is best with Harvard beets, scalloped tomatoes and mushrooms. Chicken and turkey have many affinities, but if you are serving roasted whole fowl, it is best not to duplicate any vegetable used in the stuffing, onions and celery for example.

Asparagus with Mushrooms

    1 pound fresh asparagus tips
    3 tablespoons butter
    1 (4 1/2-ounce) can sliced mushrooms and liquid
    1 small onion, chopped
      Salt and pepper to taste
  1/4 cup light cream
      Chopped parsley

Wash and trim asparagus under cold water. Combine butter with 1/4 cup mushroom liquid, and bring to boil in skillet. Add asparagus, onion and seasonings. Cook, covered, 8—10 minutes or until asparagus is tender, shaking skillet occasionally. Add mushrooms and light cream; heat thoroughly. Garnish with parsley. Serves 3—4.

Green Beans Lyonnaise

    1 pound green beans, Frenched, or 2 (10-ounce)
        packages frozen Frenched green beans
      Salted water
    1 medium onion, chopped
    2 tablespoons butter, margarine, oil or bacon fat
    1/4 teaspoon sweet basil
      Salt and pepper to taste
    2 tablespoons toasted slivered almonds or sliced
        Brazil nuts

Gently simmer beans in salted water. Drain as soon as tender. Sauté onion in fat until lightly browned; add basil, salt and pepper to taste. Pour over hot beans in serving dish, and garnish with nuts. Serves 6.

Savory Lima Beans

    1 (12-ounce) package frozen lima beans
    1 chicken-bouillon cube
    3 green onions, sliced
    2 tablespoons butter or margarine
    1 tablespoon flour
    1/4 teaspoon paprika
    1/4 teaspoon basil
    1/2 teaspoon salt
      Dash pepper

Cook lima beans as directed on package, adding chicken-bouillon cube to boiling water. Drain, reserving 1/2 cup liquid. Simmer onions in melted butter or margarine 2 minutes; stir in flour. Add bean liquid, and cook, stirring, until thickened. Add beans and remaining ingredients, and heat through. Serves 4–6.

Harvard Beets

    2 tablespoons sugar
    1 tablespoon cornstarch
    1/2 teaspoon salt
    1/4 cup vinegar
    1/2 cup beet juice
    1/4 teaspoon grated orange rind
    2 tablespoons orange juice
    2 tablespoons butter or margarine
    2–2 1/2 cups hot sliced or diced cooked beets

Blend sugar, cornstarch and salt in saucepan. Stir in vinegar, water and orange rind. Cook, stirring, until sauce is smoothly thickened and clear. Stir in orange juice, butter or margarine and beets. Cover, and keep hot over low heat 10 minutes. Serves 5–6.

Broccoli with Olives

    1 bunch broccoli (approximately 1 pound)
    3/4 cup boiling salted water
    1/4 cup *French Dressing*
      Pinch basil
    1 tablespoon lemon juice
    1/2 cup chopped ripe olives

Clean and wash broccoli; cut off tough stem ends. Cook stalks in boiling salted water about 10 minutes or until tender. Drain well. Combine French dressing with basil and lemon juice, pour over hot broccoli and add olives. Heat thoroughly. Serves 4.

Parmesan Brussels Sprouts

    2 pounds fresh Brussels sprouts or 2 (10-ounce)
        packages, frozen
      Boiling salted water
    2 tablespoons butter or margarine
    1/2 clove garlic, crushed (optional)
    2 tablespoons grated Parmesan cheese

Trim off stems of Brussels sprouts, and remove any loose or discolored leaves. Put into small amount boiling salted water, and cook, covered, about 8 minutes. Drain. Heat butter or margarine and garlic together until bubbly; strain over sprouts, turning and coating them well with sauce. Pile on heated serving dish, and sprinkle with cheese. Serves 6.

Creamed Scandinavian Cabbage

    5 cups finely shredded cabbage
    1/2 cup boiling salted water
    1/2 cup sour cream
    1/2 cup chopped dill pickles
    1/2 teaspoon caraway seeds
      Salt and pepper to taste

Cook cabbage in boiling water until almost tender, 5–6 minutes. Drain, and add remaining ingredients to pan. Heat through. Serves 4.

Cabbage with Onion Rings

    2 small onions, peeled and sliced
    1/2 cup milk
      Salt and pepper to taste
    1/4 cup fine dry bread crumbs
    1/4 cup butter or margarine
    4 cups shredded cabbage
    1/2 teaspoon salt
    2 tablespoons water
      Juice of 1/2 lemon

Separate onion slices into rings. Season milk with salt and pepper to taste. Dip onion rings into milk, then into dry bread crumbs to coat well. Melt butter or margarine in skillet over medium heat. Sauté onion rings until crisp and golden brown; lift out, and keep hot. Put shredded cabbage in same pan; sprinkle with salt, water, and lemon juice. Cover tightly, and cook 3–4 minutes over low heat, turning once. Toss with 1/2 the onion rings, and garnish with remainder. Serves 4–5.

Chinese Cabbage with Tomatoes

    5 cups shredded Chinese cabbage
      Boiling salted water
    1/2 cup canned tomatoes
    1 small onion, finely chopped
    1 teaspoon sugar
      Salt and pepper to taste
      Pinch marjoram
    1/2 bay leaf

Parboil cabbage 5 minutes, and drain. Combine tomatoes with onion, sugar and seasonings. Pour over cabbage, and cook slowly, covered, until cabbage is tender, 15—20 minutes. Remove bay leaf before serving. Serves 5—6.

Corn Fritters

    1 3/4 cups well-drained kernel corn, frozen, thawed or
              canned
        3 eggs
    1/2 teaspoon salt
    1/4 teaspoon pepper
       1 tablespoon chopped onion
    1/4 cup all-purpose flour
    1/3 cup fat

Drain corn of excess moisture; then measure 1 3/4 cups. Separate eggs; beat yolks until light and frothy. Add corn, seasonings, onion and flour. Beat egg whites until stiff but still glossy; fold into corn mixture. Heat fat in skillet, and drop mixture in by generous spoonfuls. Cook over medium heat until well browned; turn, and continue frying until thoroughly cooked. Fritters are especially good with chicken, ham or crisp bacon. Accompany fritters with maple syrup or honey. Serves 4—6.

Sautéed Cucumber

       2 firm medium cucumbers
       2 tablespoons butter or margarine
       1 teaspoon sugar
       1 teaspoon paprika
       1 teaspoon curry powder
          Salt and pepper to taste

Peel and dice cucumbers. Melt butter or margarine in skillet, and sauté cucumber over medium heat 1 minute. Turn heat low, sprinkle vegetable lightly with sugar, paprika, curry powder, and salt and pepper. Cover pan, and cook slowly about 3 minutes. Use as accompaniment for baked sausages, meat patties or fish. Serves 4.

Creamed Mushrooms with Spinach

       1 pound mushrooms, washed
    1/3 cup butter or margarine
    2 1/2 tablespoons flour
    1/2 teaspoon salt
    1/8 teaspoon pepper
    1 1/2 cups milk
       2 pounds spinach, thoroughly washed
       1 teaspoon salt
          Paprika to taste

Separate caps from stems of mushrooms. Melt butter or margarine in skillet, add stems and cook gently for 1 minute. Add caps, turning to cook both sides lightly until just tender. Blend in flour; add 1/2 teaspoon salt, pepper and milk gradually, stirring constantly until sauce is smooth and thick. Keep hot over low heat. Put spinach into saucepan, and cook in its own moisture 3—4 minutes, adding 1 teaspoon salt, and turning vegetable once. Drain well. Arrange hot spinach around sides of serving dish, and fill center with hot creamed mushrooms. Shake paprika over mushrooms. Serves 6—8.

Carrots with Green Grapes

    1/2 cup butter or margarine
    6–8 carrots, scraped and cut in 2-inch strips
       1 cup seedless green grapes
       2 tablespoons honey
       1 tablespoon lemon juice
          Salt to taste
    3–4 mint leaves, chopped

Melt butter or margarine in heavy pan, add carrots and turn over and over until well coated with butter or margarine. Cover, and cook until almost tender, about 25 minutes. Add grapes, honey and lemon juice, and cook slowly 10 minutes. Add salt, and scatter with mint leaves just before serving. Serves 6.

Celery Braised in Consommé

    2–3 small heads celery
       1 medium onion, chopped
       2 tablespoons butter or margarine
          Dash pepper
       1 (10-ounce) can consommé
       1 tablespoon chopped parsley

Scrub celery, remove top leaves and cut each head lengthwise through heart, making 4 or 5 slender sections. If very long, cut in half crosswise. Place onion in casserole, and arrange celery on top. Dot with butter or margarine, and sprinkle with pepper. Add undiluted consommé, cover and bake 1 hour at 350°F. Sprinkle with parsley before serving. Salt may be needed, depending on strength of consommé. Serves 6.

Jerusalem Artichokes

    1 1/2 pounds Jerusalem artichokes
    1/2 cup boiling water
       2 tablespoons butter or margarine
       1 teaspoon mild vinegar or white wine
       1 tablespoon chopped parsley
       2 drops hot pepper sauce

Wash and scrape artichokes, and cook in boiling water, covered, until just tender. Do not cook beyond this point, or artichokes will become tough again; test with toothpick after 15 minutes. Drain well. Melt butter or margarine, combine with remaining ingredients and pour over cooked vegetable. Serves 4–6.

VARIATIONS:

* Instead of seasoned butter, cream artichokes in 1 cup medium white sauce.

* Slice cooked artichokes, and sauté in butter.

Acorn Squash with Mushrooms and Lime

    3 medium acorn squash (approximately 3 pounds)
1 1/2 teaspoons salt
1/2 teaspoon pepper
1/2 teaspoon nutmeg
3/4 cup butter or margarine
    4 cups button mushrooms (1 pound)
    6 slices lime

Wash acorn squash. Dry, cut in half lengthwise and remove seeds. Sprinkle each squash with salt, pepper, and nutmeg. In each hollow, place 1 tablespoon butter or margarine. (Save rest for later.) Place on a shallow baking tray. Cover with foil. Bake at 400°F. for 40 minutes or until tender. Drain any butter sitting in hollows of squash into a skillet. Add rest of butter to this. Sauté mushrooms until tender, approximately 5–7 minutes. Fill each squash half with about 3/4 cup of the mushrooms. Garnish each serving with 1 slice lime. Serves 6.

Roast Corn

5–6 ears corn
1/4 cup butter or margarine, melted
    Salt and pepper to taste

Pull back husks of corn; remove silks. Brush cobs with butter or margarine, and season with salt and pepper. Replace husks, and twist ends together as tightly as possible. Wrap individually in heavy foil, and place on rack over glowing embers. Roast about 30 minutes, turning several times with tongs. Serves 4–6.

Mashed Parsnip Patties

    3 cups mashed cooked parsnips
    1 tablespoon finely chopped onion
    1 tablespoon finely chopped parsley
3/4 teaspoon salt
    Pinch poultry seasoning
    1 egg, well beaten
1/2 cup coarse bread crumbs
1/2 cup fine bread crumbs
    2 tablespoons bacon drippings or salad oil

To parsnips, add onion, parsley and seasonings; stir in egg and coarse crumbs. Shape into 8 patties, and roll in fine crumbs. Heat drippings in frying pan, and sauté until crisply brown on both sides. Serves 4.

Vegetable Soufflé

    1 cup cooked vegetables (peas, turnips, onions, carrots, broccoli, asparagus, mushrooms or mixture of several)
    1 cup thick white sauce
    2 tablespoons finely chopped onion
    1 tablespoon lemon juice
1/2 teaspoon salt
    Dash pepper
    Dash Worcestershire sauce
    2 egg yolks, beaten
    2 egg whites
1/4 teaspoon cream of tartar

Puree vegetables in blender, mash or chop fine. Combine with white sauce, onion, lemon juice, seasonings, Worcestershire sauce and egg yolks. Cool. Beat egg whites stiffly with cream of tartar. Fold into vegetables. Turn into a greased 1 1/2-quart casserole, and bake at 325°F. 1 hour or until set. This soufflé is a good accompaniment for creamed ham or chicken. Serves 6.

Scalloped Tomatoes

    2 tablespoons butter or margarine
    2 tablespoons finely chopped onions
1 1/2 cups soft bread crumbs
    1 (20-ounce) can tomatoes, drained
    1 teaspoon sugar
1/2 teaspoon salt
    Dash celery salt (optional)
1/4 teaspoon pepper

Melt butter or margarine, add onion and cook till tender. Combine with bread crumbs, mixing well. To tomatoes add sugar, salt, celery salt and pepper; mix through. Pour 1/2 the tomatoes into greased casserole; top with layer of crumb mixture using a little more than 1/2. Add remaining tomatoes, and cover with remaining crumb mixture. Bake at 375°F. about 30 minutes. Serves 4–5.

VARIATIONS:

* Instead of celery salt, add 1/4 cup chopped celery to tomatoes; increase salt to taste.

* Peel and core 1 large tart apple; slice into tomatoes before cooking; increase sugar and salt to taste.

Turnip-Potato Casserole

    1 turnip (about 1 pound)
    Boiling salted water
4–5 potatoes
    Boiling salted water
1/4 cup finely chopped onion
    2 tablespoons cream
    1 egg, beaten
    Salt and pepper to taste
1/2 teaspoon dry mustard

Peel turnip. Slice, and boil in salted water until tender but not too soft, about 15 minutes; drain, and mash. Cook potatoes in salted water in separate saucepan. Drain well, mash and combine with mashed turnip. Add remaining ingredients, and whip with egg beater or electric beater. Turn puree into buttered casserole, and bake uncovered at 400°F. 20 minutes or until firm, puffed and lightly browned on top. Serves 6—8.

Note: Grated cheese may be sprinkled over top a few minutes before removing from oven.

Sweet-and-Sour Red Cabbage

    1 small firm red cabbage (4 cups shredded)
      Boiling salted water
    2 medium tart apples, cored, peeled and sliced
    1/4 cup brown sugar, firmly packed
    1/4 cup cider vinegar
    1 tablespoon butter or margarine

Discard core and tougher white ribs of cabbage. Shred coarsely. Cook, covered, in boiling salted water about 10 minutes. Add apples, and cook until tender, about 10 minutes more. Drain. Dissolve brown sugar in vinegar, stir into cabbage mixture and add butter or margarine. Cover, and keep hot over low heat a few minutes before serving. Serves 4—5.

Eggplant Italian Style

    1/4 cup tomato paste
    1 (28-ounce) can Italian-style tomatoes, drained
      Pinch salt
    1 large or 2 small eggplants
    1 cup hot water
    3 tablespoons hot salad oil
      Salt and pepper to taste
    2 cups soft bread crumbs
    1/2 cup grated Parmesan cheese
    1 tablespoon chopped parsley
    1 clove garlic, chopped, or 2 tablespoons finely
      chopped onion
    1/2 pound mozzarella cheese, cut in thin strips

Blend tomato paste with canned tomatoes; add pinch salt, and simmer 5 minutes. Meanwhile, wash, dry and slice eggplant crosswise into 1/2-inch slices; do not peel. Place in a bowl, cover with hot water and let stand 5 minutes. Drain slices, and pat dry with paper towel. Fry in hot oil until tender and light brown, about 3 minutes each side. Sprinkle with salt and pepper to taste. Mix crumbs, Parmesan, parsley and garlic. Add spoonful of hot oil from pan. Arrange layer of eggplant slices in baking dish; cover with 1/2 crumb mixture, then with 1/2 the tomatoes. Top with another eggplant layer, remaining crumbs and tomatoes. On final eggplant layer, place mozzarella cheese. Bake in moderate oven (350°F.) until cheese is bubbly and slightly colored. Serves 5—6.

Sweet-Sour Zucchini

    6 medium zucchini
    1/2 cup salad oil
      Salt and pepper to taste
    3 tablespoons cider vinegar
    1 tablespoon sugar
    1/2 clove garlic (optional)
    1/2 teaspoon sweet basil
      Chopped parsley

Wash zucchini, and scrape lightly. Cut each into 2 or 3 lengthwise slices. Fry in salad oil about 3 minutes each side or until squash is lightly browned and tender. Sprinkle with salt and pepper. Remove from skillet, and place in hot serving dish. Mix vinegar and sugar, and add with garlic and sweet basil to remaining oil in skillet. Simmer slowly 2 minutes, remove garlic and pour sauce over zucchini. Garnish with parsley. This dish may be served hot or chilled. Serves 4—5.

Herbed Onion Casserole

    2 pounds onions
    1 teaspoon salt
    1 teaspoon paprika
    1 teaspoon celery seed
    1/4 teaspoon pepper
    1/4 teaspoon basil or sage
    1/2 cup consommé or bouillon
    3/4 cup crushed potato chips

Peel onions, and slice thick. Combine seasonings. Place layers of sliced onion in shallow greased casserole, sprinkling seasonings between layers. Add consommé, cover casserole and bake at 350°F. 45 minutes or until tender. Remove cover; scatter crushed potato chips over onions; cook another 5—10 minutes until topping is crisp and browned. Serves 4—5.

Fireside Chicken-Vegetable Stew

    4–5-pound stewing fowl
    1/2 lemon
    1/4 cup butter or margarine, melted
      Bouquet garni
    5–6 cups water
    2 chicken-bouillon cubes
    1 teaspoon salt
    1/2 cup sliced celery
    6 small carrots, scraped
    6 or more potatoes, peeled
    1 (12-ounce) package frozen lima beans
    1 cup cream or milk
    1/4 cup soft butter or margarine
    1/3 cup flour
    1 (1-pound) can small onions, drained
      Chopped parsley

Wash chicken, wipe and cut in serving pieces. Run cut surface of lemon over meat surfaces. Sauté legs, wings and breast sections slowly on both sides in melted butter or margarine until golden, watching that butter doesn't burn. Add remaining chicken pieces, including giblets from which all fat has been cut away. Add bouquet garni, water, bouillon cubes and salt. Cover tightly, and simmer until chicken is just tender, about 1 1/2—2 hours. Add raw vegetables, and simmer 20 minutes longer. Lift out, and discard large bones and pieces of skin. Pour cream and stock from chicken into double boiler. Make smooth roux by blending butter or margarine with flour and stirring into stock until thickened. Pour over cooked chicken, vegetables and drained onions. Heat until bubbly, and sprinkle with chopped parsley. Serves 6.

Note: Make a bouquet garni from 1/2 teaspoon thyme, slice of onion, few peppercorns, celery leaves and parsley sprigs, and tie all in cheesecloth bag. If chicken is fat, strain cooking stock into bowl and chill until fat comes to top; then skim. If preferred, use 1/4 cup chicken fat in place of butter or margarine for thickening stock. Cut-up frying or roasting chicken may be used in place of boiling fowl and will require less cooking time; 35 minutes for preliminary simmering or 10 minutes in pressure cooker.

Whole Cauliflower Polonaise

    1 medium head cauliflower
      Boiling salted water
    3 tablespoons melted butter or margarine
    1 teaspoon chopped parsley
    2 tablespoons toasted fine bread crumbs
    1 hard-cooked egg yolk, sieved

Trim off leaves, and cut from cauliflower as much of core as possible without harming florets. Gently boil 18—20 minutes or until tender. Drain. Place in serving dish; then, combine melted butter or margarine and parsley, and pour over cauliflower. Sprinkle with bread crumbs and egg yolk. Serves 4—5.

Vegetable Chowder

      1 cup diced carrots
    1/2 cup finely chopped onion
    2 1/2 cups boiling salted water
    2 1/4 cups chopped cabbage
      2 tablespoons butter or margarine
      2 tablespoons flour
      1 cup milk
      2 teaspoons salt
    1/8 teaspoon pepper
      1 cup cooked peas
      2 tablespoons chopped parsley

Cook carrots and onion in boiling water until almost tender. Add cabbage, and continue cooking until all vegetables are tender. Drain, and save liquid (approximately 1 1/2 cups). Melt butter or margarine in pan. And flour, milk, 1 teaspoon salt, pepper and 1/2 cup vegetable liquid. Stir until smooth. Add remaining 1 cup vegetable liquid. Stir, and cook over boiling water

until sauce thickens. Add cooked vegetables and parsley. Keep hot over simmering water till serving time. Serves 6.

ACCOMPANIMENTS FOR VEGETABLES

Special seasonings, sauces and other interesting touches can enhance plain vegetables.

Flavored Butters

Melt butter or margarine for boiled or steamed vegetables, using 3 tablespoons to 4—6 servings. Before pouring over vegetables, stir into butter 1 of the following: 1—1 1/2 teaspoons lemon juice; 1 teaspoon thick meat sauce; 1 tablespoon grated dry cheese; 1/4 teaspoon dry mustard; 1 tablespoon chopped nuts; 1/4—1/2 teaspoon Worcestershire sauce; 1/4—1/2 teaspoon beef bouillon; 1 teaspoon barbecue sauce; 1 teaspoon chopped parsley or green onions.

From the Salad Shelf

For 4—5 servings of hot cooked vegetables, toss lightly with 1 of the following: 2—3 tablespoons *French Dressing*; 1—2 tablespoons herb vinegar; 1 tablespoon *Mayonnaise* thinned with lemon juice.

Bread Acompaniments

Buttered Crumbs. Allow 1/3 cup melted bacon drippings or butter for 1 cup fine dry bread crumbs. Sauté crumbs until hot, and scatter over hot vegetable for serving. Or to buttered crumbs or croutons add 1 of the following: sprinkle of grated cheese, spoonful of finely chopped onion or scallion, diced cooked bacon, dash of curry powder, dash of paprika.

Stuffing. For 1 halved acorn squash or 4—5 onions or tomatoes, use 1 cup soft bread crumbs seasoned with grated cheese, crisp bacon pieces, grated onion or salt and pepper along with a pinch of mixed herbs or 1 favorite such as oregano.

Bread Croustades. Remove crusts from sliced bread. Brush one side with melted butter or margarine; press buttered sides into muffin tins. Toast in 350°F. oven 15 minutes or until golden. Remove from tins, keep hot and fill with creamed vegetables at serving time.

Sauce for Creamed Vegetables (White Sauce)

      2 tablespoons butter or margarine
      2 tablespoons flour
      1 cup milk or 1/2 cup milk and 1/2 cup vegetable
         water
        Salt and pepper to taste

Melt butter or margarine, and blend in flour. Stir in liquid slowly. Cook until smooth, stirring constantly, until no taste of raw starch remains. Season to taste. Makes 1 cup.

VARIATIONS:

* To basic cream or white sauce, add 1 of the following, according to kind of vegetable and to your own taste: celery salt, 1 teaspoon onion juice, 1 teaspoon sherry, 1 teaspoon lemon juice, dash Worcestershire sauce, 1/2 teaspoon curry powder, 2 teaspoons capers or chopped sweet pickle, 2 tablespoons chopped chives or parsley.

* To plain creamed vegetables in serving dish, add a last-minute grating of nutmeg, or sprinkle 2 chopped hard-cooked eggs over top.

* *Canned-soup Sauce*: Use condensed cream soup of suitable flavor—chicken, mushroom, tomato or celery. Dilute with 1/2 liquid required for soup. Heat, and pour over cooked vegetables.

* *Au Gratin Vegetables*: Add cream sauce to hot vegetable; sprinkle with fresh or dry bread crumbs, and dot with butter, margarine or grated cheese. Heat under broiler 2—3 minutes.

Sour Cream—Horseradish Sauce

    1 cup commercial sour cream
    1/2 teaspoon prepared mustard
    1/2 teaspoon horseradish
        Salt and pepper to taste

Combine ingredients, adding more horseradish if desired. Serve cold in sauceboat with hot spinach.

Glazed Vegetables

Leave parboiled, peeled vegetables such as sweet potatoes, parsnips, carrots and squash whole or in large pieces. Place in buttered baking dish. Drizzle 1 of the following glazes over pieces. Bake, basting with syrup, at 350°F. 20—30 minutes.

Sugar Glaze

    1/2 cup brown sugar, firmly packed
    1/3 cup boiling water
      2 tablespoons butter or margarine

Mix all ingredients.

Honey Glaze

    1/2 cup honey
      1 tablespoon butter or margarine, melted
    1/2 teaspoon mint

Combine all ingredients.

Orange Glaze

    1/2 cup sugar
    1/4 cup orange juice
        Dash cinnamon

Combine all ingredients.

FRUITS

A minimum of 2 servings of fruit or juice per day—1 of them a citrus fruit or tomato juice—is recommended. The 2 servings are specified because of vitamin C requirements, but oranges and tomatoes contain vitamin A as well. The mild, natural acids that such fruits provide help digestion.

In season, cantaloupe and strawberries are perfectly acceptable as the day's vitamin C ration. A normal serving of 1/2 cantaloupe supplies as much of this dietary essential as 1/2 cup fresh orange juice; in addition, the melon contains more vitamin A than does any other fruit.

There is no difference in nutritive value between canned juices and diluted frozen citrus juices; selection can be made on the basis of taste or price. To avoid a "tinny" taste, opened cans of citrus fruits and juices should be poured into another type of container, covered and kept in the refrigerator. Canned or bottled juices develop maximum flavor when aerated by pouring several times from one container to another.

All fresh, cooked, canned and frozen fruits provide a variety of vitamins, and, served whole or as unstrained juice, they provide bulk for the digestive tract and some energy, which is of course increased when sugar is added.

Fruits are low in protein and fat, except for avocados and ripe olives. With few exceptions, they are also low in minerals.

Often canned and frozen fruits and juices are less expensive than are fresh ones. And you can use the juices from canned or frozen fruits, preferably without additional cooking.

Always remember that frozen fruits should be kept at 0°F. for best flavor and texture.

Special Canned Fruits

Fruit nectars are thicker than juices. They contain some sieved pulp and pectins, which provide bulk not present in strained liquid. Sugar has generally been added, and vitamins are fewer per serving than in unsweetened juices. Fruit nectars are best used in mixed beverages or in recipes.

Don't forget that all "baby foods" are *strained* and "junior foods" *chopped*. Both can be used for special diets and recipes and for elderly people. "Baby foods" are low in bulk because they are strained. Yet they have the same food value as do regular sweetened canned fruits.

Dietetic canned fruits offer the same food values as do other canned fruits but are processed without added sugar, and instead are sweetened with non-caloric sweeteners.

Dried Fruits

Because large amounts of liquid have been removed, dried fruits are high in sugar content and therefore are an energy source. They have valuable mineral contents but are usually low in vitamins. Prunes, dates and figs encourage elimination.

Dried fruits are available the year round, are comparatively low in cost and go well with other fruits.

Prunes, raisins, apples, peaches, apricots, and pears are most common in this group; others are dates, figs and currants.

Packages labeled "tenderized" have moisture content and thus more weight. Large prunes have larger percentages of edible pulp than do smaller ones, but the volume packs of the latter are often more economical.

The three varieties of raisin most widely available are golden raisins, dark raisins, and seedless (muscats).

Preparation Tips

To halve an orange or grapefruit, cut crosswise; cut between flesh and membranes of each section. Run a sharp knife or curved grapefruit knife around edge to separate flesh from white inner rind. Center pith may be removed with scissors or knife.

To section an orange or grapefruit, slice the top and bottom rind just to flesh. Stand fruit upright. With very sharp knife, slice off skin all around, top to bottom. Trim off rind bits. Turn fruit over, and complete trimming. Cut sections free of membrane.

To prepare citrus fruit juice, halve and squeeze chilled fruit. Remove seeds, but do not strain

(except for low-bulk diet). Juice for breakfast may be prepared the night before, covered and refrigerated. There is little loss of vitamins, but flavor may not be as fresh.

The small berries, particularly raspberries, need care to avoid bruising. Spread on flat surface to pick over; remove any moldy or overripe fruit. Place in colander, and dip colander in pan of very cold water to wash fruit thoroughly. Drain; then stem or hull.

To skin peaches, work at kitchen sink. Place fruit in colander set in pan. Pour boiling water over to cover all fruit. Let stand 1 minute; put colander with fruit under tap, and run cold water over for 1 minute. Skins can then be slipped off readily.

Lemon rind and juice are often called for in recipes. It is best to grate rind before halving fruit. When "a few drops" of juice are wanted,

Three-bean Salad (p. 129) and Lentil Salad in Tomatoes (p. 129).
CREDIT: *Elbert Budin*.

it is convenient to pierce whole lemon with a skewer and even more convenient to use frozen or bottled lemon juice.

Remove apple core with an apple peeler (a slotted, rounded knife), and peel by pulling peeler toward you, holding apple over bowl. If apples are very juicy, it may be advisable to pare by pushing peeler away from you.

In making melon balls, be sure to press special scoop firmly, to its full depth, into flesh, thus ensuring well-rounded ball.

The edible part of a pomegranate is the juicy pink pulp containing the seed clusters; remove with fork. Use for garnish or fruit cups.

A pineapple needs special attention. Slice off ends. With sharp knife, pare off skin top to bottom. To remove deep "eyes" make wedge-shaped cuts along their diagonal line. Cut pineapple in crosswise slices; then quarter slices, and remove hard inner core point.

Uncooked Fruit Dishes

3-Fruit Juice

        2 cups orange juice
        1 cup apple juice
        1 cup pineapple juice

Mix, and keep covered in refrigerator. Use with any fresh-fruit appetizer or dessert to enhance flavor and prevent discoloration of cut fruits—or drink plain or with chilled soda water and ice cubes. Serves 4—5.

Melon-Ginger Mélange

    1/4 cup fresh lime juice
    1/4 cup orange juice
        3 cups cantaloupe balls
    1/3 cup preserved ginger, chopped
        1 banana, sliced
          Sugar to taste

Add juices to cantaloupe balls. Just before serving, add ginger, banana and sugar. Serves 4—5.

Honeydew Rings with Fruit

        1 ripe honeydew melon
        2 cups canned pineapple chunks, drained
        1 cup cantaloupe balls
        1 cup pitted sweet cherries
        1 cup raspberries
        1 pint lemon sherbet
        8 sprigs fresh mint

Peel melon, discard all seeds and slice crosswise into 8 1-inch thick rings. Arrange 1 ring on each individual dessert plate. Chill all other fruits ready for serving time. Place scoop of sherbet in center of each melon ring, and scatter cantaloupe balls, pineapple chunks, sweet cherries and raspberries over. Garnish with mint sprigs. Serves 8.

Watermelon Fruit Basket

    1/2 watermelon
        1 pint fresh berries
        1 dozen fresh apricots, halved
        1 cup cantaloupe balls
        1 banana, sliced
    1/4 cup fine white sugar
        2 tablespoons cherry liqueur or Cointreau (optional)
        8 sprigs fresh mint

Watermelon half may be left as cut or notched for sawtooth edge. Scoop out some of the melon center, and save removed pulp for next day's fruit cup. In hollow, arrange other fruits. Sprinkle fruit with sugar. Cherry liqueur may be drizzled over. Just before serving, decorate watermelon basket with mint sprigs. To serve, start cutting from 1 end of basket, making thick slices, and spoon mixed fruits onto each slice. Serves 8—10.

Strawberry Ice-cream Soda

        2 tablespoons mashed strawberries
        2 tablespoons sugar
        1 tablespoon cream
        1 scoop vanilla ice cream
    3/4 cup chilled soda water

Use blender, or mix in bowl with hand beater. To mashed fresh or barely thawed frozen berries add sugar and cream. Mix together, add ice cream and beat till thoroughly blended. Pour into serving glass; fill with chilled soda water, and serve at once. Serves 1.

Applesauce Delight

        2 egg whites
    1/4 teaspoon salt
        1 tablespoon lemon juice
        1 (15-ounce) can applesauce, chilled
    1/2 cup crushed almond macaroons

Beat egg whites with salt until stiff and glossy. Gradually add lemon juice and applesauce. Continue beating until mixture is very fluffy. Turn into dessert bowls, and sprinkle tops with fine macaroon crumbs. Serves 4.

Fresh Lemonade

        4 lemons
    3/4 cup sugar
        1 tray ice cubes
        2 cups cold water
        4 maraschino cherries with stems

With sharp knife, slice 3 lemons very thinly crosswise. Discard seeds and end slices. Put lemon slices into large bowl or sturdy pitcher. Add sugar. With wooden spoon, muddle until sugar is dissolved and slices are broken. Strain; then add ice cubes and cold water. Stir until very cold. To serve, pour lemonade into glasses; garnish each glass with 1 whole slice from remaining lemon and 1 cherry. Makes 4 tall glasses.

VARIATION:

* *Apricot Lemonade*: Reduce sugar to 1/2 cup, and put 2 or more tablespoons chilled apricot nectar into each glass. Fill with lemonade, and garnish with cherry.

Banana Whip

    1 egg white
    1/2 cup sugar
    1/2 cup mashed banana
         Juice of 1/2 lemon
    1/8 teaspoon salt
    1 teaspoon red currant jelly

Beat first 5 ingredients together until mixture is very light and fluffy. Heap in sherbet glasses, and garnish each with dot of jelly. Serves 2–3.

Cherry Swirl

    1 (3-ounce) package vanilla-pudding mix
       Few drops almond extract
    1 cup cherry jam

Prepare vanilla pudding according to package directions, adding almond flavoring, and allow to thicken partially. To achieve attractive diagonal stripes with red jam, proceed as follows:

Hold parfait glass at an angle, spoon in some jam, then a layer of partially thickened pudding, then another spoonful of jam and so on, ending with layer of pudding. Chill, and garnish with more jam before serving. Serves 3–4.

Banana-Pineapple Milkshake

    1 1/4 cups milk
       1 (4 3/4-ounce) can strained bananas with pineapple
    1/4 cup pineapple juice
       2 scoops vanilla ice cream

Measure all ingredients into blender; mix 1 minute. Pour into tall glasses. Serves 2.

Citrus-Plum Compote

    1 (15-ounce) can plums in heavy syrup
    1 fresh lime, grated
    3 oranges, peeled and sectioned
    2 bananas, sliced

Put plums and juice into serving bowl with rind of lime. Peel, and discard all white pith from lime; cut into small sections, and add to plums. Chill 5–6 hours. Just before serving, add fresh orange sections and sliced bananas. Serves 6.

Pears Helene

    1 (28-ounce) can Bartlett pears
    1 pint vanilla ice cream
    1/2 cup chocolate sauce

Chill pears. At serving time, drain off juice. Allow 2 pear halves for each serving; place in individual dish with scoop of ice cream between halves. Drizzle chocolate sauce over ice cream and pears. Serves 4.

Cranberry Whip

       1 (14-ounce) can cranberry sauce
       3 egg whites, beaten
       1 teaspoon grated orange rind
       1 teaspoon lemon juice
    12–18 ladyfingers

Put sauce through sieve. Beat egg whites until very stiff but not dry; fold in cranberry puree, orange rind and lemon juice. Continue beating until completely blended and mixture stands in glossy peaks. Arrange 2 or 3 ladyfingers upright in each sherbet glass, and pile whip in center. Serves 6.

Crystal Grapes

    1 large bunch seedless green grapes
    1 egg white
    1/4 cup finely granulated sugar

Cut off small clusters of firm grapes from large bunch, leaving them attached to their stems. Beat egg white slightly. Dip grapes in it, then sprinkle generously with sugar. Let dry on cake rack at room temperature.

Note: These easy-to-make novelties are great for garnishing cold-meat platters, salad plates, or cheese trays. Do not make on a humid day.

Frosted Fruit Compote

  1 (4-ounce) package cream cheese
1/2 cup mayonnaise
  2 bananas
  1 cup raspberries
  1 (10-ounce) can pineapple tidbits
1/2 pound midget marshmallows
1/2 pint heavy cream
  3 tablespoons sugar

Cream cheese with fork until softened. Blend in mayonnaise, and beat until smooth. Cut bananas into small pieces. Pick over, wash and thoroughly drain raspberries. Drain pineapple tidbits. Combine all fruits and marshmallows; then add to cheese. Whip cream until stiff, add sugar and gently fold in cheese and fruit mixture. Freeze in refrigerator trays. Thaw slightly before serving. Serves 6—8.

Fresh Fruit Whip

    2 egg whites
1/4 teaspoon cream of tartar
1/4 cup sugar
1 1/2 cups fresh fruit (peaches, pears, apples)

Beat egg whites with cream of tartar until stiff but not dry. Gradually add sugar, and beat until stiff peaks can be formed. Fold in well-drained fruit, and spoon into serving dishes. Accompany with whipped cream. Serves 4.

Note: Canned fruit or cooked prunes may be substituted if desired, and you can save drained juice for later use.

Orange-Brittle Ambrosia

2 large slabs peanut brittle
1 cup heavy cream
2 cups fresh orange, peeled and cut into small pieces

Crush sufficient peanut brittle to make 1/2 cup, using a rolling pin or blender to crush as fine as possible. Beat cream until stiff; combine with crushed brittle. Just before serving, fold in fresh chilled orange pieces. Serves 4.

Note: Ambrosia also makes a nice topping for plain cake.

Rice Cream with Cherries

1 (20-ounce) can cherry pie filling
  Few drops almond flavoring
1 cup heavy cream
1 cup cold cooked rice
1 tablespoon sugar

Sprinkle cherries with almond flavoring. Whip cream until stiff, sweeten lightly and combine with cold rice and sugar. Place spoonful of cherries at bottom of each of 4 dessert bowls, cover with thick layer of rice cream and top with remaining cherries. Chill. Serves 4.

Fruit Candy Bars

1/2 pound moist dried apricots or dates or seedless raisins
1–2 pieces preserved ginger
3/4 cup icing sugar
1/4 cup soft butter or margarine
  2 tablespoons orange juice
1/2 cup crushed vanilla wafers
  Fine white or icing sugar

Put fruit and ginger through grinder; it should be finely ground. Add 3/4 cup sugar, butter or margarine and orange juice, blending thoroughly. Gradually stir in enough wafer crumbs to make mixture sufficiently stiff to form into fingers. Coat fingers with sugar. Wrap in waxed paper, and chill in refrigerator. Makes about 3 dozen bars.

Do consider the following ideas for fruits and their juices.

Freeze them in refrigerator trays. A chilled drink becomes more tempting when there's a wedge of pineapple, lemon or orange or a whole cherry, berry or grape imprisoned in each ice cube. To hold fruit neatly in position in cube, fill tray to 1/4 depth with water, partially freeze, add the berry or piece and freeze till almost firm. Fill tray to usual level, and finish freezing. Keep temperature control at regular setting throughout; the garnished cubes may cloud with fast freezing. Fruit juices—grape, orange, berry—take to the freezing compartment as easily as does water.

Fruit sodas and milkshakes are popular among the young crowd as after-school snacks. Make milkshakes quickly with electric beater or blender, shake in cocktail mixer or stir vigorously in tall glass. For each serving use 1 scoop ice cream, 2—3 tablespoons crushed fruit or juice (not lemon) and 1 cup milk. Make fruit soda in tall glass, using peach or apricot halves or berries over ice cream, then pouring in carbonated soda water. Stir, and serve.

For garnishing, suit fruit to course; pineapple slices dipped in chopped parsley and topped with mint jelly for roast lamb; cloved canned pear or peach halves with ham, and fried apple rings prepared by cutting in 1/2-inch slices, coring and gently cooking in hot sausage fat until tender with baked or fried sausages.

Sauces for Fruit Desserts

Although the various creams–plain, whipped, ice cream, commercial sour cream–are always available, there are other excellent accompaniments as well. Choose a sauce to complement the dish's flavor: a bland sauce for a tart pudding, a sauce with special character for a mild-flavored dish.

Spicy Vanilla Sauce

> 1/3 cup sugar
> 1 tablespoon cornstarch
> Dash salt
> 1/4 teaspoon nutmeg
> 1 cup milk
> 2 tablespoons butter or margarine
> 1 teaspoon vanilla extract

Mix first 4 ingredients in small saucepan. Gradually add milk, stirring to blend, and cook over low heat until thick. Add butter or margarine and vanilla. Makes 1 1/3 cups. Chill, and serve over sliced bananas, or serve hot over *Apple Brown Betty*.

Sherry-Custard Sauce

> 4 egg yolks
> 1/4 cup sugar
> 1/8 teaspoon salt
> 1/4 cup sherry

Beat yolks until thick and lemon colored; then beat in sugar, salt and sherry. Cook over hot (not boiling) water 5 minutes, stirring constantly. Remove from heat. Serve warm or cold over fresh fruit pieces. Makes 2/3 cup.

Hard Sauce

> 1/2 cup soft butter or margarine
> 2 cups icing sugar
> 1 teaspoon vanilla extract or lemon or orange juice plus 1/4 teaspoon grated rind or brandy

Beat butter or margarine very thoroughly; add sugar, a little at a time, blending after each addition. Add flavoring. Beat well. Mound sauce on serving plate, and chill at least 1 hour. Serve with hot puddings. Makes 1 2/3 cups.

Chocolate Sauce

> 1/2 cup light corn syrup
> 1 cup sugar
> 1 cup water
> 3 ounces unsweetened chocolate
> 1 teaspoon vanilla extract
> 1 cup evaporated milk

Mix first 3 ingredients in saucepan, and boil (236°F.) until 1 drop of mixture forms a soft ball in cold water. Remove from heat, stir in chocolate until melted and add vanilla. Add milk slowly, stirring vigorously. Serve chilled with ice cream, sherbets, baked pears. Makes 2 1/2 cups.

Cooked Fruit

Some fruits should be cooked to be palatable. Green apples, rhubarb, hard little Seckel pears, quinces and red or black currants are examples. Cooking and sweetening develop the full flavors of these fruits; correct procedures make them

softer and more digestible. Cooking also prevents spoilage of perishable raw fruits and extends their many possibilities. (For long-term storage, of course, fruit must be specially handled—sterilized and sealed, as in canning, or simply frozen.)

Simple Fruit Sauces. *Applesauce* is always a favorite when well made. To achieve maximum flavor and a smooth, thick consistency, it is important to cook apples in a minimum of water and to wait until fruit is soft before adding sugar. If sugar is added at the start, more is needed and more time too, as sugar has a tendency to toughen fruit flesh and skin, thus delaying softening. Place quartered, unpared apples in saucepan with just enough water to prevent burning. Cover pan, and over medium or higher heat begin the cooking quickly; then reduce heat, and cook fruit until soft. Press through sieve at once; then stir in sugar to taste. Apples past their prime need more water than does the juicy fall crop. For extra flavor add a few drops of lemon juice or a sprinkle of cinnamon or nutmeg.

Stewed rhubarb is best when prepared without water, but some water is added at the start to draw out the abundant natural juices of this fruit. Wash rhubarb stalks, and cut in uniform 1–2-inch lengths. Use about 1/2 as much sugar as fruit. Sprinkle about 1/3 the total quantity of sugar over fruit in a saucepan, cover and cook over low heat. Do not stir. As juice is drawn out, add more sugar; when fruit is almost tender, add remainder.

Poaching. To poach fruit, stew gently, either whole or cut in fairly large pieces. The aim is to keep shape intact; the fruit is put into steadily simmering sugar-and-water syrup, a little at a time, cooked till just tender, carefully lifted out and replaced by another small batch. The smallest pieces and the softest fruits require the shortest cooking time and are added last. When all fruit is cooked, syrup is usually reduced by boiling and poured over fruit before chilling and serving.

Baked Fruits. Apples are the most frequently baked fruit, but other fruits can be baked as well. Peeled pears or peaches are baked whole or in

cored halves in shallow baking dish containing a few tablespoons of water. Sprinkle sugar over fruit, dot with butter or margarine and bake in slow oven. Peeled whole bananas are baked without water. Place in greased dish; sprinkle with lemon juice, sugar and a few grains of salt; dot with butter or margarine, and bake uncovered about 20 minutes.

Special Equipment. A pressure cooker can produce a variety of interesting cooked fruit desserts. Always follow manufacturer's directions exactly for quantities and timing, particularly with fruits that tend to froth and sputter, as do apples and cranberries.

With an electric blender, raw fruit can be pulverized for quickly assembled whips and short-

cake fillings. In less than 1 minute of blending, quartered raw apples can be transformed into very good applesauce, without heat.

Deep-dish Fruit Pie

> 1 1/4 cups sifted all-purpose flour
> 1/4 teaspoon salt
> 1/3 cup shortening
> 2–3 tablespoons cold water
>   Fruit Filling

Sift together flour and salt; cut in the shortening, using pastry blender or 2 knives; continue cutting in until mixture is in particles the size of peas. Add cold water very gradually, moistening dry areas in turn; use only enough water to bind dough. Wrap dough in waxed paper, and chill in refrigerator a few minutes while preparing filling. Roll out pastry about 1/8 inch thick on lightly floured cloth or board; make circle large enough to allow 1/2-inch margin for rim. Cut 2 or 3 small gashes in center to allow steam to escape. Now dampen the rim of the fruit-filled dish, and gently lift pastry over the top to prevent stretching. Fold overhang under the pastry edge neatly, and press against the rim with a floured fork. Start pie in hot oven, 425°F. After 15 minutes reduce heat to 350°F., and bake about 30 minutes longer. Serves 5–6.

FRUIT FILLINGS:

* *Apple Pie Filling*: Pare, core and thinly slice 6–8 tart apples. Place in 1-quart buttered dish, and sprinkle with mixture of 2 tablespoons flour, 1 cup sugar, 1/4 teaspoon salt, pinch nutmeg, and pinch cinnamon. Dot 2 teaspoons butter or margarine over top before covering with pastry.

* *Blueberry Pie Filling*: Use 4 cups fresh or just-thawed frozen berries. Follow procedure for *Apple Pie Filling* using 2 tablespoons flour, 3/4 cup sugar, and 1 tablespoon lemon juice.

Peach-Cream Pie

> 1 cup sifted all-purpose flour
> 1/2 teaspoon salt
> 1/3 cup shortening
> 1/4 cup blanched almonds, ground
> 2–3 tablespoons cold water
> 1/3 cup flour
> 1/3 cup granulated sugar
> 1/8 teaspoon salt
> 1 (20-ounce) can sliced peaches and juice
>   Water
> 3 egg yolks, slightly beaten
> 2 teaspoons lemon juice
> 2 teaspoons butter or margarine
> 1/2 teaspoon vanilla extract
> 1/4 teaspoon almond extract
> 3 egg whites
> 1/3 cup granulated sugar
> 1 teaspoon lemon juice

Sift together 1 cup flour and 1/2 teaspoon salt. Cut in shortening until quite fine; add almonds. Sprinkle cold water over until dough is moist enough to hold together. Chill; roll dough out on lightly floured board, and ease it into 9-inch pie pan. Flute edge, and bake 12-15 minutes at 450°F. Allow to cool while making filling.

Combine 1/3 cup flour, 1/3 cup sugar and 1/8 teaspoon salt in top of double boiler. Stir in peach juice plus enough water to make 2 cups, and cook over direct heat until thickened. Add a little hot filling to egg yolks, and return to hot mixture. Cook 2 minutes longer over hot water; then cool. Add 2 teaspoons lemon juice, butter, vanilla and almond extract. Turn 1/2 the mixture into cooled pastry shell; arrange peaches over filling, and add remainder of filling.

Beat egg whites until stiff; add 1/3 cup sugar, 1 tablespoon at a time, beating after each addition until all sugar is blended in. Add lemon juice. Spread meringue evenly over filling. Bake at 350°F. about 15 minutes or until meringue is golden brown. Serves 6.

Honey Fruitcake

    2 cups dried prunes
    1 cup dried apricots
      Boiling water
    1 cup seedless raisins
    1 cup slivered blanched almonds
    1 cup coarsely chopped walnuts
    1 pound mixed candied fruit, diced
    2 cups sifted all-purpose flour
    1 cup butter or margarine
    1 cup honey
    4 eggs
    1 teaspoon salt
    1 teaspoon baking powder
    1 teaspoon cinnamon
    1 teaspoon allspice
  1/4 teaspoon cloves
  1/4 teaspoon mace
    1 recipe *Honey-glazed Fruit*
    2 tablespoons chopped nuts

Cover prunes and apricots with boiling water, and let stand 10 minutes. Drain, and cool; remove pits, and chop finely. Combine all dried fruits, nuts and candied fruit. Dredge with 1/4 cup of flour. Cream butter, and add honey, then eggs, 1 at a time, beating well after each addition. Sift together remaining flour, salt, baking powder and spices. Add to creamed ingredients, and blend well. Pour batter over fruit-nut mixture, and combine thoroughly but lightly. Turn mixture into 9-inch tube pan lined with 2 thicknesses of greased brown paper and 1 of greased waxed paper. Set pan in shallow container of hot water, place on bottom rack in very slow oven (about 250°F.) and bake 3 1/2—4 hours or until a cake tester inserted in center comes out clean.

When cake has almost cooled, decorate top with *Honey-glazed Fruit* and sprinkle of chopped nuts.

Honey-glazed Fruit

    6 pitted prunes
  6–8 dried apricot halves
      Water
  1/4 cup sugar
  1/4 cup honey

Gently simmer prunes and apricots in water 10 minutes; lift out fruit. Measure 1/4 cup liquid, add sugar and honey and simmer fruit until well glazed. Allow to cool slightly before arranging on top of cake.

Cinnamon Pear Mold

  1/3 cup sugar
    2 cups water
    1 tablespoon red cinnamon candies
      Juice of 1/2 lemon
    5 fresh firm pears
    1 (3-ounce) package lemon-flavored jelly powder
    1 teaspoon plain gelatine
    1 (3-ounce) package coconut-, banana- or vanilla-pudding mix (not instant variety)
    1 cup whipped cream or whipped topping

Simmer first 4 ingredients together 10 minutes. Peel, core and quarter pears; add to syrup; cover pan, and simmer until just tender. Drain, reserving syrup; dissolve jelly powder in syrup. Slice 8 pear quarters into oiled baking dish, and cover with jelly mixture. Allow to set. Meanwhile, add plain gelatine to pudding powder, and follow package directions for pudding. Cool to room temperature, and spread over jellied pears. Chill in refrigerator at least 1 1/2 hours; then unmold. Garnish with remaining pear quarters and whipped cream. Serves 4—6.

Ginger Baked Apples

    6 large tart apples
   10 gingersnaps, crushed
    8 ounces mixed candied fruits, diced
  1/8 teaspoon salt
    2 tablespoons butter or margarine
    1 cup ginger ale
  3/4–1 cup brown sugar, firmly packed

Wash apples; core, but do not peel. Place in buttered baking dish snug enough to keep apples upright and close together. Combine gingersnaps and glacé fruits, and add salt and butter or margarine. Fill each apple center with mixture. Prick apples at several points to prevent bursting of skin. Pour ginger ale into pan, and sprinkle brown sugar over and around apples. Bake at 375°F. 1 hour or until tender, basting frequently. These baked apples are at their best when allowed to cool and served with cream. Serves 6.

Apple Brown Betty

    1 1/2 cups bread crumbs
        3 tablespoons melted butter or margarine
        4 tart apples, peeled and sliced
    3/4 cup brown sugar, firmly packed
    1/4 teaspoon salt
    1/4 cup seedless raisins
        1 tablespoon lemon juice
    2–3 tablespoons water

Mix crumbs with melted butter or margarine, and scatter 1/3 mixture over bottom of greased baking dish. Cover with about 1/2 the sliced apples; sprinkle 1/2 the brown sugar and salt over apples, and add 1/3 more crumbs. Make another layer sliced apples; add raisins and remainder of sugar and salt, and sprinkle with lemon juice and water. Top with remaining crumbs; cover dish, and bake at 350°F. about 40 minutes or until apples are tender when pierced with a fork. Uncover dish, and bake another 10–15 minutes to brown top. Serve warm with *Spicy Vanilla Sauce* or cream. Serves 4–5.

Apple Crisp

        4 large tart cooking apples
            Lemon juice (optional)
    1/2 cup flour
    1/2 cup rolled oats
    1/2 cup brown sugar, firmly packed
    1/2 cup butter or margarine

Peel and core apples, and place in greased shallow baking dish. If apples are dry and not at their prime flavor, sprinkle with a little lemon juice. Combine flour, rolled oats and sugar, and blend in butter or margarine (with 2 knives or with fingers). Mixture will have rough, crumbly appearance. Cover apples with this topping, and bake, uncovered, at 375°F. 30–40 minutes or until fruit is quite tender and top crisp and nicely browned. Serve warm with cream or ice cream. Serves 5–6.

VARIATIONS:

* Use 4 cups diced rhubarb or sliced peaches or 3 cups blueberries or blackberries.

Baked Rhubarb Compote

    1/4 cup sugar
    1/4 cup boiling water
        2 tablespoons orange juice
    1–2 drops red vegetable coloring (optional)
        4 cups washed and diced rhubarb

Dissolve sugar in water in casserole. Add orange juice and vegetable coloring. Add rhubarb, cover dish and bake at 350°F. about 20 minutes. This dish is best served chilled. Serves 4.

Broiled Grapefruit Halves

        4 grapefruit halves
    1/4 cup brown sugar, firmly packed, or honey
        4 teaspoons butter or margarine

Prepare grapefruit as for serving raw, loosening flesh from inner white rind and segment membranes. Sprinkle each half with 1 tablespoon sugar or honey and top with 1 teaspoon butter. Place fruit in pan 3–4 inches below preheated broiler. Broil about 15 minutes until topping is completely melted, skin edges begin to brown and pulp is heated through. Serve as hot appetizer in place of soup or as dessert. Serves 4.

Key-lime Sponge

        1 (3-ounce) package lime-flavored jelly powder
    1/2 cup boiling water
            Thin strip green lime rind
    1/2 cup lime juice
        2 eggs, separated
    1 1/3 cups sweetened condensed milk
            Few drops green vegetable coloring

Place first 3 ingredients in electric blender. Cover, and blend at high speed 20 seconds. Add lime juice and egg yolks, cover and resume high speed a few seconds. Add milk and coloring; blend again. Beat egg whites until very stiff, and fold lightly into lime mixture. Chill in 6 parfait glasses in refrigerator until firm; or turn immediately into deep 10-inch baked pie shell, and chill. Serves 6–8.

Grape Mallow

        1 cup grape juice
    20 marshmallows, quartered
    1/2 cup heavy cream, whipped
        1 (11-ounce) can mandarin orange sections

Heat grape juice, add marshmallows and stir until melted. Cool, and when syrupy fold in whipped cream. Set in individual molds; chill until firm. Unmold, and garnish with drained orange sections. Serves 4.

Fresh Berry Charlotte

1 1/2–2 cups washed strawberries, raspberries or black-
            berries
    1 1/2 cups soft white bread crumbs
1/2-3/4 cup sugar
        3/4 cup orange juice
    1/3 cup butter or margarine, melted
        2 egg yolks, slightly beaten
        2 egg whites
            Pinch salt
        2 tablespoons sugar

Combine first 3 ingredients; combine orange juice, butter or margarine and egg yolks, and stir into berries. Spread in greased 1 1/2-quart casserole dish. Beat egg whites and salt together until soft peaks form; then beat in 2 tablespoons sugar gradually. Spread meringue evenly over fruit mixture. Bake at 350°F. about 35 minutes. Serve warm with cream or *Custard Sauce*. Serves 6–8.

Mincemeat Puffs

>   1 (14-ounce) package raisin-bran muffin mix
> 1 1/2 cups mincemeat

Prepare batter according to package directions. Grease 8 6-ounce deep custard cups, and spoon 2–3 tablespoons mincemeat into each. Pour in batter to 2/3 depth. Distribute remaining batter among greased muffin pans and bake the 2 batches according to package directions. Invert warm puffs on individual plates, and pass hot sauce. Serves 8.

Note: By preparing full package of muffin mix you will have enough batter for 8 dessert puffs plus several plain muffins that will be useful at next day's breakfast or in the lunchbox.

Datebread Pudding

>   2 cups cubed day-old bread
>   2 cups warm milk
> 3/4 cup pitted dates, chopped
> 1/2 cup apple juice
> 1/2 cup sugar
> 1/4 teaspoon salt
>   3 eggs
> 1/2 teaspoon nutmeg
> 1/4 teaspoon cinnamon

Soak bread cubes 10 minutes in warm milk. Add chopped dates, apple juice, sugar and salt. Beat eggs well, and stir in lightly with fork. Turn mixture into greased baking dish, and sprinkle nutmeg and cinnamon over top. Set dish in shallow pan of hot water, and bake at 350°F. about 1 hour or until set. Serve warm with cream or *Hard Sauce*. Serves 5–6.

Double Strawberry Shortcake

>   1 quart strawberries
> 3/4 cup granulated sugar
>   2 cups sifted pastry flour
>   3 teaspoons baking powder
> 1/2 teaspoon baking soda
> 1/4 teaspoon salt
> 1/2 cup milk
> 1/3 cup corn oil
>   2 eggs, separated
>   2 tablespoons lemon juice
>   Grated rind of 1 lemon or 1 teaspoon dehydrated
>   grated lemon peel
>   Few drops almond extract
>   Pinch salt
> 1/4 cup sugar
> 1/2 pint whipping cream

Wash, hull and sort strawberries. Pick out and slice any that are soft or underripe. Add enough sliced good berries to make 1 cup, and spread in well-greased 8- or 9-inch ring mold. Sprinkle with 1/4 cup sugar. Halve remaining berries. Sweeten to taste with 1/2 cup sugar and refrigerate. Sift next 4 ingredients together in bowl. Combine milk, corn oil, egg yolks, lemon juice, rind and almond extract, and stir into dry ingredients. Beat until blended; then pour over berries

in prepared pan, and bake at 450°F. 25 minutes. Invert shortcake on cookie sheet. Beat egg whites and salt until soft peaks form. Add 1/4 cup sugar gradually, and continue beating until stiff. Spread over shortcake, and bake at 350°F. 5–6 minutes. Serve warm with reserved sweetened berries and whipped cream. Serves 8.

Bananas Alaska

> 4–5 medium-firm ripe bananas
> 4–5 tablespoons red currant jelly
>   3 egg whites
> 1/3 cup sugar
> 1/2 teaspoon lemon juice
> 1/4 teaspoon cream of tartar
> 1/4 cup chopped walnuts

Split bananas lengthwise and spread with jelly. Arrange in shallow baking dish. Beat egg whites until very stiff but not dry; gradually add sugar, lemon juice and cream of tartar, beating continuously. Completely cover each banana half with meringue mixture. Sprinkle with chopped nuts, and put immediately into very hot oven—500°F.—for just 3–4 minutes until meringue is golden brown. Serve with ice cream or whipped cream. Serves 4–5.

Biscuit Shortcakes

> 1 1/2 cups unsifted all-purpose flour
>   4 teaspoons sugar
>   3 teaspoons baking powder
>   1/4 teaspoon salt
>   1/4 cup hard butter or margarine
>   8–9 tablespoons milk
>   Soft butter
>   *Strawberry Shortcake Filling* or other fruit filling
>   1/2 pint whipping cream

Measure and sift flour, sugar, baking powder and salt into a bowl. Cut in the hard butter until mixture looks like coarse oatmeal. With a fork, stir in enough milk to make a soft moist dough when particles are pressed together. Knead slightly on a lightly floured pastry canvas, just until smooth. Roll out to just under 1/2-inch thickness. Cut into rounds about 3 inches in diameter with a floured cutter. Place on a small greased cookie sheet, about 1 1/2 inches apart. Bake at 425°–450°F. until well risen and lightly browned, about 12 minutes. Split and butter the halves while still hot. Put together with fruit filling on individual dessert plates. Top each with more filling and lots of lightly sweetened whipped cream. Serves 6–8.

Strawberry Shortcake Filling

>   1 quart strawberries
> 1/3 cup sugar

Wash and hull strawberries, reserving a few large ones for garnish. Slice or crush remainder, add sugar, let stand till sugar is dissolved and, just before serving, spread as directed over warm shortcake.

VARIATIONS:

* *Raspberry Shortcake Filling*: Raspberries or other suitable small berries may be used instead of strawberries.

* *Peach Shortcake Filling*: For strawberries substitute ripe peaches thinly sliced and sweetened.

* *Rhubarb Shortcake Filling*: Thick stewed rhubarb makes appropriate and tasty shortcake filling in the spring.

* *Applesauce Shortcake Filling*: Tart applesauce makes a good filling any time of year.

Cranberry Sherbet

```
      4 cups cranberries
2 1/2 cups cold water
      2 cups sugar
      1 envelope plain gelatine
  1/2 cup cold water
        Juice of 2 lemons
```

Cook berries in 2 1/2 cups water until they stop popping. Strain, add sugar to juice and simmer until sugar is dissolved. Soften gelatine in 1/2 cup water, and add to syrup, stirring well. When mixture is cool, add lemon juice. Pour into refrigerator tray, and freeze, stirring occasionally, 2—3 hours. Serves 6.

2-in-1 Custard Cream for Fruit

```
2 1/4 cups milk
  1/3 cup evaporated milk
    2 eggs, beaten
  1/3 cup sugar
    3 tablespoons flour
    2 tablespoons cornstarch
    1 teaspoon vanilla
  1/4 teaspoon salt
```

Heat milk and evaporated milk in top of double boiler over hot water. Combine remaining ingredients in small bowl, and beat until smooth. Pour into hot milk, and cook, stirring until smoothly thickened. Makes about 3 cups.

Note: This recipe makes enough thick custard to accompany dessert at 2 meals. Pour 1/2 the custard into bowl, and cover with waxed paper; chill in refrigerator. To serve, fold in 1 or 2 sliced bananas or 1 cup drained, cut-up fresh or canned fruit. For following day's use, this basic custard may be diluted with a little milk or thin cream and reheated to serve with hot dessert such as *Apple Crisp* or *Fresh Berry Charlotte*. Or use chilled without diluting over fruit-flavored molded jelly.

Arabs and Greeks in the pre-Christian era used to serve mixtures of greens and herbs with simple dressings. The Romans of Caesar's time dipped raw greens in salt ("sal") and dubbed them "salata" (salted). From these beginnings developed an ever-expanding group of tempting variations.

Appetizer salads are usually mixtures of fresh greens tossed with flavorful French or other thin dressings. They should be light and appetizing, to stimulate rather than satisfy the appetite, and can precede or follow hot main courses. Mixed fruits with their juices served in sherbet or dessert glasses are properly called "fruit cocktail" or "fruit cup," rather than "salad." Fruit salads, however, may be served as appetizers.

Accompaniment salads go with hot main dishes and should be served on separate salad plates or in individual salad bowls. With cold meats, fish, cheese and eggs, they may be placed on dinner plates. At a formal dinner, the salad sometimes becomes a separate course, following the main dish and preceding dessert. Variety can be almost endless, but the accompaniment salad should suit the main course. When the main part of the meal is light, a satisfying salad may be used: for instance, potato salad with stuffed eggs or cold cuts. To accompany a substantial main dish, the salad should be as light as an appetizer salad. Suitable types include tossed greens or coleslaw, raw-vegetable salads (sliced raw tomatoes, cucumbers, green pepper rings), asparagus tips in lettuce cups, colorful fruit salads, jellied fruit or vegetable salads.

Main course salads should include protein foods (meat, fish, seafood, eggs, cheese, nuts or dried beans). They should also be substantial enough to satisfy and provide energy material.

Dessert salads are fresh, light and satisfying without providing too many calories. They are usually made of fruits, thoroughly drained and carefully arranged in lettuce cups or on greens. The fruits may be folded lightly together and piled in lettuce cups or served as jellies in large or individual molds. Dressings may be French, special sweet fruit-salad dressing or thick dressings folded into whipped cream or commercial sour cream.

Arranged Salads

Whole or carefully cut pieces of food are set out on beds of greens. The dressing is poured carefully over the top, spooned into tiny lettuce cups at sides or passed in a bowl. Decorative placement of the food is in itself the garnish. Fruit salads are usually arranged on individual serving plates. Sometimes arranging is done after folding.

Folded Salads

For these salads the ingredients are usually very carefully cut—diced, sliced or julienned. They are combined in a large bowl, dressing and seasonings are added and all are folded together *lightly* so that the shapes of the pieces are retained. Sometimes the ingredients are gently lifted with 2 forks from the bottom of the bowl, the procedure being repeated until a uniform combination is achieved. Meat, fish and potato salads are usually prepared this way and some fruit mixtures too.

Tossed Salads

Torn or shredded greens and other items, well chilled, are sprinkled with dressing and seasonings, then lightly but thoroughly tossed with 2 forks or fork and spoon until every particle has its touch of dressing. Tossed salads are at their best when served immediately after assembling.

Jellied Salads

Many interesting mixtures can be molded in jelly form, a "make-ahead" convenience appreciated by the busy hostess. Fruit-flavored jelly powder (made tart and flavorful with the addition of vinegar or lemon juice and seasonings) or plain unflavored gelatine is used to set the mixture. In preparing a large shape for dividing into servings at the table, the solids in the mixture are finely cut or chopped. For individual jellied salads there is much greater flexibility in the sizes of cooked or raw items to be featured.

Selecting and Preparing

Buy salad greens only in quantities that can be used up within a few days. Long-stored greens become soft and watery, with a tendency to "rust" or otherwise discolor.

Look over your purchases as soon as you bring them from the store, and discard any bruised or stale parts. Wash greens well under cold running water. Do not soak. Keep bunches or heads intact until ready to use. Drain well, dry and store in refrigerator—in crisper or in plastic bags or aluminum foil. To prevent yellowing of parsley, store it well drained in tightly-covered container in refrigerator.

Before Serving. Be sure that all your salad ingredients, including dressings, are thoroughly chilled. If possible, chill salad plates too. If your cold salad course features cooked vegetables such as potatoes, beets or green peas, start preparing in time to allow complete chilling. Such extra garnishes as ripe olives, anchovies and hard-cooked eggs should also be refrigerated ahead of time.

Wash, separate and chop or shred raw salad materials, according to kind of salad planned. To make lettuce cups for individual servings, cut out core at base of lettuce head and, holding it upside down, allow cold water from tap to pour over cut area. The leaves will separate under force of the water. Drain, and shake or pat dry with towel, taking care not to break shape.

Added Dressing. Try to have all greens free of excess moisture after their final washing. Remember that an oil-base dressing cannot properly adhere to wet greens, and water in the salad bowl will thin any type of dressing. Of course, your choice of dressing will depend on the type of salad, but, unless the recipe directs otherwise, add dressing just before serving. Use just enough to season and blend ingredients.

There is a dressing to make every salad taste better. Keep several kinds ready, covered: basic *French Dressing* plus the variations your family likes best; *Mayonnaise* (refrigerated) and your favorites from among the various excellent commercial products. All these dressings store well. Homemade cooked or "boiled" dressings, however, should be used up quickly because of their milk-and-egg bases.

Note: 1/2 cup thin dressing of any kind is usually enough for 6 servings.

DRESSINGS FOR FRUIT SALADS:

* *Lemon French Dressing*: Replace vinegar in *French Dressing* with lemon juice, and increase sugar to taste.

* *French Dressing for Fruit Salads*: For use with fruit salads, omit strong flavors such as garlic and onion, and experiment instead with touches of herbs and spices—mint, sweet basil, marjoram, poppy seeds, sesame seeds, curry powder.

* *Ruby Dressing*: Beat 2 tablespoons red currant jelly until smooth; add 1/4 cup each lemon juice and salad oil and 3/4 teaspoon salt. Beat again.

* *Mayonnaise-Cream Dressing*: Combine 1/2 cup each *Mayonnaise* and heavy cream, whipped.

* *Hawaiian Dressing*: Add 2 tablespoons canned pineapple juice to 1/2 cup *Mayonnaise*.

* *Orange Whip Dressing*: To 1 cup *Mayonnaise* or "boiled" dressing, add 1/2 cup heavy cream, whipped, 2 teaspoons grated orange rind and a little sugar.

* *Velvet Dressing*: Mash 1 (4-ounce) package cream cheese; blend in 1 tablespoon lemon juice and 3 tablespoons currant jelly. Whip 1 cup heavy cream, fold into cheese mixture and chill.

Hearty Salads

Potato Salad

Allow 1 medium potato per serving. Scrub, boil in skins and do not peel until cooked unless recipe directs otherwise.

Potato Salad with Bacon Bits

Slice potatoes into bowl lined with lettuce or other greens, and sprinkle each layer with chopped onion, crumbled crisp bacon and finely chopped parsley. Pour over just enough *French Dressing* to moisten. Sprinkle freshly ground black pepper over top, and garnish with parsley.

Potatoes in Mayonnaise

Prepare required quantity of diced potatoes. For each cupful allow 1/2 cup chopped celery and 1 teasoon chopped mild onion. Combine with *Mayonnaise* to moisten. Serve on lettuce leaves, and garnish with such color contrasts as sliced stuffed olives, pimento or green-pepper strips, and sliced or chopped hard-cooked eggs. For an interesting touch, place a spoonful of chilled cooked new peas in tiny lettuce cup at side of each serving; sprinkle with *French Dressing*.

Potato Salad Vinaigrette

      1/3 cup white-wine vinegar
      1/2 teaspoon salt
      1/2 teaspoon dry mustard
      1/4 teaspoon celery seed
        6 medium potatoes, boiled and cubed
        2 tablespoons chopped onions or chives
        2 tablespoons salad oil
        2 tablespoons chopped parsley

Heat together vinegar, salt, mustard and celery seed. Pour over 6 hot coarsely cubed potatoes. Stir in onion. Let mixture cool; add salad oil and parsley. Serves 6.

Ham-Potato Salad

        2 cups diced cooked ham
        2 cups diced cooked potatoes
        2 green onions, chopped
        4 gherkins, chopped
        1 cup *Mayonnaise*
          Salt and pepper to taste
          Crisp salad greens
        3 hard-cooked eggs, sliced

Mix first 4 ingredients together; blend in *Mayonnaise* lightly, season with salt and pepper and arrange on bed of crisp salad greens. Garnish with slices of hard-cooked eggs. Serves 6.

VARIATIONS:

* Replace 1 cup cooked ham with diced cooked chicken or turkey. Use 2 cups diced cooked corned beef in place of other meat. One cup chopped celery may be added to any of these variations.

Shrimp Salad

        2 (4 1/4-ounce) cans shrimp, chilled, or 12 ounces
          frozen or fresh shrimp, cooked and chilled
        1 cup cooked peas, chilled
      1/2 teaspoon salt
          Few grains pepper
      1/2 cup chopped celery
        1 tablespoon chopped parsley
        1 tablespoon chopped green pepper
        1 tablespoon chopped green onion
      1/4 cup *French Dressing*
          Salad greens
        2 hard-cooked eggs, sliced

Rinse shrimp under cold running water, and halve if large. Combine with peas. Sprinkle with salt and pepper, and stir lightly with fork. Add celery, parsley, green pepper and onion to dressing. Pour over shrimp mixture, and toss lightly with fork. Serve on crisp greens, garnished with slices of hard-cooked egg. Serves 4.

VARIATION:

* Omit *French Dressing*, and mix first 5 ingredients with 1/4 cup *Mayonnaise*. Garnish individual salads with remaining ingredients.

Tuna Salad in Tomato Cups

        1 (7-ounce) can solid tuna
        1 cup chopped celery
      1/2 cup chopped cucumber
        1 tablespoon grated onion
      1/4 teaspoon salt
          Dash pepper
      1/3 cup *Mayonnaise*
        4 large firm tomatoes
          Watercress or other crisp greens

Drain liquid from tuna. Flake fish, and combine with celery, cucumber, onion, seasonings and enough *Mayonnaise* to hold mixture together. Slice off stem ends of tomatoes, remove a little of the plup to make "cups" and invert for a few minutes to drain. Pile tuna salad into tomatoes on individual salad plates, and surround with watercress. Serves 4.

VARIATION:

* Canned lobster, salmon or shrimp may be substituted for tuna in tomato cups or piled on salad greens. Garnish with twist of lemon peel, hard-cooked egg wedges and green-pepper rings.

Chef's Salad

    1 quart torn salad greens
    3–4 tomatoes, peeled and quartered
    1/2 cup sliced radishes
    1 green pepper, cut in strips
    1 peeled avocado, diced
    1 1/2 cups chicken or ham, in julienne strips
    6 hard-cooked eggs, sliced
    1/2 pound Swiss cheese, in strips
    1/2 cup *Italian Dressing*

Wash greens thoroughly, pat dry and place in wooden bowl rubbed with garlic. Add tomatoes and all remaining ingredients. Toss together lightly but thoroughly with dressing.

Note: For a good chef's salad choose at least 3 of the following greens: leaf or head lettuce, romaine, endive, spinach, escarole, watercress.

Curried Chicken Salad

    1/2 cup chopped raw or canned water chestnuts
    4 cups diced cooked chicken
    1/2 cup chopped celery
    1/2 cup diced green pepper
    2/3 cup *Mayonnaise*
    2 tablespoons light cream
    1 tablespoon vinegar
    1 teaspoon salt
    1 teaspoon curry powder
    6 lettuce cups
    6 pickled peaches or 1/2 cup apple jelly

Chop water chestnuts coarsely. Combine with chicken, celery and green pepper. Blend *Mayonnaise*, cream, vinegar, salt and curry powder, and combine with chicken mixture. Chill until serving time. Serve in lettuce cups on individual salad plates. Garnish with peaches. Serves 5–6.

Vegetable Salads

Relish Tray

Simple crisp relishes can be served as soon as prepared. Relishes such as *Carrot Curls* and *Celery Fans*, however, should be made at least 1 hour ahead and refrigerated in ice water so that they will hold their shapes.

* *Carrot Curls*: With vegetable parer, shave lengthwise strips from peeled long, straight carrot. Shape each strip around forefinger to make curl, secure with toothpick and place each tight curl in ice water 1 hour.

* *Celery Fans*: Cut each large tender stalk of celery into 3-inch lengths; then make several slits in each end, almost to the center. Refrigerate in ice water until ends curl.

* *Marinated Tomatoes*: Peel ripe tomatoes. (To peel, hold each tomato on fork over flame till skin wrinkles and splits; then pull off. Or dip tomatoes first in boiling then in cold water before peeling.) Slice into shallow dish. Using scissors, snip scallions over tomatoes until latter are lightly covered. Sprinkle with a little salt and dried basil. Pour *French Dressing* over all (about 1/2 cup of dressing for each 1 1/2 pounds tomatoes). Chill 1 hour. Before serving, drain off excess moisture.

Coleslaw

    1/2 cup *Mayonnaise*
    1/4 cup commercial sour cream
    1 tablespoon lemon juice
    1 tablespoon sugar
    1 tablespoon white vinegar
    1 teaspoon celery seed
    1/2 teaspoon dry mustard
    1/4 teaspoon salt
    1/8 teaspoon pepper
    6 cups finely shredded cabbage
    8 green-pepper rings
    2 pimentos, finely diced

Combine *Mayonnaise*, sour cream, lemon juice, sugar, vinegar, celery seed, mustard, salt and pepper. Chill well. Put shredded cabbage into large serving bowl, pour mayonnaise mixture over and toss lightly. Garnish with green-pepper rings; sprinkle with diced pimento. Serves 6–8.

Coleslaw with Fruits

    2 cups finely shredded cabbage
    1 cup canned pineapple tidbits
    3/4 cup seedless raisins
    2/3 cup cooked dressing
    8 large lettuce leaves
    Paprika to taste

Combine cabbage, pineapple, seedless raisins and 1/3 cup dressing. Blend lightly. Garnish 4 plates with lettuce, and top with salad mixture and remaining dressing. Sprinkle with paprika. Serves 4.

Garden Salad

    1 cup grated carrot
    1 cup grated cabbage
    1 cup chopped celery
    1 cucumber, diced
    1/3 cup sliced radishes
    1/2 cup (approximately) *Mayonnaise*
    3 tablespoons thick chili sauce
    6 lettuce cups
    12 sprigs watercress

Toss first 5 ingredients together lightly. Combine *Mayonnaise* and chili sauce, and pour over vegetables, adding only enough to moisten vegetables well. Toss lightly again. Serve in lettuce cups, and garnish with sprigs of watercress. Serves 6.

Savory Salad

    6 cups torn-up salad greens (lettuce, romaine,
        chicory, raw spinach leaves and the like)
    6 anchovies, chopped
1/4 cup diced pimento
    3 tablespoons chopped onion
1/2 cup *Italian Dressing*
    Lettuce leaves

Combine first 4 ingredients. Pour dressing over mixture, and refrigerate 1 hour. Serve on lettuce leaves. Serves 8.

Bean Salads

Three-bean Salad

    1 cup dried fava or lima beans, cooked
    1 cup white beans, cooked
    1 cup pinto or cranberry beans, cooked
1/2 cup chopped onion
1/2 cup chopped and drained bread and butter pickles
1/2 cup chopped parsley
1/2 cup salad oil
1/4 cup cider vinegar
    1 teaspoon salt
1/4 teaspoon pepper
    2 cups fresh spinach leaves

Toss together fava or lima beans, white beans, and pinto or cranberry beans with onion, pickles and parsley. Pour on dressing made from salad oil, cider vinegar, salt and pepper. Chill covered for about an hour in the refrigerator or for no more than 20 minutes in the freezer. Serve on a bed of fresh spinach leaves. Serves 6.

Lentil Salad in Tomatoes

    1 cup (1/2 pound) lentils
1/4 cup chopped onions
1/4 cup coarsely chopped radishes
1–2 cloves garlic, crushed
1/3 cup olive or salad oil
    2 tablespoons wine vinegar
1/2 teaspoon salt
1/8 teaspoon pepper
    3 large tomatoes
    Watercress

Cook lentils according to label directions. Drain well. While still hot, combine with onions and radishes. Stir in garlic, olive oil, vinegar, salt and pepper. Taste for seasoning. Chill at least 1 hour.

Cut tomatoes crosswise. Scoop out seeds and pulp. Chill. At serving time, fill each of 6 tomato halves with about 1/2 cup lentil salad. Place on platter. Garnish with watercress. Serve any remaining lentil salad separately in a bowl. Makes 6 servings.

Italian Bean and Artichoke Salad

Be careful not to marinate the beans and artichokes more than half an hour, or the green color will turn dull.

    2 (10-ounce) packages frozen green beans, cooked
    1 (10-ounce) package frozen artichoke hearts, cooked
1/4 cup diced pimentos
1/2 cup olive or salad oil
1/4 cup red wine vinegar
    1 teaspoon onion juice
1/2 teaspoon salt
1/2 teaspoon powdered oregano
1/4 teaspoon crushed rosemary
1/8 teaspoon pepper

Cook green beans and artichoke hearts separately according to label directions; then drain and cool. Add pimentos. Cover and chill. Make dressing separately by combining olive oil with wine vinegar, onion juice, salt, oregano, rosemary and pepper. Lightly toss with bean mixture and chill well. To serve: drain beans and artichoke hearts from the dressing, using a slotted spoon. Mound on serving platter. Serve extra dressing alongside, if desired. Serves 6.

Wax Beans Vinaigrette

4–5 cups cooked wax beans (fresh, frozen or canned),
        drained
    1 cup sliced fresh mushrooms
1/2 cup thinly sliced green-pepper rings
    1 cup Italian-style salad dressing
    2 small heads Bibb lettuce

Place cooked and cooled wax beans, drained, in a large bowl. Toss with mushrooms, green-pepper rings and salad dressing. Let chill at least 1 hour in refrigerator or 15 minutes in the freezer. To serve: Drain dressing from beans. Place on shallow serving platter surrounded by Bibb lettuce leaves. Serves 6.

Curried Sikh Salad

    2 (15-ounce) cans pork and beans
    4 cups cooked rice, cooled
1/4 cup chopped onions
    1 cup *Mayonnaise*
    1 teaspoon curry powder
    1 teaspoon salt
1/4 teaspoon pepper
1/2 cup shredded coconut, toasted
   12 lime slices (approximately 2 whole limes) cut in
        halves

Drain pork and beans very well. Rinse with cold water. Drain again. Place in a large bowl together with cooked, cooled rice and chopped onion. Toss gently. Fold in mayonnaise, curry powder, salt and pepper. Mound evenly on a shallow platter. Sprinkle toasted coconut to make a border around the edge. Garnish edge of platter with overlapping halved lime slices. Chill in refrigerator for at least 1 hour or in freezer for 15 minutes. Serves 6.

Fruit Salads

Caribbean Salad

    1/2 head curly endive
      2 cups salted water
      3 oranges, peeled and sliced
      1 large Spanish onion, thinly sliced
    1/2 cup *French Dressing*
      2 avocados, peeled, halved and sliced

Separate endive leaves; trim off and discard hard white ends. Put in cold water, and let stand to reduce characteristic bitter taste. Place orange and onion slices in bowl, and pour over enough dressing to cover. Chill in refrigerator. Just before serving time, drain and dry endive, and arrange on individual plates. For each serving arrange 2 or 3 orange slices with 1 onion slice on endive; surround with 1/2 slices of avocado dipped in dressing. Serves 4–5.

Florida Citrus Salad

      2 large grapefruit
      2 navel oranges
         Salad greens
      1 (4-ounce) package cream cheese
      2 tablespoons orange juice
    1/4 teaspoon grated orange rind
     12 cooked prunes, chilled
    1/2 cup *French Dressing* made with orange juice or
         Mayonnaise-Cream Dressing

Prepare grapefruit and oranges by removing peel and white rind and cutting into natural sections between membranes. Arrange on crisp salad greens on individual plates, alternating grapefruit and orange sections. Blend cream cheese with juice and grated rind. Pit prunes, and stuff with cheese, allowing 2 to each plate. Serve with dressing. Serves 5–6.

VARIATION:

* Instead of prunes, use large sweet grapes, sliced and seeded, then stuffed with cheese mixture, or fresh or canned apricot halves piled with the stuffing.

Stuffed-pear Salad

      1 (4-ounce) package cream cheese
      1 cup cottage cheese
    1/4 cup chopped nuts
    1/4 cup chopped dates
      1 tablespoon chopped maraschino cherries
         Salad greens
      8 cooked pear halves
    1/3 cup *Mayonnaise*
      2 tablespoons pear syrup
    1/2 teaspoon lemon juice

Soften cream cheese with fork, and mix with cottage cheese. Blend in nuts, dates and maraschino cherries. Arrange salad greens on four plates, and place 2 pear halves on each. Heap with cheese mixture. Thin *Mayonnaise* with syrup and lemon juice. Serve with salad. Serves 4.

VARIATION:

* This cheese mixture may also be used to stuff canned peach halves, or with pineapple slices as base.

Fruit-salad Platter

    1/2 large ripe cantaloupe, seeds removed
1 1/2–2 cups cottage cheese, drained
      2 cups fresh strawberries, raspberries or blackberries, dipped in finely granulated sugar, or 1 cup fresh or canned pineapple wedges
      2 cups watermelon balls
      8 fresh orange slices
      8 banana fingers, dipped in mayonnaise and rolled in shredded coconut
         Fresh mint leaves

Peel melon to make serving in wedges easier, and place in center of platter. Fill hollow center with cottage cheese. Heap berries in mounds at intervals around melon. Between mounds arrange separate grouping of various other fruits. Garnish platter with fresh mint leaves. Serves 8.

Citrus-Cream Dressing

      2 eggs
    1/4 cup sugar
    1/4 cup lemon juice
      2 tablespoons orange juice
    1/2 teaspoon dry mustard
    1/4 teaspoon salt
         Few grains cayenne
      1 tablespoon butter or margarine
    1/2 cup heavy cream, whipped
         Pecans, coarsely chopped
         Kumquats, coarsely chopped, or candied orange peel, coarsely chopped

Beat together in saucepan eggs, sugar, fruit juices, spices and butter or margarine. Cook, over low heat, stirring, and bring just to boiling point; then remove from stove. When cool, fold in whipped cream. Turn into serving bowl, and garnish with pecans and kumquats or candied orange peel.

Waldorf Salad

      1 cup diced tart apples
         Few drops lemon juice
      1 cup diced celery
    1/2 cup walnuts, coarsely chopped
1/2–3/4 cup salad dressing or *Mayonnaise*
    4–6 lettuce cups
    4–6 maraschino cherries

Apples may be peeled or left with skins on for color. Sprinkle with lemon juice. Combine apples, celery and walnuts; fold in dressing, and serve in individual lettuce cups. Top each with maraschino cherry. Serves 4–6.

VARIATIONS:

* Add 1/2 cup seedless raisins for extra flavor and nutrition.

* Substitute generous spoonful peanut butter for walnuts at side of plate, and sprinkle coarsely chopped peanuts over it.

Minted Fresh-fruit Salad

      4 slices fresh or canned pineapple
      2 cups whole fresh strawberries
        Honey or sugar
      1 cup heavy cream, whipped

If fresh pineapple is used, sprinkle slices with sugar or honey, and let stand at least 2 hours to absorb sweetness. Halve whole fresh berries, sprinkle with honey or sugar and let stand to absorb sweetness and draw out juice. Just before serving, mound serving of strawberries on each pineapple slice, and top with whipped cream. Serves 4.

Note: Sliced bananas may also be combined with strawberries. Sprinkle with lemon and chopped fresh mint to preserve color; do not sweeten.

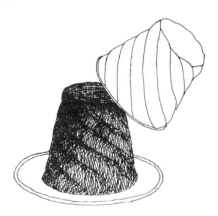

Jellied Salads

Waldorf-Cider Salad

      1 envelope plain gelatine
      2 tablespoons lemon juice
  1 3/4 cups apple cider
        Dash salt
      1 red apple
    3/4 cup diced celery
    1/2 cup diced and drained fresh or canned apricots
        Salad greens

Soften gelatine in lemon juice. Heat cider to boiling, and dissolve gelatine in it. Stir in salt, and cool until slightly thickened. Core and dice unpeeled apple. Fold apple, celery and apricots into gelatine mixture. Rinse 6 individual molds with cold water, and fill with mixture. Chill until firm, and serve unmolded on greens. Serve with *Mayonnaise* or with equal parts *Mayonnaise* and commercial sour cream beaten together. Serves 6.

Cucumber Mousse

      2 cucumbers
      1 envelope plain gelatine
    1/2 cup cold water
      1 (3-ounce) package lime-flavored jelly powder
  1 1/4 cups boiling water
    1/2 cup lemon or lime juice
      2 teaspoons onion juice
    3/4 teaspoon salt
    1/8 teaspoon cayenne
    1/2 cup chopped celery
    1/4 cup chopped parsley
    1/2 pint heavy cream, whipped
        Fish salad

Peel cucumbers, remove seeds and grate coarsely. Soften gelatine in cold water. Dissolve lime jelly powder in boiling water, and stir in plain-gelatine mixture, lemon juice, onion juice, salt, cayenne and prepared cucumbers. Chill until thickened; then fold in celery, parsley and, lastly, whipped cream. Pour into large oiled ring mold, and chill in refrigerator until set. Unmold, and fill center with fish salad. Serves 6—8.

Tomato Aspic

      2 envelopes plain gelatine
      4 cups tomato juice
      1 bay leaf
      1 celery stalk
      1 tablespoon sugar
      1 tablespoon vinegar
    3/4 teaspoon salt
        Salad greens

Soften gelatine in 1/2 cup tomato juice. Heat remaining tomato juice with bay leaf and celery, and bring to boiling point. Discard bay leaf and celery. Stir softened gelatine into hot tomato juice until completely dissolved. Add sugar, vinegar and salt. Pour into 1 large or 6 individual molds rinsed with cold water, and chill in refrigerator until firm. Turn out on crisp salad greens, and serve with *Mayonnaise*.

Note: If ring molds are used, fill centers with one of the following: cottage cheese mixed with coarsely chopped nuts, chopped celery and cucumber mixed with thick *Mayonnaise*, diced cooked chicken and diced celery mixed with *Mayonnaise*. Serves 6—8.

Frozen Cheese Salad

      2 (8-ounce) packages cream cheese
    1/2 cup stuffed olives, chopped
    1/2 cup toasted almonds, chopped
    1/4 cup lemon juice
    1/4 teaspoon salt
    1/2 cup heavy cream, whipped
        Salad greens
    1/2 cup *French Dressing*
        Fresh mint

Mash cream cheese with fork. Add olives and almonds, and stir in lemon juice and salt. Fold whipped cream into mixture. Spoon into refrigerator tray, and freeze without stirring. Cut into squares, and serve on salad greens with dressing; garnish with mint. Serves 6–8.

Orange-Cranberry Salad

    1 envelope plain gelatine
    1/4 cup cold water
    4 cups cranberries
    2 small oranges
    1 cup sugar
    1/4 cup hot water
    1 (3-ounce) package lemon-flavored jelly powder

Soak gelatine in cold water until dissolved. Meanwhile, wash cranberries, and cut oranges into pieces, leaving skins on but removing seeds. Put oranges and cranberries through meat grinder or blend in electric blender. Reserve juices from chopping. Add sugar to hot water; add lemon jelly powder, softened plain gelatine and stir until gelatine is dissolved. Stir in minced oranges and cranberries and reserved juices. Mold in wet ring mold or individual molds, and chill until firm. Serves 6.

Pineapple-Cucumber Salad

    1 envelope plain gelatine
    6 tablespoons cold water
    1/2 cup lemon juice
    1/3 cup sugar
    1/8 teaspoon salt
    1–2 drops green vegetable coloring (optional)
    1 cup crushed pineapple, undrained
    1 small cucumber

Soak gelatine in cold water, and dissolve over boiling water. Add lemon juice, sugar, salt and coloring. Mix well with pineapple. Peel cucumber, quarter lengthwise and remove seeds. Grate cucumber, and add to mixture. Pour mixture into wet mold or individual molds, and chill thoroughly. Serves 4.

Jellied Beet Salad

    1 (3-ounce) package lemon-flavored jelly powder
    1 cup boiling water
    3/4 cup beet juice
    3 tablespoons vinegar
    1 tablespoon chopped onion
    1 tablespoon horseradish
    1/2 teaspoon salt
    1 cup finely diced cooked beets
    1 tablespoon finely chopped celery
      Shredded lettuce

Dissolve jelly powder in boiling water, and add all other ingredients except beets and celery. Chill mixture until it just begins to set. Fold in beets and celery, and turn the mixture into wet mold or individual molds. Chill until very firm, and serve on shredded lettuce. Serves 4.

Jellied Avocado Salad

    1 envelope plain gelatine
    2 tablespoons cold water
    1 cup boiling water
      Juice of 1/2 lemon
    1 cup mashed avocado
    1/4 teaspoon celery salt
    1 teaspoon salt
    1/2 teaspoon Worcestershire sauce
      Few drops hot pepper sauce
    2 tablespoons chopped pimento

Soak gelatine in cold water; then dissolve in boiling water. Add lemon juice and other ingredients, blend well together, pour into wet mold or individual molds and chill until firm. Serves 4.

12 LUNCHEON MENUS STARRING VEGETABLES AND FRUITS*

Hamburgers in buns
Mustard Pickles
Applesauce Delight
Cookies

Tuna Salad in Tomato Cups
Hot bran muffins
Citrus-Plum Compote
Cheese tray

Toasted-cheese sandwiches
Coleslaw
Fresh-fruit Whip
Sponge cake

3-Fruit Juice Cocktail
Poached egg on chopped spinach
Rice Cream with Cherries

Cheese Omelets
Brown-and-serve sausages
Harvard Beets
Celery hearts
Raspberry ice and vanilla ice cream

Vegetable soup
Crusty bread
Waldorf Salad
Brownies

Quick Potato Soup
Frankfurters in buns
Stuffed-pear Salad
Cookies

Vegetable Soufflé
Crisp bacon
Melba toast
Baked apples with cream

Cream of asparagus soup
Sardine-lettuce sandwiches
Fresh-fruit cup
Gingersnaps

*Recipes are given for items printed in *italics*.

Creamed chicken and celery on toast points
Carrot sticks
Chilled stewed rhubarb

Browned corned beef hash
Tossed green salad
Cinnamon-Pear Mold

Toasted peanut butter—chopped bacon sandwiches
Fruit-salad Platter
Citrus-Cream Dressing

12 WELL-BALANCED DINNERS

Broiled Grapefruit Halves
Casserole of beef and mushrooms
Fluffy rice   Parsleyed carrots
Vanilla ice cream with maple syrup

Oven-fried Chicken
Sweet-potato Puffs   Green Beans
Raw relish platter
Strawberries and cream

Roast lamb
Minted potatoes
Asparagus
Crisp raw relishes
Fresh Berry Charlotte

Minute steaks
Baked Potatoes
Buttered onions
Pickled beets
Apricot upside-down cake

Pot roast of beef
Sour Cream—Horseradish Sauce
Riced potatoes
Baked zucchini
Cranberry Whip

Oyster stew with crackers
Chef's Salad with diced ham
Gingerbread with *Lemon Sauce*

Chilled vegetable juice
Sautéed calf liver
Baked Potatoes   String beans
Melon balls   Brown-edge cookies

Salmon steaks with *Tartar Sauce*
Au Gratin Potatoes
Head lettuce with *Roquefort Dressing*
Key-lime Sponge

Chili Con Carne
Cornbread sticks
Tossed green salad
Banana-cream pie

Breaded pork chops
Lyonnaise potatoes
Sweet-and-Sour Red Cabbage
Lemon sherbet

Curry of lamb
Rice   Pineapple rings
Green peas with almonds
Ice Cream   Coffee

Tomato juice
Swiss steak with mushroom gravy
Mashed Potatoes   Brussels sprouts
Orange-Brittle Ambrosia

MAKING JAMS AND JELLIES

Do conserve the fruits of summer in jams and jellies—to serve on breakfast toast, with dinner meat, on snack-time crackers.

Unlike canning, which is generally done speedily at the peak of the crop and in sizable quantities, making jams and jellies is best in small batches throughout the season. Or, if unsweetened fruit is first frozen, they can be made at any convenient time during the year. Blueberries, gooseberries, saskatoons, currants, peaches, plums and rhubarb are good choices for freezer storage preliminary to being made into jam. Measure fruit into cartons, and mark amounts on lids. To use, defrost almost completely; then follow any desired recipe for jams or jellies.

This type of preserving is really easy.

Jams are made by cooking together crushed or chopped fruits and sugar until thickened or set. Some jams are best with the liquid part still fluid; others have their greatest appeal when firm, as is jelly.

Conserves are a variation of jam, generally combining several fruits, including such dried varieties as raisins. Unsalted nuts are frequently added.

Marmalade is the specific term for jam made with thinly sliced citrus fruit with rind (oranges, grapefruit, lemons, limes, kumquats, tangerines or any mixture of them), though some call jam made with any type of fresh fruit prepared in thin slices "marmalade." When citrus fruit with rind is combined with other types of fruit, the product is called either "conserve" or "marmalade."

Jellies are made from the juice extracted from prepared fruit. Juice is boiled with sugar and then chilled to set or "jell."

All jellies must be set so that they retain their shapes when turned out for serving. They should be clear and quivery and should cut easily with a spoon, giving a smooth, clean edge.

For perfectly set jellies and for firm jams, there are 3 essentials: pectin, fruit acid and sugar, all in proper proportion to one another. With fruits containing enough natural pectin and fruit acid, a set jam or jelly can be produced simply by boiling fruit with sugar until mixture reaches jelling point. When fruit is deficient in either pectin or acid, jelling cannot be achieved without adding correct quantities of either.

Pectin

Pectin is a substance in fruits that, when combined with fruit acid and sugar and heated, causes juice to set. It is found in generous amounts in the fruits long known to housewives as good for jellying—apples, sour blackberries, crab apples, cranberries, currants, gooseberries, grapes, plums and citrus fruits (especially their rinds). Pectin content is highest when fruit is underripe; it decreases as fruit ripens. The fruits naturally low in pectin include apricots, cherries, peaches, raspberries and strawberries, plus most other varieties when they reach an overripe state.

A fruit lacking in pectin is often combined with another that has good pectin content. For example, raspberry juice, poor by itself, makes excellent jelly when teamed with red currant juice. Don't use fresh pineapple at all.

Commercial pectin (usually processed from underripe apples) can be combined with virtually any fruit for quickly made jellies or jams. For best results, always use quantities and times outlined by manufacturer. One advantage of commercial pectin is that fruits can be used at their full ripeness, when flavor is best but natural pectin receding.

Fruit Acids and Sugar

The acids naturally present in fruits enhance flavor and setting quality for jams and so forth. When preparing such low-acid fruits as peaches and sweet blackberries, add 1 tablespoon lemon juice to each cup fruit juice, or follow exact proportions specified in recipe.

Make a point of measuring or weighing sugar carefully. To hasten dissolving, heat sugar in shallow pan in 250°F. oven 15 minutes.

Equipment

Equipment that permits you to cook in quantities calling for no more than 5 cups fruit or juice at a time is best. In specific recipes, do not double amounts.

An electric blender crushes fruits in seconds, but if you don't have one, a potato masher can be used. For some jams, fruit can be put through food chopper.

Use wide kettle, which will allow mixture to boil freely and also will allow quick evaporation.

Use standard measuring equipment, and be accurate with measurements.

A long-handled ladle with a small bowl is useful for filling jars. Leave 1/4-inch space at tops of jars.

Sterilize all jars. Wash in sudsy water, and rinse well. Stand jars upside down in kettle containing 2 inches clean water. Bring to boil, drain and keep jars in 275°F. oven until required for filling. Or sterilize in dishwasher. If you are using cup for pouring, sterilize it along with the jars. If using ladle, scald it.

Always use fresh paraffin for sealing. Heat in small container placed in or over hot water. As paraffin is highly inflammable, *never heat over open flame or electric element.*

Cover jams and jellies while hot with 1/8-inch layer of hot paraffin. Avoid thick layer of wax, as it causes jams and jellies to break and weep.

Label and date all jars. Store jams and jellies in cool, dark dry place. Apartment dwellers will find that the coolest shelves are at the bottom of the cupboard.

Easy Methods

No-cook Method. Simply crush fruit, add sugar and pectin, pack in handy containers and store in freezer, in frozen-food section of your refrigera-

tor or on refrigerator shelves. Jams and jellies keep perfectly up to 3 months on refrigerator shelves, up to 8 months in freezer.

Quick-cook Method. Boil fruit for very few minutes before pouring into sterilized jars, sealing with paraffin, capping and storing in any cool spot in the home.

Foolproof Method. Bring jams and jellies to specified temperatures (using candy or deep-frying thermometer) during cooking, resulting in perfect consistency every time.

Choose your favorite fruit or berries, and pick a recipe that suits your taste.

To Test Jams and Jellies

For jam in which commercial pectin is not used, lift wooden spoonful of boiling mixture into saucer, and place in freezer until cold; meanwhile remove jam from heat. Within 2–3 minutes, cooled sample should set as will finished jam. If it is not sufficiently thick, further cooking of jam is necessary.

For jelly in which commercial pectin is not used, lift wooden spoonful of boiling mixture, and pour slowly back into kettle. If mixture separates at edge of spoon into *two* slow-moving clots or drips, it is ready for bottling (the saucer test may be used for jelly too).

No-cook Red Cherry Jam

      2 1/2 cups crushed pitted cherries
          4 cups sugar
          2 tablespoons lemon juice
          1 (1 3/4-ounce) package powdered pectin
        3/4 cup water

Measure cherries into bowl. Stir in sugar and lemon juice. Let stand 20 minutes, stirring occasionally. Boil pectin and water together 1 minute, and remove from heat. Stir in fruit mixture, and continue stirring 2 minutes. Ladle into 6–8 jelly glasses or freezer cartons. Let stand at room temperature 24 hours or overnight; then cover with waxed paper and metal or cardboard lids. Store in freezer or refrigerator. Makes 6–8 jelly glasses.

VARIATION:

* *No-cook Blueberry Jam*: Use 3 cups crushed blueberries, 5 cups sugar, 1/4 cup lemon juice and 1 package powdered pectin boiled with 1 cup water.

Quick-cook Red Currant Jelly

          3 quarts fully ripe red currants
          1 cup water
          6 cups sugar
             Juice of 1 lemon
        1/2 (6-ounce) bottle liquid pectin

Wash and stem currants. Crush in blender, in fruit press or with stainless potato masher. Add water, and cover. Simmer about 8 minutes. Pour into jelly bag, and squeeze out juice with back of wooden spoon. (The ready-made type jelly bag, standing on metal supports, is very convenient. Otherwise make bag of cotton flannel or several layers of cheesecloth; tie securely at top after filling.) For clearer jelly, let jelly bag drip overnight in cool place. Measure 4 cups juice into saucepan (if necessary, make up amount with water). Stir in sugar and lemon juice. Bring to full rolling boil, stirring constantly. Add pec-

tin, and boil hard 1 minute. Remove from heat, and skim. Pour into 8–10 sterilized jelly glasses or jam jars. Seal with paraffin immediately. When cool, store in cool place.

Note: If you have more than 4 cups juice, add remainder to cooling summer drinks.

Foolproof Grape Jelly

         10 cups (about 4 pounds) Concord grapes, 1/2
                underripe and 1/2 ripe
        1/2 cup water
      3 1/2 cups sugar

Crush grapes with stainless-steel potato masher in large saucepan, and add water. Cover, and simmer about 10 minutes. Pour into moistened jelly bag, and strain juice into glass bowl in cool place overnight; then strain through cheesecloth to remove tartrate crystals (which sometimes cause grape jelly to form sugar crystals around top). Measure 5 cups juice into saucepan, and add sugar. Stir and cook to boiling point. Insert candy or fat thermometer, and stir until temperature reaches 218°F., or use the "pour test" for jelly. Remove from heat. Stir and skim; then pour into 6–8 sterilized jelly glasses. Seal at once with paraffin.

No-cook Red Currant Jelly

          2 quarts red currants
          5 cups fine white sugar
        1/4 cup lemon juice
          1 (1 3/4-ounce) package powdered pectin
        3/4 cup water

Crush currants in blender for speed. Otherwise a fine sieve works well. Strain, and measure 3 cups juice into bowl; mix in sugar and lemon juice. Let stand 20 minutes, stirring occasionally. Boil pectin and water together 1 minute; remove from heat, and stir in fruit-juice mixture. Stir 2 minutes, and pour into 6–8 jelly glasses, jam jars or freezer cartons. Leave at room temperature 24 hours. Cover with waxed paper and metal or cardboard lids. Store in freezer or refrigerator.

Note: To use pulp, add 2 cups water to remaining currant pulp, and bring to boil. Simmer 5 minutes, and strain. Add sugar to sweeten. Bring again to boil, and pour into screw-top jars. Keep refrigerated, and use in combination with soda water or other carbonated beverages for cool drinks.

Crab Apple Jelly

          4 pounds crab apples
          2 cups cold water
             Sugar

Wash crab apples, remove stems and blossom ends and cut into halves. Put into kettle, and add only enough cold water to be visible under top layer of fruit. Bring to boil, and boil until apples are completely soft, 20—25 minutes. Put hot contents of kettle into moistened jelly bag. Allow juice to drip through, for several hours, into large container underneath. For sparkling, clear jelly, do not squeeze bag. Measure strained juice, and heat to boiling. Measure correct amount granulated sugar, allowing 1 cup per 1 cup juice. Add sugar to boiling juice, and continue rapid boiling until jelly stage is reached (see saucer and pouring tests at beginning of section). Remove from stove, and let stand 30 seconds. Skim off scum, and pour the jelly into hot sterilized glasses. Let cool slightly. Seal.

Note: With tart apples or crab apples, a second extraction from pulp may be made. Measure pulp, add equal amount water and cook slowly for 15—20 minutes; proceed as with first batch of juice. If less-clear jelly is acceptable, press bag with 2 wooden spoons, or squeeze and twist; flavor will still be good, but jelly will be slightly cloudy. For spiced jelly, add cinnamon stick and a few whole cloves, tied loosely in cheesecloth bag, to boiling juice.

Quick-cook Cherry-Gooseberry Conserve

    2 cups pitted cherries
    2 cups gooseberries
    7 cups sugar
    1/2 (6-ounce) bottle liquid pectin
    1 cup shredded almonds

Put fruit through mincer, or blend 2 minutes. Combine sugar and fruit in deep saucepan, and stir until sugar is dissolved. Heat to full rolling boil, and boil 1 minute. Remove from heat, stir in pectin, skim and stir 1 minute. Mix in almonds. Pour into jars immediately, and seal with hot paraffin.

Quick Orange-juice Jelly

    3/4 cup (6-ounce can) frozen orange juice
    1 (1 3/4-ounce) package powdered pectin
    2 cups water
    3 1/2 cups sugar

Thaw orange juice. Place pectin crystals and water in deep saucepan, and mix well. Place over high heat, and bring to full rolling boil. Boil 1 minute, stirring constantly. Reduce heat to low; then add thawed orange-juice concentrate and sugar. Stir until sugar is completely dissolved. Do not boil. Remove from heat, and skim if necessary. Pour into 6 or 7 sterilized jelly glasses, and cover with hot paraffin.

Port Wine Jelly

    3 cups sugar
    2 cups port wine
    1/2 (6-ounce) bottle liquid pectin

In the top of a double boiler, over rapidly boiling water, combine sugar and port wine. Mix well, and stir until dissolved—approximately 2 minutes. Remove from heat. Stir in liquid fruit pectin immediately, mixing well. Skim off any foam. Pour into hot, sterilized jars. Seal with melted paraffin. Makes 4 cups.

Crème de Menthe Jelly

    2 1/2 cups sugar
    1 cup crème de menthe liqueur (white or green)
    1 cup water
    1/2 (6-ounce) bottle liquid pectin
      Mint sprigs

In the top of a double boiler, over rapidly boiling water, combine sugar, crème de menthe liqueur and water. Stir until sugar is dissolved—approximately 2 minutes. Remove from heat; stir in liquid fruit pectin. Skim off foam if necessary. Place 1 sprig of mint, which has been plunged in boiling water for 1 minute, in each of the hot, sterilized jars. Pour jelly into jars. Seal with melted paraffin. Makes 4 cups.

Burgundy Wine Jelly

    6 cups sugar
    4 cups Burgundy
    1 (6-ounce) bottle liquid fruit pectin

In the top of a double boiler, over rapidly boiling water, combine sugar and Burgundy. Mix well, and stir until dissolved. Remove from heat. Stir in liquid fruit pectin immediately, mixing well. Skim off any foam. Pour immediately into hot, sterilized jars. Seal with melted paraffin. Makes 8 cups.

Ginger-Beet Jelly

    3 cups juice drained from canned beets
    1/4 cup fresh lemon juice
    1 (1 3/4-ounce) package powdered pectin
    4 cups sugar
    1 teaspoon ground ginger

In a large saucepan combine juice from beets, lemon juice and powdered pectin. Stir over high heat until the mixture boils hard. Stir in sugar. Bring to a full rolling boil; boil hard for 1 minute, stirring constantly. Remove from heat; skim off any foam. Stir in ginger, and pour immediately into hot, sterilized jars. Seal at once with melted paraffin. Makes 5 cups.

Quick-cook Plum Jam

    5 cups crushed yellow plums, 1/2 ripe and sweet,
      1/2 sour
    1/2 cup water
    7 cups sugar
    1/2 (6-ounce) bottle pectin

Cut plums from stones; crush in blender, or chop fine. Measure fruit into saucepan, and add water. Cover, and simmer 5 minutes, stirring occasionally. Add sugar, and bring to full rolling boil. Boil 1 minute, stirring constantly. Remove from heat, and add pectin. Stir and skim 2—3 minutes. Cool slightly, and ladle into 8—10 sterilized jam or jelly glasses. Seal at once with paraffin. When cold, store in cool place.

Ripe Cucumber Marmalade

    2 cups prepared ripe cucumbers
    4 cups sugar
  1/3 cup lemon juice
    2 tablespoons grated lemon rind
  1/2 (6-ounce) bottle liquid pectin

You will need 1 1/2—2 pounds of fully ripe yellow cucumbers. Peel, cut flesh in strips and discard all seeds. Chop cucumber very fine, or put through grinder. Measure 2 cups into large saucepan. Add next 3 ingredients, and mix well. Bring to full rolling boil, and boil hard 1 minute, stirring constantly. Remove pan from heat, and stir in pectin. Skim. Cool slightly; then ladle into jelly jars. Cover with melted paraffin. Makes about 6 (6-ounce) glasses.

Grape Conserve

    1 (6-quart) basket Concord grapes
      Sugar
    1 orange (grated rind and juice)
    1 lemon (grated rind and juice)
  1/2 pound broken walnuts

Wash grapes, and remove stems. Squeeze pulp and grape juice into saucepan. Save skins. Cover saucepan, and simmer about 10 minutes or until seeds float free. Remove seeds by pressing mixture through sieve or fruit press. Mix pulp and skins together, and measure by cups into saucepan. Add equal amount of sugar; stir, bring to boil and continue boiling 10 minutes. Add rind and juice of orange and lemon and nuts. Boil 5 minutes; then skim. Stir constantly while mixture cools slightly. Ladle into jelly glasses, and cover with melted paraffin. Makes 24 small jars.

Spiced Pickled Fruits

     1 pound dried prunes
     2 cups firm sweet or Montmorency cherries
     7 cups granulated sugar
     4 cups cider vinegar
     3 cups water
     4 (3-inch) sticks cinnamon
     1 tablespoon whole cloves
     1 tablespoon allspice
 12–16 firm peaches, peeled, halved and pitted

Soak prunes in cold water several hours, and drain; pick over cherries, and wash. Combine next 3 ingredients in large kettle; tie spices in cheesecloth bag, and add. Bring to boil, and simmer 5 minutes. Add all fruit to kettle; simmer gently 15 minutes. Remove from heat, cover ket-

tle and let stand overnight. Next morning bring to boil; remove peaches carefully, and pack in hot sterilized jars; add prunes and cherries to fill spaces around peaches. Boil syrup hard 20 minutes; discard spice bag, and pour liquid into jars, covering fruit completely. Seal. Store in cool dry place.

Peach-Raspberry Jam

    1 (15-ounce) package frozen raspberries
    2 pounds (approximately) ripe peaches
    6 cups sugar
  1/4 cup lemon juice
  1/2 (6-ounce) bottle liquid pectin

Thaw berries according to package directions. Peel, pit and crush peaches. Measure thawed berries, and add enough crushed peaches to make 4 cups fruit. Place in kettle; add sugar and lemon juice, mixing thoroughly. Bring to full rolling boil over high heat, and boil hard 1 minute, stirring constantly. Remove from heat, and add pectin, stirring vigorously. Stir and skim alternately about 5 minutes. Ladle quickly into hot sterilized glasses; cover with melted paraffin. Makes about 10 medium jars.

Strawberry Jam

    3 pints mixed ripe and underripe strawberries
    4 cups sugar
    2 tablespoons lemon juice

Crush fruit, using blender, food press or stainless-steel potato masher. Measure 4 cups into large saucepan, and stir in sugar and lemon juice. Bring to boil, stirring constantly. Continue stirring and boiling until thick, about 15 minutes. Remove from heat, and skim and stir alternately 3—4 minutes. Ladle into hot jelly glasses, and cover with melted paraffin immediately. Makes about 6 (6-ounce) jars.

Red Tomato Preserves

   12 pounds red tomatoes
    6 pounds granulated sugar
    1 (15-ounce) can crushed pineapple
    3 oranges (put through grinder)

Scald tomatoes, and peel. Cut up fine. Place all ingredients in preserving kettle, and simmer gently 2 1/2 hours or until thick. Pour into sterilized jars.

Note: A delicious soft marmalade for September, when local tomatoes are best.

Tomato Marmalade

    4 oranges
    2 lemons
  1/2 cup cold water
    8 tomatoes
      Scalding water
      Sugar

Peel oranges and lemons. Cut away white pith, and discard. Cut peel in thin strips; cover with 1/2 cup water, and bring to boil. Simmer 15 minutes; drain. Dip tomatoes in scalding water, and peel. Halve peeled oranges and lemons, and discard pits. Mince fruit pulp and tomatoes together. Add cooked peel, minced fruit pulp and tomatoes; cover, and simmer about 20 minutes. Boil uncovered 15 minutes. Measure, and add equal amount of sugar. Simmer uncovered, stirring occasionally, until ready to jell (use drip test described at beginning of section). Ladle into sterilized jars; cover with melted paraffin.

Apricot-Pineapple Conserve

        3 oranges
        1 fresh pineapple, peeled and cut in 1/4-inch dice
            (3 cups)
  1 1/4 cups water
        1 (6-ounce) bottle maraschino cherries and juice
    1/2 pound blanched almonds, halved
        6 cups chopped unpeeled apricots
        3 cups sugar

Juice oranges, and grind peel. Mix pineapple, orange juice, rind, water and cherry juice in saucepan. Cover, and simmer until pineapple and rind are tender, about 15 minutes. Add apricots and sugar. Bring to boil, stirring occasionally. Insert candy or fat thermometer, and cook, stirring until it registers 216°F., about 20 minutes; or use saucer test. Add cherries and almonds. Simmer 5 minutes. Skim, and ladle into 10—12 sterilized jelly glasses or jam jars. Cool slightly, and seal with paraffin.

Note: Heat mixture to 219°—220°F. for firm jam, 216°—217°F. for softer texture. Note temperature for consistency you like best for another year.

Ginger-Rhubarb-Pineapple Conserve

        8 cups rhubarb, cut in 3/4-inch pieces
        2 cups diced fresh pineapple, cut in 1/4-inch bits
            Grated rind and juice of 1 orange
        4 cups sugar
        2 ounces candied ginger, finely chopped

Mix the first 3 ingredients in a deep heavy saucepan, and place over low heat. Cook until juice starts flowing; then bring to a boil, and boil uncovered 15 minutes, stirring to prevent sticking. Stir in sugar, and cook 15 minutes. Add ginger, and cook to the jam stage, about 10 minutes longer. Ladle into sterilized jars and, when cooled slightly, seal with melted paraffin. Makes about 6 cups.

Note: Add 1/4 cup water to rhubarb mixture before cooking if rhubarb is not very juicy. Those who like ginger can double the quantity.

Orange-Lemon-Grapefruit Marmalade

        1 thin-skinned grapefruit
        2 thin-skinned navel oranges
        2 thin-skinned lemons
            Water
            Sugar

Wash the fruit and slice paper-thin, discarding white core and seeds. Cut the slivered fruit into pieces about 1 1/2 inches long. To save as much juice as possible, set the slicing board on a tray. Measure sliced fruit and juice. Add 3 cups water for each cup of the fruit and juice mixture. Let stand 24 hours; then bring to a boil, and boil hard, uncovered, about 25 minutes. Let stand overnight, and boil uncovered 15 minutes. Measure the mixture, and for each cup add 3/4 cup sugar. Bring to a boil, and stir until jelly point is reached. Skim, and ladle into hot sterilized jars. Seal with paraffin. Makes about 8 jars.

Spicy Green Tomato Marmalade

        10 whole medium-size green tomatoes
    3 1/2 cups sugar
            Grated rind of 1 orange
            Grated rind of 1 lemon
    1/3 cup lemon juice
        1 teaspoon ground ginger
        1 teaspoon ground cinnamon

Stem the tomatoes, cut in quarters and press through a mincer, using the coarse blade. Stir in sugar, orange and lemon rind, and let stand overnight. Bring to a boil, and simmer, uncovered, for about 30 minutes. Add lemon juice and spices, and cook at a full boil until jam stage, stirring occasionally to prevent sticking. Ladle into sterilized jars, and seal with paraffin. Makes about 6 cups.

Note: Increase spice if you like a spicier mixture, and omit if you want just a fruity flavor.

PICKLING

A wide variety of vegetables and fruits is suitable for pickling. Frequently items that are less than perfect for canning or freezing find their way into pickle jars. But in this area, as in others, the fresher the raw product, the better the result. Sound, firm vegetables and slightly underripe fruits are preferable for all pickles, with the exception of tomato ketchup, chili sauce and butters, in which the necessary boiling down plus liberal addition of seasonings may justify the use of substandard raw products.

Salt is used either for pre-preparation of ingredients or in sauce or vinegar mixtures for finishing. Coarse or pickling salt is the best choice. Iodized salt may be used; however, most packaged salt contains a free-flowing conditioner that can cause cloudiness in pickles packed in brine or syrups, such as pickled onions and dill pickles. Iodized salt may be used for sauce-type pickles, such as chili sauce, chutney and relish.

In making brine for soaking vegetables, always follow proportions exactly. If too little salt is used, pickles may become soft, with a slimy tendency; too much salt may shrivel and toughen pickles. In addition to keeping vegetables firm throughout processing and storage, the soaking procedure reduces possible bitterness.

Vinegars of high quality and strength are the best choice for fine pickling results. Remember that vinegars are stronger today than they were 20 years ago; in spite of the charm of grandmother's pickle recipes, it is better to follow up-to-date proportions and procedures and to use the exact amounts of vinegar called for.

There are 4 basic types of vinegar on the market for pickling purposes. Cider vinegar is frequently specified in fruit pickles because of its superior flavor. White vinegar is often preferred when a light color is important, as in pickling onions, cauliflower and other light-colored vegetables and fruits. Blended vinegar, a mixture of cider and white, is a good all-purpose vinegar for pickle-making. Malt vinegar, the darkest and strongest of the 4, is sometimes used for its flavor.

It is unwise to dilute vinegar for a recipe, as weakening the solution may cause stored pickles to turn soft or spoil.

Sugar in pickle recipes is generally of the standard white type, although brown may occasionally be specified for added flavor.

Spices should be purchased in fresh supply for pickling. Once opened, packaged spices can quickly lose their effectiveness.

Whole spices are frequently required in recipes. They give excellent flavor and have the advantage of not darkening the mixture as ground spices often do. For convenience, tie stick cinnamon, whole nutmeg, allspice berries, and so forth in a little cheesecloth bag loosely enough so that boiling syrup completely penetrates. Remove and discard bag and its contents before bottling pickles.

Follow spicing directions carefully. When ground spices are called for, use exact level measurements. Overspicing is one of the commonest errors in home-pickling. Always be cautious with such strong flavors as allspice, cloves, and cayenne. Add only at point specified in recipe; do not boil too long in vinegar, or flavor may be overpowering, even bitter, and pickles will darken.

Equipment for Pickling

No elaborate utensils are needed. The kitchen's usual measuring equipment and mixing bowls, a large saucepan or preserving kettle of aluminum, unchipped enamel or stainless steel, a long-handled spoon, an earthenware crock for brining if necessary and containers for bottling and storing are the items you will require.

Sealers of the type used for canned fruits are generally preferred for storage. Certain thick relishes such as *Mustard Pickles* can be stored in sterilized small glass jars and covered with hot paraffin, but this method is not so satisfactory as sealing in standard airtight containers. Sterilizing of jars is a worthwhile precaution, although it is true that pickles containing high proportions of vinegar and sugar will generally keep acceptably in well-washed and dried jars. Earthenware crocks are seldom employed for storage in the modern household because their use entails a more complicated operation and because a continuously cool atmosphere is hard to ensure. In crock storage the pickles are left in a cool place, and they should be completely covered with their own liquid to prevent spoilage. A plate or other cover that fits inside the crock should be placed over pickles and weighted down to keep them immersed. The only appropriate storage place is the refrigerator.

Small Batches in Variety

Pickles and relishes can be highly individual in character and in preparation; it is therefore better to make half-a-dozen kinds of pickles in small batches than a monotonous overlarge quantity of 1 kind.

Sweet Pickled Silver-skins

> 2 quarts silver-skin onions
> 1/2 cup salt
> 1 quart boiling water
> 1 green pepper
> 1 sweet red pepper
> 2 tablespoons salt
> 4 cups white-wine vinegar
> 1 cup sugar
> 2 sticks cinnamon, broken
> 1 piece gingerroot or a few chili peppers

Pour boiling water over onions, and leave 2–3 minutes to soften skins. Drain, and cool under cold water; then peel. Sprinkle 1/2 cup salt over onions, and add the boiling water. Let stand overnight; then drain, and rinse to remove salt. Sliver the green and red pepper into thin strips, and sprinkle with 2 tablespoons salt. Leave 1/2 hour; then rinse with cold water. Mix remaining ingredients together in a deep saucepan, and boil 3–5 minutes. Remove spices, and add the onions and slivered peppers. Bring just to a boil, stirring occasionally. Watch the edge of the pan; when bubbles break around the edge, remove from heat. Pack onions in sealers, and cover with boiling syrup. Seal. Makes about 4 pints.

Sour Silver-skin Onions

Peel skins from onions. Soak 48 hours in strong salt water (1 tablespoon salt to 1 quart water). Drain, and pack in clean jars. Fill jars with boiling white vinegar, and seal according to manufacturer's directions. Leave in a cool place a month or 2 before using.

Dark Hot Chili Sauce

> 18 large ripe tomatoes
> 4 green peppers
> 2 large onions
> 2 cups cider vinegar
> 1/2 cup brown sugar, firmly packed
> 2 tablespoons salt
> 2 tablespoons ginger
> 2 tablespoons cinnamon
> 1 tablespoon allspice
> 1 tablespoon nutmeg

Peel and cut tomatoes coarsely. Chop peppers, and dice onions. Combine vegetables with remaining ingredients, and bring to boil. Simmer uncovered about 1 hour, stirring occasionally, especially as mixture thickens. Ladle into sterilized jars, and seal. Makes 6 pints.

Note: If tomatoes are overripe or juicy, drain off some juice before cooking. Otherwise simmering time will have to be considerably extended before sauce reaches right thickness. You can use drained juice in jellied salads, gravies and the like.

Rosy Watermelon-rind Pickle

> 1 large watermelon
> 1/4 cup salt
> 3 quarts cold water
> 2 trays ice cubes
> 3 cups white vinegar
> 1 cup water
> 7 cups sugar
> 2 teaspoons whole cloves
> 4 sticks cinnamon, broken
> 2 pieces gingerroot

Slice the melon in quarters, and remove the pink pulp (see note). Cut off the hard green skin and all but a thin layer of pink pulp. Then dice in 1 1/2-inch squares. Sprinkle with salt, and add cold water and ice cubes. Drain, rinse and drain again. Drop cubes into boiling water, and cook until just tender when tested with a skewer. Drain well. Mix the next 3 ingredients together in a large kettle, and drop in the spices tied in a cheesecloth bag. Tint with rose food coloring. Bring to a boil, and boil 5—8 minutes. Add the rind, and cook gently, stirring occasionally, until transparent. Remove the bag, and let stand overnight. Next morning drain the syrup into a kettle, and boil 5 minutes. Pour over the rind, and let stand overnight. Next morning bring to a boil, and ladle into hot sterilized jars. Seal. Makes about 6 pints.

Uses for Leftover Watermelon: Scoop out melon balls, or dice the pink pulp for freezing. Remove the seeds, and pack in covered plastic or specially treated pressed paper cartons. Flavor cold thin or medium sugar syrup with a little lemon juice, and pour over the melon, leaving a 1/2-inch headspace. Crumple pieces of waxed paper, and press on top of fruit to fill the air space; then cover, and chill in the refrigerator. Freeze. You may prefer to cut out pink part for eating; then scrape out remaining pulp and juice. Discard seeds, and swish in a blender. Add chilled fruit juice or fruit-flavored carbonated beverage for a refreshing punch.

Old-fashioned Fruit Sauce

> 4 pounds (about 16) ripe red tomatoes
> 6 peaches
> 6 pears
> 6 apples
> 6 large onions
> 2–3 sweet red peppers
> 6 stalks of celery
> 4 cups vinegar
> 4 cups brown sugar, firmly packed, or white sugar
> 2 tablespoons salt
> 3 ounces mixed pickling spice, tied in a bag

Peel and chop the tomatoes and peaches. Core and chop pears and apples without peeling. Dice onions, peppers and celery. Mix together in a large kettle with remaining ingredients. Simmer uncovered until thick, stirring often to prevent sticking. Cooking time will depend on the juiciness of the fruits, but allow about 1 1/2–2 hours. Discard the bag. Ladle into hot sterilized jars, and seal. Makes about 8 (16-ounce) jars.

Dill Pickles

> 4 pounds small pickling cucumbers
> Sprigs of fresh dill
> Cloves fresh garlic or dry minced garlic (optional)
> 1/2 cup salt
> 3 cups white vinegar
> 3 cups water

Wash freshly picked firm cucumbers of uniform size, scrubbing them if necessary to remove any soil. Cover with ice-cold water, and leave overnight; then drain. Drop 1/2 clove of garlic or 1/2 teaspoon minced garlic in each clean sealer, and add a sprig of dill. Pack in the cucumbers, and place more dill sprigs on top. Bring salt, vinegar and water to a boil; when salt is dissolved, pour the boiling liquid over each jar of pickles. Seal, and store for 4–6 weeks in a cool place before using. Makes about 7 pints.

Note: If you prefer to pack quart jars, add another sprig of dill to each after jars are half-filled with cucumbers. Dill pickles may be used within 2 weeks if you process the jars in a boiling-water bath, 10 minutes for pints, 15–20 minutes for quarts.

Apple Chutney

        3 pounds (approximately 8 medium) tart cooking
            apples
        4 cups cider vinegar
        3 cups brown sugar, firmly packed
      4–5 large chopped onions
        1 pound sultana raisins
        6 chili peppers, crumbled
      1/4 pound chopped preserved ginger or 3 tablespoons
            ground ginger
        2 tablespoons salt
        1 tablespoon mustard seed
      1–2 crushed garlic cloves

Peel and dice apples into large heavy saucepan (5–6-quart size). Add remaining ingredients, and bring to boil. Cover, and turn heat low. Let mixture simmer 1 hour. Uncover, and continue cooking until thickened, stirring occasionally to prevent sticking. The time will depend on consistency you prefer; a thickish mixture will require about 3 hours. Ladle into hot sterilized preserving jars, and seal immediately; or ladle into jelly jars, and seal with melted paraffin. Makes about 4 pints or 9–10 (8-ounce) glasses.

Note: Taste mixture halfway through cooking, and if you like sweeter chutney, add 1 cup brown sugar.

Mustard Pickles

      6–7 large cucumbers
        3 cauliflowers
        2 quarts silver-skin onions
        3 quarts cold water
      3/4 cup salt
        3 sweet red peppers, diced
      4–5 cups brown sugar, firmly packed
        1 cup flour
      1/2 cup dry mustard
        1 tablespoon turmeric
        1 tablespoon salt
        1 tablespoon celery seed
      8–9 cups cider or white vinegar

Dice cucumbers into 1-inch cubes without peeling to make 2 quarts, and cut cauliflowers into small flowerets. Peel onions. Mix all together, and cover with cold water. Sprinkle with 3/4 cup salt, stir well and leave overnight. In morning scald by bringing to boil in same brine. Drain, and rinse. Add red peppers. Make sauce by mixing sugar, flour, mustard, turmeric, 1 tablespoon salt and celery seed until thoroughly blended. Add vinegar very gradually, stirring until smooth after each addition. Place over low heat, and bring to boil, stirring constantly as mixture thickens. Simmer 2–3 minutes to ensure complete cooking of flour. Drain any accumulated moisture off scalded vegetables; combine with mustard sauce. Stir, and reheat thoroughly. Ladle into sterilized jars, and seal. Makes 12–14 pints.

Note: For lighter yellow color, use 4 1/2 cups white sugar in place of brown.

4-Fruit Chutney

        3 pounds (about 10) tart apples
    1 1/2 pounds (about 6 large) peeled onions
        1 pound (about 4 large) carrots, scraped
        2 oranges
        1 lemon
        4 cups vinegar
        4 ounces crystallized ginger
      1–2 cloves garlic
      3–4 chili peppers, crumbled, or 3 hot pickled banana
            peppers
        4 cups brown sugar, firmly packed
    1 1/2 cups seedless raisins
        2 tablespoons salt
      1/2 teaspoon cinnamon
      1/2 teaspoon allspice
      1/2 teaspoon cloves

Quarter apples, onions, carrots, oranges and lemon, and grind with coarse blade of food chopper; or use blender, grinding small quantities at a time, adding some of vinegar with fruit and vegetable quarters. Grind or chop ginger and garlic. Grind hot peppers if you use them in place of chili peppers. Mix all ingredients in large saucepan, and bring to boil. Simmer until mixture thickens, stirring occasionally to prevent sticking, about 1–1 1/2 hours. Ladle into sterilized jars, and seal. Makes 10–12 (8-ounce) jars.

Bread-and-Butter Pickles

        1 (6-quart) basket small young cucumbers (dill size)
        8 small white onions
        3 green peppers
        2 sweet red peppers
        1 cup table salt
        2 quarts water
        8 cups blended vinegar
    3 1/2–4 cups white sugar
        1 tablespoon turmeric
        2 tablespoons mustard seed
        1 tablespoon celery seed
        1 teaspoon allspice berries (optional)

Wash and slice cucumbers 1/8–1/4 inch thick. Peel and slice onions the same thickness as cucumbers. Remove seeds from peppers, and cut into strips. Boil salt and water together, and cool. Pour over vegetables, and let stand overnight. Next morning drain well. Measure remaining ingredients into a large saucepan, and bring to a boil. Add drained vegetables, and stir. Heat through thoroughly without cooking; then pack immediately into hot sterilized jars, and seal. Makes 6–7 quarts.

Pickled Seckel Pears

        8 pounds (6 quarts) Seckel pears
        3 quarts boiling water
       10 sticks cinnamon
        2 tablespoons whole cloves
        2 tablespoons whole allspice
        8 cups sugar
        1 quart cider vinegar
        1 quart water

Seckel pears are small, hard and rather tough-skinned. Rub off blossom ends, but leave stems and skins intact. Cover with boiling water; simmer 10 minutes, and drain. Tie spices in bag, and add to sugar, vinegar and 1 quart water. Stir, and bring to boil. Simmer 5 minutes. Drain accumulated moisture from pears; pour hot syrup over them, bring to simmer and cook 15 minutes. Let stand overnight. In morning, drain, discarding spice bag. Pack pears in sterilized jars, reheat syrup, and fill jars with it. Seal. Makes about 8 pints.

VARIATION:

* *Pickled Crab Apples*: Use 8 pounds crab apples in place of pears. Do not parboil, but add raw to hot vinegar syrup. If deeper tone is desired, add a little red vegetable coloring to syrup before pouring over apples in jars.

Corn Relish

  3 cups raw kernel corn, cut from cobs
  2 cups diced onion
  2 cups diced celery
  1 cup diced green pepper
  1 cup diced red pepper
  2 cucumbers, chopped
  4 firm red tomatoes, diced
  4 teaspoons salt
  2 tablespoons dry mustard
  1 1/2 teaspoons turmeric
  3 cups vinegar
  1 3/4 cups light brown sugar, firmly packed

Mix all ingredients together in a large saucepan, and simmer without a cover until thickened, about 1 hour. Stir frequently to prevent sticking. Ladle into sterilized jars, and seal. Makes 4–5 pints.

Chili Sauce

  24 large ripe tomatoes
  6 large onions, peeled and diced
  3 sweet red peppers, diced
  1 hot red pepper, diced
  6 large outside stalks of celery, diced
  2 tablespoons salt
  3 1/2 cups cider or blended vinegar
  1 1/2 cups white or brown sugar
  3/4 cup mixed pickling spice, tied in a bag

Blanch and peel tomatoes. Cut into pieces, and add remaining ingredients. Bring to a boil; then simmer, uncovered, on medium heat until quite thick, 2–3 hours. Stir frequently to prevent sticking. Lift out spice bag, and ladle into hot sterilized jars. Seal.

Note: During cooking, taste and increase sugar if you like a sweeter mixture.

VARIATIONS:

* For spicier sauce, add 1 stick of cinnamon, 3 allspice berries and 2 cloves, tied in a cheesecloth bag; remove before packing.

* Add 1 teaspoon dry mustard and 1 tablespoon Worcestershire sauce.

Antipasto (Preserved)

  6 carrots
  1/2 pound silver-skin onions
  1 small cauliflower
  3 green peppers
  3 sweet red peppers
  3/4 pound mushrooms
  1 small eggplant
  2 cloves garlic, crushed
  3/4 cup olive oil
  1 cup vinegar
  5 cups ketchup
  1 tablespoon monosodium glutamate (optional)
  1 can or jar black olives, drained
  2 jars stuffed olives, drained
  1 can cut green beans, drained

Scrape carrots, and slice or cut into fingers. Peel onions. Cut out and discard the core of the cauliflower, and separate the head into small flowerets. Slice peppers in half, and remove seeds and pulp; then dice in large cubes or cut in strips. Trim mushrooms, and cut in halves. Peel eggplant; then slice and cube. Bring 2 quarts salted water to a boil, and add carrots and onions. Bring to a boil. Add cauliflower and peppers, and bring to a boil; then stir in mushrooms and eggplant. Boil up again, and test for tenderness with a skewer. If barely tender, drain the vegetables well, and add remaining ingredients. Bring to a boil, stirring gently to prevent breaking the vegetables. Ladle into hot sterilized sealers, and cover. Process in a boiling-water bath 10 minutes for pints, 15 minutes for quarts. Cool, and store in a cool place. Makes 10–12 (16-ounce) sealers.

To serve as an appetizer, chill and spoon into crisp dry lettuce cups. Garnish with sardines, shrimp, chunks of tuna, anchovies or rolls of salami and celery curls, lemon wedges and parsley sprigs.

Note: Because fresh silver-skin onions are a nuisance to peel, you may prefer to use drained, small, pickled onions or mixed pickles, either sweet or sour. Add the pickled variety with the drained olives and beans. Fresh green beans may be used in place of canned. Cook them for a short time with the fresh vegetables.

Chowchow

  20 green tomatoes
  1/3 cup salt
  10 onions
  6 large cucumbers
  1/2 cauliflower or cabbage
  4–5 sweet red or green peppers
  1 hot red pepper
  7 cups vinegar
  3 cups sugar
  2 teaspoons celery seed
  4 tablespoons mixed pickling spice, tied in a bag

Grind the green tomatoes with the coarse blade of a food chopper, and stir in the salt. Let stand 30 minutes. Drain in a colander for several hours or overnight. Coarsely grind onions, unpeeled cucumbers, cauliflower and seeded peppers with the food chopper, and mix with the green tomatoes and remaining ingredients. Bring slowly to a boil, and cook, uncovered, until vegetables are tender. Remove the bag, and pack in hot sterilized sealers. Seal. Makes about 7 (16-ounce) jars.

Sweet Green Tomato Pickles

    8 pounds (about 32) green tomatoes
    6 large onions
    3 cups vinegar
    3 cups brown sugar, firmly packed
    1 tablespoon salt
    1 teaspoon cloves
    1 teaspoon cinnamon
    1 teaspoon mace

Chop or grind tomatoes and onions, and bring to boil in their own juices. Turn heat low, and simmer 30 minutes. Add remaining ingredients, and simmer, uncovered, until thick, stirring occasionally. Ladle into hot sterilized jars, and seal. Makes 8 pints.

Prune-Apple Chutney

    2 pounds dried prunes
    3 cups peeled, chopped onions
    2 cups peeled, chopped, tart apples
    3 cups blended vinegar
    1 lemon, thinly sliced
    1 1/2 cups brown sugar, firmly packed
    1/2 cup seeded raisins
    2 teaspoons salt
    1 teaspoon mustard seed
    1 teaspoon cayenne
    1 teaspoon ground ginger

Soak prunes overnight in water to cover. Drain, remove pits and cut prunes into coarse pieces. Turn all ingredients into preserving kettle, bring to boil, reduce heat and simmer, uncovered, at least 2 hours. Stir from time to time, especially when mixture starts to thicken. Ladle into hot sterilized jars, and seal. Makes 3–4 pints.

Rhubarb Relish

    6 cups rhubarb, cut fine
    4 cups chopped onions
    4 cups brown sugar, firmly packed
    4 cups vinegar
    4 teaspoons salt
    1 teaspoon cinnamon
    1 teaspoon cloves
    1 teaspoon ginger
    1 teaspoon allspice
    1/4 teaspoon cayenne

Mix all ingredients together and cook until thick, about 1 hour, stirring from time to time. Ladle into hot sterilized jars, and seal. Makes 8 pints.

Sweet Pepper Relish

    1 dozen large sweet red peppers
    1 dozen large green peppers
    1 dozen medium onions
    4 cups white-wine vinegar
    1 cup sugar
    2 tablespoons salt
    1 tablespoon dry mustard
    1 tablespoon celery seed
    1 teaspoon mustard seed

Wash and stem peppers; remove seeds and white membrane. Peel onions. Put vegetables through meat grinder, using coarse blade. Cover with boiling water, and let stand 5 minutes. Drain thoroughly. Add remaining ingredients, bring to boil, reduce heat and simmer, stirring several times, until vegetables are tender, about 10 minutes. Pack in hot sterilized jars, and seal. Makes about 6 pints.

Mustard-pickled Wax Beans

    2 pounds wax beans
    1–2 sweet red peppers
    2 cups light brown sugar, firmly packed
    2/3 cup dry mustard
    1/2 cup flour
    2 teaspoons turmeric
    1 tablespoon celery seed
    1 teaspoon dill seed (optional)
    2 teaspoons salt
    3 cups vinegar
    1 cup water

Wash the beans, and trim off the tops and tips; then cut diagonally into 1-inch pieces. Dice the peppers. Cook the beans in boiling salted water until barely tender. Stir in diced pepper, and cover. Cook 1 minute. Drain. Mix the next 7 ingredients together in a large kettle, and slowly stir in the vinegar and water. Cook and stir until thickened and smooth. Taste for salt, and add the drained vegetables. Cook slowly 4 minutes. Ladle into sterilized sealers and seal. Makes 4 (16-ounce) sealers.

HOME FREEZING OF FRUITS

At the beginning of summer, make a rough plan of the foods you intend to freeze, so that you can make full use of your equipment and leave space for items available late in the season.

Label each package with full information—date, kind, sugar, no sugar, and so forth. Hang an inventory pad and pencil on the wall near the freezer, and cross off all items as they are taken out.

Keep the thermometer in the center of the freezer, and check often to see that it registers the correct 0°F. In case of power failure, remember that a well-filled freezer requires 2—3 days for the temperature to rise to a dangerous level.

Thawed fruits can be refrozen if the temperature has not risen above 40°F. (Never refreeze thawed vegetables).

As fruits cannot "improve" during storage, select only choice ripe products for freezing. Some fruits, notably pears and apples, do not freeze well. See Freezing Guide for Fruits in this section, for dependable varieties.

As *fast* freezing is always desirable, freeze in reasonably small quantities at one time, using small rather than large packages. Spread containers here and there over the bottom or floor of a freezer chest, or on the metal shelves of an upright freezer cabinet. Group packages later for convenience.

Most home freezers can, in 24 hours, freeze 2—4 pounds of foodstuffs for each cubic foot of freezer capacity.

Which Packaging Materials?

The importance of proper packaging cannot be overemphasized. The fresh flavor, color, texture and nutritive value of foods that are frozen will reach the table only if they are properly protected during storage. Use only packaging material that seals in the natural moisture of the food and keeps out the air. Ordinary waxed paper will not do as moisture can seep through.

Here is a list of various satisfactory moisture-vapor proof containers for home freezing of fruits: firm polyethylene containers with snap-on or squeeze-in lids; heavily waxed cartons (although round shapes waste freezer space); plastic containers (more costly but reusable, with the additional advantage of transparency); polyethylene freezer bags (excellent for dry-packing fruits); and folding cartons (best for vegetables but sometimes used for dry-packing fruits).

Pint packages are good for sliced strawberries, small boxes for perfect whole berries to be used as garnishes. Packaging in different sizes according to purpose permits you to thaw only what you need.

Pack with or without Sugar

Fruits can be packed in any of 4 ways, depending on variety and intended use.

Dry Sugarless Pack. Some fruits (blueberries, cranberries, raspberries, whole strawberries and so forth) can be frozen without sweetening. Berries intended for later jam-making should be frozen without sugar.

Wet Sugarless Pack. For special diets in which sugar is restricted, this method is useful. Use fully ripe fruit; crush enough fruit to extract sufficient juice to cover fruit in container; then pour crushed fruit over cut-up pieces to fill package to correct level. If diet permits a calorie-free sweetener, it may be added.

Dry Sugar Pack. Sift sugar over small amounts of fruit at a time, using bowl and stirring carefully so as not to break fruit. Or add sugar by the tablespoon, in alternate layers with fruit. Use this guide for proportions:

* 1 pound sugar to 5 pounds blueberries
* 1 pound sugar to 3—5 pounds sour cherries
* 1 pound sugar to 4 pounds peaches or plums
* 1 pound sugar to 4 pounds strawberries (a little more sugar for 4 pounds raspberries)

Syrup Pack. Use firm containers only. Sweeten each specific fruit according to taste. Prepare syrup the day before, and chill overnight. Allow 1 cup syrup for pint carton, 1 1/2 cups for quart carton. Place fruit in containers, and cover with syrup, leaving 1-inch space at top. Place crumpled clean waxed paper on fruit to keep it under syrup.

For proportions of sugar to water in thin, medium and thick syrups, see recipes for canning later in chapter.

To Prevent Darkening

Vitamin C (ascorbic acid) can be used to prevent darkening of frozen apricots and peaches. Buy it at a drugstore or locker plant, and follow instructions on package. Generally 1/4 teaspoon of ascorbic acid powder is allowed for each pint of fruit. Sprinkle it in with sugar, or add to syrup.

Important: In packaging sweetened fruits for freezing, work quickly. Never let filled packages stand at room temperature for any length of time. Transfer immediately to freezer, or place in refrigerator until all packages are ready.

Using Frozen Fruits

As thawed fruit quickly deteriorates, it should be used at once. It may be thawed at room temperature or in refrigerator; the latter is better when fruit is to be served cold. Or container may be placed in lukewarm water and fruit removed as soon as it has defrosted.

FREEZING GUIDE FOR FRUITS

FRUIT	NOTES	TO PREPARE FOR FREEZING
Sliced apples	Slice apples into weak brine (1 teaspoon salt to 1 quart cool water); drain well.	Parboil 2 minutes; cool quickly over ice; pack and label.

FRUIT	NOTES	TO PREPARE FOR FREEZING
Blackberries	Must be fully ripe; otherwise they change color and become sour.	Crush gently with dry sugar, and seal; or pack in thin-to-medium syrup, and label.
Cantaloupe and watermelon	Use fully ripe, deep-colored fruit.	Slice, seed, peel and dice in 1/2- or 3/4-inch cubes, or use melon-ball cutter; pack, cover with thin syrup and label.
Sour cherries	Frozen cherries make an excellent pie filling.	Pit, and sugar, stir frequently until all sugar is dissolved; pack, press waxed paper over and seal.
Blueberries	Pick over; wash, and drain carefully.	Pack dry, or add thin syrup to cover.
Red and black currants	Good for later jelly-making.	Pack sugarless in freezer bags; label with exact quantities.
Cranberries		Use dry sugarless method; label freezer bags.
Gooseberries	Do not use under-ripe fruit.	May be frozen "as is," in dry sugar pack or in medium-to-heavy syrup.
Grapes	Freeze for jelly later on if desired.	After stemming, freeze "as is."
Peaches	Note variety for next season's guidance.	Scald, cool and peel; halve, pit and pack; cover with thin, medium or heavy syrup; add ascorbic acid; seal.
Plums	Must be fully ripened.	Remove pits; pack, and cover with light syrup. Seal.
Raspberries	Only first-quality fruit should be used.	Dry-pack, with or without sugar.
Rhubarb	Use tender stalks.	Cut into 1-inch pieces; freeze "as is," in dry sugar pack or stewed for table use.
Strawberries	Wash under very cold water; drain well, and hull.	Slice each berry into 2 or 3 pieces; use dry sugar pack.

FREEZING GUIDE FOR SPECIAL FRUIT DISHES

FRUIT	PREPARATION FOR FREEZING	NOTES ON USE
Baked apples	Select best varieties for baking, and bake as usual; cool quickly in basin surrounded by cold water; pack in container with 2 pieces of foil between apples.	Reheat without thawing in 350°F. oven.
Applesauce, cranberry-sauce and the like	Prepare and sweeten as for immediate use; cool, pack and label.	Thaw at room temperature.
Uncooked jams	See instructions in section on jams and jellies.	
Purees (fresh apricots, cantaloupe, berries, peaches, plums)	Choose well-ripened fruit; puree in electric blender; 1 1/2 cups sugar to 6 cups fruit; or simmer fruit until soft, add sugar, cool and pack in containers.	For dessert sauces.

Note: For full freezing instructions, see *Freezing Guide for Fruits*. Do not overcook fruits for freezing, and do not refreeze.

FREEZING VEGETABLES

Freezing has a number of advantages over other methods of long-term storage of vegetables. With a home freezer, preparation is quick and convenient and calls for little equipment beyond that usually available in the kitchen. Vegetables retain fresh color and flavor, and, when freshly gathered and quickly and correctly processed, their high food value is also retained.

For best results, use only highest quality fresh vegetables, and follow instructions carefully.

Freeze Only the Best

Vegetables that freeze with greatest success include asparagus, broccoli, corn, green peas, squash (cooked), spinach and similar greens. Green and wax beans also freeze well, although the flavor tends to be weak.

Cucumbers, lettuce and radishes are not suitable for freezing. Chopped celery, tomatoes, green peppers and onions may be frozen without blanching and used in making cooked sauces or for frying. Try to use them within 3—4 weeks.

Choose fresh, high-quality vegetables that are tender and succulent, just right for table use. Not-quite-ripe vegetables soften and are rather flavorless after freezing. Overripe vegetables tend to become tough.

Blanching Before Freezing

Rules given for home-freezing fruits apply equally to vegetables, except that, whereas fruits are usually frozen raw, vegetables must be "blanched," that is scalded in boiling water, before packing.

Blanching destroys enzymes that would otherwise affect quality during storage. It also "sets" natural colors, partially sterilizes vegetables and softens them for closer packing.

You will need a kettle (at least 6-quart) and a long-handled sieve or wire basket or a large double square of cheesecloth. Blanch only about 1 pound of prepared vegetables at a time, so that water can be quickly brought back to boil after vegetable is added. Have at least 1 gallon of water boiling rapidly over high heat (2 gallons for 1 pound of leafy vegetable). Place vegetable in sieve, basket or cheesecloth. Immerse vegetable in water, bring very quickly to boil again and start counting the blanching time. Watch a clock with a second hand, or set a timer—*blanching time must be exact* (see tables for specific vegetables). Move container of vegetable through water to help heat penetration.

Immediately after blanching, lift container of vegetable to tray, and transfer to sink. Turn vegetable into colander under running cold water, or immerse in ice water. Vegetable takes as long to cool as to blanch. To check, bite a piece; it should not feel hot to the tongue.

Drain quickly and thoroughly. The vegetable is now ready for packaging.

The Right Packaging Materials

As for all frozen foods, packaging material for vegetables must be moisture-vapor proof.

Suitable containers for home freezing of vegetables include polyethylene or plastic-film freezing bags; heavily waxed rectangular cardboard cartons with heat-sealed inner bags or heat-sealed overwraps; and firm polyethylene containers with snap-on or squeeze-in lids.

The first 2 mentioned are probably the most convenient for home use, as they are easy to handle and take relatively little freezer space. Remember, smaller containers freeze more quickly, thus giving better results. For convenience at serving time, a container that holds the right amount for your family at 1 meal is ideal. If larger quantities are stored in freezer bags, it is important to remove needed amounts quickly;

then tie down wrap, or secure it with rubber band to exclude air from remainder while stored in the freezer.

Step-by-Step Procedure

1. Plan to freeze only amount of vegetable that will be used in 1 season.
2. Assemble necessary utensils and equipment. Be sure to have on hand right sizes, types and number of containers and labels, as well as an inventory pad.
3. Select best vegetable variety for freezing. If in doubt about varieties, pack small sample, freeze overnight and test next day.
4. Reorganize freezer to leave space for scattering packages through it against the metal walls or shelves. Plan also where packages will be assembled after they are completely frozen.
5. Make space in refrigerator, if necessary, to "hold" packages briefly before you transfer them to freezer.
6. Vegetables should be frozen the day they are bought or gathered, preferably within a few hours of gathering. If preparation must be postponed, store vegetables in refrigerator. Or place in pan or pail, cover and immerse in larger container of ice water up to level of vegetables.
7. Sort vegetables, setting aside any of inferior quality for immediate use.
8. Prepare carefully and quickly. Wash very thoroughly, remove bruised or blemished parts and, when necessary, cut in serving sizes (prepare as for table use). Be sure to have clean hands, clean utensils and frequent changes of clean water, as the next step, blanching, does not heat the product sufficiently to sterilize before freezing.
9. Blanch, cool, and drain vegetables as already outlined.
10. Pack in moisture-vapor proof containers. Leave 1-inch space at top to allow for expansion in freezing. Neither salt nor brine is used, as they delay freezing and thawing.
11. Seal, according to type of container employed; with moisture-vapor proof bags, press out as much air as possible. Twist top, and secure with metal or paper closures or with rubber band.

    With rectangular cartons, press air out of inner container. If carton has heat-sealed inner bag, seal bag and close the carton. If the carton has heat-sealed outer wrap, close carton, wrap closely and heat-seal. Use your electric iron set at "warm" to heat-seal; press top inch of container edges together with iron.

    With polyethylene containers, adjust covers, and, if desirable, seal with freezer tape.

12. Label cartons with names of vegetables, special details of preparation and date of freezing.
13. Store each group of 2 or 3 packages in the refrigerator as it is filled and labeled, or place in freezer immediately if convenient.
14. Freeze promptly at 0°F. or lower temperature. If packages are to be taken to a freezer plant, place in carton lined with newspaper.
15. Make complete inventory listing, which you will keep handy to freezer.
16. Postpone stacking of home-frozen vegetables for 1—2 days. Remember, do *not* refreeze after thawing.

HOME-CANNED FRUIT

Home canning of fruits is most satisfying and profitable when fresh, fully ripened fruit is readily obtainable. Avoid overripe or underripe products, and plan to can fruit as quickly as possible to ensure maximum flavor and texture.

It is necessary to destroy organisms that cause ripening and, if allowed to continue working, produce spoilage. You must also provide a perfect seal, which will prevent entrance of spoilage-producing organisms. You can destroy the organisms and provide a perfect seal by heat sterilization and by airtight sealing of filled jars or cans.

Unlike non-acid vegetables, fruits (including tomatoes) may be home canned even without the aid of a pressure cooker, for fruits and tomatoes contain organic acids that help prevent spoilage. Also, fruits are usually sweetened, which further helps preservation. (Vinegar and spices, when suitable, are additional aids in preventing spoilage of home-processed foods.)

Equipment for Home Canning

Check carefully the day before canning, and be sure your supplies are in satisfactory condition.

Jars. Jars must be sound, airtight and without the slightest crack, chip or dent. Styles in jars have changed slightly over the past years, but the types listed here are basic and include those now generally available. Jars with 3-piece tops are the familiar containers that are closed with rubber rings, glass covers and metal sealing rings. Jars may be squat or tall. Today's Mason jar has sides of rounded-square shape and a 2-piece top, consisting of a metal cover with a rubber gasket and a metal screw-on ring. Variations of these 2 types may be on the market in some localities.

Rubber Rings. Never use old or once-used rubber rings; they lose their springinesss and provide poor protection. If your jars require separate rings, buy as required, and be very sure that they are the right size for the jars you use. Be sure they are of the current year's production, but do not test by stretching.

Screw Tops. Screw tops should be free of corrosion and should perfectly fit jars.

Metal Cans. If you process large amounts of home-canned fruits and vegetables, you will probably find metal cans useful and convenient. For most products, plain tin cans are satisfactory. Enameled cans are recommended for some fruits and vegetables (red berries, red and black cherries, plums, rhubarb and pressure-canned corn, beets, pumpkin and winter squash). Enamel lining prevents discoloration of food; it is not essential for safety.

Kitchen Utensils. The following utensils are required: 2 large bowls, large kettle, saucepan and dependable container—hot water bath or steam-pressure cooker. For various reasons, including the danger of exploding jars, oven canning is no longer recommended.

A colander or large sieve will be needed, as well as measuring cups, towels, potholders, a wide-mouthed funnel, pie plate, long knife, peeler and spoon. Handy additions to your canning equipment are paper toweling, small brush, jar lifter and metal tongs.

Water-bath Processor. Use large clean kettle or other container with cover. Container should be deep enough to allow 2 inches or more space above tops of jars. To keep jars off bottom of container, a rack, preferably of wire or wood, is essential. Overlapping cake coolers may be used.

Pressure Canner. For the general procedure, see section on pressure canning. Always consult instructions given by manufacturer. If you have a pressure saucepan large enough to take several jars at a time, it can substitute for large canner. Consult your instruction booklet for specific use.

Preparing Jars and Rings

1. Test seal. Put about 2 inches of water in jar; fit with rubber ring and glass top, and invert. If water leaks out, it is not airtight and should be refitted or discarded.
2. Wash jars and glass lids (except those with sealing compound) in hot sudsy water. Rinse, and scald.
3. Sterilize jars and lids (except those with sealing compound) in kettle of water, dishwasher or oven. Place jars in kettle, half-fill with water and cover with glass lids, if latter are to be used. Pour around them 3 inches or more

warm water. Add 1 tablespoon vinegar (to prevent lime coating). Bring water to boiling, and leave jars in water until ready to fill. Or place empty jars on rack in cold oven. Cover each with its glass top, if glass tops are to be used, or with foil. Heat oven slowly to 200°F. Remove jars as needed, and place on folded paper or dry cloth for filling.

Dip rubber or metal rings in boiling water just before using. To use sealing compound, follow instructions of the manufacturer.

Preparing Metal Cans

See that cans, lids and gaskets are perfect. Discard any that are bent, dented or rusted or have damaged gaskets. To protect lids from dust and moisture, leave in paper packing until required.

Just before using, wash cans in sudsy hot water, and rinse in boiling water. Invert to drain until required. Do not wash lids, as washing damages gaskets; simply wipe with damp cloth if dirty before putting on cans.

Follow manufacturer's sealing instructions.

Use only standard enamel cans for tomatoes or fruits.

It will speed your canning preparations if you know how to do quick translation of pounds or quarts into cups. You should also have a good approximate idea of the number of pint or quart containers that will be needed for a given quantity of the finished product.

CONVERSION TABLE FOR FRUITS

FRUIT	AS PURCHASED	QUANTITY
Apricots, small	1 pound	18 apricots
Blackberries	1 quart	1 3/4 pounds or 4 1/2 cups
Blueberries	1 quart	1 3/4 pounds or 4 1/2 cups
Blue grapes	1 quart	2 pounds or 5 cups
Cherries	1 quart	1 3/4 pounds or 4 1/2 cups
Gooseberries, whole	1 pound	1 heaping pint or 2 cups or 1 3/4 cups crushed
Plums, small yellow	1 pound	18 plums
Peaches	1 pound	4 medium peaches
Strawberries	1 quart	1 1/2 pounds or 4 1/2 cups or 2 1/2 cups crushed
Tomatoes	1 pound	4 medium tomatoes

TABLE OF YIELDS FOR FRUITS

FRUIT	QUANTITY RAW	YIELD IN QUART JARS
Apricots	15 pounds	9
Berries, general	12 quarts	12
Strawberries	12 quarts	9–10
Cherries	6 quarts	5
Peaches	6 quarts	4
Plums, pears	6 quarts	5

Before proceeding with either cold- or hot-pack methods, it is necessary to know the type of syrup required for particular fruit and estimate amount needed. For type of syrup best suited to canning each type of fruit, see charts with discussions of packs.

To Make Syrup

Measure sugar and water according to type of syrup specified (see following list of proportions). Stir in saucepan until sugar dissolves; then heat to boiling. Should scum form, skim it off. Always use syrup boiling hot in either cold- or hot-pack procedures.

* For 2 1/2 cups thin syrup, 1 cup sugar to 2 cups water
* For 2 cups moderately thin syrup, 1 cup sugar to 1 1/2 cups water
* For 1 1/2 cups medium syrup, 1 cup sugar to 1 cup water
* For 1 1/4 cups heavy syrup, 1 cup sugar to 3/4 cup water

Allow ample syrup. For cold-pack method, you should estimate 1–1 1/2 cups syrup for each quart of raw berries, strawberries, cherries or rhubarb; 1 1/2–2 cups syrup for larger fruits such as apricots, peaches, plums and pears. The size of the fruit or cut pieces has a bearing on the amount of syrup. For example, 12 cups of syrup may be sufficient to do a crate of good berries, whereas 10 cups may be needed for a 6-quart basket of peaches, especially if they are prepared in halves.

The hot-pack method uses less syrup than does the cold-pack method. Allow about 1/2 less syrup for each quart of raw fruit to be canned in this way.

Sort fruit under a good light. Set aside and refrigerate for jam, relish or similar purposes any with blemishes or spots, cutting out bad patches. Carefully wash small amounts of sound fruit in sieve under gently running water. Fruits such as raspberries and cherries should be lifted from first rinse to another.

To skin peaches or tomatoes, first scald by pouring boiling water over them; let stand 1 minute. Drain, cover with cold water and peel.

Lemon-water dip, known as acidulated water, or simple salt and water brine will prevent peaches, pears, and apples from darkening during preparation. As fruits are peeled, slip pieces into lemon-water, made with 1 cup lemon juice to 5 cups cold water, or brine of 1 teaspoon salt to 5 cups water. Put only enough fruit for 3 jars in at a time, and work quickly. Lift out fruit, and drain well before precooking or packing. Change acidulated water or brine if it becomes discolored.

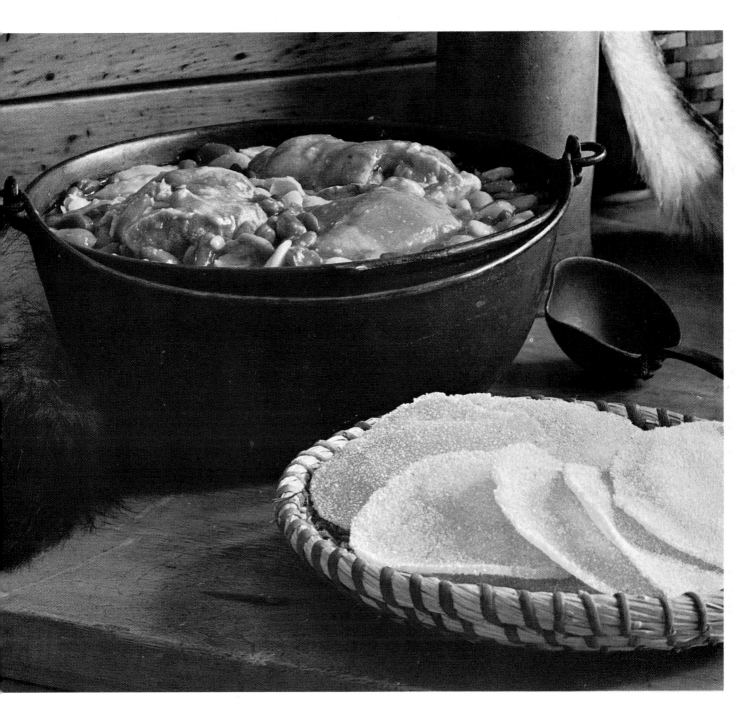

Maple Baked Beans (pp. 272-273).
CREDIT: *Ray Webber*.

Italian Bean and Artichoke Salad (p. 129), Wax Beans Vinaigrette (p. 129) and Curried Sikh Salad (p. 129).
CREDIT: *Elbert Budin.*

A special powdered ascorbic acid can be purchased to mix into water to prevent discoloration of fruit. Use according to manufacturer's directions.

BOILING BATH METHOD

FRUIT	PREPARATION	MINUTES OF PROCESSING*	
		PINTS	QUARTS
Apples	Use thin syrup. Hot pack: Wash, peel, core and slice or quarter; drop in acidulated water or brine bath; drain; bring to boil in syrup, and simmer 3 minutes; pack hot in hot jars, leaving space at top.	15	15
Applesauce	Make applesauce as usual; pack hot in hot jars, leaving space at top.	15	15
Apricots	Use moderately thin syrup. Cold pack: Wash, but do not peel; halve and pit, or leave whole; pack "cups" down if halved; add boiling syrup, leaving space at top.	20	25
	Hot pack: Prepare fruit; bring to boil in syrup, simmering 2–3 minutes; pack hot, leaving space at top.	15	15
Small berries	Use thin syrup for blueberries, blackberries, saskatoons; moderately thin or medium syrup for raspberries; medium or heavy syrup for gooseberries or loganberries. Cold pack: Wash, and pick over (remove ends of gooseberries); pack, cover with boiling syrup, leaving space at top.	15	20
Strawberries	Use moderately thin or medium syrup. Cold pack: Wash, and hull; bring slowly to boil in syrup, and simmer 1 minute; cover, and let stand off heat 1 hour; pack, leaving space at top.	15	20

*If you live at an altitude over 2,000 feet, the processing times for canning by boiling-bath method will have to be increased by 1/5 for each additional 1,000 feet. For example, if processing time is listed in this chart as 20 minutes, add 4 minutes, if you live at an altitude 2,000–3,000 feet; above 3,000 feet add 2/5 of 20 minutes, or 8 minutes, to processing time.

FRUIT	PREPARATION	MINUTES OF PROCESSING*	
		PINTS	QUARTS
Strawberries (cont'd.)	Hot pack: Add hulled berries to boiling syrup; cover, and let stand off heat 1 hour; bring to boil; pack, leaving space at top.	10	10
Cherries	Use thin syrup for sweet cherries; medium or heavy for sour cherries. Cold pack: Wash, stem and pit (optional); pack, and cover with boiling syrup, leaving space at top.	20	25
	Hot pack: Wash, stem, and pit (optional); bring to boil in syrup, and simmer 3 minutes; pack hot, leaving space at top.	15	15
Peaches	Use moderately thin syrup. Cold pack: Peel, and pit after blanching 1 minute or less and then cold-dipping; drop in acidulated water or brine; drain; pack as slices or halves, the latter "cup" down; add boiling syrup, leaving space at top.	20	25
	Hot pack: Prepare fruit as for cold pack; bring slices or halves to boiling point in syrup, and simmer 3 minutes; pack hot, leaving space at top.	15	15
Pears	Use thin syrup. Cold pack: Wash, peel, and core; halve or quarter; drop in acidulated water or brine, and drain; pack halves "cup" side down; cover with boiling syrup, leaving space at top.	20	25
	Hot pack: Prepare fruit as for cold pack; bring to boil in syrup, simmering 3–5 minutes, depending on hardness of pears; pack hot, leaving space at top.	10	10
Plums	Use moderately thin syrup for tart plums; thin syrup for prune plums. Cold pack: Wash, and leave whole, or halve and pit; pack, and cover with boiling syrup, leaving space at top.	15	20
	Hot pack: Prepare fruit as for cold pack; bring	10	10

FRUIT	PREPARATION	PINTS	QUARTS
Plums (cont'd.)	to boil in syrup, simmering 2 minutes; pack hot, leaving space at top.		
Tomatoes	*Cold pack*: Peel, and cut out stem ends, after blanching 1/2 minute and then cold-dipping; pack, and add 1 teaspoon salt per quart, 1/2 teaspoon per pint; cover with heated tomato juice; leave space at top. Or press down on tomatoes in jar until covered with their own juice; add salt, leaving space at top, and add extra 5 minutes to processing time.	25(30)	30(35)
	Hot pack: Prepare tomatoes as for cold pack; heat, whole or quartered, to boiling point; pack hot, adding 1 teaspoon salt per quart; leave space at top.	15	15
Grape juice	*Hot pack*: Wash grapes; stem, and crush well; add 2 1/2 cups water per 6-quart basket; bring to boil, and simmer, covered, 15 minutes; strain through moistened jelly bag; add sugar if desired; heat to boiling point, and pour into hot jars, leaving space at top.	10	10
Tomato juice	*Hot pack*: Wash tomatoes, cut out ends and cut in pieces; bring to boil; simmer, covered, 5 minutes; press through sieve; heat to boiling point; pour into hot jars, leaving space at top; add 1/2 teaspoon salt per pint. Or obtain juice by using juice extractor; bring juice to boiling point, and pour into hot jars, leaving space at top; salt as in first method.	15 / 15	15 / 15

Cold-pack Method

Fill sterilized jars with cold raw fruit (see recipe chart for specific fruits). Cover with boiling syrup. Leave a 1/2-inch space at top. Adjust tops correctly, according to type of jar (see jar-closure directions that follow). Process in hot-water bath.

The cold pack is often preferred because with it fruits (especially berries, though not strawberries) retain their shapes and food values better.

The disadvantages of the cold pack are the higher proportion of syrup to fruit in each jar and the sometimes excessive space between processed fruit and lid, although the latter does not affect the keeping qualities.

Hot-pack Method

By this method the fruit is precooked in syrup for a few minutes (see recipe chart). It is then packed in sterilized jars and covered with hot syrup, leaving 1/2-inch space below rims. Tops are correctly adjusted (see jar closures), and jars are ready for processing in hot-water bath. The hot-pack method has certain advantages. It prevents floating fruit, especially strawberries; more fruit may be packed in each jar; processing time is shorter; fruit color stays truer. The chief disadvantage is that more preparation time is required because of precooking.

To Fill Containers

Do not fill more containers than your hot-water processing bath will hold. With the hot-pack method, precook only sufficient fruit to fill 3–5 jars at a time.

Place hot empty jars on trivet or cake rack, covered with folded newspaper or towels, to prevent cracking glass.

Fill each container to within 1/2 inch of rim (or 1/4 inch, when using tin cans and sealing machine). Insert knife to bottom of jar to let out air bubbles or tilt jar before sealing. Work quickly.

Adjusting Jar Closures

Two of the most familiar types of jars are sealed only partially before processing. They are the standard glass design with 3-section top and the bail or spring-type jar.

For 3-section top, dip new rubber ring into boiling water; then fit onto jar. Fill jar with fruit and syrup (if necessary, wipe ring and rim clean; a spilled bit of fruit will break seal). Place on glass cap, and screw on metal band firmly as far as it will go; then turn band back about 1/2 inch but not more than 1 inch.

With bail or spring-type closure, click longer wire into place over glass cup, but leave shorter wire *up*.

In other types of containers—those with flat metal lids or tin cans for machine sealing—sealing is completed before processing. Follow manufacturer's instructions carefully in each case.

Processing in Hot Bath

Have your big kettle ready with several inches of hot—not boiling—water. To prevent cracking of glass, temperature of water should be as close as possible to that of filled jars. Carefully lower jars into water. They should be standing upright, not touching and supported on rack or in basket to permit water to circulate underneath and around. Add enough hot water to cover jars by at least 2 inches. Cover kettle, and place over heat. Count processing time from minute water is actually boiling vigorously. Keep water boiling, and boil only as long as specific recipe directs (see chart).

Remove jars at end of processing time. (A large baster or small dipper is handy to scoop out excess water; canning basket with handles is also ideal at this point.) Place hot jars on layer of newspapers or crumpled towels. When contents have ceased bubbling, *complete seal* on regular or bail-type jars. Screw metal ring tight on 3-section tops. Push short wire down on spring-top jars.

Do not touch top again until opening for table use. To retighten top after jar has cooled can break seal and spoil contents. Do not be concerned about empty space at the top, as everything inside the container has been sterilized. Never attempt to open a jar after processing in order to "fill it up."

Let jars cool in upright position; do not cover them. Let tin cans cool in cold water, and keep adding cold water to hasten cooling.

When cool, test for leakage by inverting each screw-top or spring-top jar for 2—3 minutes. If a jar leaks, do not attempt to reprocess, but use contents within a few days. On the vacuum-type jar a complete seal is identified by a ringing sound when the lid is tapped with a spoon.

Wipe all containers with a damp cloth; then dry and label.

Store in cool, dark place. Cover canned fruit with pad of newspaper, if necessary, to absorb dampness in the atmosphere and to keep out light. With this protection, the metal bands will not corrode, and the fruit will not fade.

In home canning do not use canning compounds, sulphur compounds or chemicals such as boracic acid or salicylic acid. Such additions can be harmful.

Vitamin C (ascorbic acid) is sometimes used in canning peaches and pears, in order to prevent discoloration in canned fruit during storage. This additive is obtainable from the drugstore. Place powder or tablet in bottom of each jar before filling with fruit and syrup. Allow 1/16 teaspoon powder or one 25-milligram tablet for each jar (pint or quart).

PRESSURE CANNING

Pressure canning is the only safe way to preserve the nonacid vegetables, because it ensures a high enough temperature to destroy organisms.

The warning cannot be repeated too often: *do not* attempt home canning of nonacid vegetables without a pressure cooker. It is true that tomatoes, because of their high acid content, may be safely processed in jars in a hot-water bath (see preceding section for full directions). But such vegetables as asparagus, beans, corn, peas and squash must be raised to temperatures above that of boiling water; otherwise harmful microorganisms that can cause illness, and even death, may continue to live and grow in the stored product. A pressure cooker, properly used, gives temperatures necessary to assure destruction of harmful organisms in nonacid vegetables.

A few jars at a time may be canned in the regular pressure saucepan, but homemakers who wish to can frequently and in quantity would be wise to invest in a pressure canner.

In addition to pressure equipment, you will need some of the utensils outlined for home canning of fruits.

Choose fresh, firm, tender vegetables, free from blemishes. Wash, and sort for size and quality; then peel, trim, shell or husk. Cut, and precook according to kind (see chart on *Pressure Canner Method*).

Packing

Have hot sterilized jars ready. Pack hot vegetables quickly, and cover with boiling water, leaving 1/2—1-inch space at top—the larger allowance for corn and peas, the lesser for other vegetables (in using tin cans, allow 1/2-inch space at top for corn and peas, 1/4-inch for other vegetables). Add 1 teaspoon salt to each quart container, 1/2 teaspoon to each pint. Work out air bubbles by running knife blade around inside of jar.

Pressure Canning Procedure

1. Check cleanliness of petcock and safety valve by running toothpick around them. Do not put gauge in water. Make sure gasket fits snugly; replace when necessary.

2. Pour 2 inches hot water into canner. Place filled containers on rack, allowing space around each. If canning only 4 or 5 jars, add 3 extra cups hot water. You must have 2 quarts water in the canner.

3. In using machine-sealed tin cans, a second row of tin cans may be added, preferably on a cake rack and arranged for uneven distribution (not directly on top of one another).

4. Fasten lid on securely. Keep petcock open until steam escapes in steady stream with hissing sound, 5—10 minutes.

5. Close petcock, and allow pressure to rise slowly until gauge indicates required pressure, usually over medium or low heat (not high). Set a "minute minder" as soon as desired pressure is reached.

6. Turn heat low, but not off, to maintain constant pressure.

7. At end of specified canning time, move canner to a board, and allow pressure to drop gradually to 0.

8. Slowly open petcock. Let canner cool about 2 minutes longer.

9. Remove lid, tilting it away from face. Place towel over canner to absorb excess steam 2 minutes; then remove towel.

10. Leave containers in canner until bubbling ceases; lift out, and complete jar seals. Let cool. Label, and store. (Tin cans should be placed in cold water immediately. Leave cans in cold water until cold. Label, and store.)

A pressure saucepan equipped with accurate indicator or gauge for controlling pressure at 10 pounds (240°F.) may be used as a steam-pressure canner for processing vegetables in pint jars or 20-ounce tin cans. *If you use a pressure saucepan, add 20 minutes to processing times listed on* Pressure Canner Method *chart for pint containers.*

Never place pressure pan or cooker in cold water to reduce pressure.

All home-canned vegetables except tomatoes should be opened and boiled 10 minutes before they are tasted and served.

PRESSURE CANNER METHOD

VEGETABLE	PREPARATION	MINUTES OF PROCESSING*	
		PINTS	QUARTS
Asparagus	Wash, and break off tough ends of stalks; remove scales if necessary to help wash away sand; cut into lengths to fit containers; tie in uniform bundles, and stand	30	35

*At 10-pound pressure; increase pressure 1 pound for each additional 1,000 feet after 2,000 feet above sea level.

VEGETABLE	PREPARATION	MINUTES OF PROCESSING*	
		PINTS	QUARTS
Asparagus (cont'd.)	upright in sufficient boiling water to come 1/2 way up stalks; cover, bring to boil and boil 3 minutes; pack hot, all tips up except a few in center, to help keep stalks upright.		
Beans, green or wax	Wash young tender beans; trim ends and string if necessary; leave whole or cut in pieces; cover with boiling water; bring to boil and boil, covered, 3 minutes; pack hot; add salt; cover with hot cooking liquid from beans, leaving space at top.	30	35
Beets	Wash small young beets; leave on roots and 2 inches of stem; cover with boiling water; bring to boil, and boil, covered until skins slip off easily, about 20 minutes; remove skins and roots; pack hot, adding salt; cover with boiling water, leaving space at top.	30	35
Greens: spinach, chard, beet tops	Wash thoroughly; cook, covered, in very little water until thoroughly wilted, 5–8 minutes, turning several times during cooking; pack hot, loosely; cut greens crosswise with sharp knife to bottom of container; add salt; cover with boiling water, leaving space at top.	50	60
Peas	Shell and wash young tender peas; cover with boiling water; bring to boil, and boil, covered, 1 minute; pack hot, loosely; add salt; cover with hot cooking liquid from peas, leaving space at top.	40	45
Pumpkin and squash	Cut or break apart; remove seeds and stringy fibers; cut into pieces; steam, bake or boil in small amount of water until tender; scrape from skins, and mash or sieve; bring to boiling point, adding little water, if necessary, to prevent scorching; pack hot, leaving space at top.	70	80
Tomatoes	See *Boiling-Bath Method* chart.		

❦ CHAPTER FOUR ❦

Creative Baking

❦

Baking is the test of delicate cookery—an imaginative art and a careful science.

Today's kitchen makes baking easier than ever before. And, with freezers, what you bake today can be stored for later use.

If you don't have time to bake a fancy cake all at once (which means baking cake, making filling, making icing—3 distinct operations) you can make a batch of fillings and icings 1 day, and refrigerate them. Another day, you can make cake layers. Or turn out a recipe of tiny tart shells or some *vol-au-vent* shells which can be filled with either sweet or savory mixtures. But whenever you do bake make sure you measure accurately and time carefully. Recipes offer directions for achieving perfect products, so follow them.

Ingredients

Know the characteristics of various flours, fats, leaveners and liquids, how to measure each and how to adjust for substitution.

Flour is the essential ingredient of all baked products, and there are different flours suited to different types of baking. Flour made from soft wheat is excellent for cakes and is called cake or cake and pastry flour. Hard-wheat flour, known as all-purpose flour or bread flour, contains the strong gluten necessary for yeast products but

may also be used for cakes and pastry when called for in recipes. Self-raising flour, as its name indicates, contains a leavening agent. Use the recipes in the package or tested recipes asking for this special type of flour. In following any baking recipe, the most satisfactory results will be achieved if you use the type of flour called for. If it is necessary to substitute all-purpose for cake flour, reduce quantity, using 7/8 cup sifted all-purpose flour for 1 cup sifted cake flour. (A quick and easy way to measure 7/8 cup of flour is to fill 1 cup level and then to remove 2 level tablespoons.) But if possible it is best to avoid such substitutions. When a recipe states sifted flour, first sift the flour onto a sheet of waxed paper; then lightly spoon into a standard dry measuring cup, heaping the flour slightly above the rim. Cut off excess with a straight-edged knife or metal spatula. Many recipes today call for unsifted or presifted flour. To measure, spoon flour directly from package, bag or cannister into a standard dry measuring cup. Heap above rim, and cut off excess as for sifted flour. The important point to remember is *never* to pack flour into measuring cup or to bang cup on table to shake down flour.

Use granulated *sugar* for most baking. Choose the finest grind of sugar or fruit sugar for delicate textured cakes such as angel food cake, chiffon cake or sponge cake. Brown sugar is moist, and some recipes call for firmly or lightly packed amounts. To pack firmly, spoon brown sugar into a cup, and press down so that sugar holds its shape when cup is inverted. For lightly packed, spoon into cup and just level with the back of a spoon without pressing firmly. Icing sugar may be listed in recipes without the words sifted or unsifted. In such cases, measure first without sifting, but sift before using to remove any lumps.

Leavening action causes dough to rise, making it lighter, more digestible and more palatable. Rising may be achieved in several ways. One is by incorporation of air, as in beating egg whites for angel food cake in which no other leavening is used. Another is by quick formation of steam, as in popovers or cream puffs. A third is by the addition of baking powder, baking soda or yeast.

There are 2 kinds of *baking powder*: quick-acting and double-acting. The first starts its function on contact with the moisture in the mixture and slowly continues its action. The second, as its name implies, works in 2 stages: first, on contact with liquid ingredients and, second, when subjected to heat. Nevertheless these 2 types of baking powder are usually interchangeable in practically all kinds of home baking. Baking powder should be stored covered and dry in a cool place. A combination of moisture and heat will cause it to deteriorate in leavening ability.

Yeast is a tiny living plant that produces carbon dioxide gas, causing dough to rise. There are 2 kinds of yeast available today: active dry yeast, granulated in form, and cakes of compressed fresh yeast. Dry yeast needs no refrigeration. The 2 kinds of yeast may be used interchangeably. One envelope of active dry yeast is equal to 1 (1/2-ounce) cake of compressed fresh yeast. To substitute fresh yeast for active dry yeast, crumble yeast cake over water as directed on package.

Skim and whole *milk* may be used interchangeably. When using instant nonfat dry milk, follow manufacturer's directions. Sour milk and buttermilk are interchangeable. To sour sweet milk, measure 1 tablespoon vinegar or lemon juice into a cup, and fill to the 1-cup line with sweet milk. Let stand a few minutes before using.

To measure liquids accurately, use liquid measuring cup. Set measuring cup at eye level, and fill it exactly to measuring mark. Do not dip measure *into* honey, molasses or other thick liquids; instead, pour from container into measuring spoon or cup. If you lightly grease or wet measure, sticky liquids will not cling.

Shortening is often used as a general term for any type of fat. When specified in a recipe however, it refers to emulsified shortening, which may be all vegetable or a mixture of vegetable and animal. Butter and margarine may be used interchangeably, but if you substitute shortening for butter or margarine, use 7/8 cup of shortening for each cup of butter, and add 1/2 teaspoon of salt. Some tested recipes call for butter or shortening and have been developed with a special tolerance to make an equal amount of one or the other type of fat successful in the finished product.

There are several ways to measure shortening:

1. Press fat (at room temperature) firmly into standard measuring cup or individual measures.
2. Use water-displacement method when shortening is cold and hard. To measure 1/2 cup shortening, fill 1-cup measure to the 1/2-cup mark with water. Add shortening in pieces until water reaches 1-cup level.
3. The 1-pound packages of various emulsified shortenings and lard generally have printed measuring marks, and these are helpful. Notice the package yields 2 1/3 cups.

Recipe for Successful Baking

1. Assemble all necessary ingredients and utensils.
2. Preheat oven to required temperature.
3. Measure each ingredient in advance; then you will be ready to combine them at the right moment in your recipe.

TABLE OF MEASURES

1 pint	=	20 ounces (2 1/2 cups)
1 quart	=	40 ounces (5 cups)
1 gallon	=	160 ounces (20 cups)
1 tablespoon	=	3 teaspoons
16 tablespoons	=	1 cup
1 cup	=	8 ounces
1/2 cup	=	8 tablespoons
1/3 cup	=	5 tablespoons plus 1 teaspoon
1/4 cup	=	4 tablespoons
1 pound	=	16 ounces (dry measure)

TABLE OF EQUIVALENTS*

Butter, margarine	1 pound = 2 cups
	1 ounce = 2 tablespoons
Cheese, shredded	1 pound = 4 cups
Cornmeal	1 pound = 3 cups
Heavy cream, unwhipped	1 cup = 2 cups whipped
Currants, seedless raisins	1 pound = 3 cups
Dates, pitted and chopped	1 pound = 2 cups
Egg whites	8–11 = 1 cup
Egg yolks	12–14 = 1 cup
Flour, cake and pastry, sifted	1 pound = 4 cups
all-purpose, sifted	1 pound = 3 3/4 cups
whole wheat, unsifted	1 pound = 3 2/3 cups
Lemons, juice from 1 medium	= 3 tablespoons
grated rind from 1 medium	= 1 tablespoon
Almonds, shelled	1 pound = 3 1/2 cups
Walnuts, whole, shelled	1 pound = 4 cups
finely chopped	1 pound = 1 3/4 cups
Marshmallows	8 ounces = 32 large
Sugar, brown, lightly packed	1 pound = 3 cups
granulated	1 pound = 2 1/4 cups
icing, sifted	1 pound = 3 1/2 cups

*Equivalent amounts are approximate.

SUBSTITUTIONS*

1 teaspoon baking powder = 1/4 teaspoon baking soda plus 1/2 teaspoon of cream of tartar

1 ounce (1 square) chocolate = 3 tablespoons cocoa plus 3/4 tablespoon fat

1 tablespoon cornstarch = 2 tablespoons flour or 2 tablespoons quick-cooking tapioca (for thickening)

1 cup all-purpose flour = 1 cup plus 2 tablespoons cake and pastry flour

1 whole egg = 2 egg yolks (in custards) or 2 egg yolks plus 1 tablespoon water (in cookies)

1 cup whole milk = 1/2 cup each evaporated milk and water or 4 tablespoons powdered milk plus 1 cup water

1 cup sour milk = 1 tablespoon lemon juice or vinegar with enough sweet milk to make 1 cup

1 cup honey = 1 cup sugar plus 1/4 cup liquid

*As mentioned previously, it is best to use the ingredients called for in the recipe.

QUICK BREADS

Quick breads are so called because they are made with quick-acting leavening agents: baking powder, baking soda or steam as distinct from those leavened with yeast. There are many varieties and many different methods of cooking. Quick breads may be baked in the oven, as with muffins, popovers, baking-powder biscuits and tea breads; deep-fried, as with fritters and doughnuts; steamed, as with dumplings, Boston steamed bread and steamed puddings; cooked on a griddle, as with pancakes; cooked in a frying pan, as with crêpes, or cooked on waffle iron as with waffles. All can be made quickly, shortly before the meal, and served hot, except for the tea breads, which are better if sliced cold.

For speed, keep on hand a few packages of mixes for muffins, breads, pancakes and biscuits; refrigerated biscuits, ready to slice and bake; or frozen waffles and doughnuts.

Biscuits

Biscuit dough has many uses. It may be the foundation for berry shortcakes or fruit cobblers. You can use it to make topping for savory meat pie, either whole topping or cut into rounds, or to cover individual casseroles or meat pies. And you can vary the flavor to complement other foods served. To make biscuits and toppings light and flaky *cut* rather than mash shortening into flour mixture. Add liquid *all at once*, and stir mixture quickly with fork to make a soft dough. Knead very gently on lightly floured surface to smooth the dough. Roll or pat dough gently to desired thickness—good biscuits will double in height during baking.

Baking-powder Biscuits

> 2 cups unsifted all-purpose flour
> 4 teaspoons baking powder
> 1 teaspoon salt
> 1/3 cup shortening
> 3/4 cup (approximately) milk

Sift flour, baking powder and salt into mixing bowl. Cut in shortening with pastry blender or 2 knives until mixture has texture of quick-cooking oatmeal. Add milk; stir with fork to make soft dough. An extra tablespoon of milk may be used if mixture seems too stiff. Place on lightly floured board, and knead gently 8—10 times. Roll or pat dough to desired thickness, and cut with floured cutter. Pat leftover dough together, and cut again. Place biscuits on ungreased baking sheet, close together for soft-sided biscuits or about 1 inch apart for crusty ones. Bake 12—15 minutes at 450°F. Makes 18—20 biscuits (approximately 1 3/4 inches in diameter).

VARIATIONS:

* *Sour-milk Biscuits*: Replace milk with sour milk or buttermilk; substitute 1/4 teaspoon baking soda for 1 teaspoon baking powder.

* *Savory Biscuits*: Add 1 teaspoon poppy seeds, 1/2 teaspoon sage and 1/4 teaspoon dry mustard to flour mixture.

* *Cheese Biscuits*: Add 3/4 cup grated Cheddar or Swiss cheese to flour mixture.

* *Vegetable Sticks*: Add 1 teaspoon celery salt and 1 teaspoon parsley flakes to flour mixture. Roll dough 1/4 inch thick; cut into fingers 5 inches long, 1/2 inch wide. Place on ungreased baking sheet. Brush with butter or margarine. Sprinkle with sesame seeds before baking.

* *Drop Biscuits*: Add 1/3 cup additional milk. Drop dough from tablespoon onto greased baking sheet.

* *Butterscotch Pinwheels*: Cream 1/3 cup butter or margarine, blend in 2/3 cup brown sugar. Set aside. Roll out dough into 9-inch square. Spread sugar mixture over it; roll up as for jelly roll. Dampen edges to seal. Slice into 3/4-inch pieces; place, cut side down, in well-greased muffin pans. Bake in preheated 450°F. oven 12—15 minutes. To remove, invert pan immediately. Makes 12 biscuits.

* *Spicy Fruit Pinwheels*: Add 1/2 cup raisins and 1 1/2 teaspoons cinnamon to brown-sugar mixture when making *Butterscotch Pinwheels*.

* *Whole Wheat Biscuits*: Substitute 1 cup whole wheat or graham flour for 1 cup all-purpose flour, and mix with dry ingredients.

Scones

> 1 3/4 cups unsifted all-purpose flour
> 1 tablespoon baking powder
> 2 tablespoons sugar
> 3/4 teaspoon salt
> 1/4 cup shortening
> 1/2 cup raisins
> 2 eggs, beaten
> 1/2 cup milk or cream

Sift flour, baking powder, sugar and salt into a large bowl. Cut in shortening with blender or 2 knives until mixture resembles coarse oatmeal. Add raisins. Reserve 1 tablespoon of beaten egg, and mix remainder with milk. Make well in dry

ingredients, and add milk mixture. Stir quickly with fork. Place dough on lightly floured surface. Knead gently 8–10 times. Cut dough in half. Form into 2 balls. Pat or gently roll each out to a

1/2-inch-thick round. Transfer to greased cookie sheet. Brush with remaining egg. Score into wedge-shaped pieces. Bake 12–15 minutes at 450°F.

Orange-glazed Biscuits

        1/4 cup butter or margarine
        1/2 cup orange juice
        1/2 cup sugar
          2 teaspoons grated orange rind
          2 cups sifted all-purpose flour
          1 tablespoon baking powder
        1/2 teaspoon salt
        1/4 cup shortening
        3/4 cup (approximately) milk
          2 tablespoons melted butter or margarine
        1/3 cup sugar
        1/2 teaspoon cinnamon

Combine first 4 ingredients, and cook 2 minutes; pour into 9 greased muffin cups. Sift together flour, baking powder and salt; cut in shortening. Add milk, and stir with fork to make soft dough. Place on lightly floured board, and knead gently 4–5 times. Roll out to 1/4-inch thickness. Brush with melted butter or margarine; mix sugar and cinnamon, and sprinkle over dough. Roll up as for jelly roll, cut in 1-inch slices and place, cut side down, over orange mixture in muffin pans. Bake at 450°F. 20–25 minutes.

Popovers, Corn Bread and Similar Batters

Popovers

          1 tablespoon oil or melted shortening
          1 cup unsifted all-purpose flour
        1/4 teaspoon salt
          2 eggs
          1 cup milk
          1 tablespoon vegetable oil or melted shortening

Preheat oven to 450°F. Brush muffin pans well with 1 tablespoon oil, and heat pans in oven while preparing batter. Sift flour and salt into a bowl. Beat eggs well; then stir in milk and vegetable oil. Make well in flour, pour in egg mixture and beat until smooth. Pour batter into hot pans, filling them 1/2 full. Bake at 450°F. 20 minutes; reduce heat to 325°F. and bake 10 minutes longer. Serve at once. Makes 6–8 popovers.

Note: To prevent sogginess, remove baked popovers from pans as soon as they come from oven, and insert knife in side of each to let out steam. They should be served at once.

VARIATION:

* *Yorkshire Pudding*: Remove roast beef from pan, and keep warm. Raise oven temperature to 450°F. Pour 3 tablespoons beef drippings into an 8-inch square baking pan, and heat in oven while preparing batter. Pour popover batter into hot pan; bake at 450°F. about 35 minutes. Cut in squares, and serve immediately with roast beef.

Corn Bread (Johnnycake)

        3/4 cup unsifted all-purpose flour
        1/4 cup sugar
          4 teaspoons baking powder
        1/2 teaspoon salt
          1 cup yellow cornmeal
          1 egg, beaten
          1 cup milk
        1/4 cup vegetable oil or melted shortening

Preheat oven to 375°F. Combine flour, sugar, baking powder and salt. Mix in cornmeal, and make well in center. Combine egg, milk and vegetable oil; then stir quickly into dry ingredients until combined. Pour into greased 8-inch square cake pan. Bake 25—30 minutes at 375°F. Cut into squares. Or bake in corn-stick pans 15 minutes. Serve warm. Makes 16 squares.

VARIATION:

* *Onion Corn Bread*: Add 1/2 cup diced, sautéed onion to batter.

Pancakes, Waffles and Crêpes

The general term "pancakes" includes 3 basic types. The thin, rich pancakes that the French call "crêpes" are usually served as dessert, with sugar sprinkled over them and wedges of lemon, rolled up with jam or with various sauces. For crêpes suzette, pour a liqueur sauce over pancakes and set aflame.

We are more familiar with the kind called "hotcakes" ("griddle cakes," "flapjacks"), which are a heartier version of the Scottish griddle cake. Then there are waffles, which are lighter and crisper, made from thinner batter in an iron designed to expose more of the surface to the heat and develop more crustiness.

All these pancakes are made with pouring batters, made by adding liquids to dry ingredients and beating only until flour is incorporated. The batter may be lumpy. Waffle and French pancake batters, however, should be beaten until smooth.

To bake pancakes, heat griddle or electric frying pan to 350°F. or until a drop of cold water will "dance" across it. Grease lightly with unsalted fat, unless you have a special grill that does not require greasing. Bake pancake on the first side until its top is covered with bubbles and edges start to lose their gloss. Using spatula, turn cake, and bake other side until golden brown. If batter thickens as it stands or if a very thin pancake is preferred, add more liquid.

To keep pancakes hot, place between folds of a towel in a warm oven as soon as they are cooked. Do not stack pancakes while you keep them hot; stacking causes sogginess.

For waffles, preheat waffle iron as directed (greasing is usually not necessary), and pour required amount of batter in center. Close iron, and bake until waffle stops steaming. Lift out carefully with fork. A 9-inch square waffle iron requires about 1 cup batter; a 7-inch round iron takes about 1/2 cup batter. To keep waffles warm, place on cookie sheet (do not stack) in warm oven.

Pancakes

> 1 1/2 cups sifted all-purpose flour
> 2 tablespoons sugar
> 1 tablespoon baking powder
> 1/2 teaspoon salt
> 1 egg, beaten
> 1 1/2 cups milk
> 3 tablespoons melted butter or margarine

Mix flour, sugar, baking powder and salt together in bowl. Combine egg, milk and oil. Make well in dry ingredients, and pour in egg mixture. Beat only until combined. Heat griddle or frying pan to 350°F. or until drop of cold water will dance across the surface. Grease with unsalted oil or shortening if necessary. Allow about 1/4 cup batter (use individual measure) for each 4-inch pancake. Bake until top of pancake is covered with bubbles and edges begin to lose their gloss. Turn cakes, and bake until golden brown. Makes 12—14 pancakes.

VARIATIONS:

* *Corn Pancakes*: Add 1/2 cup well-drained corn kernels to batter.

* *Nut Pancakes*: Add 1/4 cup chopped nuts to batter.

* *Ham Pancakes*: Omit sugar, and add 1/2—1 cup chopped ham to batter.

* *Blueberry Pancakes*: Fold 1/2 cup fresh blueberries into batter.

* *Pineapple Pancakes*: Add 1/2 cup drained crushed pineapple to batter. Serve with butter or margarine and honey.

Sour-milk Pancakes

> 1 egg
> 1 1/4 cups sour milk
> 1/2 teaspoon baking soda
> 1 1/2 cups sifted all-purpose flour
> 2 teaspoons sugar
> 2 teaspoons baking powder
> 1/2 teaspoon salt
> 2 tablespoons melted butter or oil

Beat egg well. Stir sour milk and soda together, and add mixture to egg, blending well. Sift flour with sugar, baking powder and salt, and stir into milk mixture; add shortening. Beat mixture well until smooth; pour from tablespoon onto greased griddle, and bake as directed above. Makes 12–14 pancakes.

Fluffy Breakfast Pancakes

>   3 egg yolks
> 1 1/2 cups sour milk or buttermilk
>   1 teaspoon baking soda
> 1 1/4 cups unsifted all-purpose flour
>   2 teaspoons sugar
>   1 teaspoon baking powder
>   1/2 teaspoon salt
>   3 tablespoons soft butter or margarine
>   3 egg whites

Beat egg yolks well; stir sour milk and soda together, and stir into egg yolks. Sift flour with sugar, baking powder and salt, and add to milk mixture. Then beat in butter or margarine. Beat egg whites until they hold stiff peaks, and fold into batter. Drop from tablespoon onto hot greased griddle, and bake as directed above. Makes 14–16 pancakes.

Waffles

> 1 1/2 cups unsifted all-purpose flour
>   2 tablespoons sugar
>   1 tablespoon baking powder
>   1/4 teaspoon salt
>   2 eggs, separated
> 1 1/2 cups milk
>   1/2 cup vegetable oil or melted shortening

Heat waffle iron. Sift flour, sugar, baking powder and salt into bowl. Beat egg whites to form soft peaks. Beat yolks; add milk and oil, and beat to blend. Make well in flour mixture, pour in milk mixture and beat until smooth; then fold in beaten whites. When waffle iron is hot enough, pour batter into center of griddle and cook, following manufacturer's directions. Do not raise

cover until waffle stops steaming. When done, loosen waffle with fork, and serve hot with butter or margarine and warm maple syrup. Makes about 6 7-inch waffles.

VARIATIONS:

* *Apple Waffles*: Fold 1/2–1 cup grated apple into batter. Serve with sausages or alone.

* *Cheese Waffles*: Add 1/2 cup shredded aged Cheddar cheese to batter. Serve topped with creamed ham and mushrooms or creamed asparagus.

* *Spice Waffles*: Add 1 teaspoon cinnamon and 1/2 teaspoon nutmeg to dry ingredients. Serve topped with ice cream and *Butterscotch Sauce*.

Dessert Crêpes

>   4 eggs
> 1 1/2 cups milk
> 1 1/3 cups sifted all-purpose flour
>   2 tablespoons sugar
>   1/4 teaspoon salt
>   1/4 cup butter or margarine, melted and cooled
>   1 teaspoon vanilla extract
> 1/2–1 teaspoon grated orange or lemon rind
>   1 teaspoon butter or margarine
>   Sifted icing sugar

Beat eggs in small bowl, and stir in dry ingredients. Add milk and next 3 ingredients. Strain, and allow batter to stand at least 30 minutes or as long as 2 hours. Melt 1 teaspoon butter or margarine in frying pan of 5-inch diameter; when hot, pour in about 2 tablespoons batter or enough to cover thinly the bottom of the pan. Cook 1 minute; then turn, and cook other side. Lift out, and keep warm; sprinkle with sifted sugar. Proceed until all batter is used. Accompany with crushed or sweetened fresh fruit and whipped cream. Makes approximately 16–18 crêpes. (Allow 3 or 4 to a serving).

Note: These French dessert pancakes have a characteristic texture: delicate, almost like custard; and because they roll or fold without cracking they are often served with filling. Be careful to beat batter just until smooth, as overbeating toughens mixture. To cook crêpes evenly, use heavy small pan that is flat on bottom. Cook just 1 crêpe at a time in butter heated until bubbly but not allowed to burn dark. Tilt pan after adding measured batter, so that crêpes will be uniformly round. Turn them just once. Keep warm until all are cooked and ready to serve. Crêpes freeze well and can be quickly defrosted and reheated in dessert sauce. To freeze, leave flat or fold as desired; let cool completely. Then stack with waxed paper between layers. Wrap airtight and freeze.

VARIATIONS:

* *Plain Crêpes*: Omit sugar, vanilla and orange rind from the batter. Fill with savory stuffing mixture.

* *Crêpes with Apricot Sauce*: Combine in saucepan 1 cup apricot nectar, 1/4 cup sugar, 1 tablespoon each lemon juice and brandy. Heat crêpes in this mixture.

* *Crêpes with Jam*: When each pancake is cooked, spread with jam, roll as for jelly roll,

dust with icing sugar and keep hot. Or spread each pancake with jam, do not roll but stack 6

or 8. To serve, cut into wedges as you would a pie.

Crêpes Gismonda

    2 cups medium-thick white sauce
    2 tablespoons grated cheese
    2 (10-ounce) packages frozen spinach, cooked, drained and chopped
    2 tablespoons chopped onion
    2 tablespoons butter or margarine
    1 cup sliced mushrooms
    12 8-inch *Plain Crêpes*
    1/2 cup grated Swiss cheese

Prepare white sauce, adding at least 2 tablespoons grated cheese. To the spinach, add the chopped onion and mushrooms, previously sautéed in the butter or margarine. Cook 5 minutes. Fill the crêpes. Arrange, seam side down, in shallow buttered baking dish. Coat with sauce. Sprinkle with grated Swiss cheese. Bake at 350° 10 minutes. Then broil until cheese is golden. Serves 6.

Chicken Crêpes

    1/4 cup butter or margarine
    5 tablespoons all-purpose flour
    2 cups milk
    1/2 teaspoon salt
    2 cups diced cooked chicken
    1 cup diced sautéed mushrooms
    12 thin *Plain Crêpes*
    2 cups seasoned cooked spinach
    1 cup whipped cream
    1/2 cup grated Parmesan cheese

Melt butter or margarine in saucepan, and stir in flour. Mix well, and add milk gradually. Add salt, and stir constantly until mixture comes to a boil; then stir quickly, and cook over low heat 10 minutes or until thick and smooth. Divide sauce in 1/2. Mix chicken and mushrooms with 1/2 the sauce. Taste for seasoning. Spread each crêpe with chicken mixture, and roll up. Butter 12-inch baking dish, and spread bottom with bed of cooked spinach. Set filled pancakes on spinach, and spread with remaining sauce. Top with thin layer of whipped cream, and sprinkle with Parmesan cheese. Bake at 450°F. 10 minutes; then broil quickly until top is glazed. Serves 8.

Hot Milk Crêpes

    1 cup milk
    2 tablespoons butter or margarine
    2 eggs, beaten
    1/2 cup unsifted all-purpose flour
    2 teaspoons sugar
    1 teaspoon baking powder
    1/2 teaspoon salt
    Jelly (optional)
    Icing sugar

Heat milk and butter or margarine in saucepan, and cool slightly. Add eggs, and beat well. Sift next 4 ingredients together, and add to egg mixture. Use small frying pan about 5 or 6 inches across. Pour in only enough batter to coat bottom of pan thinly, tipping frying pan so that batter runs around. Cook each side 1 minute, and turn cakes again if not sufficiently browned. Makes 14—16. Serve rolled, with jelly filling if desired, and dusted with icing sugar.

Doughnuts

Perfect doughnuts have a crisp, thin, golden crust and are tender and moist inside. For best results, always have the cooking fat at the right temperature. If temperature is too low, the fat will permeate the dough and make it soggy; if too high, the outside may be well browned, but the inside raw. To maintain the correct temperature, an electric control is best. Doughnuts and fritters can be cooked easily in an electric frying pan and even better in an electric deep-fryer.

Without these conveniences, your deep-frying can be successful if the fat is kept at a constant 375° F. throughout the frying. When you drop cold, uncooked foods into hot fat, the temperature immediately falls. So have the temperature slightly over 375°F. *before* you start frying, and fry only a few pieces at a time. Then the temperature will not fall below 375°F. during the frying.

Doughnuts

    1 cup sugar
    1/4 cup soft shortening or butter
    2 eggs
    3/4 cup sour milk or buttermilk
    3 3/4 cups unsifted pastry flour
    3 teaspoons baking powder
    1 teaspoon baking soda
    1 teaspoon salt
    1/2 teaspoon nutmeg
    1/2 teaspoon cinnamon

Beat sugar, shortening and eggs together until very fluffy. Add sour milk and sifted dry ingredients, alternately. Dough will be soft. Coat dough with flour, and knead slightly. Roll or pat out to 3/8-inch thickness. Cut with floured doughnut cutter. Fry in deep fat at 375°F. about 1 minute on each side. Drain on absorbent paper. Makes 28 doughnuts (2 1/2-inch cutter size).

Note: To sugar, shake hot doughnuts in brown paper bag with 1/2 cup sugar and 1/2 teaspoon cinnamon. *To glaze,* gradually add 1/3 cup boiling water to 2 cups sifted icing sugar, mixing well; dip one side of warm doughnut into glaze, and set on cake rack to drain.

Fritters: Savory or Sweet

Fritters are made by coating fruit or vegetable pieces in thin batter and frying them in deep fat. Similar batters may be used to coat seafoods or chicken pieces for deep frying. Sometimes a thicker batter is used, and chopped foods mixed into it, to make a fritter that may be served as a main course.

Savory Fritter Batter

    1 cup unsifted all-purpose flour
    2 teaspoons baking powder
    1 teaspoon salt
    2 eggs
    2/3 cup milk
    1 tablespoon vegetable oil or melted shortening

Sift together flour, baking powder and salt. Beat eggs; add milk and oil. Make well in dry ingredients; blend in liquid, and beat well until smooth. Use as directed to coat foods for deep-frying. Makes about 1 3/4 cups.

* *Chicken in Batter*: Partially cook chicken pieces by simmering. Cool, and pat dry. Dip each piece in batter, and fry in deep fat at 375°F. 6—8 minutes or until crisp and golden brown.

* *Shrimp in Batter*: Peel and devein 1 pound fresh (or defrosted frozen) shrimp, and pat dry. Prepare 1/2 the recipe for *Savory Fritter Batter* for this amount of shrimp, and proceed as for chicken in batter, cooking only 3—4 minutes.
Note: It is important not to overcook shrimp.

* *French-fried Cauliflower*: Cook 1 medium cauliflower until just tender; cool, and separate into flowerets. Prepare 1/2 *Savory Fritter Batter* recipe; dip cauliflower pieces in batter, and fry at 375°F. 3—4 minutes or until evenly browned. Serve as is or with cheese sauce.

* *French-fried Onion Rings*: Slice medium-size onions about 1/3 inch thick, and separate into rings. Prepare 1 recipe *Savory Fritter Batter,* less if only a few onions are to be used. Dip each ring into batter, shaking gently to remove excess; fry a few at a time in deep fat preheated to 375°F. Drain well, and keep warm (place rings on a cake rack to prevent steaming).

Sweet Fritter Batter

    1/2 cup unsifted all-purpose flour
    1 tablespoon sugar
    1 teaspoon baking powder
    1/4 teaspoon salt
    1 egg
    1/3 cup milk
    1 1/2 teaspoons vegetable oil or melted shortening

Combine flour, sugar, baking powder and salt. Beat egg; add milk and oil. Make well in dry ingredients, blend in liquid mixture and beat until very smooth. Use as directed to coat foods for deep-frying. Makes about 1 cup.

Note: Halved bananas and fresh or canned (drained) peaches or pears in suitably sized pieces may be cooked in this batter.

Apple-ring Fritters

    4–5 apples, unpeeled and cored
    1 tablespoon lemon juice
    1/4 cup sugar
    1 recipe *Sweet Fritter Batter*
    1 tablespoon sugar
    1 teaspoon cinnamon

Slice apples crosswise 1/4—1/3 inch thick. Sprinkle with lemon juice, and let stand while preparing batter. Dust slices with 1/4 cup sugar; dip each in batter. Shake off any excess batter, and drop in deep fat preheated to 375°F. Cook 3—4 minutes, turning so that slices brown evenly.

Keep fritters warm in 300°F. oven until all apple rings are cooked. Sprinkle with 1 tablespoon sugar and cinnamon, and serve as accompaniment for meat or as a dessert with *Lemon Sauce* or cream. Makes 4—5 servings.

Note: Canned pineapple rings or apricot halves can be substituted for apples.

Muffins

The secret of tender muffins lies in the mixing. Always stir dry ingredients and liquids together only until flour is dampened. Batter will be lumpy. Overmixing or beating causes unattractive peaked tops and large tunnels inside. Line muffin pans with paper baking cups, or grease well. Fill cups only 2/3 full with batter. The variation of 5 minutes or so in baking times in the following recipes allows for difference in muffin pan sizes. The yield from each recipe will also vary depending on size of your muffin tins. Pour 2—3 tablespoons water into any leftover greased muffin cups to prevent burning.

To keep muffins warm, tilt baked muffins in pan (to prevent sogginess), and place in warm oven.

To reheat, place muffins in brown paper bag, sprinkle bag with water and warm in oven. Or wrap in foil.

Plain Muffins

```
    2  cups unsifted cake and pastry flour
    3  teaspoons baking powder
 1/2  teaspoon salt
 1/3  cup sugar
    1  egg, beaten
1 1/4  cups milk
 1/4  cup melted butter or margarine
    1  teaspoon vanilla (optional)
```

Measure and sift dry ingredients into a bowl, and make a well in the center. Combine the remaining liquid ingredients, and pour into the well. Stir only until flour mixture is dampened; then fill lined or well-greased muffin cups 2/3 full. Bake about 20 minutes at 425°F. Makes about 12 muffins.

VARIATIONS:

* *Bacon Muffins*: Omit sugar, and add 1/4 cup diced crisp bacon to dry ingredients. Bacon fat can be used in place of oil or melted shortening, or partially cooked thin bacon can be used to line muffin pans before pouring batter in.

* *Fruit Muffins*: Add 1 cup currants, raisins or chopped dates to dry ingredients, or fold 1 cup fresh blueberries into batter.

* *Whole Wheat Muffins*: Decrease flour to 1 cup; increase sugar to 1/4 cup. Add 1 cup whole wheat flour to sifted dry ingredients, and blend.

* *Cinnamon Muffins*: While muffins are hot, dip tops in mixture of 1/2 cup sugar and 1 teaspoon cinnamon.

* *Streusel-topped Muffins*: Sprinkle mixture of 1/2 cup chopped walnuts, 1/2 cup brown sugar, 2 tablespoons each flour and melted butter or margarine and 1 teaspoon cinnamon over batter in tins.

Pineapple Muffins

```
    1  cup canned unsweetened pineapple juice
    1  egg, slightly beaten
 1/4  cup melted shortening
1 3/4  cups sifted all-purpose flour
 1/4  cup sugar
    4  teaspoons baking powder
 1/2  teaspoon salt
    2  tablespoons sugar
    1  teaspoon grated orange rind
```

Beat pineapple juice into slightly beaten egg. Add shortening. Sift flour with 1/4 cup sugar, baking powder and salt, and add to egg mixture. Stir quickly until dry ingredients are just moistened. Fill greased muffin pans 2/3 full. Mix 2 tablespoons sugar and orange rind, and sprinkle over muffins. Bake at 400°F. 20—25 minutes. Makes 10—12 muffins.

Note: Add 1/4—1/3 cup well-drained crushed pineapple if you wish.

Oatmeal Muffins

```
    1  cup sifted all-purpose flour
 1/4  cup brown sugar, firmly packed
    1  tablespoon baking powder
 1/2  teaspoon salt
    3  tablespoons shortening
    1  cup rolled oats
 1/3  cup seedless raisins
    1  egg, beaten
    1  cup milk
```

Sift together flour, sugar, baking powder and salt, and cut in shortening. Stir in rolled oats and raisins, and add egg and milk, stirring just enough to dampen dry ingredients. *Do not overstir.* Fill greased muffin cups 2/3 full, and bake at 425°F. 15—25 minutes. Makes 12—14 muffins.

Spiced Apple Muffins

      2 cups sifted all-purpose flour
  1/3 cup sugar
      4 teaspoons baking powder
      1 teaspoon cinnamon
  3/4 teaspoon salt
  1/4 teaspoon nutmeg
  3/4 cup shredded peeled apple
      1 egg, beaten
      1 cup milk
  1/4 cup melted shortening

Sift together first 6 ingredients; stir in apple. Make well in center. Combine egg, milk and shortening, and add to dry ingredients. Stir only until combined; the batter should be lumpy. Fill greased muffin pans 2/3 full, and bake at 400°F. 20—25 minutes. Makes 14—16 muffins.

Bran Muffins

  1/4 cup soft butter or margarine
  1/2 cup brown sugar, firmly packed
      2 tablespoons dark molasses
      1 egg
  3/4 cup sour milk or buttermilk
      1 cup natural bran
      1 cup unsifted all-purpose flour
  1/2 teaspoon soda
      2 teaspoons baking powder
  1/2 teaspoon salt
  2/3 cup raisins or chopped dates

Beat butter, brown sugar, molasses and egg together until very fluffy. Stir in sour milk and bran. Let stand 15 minutes to soak; then lightly stir in sifted dry ingredients. Add raisins, and spoon into 12 lined or greased muffin cups, filling 2/3 full. Bake at 425°F. about 20 minutes. Makes 12 or more muffins.

Quick Loaves

The method of mixing these breads varies with the recipe, but many recipes call for the muffin method of combining ingredients with a minimum of stirring. To help prevent cracking along top of the loaf, after spreading batter in pan, let stand about 20 minutes before baking.

Nut Bread

      2 cups sifted all-purpose flour
  1/2 cup sugar
      4 teaspoons baking powder
      1 teaspoon salt
      1 cup finely chopped walnuts
      1 egg, beaten
  1 1/4 cups milk
      4 tablespoons melted shortening

Sift flour, baking powder, sugar and salt into mixing bowl. Add nuts. Combine egg, milk and shortening. Make well in dry ingredients, and add egg mixture. Stir quickly until flour is absorbed. Scrape into greased 9″ x 5″ x 3″ loaf pan, and bake 50—60 minutes at 350°F. Makes 1 loaf.

Date-Nut Loaf

      2 cups chopped dates
      1 teaspoon baking soda
  3/4 cup boiling water
  3/4 cup sugar
      2 tablespoons shortening
      1 egg, beaten
      1 teaspoon vanilla extract
  1 3/4 cups sifted all-purpose flour
  1/2 cup chopped walnuts
  1/2 teaspoon salt

Combine dates and baking soda; cover with boiling water, and let stand until cool. Cream sugar and shortening together, add egg and vanilla and beat until combined. Add cooled date mixture, flour, walnuts and salt; stir until just combined. Do not beat. Scrape mixture into greased 9″ x 5″ 3″ loaf pan, and bake at 350°F. 60—70 minutes. Makes 1 loaf.

Banana-Gumdrop Loaf

  1 3/4 cups unsifted all-purpose flour
  1/2 teaspoon baking soda
  1 1/2 teaspoons baking powder
  3/4 teaspoon salt
  3/4 cup sugar
  4—5 ounces gumdrops, cut in pieces
      1 egg, beaten
  1/4 cup oil
      1 cup mashed banana
  1/2 cup milk
      2 teaspoons grated orange rind

Measure and sift the first 5 ingredients into a bowl, and stir in gumdrop pieces. Combine remaining ingredients, and stir into the dry mixture. Stir until blended, and scrape into a greased 9″ x 5″ pan. Bake at 350°F. 50 minutes. Makes 1 loaf.

3-Fruit Loaf

      2 cups biscuit mix
  1/2 cup sugar
  1/3 cup chopped glacé cherries
      1 egg, beaten
      2 tablespoons salad oil
  1 1/2 teaspoons grated orange rind
  1/2 cup crushed pineapple and juice
  1/3 cup orange juice

Combine biscuit mix and cherries. Mix remaining ingredients together, and stir into the dry mixture. Scrape into a greased 8 1/2″ x 4 1/2″ loaf pan, and bake at 375°F. 45—50 minutes. Cool, and remove from pan. Makes 1 loaf.

Maraschino Loaf

1 3/4 cups unsifted all-purpose flour
4 teaspoons baking powder
1/2 teaspoon salt
3/4 cup sugar
1 (6-ounce) bottle red maraschino cherries
2 teaspoons grated orange rind or 1 teaspoon grated lemon rind
2 eggs, beaten
1 cup milk
3 tablespoons salad oil

Sift dry ingredients into a bowl. Drain cherries, and dry well on paper towels. Cut cherries in small pieces, and toss into dry ingredients. Combine remaining ingredients, and stir into the dry mixture. Scrape into a greased 8 1/2″ x 4 1/2″ loaf pan, and bake at 375°F. 50 minutes. Cool, and remove from pan. Makes 1 loaf.

Tomato Soup–Spice Loaf

1 2/3 cups unsifted all-purpose flour
1 teaspoon baking soda
1 1/2 teaspoons baking powder
1 1/2 teaspoons mixed spice
3/4 cup brown sugar, lightly packed
1/2 cup raisins
1/2 cup chopped nuts
1 (10-ounce) can tomato soup
2 tablespoons salad oil
2 tablespoons milk

Sift the first 4 ingredients into a bowl. Add the sugar, raisins and nuts; then stir in a mixture of soup and oil. Mix thoroughly, and scrape into a greased 8 1/2″ x 4 1/2″ loaf pan. Bake at 350°F. 50 minutes. Cool, and remove from pan. Makes 1 loaf.

Note: Substitute sweetened applesauce for tomato soup if you wish, using 1 1/4 cups.

Orange Bread

2 cups sifted all-purpose flour
3/4 cup sugar
2 teaspoons baking powder
3/4 teaspoon salt
1/2 teaspoon baking soda
3/4 cup chopped nuts
1/2 cup raisins
2 tablespoons grated orange rind
1 egg, well beaten
1/2 cup milk
1/2 cup orange juice
3 tablespoons shortening, melted

Sift dry ingredients together. Add nuts, raisins and orange rind. Combine egg with milk, orange juice and shortening, and stir into flour mixture. Turn batter into greased 9″ x 5″ x 3″ loaf pan, and bake at 350°F. 60 minutes or until done. Makes 1 loaf.

Whole Wheat–Nut Bread

1 cup unsifted all-purpose flour
2 teaspoons baking powder
1/2 teaspoon baking soda
3/4 teaspoon salt
2 teaspoons mixed spice
1 cup whole wheat flour
2/3 cup brown sugar, firmly packed
1/2 cup chopped pecans or walnuts
3/4 cup sultana raisins
1 egg, beaten
3/4 cup milk
1/4 cup fancy molasses
1/4 cup salad oil

Sift the first 5 ingredients into a bowl, and stir in whole wheat flour, brown sugar, nuts and raisins. Make a well in the center, and pour in the combined liquids. Mix thoroughly, and scrape into a greased 9″ x 5″ loaf pan. Bake at 350°F. 55 minutes. Makes 1 loaf.

Peanut Butter Bread

2 cups sifted all-purpose flour
1/2 cup granulated sugar
1 tablespoon baking powder
1/2 teaspoon salt
1/2 cup peanut butter
2 eggs, well beaten
1 cup milk
1 teaspoon grated lemon rind or orange rind
1/3 cup chopped salted peanuts
1 tablespoon melted butter or corn syrup

Place first 4 ingredients in bowl. Rub in peanut butter until mixture is crumbly. Combine eggs, milk and lemon rind, and stir quickly into flour mixture. Scrape into greased 9″ x 5″ x 3″ loaf pan. Sprinkle with peanuts. Bake at 325°–350°F. 50–60 minutes. While still hot, brush top with melted butter. Cool, and remove from pan. Slice second day. Makes 1 loaf.

Cranberry Bread

Juice and grated rind of 1 orange
3 tablespoons salad oil
Boiling water
2 cups unsifted all-purpose flour
2 teaspoons baking powder
1/2 teaspoon baking soda
1/2 teaspoon salt
1 cup sugar
1 egg, beaten
1 cup chopped or minced raw cranberries
2/3 cup chopped walnuts

Pour orange juice into a measuring cup, and add grated rind, oil and enough boiling water to make 3/4 cup. Set aside. Sift dry ingredients into a bowl, and make a well in the center. Pour in the liquids and beaten egg. Stir until blended. Fold in cranberries and nuts. Bake in a greased 9″ x 5″ x 3″ loaf pan at 325°F. 60–70 minutes or until center is set. Cool in the pan. Store 24 hours before slicing.

Onion Quick Bread

    1 1/2 cups unsifted all-purpose flour
        1 cup whole wheat flour
        1 tablespoon baking powder
    1 1/2 teaspoons salt
        1 teaspoon baking soda
    1 1/2 cups buttermilk or sour milk
        1/2 cup light molasses
        1/4 cup melted shortening or oil
        1/2 cup finely chopped onion
        2 teaspoons caraway seeds or sesame seeds

Combine dry ingredients, and add buttermilk, molasses and shortening. Mix thoroughly but lightly. Add onion; sprinkle 2 teaspoons caraway seeds over batter, and fold in. Scrape into well-greased 9″ x 5″ x 3″ loaf pan. Top may be sprinkled with additional caraway and sesame seeds. Bake at 350°F. 60 minutes or until done. Unmold on rack. Serve when still slightly warm with butter and cottage cheese, sliced apples, pears or bunches of grapes. Makes 1 loaf.

Note: If well wrapped, bread will keep moist for days, and freezes extremely well.

BAKING BREAD

Baking bread is easier than you think. Here are the basic ingredients. You can buy cakes of compressed fresh yeast or, more commonly, envelopes of activated dry yeast. The two may be used interchangeably. To substitute fresh yeast for dry yeast, crumble yeast cake over required amount of *unsweetened* lukewarm water, and let stand 10 minutes. Yeast works best at about 85°F. For very fast results the temperature can be 115°F., but no higher. A lower temperature slows down production of gases, and too high a temperature kills yeast. All ingredients must therefore be lukewarm during mixing and rising of dough. For best results, prepare bread dough in a draft-free room.

Sugar provides food for the yeast, whereas *salt* helps to control the action of the yeast. Both ingredients must be used in the right proportions.

The *liquid* may be milk, water, potato water or a mixture of them. Milk gives finer crumbs and more tender crust. When fresh milk is used, it must first be scalded to destroy enzymes that would otherwise interfere with the yeast.

Hard-wheat or all-purpose *flour* must be used for bread, as it contains gluten, which is nessary to give bread dough an elastic quality, enabling it to hold gases produced by the yeast and to expand or rise. Such other flours or cereals as whole wheat or cracked wheat and rolled oats may be used for bread, but the flour content of the recipe should include 40–50 percent all-purpose flour in order to supply the necessary gluten.

Note: Rye flour has a higher percentage of gluten than oats, cracked wheat or whole wheat. Therefore some recipes for rye bread may contain less than 40 percent all-purpose flour.

Yeast Dough

There are 3 basic methods for making yeast breads.

1. *Sponge Method*: A batter, made from yeast, lukewarm liquid, sugar and some flour, is allowed to rise until light and bubbly; texture resembles that of sponge. Then the remaining flour and other ingredients are added, and dough is allowed to rise as directed in recipe. Next it is divided into loaves or rolls and left again to rise before baking.

2. *Straight-dough Method*: This method is now the most commonly used. The softened yeast is combined with sugar, salt, liquids and shortening. Flour is then added to make a soft but not sticky dough, which is kneaded and allowed to rise according to requirements of recipe. When it is ready, the dough is shaped into loaves or rolls and allowed to rise again before baking.

3. *Quick Method*: To make rolls or sweet dough quickly, ingredients are combined and beaten, rather than kneaded. A fairly high proportion of yeast is used in batter-type recipes, as well as more liquid. The finished product has a lighter, more open texture, but it lacks the keeping quality of breads made by the straight-dough method. However, as dough is soft enough to be beaten by electric mixer, there is some saving of time and effort. No kneading is required because beating serves to develop gluten sufficiently.

Basic Steps for Making Bread

A firm working of dough with your hands is essential (except in quick method) to develop gluten and to distribute gas bubbles evenly throughout dough. Kneading is a simple, 3-step action. First, fold far side of dough toward you. Then push dough away from you, pressing it firmly with "heels" of your hands. Finally give dough a 1/4 turn. Repeat this folding, pressing and turning with rhythmic motion until dough is satin-smooth and elastic. Kneading usually requires 8—10 minutes for bread, about 5 minutes for sweet dough. Use only enough flour on board to keep dough from sticking. Flour your hands, too, to prevent sticking.

The First Rising. Place kneaded dough in lightly greased bowl. Grease top of dough slightly to prevent dry crust from forming. For white bread and rolls, allow dough to rise until it has doubled in bulk, which takes about 1 1/2 hours. To test dough, push 2 fingers deep into it and withdraw them at once. If indentations remain, dough has risen enough. For dark bread and rolls, dough must rise only until it is 1/2 more than its original volume, as whole wheat, rye, and similar cereals make a heavier mixture.

Rising times will vary, depending on amount of yeast and whether or not dough is kept at fairly uniform temperature of 85°F. To keep temperature constant, set bowl of dough in pan of lukewarm water, and cover it with cloth. Always keep dough away from direct heat and cold drafts.

Once dough has risen enough, punch it down to expel air. Allow it to rise again if recipe requires it. Otherwise, divide dough into required portions, shape into smooth balls, cover with cloth and allow to "rest" about 15 minutes, in order to make dough easier to shape into loaves or rolls.

TO SHAPE LOAVES:

* *Method 1*: Roll or press dough out lightly into a rectangle; then roll up tightly like a jelly roll. Turn ends under or pinch together, and place seam edge down in greased loaf pan.

* *Method 2*: Roll dough out into a long rectangle about twice the length of the loaf pan. Fold ends toward the center, and press down where they meet. Lift up for side of rectangle, and fold toward you. Seal front edges together with palms of hands. Place edge down in prepared loaf pan. Grease tops of loaves lightly.

Second Rising. Place pans in warm place free from drafts or direct heat. Cover with cloth. For white bread, let dough rise until it fills pan and center is rounded slightly above top edge. To test, press dough gently with fingertips. If slight impression remains, dough is ready for oven. For dark bread, dough should be allowed to rise until rounded center of loaf is about level with top edge of pan. This rising time for bread in pan varies with recipe and room temperature.

To Bake. Bread is sufficiently baked when loaves lift free from the pan and when they sound hollow if tapped on bottom crust. Remove baked bread from pans at once, and stand on rack to cool. Keep them away from drafts to prevent crust cracking. For softer crusts, brush warm loaves with softened butter or margarine.

The following recipes can be halved. Use 1/2 the ingredients called for, but otherwise prepare dough exactly as directed for full recipe, allowing same baking times. Shape into 2 loaves when 4 are given in recipe, 1 loaf when 2 are given.

White Bread

      2 cups milk
    1/4 cup sugar
    1/4 cup shortening
      4 teaspoons salt
      2 cups lukewarm water
      2 envelopes dry yeast
      2 teaspoons sugar
  10–11 cups (approximately) all-purpose flour

Scald milk, and add 1/4 cup sugar, shortening and salt. Stir in 1 cup lukewarm water, and cool until whole mixture is lukewarm. Sprinkle yeast into other cup lukewarm water with 2 teaspoons sugar (if yeast cakes are used, omit sugar). Let stand 10 minutes. Stir yeast, and mix into milk mixture. Add 1/2 the flour, and beat until almost smooth. Add remaining flour gradually, mixing thoroughly. Use enough to prevent dough clinging to bowl. When dough is stiff, turn out on lightly floured board; flour your hands, and knead about 10 minutes. Shape into ball, and place in greased bowl. Grease top slightly to prevent crust from forming. Cover, and let rise in warm place until dough doubles in bulk. Punch dough, and fold into center. Turn onto lightly floured board, and shape dough into mound. Cut into 4 equal pieces, and shape each into 2 balls. Cover balls with clean tea towel, and let rest 10 minutes. Shape into 4 loaves. Place in greased 9″ x 5″ x 3″ loaf pans, and bake at 425° F. 15–20 minutes; reduce heat to 350°F. and continue baking 20–30 minutes. Makes 4 loaves.

VARIATIONS:

* *Bran Bread*: Use 1/2 cup fancy molasses in place of sugar. Use 2 cups natural bran in place of 2 cups flour plus a little extra flour if necessary.

* *Cheese Bread*: Mix in 1 cup finely shredded Cheddar cheese after the first 1/2 of the flour has been added.

* *Rye Bread*: Substitute brown for granulated sugar. Mix in 6 cups all-purpose flour and enough rye flour (about 4 cups) to make dough that comes clean from bowl and is not sticky.

Whole Wheat Bread

  1 1/2 cups milk
    1/2 cup brown sugar, firmly packed
    1/2 cup shortening
      3 teaspoons salt
      3 cups lukewarm water
      2 teaspoons sugar
      2 envelopes dry yeast
      6 cups whole wheat flour
  4 1/2–5 cups (approximately) all-purpose flour

Scald milk, and pour into large mixing bowl. Add brown sugar, shortening and salt, and stir until shortening melts. Stir in 2 cups luke-warm water, and cool until whole mixture is lukewarm.

Dissolve white sugar in 1 cup lukewarm water, sprinkle yeast over it and let stand 10 minutes at about 85°F. Stir yeast mixture with fork, add to lukewarm milk mixture and stir again. Beat in whole wheat flour gradually; then add all-purpose flour. Turn dough onto floured board, and knead 8—10 minutes. Shape into smooth ball. Place dough in lightly greased bowl, and grease top a little to prevent crust from forming. Cover, and allow to rise in warm place until almost doubled in bulk, about 1 1/4 hours. Punch down, and turn out again on floured board. Cut into 4 equal portions, and form each into a smooth ball. Cover balls, and allow to rest about 15 minutes before shaping into loaves. Place loaves in greased 9″ x 5″ x 3″ loaf pans; grease tops lightly, cover and let rise 1 hour or until nearly doubled in bulk. Bake at 425°F. 20—25 minutes; then reduce heat to 375°F. and continue baking 25 minutes longer.

VARIATION:

* *Molasses—Whole Wheat Bread*: Instead of brown sugar, use 1/2 cup fancy molasses.

Plain Batter Bread

```
      2 teaspoons sugar
1 1/4 cups lukewarm water
      1 envelope dry yeast
      2 tablespoons soft shortening
      2 tablespoons sugar
1 1/2 teaspoons salt
      3 cups unsifted all-purpose flour
```

Add 2 teaspoons sugar to water in mixing bowl. Dissolve yeast in this water, and let stand 10 minutes. Add shortening, 2 tablespoons sugar, salt and 1 1/2 cups flour. Beat 2 minutes in electric mixer at medium speed or 300 strokes by hand. Scrape sides and bottom of bowl frequently. Add remaining flour, and beat with spoon until smooth, about 1 1/2 minutes. Scrape batter from sides of bowl frequently. Cover bowl with cloth, and let rise in warm place until doubled in bulk, about 1/2 hour. Beat down, about 25 strokes. Spread batter evenly in greased 9″ x 5″ x 3″ loaf pan. Smooth top by patting into shape with floured hands as batter will be sticky. Let rise in warm place until edge of batter is within 1/4 inch of top of pan, about 40 minutes. Bake at 375°F. 45—50 minutes. When baked, remove from pan, and brush top with melted butter or margarine. Makes 1 loaf.

VARIATIONS:

* *Herb Bread*: Into first 1 1/2 cups flour, mix 1 teaspoon caraway seeds and 1/4 teaspoon each nutmeg and powdered sage.

* *Whole Wheat Batter Bread*: Substitute firmly packed brown sugar for 2 tablespoons granulated sugar and 1 cup whole wheat flour for 1 cup all-purpose flour. Add 1/2 cup whole wheat flour in first 1 1/2 cups flour; add remaining 1/2 cup whole wheat flour at the end of the mixing.

* *Festive Bread*: To second 1 1/2 cups flour add 1/4 cup each chopped candied peel, raisins and nuts and 1/2 teaspoon each almond and vanilla extracts. Spread batter in 2 greased 1-pound coffee cans. Let rise until batter is 1/2 inch from top. Bake about 40 minutes.

Quick Oatmeal Bread

```
      1 teaspoon sugar
  1/2 cup warm water
      1 envelope dry yeast
  1/2 cup boiling water
  1/2 cup rolled oats
  1/4 cup fancy molasses or honey
      2 tablespoons soft shortening
1 1/2 teaspoons salt
      1 egg
2 3/4 cups all-purpose flour
```

Add sugar to warm water, and sprinkle yeast over; let stand 10 minutes. Mix boiling water, oats, molasses, shortening and salt in large mixing bowl, and let mixture cool to lukewarm. Add yeast mixture, egg and 1 1/2 cups flour to lukewarm mixture. Beat 2 minutes in electric mixer at medium speed or 300 strokes by hand. Scrape sides and bottom of bowl frequently. Add remaining flour, and blend with mixing spoon until smooth. Spread batter evenly in greased 9″ x 5″ x 3″ loaf pan. Smooth top of loaf with floured hands, and pat into shape. Let rise in warm place (85°F.) until batter is 1 inch from top of pan, about 1 1/2 hours. Bake at 375°F. 50—55 minutes. Crust will be dark brown. To test, tap bottom crust; it should sound hollow. After removing from pan, brush top with melted butter or margarine. Makes 1 loaf.

Cheese Pan Bread

```
  1/2 cup milk
  1/2 cup butter or margarine
      3 teaspoons sugar
      1 teaspoon salt
  1/2 cup lukewarm water
      1 teaspoon sugar
      1 envelope dry yeast
      3 eggs, well beaten
2 3/4 cups (approximately) all-purpose flour
1/3—1/2 cup grated Parmesan or Romano cheese
  1/4 teaspoon dry mustard
      Few grains pepper
```

Scald milk; stir in butter or margarine, 2 teaspoons sugar and salt. Cool to lukewarm. Meanwhile, measure lukewarm water into large bowl; stir in 1 teaspoon sugar. Sprinkle with yeast. Let stand 10 minutes; then stir. Stir in lukewarm milk mixture, eggs and 1 3/4 cups flour. Beat until smooth and elastic. Combine cheese, mustard and pepper, and stir into batter. Work in sufficient additional flour to make thick batter, about 1 cup more. Cover with damp towel. Let rise until doubled in bulk, about 1 1/4 hours. Stir down batter. Divide between 2 greased 8-inch layer-cake pans, and spread evenly. Cover loosely with waxed paper or plastic wrap. Let rise until almost doubled in bulk, about 45 minutes. Bake at 375° F. 25—30 minutes. Makes 2 loaves.

Challah (Egg Bread)

    1/3 cup warm water
      2 tablespoons sugar
      1 envelope dry yeast
      1 cup lukewarm scalded milk
    1/4 cup soft butter or margarine
      2 eggs, unbeaten
      2 teaspoons salt
  5—5 1/2 cups (approximately) all-purpose flour
      1 egg yolk
      2 tablespoons water

Combine water, sugar and yeast in warm mixing bowl, and stir until dissolved. Add lukewarm milk, butter or margarine, 2 eggs, salt and 2 1/2 cups flour. Using electric mixer, beat slowly at first until ingredients are well combined; then increase speed to medium, and beat until smooth. Continue adding flour until batter begins to creep up beaters. Remove and scrape beaters, and work in as much remaining flour as you can with wooden spoon, then by hand. Turn dough onto floured board, and knead until smooth, working more flour in until dough loses its stickiness. Place in lightly greased bowl, and oil top. Cover, and let rise until doubled in bulk. Punch down, and cut dough into 2 pieces, one slightly smaller than the other. Cut larger piece into 3 equal parts, and shape each into a strand about 12 inches long and 1 inch in diameter. Roll back and forth on board to form evenly shaped ropes. Make 3 strands 10 inches long out of remaining dough. Braid longer strands loosely on greased cookie sheet, and tuck ends under neatly. Braid shorter strands, and center on top of first braid, tucking ends under. Brush with salad oil, and cover with damp cloth. Let rise until doubled in bulk. Beat egg yolk with 2 tablespoons water, and brush over loaf. Bake at 425°F. 25 minutes; reduce heat to 350°F. and bake 10 minutes longer. Makes 1 loaf.

Onion Bread

      1 envelope dry yeast
      1 teaspoon sugar
    1/2 cup lukewarm water
      1 cup scalded milk
      2 tablespoons sugar
      2 tablespoons shortening
      2 teaspoons salt
      3 cups sifted all-purpose flour
      3 tablespoons chopped onion
      5 teaspoons caraway seeds
  1 1/2 cups (approximately) unsifted rye flour

Dissolve yeast and 1 teaspoon sugar in lukewarm water. Mix milk, sugar, shortening and salt together, and cool to lukewarm. Add yeast mixture, and stir in all-purpose flour. Mix until smooth. Add onion and caraway seeds, then enough rye flour to make firm dough. Knead until smooth on rye-floured board. Brush top with salad oil, and cover. Let rise until doubled. Knead again until free of large air bubbles, and shape into 2 small loaves or 1 large one. Place in 2 small or 1 large well-greased loaf pan, and brush tops with oil. Let rise again until doubled, and bake in a 350°F. oven 45—50 minutes. Makes 2 small loaves or 1 large loaf.

Dill Bread

    1/2 cup lukewarm water
      2 envelopes dry yeast
      2 cups creamy cottage cheese
    1/4 cup chopped onion
    1/4 cup melted butter or margarine
      2 teaspoons salt
      2 eggs
      5 cups sifted all-purpose flour
      2 tablespoons dried dill weed or 2 teaspoons
           dill seed
      2 thin slices onion

Pour water into jar of electric blender. Add dry yeast, stir and let stand 5 minutes. Blend at high speed 10 seconds. Add cottage cheese, onion, butter or margarine, salt and eggs; blend at high speed 20 seconds. Sift flour into large mixing bowl; add dill. Add blender mixture. Mix with spoon until dough falls away from sides of bowl. Place in a large, lightly greased bowl, cover with a damp cloth and let rise until double. Punch down. Put into 2 well-greased 9″ x 5″ x 3″ pans. Separate onion slices into rings and arrange over top of loaf. Let rise again until double. Preheat oven to 350°F. Bake 1 hour, 15 minutes.

Saint's Loaf

  1 1/2 cups boiling water
    1/2 cup honey
    1/3 cup vegetable shortening
      1 tablespoon salt
      2 envelopes dry yeast
    1/2 cup lukewarm water
      1 teaspoon sugar
      2 eggs
    1/2 cup wheat germ
  2 3/4 cups flour
  1 3/4 cups whole wheat flour
      1 cup coarsely chopped walnuts
    1/4 cup water
    1/4 cup sugar
    1/4 cup coarsely chopped walnuts

In large bowl of an electric mixer, combine water, shortening, honey and salt. Stir until shortening melts. Cool to lukewarm. Dissolve yeast in lukewarm water with 1 teaspoon sugar. Add to honey mixture along with eggs, wheat germ and 1 1/2 cups flour. Beat with mixer 2 minutes at medium speed. Stir in remaining flour, whole wheat flour, and 1 cup coarsely chopped walnuts. Mixture will be sticky. Shape into 2 loaves, and place in 2 well-greased 9″ x 5″ x 3″ loaf pans. Cover with a damp cloth, and let rise until 1 inch from top of pan.

Preheat oven to 375°F. Bake loaves 40—50 minutes. Meanwhile make topping: in small saucepan combine 1/4 cup water and 1/4 cup sugar. Both until slightly syrupy (about 2 minutes). Brush tops of loaves with syrup, and sprinkle with coarsely chopped walnuts after loaves are baked.

Golden Corn Loaf

    2 medium potatoes, peeled and quartered
1 1/2 cups water
    1 cup cornmeal
    1/4 cup corn syrup
    1/4 cup shortening
    2 teaspoons salt
    1/2 cup warm water
    1 teaspoon sugar
    1 envelope dry yeast
4–4 1/3 cups all-purpose flour

Simmer potatoes and water together in a covered pan until potatoes are very tender. Remove from the heat, and mash without draining; then stir in the next 4 ingredients. Let cool to lukewarm. Combine the warm water, sugar and yeast, and let stand until yeast dissolves, about 10 minutes. Then add the potato mixture and about 2 cups of the flour. Beat until smooth. Work in another 1 1/2 cups of flour with a wooden spoon, then by hand. Knead in remaining flour until dough is smooth, about 5 minutes. Let rest for 10 minutes; then cut in half, and shape into 2 loaves. Press into 2 oiled 8″ x 4″ x 3″ loaf pans, and cover. Let rise until pans are full. Brush with egg white, and sprinkle with sesame seeds. Bake at 400°F. 15 minutes; then reduce heat to 350°F., and continue baking 20–25 minutes.

Garlic Puffs

    1 (13 3/4-ounce) package hot-roll mix
    1 egg
    1 tablespoon water
    1 clove garlic, crushed
    1 tablespoon coarse crystal salt

Prepare dough from hot-roll mix, following package directions through first rising. Punch dough down, and roll out into 4″ x 18″ oblong. Cut in half lengthwise, making two strips; then cut each strip into 9 2-inch squares. Form each square into a ball; place in well-greased muffin pans. Brush with egg wash made by beating 1 egg with 1 tablespoon water. Mix crushed garlic with salt, and sprinkle over tops of rolls.

Let rise until double. Preheat oven to 375°F. Bake 15—18 minutes. Makes 18 puffs.

Quick Brioches

    1/3 cup warm water
    1 teaspoon sugar
    1 envelope dry yeast
    1/2 cup sifted all-purpose flour
    1 bowl lukewarm water
    4 eggs
    3/4 cup soft butter or margarine
    1 tablespoon sugar
    3/4 teaspoon salt
    1/2 teaspoon lemon extract (optional)
2 3/4 cups unsifted all-purpose flour
    1 egg yolk, slightly beaten
    2 tablespoons water

Measure 1/3 cup water and sugar into small bowl, and add yeast. Let stand 10 minutes or until dissolved; stir in 1/2 cup flour. Knead slightly until smooth, and shape into soft ball. Gash top, and drop into bowl of lukewarm water. Let dough rise to top of water before removing from water and adding to other ingredients. Meanwhile, beat 4 eggs slightly in large bowl. Add next 4 ingredients, and beat in 1 1/2 cups flour and risen yeast ball. Scrape and remove beaters, and add remaining flour with wooden spoon and then by hand. Knead slightly just until smooth, about 1 minute. Dough will be soft. Place in warm oiled bowl, and cover. Let rise until puffy (about 1 hour); stir down, and scrape into oiled 8-inch square pan. Chill in freezer 30 minutes or until dough is firm enough to handle. Oil 2 1/2 dozen fluted tart pans or muffin pans. Cut off small pieces of dough, and turn edges under to form smooth balls 1/3 the size of the tart pans. Press thumb or finger into center of each ball; mold tiny balls of dough, and place in the depressions. Cover, and let rise about 45 minutes or until doubled in bulk. Make solution of egg yolk and 2 tablespoons water, and brush carefully over brioches. Bake at 400°F. 15—20 minutes, depending on size. Makes 2 1/2 dozen.

Oatmeal-Honey Bread

    1/2 cup warm water
    1 teaspoon sugar
    1 envelope dry yeast
    1 cup commercial sour cream
    1 cup quick-cooking oats
    3 tablespoons honey
    1 teaspoon salt
    1/4 teaspoon baking soda
2 1/3 cups unsifted all-purpose flour
    1 tablespoon honey

Combine warm water, sugar and yeast in mixing bowl, and stir or let stand 10 minutes to dissolve. Heat sour cream until warm, but not hot, and remove from heat. Stir in oats, 3 tablespoons honey, salt and baking soda. When cooled to lukewarm, add yeast mixture and 1 cup flour, and beat well. Mix in 1/2 cup flour with wooden spoon. Knead lightly on board to work in remaining flour until dough is smooth, about 5 minutes. Place ball of dough in warm oiled bowl, and turn it over once to oil top. Cover, and let rise 30 minutes. Punch down and shape into round loaf. Place in greased round pan, 7 inches in diameter and 3 inches deep. Cover, and let rise until dough fills pan. Bake at 400°F. 15 minutes; then reduce heat to 350°F., and bake 35 minutes. Brush with 1 tablespoon honey while loaf is still hot. Makes 1 round loaf.

French Bread

    1 1/2 cups warm water
        2 envelopes dry yeast
        1 teaspoon sugar
    4–6 cups all-purpose flour
    1 1/2 teaspoons salt
        1 egg white
        1 tablespoon water

Measure 1 1/2 cups water into large bowl, and add yeast and sugar. Stir, and let stand until yeast is dissolved. Sift 1 1/2 cups flour with salt, and add to yeast. Beat until mixture is smooth. Stir in more flour (about 2 cups) with wooden spoon, then by hand. Knead in remaining flour until dough is smooth and elastic (about 6 minutes). Place ball of dough in warm oiled bowl, turning it over once to oil top. Let rise until doubled (about 1 hour). Punch down, and roll into 2 rectangles—6″ x 10″. Roll each tightly as for jelly roll, rolling up from the long side. Dampen and seal edges. Roll back and forth to lengthen loaf and taper ends. Loaves should be about 12 inches long and 2 1/2 inches thick. Place side by side 2 inches apart on lightly greased 15″ x 10″ cookie sheet that has been sprinkled with cornmeal. For appearance, gash tops in several places, cutting 1/4 inch deep. Brush with cold water, and let stand uncovered in warm place 1 hour or until doubled. Brush again with water, and bake at 375°F. 15 minutes. Beat 1 egg white slightly with 1 tablespoon water, and brush 1/2 of mixture over loaves. Continue baking 10 minutes. Brush again with egg-white mixture, and bake until golden brown (about 10 more minutes). Makes 2 loaves.

VARIATION:

* *Sesame French Bread*: After brushing the partially baked loaves with egg white—water mixture, sprinkle generously with sesame seeds, and continue baking.

Note: The secret of the crustiness so characteristic of French bread lies in slower baking than usual. If you bake at 25°F. less than temperature given in recipe, you will have an even thicker crust.

Rolls

The dough for rolls is prepared and allowed to rise in the same way as bread dough. When dough has been punched down after first rising, divide it into smooth balls, and let rest a few minutes. Then proceed according to shape desired.

As with bread, after shaping, rolls are left to rise again. Press them with a finger. If a slight impression remains, rolls are ready for oven.

Dark rolls are ready for oven when they have risen to 1/2 more than their original size. White rolls are allowed to double in bulk before they are baked.

As with any yeast dough, rising should take place in a warm room (75°–85°F.) free from drafts.

A 375°F. oven is usually best for sweet rolls, as the sugar in them makes them brown more quickly. Rolls made from bread dough may be baked along with bread. Rolls are done when they are light and nicely browned.

If you wish to postpone baking for more than a short time, it is best to use a refrigerator-dough recipe. Because cold retards the action of yeast, dough may be kept refrigerated 2—3 days before baking. Special proportions of sugar and salt help to control yeast during waiting period. Regular dough should not be refrigerated, as it does not have these proportions.

Shaping Rolls. Mold rolls into any shape you wish. Then cover again, and allow to rise until doubled in bulk once more. Rising will take 45—60 minutes.

As size of rolls will vary according to shapes you decide to make, baking times will also vary. Generally, they will take 12–20 minutes at 375°–400°F.

Pan Rolls

Form each ball of dough into a cylindrical shape about 1 1/2 inches in diameter. Cut into 1-inch lengths and form into balls, tucking under any uneven edges. Place 16 rolls in each greased 8- or 9-inch square pan, and brush with melted butter or margarine. Cover with cloth, let rise and bake at 375°F. 25—30 minutes.

Cloverleaf Rolls

Shape balls of dough into cylinders, about 1 1/2 inches in diameter. Cut into 1-inch lengths, then cut each into 3 parts again. Form each small piece into a ball, tucking edges under. Brush with melted butter or margarine, and place 3 balls in each greased medium-sized muffin cup. Cover, let rise and bake at 375°F. 18—20 minutes.

Parker House Rolls

Roll balls of dough to 1/4-inch thickness. Cut with floured 2-inch round or oval cutter. Brush with melted butter or margarine. Crease each deeply, just off center, with back of knife. Fold each over, with wider half on top. Lightly press edges together. Turn over, and place on greased baking sheets; cover, let rise and bake at 375°F. 10–20 minutes.

Crescent Rolls

Roll balls of dough into circles, about 8 inches in diameter and about 1/4 inch thick. Cut each into 8 triangular wedges. Roll up each wedge toward pointed end. Place on greased baking sheet, with point underneath. Brush with melted butter or margarine, and curve each slightly, to form crescent shapes. Cover, let rise and bake at 375° F. 18–20 minutes.

Dinner Rolls

Divide dough into 8 equal parts. Roll each piece into cylindrical shape. Then taper each end to make roll lemon-shaped. Brush with melted butter or margarine, and place on cookie sheet. Cover, and let rise. Bake at 375°F. 25–30 minutes.

Butter Rolls

Roll dough to 1/8-inch thickness, forming into oblong about 9 inches wide. Spread dough with softened butter or margarine. Cut 6 long strips about 1 1/2 inches wide. Stack strips on top of one another, and cut straight down through all layers at about 1-inch intervals. Place each 1-inch section, cut side down, in greased muffin cups, cover and let rise; bake at 375° F. 15–20 minutes.

Twisted Rolls

These rolls may take many shapes, but you begin by rolling out dough to a little less than 1/2-inch thickness, making an oblong about 12 inches wide. Spread dough with soft butter or margarine and fold in half over butter or margarine. Trim edges to make corners even, and cut into strips, each 1/2 inch wide and about 6 inches long. Make figure 8s by holding 1/2 end of each strip, twisting other end and stretching it so that when the 2 ends are brought together on greased baking sheet, a figure 8 is formed. Make whirls by holding 1 end of each strip on baking sheet and winding strip around it in circles. Tuck other end of strip under.

Make knots by first rolling each strip of dough lightly under hands, then tying each into a knot by pulling end through. Cover, and let rise. All these "twists" should be baked on a greased baking sheet at 375°F. 18–20 minutes.

Basic Sweet Rolls

    1 1/2 cups milk
      1/3 cup sugar
      1/4 cup shortening
        2 teaspoons salt
        1 teaspoon sugar
        1 envelope dry yeast
      1/2 cup lukewarm water
        2 eggs, well beaten
      6–7 cups (approximately) all-purpose flour

Scald milk, and pour into large bowl. Add 1/3 cup sugar, shortening and salt, and stir till shortening is melted. Cool to lukewarm. Meanwhile, sprinkle 1 teaspoon sugar and yeast in lukewarm water. Let this mixture stand 10 minutes. Stir it with fork, and add with eggs to lukewarm milk mixture. Stir well; then beat in 3 cups flour. Add remaining flour, working in the last of it by hand. Turn dough onto lightly floured board. Knead until smooth, about 5 minutes. Shape dough into ball, and place in lightly greased bowl. Grease top slightly to prevent drying; cover, and let stand in warm place until doubled in bulk, about 1 1/2 hours. Punch dough down after it has risen, and turn onto lightly floured board. Divide into 4 equal parts. Form each into 2 smooth balls, cover and let rest for 10 minutes to make dough easier to work. Shape, let rise and bake according to previous directions.

3-Day Refrigerator Rolls

    1 3/4 cups hot water
        1 tablespoon salt
      1/2 cup granulated sugar
      1/3 cup butter or margarine
      1/2 cup lukewarm water
        2 teaspoons granulated sugar
        2 envelopes dry yeast
        2 eggs, well beaten
    8 1/2 cups (approximately) all-purpose flour

Measure hot water into large bowl. Stir in 1/2 cup sugar, butter or margaine and salt. Cool to lukewarm. Meanwhile, measure lukewarm water into very large mixing bowl. Stir in 2 teaspoons sugar, and sprinkle with yeast. Let stand 10 minutes; then stir well. Stir in butter mixture and eggs. Stir in 4 cups flour, and beat until smooth and elastic. Stir in sufficient additional flour to make soft dough. Work dough in bowl with floured hands to make a smooth ball. Grease top. Cover tightly with foil or plastic film, and refrigerate. To bake, use 1/3 the dough on each of 3 ensuing days. Form portion of dough into smooth ball on lightly floured board. Form ball of dough into 12-inch roll, and cut crosswise into 1-inch lengths. Shape each length into smooth ball, and place in greased muffin cup, 1 ball to each. Grease tops, cover and let rise in warm place, free from drafts, until doubled in bulk. Rising time will depend upon temperature of dough. Bake in hot oven, 400°F. about 15 minutes. Makes 3 dozen.

Homemade Brown-and-Serve Rolls

    1/2 cup milk
    3/4 cup water
      3 tablespoons sugar
      1 envelope dry yeast
      2 tablespoons soft shortening
      2 teaspoons salt
      1 egg, well beaten
  4 1/2 cups (approximately) all-purpose flour

Scald milk; add cold water. When milk and water are lukewarm, stir in 1 teaspoon sugar, and sprinkle yeast on top. After 10 minutes, stir, and add remaining sugar, shortening, salt and egg. Add flour, and stir until liquid is absorbed. By hand, mix dough in bowl to a ball. Knead on greased board until smooth (5 minutes). Place in greased bowl. Cover, and let rise at warm temperature until double in bulk. Punch down. Divide dough in 2, and let rest 15 minutes. Cut each portion into 16 pieces, and form each piece into a ball. Space evenly in 2 well-greased 8-inch square pans. Cover with greased waxed paper, and let rise in warm place until doubled. Bake in slow oven, 275°F. 40 minutes. Remove from pans, and cool on wire racks. When cold, wrap securely. To brown and serve, heat in hot oven 450°F. about 7 minutes.

Hot Cross Buns

        2 teaspoons sugar
        1 envelope dry yeast
    1/2 cup lukewarm water
    3/4 cup milk
    1/4 cup soft butter or margarine
    1/2 cup sugar
      1 egg, beaten
  1 1/2 cups unsifted all-purpose flour
      1 teaspoon salt
      1 teaspoon cinnamon
    1/2 teaspoon nutmeg
1/4–1/2 teaspoon cloves
1/2–3/4 cup raisins or currants
2–2 1/4 cups (approximately) unsifted all-purpose flour
      1 egg white
      1 teaspoon water

Sprinkle 2 teaspoons sugar and the yeast over the lukewarm water. Let stand until dissolved.

Scald milk, and pour into a bowl. Add butter and sugar. Stir, and cool to lukewarm. Add egg and yeast mixture. Beat in the next 5 ingredients sifted together. Add raisins, and work in enough remaining flour to form a soft firm dough. Knead 3–4 minutes or until smooth on a floured board. Form into a ball, and let rise in a greased bowl until doubled, about 1 hour. Punch down, and cut into 2 equal pieces. Form into 2 balls, and cut each into 8 equal wedges. Form into round buns. Roll each with a rolling pin to flatten slightly. Place on 2 small greased cookie sheets. Gash the tops to form crosses. Cover, and let rise until puffy and light. Brush with a mixture of slightly beaten egg white and water. Bake at 400°F. 15–18 minutes. Crosses may be filled in with confectioners' icing. Makes 16.

Note: If you have no immediate use for the leftover egg yolk, beat it into the butter-sugar-egg mixture in the dough recipe.

French Croissants

      1 cup milk
      2 tablespoons sugar
      2 tablespoons shortening
      1 teaspoon salt
      1 envelope dry yeast
      1 teaspoon sugar
    1/2 cup lukewarm water
      2 eggs, beaten
      1 teaspoon grated lemon rind
      5 cups (approximately) all-purpose flour
      1 cup butter or margarine
      1 egg yolk
      2 tablespoons cream

Scald milk; add 2 tablespoons sugar, shortening and salt, and stir until shortening is melted. Cool to lukewarm. Sprinkle yeast and 1 teaspoon sugar over water; let stand to dissolve, and add to milk mixture. Add eggs and lemon rind, and stir well. Add flour to make soft dough, turn onto floured board and knead lightly. Dough should be smooth but not elastic; kneaded too long, croissants will not be tender. Chill dough in refrigerator until firm. Shape butter or margarine into flat brick, roll it in some of remaining flour to keep it from sticking and place it between 2 sheets of waxed paper. Then roll it out into a square 1/4 inch thick. Divide square in 2 oblong pieces. Wrap in waxed paper, and chill. Take dough from refrigerator, and roll out on well-floured cloth until you have a rectangle about 3 times longer than its width. Brush off any excess flour; then place on it 1 slab of chilled butter or margarine. Fold right edge of dough over butter or margarine. Place other slab of butter or margarine on top of this flap of dough, and fold left edge of dough over butter or margarine. Press edges together to seal. Place dough on cloth so that short end is toward you. Roll out into long rectangle as before. Brush off excess flour; fold each side in to meet center. Then fold once more, in half, to make a "book" of 4 layers. Press all edges together again, wrap dough in waxed paper and chill 1 hour. Place dough again on floured cloth, again with short end toward you. Roll out dough into rectangle, and fold, as before. Wrap dough, and chill again, this time 2—3 hours at least. Cut dough into 4 parts. Roll out each piece separately until it is 1/8 inch thick. Cut into strips about 5 inches wide, and divide strips into triangles. Roll triangles, starting with widest edge and working toward point. Roll fairly tightly, stretching dough a little to make them longer. Chill rolls in freezing compartment 1/2 hour.

Take rolls from freezer no more than 1/2 dozen at a time so that they can stay well chilled. Roll them on the pastry cloth under palm of 1 hand until they are thinner and firmer in shape. Place rolls on greased baking sheet, and curve into crescent shapes. Chill again until very cold before placing in oven. Brush with egg yolk and cream, and bake at 475°F. 5 minutes; reduce heat to 400°F., and bake about 8 minutes longer or until golden brown. Makes 3—4 dozen.

Note: If frozen immediately after cooling, croissants will keep for months. The recipe may be halved, but follow chilling and baking times exactly as specified for full amount.

Sour Cream Twists

     1 envelope dry yeast
   1/4 cup lukewarm water
     1 teaspoon sugar
     4 cups unsifted all-purpose flour
     1 teaspoon salt
     1 cup butter or margarine
   3/4 cup sour cream
     2 eggs, well beaten
     1 teaspoon vanilla extract
   1/2 teaspoon grated lemon rind
 1 3/4 cups granulated sugar

Dissolve yeast in water with 1 teaspoon sugar. Combine flour and salt; cut butter or margarine in with pastry blender. Add dissolved yeast, sour cream, eggs, vanilla and lemon rind, and stir thoroughly. Cover with damp cloth, and refrigerate 2 hours or overnight. Roll 1/2 the dough out on well-sugared board (use 3/4 cup) into rectangle 8″ x 16″. Fold ends toward center, and sprinkle with 1 tablespoon sugar. Repeat rolling and sprinkling twice. Roll about 1/4-inch thick, and cut into strips 1″ x 4″. Twist ends in opposite directions, stretching dough slightly. Place in shape of horseshoes on greased cookie sheets. Repeat with remaining dough. Cover, and let rise until doubled in bulk. Bake at 400°F. about 15 minutes. Remove from pans immediately. Makes 5 dozen twists.

Festive Breads

Many festive breads come to us from other countries. Each recipe should be followed carefully, but once you have experimented a little you can, if you wish, use a basic dough, either plain or rich, and vary the way you shape it. Most of these doughs may be either baked in pans or shaped in special ways and baked on cookie sheets.

Sweet Bread Dough

     1 cup milk, scalded
   1/2 cup shortening
   1/3 cup sugar
 1 1/2 teaspoons salt
     1 teaspoon sugar
     1 envelope dry yeast
   1/2 cup warm water
     1 egg, well beaten
4–4 1/2 cups unsifted all-purpose flour

To scalded milk add shortening, 1/3 cup sugar and salt. Sprinkle 1 teaspoon sugar and yeast over water, and let stand 10 minutes in warm place (85°F.). Stir yeast briskly, and add to milk mixture. Add egg. Beat in 2 cups flour. Combine remaining flour with batter by stirring with hand. Turn dough onto lightly floured board, and knead 5 minutes or until elastic. Shape into smooth ball, place in greased bowl and grease top slightly. Cover, and let rise until doubled in bulk, about 1 1/2 hours. Punch down, and turn onto lightly floured board. Divide into 2 pieces. Form each into a ball. Cover, and let rest 10 minutes. Use 1 ball of dough for each variation.

* *Swedish Tea Ring*: Roll out 1 ball of dough to make rectangle about 9″ x 16″. Brush with melted butter or margarine to within 1/2 inch of edge. Combine 1/2 cup chopped nuts, 1/3 cup brown sugar, 1/4 cup raisins and 1/2 teaspoon cinnamon. Sprinkle this mixture over dough, and roll as for jelly roll. Seal edges well, and shape into circle on greased baking sheet. Dampen, and seal seam. With scissors, snip dough about 3/4 of the way through at 1-inch intervals. Turn each section on its side. Cover, and let rise about 45 minutes, or until doubled in bulk. Bake at 375°F. 25—30 minutes. Glaze, and serve warm. To make glaze, add sufficient milk (about 2 teaspoons) to 1 cup sifted icing sugar to bring the mix to spreading consistency. Flavor with 1 teaspoon vanilla and a few grains salt. Makes 1 tea ring.

* *Cinnamon Buns*: Combine 1/3 cup melted butter or margarine and 1/2 cup brown sugar. Spread in pan about 8 inches square. Sprinkle with pecan halves. Roll dough to rectangle about 8″ x 13″. Brush with melted butter or margarine, and sprinkle with mixture of 1/3 cup granulated sugar, 1/3 chopped walnuts or pecans and 1 teaspoon cinnamon. Roll as for jelly roll, and seal edges. Cut with sharp knife into 12 1-inch slices, and place, cut side down, in prepared pan. Cover, and let rise until doubled in bulk. Bake at 375°F. 25—30 minutes. Turn out and serve at once, with sugary topping up. Makes 1 dozen.

Fruited Coffee Braid

    1 1/4 cups hard butter or margarine
        2 envelopes dry yeast
        2 teaspoons sugar
    3/4 cup lukewarm water
        2 eggs, well beaten
    4 1/2 cups sifted all-purpose flour
    1/2 teaspoon salt
    1/3 cup white sugar
    1/2 cup chopped nuts
    1/2 cup raisins
        3 tablespoons chopped candied peel
        Confectioners' icing (optional)

Measure and chill butter in the freezer until very hard. Sprinkle yeast and 2 teaspoons sugar into the lukewarm water, and let stand until dissolved, about 10 minutes. Add eggs, and set aside. Sift flour, salt and 1/3 cup sugar into a large bowl. Hold butter with a small piece of waxed paper, and shred on a medium-to-coarse grater into the flour mixture. Or cut butter into pieces; then cut into the dry ingredients with a pastry blender until butter is about the size of peas. Stir lightly with a fork to distribute the butter bits evenly. Then stir in the nuts and fruits. Pour in yeast-egg

mixture. Stir with a fork; then knead quickly until all particles stick together and dough cleans the sides of the bowl. Press out into a flat oblong on waxed paper, and chill until evenly firm. Cut dough in half, and roll each piece out into a 12″ x 3″ rectangle. Cut each rectangle lengthwise into 3 strips 1 inch wide. Roll strips lightly back and forth to smooth edges; then braid each group of 3 strips together. Place on lightly greased baking sheets. Tuck ends under neatly, and cover. Let rise in a warm place until light and puffy, about 1 1/2—2 hours. Bake at 350°F. 30—40 minutes. Cool slightly, and drizzle with confectioners' icing if you wish.

* *Fruit-filled Braid*: In a saucepan mix 1 1/2 cups grated raw peeled apple, 2/3 cup chopped cooked prunes, 2/3 cup brown sugar and 1/2 cup water. Add 1 tablespoon lemon juice, 1/2 teaspoon cinnamon and 1/4 teaspoon salt. Boil gently, and stir until mixture is thick, about 8 minutes. Cool to room temperature before using. Prepare and chill the rich dough for *Fruited Coffee Braid*, but omit the nuts and fruits. Divide dough in half, and roll each piece out into a 9″ x 14″ rectangle. Place rectangles on 2 greased baking sheets. Spoon the fruit filling along the center of each rectangle. Slash dough at 1-inch intervals from outer edges in, not quite to the filling; then fold strips over filling, first 1 side, then the other. Cover, and let rise until light and puffy. Bake as for *Fruited Coffee Braid*.

* *Spice or Chocolate Almond Coffee Bread*: Prepare the rich dough for *Fruited Coffee Braid*, but omit the nuts and fruits. Before chilling, divide dough in half. Press one half out on a square of waxed paper into a 10-inch square, and chill. Place second half of dough on unfloured pastry board, and lightly knead in 2—3 tablespoons cinnamon-sugar (cinnamon toast mix) or 2—3 tablespoons sweetened chocolate

drink powder. Divide flavored dough into 4 parts, and roll each part between the hands to form 4 rolls 10 inches long and about 1 inch in diameter. Chill the rolls until firm. Meanwhile, cut the square of chilled plain dough in half to make 2 10″ x 5″ rectangles. Roll each out on a lightly floured board into 10-inch squares. On one half, horizontally place a flavored roll, and brush the top with slightly beaten egg white; then lift the front edge up over the roll. Press edge firmly against the roll. Flip or invert the entire arrangement, and place another flavored roll horizontally on the second half of dough. Brush top of roll with slightly beaten egg white, and bring far edge of plain dough up over the roll. Press the 2 covered rolls together. Arrange on a greased baking sheet. Prepare the second long loaf in the same way. Cover, and let rise until light and puffy, about 1 1/2–2 hours. Brush tops with slightly beaten raw egg white, and sprinkle generously with sliced blanched almonds and white sugar. Bake as for *Fruited Coffee Braid*.

Apricot-Almond Savarin

  1/2 cup chopped blanched almonds
    2 envelopes dry yeast
    1 tablespoon sugar
  3/4 cup lukewarm scalded milk
  3/4 cup soft butter or margarine
  1/2 cup sugar
    4 eggs
    1 teaspoon vanilla extract
    1 teaspoon grated lemon rind
  3/4 teaspoon salt
3 1/2 cups sifted all-purpose flour
  2–3 tablespoons chopped orange peel
  2–3 tablespoons raisins
    1 recipe *Rich Apricot Glaze*
      Toasted almond halves
      Candied fruits or cherries

Butter 9-inch ring mold generously, and sprinkle bottom and sides with 1/2 cup blanched almonds. Dissolve yeast and 1 tablespoon sugar in milk for about 10 minutes. Beat butter or margarine, remaining sugar and eggs together until fluffy. Stir in vanilla, lemon rind, salt and yeast mixture. Add sifted flour, and beat until smooth. Fold in orange peel and raisins. Scrape into prepared tube pan, and set in bowl of warm water. Cover with warm wet cloth, and let rise until batter almost fills pan. Bake at 350°F. for about 30 minutes. Remove cake from pan, and pour 1/2 the glaze over bottom of pan. Return cake to pan, and pour remaining glaze over top and sides. Let marinate several hours. Invert on serving plate, and stick with toasted almonds. Garnish with candied fruits. Slice, and serve plain, or fill hollow with sauce made by blending 1 package frozen raspberries (without defrosting) and folding in 1 cup whipped cream. Savarin may be served warm after marinating for 20 minutes, or cooled, wrapped and frozen. Makes 16 servings.

Rich Apricot Glaze

  1/2 cup apricot jam
  1/2 cup water
  1/2 cup dry sherry, rum or brandy
  1/4 cup sugar

Combine all ingredients in saucepan, and simmer about 3 minutes. Makes 1 1/2 cups.

German Apple Cake

    1 envelope dry yeast
    1 teaspoon sugar
  1/2 cup lukewarm water
    2 eggs, beaten
    2 tablespoons sugar
    1 teaspoon salt
    1 teaspoon grated lemon rind
  1/3 cup melted butter or margarine
2 3/4 cups unsifted all-purpose flour
    6 tablespoons melted butter or margarine
    6 cooking apples, peeled and cored
3/4–1 cup granulated sugar
  1/3 cup unsifted all-purpose flour
    2 teaspoons cinnamon

Sprinkle yeast and 1 teaspoon sugar over the warm water, and let stand 10 minutes or until yeast is dissolved. Meanwhile, combine the next 5 ingredients in a large bowl. Stir in the dissolved yeast; then beat in 1 1/2 cups of the flour to make a smooth batter. Work in remaining flour to form a soft sticky dough. Knead lightly, just until smooth, on a floured board, using 2–3 tablespoons additional flour. Place dough in a greased bowl, and turn to grease the top. Cover, and let rise until doubled, about 1 1/4 hours. Punch down, and cut dough in half. Press out in 2 greased 8-inch square pans so that dough has a 1/2-inch raised edge around the pans. Brush dough with 2 tablespoons of the melted butter; then cover with waxed paper and a towel. Let rise again until light, about 45 minutes. Meanwhile, cut apples into 12 sections each, and drop into a medium size saucepan. Add 2 tablespoons water and 2 tablespoons melted butter. Cover, and steam-cook just until edges are transparent. Stir once or twice for even steaming; then cool. Do not cook until tender. Mix 3/4–1 cup sugar, 1/3 cup flour and the cinnamon together with remaining 2 tablespoons butter. Use the smaller amount of sugar for sweet ripe apples. Measure out about 1/2 cup of the mixture, and stir remaining sugar-spice combination into the apples. Spread apple mixture evenly over the risen dough. Sprinkle with reserved sugar-spice mixture. Bake at 375°F. about 30 minutes. If apples are firm, even after steaming, cover the cakes with foil for the first half of the baking; then uncover, and continue baking until tops are golden brown. Serve warm in squares or oblongs with whipped cream or ice cream.

Note: For extra tartness, steam apples with 2 tablespoons lemon juice rather than water.

Rich Refrigerator Dough

```
2 1/4  cups lukewarm water
    2  envelopes dry yeast
  1/2  cup sugar
    8  cups (approximately) all-purpose flour
    2  teaspoons salt
  1/3  cup soft butter, margarine or vegetable
          shortening
    3  eggs, well beaten
```

Measure 1 cup lukewarm water into small bowl; over it sprinkle yeast, and add 2 teaspoons sugar. Let stand 10 minutes to dissolve; then stir with fork. Measure 7 cups flour into large mixing bowl, and make well in center. To remaining lukewarm water add remaining sugar, salt and butter or margarine. Stir gradually into beaten eggs. Add dissolved yeast, and mix thoroughly. Pour mixture into center of flour, and stir until liquid is absorbed, about 1/3 minute. With 1 hand mix dough in bowl, using swinging rotary motion, adding more flour if needed. Gradually form dough into smooth ball; knead in bowl 2 minutes. Transfer dough to greased bowl, large enough to allow at least 1/3 free space for rising (which will take place in refrigerator). Brush top with melted butter, and cover bowl with well-greased waxed paper and tight-fitting lid or refrigerator-bowl cover to prevent formation of crust. Place in refrigerator. Dough may be used after 8 hours or any time within 1 week. If dough rises too much in refrigerator, punch down occasionally. When ready to bake, remove just enough dough from bowl for your recipe. Form piece into ball, turning cut surface under to prevent escape of gases, and allow to rest at room temperature 15 minutes. Then shape according to recipe instructions. Cover remaining dough as before, and store immediately in refrigerator.

Streusel Coffee Cake

```
1/4  recipe Rich Refrigerator Dough
  1  egg yolk
  2  teaspoons milk
1/3  cup brown sugar, firmly packed
1/3  cup flour
1/2  teaspoon cinnamon
  3  tablespoons butter or margarine, melted
```

You will need an 8″ x 8″ x 2″ square pan or 8″ x 2″ round pan. Using greased rolling pin, roll out rested ball of dough into square or round to fit nicely into pan. Cover with dampened cloth and with dry cloth over that; allow dough to rise at warm room temperature until doubled in bulk (up to 2 hours). When risen, prick top lightly with fork. Combine egg yolk and milk, and brush over dough. Mix brown sugar, flour and cinnamon; add butter or margarine, and combine thoroughly with fork. Sprinkle mixture over dough; then put to rise under damp and dry cloths another 30 minutes. Meantime heat oven to 375°F. Bake coffee cake 25–30 minutes. Loosen edges with spatula. Serve warm, cut in squares or wedges. Makes 1 cake.

Butterscotch Rolls

```
3/4  cup brown sugar, firmly packed
1/4  cup butter or margarine, melted
  3  teaspoons water
1/3  cup whole pecans or walnuts
1/4  recipe Rich Refrigerator Dough
```

Mix brown sugar, butter and water together. Grease 12 medium-size muffin cups (2 1/2 inches top diameter). Cover bottom of each cup with about 1 1/2 teaspoons of the sugar mixture. Place 3 or 4 nut meats on each. Using greased rolling pin, roll out rested ball of dough to make rectangle 9″ x 12″. Spread with remaining sugar mixture. Roll dough lengthwise as for jelly roll. Seal edge of roll firmly with fingers. Using sharp knife, slice roll into 12 1-inch pieces. Place, cut side down, in prepared muffin tins. Cover pans with dampened cloth, with dry cloth over that. Allow to rise at warm temperature, 75–80°F., away from any drafts, until doubled in bulk (about 2 hours). About 20 minutes before rolls are ready to bake, heat oven to 375°F. When rolls have risen almost level with tops of containers, bake 15–20 minutes. Invert tins on cake rack; let stand 5 minutes so that butterscotch mixture will run down over each roll. Turn out rolls, and serve warm or cold. Makes 1 dozen rolls.

Hungarian Coffee Cake

```
1/4  recipe Rich Refrigerator Dough
  3  tablespoons butter or margarine, melted
1/3  cup granulated sugar
  1  teaspoon cinnamon
  3  tablespoons chopped walnuts or pecans
  5  maraschino cherries, sliced
  3  tablespoons whole seeded raisins, washed and
        dried
```

Generously grease a tube pan 9 inches in diameter. Form dough into ball, cover and let stand until other ingredients are ready. Have ready several small bowls, 1 for melted butter, 1 for combined sugar and cinnamon, 1 for chopped nuts, 1 for cherries and raisins. Strew a few chopped nuts, cherries and raisins in bottom of greased pan. Roll dough with hands to form cylinder about 20 inches long. Cut dough with greased knife into 20 1-inch pieces. Form pieces into little balls. Brush each all over with melted butter or margarine, using pastry brush; then dip into sugar and cinnamon mixture. Place some balls in bottom of pan; they should barely touch one another. Strew with 1/2 the nuts, and add a few raisins and cherries in spaces between balls, pressing fruit in slightly. Add second layer of dough balls, covering lower spaces. Strew with remaining nuts, and add rest of raisins and cherries, pressing slightly as before. Cover pan with damp cloth, and top with dry towel. Allow dough to rise at warm temperature, 75°–85°F. until doubled in bulk, about 2 hours. Bake in preheated 375°F. oven about 35 minutes. When cake comes from oven, use spatula to loosen it from sides of pan. Invert on rack; cool 10 minutes before removing. Serve warm, breaking cake apart with 2 forks. Makes 1 cake.

German Coffee Cake

       1 envelope dry yeast
       1 teaspoon sugar
     1/3 cup lukewarm water
     1/3 cup soft butter or margarine
     1/3 cup fine white sugar
       2 eggs
   2 1/4 cups sifted all-purpose flour
       1 teaspoon grated orange rind
     1/2 teaspoon salt
     1/2 teaspoon ground cardamom
     1/8 teaspoon mace
     2/3 cup lukewarm milk
     1/2 cup chopped almonds
     1/4 cup raisins
     1/4 cup chopped candied fruit peel
       2 tablespoons icing sugar
     1/2 cup whole blanched almonds, split

Dissolve yeast and 1 teaspoon sugar in water. Leave about 10 minutes. Beat next 3 ingredients together, and beat in 1 cup flour. Add orange rind, flavorings, yeast mixture, milk, almonds, raisins, peel and remaining flour. Beat until smooth. Cover, and let rise 45 minutes. Line buttered gugelhupf mold (a 2-quart ring mold or small angel food cake pan will do) with split almonds. Beat dough down, and pour into mold. Cover, and let rise until mixture fills pan, about 1 hour. Bake at 350°F. 45 minutes. Unmold, and dust with icing sugar. Makes 1 9-inch cake.

Chelsea Buns

     1/4 recipe *Rich Refrigerator Dough*
     1/4 cup butter or margarine, melted
       1 cup brown sugar, lightly packed
     1/2 teaspoon cinnamon
     1/3 cup seedless raisins, washed and dried
     1/3 cup chopped nuts

Grease a deep 8-to 9-inch square pan. Roll dough with a greased rolling pin to form rectangle about 3/8 inch thick. Brush top surface with a little melted butter or margarine. Mix 1/2 cup brown sugar with cinnamon, and sprinkle evenly over dough. Strew raisins over sugar. Roll dough as for jelly roll. Seal edge of roll firmly,

pinching with fingers. Using sharp knife, cut into 12 slices. Combine remaining butter or margarine and brown sugar with nuts. Spread mixture over bottom of greased pan. Arrange dough slices on top, cut side down. Cover with damp cloth, and top with dry towel; allow buns to rise at warm temperature, 75°–85°F., until doubled in bulk, about 2 hours. Preheat oven to 375°F. Bake buns 30 minutes. Remove, and invert pan on cooling rack; let stand 10–25 minutes to allow syrup to run down over buns. Turn out. Serve warm or cooled. Makes 12 medium buns.

Stollen

       3 envelopes dry yeast
       1 tablespoon sugar
   1 1/2 cups lukewarm scalded milk
   7 1/4–8 cups (approximately) all-purpose flour
   1 1/2 cups butter or margarine
     3/4 cup sugar
       3 eggs
   1 1/2 teaspoons salt
       2 teaspoons grated lemon rind
   1 1/3 cups seedless raisins, washed and dried
       1 cup blanched almonds, chopped
       3 tablespoons butter or margarine, melted
   1 1/2 cups icing sugar
       2 tablespoons (approximately) boiling water
       1 tablespoon lemon juice

Dissolve yeast and 1 tablespoon sugar in milk. Beat in 1 1/2 cups flour; cover, and let rise in warm place several hours. In large bowl, beat butter or margarine until soft, and add sugar, blending until very creamy. Add eggs, 1 at a time, beating well after each addition. Add salt and grated rind. Turn into yeast batter, and beat to incorporate. Sprinkle a little of the remaining flour over raisins and almonds, and stir into the batter. Add remaining flour gradually to main mixture. Knead until dough is smooth and elastic. Cover dough, and let rise until doubled in bulk. Remove to floured board; divide into 4 parts, and shape each into a uniform oval 1/3 inch thick. Fold each almost in half (as in a *Parker House Roll*). Lightly roll the folded dough to set fold. Place well apart on lightly greased baking sheets, and brush with melted butter or margarine. Again let rise until doubled. Bake in preheated 375°F. oven about 30–35 minutes. Let stand about 15 minutes; then remove to cooling rack. When loaves are quite cool, spread icing on tops and sides. Makes 4 loaves.

To icing sugar add boiling water and lemon juice to make icing of spready type.

Note: *Stollens* are old-fashioned European yeast and raisin cakes, always topped with icing.

Danish Pastries

The rich yeast dough used for Danish pastry is prepared and rolled to about 1/4-inch thickness. Sweet butter, shortening or regular butter or margarine is then dotted over dough. Or paste can be made by mixing shortening with flour, which is the method used in the following recipes. The dough is then folded over, rolled and chilled. This process of rolling, dotting with fat, folding, rolling and chilling is usually repeated 3 or 4 times, so that finally many layers of pastry are built up. The butter or shortening must be soft enough to roll between layers of dough without breaking through, but not soft enough to soak into dough. When all fat has been used, dough is chilled thoroughly before shaping, rising and baking.

Note: If sweet butter or shortening is used, add at least 1 teaspoon salt to the pastry dough.

Danish Pastry

    1 1/2 cups butter or margarine
    1/3 cup all-purpose flour
    1 envelope dry yeast
    1 teaspoon sugar
    1/2 cup lukewarm water
    1 cup lukewarm scalded milk
    1 egg, beaten
    1/4 cup sugar
    3 1/2 cups all-purpose flour
    3/4–1 cup thick applebutter, jam or preserves
    1 egg, beaten

Prepare butter dough by cutting butter into 1/3 cup flour until grains are the size of marbles. Chill. Combine yeast, 1 teaspoon sugar and water according to directions on yeast package; let stand until dissolved. Beat milk, 1 egg and 1/4 cup sugar together. Stir in enough flour to make batter. Add yeast, and beat until foamy. Add remaining flour to make stiff dough. Shape into loaf, and chill 1 hour. Then roll dough into oblong 1/4 inch thick and twice as long as it is wide. Sprinkle 1/4 chilled butter crumbs over 2/3 the length of yeast dough. Fold unsprinkled piece over middle section, then over again. Roll out again as before. Sprinkle with 1/4 butter crumbs, fold in 3 lengthwise and chill 1 hour. Repeat this rolling and folding process until all butter crumbs have been used. Chill pastry at least 3 hours. Roll dough thinly, and cut in 4-inch squares. Place 1 tablespoon of applebutter in center of each. Bring corners into center, pressing edges to make them stay in place. Brush with beaten egg. Let rise on greased baking sheet in cool place. Bake at 425°F. 10 minutes; reduce heat to 300°F. until done, 10–15 minutes. Makes 2 dozen.

Note: To serve, cover with lemon-cream icing or apricot glaze (1 cup sieved apricot jam, heated to boiling and spread hot over baked pastries).

CAKE MAKING

Basically, there are 3 types of cakes.

Butter cakes include all those made with a solid fat—butter, margarine, lard or shortening. A simple 1-egg cake and an extravagant 3-tiered wedding cake both belong in this category, and there are dozens of other versions—dark and light, rich and plain—ranging between the 2 extremes. All butter cakes, however, have a common richness of flavor and moist texture because of the ingredients they share.

The usual method for preparing butter cakes involves creaming shortening and sugar together until very light and fluffy, with an electric beater or by hand. If using an electric beater, eggs may be added to the creamy butter-sugar mixture without first beating them in a separate bowl. When creaming by hand, beat eggs separately before adding them to the butter-sugar mixture unless recipe states otherwise. If yolks and whites are beaten and added separately, the cake texture will be softer and fluffier. Dry ingredients are mixed and sifted together, so that salt and baking powder (or soda) will be evenly distributed throughout batter. A further means to achieve smooth texture is to alternate the addition of dry ingredients and liquids, preferably beginning and ending with the dry. Mix in sifted dry ingredients and liquids by hand unless you are using a 1-bowl cake recipe or the recipe states otherwise.

Always have cake-making ingredients at room temperature. Eggs will beat more quickly to a greater volume, and soft fats to a creamier consistency. Chilled liquids such as milk and fruit juices tend to curdle a cake batter. Measure and let liquids stand at room temperature for 20–30 minutes before mixing the batter.

For butter cakes grease the inside bottom of baking pan, and sprinkle about 1 teaspoon flour lightly over grease; to insure a smooth surface on your cake turn pan upside down to dislodge any surplus. Or cover pan bottom with greased waxed paper, cut to fit smoothly. Unsalted shortening or oil is best for greasing.

Stand freshly baked hot butter cakes on a cake

rack, and let cool about 10 minutes before removing from the pan. Run a knife around the edge, and invert cakes onto greased cake racks or a towel. Greasing racks slightly helps to prevent the soft warm cake top from sticking to the rack. Cool cakes completely before frosting if using a butter-type, gelatine-base or whipped-cream icing. Cakes may be filled and frosted while still warm with a double-boiler or boiled-type icing.

Sponge cakes of the true type consist of flour, sugar, eggs and flavorings; the principal leavening agent is air beaten into the eggs. Yellow sponge and angel food are the leading types, but there are also modified sponge mixtures, which supplement the leavening with baking powder and the like. They may or may not contain fat or liquid. If fat is included, it will be in much smaller amounts than in butter-type cakes.

Chiffon cakes, a mid-20th century development, have fairly large amounts of beaten egg whites incorporated into the batter. They are often grouped with sponge cakes under the general heading "foam-type cakes." All such types should be baked in *ungreased pans*.

General Hints

Whatever type of cake you plan to make, study the recipe, check ingredients and bring all ingredients to room temperature before starting to mix.

It is not generally advisable to substitute ingredients or to double a recipe, as this may prevent proper blending. A special cake flour milled from soft wheat is best unless recipe specifies differently. All-purpose flour gives firmer texture and slightly smaller volume, but it is quite often preferred for cakes that contain high proportions of fruit.

Before you begin to mix your cake, preheat oven to required temperature. Be sure it has reached correct temperature before cake goes in. Place cake pan as near as possible to center of oven. *Do not open door* until at least 2/3 the recommended baking time has elapsed. Check cake for doneness at minimum time specified in recipe; that is, if recipe says "bake 25–30 minutes," it is advisable to check at the 20–25-minute point. If inserted cake tester or toothpick comes out with sticky crumbs adhering, the cake needs an extra 5 minutes. This leeway of 5–10 minutes in recipe baking times is simply a safeguard to allow for differences in oven temperatures.

To store fruitcakes wrap each cake in a clean cloth dipped in brandy or wine; overwrap in foil or plastic wrap; place in tightly covered container such as a breadbox, and store in cool dry place.

Remoisten cloth as necessary. Fruitcake stores well in refrigerator or freezer, after a mellowing period of 2–3 weeks.

Cake Pans

It is important to use correct-size pan. The batter itself should fill pan approximately 1/2 full. Some pans have measurements embossed in the metal, which is helpful. To measure pans that do not have embossed measurements, check inside top dimensions with a ruler.

Shiny metal gives a better result than darkened, warped pans. To prevent uneven browning or overbrowning, line dark pans with foil or bake at 25°F. lower than recipe calls for.

Glass is great for baking, but usually requires an oven temperature about 25° lower than that specified in recipe because it absorbs rather than reflects heat.

When making cupcakes, grease muffin cups or line with paper cups or liners. Fill each cup only about 2/3 full of any butter-type cake batter. Bake at 375°F. about 20 minutes. A cake recipe containing 2 cups of flour will yield about 18 medium cupcakes.

Generally speaking, the pan size specified in a recipe is ideal for that particular cake. But it is possible in many cases to use a pan other than the one called for. The amount of batter for 2 8-inch layer pans of shallow depth will generally be successful in 1 8-inch square pan, with extra baking time. A recipe specifying a loaf pan 9″ x 5″ x 3″ can be baked in a 9″ x 9″ x 2″ square pan. Note that for pound cake, though, such a substitution is not advisable: This fine cake should be baked in a loaf or tube pan. The shape and size of a tube pan has been designed with angel food cake in mind, but other sponge cakes may be baked in it if you follow guide to approximate capacities at end of this chapter.

Basic Butter Cake

In the practical art of baking, the best way to learn is not only by "doing" but also by knowing some of the reasons for the various steps that you take toward your goal, which is the perfect butter cake.

The following basic steps for *2-Egg Cake* are taken from the first recipe in this section. You'll be able to follow any recipe for a cake calling for solid shortening, whether butter, margarine or vegetable shortening.

Note: Butter and margarine should be well beaten to a creamy consistency before adding the sugar. However, homogenized shortening is made airy and light by the manufacturer and needs only sufficient creaming or beating to spread around the sides of the bowl before adding the sugar.

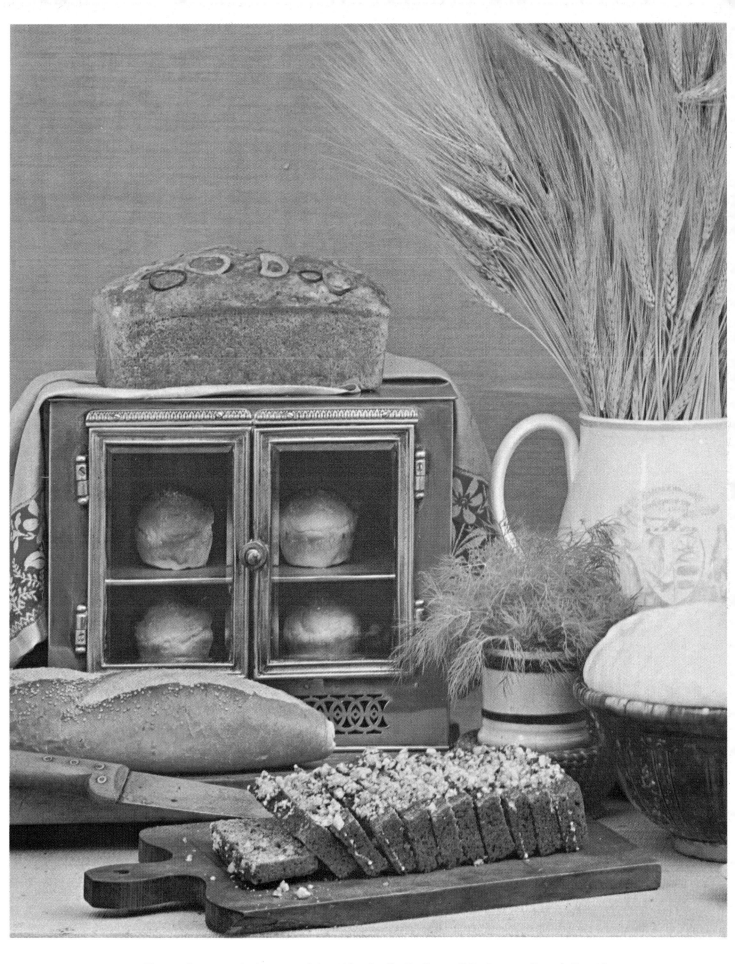

Top to bottom: Onion Bread (p. 169), Garlic Puffs (p. 170), Sesame French Bread (p. 171) and Saint's Loaf (pp. 169-170).
CREDIT: *Faulconer/Fenn*.

Rosette Churos (pp. 250-251) and Candied Apple (p. 312).
CREDIT: *Bernard Gray.*

1. Read through recipe, and obtain all the ingredients. For this *2-Egg Cake* you'll need butter or other shortening, sugar, eggs, suitable flour, salt, baking powder, milk and flavoring.

2. Assemble the necessary utensils. You'll need the right kind of baking pan, in this case an 8-inch square pan or 2 matching round pans 8 inches across by 2 inches deep. You'll also need a large mixing bowl, measuring cups (1 for liquids, nesting set for dry ingredients), measuring spoons, a flour sifter, a wooden spoon or electric mixer, a narrow spatula and a wire rack for cooling the cake after baking.

3. Have all ingredients at room temperature, and measure carefully. Our *2-Egg Cake* calls for unsifted cake and pastry flour. Spoon flour directly from the bag or cannister into a 1-cup dry measuring cup, and when heaped, cut off excess with a spatula. Empty into a sifter or fine mesh sieve that is resting on a square of waxed paper or foil. Measure the additional 3/4 cups flour in the same way using the 1/2-cup and 1/4-cup dry measuring cups of the set. With measuring spoons, measure the baking powder and salt into the sifter or sieve; then sift through on the paper.

4. Grease bottoms of cake pans lightly. As salted butter may make cake stick to bottom, use bland shortening. Sprinkle a little flour over the grease; then shake pan to distribute flour evenly. Turn pan upside down, and tap it on sides to dislodge any surplus flour. Do not grease sides of pan; your cake will rise better if it can "climb" the sides. As an alternative, cut a piece of waxed paper to fit bottom of pan, and grease paper lightly.

ELECTRIC MIXER METHOD:

1. Measure soft shortening or butter into a small mixing bowl, and beat with electric mixer until creamy.

2. With mixer on medium speed gradually add the sugar, and continue beating and adding until you have incorporated the entire measured amount. Stop the beater occasionally, and scrape sides of the bowl.

3. Add unbeaten eggs 1 at a time, beating on medium to high speed after each addition and again scraping the bowl occasionally. When mixture is very fluffy, beat in the flavoring.

4. Remove beaters, and scrape them with a rubber spatula. Transfer creamed mixture to a large bowl.

5. With a wooden spoon or wire whisk stir in the sifted dry ingredients alternately with the milk, making 3 or 4 additions beginning and ending with dry ingredients.

6. When smoothly blended, pour into prepared pan or pans, using a rubber spatula to clean the sides of the bowl. Spread batter evenly in the pan or pans; then push well into the corners or up the edge so that cake tops will be more level after baking. Bake according to recipe directions.

HAND METHOD:

1. Measure soft shortening or butter into a large bowl; using the back of a wooden spoon, press and beat the fat against the sides of the bowl until very creamy.

2. Add measured sugar gradually, 2—3 tablespoons at a time, beating well after each addition so that sugar will dissove in the butter. Continue working with the spoon until mixture is light and creamy. Beat in the flavoring.

3. In a separate small bowl, beat eggs with a rotary beater until lemony in color.

4. Stir beaten eggs gradually into fat and sugar mixture, and again beat well.

5. Stir in sifted dry ingredients alternately with the milk as in the mixer method, beginning and ending with dry ingredients.

6. When smoothly blended, pour into prepared pans.

Baking and Cooling. Set square pan on rack as near center of oven as possible. Set layer pans similarly, but leave some free space around each. Cake is done when it has drawn away from sides of pan, when the top surface springs back when pressed lightly with a finger or when toothpick or metal tester inserted into middle of cake comes out clean, with no dough adhering to it. If the cake needs a few minutes more, shut oven door, and continue baking longer.

After removing from oven, stand pan on wire cake-cooling rack 10—15 minutes. Loosen cake by running a spatula around the edge, between cake and pan. Place clean towel over top of the cake, and quickly invert covered pan over cake rack. Lift off pan gently. Strip away any lining paper, being careful not to tear cake. Cake may be turned right side up for cooling; or, if cake bottom appears more level than top, you may decide to make it your surface for filling or icing.

Checking the Finished Cake. Is the cake of uniform depth all around? If not, perhaps the batter was not spread evenly; or your oven may not be heating properly.

Is the texture fine and even throughout? Unevenness of texture, with some large air holes, is generally caused by failure to cream butter and sugar sufficiently or to mix in other ingredients thoroughly at the proper time.

Is there heaviness or thickening near the bottom of the cake? It could mean that the sugar was coarse or that the butter-sugar mixture was not sufficiently worked to dissolve sugar. Or your oven temperature may have been too low.

Did your cake crack on top? Cracking may be traced to the wrong kind of flour or too much flour. Or the oven temperature may have been too high.

2-Egg Cake (Basic Butter Cake)

        1/2 cup shortening
          1 cup fine white sugar
          1 teaspoon vanilla extract
          2 eggs
    1 3/4 cups unsifted cake and pastry flour
    2 1/2 teaspoons baking powder
        1/2 teaspoon salt
        3/4 cup milk

Arrange oven rack about halfway up in the oven or close to the center position. Preheat oven to 350°F. Follow *Electric Mixer Method* or *Hand Method* of mixing. Set filled cake pan or pans on the oven rack, bake for about 45 minutes for 1 8-inch square pan and 25—30 minutes for 8-inch layer pans.

VARIATIONS:

* *Spice Cake*: Add 1 teaspoon cinnamon and 1/2 teaspoon each allspice and nutmeg to dry ingredients when sifting.

* *Nut Cake*: Add 1/2 cup finely chopped walnuts to sifted dry ingredients when incorporating with creamed mixture.

Fudgy Chocolate Cake

          3 squares unsweetened chocolate
        2/3 cup brown sugar, firmly packed
          1 (6-ounce) can evaporated milk
        1/2 cup soft shortening
        3/4 cup white sugar
          2 egg yolks
          1 teaspoon vanilla
    1 3/4 cups unsifted all-purpose flour
          1 teaspoon baking powder
          1 teaspoon baking soda
        1/2 teaspoon salt
        3/4 cup milk
          2 egg whites

Grease the bottoms of 2 deep 10-inch layer cake pans; then line with circles of greased waxed paper. Mix chocolate, brown sugar and evaporated milk together in the top part of a double boiler. Cook and stir over boiling water until chocolate melts and mixture is smooth. Remove from heat. Cool to room temperature. Beat shortening, 1/2 cup white sugar, egg yolks and vanilla together until light. Stir in chocolate mixture. Sift and add 1/2 the dry ingredients; then add milk and remaining sifted ingredients alternately. Beat egg whites until peaked, but moist; then beat in remaining white sugar. Fold into the chocolate batter. Divide between prepared pans, and bake at 350°F. 35—40 minutes. Cool 10 minutes. Cut around the edges. Invert on towels over a cake rack. When cold, fill with a date filling, and frost with your favorite chocolate butter icing.

Silver Cake

        2/3 cup soft shortening
          2 cups fine white sugar
          1 teaspoon almond extract
          3 cups sifted cake and pastry flour
          1 teaspoon salt
          3 teaspoons baking powder
          1 cup water
          4 egg whites

Beat shortening and sugar together thoroughly; add almond extract. Sift together flour, salt and 2 teaspoons baking powder. Add to creamed mixture alternately with water, beating well after each addition. Beat egg whites with remaining teaspoon of baking powder until stiff; fold into first mixture. Pour batter into 2 deep 9- or 10-inch layer-cake pans, and bake at 350°F. for 30 minutes. Fill and frost.

Gold Cake

        1/2 cup butter or margarine
          1 cup sugar
          3 egg yolks
          2 cups sifted cake and pastry flour
          3 teaspoons baking powder
        1/4 teaspoon salt
        3/4 cup milk
          1 teaspoon grated orange rind
          1 teaspoon vanilla extract

Beat butter or margarine, gradually add sugar and beat until mixture is light and fluffy. Beat in egg yolks 1 at a time, beating thoroughly after each addition. Sift together flour, baking powder and salt 3 times; add dry mixture alternately with milk to creamed mixture, beating well after each addition. Stir in orange rind and vanilla. Pour into 2 8-inch layer pans, and bake at 375°F. 25—30 minutes or until cake tests done. Fill and frost.

VARIATION:

* *Orange-Mace Layer Cake*: Omit vanilla. Add 1/4 teaspoon mace to dry ingredients before sifting. Replace 1/4 cup milk with fresh orange juice. Fill layers with sieved orange marmalade; frost sides and top with boiled butter icing.

Rich Butter Cake

          1 cup butter or margarine
          2 cups sugar
          4 eggs, separated
          1 teaspoon vanilla extract
          3 cups sifted cake and pastry flour
          3 teaspoons baking powder
        1/2 teaspoon salt
          1 cup milk

Beat butter or margarine, add sugar gradually and continue to beat until very smooth and creamy. Beat in egg yolks and vanilla. Beat well. Sift together dry ingredients, and stir in by hand a little at a time, alternately with milk; beat after each addition. Beat egg whites until stiff but not dry; fold them into mixture. Divide batter among 3 greased 8-inch layer-cake pans; bake in pre-heated 350°F. oven 30 minutes. Or bake in rectangular pan, 13″ x 9″ x 2″, about 40 minutes or until toothpick or tester comes out clean.

Apricot-Pecan Torte (Electric Mixer Method)

    2 1/2 cups sifted cake and pastry flour
    3/4 cup finely chopped pecans
    1 1/2 cups sugar
    1 1/2 teaspoons baking powder
    1 teaspoon baking soda
    1/2 teaspoon salt
    2/3 cup soft shortening
    2 (4 3/4-ounce) jars strained apricots
    2 large eggs
    1/2 teaspoon almond extract

Stir 2 tablespoons of the flour into nuts; set aside. Sift remaining flour, sugar, baking powder, baking soda and salt into large mixer bowl. Add shortening and 2/3 the apricots. Beat at medium speed 1 1/2 minutes. Add eggs, remaining apricots and flavoring. Beat another 1 1/2 minutes.

Fold in floured nuts. Pour batter into 2 deep 9-inch round cake pans lined with greased waxed-paper circles. Bake in 350°F. oven 35—40 minutes. Loosen edges of cake, and cool in pans. The cake may be filled and frosted with orange-flavored boiled icing, or with *Caramel-Cheese Frosting*, which will require that cake be refrigerated until serving time.

Caramel-Cheese Frosting

    1/2 cup sugar
    1/4 cup hot water
    1 (8-ounce) package cream cheese
    1 teaspoon grated orange rind
    4 cups (or slightly more) sifted icing sugar

Melt sugar in small frying pan over low heat until it turns rich golden brown. Add hot water; heat, and stir until smooth. Cool. Blend cream cheese with 2 tablespoons cooled syrup; add orange rind, and blend in icing sugar.

Crumb Cake

    3/4 cup butter or margarine
    1 cup sugar
    2 cups sifted all-purpose flour
    1 teaspoon cinnamon
    1/4 teaspoon nutmeg
    1/4 teaspoon ground cloves
    1/4 teaspoon salt
    1 teaspoon baking soda
    2 eggs
    3/4 cup sour milk

Prepare 9-inch square pan. Cream butter or margarine, and gradually blend in sugar, beating until light and fluffy. Sift together flour, spices and salt; add to creamed mixture by cutting in with pastry blender or 2 knives. Mixture should be worked until it resembles cornmeal. Measure 1 cup flour mixture, and set aside. To remainder add baking soda, stirring in thoroughly. Beat eggs until foamy; then beat in sour milk. Make well in center of baking-soda mixture, add liquid and combine very thoroughly. Pour batter into prepared pan. Sprinkle reserved crumbs over top, and lightly press into cake top. Bake in 350°F. oven 40—50 minutes. No icing is required.

Butterscotch Coffee Cake

    1/4 cup butterscotch sundae topping
    1/4 cup brown sugar, firmly packed
    2 cups sifted all-purpose flour
    1/3 cup white sugar
    4 teaspoons baking powder
    1/2 teaspoon salt
    1/2 teaspoon nutmeg
    1/3 cup butter or margarine
    1 egg, beaten
    1 cup milk
    1 teaspoon vanilla extract
    1 recipe *Streusel Filling*
    1/4 cup chopped walnuts
       Candied cherries, sliced (optional)

Grease 8-inch square pan; spread butterscotch topping and brown sugar in bottom of pan. Sift together next 5 ingredients. Cut in butter or margarine. Combine egg with milk and vanilla, and stir into dry mixture. Drop 1/2 the batter by the tablespoon into prepared pan. Sprinkle streusel filling over batter; cover with remaining batter. Bake at 400°F. 30 minutes. Cool in pan 5 minutes; invert cake on rack. Decorate butterscotch surface with nuts, plus sliced candied cherries if desired. Makes 1 8-inch square cake.

Note: The European type of coffee cake is generally made with yeast, but a very satisfactory quick version can be produced with baking powder, as in this recipe.

Streusel Filling

> 1/3 cup brown sugar, firmly packed
> 1/4 cup chopped walnuts
> 2 tablespoons flour
> 1 teaspoon cinnamon
> 2 tablespoons butter or margarine, melted

Combine all dry ingredients. Sprinkle melted butter or margarine over. Toss to combine.

Quick Coffee Cake

> 2 cups biscuit mix
> 1/4 cup white sugar
> 1/2 teaspoon cinnamon
> 1/4 cup milk
> 1 (4 3/4-ounce) jar strained apricots
> 1 egg, beaten
> 1/2 cup raisins
> 1/3 cup brown sugar, firmly packed
> 1/3 cup melted margarine
> 2 tablespoons flour

Grease 8-inch square cake pan. Combine biscuit mix, sugar and cinnamon. Combine milk, apricots and egg, and stir into dry ingredients. Spread batter in prepared pan. Combine remaining ingredients, and spread over batter. Bake at 400°F. 25 minutes; let coffee cake cool before cutting and serving. Makes one 8-inch square cake.

Pineapple Upside-down Cake

> 1/4 cup plus 1 tablespoon shortening or butter
> 1/4 cup brown sugar, firmly packed
> 6 canned pineapple slices
> 8 maraschino cherries
> 2/3 cup white sugar
> 1 egg, beaten
> 1 1/4 cups sifted all-purpose flour
> 1 1/2 teaspoons baking powder
> 1/4 teaspoon salt
> 1/2 cup milk
> 1/2 teaspoon almond extract
> Grated rind of 1 orange

Melt 1 tablespoon shortening (or butter) in bottom of an 8″ x 8″ x 2″ cake pan, and sprinkle with brown sugar. Arrange pineapple slices, either whole or cut in halves or wedges, with cherries in pattern over brown sugar. Beat 1/4 cup shortening; add white sugar gradually, continuing to beat mixture until fluffy. Add egg, and beat well. Sift next 3 ingredients together. Combine milk and almond extract. Add flour and milk mixtures alternately beating after each addition. Add orange rind. Pour over fruit, and spread evenly. Bake at 350°F. 40 minutes. To serve, turn out, fruit side up, and cut in squares. Can be served warm or cold, with or without cream. Serves 6.

* *Peach or Apricot Upside-down Cake*: Substitute canned peaches or apricot halves for pineapple.

Orange Cake

> 1/4 cup butter or margarine
> 1/2 cup fine white sugar
> 1 egg plus 1 egg yolk
> Grated rind of 1/2 orange
> 1/4 teaspoon salt
> 1 1/2 cups sifted cake and pastry flour
> 1/2 teaspoon baking powder
> 1/2 teaspoon baking soda
> 1/2 teaspoon cream of tartar
> 1/2 cup milk
> 1/2 cup sugar
> 1/4 cup orange juice
> 2 tablespoons lemon juice

Cream butter or margarine and 1/2 cup sugar together; add egg and egg yolk, and beat until mixture is very light. Add orange rind. Sift dry ingredients together, and add alternately with milk to creamed mixture. Scrape into well-buttered small 8-inch angel-cake pan, and bake at 350°F. 30–40 minutes. While cake is baking, make syrup of 1/2 cup sugar and juices. Pour over hot cake fresh from oven. Let cake stand until syrup is absorbed; then invert cake onto serving plate. Serve warm or cold.

Applesauce Cake

> 1/2 cup shortening
> 1 1/2 cups brown sugar, lightly packed
> 2 eggs
> 1 teaspoon lemon extract
> 1 2/3 cups sifted all-purpose flour
> 3 teaspoons baking powder
> 1 teaspoon cinnamon
> 1 teaspoon nutmeg
> 1/2 teaspoon salt
> 1 cup thick applesauce, sweetened and sieved

Prepare 2 round layer-cake pans, 8 or 9 inches across top. Cream shortening thoroughly. Add brown sugar very gradually, creaming and beating after each addition, to make mixture as light and fluffy as possible. Add eggs and lemon flavoring; again beat thoroughly. Sift dry ingredients together, and add alternately with applesauce to creamed mixture, adding just a little at a time and blending well after each addition. Divide batter evenly between pans. Bake in 350°F. oven 30–40 minutes.

Banana Cake (Electric Mixer Method)

> 2 1/4 cups sifted cake and pastry flour
> 1 1/4 cups sugar
> 2 1/2 teaspoons baking powder
> 1/2 teaspoon baking soda
> 1/2 teaspoon salt
> 1/2 cup vegetable shortening
> 2 eggs
> 1 1/2 cups (4–5) mashed bananas
> 1 teaspoon vanilla extract

Prepare 2 8-inch layer-cake pans or 1 9-inch square pan. Sift together flour, sugar, baking powder, baking soda and salt in larger mixer bowl. Add shortening, eggs and 1/2 cup banana pulp. Beat 2 minutes at medium speed. Scrape bowl often. Add remaining banana and vanilla. Beat 1 minute. Turn into pan(s). Bake in preheated 350°F. oven 30—35 minutes for layers or 50—55 minutes for square cake. Cool. Fill and frost as desired. Or top with sweetened whipped cream and sliced bananas.

Maple-syrup Gingerbread

       2 eggs
       1 cup sour cream
       1 cup maple syrup
     1/2 cup brown sugar, firmly packed
     1/2 cup shortening, melted
   2 1/2 cups unsifted cake and pastry flour
       3 teaspoons ground ginger
       2 teaspoons cinnamon
       1 teaspoon baking soda
       1 teaspoon baking powder
     1/2 teaspoon salt
     1/2 teaspoon ground cloves
     1/2 teaspoon nutmeg
       1 tablespoon finely chopped candied orange peel

Beat eggs until light, and add sour cream, syrup, brown sugar and shortening. Sift dry ingredients together; add to egg mixture, and beat until smooth. Add orange peel. Batter will be thin. Grease deep 8 1/2—9-inch square pan, and line bottom with waxed paper. Pour batter in, and bake at 350°F. for 35—40 minutes or until center is set. Serve with chilled applesauce and whipped cream.

Lemon Cheesecake

      36 vanilla or chocolate wafers, crushed
     1/3 cup fine white sugar
     1/3 cup soft butter or margarine
       1 teaspoon grated lemon rind
       2 pounds creamed cottage cheese
   1 1/2 cups fine white sugar
       5 eggs, separated
     1/3 cup sifted cake flour
         Juice of 3 lemons
     1/4 cup heavy cream or evaporated milk
     2—3 teaspoons grated lemon rind
       1 tablespoon fine white sugar
         Shaved chocolate or chocolate curls

Mix wafers, 1/3 cup sugar, butter or margarine and 1 teaspoon lemon rind together, and press thinly into bottom and halfway up sides of 10-inch spring-form pan. Bake at 325°F. 10 minutes to prevent sogginess. Beat cheese until creamy in large mixing bowl. Beat in 1 1/2—2 cups sugar, egg yolks, flour, lemon juice, heavy cream and 2—3 teaspoons lemon rind. Beat egg whites with 1 tablespoon sugar until stiff, and fold into cheese mixture very gently. Batter will be thick. Pour into prepared crust. Bake in preheated oven at 250°F. 1 1/2—2 hours. Turn heat off, and leave cake in oven 1 hour. Cool at room temperature 4—6 hours. Chill in refrigerator overnight. Before serving, sprinkle top with shaved chocolate or chocolate curls. Cut in small wedges with sharp knife, wiping knife after each cut. Serves 16.

Note: To halve recipe, use same-size pan and all the crumb-crust mixture. Follow procedures for full recipe, using 1 pound cottage cheese, 3/4 cup sugar, 3 eggs, 2 tablespoons flour, juice of 1 1/2 lemons, 2 tablespoons heavy cream, 1 1/2 teaspoons grated lemon rind and 1 1/2 teaspoons sugar. Bake 1 hour at 250°F.

Christmas or Wedding Cake

       1 pound seeded muscat or lexia raisins
       1 pound seedless raisins
       1 pound currants
     1/2 pound soft butter or margarine
     1/2 pound soft shortening
       2 cups sugar
       1 tablespoon vanilla extract
       1 tablespoon almond extract
      12 eggs
       1 cup brandy or grape juice
     1/2 cup honey
   4 1/2 cups unsifted all-purpose flour
       2 teaspoons cinnamon
       2 teaspoons baking powder
       1 teaspoon baking soda
       1 teaspoon salt
       1 teaspoon nutmeg
     1/2 teaspoon ground cloves
     1/2 pound pitted dates, cut up
       1 pound chopped mixed candied peel
       1 pound candied cherries, halved
     1/2 pound blanched almonds, halved

Use 2 tube pans 10″ x 4″ each, or 5 8 1/2″ x 4 1/2″ loaf pans or 3 graduated cake pans, round or square, plus 1 loaf pan. Line pans with 2 or 3 thicknesses of brown paper or 1 thickness of heavy foil; grease well with unsalted shortening.

Wash raisins and currants; dry thoroughly between paper towels. Beat butter and shortening together very thoroughly; when smooth and fluffy, add sugar gradually, beating continuously. Blend in vanilla and almond extract. Add eggs, 1 at a time, beating after each addition. Beat in brandy and honey; they may cause batter to appear separated, but it will not affect results. Sift together remaining dry ingredients. Mix prepared fruits and almonds in large mixing bowl; add sifted dry ingredients, and mix well to coat pieces. Scrape egg-and-butter mixture into bowl, and, using hands, combine very thoroughly. Fill each pan 3/4 full. Preheat oven to 275°F. Bake cakes 1 1/2—3 1/2 hours, depending on size of pans used. After first hour or so, place pan of water on bottom of oven to prevent cakes from drying out. When cakes test done, remove from oven, and let pans stand on racks until contents are completely cooled. Remove from pans, and peel off paper linings. Let ripen 4–5 weeks before serving. See beginning of cake section for storage information.

Note: This recipe makes dark moist cake, rich with fruits and mingled flavors of spices, honey, brandy, and the like. If desired, recipe may be halved with good results.

Old-fashioned Pound Cake
(Electric Mixer Method)

      2 cups soft butter or margarine
      2 cups sugar
      8 eggs
      1 teaspoon vanilla extract
      4 cups sifted cake and pastry flour
    1/2 teaspoon salt
    1/2 teaspoon mace

Beat butter very thoroughly, using largest bowl. Add sugar, a very little at a time, continuing beating and creaming action. Scrape bowl often. After all sugar has been added, beat 1 minute at high speed. Add eggs, 1 at a time, beating 1 minute after each addition. Scrape bowl, and add vanilla. Sift dry ingredients together, and sprinkle very slowly into butter mixture, operating mixer at lowest speed. When last of flour has been added, pour batter at once, with no further beating, into 2 9″ x 5″ x 3″ loaf pans lined with greased heavy waxed paper. (For convenience in removing cake, let paper extend over sides of pan.) Bake in preheated 325°F. oven 1 1/4 hours or until cake has drawn away from sides of pans. Let pans stand on rack 20 minutes; turn out cakes carefully to finish cooling. Store cakes in covered container at least 24 hours before cutting.

Note: This cake freezes well.

VARIATIONS:

* *Seed Cake*: Add 2 teaspoons caraway seeds before turning batter into pan.

* *Special-occasion Cake*: Add 2 tablespoons brandy with vanilla and 1 cup finely chopped candied cherries and pineapple, dusted with a little flour, just before pouring batter into pans.

Foam-type Cakes

The cakes that follow shoud be cooled completely in pans to prevent shrinkage. Turn pan upside down on cake rack or, if more convenient, suspend from 2 even supports at sides. To remove, run long thin spatula around edge of cake; then tap pan sharply.

Basic Sponge Cake

      4 egg whites
    1/4 teaspoon cream of tartar
    1/4 teaspoon salt
    2/3 cup fine white sugar
      4 egg yolks
      2 teaspoons lemon juice
    1/2 teaspoon grated lemon rind
    3/4 cup sifted cake and pastry flour

Beat egg whites with cream of tartar and salt until very stiff but not dry; gradually beat in 1/3 cup sugar and set aside. Beat egg yolks until thick and lemon-colored; then beat in 1/3 cup sugar, lemon juice and rind. Fold this mixture into beaten whites, only until just combined. Sift 1/3 cup flour over fluffy mass, and fold until flour is absorbed; add remaining flour in same manner. Pour into ungreased tube pan 8 or 9 inches in diameter. Bake 45–55 minutes in 325°F. oven. Invert pan until cake is cooled; then remove.

VARIATION:

* *Spice Sponge Cake*: To flour add 1 teaspoon cinnamon and 1/4 teaspoon each nutmeg and allspice. Omit orange juice and rind.

Angel Food Cake

      1 cup sifted cake and pastry flour
    1 3/4 cups sugar
      12 eggs whites (1 1/2 cups)
    1 1/2 teaspoons cream of tartar
    1/4 teaspoon salt
    1 1/2 teaspoons vanilla extract
    1/4 teaspoon almond flavoring

Use 1 10-inch tube pan. Sift flour and 1 cup sugar together 3 times. Measure egg whites, cream of tartar and salt into large mixing bowl; beat until foamy. Gradually add 3/4 cup sugar, sprinkling 1 tablespoon at a time over froth. Continue beating until meringue will hold very stiff peaks. Fold in flavorings. Gradually sift flour-sugar mixture over meringue. Fold in gently, just until flour is absorbed. Pour batter into ungreased pan. Gently cut through batter with knife to remove any air pockets. Bake at 375°F. 30–35 minutes, until top springs back when touched lightly. Invert pan, cool completely and remove cake.

VARIATIONS:

* *Coconut Angel Food Cake*: Fold 1 cup flake coconut into meringue when adding flour-sugar mixture.

* *Mocha Angel Food Cake*: Omit almond flavoring. Substitute 1/4 cup cocoa and 2 teaspoons instant coffee powder for 1/4 cup flour, and sift with sugar and remaining flour.

* *Cherry Angel Food Cake*: Pat dry 1/3 cup finely chopped maraschino cherries, and fold into batter before pouring into pan.

Chiffon Cake

    2 1/4 cups sifted cake flour
    1 1/3 cups sugar
        1 tablespoon baking powder
        1 teaspoon salt
        1/2 cup vegetable oil
        5 egg yolks
        3/4 cup cold water
        2 teaspoons vanilla extract
        2 teaspoons grated lemon rind
        7–8 egg whites (1 cup)
        1/2 teaspoon cream of tartar

Use 1 10-inch tube pan. Sift flour, sugar, baking powder and salt into bowl. Make well in center, and add, in order, oil, yolks, water, vanilla and lemon rind. Beat until smooth. Measure egg whites and cream of tartar into large mixing bowl; beat until stiff peaks are formed. Pour yolk mixture gradually over beaten whites, folding with whisk or rubber scraper just until blended. Pour into ungreased pan. Bake at 325°F. 60–75 minutes. Invert pan until cake is cool. Loosen with spatula to remove from pan.

VARIATIONS:

* *Confetti Chiffon Cake*: Add 1/2 teaspoon cinnamon to dry ingredients. Before pouring batter into pan, sprinkle in 3/4 cup finely chopped red and green cherries and 1/4 cup finely chopped candied fruit peel. Fold in gently with a few strokes.

* *Candy-stripe Chiffon Cake*: Omit lemon rind and vanilla. Add 1 teaspoon peppermint flavoring. Shake in 3–4 drops red vegetable coloring during final folding to give striped effect.

* *Dot Chiffon Cake*: Omit lemon rind. Fold 1/2 cup chopped semisweet chocolate bits into batter with egg yolk mixture.

* *Pink Chiffon Cake*: Omit vanilla. Substitute 1/4 cup maraschino cherry juice for 1/4 cup water. Fold in 1/2 cup finely chopped maraschino cherries (first patted dry) and 1/4 cup finely chopped pecans with egg yolk mixture.

Cocoa Chiffon Cake

        1/4 cup cocoa
        6 tablespoons boiling water
        3/4 cup plus 2 tablespoons sifted cake and pastry
            flour
        3/4 cup sugar
    1 1/2 teaspoons baking powder
        1/2 teaspoon salt
        1/4 cup cooking oil
        4 egg yolks
        1/2 teaspoon vanilla extract
        4 egg whites
        1/4 teaspoon cream of tartar

Mix cocoa with boiling water, and set aside to cool. Sift together into mixing bowl flour, sugar, baking powder and salt. Make well in center, and pour in oil, unbeaten egg yolks, and cooled cocoa. Add vanilla, and beat until mixture is smooth. In large bowl beat egg whites with cream of tartar until very stiff and dry. Pour first mixture gradually over top of egg whites, and gently fold until 2 mixtures are completely blended. Pour into ungreased 9-inch tube pan or 9″ x 5″ x 3″ pan, and bake at 325°F. 50—55 minutes or until cake tests done. Remove from oven, invert immediately on cake rack and let hang until cooled.

Génoise

        1/2 cup sweet butter
        4 eggs
        1/2 cup fine white sugar
        1 cup sifted cake and pastry flour
        1/2 teaspoon baking powder
        1/4 teaspoon salt
        1 teaspoon vanilla extract
        1/2 teaspoon grated lemon or orange rind

Oil bottom of 9-inch tube pan. Preheat oven to 350°F. Melt butter slowly until it froths; remove from heat and set aside. Beat eggs at high speed 25 minutes or until very thick. Then add sugar, and continue beating about 10 minutes. Meanwhile sift flour, baking powder and salt together. Fold into egg mixture 1/4 at a time. Fold in vanilla and lemon rind. Pour butter in last, drizzling it over batter slowly, folding as you pour. Stop when you reach sediment and water at bottom of pan (about 2 tablespoons), and discard them. Lift batter up each time you fold to be sure butter has not settled to bottom. Scrape into prepared pan, and bake 35—40 minutes or until set. Cool upside down; loosen edges with knife, and remove from pan. Slice horizontally through center, and fill and frost with your favorite butter cream frosting. Serves 10.

Chocolate-Rum Sponge Cake

    1 3/4 cups sifted cake and pastry flour
        1/4 cup cornstarch
        2 teaspoons baking powder
        1/4 teaspoon salt
        4 eggs, separated
        2 cups fine white sugar
        1 teaspoon vanilla extract
        1 cup milk
        2 teaspoons butter or margarine
    1/3–1/2 cup light rum
        1 recipe *Chocolate Cream Filling*
        1/4 cup toasted almonds

Grease and line bottom of deep 9″ x 13″ x 3″ pan with waxed paper. Sift first 4 ingredients together. Beat egg whites until stiff; gradually add 1 cup sugar, and continue beating until very stiff, about 15 minutes. Set aside. Beat egg yolks until thick, and add remaining sugar and vanilla. Continue beating until smooth and cream-colored. Scald milk and butter or margarine together; fold alternately with sifted ingredients into egg yolk mixture, using wire whisk or spatula. Fold into egg whites. Scrape into pan, and bake at 350°F. 50–55 minutes. Cool 5 minutes, and run spatula around edge of pan. Invert, and cool completely. Slice cake horizontally through center to make 2 layers. Sprinkle each layer with rum. Fill and frost with filling. Sprinkle with toasted almonds, and refrigerate until serving time (cake can be made the day before serving).

Chocolate Cream Filling

> 4 squares semisweet chocolate
> 1/4 cup sugar
> 1/4 cup milk
> 1/8 teaspoon salt
> 2 egg yolks, slightly beaten
> 1 teaspoon vanilla extract
> 1 1/2 cups whipped cream
> 2 eggs whites, stiffly beaten

Combine chocolate, sugar, milk and salt in top of double boiler. Heat and stir until blended. Add egg yolks, and cook, stirring, 3 minutes. Remove from heat, and add vanilla. Stand in bowl of ice cubes, and stir occasionally until cool and thick. Fold in stiffly beaten cream and egg whites. Chill to spread easily.

COOKIES

For best results use a bright, shiny baking sheet to reflect heat. Darkened metal lets cookies brown too quickly. Grease sheets with shortening to prevent sticking. Place baking sheet in oven so that 2 inches of oven rack show all around it, for proper circulation of heat. The oven rack should be placed almost in center of oven. If 2 racks are used, divide oven into thirds, and stagger baking sheets so they are not directly above one another. When 2 baking times are listed, always check to see if cookies are done at shortest time given. Let delicate cookies cool slightly before lifting, and cool them thoroughly on cake rack.

Soft cookies keep best in airtight containers. Crisp ones need a little air circulation around

them and are thus best stored in loosely covered containers.

Unbaked cookie doughs freeze well as do baked cookies if properly packed.

Drop Cookies

Drop cookies are easily and quickly made; the mixture is simply dropped from the tip of a spoon onto a greased cookie sheet. Space cookies about 2 inches apart to allow for spreading. Some drop cookies have soft cake-like texture, others may be firm and macaroons (which are part of this group) have their own distinctive consistency.

Rich Drop Cookies

> 1/2 cup shortening
> 1 cup brown sugar, firmly packed
> 2 eggs, beaten
> 1/2 teaspoon vanilla extract
> 1 3/4 cups unsifted all-purpose flour
> 1 teaspoon baking powder
> 1 teaspoon baking soda
> 1/2 teaspoon salt
> 1/3 cup sour milk
> 1/2 cup raisins

Cream shortening, and add sugar. Add eggs and vanilla, and beat until fluffy. Sift flour, baking powder, baking soda and salt together; add alternately with sour milk. Fold in raisins. Drop by teaspoonfuls onto greased cookie sheet, about 2 inches apart. Bake about 12 minutes at 350°F. Makes 4 dozen.

VARIATIONS:

* *Hermits*: Add 1 teaspoon cinnamon, 1/2 teaspoon cloves and 1/2 teaspoon nutmeg with dry ingredients, Fold in 1 cup chopped nuts with raisins.

* *Date-Almond Drop Cookies*: Add 1/2 teaspoon almond flavoring with vanilla. Add 1 1/2 cups chopped dates and 1/2 cup chopped almonds in place of raisins.

* *Christmas Drop Cookies*: Add 1 cup light golden raisins, 1 cup finely chopped cherries, 1/2

cup sliced blanched almonds, 1/2 cup finely chopped orange peel and 1 teaspoon almond flavoring.

* *Marmalade Drop Cookies*: Add 1/2 cup thick orange marmalade, and reduce sour milk to 1/4 cup.

* *Cereal Drop Cookies*: Use 1/4 cup less flour. Add 1 cup crushed ready-to-eat cereal, 1 cup chopped dates, 1/2 cup chopped walnut meats and 1/4 teaspoon cinnamon.

* *Coconut Drop Cookies*: Add 1 cup dessicated or flake coconut.

Chocolate Dot Cookies

```
1/2  cup shortening
1/2  cup white sugar
1/4  cup brown sugar, lightly packed
  1  egg, beaten
  1  teaspoon vanilla extract
  1  cup sifted all-purpose flour
1/2  teaspoon salt
1/4  teaspoon baking soda
  1  cup (6-ounce package) semisweet
       chocolate chips
1/2  cup chopped walnuts
```

Cream shortening, add all sugar and continue to cream until thoroughly blended. Add egg and vanilla; beat mixture. Sift flour, salt and baking soda together, and add to creamed mixture, combining well. Fold in chocolate bits and walnuts. Drop by teaspoonfuls onto greased baking sheets. Bake in 350°F. oven 10—12 minutes. Makes 3 dozen cookies.

Nut Meringues

```
      1  cup finely chopped dates
      1  cup icing sugar
      2  egg whites
1 3/4  cups finely chopped Brazil nuts
    1/4  teaspoon salt
      1  teaspoon vanilla
```

Combine dates and 1/2 cup sugar. Beat egg whites until softly peaked, and add remaining sugar very gradually, beating until very stiff. Fold in dates and nuts. Drop by teaspoonfuls onto baking sheets covered with brown paper. Bake in 275°F. oven 20 minutes or until set. Cool on paper; then peel off. Makes 4 dozen meringues.

Molasses Cookies

```
      3  cups unsifted all-purpose flour
1 1/2  teaspoons baking soda
      1  teaspoon ginger
      1  teaspoon cinnamon
    1/2  teaspoon salt
    1/2  cup butter or margarine
      1  cup sugar
      1  egg
    1/2  cup dark molasses
      1  cup buttermilk or sour milk
    1/2  teaspoon vanilla extract
```

Combine flour, soda, spices and salt. Cream butter or margarine until fluffy, and add sugar gradually, continuing to cream. Add egg, and beat well. Stir in molasses. Add sifted dry ingredients alternately with buttermilk, a little at a time, incorporating thoroughly after each addition. Add vanilla. Place bowl of batter in refrigerator 1—2 hours to firm dough. Drop by teaspoonfuls onto lightly greased sheets. Bake in 375°F. oven 8—10 minutes. Makes about 6 dozen cookies.

Coconut Macaroons

```
      3  egg whites
    1/4  teaspoon salt
      1  cup sugar
3 1/2  cups shredded coconut
      1  teaspoon vanilla extract
```

Beat egg whites and salt to soft peaks; gradually beat in sugar until very stiff. Stir in coconut and vanilla. Drop by teaspoonfuls onto greased and floured cookie sheets. Bake at 325°F. 15—20 minutes. Makes 3 dozen macaroons.

Anytime Cookies

```
      1  cup butter or margarine
      1  cup light brown sugar, firmly packed
      2  eggs
      2  teaspoons rum extract
         Grated rind of 1 orange
      1  cup finely chopped dates
         Juice of 1 orange
    1/2  cup chopped walnuts
    1/2  cup fancy molasses
    1/2  cup peanut butter
      2  cups sifted all-purpose flour
      1  teaspoon baking powder
      1  teaspoon salt
    1/2  teaspoon baking soda
      2  cups bran
```

Cream butter or margarine and sugar together. Add eggs, rum flavoring and orange rind. Soak dates in orange juice a few minutes, and add to butter mixture. Add nuts, molasses and peanut butter. Sift next 4 ingredients together, and add with bran. Drop from teaspoon onto greased cookie sheets. Bake at 375°F. 10 minutes. Makes 6 dozen.

Chocolate-Orange Cookies

```
      1  cup shortening (part butter or margarine)
      1  (4-ounce) package cream cheese
      1  cup sugar
      2  eggs
      2  cups unsifted all-purpose flour
      1  tablespoon grated orange rind
      1  teaspoon vanilla extract
      1  teaspoon salt
      1  cup (6-ounce package) semisweet chocolate chips
      1  recipe *Orange Icing*
```

Cream shortening and cheese together. Add sugar, then eggs, beating until light and fluffy. Stir in flour, orange rind, vanilla and salt, mixing well. Fold in chocolate chips. Drop by teaspoonfuls about 1 inch apart on lightly greased cookie sheet. Bake at 350°F. about 15 minutes. Cookies should be only very lightly browned. While warm, frost with icing. Makes 5—6 dozen.

Orange Icing

>2 teaspoons butter or margarine
>1 cup sifted icing sugar
>2 teaspoons orange juice
>1/8 teaspoon grated orange rind
>Dash salt

Cream butter or margarine with 1/4 cup sugar. Add orange juice, orange rind and salt. Stir in remaining sugar. Beat until smooth. If mixture is too dry, add a few drops more orange juice. A very small amount will glaze top of each cookie.

Ragged Robins

>1 cup soft butter or margarine
>2 cups brown sugar, lightly packed
>3 cups sifted all-purpose flour
>1 cup chopped walnuts
>1/2 cup finely chopped mixed candied fruit
>2 eggs
>2 tablespoons water
>2 teaspoons baking soda
>1 teaspoon vanilla extract
>1/2 teaspoon salt
>1/2 cup chopped glacé cherries

Cream butter or margarine with sugar. Add all ingredients (except cherries). Drop by spoonfuls onto greased cookie sheet; center each with cherry, and bake at 350°F. 12 minutes or until light brown. Makes 8 dozen or more, depending on size.

Melting Moments

>2/3 cup soft butter or margarine
>2/3 cup fine white sugar
>2 eggs
>1 cup sifted all-purpose flour
>1/2 cup cornstarch
>2 teaspoons baking powder
>1 teaspoon grated lemon rind or vanilla extract
>1 cup flaked coconut or chopped roasted almonds

Beat butter or margarine, sugar and eggs together until very fluffy. Sift dry ingredients together, and stir in butter mixture. Add lemon rind and coconut. Grease cookie sheets with salad oil or unsalted fat to prevent burning, and drop mixture 2 inches apart by small teaspoonfuls. Bake at 350°F. 10—12 minutes or until centers are set and edges golden brown. Makes 6 dozen.

Note: For fruit-flavored drops, add 1/2 cup finely chopped candied fruit and 1/2 the coconut or almonds.

Refrigerator Cookies

Any cookie dough stiff enough to hold its shape may be formed into a long roll and refrigerated for baking at a later time. Wrap securely in waxed paper, and store in refrigerator. It will keep 3—4 weeks. If you freeze wrapped dough, it will keep 6 months.

You will notice that a rich dough made with butter will chill to a firmer texture than the same dough made with homogenized shortening. Prepare shorter rolls of dough if shortening is used to reduce the time of slicing. The ends of long rolls of shortening dough will soften before slicing is completed.

In slicing refrigerator cookies, always use a sharp thin or serrated knife. Dip in hot water, and wipe dry; the warm metal will cut more easily.

Cookies sliced very thin will be crisp; thicker slices tend to be softer after baking. Always allow 2—3 minutes additional baking time for thicker ones.

Cherry Refrigerator Cookies

>1/2 cup shortening
>1 1/4 cups white sugar
>2 eggs, well beaten
>Juice and grated rind of 1/2 lemon
>1/4 teaspoon almond extract
>2 1/4 cups sifted all-purpose flour
>1 1/2 teaspoons baking powder
>1/2 teaspoon salt
>2/3 cup chopped candied cherries
>1/2 cup chopped almonds or filberts
>1/3 cup chopped candied pineapple (optional)

Cream shortening and sugar together. Add eggs, lemon juice, rind and almond extract. Sift dry ingredients together, and stir in; add fruit and nuts. Mix well. Chill dough. Form into 1 1/2-inch rolls. Wrap in waxed paper; chill again. Slice 1/4 inch thick, and place on greased cookie sheets. Bake at 375°F. 10 minutes. Makes 5 dozen.

Butterscotch Cookies

>1/2 cup butter or margarine
>2 cups brown sugar, lightly packed
>2 eggs, beaten
>1/2 teaspoon vanilla extract
>3 cups sifted all-purpose flour
>1 teaspoon baking soda
>1/2 teaspoon cream of tartar
>1/4 teaspoon salt
>1/2 cup chopped walnuts

Cream butter or margarine until soft and fluffy; add brown sugar, continuing to cream. Add eggs and vanilla. Sift dry ingredients together. Blend into egg mixture gradually. When mixture is smooth, add walnuts. Have ready several layers of waxed paper; turn dough onto paper, and shape into roll of uniform thickness, about 2 inches in diameter. Wrap tightly in waxed paper, and store in refrigerator. When ready to bake, preheat oven to 375°F. Cut slices from chilled dough, arrange on greased cookie sheet, leaving space between, and bake. Slices 1/4 inch thick will bake in 5–7 minutes. Keep remainder of dough well-wrapped in refrigerator. Makes 5 dozen.

Orange Cookies

        1 cup soft butter or margarine
        1 cup sugar
        1 egg, beaten
    1/3 cup orange juice
        2 tablespoons grated orange rind
    1/2 teaspoon vanilla extract
2 3/4 cups unsifted all-purpose flour
1 1/2 teaspoons baking powder
    1/2 teaspoon salt

Cream butter or margarine, add sugar and continue creaming until fluffy. Add egg, orange juice, orange rind and vanilla; beat mixture until smooth. Sift together flour, baking powder and salt; blend into first mixture thoroughly. Place dough on waxed paper, and shape into 1 or more rolls about 2 inches in diameter. Wrap securely. Refrigerate until needed. Slice 1/4 inch thick, and place on greased cookie sheets. Bake at 350°F. 10–12 minutes. Makes about 5 dozen.

VARIATIONS:

* *Orange-Nut Cookies*: Add 1 cup finely chopped nuts to dough before shaping.

* *Chocolate-Orange Pinwheels*: Divide dough in 1/2. To 1 portion add 1 square unsweetened chocolate, which has been melted and cooled. Roll each piece of dough to a uniform oblong. Place chocolate dough on top of plain dough, and roll together firmly. Chill very thoroughly before slicing.

Rolled Cookies

Roll out on lightly floured pastry cloth or board; then cut into desired shapes. The dough should be well chilled; otherwise more flour will be needed, and cookies will be heavier. Part of dough may be rolled out as needed and remainder left in refrigerator for later use.

Roll dough about 1/4 inch thick. Cut out with floured cutter in plain rounds, or use fancy cutter shapes. Gather up remaining scraps of dough, combine, roll out again and cut. Second and third rollings will result in somewhat less tender cookies.

Sugar Cookies

        1 cup butter or margarine
    1 1/2 cups sugar
        2 eggs
        1 teaspoon vanilla extract
        4 cups unsifted cake and pastry flour
    2 1/2 teaspoons baking powder
    1/2 teaspoon salt
        2 tablespoons cream or 1 egg white

Cream shortening, and add sugar gradually, continuing to cream. Add eggs and vanilla; beat until light and fluffy. Sift dry ingredients together. Blend into creamed mixture thoroughly. Chill dough. When ready to bake, roll dough 1/4 inch thick for soft cookies and about 1/8 inch thick for crisp cookies. Cut in any desired size or shape. Use broad spatula to transfer cookies to greased baking sheet. Leave about 1/2 inch between cookies. Brush lightly with cream. Decorate as desired with nutmeats, sprinkles of colored sugar and the like. Bake in 375°F. oven 8—10 minutes. Makes about 6 dozen cookies.

VARIATIONS:

* *Lemon Sugar Cookies*: Omit vanilla. Add 2 tablespoons finely grated lemon rind and 1 tablespoon lemon juice.

* *Butterscotch-Almond Cookies*: Use brown sugar in place of white sugar. Add 1/3 cup finely ground blanched almonds.

* *Chocolate Sugar Cookies*: Add 3 squares unsweetened chocolate, melted and cooled, to creamed shortening-egg mixture.

Date Turnovers

       1 cup soft margarine
       1 cup brown sugar, firmly packed
       1 egg
       1 teaspoon vanilla
   2 1/4 cups unsifted all-purpose flour
     3/4 teaspoon salt
       2 teaspoons baking powder
     1/2 teaspoon baking soda
     1/4 teaspoon mace (optional)
     1/4 cup buttermilk or sour milk
       2 cups rolled oats
         Homemade or canned date filling

Beat the first 4 ingredients together; then stir in sifted dry ingredients alternately with milk. Add the oats, and chill until firm enough to roll. Roll out on a floured board to 3/8-inch thickness, and cut into circles, 3—4 inches in diameter. Dampen the edge of each round. Dab center with date filling, and fold over. Press edges together with a fork. Prick the top with a fork. Bake on a greased cookie sheet at 375°F. 10 minutes or until edges are light brown. Makes 3 dozen.

Old-timers

     3/4 cup lard
     3/4 cup granulated sugar
     3/4 cup molasses
     3/4 cup sour cream
       2 eggs, well beaten
   4 1/2 cups sifted all-purpose flour
       2 teaspoons baking soda
       2 teaspoons cinnamon
   1 1/2 teaspoons salt
       1 teaspoon ground ginger

Cream lard and sugar together well. Add molasses and cream, then eggs. Sift dry ingredients together, and stir in. Dough will be soft. Chill in refrigerator overnight. Use 1/2 the dough at a time. Roll out lightly, 1/4 inch thick, on floured cloth. Cut rounds 2 1/2—3 inches in diameter.

Place on greased cookie sheets, and bake at 350°F. 15—20 minutes. These cookies are good warm, spread with butter or eaten with cheese. Makes 4 dozen.

Crisp Oatmeal Cookies

       1 cup shortening, butter or margarine
       1 cup brown sugar, firmly packed
       2 eggs, beaten
       2 cups sifted all-purpose flour
       1 teaspoon baking soda
     1/2 teaspoon salt
       2 cups rolled oats
       1 teaspoon vanilla extract

Cream shortening, add sugar and continue creaming. Beat in eggs. Sift together flour, baking soda and salt; add to egg mixture. Stir in oats and vanilla; blend well. Chill. Divide dough into sections for easy handling, and roll out very thin on floured pastry cloth. Cut with 2 1/2-inch floured cookie cutter, and place on lightly greased sheet. Bake at 375°F. 6—8 minutes. Cooled baked cookies can be put together in sandwich fashion with jam or date fillings. Makes 6 dozen single cookies.

Scottish Shortbread

       1 cup butter or margarine
     1/2 cup brown sugar, firmly packed
       1 egg yolk
       1 teaspoon vanilla extract
       2 cups unsifted all-purpose flour

Cream butter or margarine. Add brown sugar, and continue to cream thoroughly. Add egg yolk and vanilla, and beat mixture by hand until light and fluffy. Add gradually to creamed mixture, and combine completely. Turn out dough onto lightly floured board. Roll 1/4 inch thick. Cut in strips, squares or fancy shapes. Bake on ungreased sheet in 300°F. oven 18—20 minutes.

Note: If desired, decorate shortbread tops with halved nuts, candied cherries or angelica.

Coffee Shortbread Fingers

       1 cup soft butter or margarine
     2/3 cup brown sugar, firmly packed
       1 teaspoon instant coffee powder
   2 1/2 cups sifted cake flour
       1 egg white, slightly beaten
       1 cup finely chopped nuts

Cream butter or margarine and sugar together. Blend in coffee; add flour gradually, and mix thoroughly. Chill dough. Roll out 1/2 inch thick, and cut into fingers. Dip fingers in egg white; then roll in finely chopped nuts. Place on ungreased baking sheets. Bake at 300°F. 20—25 minutes. Cool; store in covered tin, with waxed paper between each layer of cookies. Makes about 4 dozen.

Apricot Dream Squares

    1 cup crushed graham crackers
    1 cup sifted all-purpose flour
    1 cup shredded coconut
    1 cup brown sugar, firmly packed
    1/2 teaspoon salt
    1/2 cup butter or margarine, melted
    1 cup dried apricots
    1 cup water
    2 eggs
    1 cup brown sugar, firmly packed
    1 tablespoon lemon juice
    1/3 cup sifted all-purpose flour
    1/2 teaspoon baking powder
    1/4 teaspoon salt

Combine first 5 ingredients. Add butter or margarine, and mix well. Reserve 1 cup mixture for topping. Pack remainder in bottom of 9-inch square cake pan. Bake 10 minutes at 350°F. Cover apricots with water. Simmer until tender, approximately 15 minutes. Drain, chop and set aside. Beat eggs until light, and add brown sugar and lemon juice. Sift remaining ingredients together, and stir into eggs; add apricots. Spread over bottom layer. Sprinkle with topping. Bake 30—35 minutes at 350°F. Cool. Cut into 20 squares.

Marshmallow-Fudge Squares

    2 cups graham cracker crumbs
    1/2 cup chopped walnuts
    3 squares unsweetened chocolate, melted
    1 (14-ounce) can sweetened condensed milk
    1/2 teaspoon vanilla extract
       Pinch salt
    18 large marshmallows, halved
    1 package chocolate frosting mix, made according to
       directions

Mix first 6 ingredients together, and spread in greased 8-inch square pan. Bake at 325°F. 25 minutes. Cover with marshmallows; cut sides down, and cool. Drizzle with frosting. When completely cold, cut into 30 small squares with a warm wet knife.

Fruit Squares

    1/2 cup soft butter or margarine
    3 tablespoons brown sugar, firmly packed
    1 cup sifted all-purpose flour
    1/2—3/4 cup raspberry jam
    1/3 cup butter or margarine
    1/2 cup sugar
    1/2 teaspoon salt
    2 eggs
    1 1/2 cups stale white-cake crumbs
    1/2 cup raisins
    1/2 cup chopped mixed candied fruit peel
    1/4 cup milk
    1/2 teaspoon rum extract
    1/4 cup chopped walnuts

Cream first 2 ingredients together, add flour and spread in greased 8-inch square pan. Bake at 350°F. 10—12 minutes. Remove from oven, and spread with jam. Beat next 4 ingredients together until fluffy, and stir in all remaining ingredients except nuts. Spread over jam. Sprinkle with nuts. Bake at 350°F. 40—45 minutes. When thoroughly cool, cut into 24 squares.

Chocolate-Prune Bars

    1 cup pitted cooked prunes
    1/3 cup granulated sugar
    1/4 cup water
    1/4 cup orange juice
    1 cup sifted all-purpose flour
    1 cup brown sugar, firmly packed
    1/2 teaspoon salt
    1/4 teaspoon nutmeg
    1/2 cup soft shortening
    1 1/2 cups uncooked rolled oats
    1 cup (6-ounce package) semisweet chocolate chips
    1 tablespoon grated orange rind
    1/4 cup milk

Combine first 4 ingredients, and cook in saucepan until mixture thickens, about 10 minutes. Cool. Measure flour, sugar, salt and nutmeg into bowl, and cut in shortening until texture is that of coarse meal. Add oats, chocolate chips, rind and milk. Mix lightly. Pack 1/2 the oat mixture into greased 8-inch square pan. Cover with prune mixture, and spread remaining oat mixture over top. Press down well, and bake at 325°F. 50—60 minutes. Cool, and cut in bars. For thinner bars use 8″ x 10″ pan, and bake at 350°F. 35—40 minutes.

Cherry-Nut Treats

    1/2 cup margarine
    1/4 cup granulated sugar
    1 egg, separated
    1 tablespoon lemon juice
    1 teaspoon grated lemon rind
    1 teaspoon grated orange rind
    1/2 teaspoon almond extract
    1 cup sifted cake flour
    3/4 cup chopped walnuts
    6 candied cherries, coarsely chopped

Cream margarine, sugar and egg yolk together until fluffy. Add lemon juice, lemon rind, orange rind and extract. Add flour, and mix well. Wrap in waxed paper, and chill several hours. Roll into small balls. Beat egg white slightly, and dip balls in it, then in chopped nuts. Place on greased cookie sheet. Press small piece of cherry into each. Bake at 350°F. 12—15 minutes. Makes approximately 3 dozen.

Salted Peanut Sticks

        1/2 cup soft butter or margarine
          1 cup brown sugar, firmly packed
          1 egg
          1 teaspoon vinegar
          1 teaspoon grated lemon rind
        1/2 teaspoon allspice
          2 cups sifted all-purpose flour
      1 1/2 cups salted peanuts, chopped

Cream first 4 ingredients together until fluffy. Add lemon rind and allspice. Work in flour and peanuts. Press mixture firmly and evenly into 8-inch square pan lined with waxed paper. Chill in freezer until firm. Remove from pan, and peel off paper. Cut square in half; then slice each rectangle into 1/4-inch slices to make fingers 4 inches long and 1/2 inch wide. Place on oiled cookie sheets, and bake at 325°F. 25—35 minutes or until lightly browned. Makes 5 dozen.

Date Squares

          1 cup butter or margarine
          1 cup brown sugar, firmly packed
      1 3/4 cups sifted all-purpose flour
          1 teaspoon salt
        1/2 teaspoon baking soda
      1 1/2 cups rolled oats
          1 egg, beaten
          1 recipe Date Filling

Cream shortening and sugar well. Sift flour, salt and baking soda together, and stir in. Mix in rolled oats and egg. Place 1/2 mixture in greased 13″ x 9″ cake pan or 2 8-inch square pans, and pat down firmly. Spread with filling. Cover with remaining crumb mixture, and pat lightly. Bake at 350°F. 35 minutes or until lightly browned. Cool, cut in squares and remove from pan. Makes 2 1/2 dozen medium bars or 4 dozen smaller ones.

Date Filling

          3 cups dates, cut up
      1 1/2 cups boiling water
        1/4 cup brown sugar, firmly packed
          1 teaspoon vanilla

Combine all ingredients in saucepan. Cook about 10 minutes until mixture takes on consistency of jam, and cool thoroughly.

Molded Peanut Butter Cookies

          1 cup shortening
          1 cup brown sugar, firmly packed
          1 cup white sugar
          2 eggs
          1 cup peanut butter
          1 teaspoon vanilla extract
      2 1/2 cups unsifted all-purpose flour
          1 teaspoon baking soda
          1 teaspoon baking powder
        1/2 teaspoon salt

Cream shortening; add all sugar, and continue creaming until fluffy. Beat in whole eggs. Stir in peanut butter and vanilla; beat mixture very thoroughly. Sift together flour, baking soda, baking powder and salt. Add dry ingredients, a little at a time, to batter, and mix until well blended. Pinch off pieces of dough, and roll into balls the size of walnuts. Arrange on greased baking sheet, and flatten each ball by pressing with fork; let tines make criss-cross pattern. Bake in 375°F. oven 10—12 minutes. Makes about 6 dozen.

Dream Bars

        1/3 cup shortening
        1/3 cup icing sugar
          1 teaspoon vanilla extract
          1 egg yolk
      1 1/3 cups sifted cake and pastry flour
        1/4 teaspoon salt

Cream shortening and 1/3 cup icing sugar together; stir in 1 teaspoon vanilla and egg yolk. Add flour and salt; mix well. Press dough into 8-inch square pan lined with waxed paper. Bake at 350°F. 12 minutes.

        1/2 cup strawberry jam
          1 egg plus 1 egg white
          1 cup brown sugar, firmly packed
          2 tablespoons flour
        1/2 teaspoon salt
        1/4 teaspoon baking powder
          1 cup chopped nuts
        1/2 cup flaked coconut
          1 teaspoon vanilla extract

Spread jam over baked crust. Beat egg and egg white until light; add brown sugar, and beat until thick. Stir in remaining ingredients. Spread over jam; bake 25—30 minutes at 350°F.

          1 cup icing sugar
          2 tablespoons hot milk
        1/4 teaspoon vanilla extract

Combine 1 cup icing sugar, milk and 1/4 teaspoon vanilla. Frost baked bars in pan while still warm, and cool in pan. Cut into 24 squares or bars.

Cherry Meringue Squares

    1/2 cup butter or margarine
    1/4 cup brown sugar, firmly packed
      1 cup sifted cake and pastry flour
    1/2 teaspoon baking powder
    1/2 teaspoon salt
      1 (6-ounce) jar maraschino cherries, drained and
          quartered
      2 egg whites
    1/4 teaspoon cream of tartar
  1 1/4 cups brown sugar, firmly packed
    1/2 teaspoon vanilla extract

Cream butter or margarine and 1/4 cup brown sugar together. Sift flour, baking powder and salt, and blend thoroughly with sugar mixture. Pat into 8-inch square pan, and bake at 350°F. 15 minutes. Sprinkle with quartered maraschino cherries. Beat egg whites until frothy; add cream of tartar, and beat until soft peaks form. Gradually add 1 1/4 cups brown sugar, and continue beating until stiff. Fold in vanilla. Spread meringue evenly over baked layer, and bake 25 minutes at 350°F. When cool cut into 24 squares.

Dutch Cookies

  2 2/3 cups unsifted cake and pastry flour
      1 teaspoon cinnamon
    1/2 teaspoon baking soda
    1/4 teaspoon salt
      1 cup butter or margarine
      1 cup brown sugar, firmly packed
    1/2 teaspoon almond extract
      1 small egg
      1 teaspoon cold water
    1/2 cup blanched almonds, chopped or slivered
    1/3 cup white sugar

Sift first 4 ingredients together, and knead in butter or margarine and brown sugar. Add almond extract. Divide dough in half, and press out very thinly on 2 ungreased 15″ x 10″ cookie sheets (press out to edges of pans with sides or 1/2 inch from edge on flat sheets). Beat egg, and add water. Brush over dough. Sprinkle with almonds and white sugar. Bake at 350°F. 15—17 minutes. Cool 2 minutes; cut into 4″ x 2″ rectangles. Makes 6—7 dozen.

No-bake Confections

Fruit Balls

  1 1/2 cups mixed dried fruits
    1/2 cup dried figs
    1/2 cup sultana raisins
    1/4 cup walnuts
      2 tablespoons honey
    1/2 teaspoon almond extract
      1 cup toasted coconut

Wash fruits and dry well. Put fruits and walnuts through food grinder. Combine with honey and almond flavoring, mixing well. Shape into balls about the size of walnuts. Roll in toasted coconut. Chill at least 1 hour. Makes 3 dozen balls.

Brandy Balls

      1 cup (6-ounce package) semisweet chocolate chips
    1/2 cup sugar
      3 tablespoons corn syrup
    1/2 cup brandy
  2 1/2 cups (about 5 dozen) finely crushed vanilla wafers
      1 cup finely chopped walnuts
    1/4 cup fine white sugar

Melt chocolate in top of double boiler over hot (not boiling) water. Remove from heat. Stir in 1/2 cup sugar, corn syrup and brandy. Blend in wafer crumbs and nuts. Mix thoroughly. Chill until firm enough to form into balls. Shape into 1-inch balls. Roll in fine sugar. Let ripen in covered container 2—3 days. Makes about 4 1/2 dozen.

TIPS ON FROSTINGS AND FILLINGS

If you use a cooked filling, let it cool a little. Spread it over bottom layer; then let filling set slightly before placing second layer on top. Butter icings are easy to make and use. Be sure to sift icing sugar, so that frosting will be smooth and creamy. Cooked icings will be perfect every time if syrup is cooked to exact temperature specified in recipe. You can test with a candy thermometer.

It is best to ice sides of cake before doing top. Swirl icing lightly upward from bottom edge to top to assure well-shaped finished cake. A tablespoon or spatula is good for swirling. If you like tinted icing, add only a few drops of vegetable coloring.

Cake crumbs won't get mixed in with creamy frosting if you brush them off with a soft pastry brush beforehand.

For smooth icing on which you plan to write "Happy Birthday" or a similar message, make a special effort to hold spatula straight while applying. Use plenty of icing mixture, and scrape it over contours of cake; then dip knife in hot water, and smooth any ridges or dents.

Double-boiler icings sometimes lose their smooth appearance while you are busy with the first spreading. Just beat them up again over hot water, and continue.

Frostings made with butter or shortening will stiffen to good spreading consistency if you place them over a bowl of ice and beat them well.

For really fast finishing touches, decorate iced cake with thin, colored fondant patties cut in half, crushed peppermint candies, crushed and sifted peanut brittle, small marshmallows dipped in delicate food coloring and cut in half or halved thin chocolate wafers stuck into frosting at an angle to make an attractive pattern.

If you have a cookie press, use it for finishing touches. Prepare a thick butter-type frosting of about the same consistency as cookie dough. Put it into press, and produce star, wreath or petal shapes, keeping gadget upright just as you would when pressing out cookies. If basic frosting is sticky, it is best to press shapes out on waxed paper, and let them set a little; then with a knife lift them to positions on the cake. Bits of candied fruit or gumdrops may be dropped onto the various shapes.

For tinted coconut or sugar crystals, half-fill a small jar; then add a few drops of food coloring, cover and shake well.

Dip blanched almonds in vegetable coloring or melted chocolate, and allow to dry. They make attractive touches as edgings around a cake or as petals when arranged in flower formations.

Large curls of Brazil nuts make an impressive garnish on chocolate or mocha frosting. To prepare them, use a sharp vegetable scraper or peeler, and pull it toward you the full length of the nut. Try to have each curl about 1/8 inch thick. For chocolate curls, let 1 square semisweet chocolate soften slightly; then scrape with vegetable peeler in the same way.

For swirls on fluffy frostings, drop a little thick butterscotch or chocolate ice cream sauce here and there on the topping; swirl each blob gently with back of spoon.

For the easiest possible garnish, try fruit-flavored jelly powder straight from the package, sprinkled on a plain whipped-cream topping.

Plain Butter Icing

    1/4 cup butter or margarine
        Dash salt
    2 cups sifted icing sugar
    3 tablespoons cream or milk
    1 teaspoon vanilla extract

Cream butter or margarine until very fluffy. Add salt and, very gradually, about 1/2 cup sugar, continuing to cream. Add remaining sugar alternately with cream, beating after each addition. When mixture is smooth, add vanilla. Spread on 8-inch square cake or over top and sides of 2 8-inch layers.

Rich Butter Icing

    1/4 cup butter or margarine
    2 cups sifted icing sugar
    1 egg yolk
    1 teaspoon vanilla extract
    1 tablespoon cream

Thoroughly cream butter or margarine with 1 cup sugar. Stir in unbeaten egg yolk and vanilla.

Add remaining sugar and cream. Beat to a spready consistency. Spread on top and sides of 9-inch square cake.

VARIATIONS:

* *Chocolate Butter Icing*: Add 1 1/2 squares melted unsweetened chocolate to butter after first 1/4 cup sugar has been added. Beat until well blended before adding remaining sugar.

* *Lemon-Banana Butter Icing*: Substitute 3 tablespoons mashed bananas and 1 tablespoon lemon juice for cream and vanilla.

* *Orange Butter Icing*: Substitute orange juice for cream and 1 teaspoon grated orange rind for vanilla.

* *Mocha Butter Cream Icing*: Sift 3 tablespoons cocoa and about 1/4 teaspoon instant coffee powder with sugar.

Seven-minute Frosting

    1 1/2 cups white sugar
        2 egg whites
    1/3 cup cold water
        2 teaspoons light corn syrup
    1/4 teaspoon cream of tartar
    1/8 teaspoon salt
        1 teaspoon vanilla extract

Place all ingredients except vanilla in top of double boiler. Beat 1 minute with electric mixer or rotary beater. Set over boiling water, and beat constantly with rotary or electric beater until mixture forms peaks, about 7 minutes. Remove from heat, and add vanilla. Beat until mixture is of spreading consistency. This amount will frost top and sides of 2 9-inch layers or 1 10-inch tube cake. For smaller amount, halve all ingredients, and cook about 4 minutes. Frost top of average loaf cake, top and sides of 8-inch tube cake or 8–10 cupcakes.

VARIATIONS:

* *Chocolate Seven-minute Frosting*: Fold 1 (1-ounce) square melted and cooled unsweetened chocolate into finished frosting; do not beat.

* *Ivory Seven-minute Frosting*: Substitute brown sugar for white sugar.

* *Peppermint Seven-minute Frosting*: Add 2 drops of peppermint and 4 drops green vegetable coloring.

* *Pineapple Seven-minute Frosting*: Substitute canned pineapple juice for water. Omit vanilla; add 1 teaspoon grated lemon rind. Tint yellow if desired.

Broiled Frosting

    1/2 cup brown sugar, firmly packed
    1/3 cup soft butter or margarine
      2 tablespoons evaporated milk or cream
    1/2 cup chopped nuts or coconut

Beat first 3 ingredients together. Fold in nuts. Spread on top of warm 9-inch square cake. Place on broiler rack so that top is 4 inches from heat. Broil 3 minutes or until frosting bubbles.

VARIATION:

* *Broiled Peanut Butter Frosting*: Add 1/3 cup peanut butter and extra 1/4 cup chopped peanuts.

Pastel Icing for Petits Fours

      2 tablespoons red currant jelly
        Sifted icing sugar
    1–2 drops red vegetable coloring

Heat jelly in small saucepan until melted. Remove from heat, and stir in enough sugar to make smooth, runny consistency. Add coloring for a pretty shade. Have ready your little petits fours; cut in squares or diamonds about 1-inch thick. Put 1 small cake on fork, and spoon icing over it. Let drip for a moment. If icing runs off completely, letting cake show through, add a little more sugar to the mixture. Keep icing soft over hot water while you frost. If it thickens, add a few drops boiling water. Set each frosted cake, as done, on a rack over waxed paper to catch drips that can be reused. Decorate tops with candied cherries, halved almonds and so forth.

Note: To vary color and flavor, substitute mint, apple, cherry or grape jelly for red currant jelly.

Orange Glaze

    1 cup sifted icing sugar
    2 tablespoons orange juice
    1 teapoon lemon juice
    1 teaspoon grated orange rind
    1 teaspoon grated lemon rind

Mix all ingredients, blending to a smooth, spready consistency. Use on sponge cake, angel cake and tea breads.

Cream Filling

    1/4 cup white sugar
      3 tablespoons flour
    1/4 teaspoon salt
      1 cup milk
      1 egg, slightly beaten
    1/2 teaspoon vanilla extract
      1 tablespoon butter or margarine

Combine sugar, flour and salt. Scald milk, and carefully pour and stir into dry ingredients. Cook in top of double boiler over hot water 15 minutes

or until thick. Add a little hot mixture to egg; then stir back into hot mixture. Continue cooking 3 minutes, and add vanilla and butter. Cool. Makes about 1 cup.

VARIATIONS:

* *Butterscotch Filling*: Use 1/3 cup brown sugar in place of white sugar. Add 2 tablespoons butter or margarine at end of cooking.

* *Chocolate Filling*: Melt 1 square unsweetened chocolate in milk, and increase sugar to 1/2 cup.

* *Pineapple Filling*: Substitute 1/2 teaspoon lemon juice for vanilla. Add 1/3 cup drained crushed pineapple to cooled filling.

Lemon Filling

    3/4 cup white sugar
      2 tablespoons cornstarch
        Few grains salt
      1 egg yolk, slightly beaten
    3/4 cup water
      3 tablespoons lemon juice
      1 tablespoon butter or margarine
      1 teaspoon grated lemon rind

Mix sugar, cornstarch and salt; blend in water and egg yolk. Cook until thick and clear, stirring constantly. Remove from heat, and add lemon juice, butter or margarine and lemon rind. Cool before spreading on cake. Makes about 1 1/2 cups.

Orange Filling

    3/4 cup white sugar
      2 tablespoons cornstarch
        Few grains salt
    3/4 cup orange juice
      1 tablespoon lemon juice
      1 tablespoon grated orange rind
      1 tablespoon butter or margarine
      2 egg yolks, beaten

Combine sugar, cornstarch and salt. Add juices gradually, and blend well. Add orange rind and butter or margarine. Cook over medium heat, stirring constantly, until thick and clear. Add small amount of hot mixture to egg yolks, and stir into hot mixture. Cook over low heat about 3 minutes, stirring constantly. Cool before using. Makes about 1 cup.

Tutti-frutti Filling or Frosting

      1 cup plus 2 tablespoons white sugar
    1/3 cup water
      1 tablespoon corn syrup
      2 egg whites
    1/4 teaspoon salt
    1/3 cup finely chopped candied pineapple
    1/3 cup finely chopped candied cherries
    1/2 teaspoon rum extract

Cook sugar, water and syrup to soft-ball stage (236°F.). Beat egg whites and salt slowly until stiff, and pour sugar syrup over them, beating constantly. Continue beating until mixture is of spreading consistency; then fold in fruits and rum extract. Makes enough to fill and frost a 9-inch layer cake.

Swiss Frosting

> 3 squares unsweetened chocolate
> 1/4 cup white sugar
> 3 tablespoons cornstarch
> 1 teaspoon instant coffee powder
> 1/4 teaspoon salt
> 1 egg
> 3/4 cup water
> 2 cups sifted icing sugar
> 1/2 cup butter or margarine
> 1 teaspoon vanilla extract

Melt chocolate in the top of a double boiler. Pour in a smooth mixture of the next 5 ingredients. Cook and stir until thick and smooth. Stir a little of the hot mixture with the egg, and return to double boiler. Cook and stir 3 minutes. Cool completely. Meanwhile, cream icing

sugar with butter or margarine until light. Add vanilla, and beat in chocolate custard. Refrigerate until completely cold and butter or margarine starts to stiffen. If necessary add additional sifted icing sugar to make a spready consistency. Fill layer cake, and swirl remaining icing over top and sides. Chill cake before serving to firm the icing.

French Mocha Frosting

> 3 squares sweet chocolate, melted
> 2 teaspoons instant coffee powder
> 1 tablespoon hot water
> 3/4 cup icing sugar
> 2 eggs
> 1/2 cup soft butter or margarine

Mix chocolate, coffee and water in small beater bowl. Beat in sugar and eggs; add butter or margarine, 2 tablespoons at a time, and continue beating until mixture is thick. Chill to spready consistency. Fill and frost an 8- or 9-inch layer cake. Chill until icing is set.

Thick Butter Cream

> 1/2 cup soft sweet butter
> 1/3 cup cold *Simple Syrup*
> 1/2 teaspoon vanilla
> Pinch salt

Measure butter into blender, and add syrup, vanilla and salt. Blend until smooth. Stop blender, and scrape sides once or twice. Use as filling and frosting or to decorate icing for cakes that are not rich. Chill after spreading.

Note: Butter cream freezes well.

VARIATION:

* *Chocolate Butter Cream*: Add 2 squares melted semisweet chocolate and 2 egg yolks to blender with syrup. Makes 1 1/3 cups.

Simple Syrup

> 1 1/4 cups white sugar
> 1/3 cup corn syrup
> 2/3 cup water

Put sugar, corn syrup and water into small saucepan. Bring to boil, and cover. Simmer 5 minutes; uncover, and simmer 4 minutes longer. Cool, pour into screw-top jar and refrigerate. Makes about 1 1/4 cups.

Sauces

Baked or steamed puddings often have their own sauces: the fruit or sugar mixture in the bottom of the pan or mold. But often you will wish to serve a separate sauce, one that complements the pudding. A plain pudding can take a rich sauce; a rich pudding needs a simple bland sauce. There are creamy custard sauces, fruit sauces and sugar sauces, and you can experiment with different flavors in all of them. Try adding a few drops of any liqueur to whipped cream: crème de menthe for a cool minty flavor, rum for a rich one.

Fluffy Orange Sauce

    2 eggs, separated
    1/2 cup orange juice
    1 teaspoon lemon juice
    1/2 teaspoon grated lemon rind
    1/2 teaspoon grated orange rind
    1/3 cup sugar
       Pinch salt
    1/2 teaspoon vanilla extract

Beat egg yolks. Combine juices and rinds with sugar and egg yolks, and stir over low heat until slightly thickened. Remove pan from the heat, and cool slightly. Beat egg whites and salt until stiff; add vanilla. Then fold in sauce mixture. May be served hot or cold. Makes about 1 1/2 cups.

Brandy Sauce

    1/4 cup soft butter or margarine
    1 cup fine white sugar
    2 tablespoons brandy
    2 eggs, separated
    1/2 cup light cream

Beat butter, sugar, brandy and egg yolks together until creamy. Then add cream. Scrape into the top of a double boiler. Set mixture over hot (not boiling) water; cook, stirring, until thickened. Beat egg whites until stiff. Pour hot mixture gradually over egg whites. This sauce is best when used warm with hot pudding. Makes about 1 1/4 cups.
Note: Rum may be used in place of brandy.

Brandied Cream Sauce

    1/2 pint light cream
    5 egg yolks, beaten
    1/4 cup white sugar
    1/8 teaspoon salt
    1/4 cup brandy
    1/2 teaspoon vanilla extract
    1/2 pint heavy cream, whipped

Mix first 4 ingredients together in top of double boiler. Cook, stirring over hot (not boiling) water until mixture coats spoon. Remove from heat, and stir in brandy and vanilla. Cover, and chill. Fold in whipped cream just before serving. Makes 3 1/2 cups.

Easy Chocolate Sauce

    1 1/4 cups instant chocolate milk powder
    3/4 cup milk
    1/4 cup granulated sugar

In saucepan combine all ingredients. Bring to boil; lower heat. Cook 3 minutes, stirring constantly. Cool, and pour into a jar and cover. This sauce keeps well in the refrigerator. Use evaporated milk for richer sauce. If sauce is too thick after standing, dilute slightly with fresh milk. Makes about 1 cup syrup.

Sabayon Sauce

    4 egg yolks
    2/3 cup granulated sugar
    1 cup dry white wine
       Pinch salt
    1 tablespoon rum

Beat egg yolks until thick, and add sugar gradually. Continue to beat until fluffy. Add wine and salt. Pour into top of double boiler, and set over hot water; water must not touch bottom of top section. Beat until mixture is light, creamy and thickened. Stir in the rum. Serve over hot puddings and baked fruit dishes. Makes about 1 1/2 cups.

Special Cake Decoration

Dozens of party events during the year are extra special when you present a beautifully decorated cake. For best results in decorating, choose a good quality cake-decorating set, consisting of a cloth or plastic bag and variously shaped metal tips that make rosettes, shells, leaves, flowers, ruchings, swags and so on. Full instructions for use are packed with the bag; follow them closely, and be sure to practice first on an inverted pie plate or cake pan.

A special frosting will be needed, soft enough to press through a pastry bag and assume desired shapes, yet sufficiently stiff to hold form.

Pastry-tube Frosting

    1/4 cup shortening
    2 cups sifted icing sugar
    1/2 teaspoon vanilla extract
    1/4 teaspoon salt
    3 tablespoons water

Cream shortening, and gradually add 1 cup sugar, continuing to cream and beat after each addition. Add vanilla and salt. Add remaining sugar, alternately with just enough water to form a thick smooth mixture suitable to force through a cake-decorating bag. Makes 3/4 cup.

ALL ABOUT PASTRY-MAKING

The "pyes" of Merrie England were, for the most part, filled with meat, "fysche or fowle," until a certain June day in Elizabeth I's reign, when the Queen ordered fresh stewed cherries baked in a pie. The sweet pie was thus launched.

Basically, pastry is a mixture of flour, fat, salt and liquid. Sometimes other ingredients are specified—egg yolks, baking powder and sugar—for particular textures. The character of the finished product and its success will depend upon proportions of various ingredients, methods of mixing and handling, and baking times and temperatures.

There are 3 modern *flours* suitable for pastry-making: cake flour, cake and pastry flour and all-purpose flour. The first 2 will produce a very light tender crust, whereas all-purpose flour tends to give a flakier pastry. Puff pastry, made with a high proportion of shortening, requires the elastic qualities of all-purpose flour for best results.

In substituting all-purpose flour in a recipe designating cake flour, reduce each cup called for to 7/8 cup. Simply measure out sifted all-purpose flour to 1 even cup; then remove 2 level tablespoons flour, and proceed.

Various types of *fat* may be used: shortenings, which may be all-vegetable or combinations of vegetable and animal fat; lard; liquid cooking oils; butter or margarine.

Cold water is the *liquid* required for most pastries, the one exception being *Hot-water Pastry*, which is made with boiling water. Many of today's recipes are deliberately not specific about the amount of liquid to add, simply because the moisture content of the various flours on the market varies considerably, and this factor has an important influence on the liquid used. If your recipe gives a quantity range such as "5–6 tablespoons water," use only *minimum* amount stated, and then judge whether the mixture is moist enough to form into a ball or whether it needs a few drops more.

Utensils

In addition to standard measuring cups, mixing bowls and the like, you will need a board that provides an even surface for rolling pastry. A canvas pastry cloth and a stockinette cover for the rolling pin are also helpful; they will ensure that only a minimum amount of extra flour need be sprinkled on surface to prevent dough from sticking during rolling.

There are other handy small gadgets to speed the job. A pastry wheel is nice to have and easy to use for cutting out rounds for tarts, turnovers, top crusts and lattice-top strips or to make attractive edgings. A pastry brush is helpful for glazing.

The most satisfactory materials for pie plates are oven glass, aluminum and good quality tinware. The most popular sizes are the 8-inch and 9-inch plates—the former dividing into 4–6 portions, the latter 6–8.

Basic Pastry

Plain pastry is the most frequently used for dessert pies, tarts, toppings for savory mixtures, and turnovers. (Puff pastry, sweet pastry and certain others are generally reserved for specific dessert purposes other than the family-size pie.) The standard method can be mastered with practice, and the hot-water method is especially recommended for beginners.

Success requires following directions—adding water sparingly as advised, chilling dough if possible before rolling out and handling lightly during rolling and shaping.

Plain Pastry

USING CAKE AND PASTRY FLOUR:

  2 cups sifted cake and pastry flour
  1 teaspoon salt
  2/3 cup shortening
  4–5 tablespoons cold water

USING ALL-PURPOSE FLOUR:

  2 cups sifted all-purpose flour
  1 teaspoon salt
  3/4 cup shortening
  4–5 tablespoons cold water

Measure and sift flour and salt into bowl. Add shortening. Cut in with pastry blender or 2 knives until mixture resembles oatmeal, with some pieces

slightly larger. Add water, 1 tablespoon at a time. Sprinkle over surface of the flour mixture, and mix lightly after each addition until mixture is then, using lightest possible pressure, roll with the floured pin, rolling away from you. Roll from center to edge each time. Lift pastry occasionally during rolling process to make sure that dough is not sticking. An extra sprinkle of flour may be

dampened. Turn onto piece of waxed paper, and form into a ball, using the paper to press pastry firmly together. Chill 1 hour if time permits, but

let pastry stand at least 5 minutes for ease in rolling.

Lightly and evenly flour pastry cloth and rolling-pin cover. To make 2 single shells or a batch of tart shells, cut chilled ball of dough in half.

needed on pastry cloth or board, but *avoid excessive flouring* as a quantity of extra flour can toughen the dough. When rolled circle is about 1 inch larger than pie plate and about 1/8 inch thick, it is ready for next step.

Fold circle of pastry in half, and transfer quickly to center of pie plate. Or roll circle around pin; place pin over pie plate, and unroll circle of dough. In either case, unfold dough carefully, and ease into plate; then press lightly to exclude any air bubbles.

Do not stretch pastry, either while rolling it or while fitting into plate, especially if making single baked pastry shells. Stretched pastry will shrink during baking and spoil the appearance of your pie.

Waxed-paper Method: Set dough on a large square of lightly floured waxed paper, placed on a dampened table to prevent slipping, and flatten with a rolling pin to about 5 inches diameter. Cover with more waxed paper; then roll dough to required size, starting each rolling movement at the center and continuing to the edges. Peel off top square of paper, invert pan over dough and turn right-side-up. Peel off second square of paper; gently fit dough into pan. (This method requires less flour than rolling on a floured board, so there is less chance that the pastry will become tough.)

For double-crust pie, cut ball into 2 slightly unequal pieces, the larger to be rolled out for the bottom crust. Flatten larger piece into round disc;

Trim pastry in pie plate flush with edge, using knife. Roll out second ball of dough to size about 1 inch more than width of pie plate, rim to rim. Cut out with knife or pastry wheel; fold over, and make decorative slits at center to allow steam to escape during baking.

Fill pastry-lined plate with fruit filling or other desired mixture. Moisten edge of bottom crust. Place folded pastry circle over filling; or roll it around pin, and set in position. Unfold, and fit cover evenly over filling. Trim off any ragged edges neatly, and fold overhang *under* edge of bottom crust. Seal by pressing 2 crusts together against edge of pie plate, using tines of fork or crimping between finger and thumb. Bake according to the directions in your recipe.

Note: 1 recipe for plain pastry makes 2 9-inch shells, double-crust 9-inch pie, 12—14 medium shells or 20—24 small tart shells.

VARIATIONS:

* *Single Unbaked Pie Shell*: Line pie plate with pastry, leaving an overhang of 1/2 inch. Fold pastry overhang back and under, making it stand upright. Flute edge with fingers. *Do not prick*. Pour in filling. (An unbaked shell is usually used for pumkin, custard, pecan or any kind of pie in which filling and pastry should be baked together.) To avoid spills between work surface and oven, fill shell 3/4 full, and pour in remainder when pie plate is on oven rack. Bake as directed in recipe.

* *Single Baked Pie Shell*: Line pie plate with pastry. Prick with fork at 1-inch intervals. Bake at 450°F. 10—12 minutes. If, after 5 minutes' baking, pastry puffs up, prick it again. Another way to avoid shrinkage is to set empty pie plate the same size in pastry shell before baking. Bake as usual, but remove empty pie plate 3—4 minutes before end of baking time to allow inside of shell to brown lightly. Cool shell. Fill as directed in recipes.

* *Flaky Pastry*: To make rich pastry with flaky texture, use additional fat. Roll out entire pastry 1/4 inch thick, making shape as square as possible. Cut 2 tablespoons well-chilled fat into small pieces. Dot these pieces over 1/2 the square of pastry, keeping fat 1/2 inch away from edges. Fold other 1/2 of pastry over to cover fat. Dot on 2 more tablespoons of fat, and fold in half once more. Then roll pastry into square, 1/4 inch thick. Fold in half and then in half again, to make quarters. Chill well before using. Divide pastry into parts, roll out 1/2 for bottom crust and other 1/2 for top; bake as 2 pie shells, or use for tart shells.

* *Flavored Pastry*: To measured flour (before cutting in fat) add 3 tablespoons finely ground nuts for pumpkin or squash fillings, 2 tablespoons finely grated mild cheese for apple pie; 1/2 teaspoon finely chopped mint for chicken pie. Or add with cold water 1/4 teaspoon almond extract for cherry pie; 4 tablespoons orange juice and 1/2 teaspoon grated orange rind for custard pies.

* *Packaged Pie-crust Mix*: Add only water before rolling out; for single-shell pie, use 1/2 the amount in package plus 1/2 the suggested proportion of water.

Hot-water Pastry

USING CAKE AND PASTRY FLOUR:

2 1/4 cups sifted cake and pastry flour
1 teaspoon salt
1/2 teaspoon baking powder
2/3 cup shortening
1/3 cup boiling water

USING ALL PURPOSE FLOUR:

2 cups unsifted all-purpose flour
1 teaspoon salt
1/2 teaspoon baking powder
3/4 cup shortening
1/3 cup boiling water

Sift flour, salt and baking powder together. Melt shortening in boiling water over very low heat. Cool, and beat in sifted dry ingredients. Turn dough onto waxed paper, and form into ball. Chill. Roll out as directed for *Plain Pastry*. Use in any recipe requiring plain pastry.

Easy Pastry Shell

1 cup sifted all-purpose flour
1/2 teaspoon salt
1/3 cup cooking oil
4 1/2 teaspoons cold milk

Sift flour and salt into pie pan. Mix oil and milk, stir and pour into flour all at once. Stir with fork until all ingredients are blended; shape crust by patting and tamping dough with your fingers so that it comes up around sides of pan. Bake at 425°F. 12—15 minutes, and cool before filling. The texture will be crumbly rather than flaky.

Butter-Crumb Crust

1 1/4 cups sifted cake and pastry flour
1/4 cup brown sugar, firmly packed
1/4 cup chopped walnuts
1/3 cup melted butter or margarine

Mix flour, brown sugar and nuts together. Stir in the melted butter or margarine with a fork, then with fingertips, to form a crumbly mixture.

Press into bottom and sides of a deep 9-inch pie plate, and prick here and there. Bake at 300° F. 30–35 minutes. Cool, and fill with your favorite cooked or chill-type filling.

Double-crust Pies

These pies usually have fillings of fruits (fresh, canned or dried) by themselves or combined. They may be stored, covered, at room temperature. If desired, give them a fresh-baked texture by reheating in slow oven about 15 minutes before serving.

Spicy Apple Pie

> 4–5 medium-size tart apples (approximately 5 cups peeled apple sections)
> 4 teaspoons lemon juice
> 1 1/2 teaspoons flour
> 1/3 cup white sugar
> 1/3 cup brown sugar, firmly packed
> 1/2 teaspoon cinnamon
> 1/4 teaspoon nutmeg or mace (optional)
> 3–4 teaspoons butter or margarine
> Pastry for double-crust pie

Sprinkle apples with lemon juice; roll out 2/3 of the pastry between sheets of floured waxed paper. Peel off top paper, and invert over a deep 9-inch juice-saver pie plate. Trim the edge. Sprinkle bottom with about 1 1/2 teaspoons flour; then add half the apples. Mix sugars and spices together, and sprinkle half over the apple layer. Pile remaining apples on top, and cover with remaining sugar mixture. Dot with butter; then dampen edges. Cover with rolled-out top crust. Press edges together. Prick, and bake at 450°F. 20 minutes; then lower heat, and bake 25 minutes or until apples are tender.

Note: If apples are tart, increase sugar to 1 cup. If they are juicy, add 1 extra tablespoon flour to sugar. If fruit is quite dry, as with some winter-stored apples, sprinkle with 1–2 tablespoons water; a dash of lemon juice will help sharpen the flavor.

Berry Pie

> Pastry for double-crust pie
> 1/4 cup flour or 2 tablespoons quick-cooking tapioca or cornstarch
> 3/4 cup sugar
> 1/8 teaspoon salt
> 4 cups fresh strawberries, raspberries, blackberries or loganberries, washed and hulled
> 1 tablespoon butter or margarine

Prepare pastry, and line a 9-inch pie plate. Combine flour, tapioca or cornstarch with sugar and salt. Sprinkle mixture over berries, and toss lightly with a fork. Scrape into prepared pie shell. Dot with butter. Dampen edges, and cover with rolled-out top crust. Press edges together. Prick, and bake at 450°F. 20 minutes. Reduce heat to 350°F., and continue baking 20–25 minutes.

VARIATIONS:

* *Blueberry Pie*: Add 2 teaspoons lemon juice and 1/2 teaspoon lemon rind to sugar mixture.

* *Cherry Pie*: Stem and pit cherries; increase sugar to 1 1/3 cups or more, depending on tartness of fruit.

Old-fashioned Mincemeat

> 1/2 pound ground beef
> 1 cup water
> 3 cups cider
> 3 pounds brown sugar, firmly packed
> 1 1/2 teaspoons cinnamon
> 1 teaspoon mace
> 1 tablespoon salt
> 1 pint molasses
> 1 (6-quart) basket tart apples
> 1 1/2 pounds seeded lexia or muscat raisins
> 3 pounds currants
> 1 pound sultana raisins
> 3/4 pound chopped mixed peel
> 1/4–1/2 pound blanched almonds, cut fine
> Juice and grated rind of 3 lemons
> Juice and grated rind of 3 oranges
> 1/2 pound ground suet

Combine meat and water in a saucepan. Bring to a boil; then cover, and simmer 10 minutes. Drain meat, and reserve juice. Refrigerate meat. Combine meat juice, cider, 2 pounds of the sugar and the next 4 ingredients. Bring to a boil, and simmer for 15 minutes. Remove from heat. Peel and dice the apples into a large kettle. Add the meat, remaining sugar and other ingredients. Add molasses-syrup mixture, and stir well. Cook for 20 minutes. Ladle into sterilized sealers, and process in a boiling-water bath for 30 minutes.

Rhubarb Pie

        Pastry for double-crust pie
    4 tablespoons flour
    3/4 cup sugar
    1/2 teaspoon grated orange rind
3 1/2–4 cups pink rhubarb cut in 1/2-inch pieces (about
            1 pound)
    1 tablespoon frozen undiluted orange juice
    1–2 tablespoons butter
        Sugar

Roll out 2/3 of the pastry, and fit into a deep 9-inch pie plate. Trim the edge. Combine flour thoroughly with the sugar and orange rind. Pour over the rhubarb, and toss with a fork. Scrape into the prepared pie plate. Spread evenly, sprinkle with orange juice and dot with butter. Dampen pastry edge. Roll out remaining pastry into a 10-inch circle, and with a 1/2- to 3/4-inch cutter cut out evenly spaced fancy openings. Save the cutouts. Fold pastry in half, and lift to the center top of the pie. Flip folded part over remaining exposed fruit, and press edges together. Fold edge under bottom crust. Lift up the pressed edges, and fold the overhanging 1/2 inch of pastry under. Flatten the edge slightly, and flute or crimp. Brush the top with ice water, and set a few of the reserved cutouts on solid sections of the top. Sprinkle with sugar. Bake at 425°–450° F. 25 minutes; then reduce heat to 350°F., and bake 20–30 minutes longer or until rhubarb is tender. Cool slightly before cutting.

Note: For a clear thickened juice, use 2 tablespoons cornstarch in place of flour.

Sherried Raisin Pie

    1 1/4 cups water
    2/3 cup sherry or apple juice
    2 1/4 cups sultana raisins
    1/2 cup brown sugar, firmly packed
    5 teaspoons cornstarch
    1/4 cup cold water
1/4–1/2 teaspoon cinnamon
    1 teaspoon vanilla
    2 tablespoons butter

Pour 1 1/4 cups water and sherry over the raisins. Bring to a boil; then cover, and simmer for 5–6 minutes. Stir in the brown sugar and the cornstarch mixed smoothly with 1/4 cup cold water. Stir, and cook until thickened and clear. Add cinnamon, vanilla and butter. Taste, and if sweet, add 1 or 2 teaspoons of vinegar or lemon juice. If not sweet enough, stir in 1 or 2 tablespoons brown sugar. Cool, and scrape into a 9-inch unbaked pie shell. Cover with pastry top, and bake at 425°F. 35–40 minutes or until pastry is golden.

Mince Pie

    3 cups mincemeat
    1 cup drained crushed pineapple
        Pastry for double-crust pie

Combine mincemeat and pineapple. Line 9-inch pie plate with pastry; fill; adjust top pastry cover, and seal edges. Bake in 425°F. oven about 30–35 minutes or until pastry is golden brown.

Note: To reheat, place in 300°F. oven about 20 minutes.

Frosted Cherry Pie

    1 (20-ounce) can pitted sweetened cherries
    4 teaspoons cornstarch
    2 tablespoons sugar
    2 tablespoons maraschino cherry juice or 2–3 drops
        almond flavoring and 2 tablespoons hot water
    1–2 teaspoons lemon juice
        Few drops red food coloring
        Pastry for double-crust pie
    1/2 cup sifted icing sugar
        Orange juice
    1/4 cup slivered toasted almonds

Drain the cherries. Mix the juice smoothly with the cornstarch and sugar, and cook and stir until clear. Add maraschino juice, lemon juice, a few drops food coloring and the cherries. Taste, and add a little more sugar if you wish. Cool. Spread in prepared bottom pie shell after sprinkling it lightly with flour. Cover with top pastry, and bake at 425°F. 35–40 minutes or until golden. Cool to warm. Mix icing sugar with a very little orange juice to form a thin glaze-type icing, and spread over the top. Sprinkle with slivered almonds; then cool completely before serving.

Fresh Cherry Pie

    4 cups pitted sour cherries
2 1/2 tablespoons cornstarch
1 1/4 cups white sugar
        Pastry for double-crust pie
    2 drops almond extract
    2 tablespoons butter
        Cold milk
        Sugar

Sprinkle cherries with a mixture of cornstarch and sugar. Stir lightly. Spread in unbaked pie shell. Sprinkle with almond extract, and dot with butter. Cover with top crust. Trim and crimp edges. Gash top, and brush with cold milk. Sprinkle with sugar. Bake at 450°F. 20 minutes; then reduce heat to 350°F., and bake 20 minutes or until juice thickens clearly.

Single-crust Pies

There are several kinds of single-crust pies. With pumpkin, custard and certain fruit fillings, shell and contents are baked together. Other types, notably lemon pie, require a pre-baked and cooled shell. A deep-dish fruit pie uses a top cover only, which, of course, is baked along with the filling.

Deep-dish Fruit Pie

1–1 1/2 cups sugar
    2 tablespoons quick-cooking tapioca or 3 table-
      spoons flour
1 1/2 teaspoons grated lemon or orange rind
   1/4 teaspoon salt
    6 cups prepared fruit (apples, peaches, berries or
      plums)
    1 tablespoon butter or margarine
  1/2 recipe *Plain Pastry* or *Flaky Pastry*

Combine sugar, tapioca, grated rind and salt. Grease baking dish or casserole 7 inches in diameter. Turn in prepared fruit, and stir in sugar mixture until well distributed. Add water or lemon juice if necessary. Dot with butter or margarine. Roll out pastry to 1/4-inch thickness and about 8-inch diameter. Prick dough. Place over filling, folding edge under and fluting with thumb and forefinger. Bake in 450°F. oven 10 minutes; reduce oven setting to 350°F., and continue baking 35–40 minutes.

Note: Peel and slice apples or peaches; wash and hull berries; or halve and stone plums. The amount of sugar will depend on tartness of fruit being used; if using blueberries or winter-stored apples, include 1 tablespoon lemon juice in filling for better flavor; if fruit is dry, sprinkle with 2 tablespoons water. For such juicy fruit as fresh berries, prevent boiling over by inserting small foil funnel or cone at center. Remove before serving pie.

Apple-crumble Pie

      Pastry for single-crust pie
    4 cups peeled sliced apples
    2 teaspoons lemon juice
  1/2 cup brown sugar, firmly packed
  1/3 cup sifted all-purpose flour
  1/4 cup butter or margarine
  1/4 teaspoon mixed nutmeg and cinnamon

Line 9-inch pie plate. Arrange apples in pastry, and sprinkle with lemon juice. Make crumble topping by blending sugar, flour, butter or margarine and spices together until fat is well distributed. Sprinkle over apples. Bake at 425°F. 20 minutes. Reduce heat to 350°F., and bake until apples are tender, about 20 minutes.

VARIATIONS:

* *Mincemeat–Apple-crumble Pie*: Combine 2 cups canned or homemade mincemeat with 2 cups sliced apples.

* *Peach-crumble Pie*: Sprinkle 1 tablespoon quick-cooking tapicoa over pastry-lined pie plate. Use 4–5 cups peeled sliced peaches.

Custard Pie

    3 eggs
  1/3 cup sugar
  1/4 teaspoon salt
    2 cups milk, scalded
      Pastry for single-crust pie
    1 teaspoon vanilla extract
      Freshly grated nutmeg

Beat eggs just enough to mix. Add sugar and salt, and slowly stir in milk. Strain mixture, and allow to cool while preparing pastry and lining 9-inch pie plate. When milk mixture is completely cool, add vanilla, and pour into pastry shell. Sprinkle top with freshly grated nutmeg. Place pie in oven preheated to 450°F.; after 10 minutes reduce heat setting to 325°F. Bake 35 minutes. Test filling with silver knife; if it comes out without custard adhering, pie is done. If not, leave another 5–10 minutes to complete baking.

Note: With this method, pastry will start to cook immediately at high heat, thus preventing soggy crust; liquid mixture, slower to heat up, will bake at reduced temperature and form smooth firm custard.

Apple-Butter Single-crust Pie

    3 tart juicy apples, peeled and cut in twelfths
  1/4 cup raisins
    3 tablespoons water or apple juice
      Pastry for single-crust pie (unpricked)
    2 tablespoons flour
  1/4 teaspoon nutmeg
  1/4 cup soft butter
  1/4 cup corn syrup
    1 egg, beaten
    1 teaspoon vanilla

Place apples, raisins and water in a saucepan, and cover. Steam-cook until apples are just tender, 3–5 minutes depending on variety. Scrape into unbaked pie shell, and spread evenly. Combine remaining ingredients, and pour over the apples. Bake at 450°F. 20 minutes; then reduce heat to 350°F., and bake 25–30 minutes longer or until butter filling is set. Cool before serving, just as you would for butter tarts, and serve with ice cream or whipped cream.

Pumpkin Pie

    2 eggs
  1/2 cup milk
1 1/2 cups mashed cooked or canned pumpkin
  2/3 cup evaporated milk or light cream
  2/3 cup brown sugar, lightly packed
  3/4 teaspoon cinnamon
  1/2 teaspoon ground ginger
  1/2 teaspoon salt
  1/4 teaspoon nutmeg
      Pastry for single-crust pie

Beat eggs well, and stir in milk. Combine all remaining ingredients, except pastry, and stir in milk mixture. Line 9-inch pie plate with pastry, and pour in filling. Place in 450°F. oven; after 10 minutes reduce temperature setting to 350°F. Bake 40—50 minutes or until silver knife inserted in center comes out clean.

Lemon Meringue Pie

1 1/4 cups sugar
3 tablespoons cornstarch
1/4 cup flour
1/8 teaspoon salt
1/3 cup cold water
3 egg yolks
2 cups boiling water
1/2 cup lemon juice
Grated rind of 1 lemon
2 tablespoons butter or margarine
1 baked 9-inch pie shell, cooled
3 egg whites
Pinch salt
6 tablespoons sugar

Sift the first 4 ingredients together; then stir lightly. Beat cold water and egg yolks together in the top of a double boiler, and add dry ingredients. Stir until smooth. Add the boiling water, and set pan over boiling water. Cook and stir until thick and smooth, about 15 minutes or until no raw starch flavor is present. Whisk in lemon juice, rind and butter. Remove from heat, and cool to room temperature, stirring occasionally. Spread in a baked pie shell. Beat 3 egg whites with a pinch of salt until fluffy moist peaks form. Beat in 6 tablespoons sugar, a little at a time, and beat until stiff. Cover filling with meringue. Swirl with the back of a spoon. Sprinkle with sugar to make cutting easier. Bake at 375°F. 10 minutes or until lightly browned. Cool completely.

Lemon Chiffon Pie

1 envelope plain gelatine
1/4 cup cold water
3/4 cup sugar
2 teaspoons grated lemon rind
1/2 teaspoon salt
2/3 cup boiling water
3 egg yolks, beaten
1/2 cup lemon juice
3 egg whites
1 baked 9-inch pie shell, cooled

Soften gelatine in cold water. In top of double boiler combine 1/2 cup sugar, lemon rind and salt; stir in boiling water, then softened gelatine, stirring to dissolve. Add a little of this mixture to beaten egg yolks; then return to double boiler, and cook over simmering water, stirring constantly until mixture coats spoon. Remove from heat, and stir in lemon juice. Pour into bowl, and place in refrigerator or in pan of ice water; let stand, stirring occasionally, until thickened. Beat egg whites to glossy peaks, and gradually add remaining sugar. Fold meringue into gelatine mixture. Pile into pastry shell, and chill in refrigerator for several hours until firm.

Strawberry Chiffon Pie

1 envelope plain gelatine
1/4 cup cold water
2 cups strawberries, washed and hulled
2/3 cup fine white sugar
2 teaspoons lemon juice
1/2 teaspoon salt
2 egg whites
1/2 cup heavy cream
1 baked 9-inch pie shell, cooled

Soften gelatine in cold water. Reserve about 1/2 cup of choicest strawberries for garnish. Mash remainder, adding sugar, and let stand until sugar melts. Dissolve gelatine over boiling water; add lemon juice, salt and mashed berries. Place mixture in refrigerator or pan of ice water until thickened, stirring occasionally. Beat egg whites to glossy peaks; then beat into mixture. Whip cream, and fold in. Pile into pastry shell, and chill in refrigerator until filling is firm. Garnish with whole berries before serving.

Cream Pie

2 cups milk
1/2 cup sugar
2 tablespoons flour
2 tablespoons cornstarch
1/2 teaspoon salt
3 egg yolks, beaten
2 tablespoons butter or margarine
1 teaspoon vanilla extract
1 baked 9-inch pie shell, cooled

Scald 1 1/2 cups milk. Combine dry ingredients in top of double boiler, and gradually add 1/2 cup cold milk, blending until smooth. Stir in scalded milk. Set directly over moderate heat, and let come to boil, stirring constantly. Remove from heat. Stir thick sauce very gradually into beaten egg yolks; then return all to double boiler, and cook over hot water about 2 minutes, stirring constantly. Remove from heat, and add butter or margarine and vanilla. Cool almost completely before pouring into pastry shell. Top with meringue, whipped cream, toasted shredded coconut or whole strawberries.

VARIATIONS:

* *Butterscotch Cream Pie*: Replace sugar with 2/3 cup dark brown sugar, and add 1 extra tablespoon butter or margarine.

* *Chocolate Cream Pie*: Melt 2 (1-ounce) squares unsweetened chocolate in scalded milk; increase sugar to 2/3 cup.

Pecan-Syrup Pie

```
1/2 cup butter or margarine
1/3 cup sugar
3/4 cup corn syrup
1/4 cup maple syrup
  3 eggs
  2 cups pecan halves
  1 teaspoon vanilla extract
  1 unbaked 9-inch pie shell
    Whipped cream
```

Cream butter or margarine thoroughly; add sugar gradually, continuing to cream. Stir in syrups, a little at a time. Beat eggs slightly, and add to mixture. Stir in nuts and vanilla. Combine well. Turn into pastry shell. Bake at 450°F. for 10 minutes. Reduce heat to 350°F., and bake 20 minutes or until almost set. Cool. Before serving swirl whipped cream on top.

Meringue for Pies

FOR 8-INCH PIE:

```
    Few grains salt
  2 egg whites
  4 tablespoons sugar
1/4 teaspoon vanilla
```

FOR 9-INCH PIE:

```
1/4 teaspoon salt
  3 egg whites
  6 tablespoons sugar
1/2 teaspoon vanilla
```

Add salt to egg whites, and beat until rounded peaks are formed. Add sugar very gradually, about 1 tablespoon at a time, continuing to beat after each addition. After all sugar has been beaten in, continue beating until mixture is stiff but still glossy. Beat in vanilla. Pile meringue on top of pie filling that has been allowed to cool completely. Spread meringue right to the pastry edge. Do not leave any space between meringue and rim; otherwise topping may shrink or "weep." Swirl into crests or peaks for attractive effect. Put pie into preheated 375°F. oven, and bake for 10–12 minutes until meringue is delicately browned. Let pie cool at room temperature away from drafts. To cut meringue topping easily, dip sharp thin knife in water or butter before inserting. Or sprinkle raw meringue lightly with sugar before baking.

Note: Do not bake meringue on instant pudding- or pie-mix fillings. Vary your meringue flavoring according to filling being used; for lemon pie substitute lemon juice for vanilla.

Maple Cream Pie

```
  2 tablespoons soft butter or margarine
  2 egg yolks
  1 cup maple syrup
1/2 cup commercial sour cream
1/4 cup flour
  1 teaspoon vinegar
  1 teaspoon vanilla
  1 unbaked 8-inch pie shell
  2 egg whites
1/4 teaspoon salt
  4 tablespoons sugar
```

Beat the first 7 ingredients together. Pour into pie shell, and bake at 425°F. 20 minutes. Lower heat to 325°F., and cook 30 minutes more or until set (metal skewer should come out clean). Beat egg whites, salt and sugar until very stiff, and swirl over pie. Bake at 350°F. 15 minutes or until lightly browned. Serve at room temperature.

Eggnog Pie

```
  1 envelope plain gelatine
1/2 cup milk
1 1/2 cups commercial eggnog
    Vanilla, brandy or rum extract to taste
  1 cup heavy cream, stiffly beaten
  1 9-inch Simple Crumb Crust or baked pastry shell
1/2 cup chopped nuts
  2 tablespoons chopped candied pineapple
```

Soften gelatine in milk, and heat over hot water until melted. Remove from heat; don't worry if it curdles. Whisk in eggnog and vanilla slowly. Chill until mixture thickens. Fold in 3/4 cup whipped cream. Pour into pie shell, and chill until set. Sprinkle center with nuts, and garnish edge with remaining whipped cream and bits of pineapple.

Sherry Chiffon Pie

```
    Dash salt
  3 eggs, separated
2/3 cup sherry
1/3 cup sugar
  2 teaspoons plain gelatine
1/4 cup cold milk
1/4 cup sugar
1/2 teaspoon vanilla
  1 9-inch Simple Crumb Crust or baked pastry shell
3/4 cup whipped cream
```

Add salt to egg yolks, and beat until thick. Add sherry and 1/3 cup sugar, and beat well. Cook in double boiler until mixture coats spoon; remove from heat. Soften gelatine in cold milk; add to hot mixture. Stir until gelatine dissolves. Chill until partially set. Stiffly beat egg whites, and slowly beat in 1/4 cup sugar and vanilla. Fold into custard, and pour into crust. Chill until set. Spread with whipped cream.

FANCY PASTRIES

Fancy pastries range from choux and sweet pastry to crumb and nut crusts.

Crumb and Nut Crusts

These pie shells are quickly made and often require only a quick chilling, rather than baking. Fill with cooked and cooled cream fillings, instant pudding and pie mixtures and whipped cream and gelatine combinations. Crush crumb ingredients such as wafers and cereal flakes in a blender, or drop into a plastic or paper bag and roll with a rolling pin. For finely pulverized nuts, use a blender or fine blade of a mincer, or crush in a plastic bag with a rolling pin.

Simple Crumb Crust

    1 1/2 cups crumbs (1 cup graham cracker crumbs,
            1/2 cup crushed cornflakes)
      1/3 cup sugar
      1/2 cup butter or margarine, melted

Mix crumbs, sugar and butter or margarine together. Press firmly into 9-inch pie plate. Chill about 1 hour before filling.

Graham Cracker Crust (Baked)

    1 1/3 cups graham cracker crumbs
      1/4 cup sugar
        1 teaspoon cinnamon
      1/3 cup butter or margarine, melted

Combine fine crumbs, sugar and cinnamon, and stir in butter or margarine. Reserve 3 tablespoons mixture for topping. Press crumbs into 9-inch pie pan, covering bottom and sides evenly and building up the edge slightly. Bake in 350°F. oven 5–10 minutes. Cool completely. Fill with cream or chiffon filling, and sprinkle with reserved crumbs. Chill in refrigerator several hours before serving.

VARIATIONS:

* Use gingersnaps or chocolate or vanilla wafers in place of graham crackers, and reduce sugar to 2 tablespoons or less. A tangy lemon filling is particularly good in gingersnap-crumb crust.

Cereal Crumb Crust

    4 cups cornflakes
    1/4 cup sugar
      1 tablespoon all-purpose flour
    1/4 cup butter or margarine, melted

Crush cornflakes very fine; then measure 1 cup. Combine with sugar and flour, and blend in melted butter or margarine. Spread over 9-inch pie pan, allowing greater thickness over bottom than against sides. Bake in 350°F. oven 8–10 minutes. Cool completely before filling; keep chilled until serving.

Crisp Coconut Crust

    2 tablespoons soft (not melted) butter or margarine
    1 1/2 cups flaked or shredded coconut

Spread or brush butter evenly over bottom and sides of 9-inch pie plate. Pat coconut into butter or margarine. Bake in 350°F. oven 8–10 minutes or until shell is crisp brown. After filling with cream or chiffon mixture, refrigerate several hours before serving. Or fill with vanilla ice cream just at serving time; drizzle butterscotch sauce on top, and sprinkle with toasted coconut.

Brazil Nut Crust

    1 1/2 cups (about 3/4 pound) finely ground Brazil nuts
        3 tablespoons sugar

Combine nuts and sugar in 9-inch pie pan. Press mixture with back of spoon over bottom and sides to cover evenly. Bake in 400°F. oven 6–7 minutes or until lightly browned. Cool completely before filling; keep chilled until serving.

Meringue Pie Shell

    1/2 cup (about 4) egg whites
      1 cup fine white sugar
    1/4 teaspoon cream of tartar
        Pinch salt

Beat egg whites until stiff but not dry. Combine sugar, cream of tartar and salt. Add mixture 1 tablespoon at a time to egg whites, beating after each addition. After all mixture has been added, continue beating until very stiff but still glossy. Grease 9-inch pie plate, and sprinkle lightly with flour, shaking off excess. Turn in meringue, and spread just to rim. Mound meringue slightly at center. Bake in 275°F. oven for 1 hour or until delicately browned and crisp to the touch. Set pie plate on cooking rack in place away from drafts but at room temperature. Meringue will crack and fall in center, but that is the way it should be, in order to make shell suitable for filling. If cooled pie is not to be used immediately, store in covered container in cool, dry place. If shell becomes sticky from moisture, reheat in 250°F. oven 15 minutes. Cool before filling, and fill just before serving.

Note: Fill with drained, diced fruits, fresh or canned, with whipped-cream topping, or with well-thickened, cooled filling for *Lemon Chiffon Pie*, to which 1 cup whipped cream has been added, or with sliced fresh strawberries lightly folded into sweetened whipped cream.

To Make Puff Paste

Puff paste consists of hundreds of layers of paper-thin dough, which remain separate because of the many thin layers of fat interspersed. During baking, moisture trapped in the layers becomes steam, forcing dough to rise. After baking, steam evaporates, leaving pastry high, crisp and flaky.

Older recipes for puff pastry involve washing butter to remove salt and to obtain plastic, waxy consistency. With unsalted (sweet) butter, however, washing is not necessary. But the consistency of the butter is extremely important; if too cold and hard, it will break up dough when rolled; if too soft, it will ooze out. Butter should be of about the same consistency as the dough.

Do not try to make puff paste during hot weather unless your kitchen is air-conditioned.

Puff Paste

    3 cups unsifted all-purpose flour
1 1/2 teaspoons salt
    1 pound unsalted (sweet) butter
1 1/4–1 1/3 cups ice water

Sift together flour and salt. Cut in 2 tablespoons butter with pastry blender. Sprinkle with a little ice water, adding it gradually and mixing in lightly with fork. Continue sprinkling and mixing in ice water until 1 1/4 cups have been added. If dough is firm and slightly sticky, as it should be, don't add any more water. Turn dough onto lightly floured board, and knead 5–8 minutes or until very elastic and smooth. Cover with cloth; invert large bowl over it, and let stand 10 minutes. While dough is resting, flatten block of butter into oblong about 3″ x 6″ x 1 1/2″.

Roll dough to 1/8-inch thickness, into an oblong about 3 times as long as wide. Place flattened butter at center of 1/2 dough. Fold other 1/2 over butter. Seal edges of dough to enclose as much air as possible. Pat down until enclosed butter spreads to within 1/2 inch of all edges. Fold one end under and other end over, to form 3 layers of pastry. Wrap, and chill about 20 minutes.

Now roll out pastry evenly to 1/8-inch thickness, keeping it longer than it is wide. Lift pastry from board frequently to prevent sticking; dredge board with flour if necessary. Fold each end of dough rectangle to meet in center. Give dough 1/4 turn, and repeat rolling and folding in thirds as before. Chill. Repeat rolling, folding and chilling 3 more times. Then roll and fold ends to center, and double parcel again, making 4 layers. Chill until dough is stiff before using.

Note: For fast chilling, place dough in freezer after each rolling, chilling only until firm.

Patty Shells

    1 recipe *Puff Paste*

Roll well-chilled dough to 1/4-inch thickness. Cut 3-inch rounds with cookie cutter. Remove 2-inch centers from 1/2 the rounds. Moisten edges of full rounds, and lightly press 1 ring shape on top of each. Place well apart on ungreased cookie

sheet. Bake in 500°F. oven 5 minutes; then lower heat by 50°F. at 5-minute intervals until temperature is down to 350°F. Bake about 10 minutes at 350°F. Makes 12–16 large patty shells or 24–30 small shells.

Note: The cut-out centers from the rings may be baked and used as lids for filled patty shells.

Napoleons or Cream Slices

> 1 recipe *Puff Paste*
> 2 cups whipped cream, sweetened and flavored, or 1
> recipe *French Cream Filling*
> 1/2 cup icing sugar or confectioners' icing
> 1/2 cup chopped nuts

Roll out puff paste to 1/8-inch thickness to fit a 10 1/2″ x 5″ ungreased cookie pan with an edge, or a shallow jelly roll pan. Let stand on sheet in refrigerator 15 minutes. Prick paste all over with fork. Bake in 400°F. oven about 15 minutes; lower heat to 300°F., and continue baking 40 minutes. Pastry should be well puffed and light brown. Allow it to cool thoroughly. Trim off all edges with serrated knife, and split pastry horizontally, making 2 layers. Lay bottom 1/2 on flat surface, spread with stiffly beaten cream (or filling); cover with remaining 1/2. Sprinkle with icing sugar or spread with icing and chopped nuts. Chill 1 hour before cutting into strips 3 inches wide and then into 1 1/2-inch slices. Makes 18–24 Napoleons.

French Cream Filling

> 1 cup milk
> 1/3 cup sugar
> 2 tablespoons flour
> Pinch salt
> 3 egg yolks, beaten
> 1 teaspoon vanilla extract

Heat 3/4 cup milk in saucepan over medium heat. Combine sugar, flour and salt; add remaining 1/4 cup milk, and blend to a smooth paste. Stir paste into hot milk, and cook, stirring constantly, until mixture thickens. Remove from heat. Add hot mixture, a little at a time, to egg yolks; then return to saucepan. Place over low heat. Cook a few minutes longer, stirring well, but do not boil. Add vanilla, and cool as quickly as possible. Refrigerate. Stir well before using. Mixture may be thinned if desired by beating in a few spoonfuls of rich milk.

VARIATIONS:

* *Chocolate Cream Filling*: Melt 1 1/2 squares unsweetened chocolate, and beat thoroughly into mixture after removing from stove.

* *Deluxe Cream Filling*: Soften 1 envelope plain gelatine in 1/4 cup cold water; set container in hot water to dissolve; stir into cooled filling, and fold in 1 cup heavy cream, stiffly beaten; flavor as desired. Chill before using.

Cream Puffs, Eclairs, Bouchées

These pastries are easier to make than you think. They're made from basic *Choux Paste*. They keep well if stored in a closed container.

During hot humid weather they may soften somewhat but will be completely restored if reheated at 350°F. about 10 minutes.

A pastry bag equipped with a plain round tube about 3/4 inch in diameter is a handy utensil to prepare pastry for baking. But a tablespoon or teaspoon, depending on the size wanted, can be used with complete success. Follow specific baking instructions in recipe. Puffs will collapse if they are not baked long enough; or they may be soft instead of crisp. In that case, just return them to oven, and continue baking until they become crisp.

Filling should not be added until just before serving. Split puffs, and fill with sweetened whipped cream, *French Cream Filling*, or ice cream. Top with sifted icing sugar, sweetened fresh fruit or sundae sauce. Tiny bouchées are generally filled with savory mixtures such as chicken salad or hot creamed lobster.

Choux Paste

> 1/2 cup butter or margarine
> 1 cup boiling water
> 1 cup unsifted all-purpose flour
> 1/4 teaspoon salt
> 4 whole eggs, unbeaten

Bring butter or margarine and water to boil in saucepan. Add flour and salt all at once. Beat vigorously over low heat until mixture leaves side of pan and forms a ball. Remove from heat; beat in 1 whole egg at a time, and after each addition beat until smooth. Or transfer the hot paste to a beater bowl, and beat in 1 egg at a time. When all eggs have been added, continue beating until mixture is glossy.

VARIATIONS:

* *Cream Puffs*: Drop paste by spoonfuls on a greased cookie sheet, using tablespoon for large puffs, teaspoon for small ones. Or press through

pastry bag, fitted with plain round tube. Space puffs about 2 inches apart. Mound paste, and swirl tops. Bake at 400°F. for about 30 minutes for large puffs and about 15 minutes for small or until light and crusty. Remove from oven, and cut 2 slits on sides of each puff. Turn off oven heat and return puffs to oven about 10 minutes to dry out centers. Cool, and when cold

fill with whipped cream or other filling. Spread with *Apricot Glaze* or other appropriate glaze.

Makes about 18 medium puffs. Recipe can easily be halved for smaller quantities.

* *Eclairs*: Shape paste into rectangles, about 1″ x 4″, using pastry bag or spoon. Round sides and top. Bake as for *Cream Puffs*.

* *Bouchées*: For each tiny bouchée, use 1 scant teaspoon of paste. Drop onto greased cookie sheet, and shape into high mound with spoon. Bake at 400°F. 15—18 minutes. Cut slits, and return to oven 10 minutes after heat has been turned off. Cool.

Apricot Glaze

> 1 cup sieved apricot jam
> 1 tablespoon orange curaçao or apricot brandy

Heat jam in saucepan; when it reaches simmering point, add curaçao. Spread while still warm over filled cases. Makes 1 cup.

VARIATIONS:

* *Currant Glaze*: Use 1 cup red currant jelly, and flavor with a little wine or brandy.

* *Chocolate Glaze*: Instead of jam melt semi-sweet chocolate, and add 1 tablespoon hot water or rich milk.

To Make a Fruit Flan

Fruit flan is a European dessert. Its special sweet pastry has a tender, crumbly consistency, because of the egg. The pastry is prebaked in a flan ring. The utensil is a straight-sided hoop of metal into which the rolled circle of dough is fitted. The pastry-lined ring rests on a cookie sheet while baking. After cooling, the shell is removed from the supporting ring and filled, generally first with thick custard or cooked cream mixture and then with lightly stewed or fresh or canned fruit arranged in decorative pattern. For topping, melted red currant jelly is frequently poured over fruit, or meringue is swirled on and baked until delicately colored and set.

Instead of the flan ring, a 9-inch layer-cake pan can be used. In order to get the necessary depth for a special filling, the sides can be built up slightly higher by means of a band of heavy aluminum foil fitted around the inside of the pan before putting in the pastry.

Note: Flan rings are available in different diameters at gourmet houseware stores and some department stores.

Sweet Pastry

> 2 cups sifted all-purpose flour
> 2 tablespoons sugar
> 1 teaspoon salt
> 3/4 cup butter or margarine or mixture of 1/2 butter and 1/2 shortening
> 2 egg yolks, slightly beaten
> 1 tablespoon water
> 1 tablespoon lemon juice

Sift flour, sugar and salt into mixing bowl. Cut in butter or margarine (which should not be ice-cold) with pastry blender, or work it in with fingers until mixture resembles cornmeal. Combine egg yolks, water and lemon juice thoroughly; sprinkle over flour mixture, and toss lightly to make soft dough. Work quickly so that butter does not become too oily. Turn out on floured board, and knead gently 5 or 6 times; wrap tightly in waxed paper, and chill in freezer or refrigerator until just firm. (It should still give when pressed with the fingers.) Roll out on lightly floured surface to 3/8-inch thickness, slightly thicker than for plain pastry. Then cut and shape according to your requirements for flan or regular pie shell or tart shells. Makes 1 9-inch shell (with leftover trimmings) or 10—12 medium tart shells.

Note: *Sweet Pastry* may also be baked along with filling, as in *Mince Pie, Custard Pie* and fresh-fruit pies.

Cream Cheese Pastry

    1 cup sifted all-purpose flour
    1/4 teaspoon salt
    1/2 cup butter or margarine
    1 (4-ounce) package plain cream cheese

Sift together flour and salt. With pastry blender or 2 knives cut in butter or margarine and cheese. When well blended, wrap in waxed paper, and chill until firm. Roll to 1/8-inch thickness, and cut according to desired use. Bake at 450°F. 12 minutes.

Note: This pastry can be used as the base for *Apple-Crumble Pie*, as small tart shells, for turnovers filled with jelly, or plain in dainty rounds, diamonds and strips served warm with a soup or salad course.

Tarts

Fill baked tart shells with a variety of fillings; chiffon cream pie mixtures, cooked fruit fillings or jam. Prepare cook-type fillings several hours before serving time. Cool; then fill shells. Top with meringue, and bake until delicately colored. Or just before serving, top tarts with whipped cream or sprinkled coconut, chopped nuts, orange rind or shaved chocolate. Fill unbaked tart shells with the same fillings used in unbaked pie shells; fresh fruit, pumpkin, custard, pecan or butter tart mixtures.

The fluted or plain tart tins or muffin pans used in preparing tarts vary greatly in size and shape. To determine the size of pastry circles for tarts, invert the tart tins, and measure the bottom with a piece of string, holding the string across the center of the bottom and up both sides. The length will be close to the diameter of pastry circles you will need for your pans.

Plain Pastry, Flaky Pastry, Sweet Pastry or *Cream Cheese Pastry* may be used for tart shells.

Roll pastry to 1/8-inch thickness, and cut in desired size with pastry cutter or sharp-edged tin or lid. Fit pastry into tart tins, and fill 2/3 full with prepared filling. Bake as directed in specific recipe.

To keep small tart shells nicely shaped and prevent shrinkage, fit pastry circles over outside of inverted tart tins. Prick with fork to prevent puffing. Bake at 450°F. 10—12 minutes. Cool thoroughly before removing from pans.

Note: Place individual tart tins or pressed foil tins lined with pastry on a cookie sheet before baking.

Lemon Filling

    3 eggs
    3/4 cup sugar
    1/3 cup butter or margarine
    3 tablespoons grated lemon rind
    1/3 cup lemon juice

Beat eggs in top of double boiler; then beat in sugar, butter or margarine and lemon rind. Place over boiling water, and cook 5 minutes. Add lemon juice, and continue cooking 5 minutes, stirring until thickened. Remove from hot water. Chill mixture thoroughly. Fill medium tart shells, and refrigerate until shortly before serving time. Fills 10—12 medium shells.

Glazed Fruit Filling

    1 (4-ounce) package plain cream cheese
    1 teaspoon orange or pineapple juice
      Fine white sugar
      Prepared peaches, sweet cherries and raspberries
    1/2 cup red currant jelly
    1 tablespoon hot water

Blend cream cheese and orange juice together. Sweeten lightly to taste. Spread thin layer of mixture in bottom of cooled, baked tart shells. Fill with well-drained fresh or frozen fruit. Prepare glaze by melting jelly and mixing with hot water. Spoon over fruit in tarts.

Strawberry-Cream Filling

    1/2 cup milk
    1/4 cup sugar
    1 tablespoon flour
    1 egg, well beaten
    1/8 teaspoon salt
    1/2 teaspoon vanilla extract
    1/4 cup whipped cream
    1 1/2 cups strawberries, washed, hulled and drained
    1/4 cup (or more) red currant jelly

Scald milk in top of double boiler. Combine sugar, flour, beaten egg and salt. Pour hot milk slowly over egg mixture. Stir, and return to double boiler; cook over boiling water until thick,

Croquembouche (p. 246).
CREDIT: *Bernard Gray*.

Chocolate Almond Coffee Bread (pp. 175-176).
CREDIT: *Henry Sandbank.*

Panettone (p. 255).
CREDIT: *Henry Sandbank.*

stirring constantly. Add vanilla, and chill. Just before using, fold in whipped cream. Fill tart shells half full of mixture. Arrange layer of strawberries on top of each. Heat currant jelly until it melts, and pour a spoonful on top of each tart. Fills 6 large tarts. Chill until serving time.

MAIN DISH PASTRIES

For savory pies with the sort of fillings that might be absorbed by the pastry—*Beefsteak-and-Kidney Pie* for example—use a plain pastry or the special type called *Rough Puff Pastry*. *Rough Puff Pastry* is flaky and many-layered like *Puff Paste*, but is not so rich or delicate. This kind of pastry may be used to make *Vol-au-Vent Shells*, which can be filled with creamed chicken, sweetbreads and mushrooms and so forth, as luncheon dishes.

Rough Puff Pastry

     2 cups sifted all-purpose flour
   1/2 teaspoon salt
     6 tablespoons hard lard
     6 tablespoons hard sweet butter
   1/2 teaspoon lemon juice
     6 tablespoons ice water

Sift flour with salt. Cut lard and butter or margarine into 1-inch cubes. Cut lightly into flour mixture so that fat is in about 1/4-inch pieces. Add lemon juice to ice water, and mix in lightly. Continue to blend in water gradually until all has been added. Dough should be fairly stiff. Roll dough into oblong shape. Fold in 3. Turn so that folded edges are at right and left. Roll out away from you, fold and turn again. Repeat this process 4 times. Then allow dough to rest at least 1/2 hour and preferably 1 hour in refrigerator. Then roll it out, and shape to make single top crust for 9-inch pie or in any other suitable shape or size.

Vol-au-Vent Shells

These shells may be made of *Puff Paste* or *Rough Puff Pastry*, depending on type of filling you wish to use. Make pastry as directed; roll out, and cut dough into circles. Size will vary according to your needs. For bouchées and cocktail-hour specialties, make very small; for a luncheon dish you will need larger shapes, about 3 inches in diameter. Set enough aside for number of servings planned. With remaining dough circles, cut a round out of each center, leaving rings like doughnuts. These rings will be used to make "walls" on complete circles and will hold filling in place. Set whole circles on baking sheet; on each stack 2 rings. Bake at 450°F. 8—14 min-

utes or until done; baking time will depend on size. On separate sheet bake small rounds cut from rings. As they are small, they will bake in less time. When all are baked and out of the oven, fill shells, and place 1 small round on top.

Beefsteak-and-Kidney Pie

   1 1/2 pounds round or chuck steak
     1/2 pound lamb kidneys
     1/4 cup all-purpose flour
   1 1/2 teaspoons salt
     1/2 teaspoon thyme
 1/8–1/4 teaspoon pepper
       3 tablespoons shortening or cooking oil
       1 tablespoon Worcestershire sauce
       1 tablespoon chopped parsley
     5–6 small onions, peeled
   2 1/2 cups boiling water
         Flaky Pastry or *Rough Puff Pastry* for single-crust pie, chilled

Cut beef into 1-inch cubes, trimming away all fat. Wash kidneys; trim away outer skin and any fat or tubes, and slice. Mix flour, salt and spices; combine with meat, coating all sides. Heat shortening in skillet, and put in meat and seasoned flour. Cover, and brown thoroughly; turn meat several times so that all sides are brown. Reduce heat, and add remaining ingredients except pastry, stirring to blend water with flour and fat mixture. Cover, and simmer about 1 hour. Turn into casserole. Roll out pastry to fit top generously; slash for steam vents; arrange over top, pressing to seal edge against moistened rim of dish. Bake in 425°F. oven 35—40 minutes. Serves 5—6.

Tourtière

   1/2- inch slice salt pork, diced, or 3 slices bacon, diced
     1 small onion, chopped
   1/2 clove garlic, crushed (optional)
     2 pounds lean shoulder pork, ground
   3/4 cup meat stock, bouillon or consommé, or 2/3 cup water and 2 tablespoons meat glaze
     2 tablespoons chopped celery leaves
     2 tablespoons chopped parsley
 1 1/2 teaspoons salt
   1/2 bay leaf
   1/8 teaspoon mace
   1/8 teaspoon chervil
       Pinch ground cloves
       Pinch cayenne
     1 slice day-old French bread
     2 recipes *Plain Pastry* or *Rough Puff Pastry* for double-crust 8-inch pie

In large skillet sauté salt pork over low heat until crisply browned. Add onion and fry, stirring until it is transparent; add remaining ingredients, except bread and pastry. Simmer, stirring occasionally, about 45 minutes. Crumble French bread into mixture to absorb some of juice and keep meat mixture from spreading out of hot pastry when you cut it later. (If pie is to be served cold, omit bread.) Let mixture cool before turning into pastry. Roll out 1/2 the pastry, and line 2 8-inch pie pans. Trim edges, and add filling. Dampen rims, and roll out remaining pastry for top crusts; put in place, and seal edges. Bake at 425°F. 15 minutes; reduce heat to 350° F., and continue baking 25–30 minutes. Serves 6–8.

Onion-Custard Pie

> *Plain Pastry* for single-crust 9-inch pie shell
> 5 medium onions
> 2 tablespoons butter or margarine
> 1 cup commercial sour cream
> 3 eggs, slightly beaten
> 2 tablespoons dry sherry
> 1 teaspoon salt
> 1/4 teaspoon black pepper
> 1/2 teaspoon celery seed
> 1 tablespoon chopped parsley
> 1/4 teaspoon sage
> 2–3 bacon strips, lightly fried
> 1 tomato, sliced

Line 9-inch pie plate with pastry, and chill. Slice onions thinly, and sauté gently in butter or margarine until transparent but not browned.

Heat sour cream, and stir gradually into eggs. Add sherry and seasonings, mixing well. Turn cooked onion into lined pie plate, and pour egg

mixture over. Bake at 450°F. 10 minutes. Reduce heat to 350°F., and continue to bake another 1/2 hour or until filling is set. About 15 minutes be-

fore end of cooking time, arrange bacon strips in diagonal effect on top, with slice of tomato between strips. Serves 4–5.

Oyster Pie

> 1 1/2 cups combined oyster liquor and rich milk
> 2 tablespoons butter or margarine
> 2 tablespoons chopped celery
> 1 tablespoon chopped parsley
> 2 egg yolks beaten
> 2 tablespoons fine bread crumbs
> 1/2 teaspoon salt
> Dash paprika
> Dash Worcestershire sauce
> 2 cups oysters, fresh or canned
> *Plain Pastry* for single-crust 8-inch pie
> 1 tablespoon milk

Heat oyster liquor and milk mixture in saucepan, and add butter or margarine, celery and parsley. When hot, pour gradually into egg yolks. Add crumbs, seasonings and Worcestershire sauce; stir thoroughly. Arrange oysters in greased shallow baking dish, and cover with hot sauce. Roll out pastry, prick and cover dish. Seal edge, and brush top with 1 tablespoon milk. Bake at 375°F. 30 minutes or until pastry is golden. Serves 4.

Savory Turnovers

    1 recipe *Plain Pastry* or *Rough Puff Pastry*
        for single-crust 8-inch pie
    1 egg white, slightly beaten (optional)

Roll out pastry to about 1/8-inch thickness, and cut into 4-inch squares. Place 2 or more tablespoons suitable savory filling just off center of each square. Brush edge of each square with water, and fold pastry over to make a triangle; press edges together with fork tines. Place on cookie sheet; brush with egg white, and bake in 450°F. oven about 20 minutes. Makes 4.

Note: Fill with about 3/4 cup finely ground cooked meat moistened with gravy, slightly diluted canned mushroom soup or chili sauce and seasoned to taste; or with 3/4 cup finely flaked and cooked fish (all bones removed) moistened with cream and sprinkled with chopped stuffed olives.

Chicken Pie

    4- pound stewing chicken
    3–4 cups boiling water
    1 large onion, sliced
    2 stalks celery, diced
    1/4 teaspoon paprika
       Salt to taste
    5–6 carrots, sliced
    2 tablespoons flour
    2 tablespoons soft butter or margarine
       Plain Pastry or *Rough Puff Pastry* for single-crust
          9-inch pie

Cut chicken in serving pieces, and cover with boiling water. Add onion, celery, paprika and salt. Bring to boil. Reduce heat, and simmer about 2 hours until chicken is tender, adding carrots for last 1/2 hour of cooking time. Strain off stock, and chill chicken and stock quickly, uncovered. Cut chicken meat from bones into large pieces. Scrape fat from stock. Heat 3 cups chicken stock (water or milk may be added if necessary to make up quantity). Blend flour and butter or margarine, and use to thicken hot broth,

continuing to stir until sauce is thick and smooth. Add diced meat and additional seasoning to taste. Cool again. Fill large or individual casseroles with chicken mixture. Cover with sheet of pastry; cut slits to release steam. Flute edge, and bake, allowing 12—15 minutes at 475°F. for small pies and 20—25 minutes at same heat for 2 large ones, or bake until pastry is golden brown. Serves 4.

Note: A roasting chicken or 2 small fryers may be used, but add 1—2 chicken-bouillon cubes during cooking, and simmer only until tender. Suitable pre-cooked vegetables may be added: green peas, mushrooms or tiny new potatoes. The chicken filling can be served as stew without pastry.

Chicken à la King in Pastry Shells

    2 tablespoons butter or margarine
    1/2 cup chopped sweet red or green pepper
    3 tablespoons flour
    1 cup chicken stock or consommé
    1 cup rich milk
    1/2 teaspoon salt
       Dash pepper
       Dash paprika
    2 egg yolks
    1/4 pound mushrooms
    1 tablespoon butter or margarine
    3 cups diced cooked chicken
    1 teaspoon lemon juice
    4–6 *Patty Shells*

In top of double boiler over direct medium heat melt 2 tablespoons butter or margarine. Add sweet pepper, and sauté until tender. Blend in flour, and gradually add stock and milk, stirring constantly until thick and smooth. Add salt, pepper and paprika to taste. Beat egg yolks until thick and lemon-colored. Stir hot mixture very slowly into eggs; return to double boiler, this time over hot water. Sauté mushrooms lightly in 1 tablespoon butter or margarine; add, along with chicken, to hot mixture. Just before serving stir in lemon juice. Spoon into patty shells. Serves 4—6.

Do not freeze custard pies, cream fillings and puddings, unwhipped gelatine desserts, unwhipped heavy cream and boiled or double-boiler icings. Most baked goods, however, freeze very well. A major factor is proper packaging—poorly wrapped cakes and breads will take on an undesirable freezer flavor. Detailed instructions on wrapping and storing will be found in your freezer manufacturer's booklet.

How To Freeze Breads

All yeast breads and quick breads can be frozen very successfully. Prepare and bake as usual, and let cool to room temperature. If desired, frost buns or fancy breads before freezing; or leave frosting until after thawing.

To Package. Wrap in freezer wrappings (foil, plastic film, freezer paper), or insert in plastic bags, excluding as much air as possible. Seal. Items that you like to reheat before serving—rolls, French bread or coffee cakes—should, for later convenience, be wrapped in foil, so that they are ready to warm in the oven. Such reheating must never be done in waxed or plastic wrappings, which will melt. The inexpensive aluminum-foil baking pans are useful in their various sizes for wrapping complete with contents for freezer storage.

To Thaw. Allow frozen baked goods to thaw in their wrappings at room temperature. If they are foil-wrapped and you wish to serve warm, place parcels in preheated 300°F. oven 15—30 minutes, depending on size. Unwrap as soon as heated through; otherwise they may develop a steamed texture. Allow 2 hours thawing time at room temperature for yeast breads, tea breads and square quick breads such as coffee cakes. Allow 1 hour or less for thawing rolls, muffins, scones and sweetened mixtures. Waffles, pancakes and presliced bread will thaw when toasted or heated under broiler.

How To Freeze Cakes

All kinds of cakes can be frozen—fruit, sponge, angel food, chiffon and butter cakes. Prepare and bake as usual; cool to room temperature.

Cakes may be frosted before freezing. The uncooked butter frostings are best for this purpose, as boiled or 7-minute frosting tends to become gummy when frozen, and the fudge type will crumble.

Fill large iced layer cakes with butter icing, jam or cooked fruit fillings such as date or raisin.

Fill and frost cooled cake. Place it unwrapped in freezer 2 hours to set icing; then wrap.

To Package. Place cake, frosted or unfrosted, on piece of foil-covered cardboard; wrap with freezer wrappings (foil, plastic wrap), or insert in plastic bag, excluding as much air as possible; seal. Freeze; then place cake in cardboard bakery carton or any firm container to protect cake from other packages during storage period.

For luncheon, cut cakes into halves, quarters or slices. Wrap securely in individual portions, according to your requirements, and freeze.

To Thaw. Always leave cake in freezer wrappings during thawing period. Allow 2—3 hours for square or loaf cakes; 1—1 1/2 hours for layers, and as much as 4—5 hours for large iced layer cake. Fruitcakes, being quite solid, require about 1 hour per pound. Rich fruitcakes slice neatly when they are still icy cold. To speed thawing of any cake, place package in stream of air blown from electric fan.

How To Freeze Cookies

Cookies of standard types may be frozen baked or unbaked. It will save space in your freezer to store dough and bake as needed. Generally, bars and squares must be baked before freezing.

To Prepare Dough. Refrigerator-cookie dough can be shaped into roll and wrapped as usual, then placed in plastic bags and sealed before storing in freezer. Drop or molded cookie doughs may be handily packed in bulk in airtight freezer containers. Another way is to drop batter by spoonfuls or in balls onto a baking sheet and freeze 1 hour. Transfer frozen shapes to rigid container, placing a couple of sheets of waxed paper between layers.

To Thaw Cookie Doughs. Thaw refrigerator-type dough slowly in the refrigerator overnight, rather than at room temperature. The dough will be a uniform firmness for slicing, instead of soft on the outside and hard on the inside. Other bulk cookie dough should stand at room temperature and be used when soft enough to handle. Preshaped cookies should be placed in their unthawed state on greased baking sheet and placed into oven immediately. Allow longer baking time and slightly lower temperature.

To Package Baked Cookies. If you wish to freeze cookies, let them cool thoroughly; pack in firm containers with lightly crushed waxed paper between layers; overwrap tightly with freezer wrapping. For such special occasions as Christmas, decorated fancy cookies can be arranged on trays with waxed paper between layers and the trays overwrapped before storing.

To Thaw Baked Cookies. Leave in freezer wrapping at room temperature; time will depend upon size of container and type of cookies. Date and oatmeal cookies and brownies require longer thawing time than do rolled sugar cookies.

How To Freeze Pies

Double-crust fresh fruit pies and mince pies are better frozen *unbaked*, with special preparation. On the other hand, pies and tarts with pecan-syrup or butter-tart fillings or fruit and sponge-cake fillings should be baked and cooled before freezing. *Do not freeze custard or cream-filled pies*, baked or unbaked.

To Prepare Fruit and Mince Pies. Use regular or foil pie pans. When preparing filling allow 1/3 more thickener (flour, cornstarch or tapioca) to control extra juices of frozen fruit. For example, if berry-pie recipe specifies 3 tablespoons flour, increase amount to 4. Do not make slits in top crust. Put unwrapped pie into freezer; package after it has frozen firm. Use cardboard bakery cartons, or cover top with inverted foil pie pan; overwrap with freezer wrappings.

Note: On a real baking day, you will probably have a fair amount of pastry trimmings after cutting out pie shapes. Why not cut out these scraps in fancy shapes with a cookie cutter and freeze them for elegant decorations on a casserole or a pudding a month from now?

To Bake Frozen Fruit Pies. Remove unthawed fruit or mince pie from wrappings. Place immediately in preheated 450°F. oven. After first 15 minutes of cooking cut 2 or 3 slits in top crust. Reduce heat to 375°F., and bake 50–70 minutes more, depending on type of pie.

To Freeze Baked Pies. Prepare pies according to your recipe; cool. Freeze 1 hour; remove from freezer, and press circular foil or plastic wrap over filling. Package as for unbaked fruit pies.

To Thaw Baked Pies. Leave in freezer wrappings at room temperature 30–60 minutes.

How To Freeze Pastry

As bulk pastry dough takes a long time to thaw, it is advisable to roll it out before freezing. After rolling, cut into circles of size required to fit your pie pans. Have ready a heavy cardboard circle about 3/4 inch larger than pastry round; cover cardboard with aluminum foil; on top of it stack pastry circles, separating each layer with 2 thicknesses of waxed paper. Wrap and stack in freezer wrapping, and store in freezer.

To Thaw Pastry Dough. Leave wrapped stacks of pastry circles at room temperature until dough is soft enough to fit into pie pans.

Freezer Storage Life for Baked Goods

The following suggested periods for freezer storage of various home-baked products are conservative and must be considered only approximate (they are maximums for well-packaged foods held continuously at 0°F. or below). It is always desirable, however, to use items from freezer regularly and replace them as soon as convenient.

Yeast breads and quick breads, 3 months
Angel food and chiffon cakes, 2 months
Chocolate layer cakes, 4 months
Yellow pound cakes, 6 months
Fruitcakes, 12 months
Unbaked cookies, 6–8 months
Baked cookies, 12 months
Unbaked fruit and mince pies, 8 months
Chiffon and other baked pies, 2 months
Unbaked pastry, 6 months

APPROXIMATE BAKING TIMES AND TEMPERATURES

1 loaf bread, 45–60 minutes at 375°–400°F.
Sweet rolls, 15–30 minutes at 350°–400°F.
Baking-powder biscuits, 10–15 minutes at 450°F.
Tea breads, about 60 minutes at 350° F.
Coffee cakes with baking powder, about 25 minutes at 375°F.
Coffee cakes with yeast, about 25 minutes at 400°F.
Layer cakes, about 30 minutes at 375°F.
Rectangular cakes, 30–45 minutes at 375°F.
Cupcakes, about 20 minutes at 400°F.
Sponge cakes, 50–60 minutes at 300°–325°F.
Pie shells, about 15 minutes at 450°F.
Double-crust pies, 15 minutes at 425°F., then 30–45 minutes at reduced heat according to filling

APPROXIMATE SIZES OF CAKE PANS*

Round layer pans, 8″ or 9″ x 1 1/2″ deep
Square cake pan, 8″ x 8″ x 2″ or 9″ x 9″ x 2″
Oblong cake pan, 13″ x 9″ x 2″
Sheet pan (for jelly rolls), 15″ x 10″ x 1/2″
Loaf pan, 9″ x 5″ x 3″ or 8″ x 4″ x 3″
Tube pan, 8″ x 3 1/2″ deep or 10″ x 4 1/2″ deep
Spring-form pan, 9″ x 3 3/4″ deep or 10″ x 4 1/2″ deep

*Sizes for most frequently used pans.

CHAPTER FIVE

An Introduction to Gourmet Cookery

✿

A gourmet evaluates cooking critically and is an epicure, or lover of good eating. The person who is a gastronome practices the art of preparing fine foods. Although the controversy over whether gastronomy is an art or a science has not been resolved, we fortunately remain free to explore all possibilities for fine cooking. The recipes in this chapter range from simple to complex. In all of them always assemble materials and utensils before starting preparation, and follow procedures, times and temperatures given. Omit or replace certain seasonings or flavors to suit your taste.

It is wise to try these recipes privately before serving to guests. Gourmet cooking more than any other kind improves with practice.

Equipment

A selection of good sharp knives is essential for slicing, dicing, chopping, boning and skinning. If you happen to find the type known as a "French chef's knife," buy it. It has a carbon-steel blade, which can be sharpened more quickly and easily than can a hard stainless-steel edge.

A heavy chopping board of good size—at least twice as large as an ordinary bread board—is another essential. There should be surface enough to let you undertake several cutting jobs at one time without overlapping, and the board should rest firmly, flat and even, on your kitchen counter or table.

Whisks, or wire whips for beating eggs and sauces, are not easy to find, but when you acquire one you will find it as indispensable as the European cook does. They are made in various sizes, with short or long handles, so try them out for feel and choose 2 or 3—perhaps 1 in the true whisk shape and the others with continuously coiled wire around an oval stirrer. Without these simple devices, intended for brisk whipping and beating by the right hand while the left is add-

ing ingredients, the encyclopedia of French sauces could never have been achieved.

A rubber scraper is a great tool for folding, creaming, stirring and scraping. And a food mill, of the kind used to strain mixtures for a baby's diet, is frequently in use in gourmet kitchens for pureeing soups and other mixtures; an electric blender is generally a quicker, easier, neater substitute. The original blender, used in the days of Escoffier and for centuries before him, was the mortar and pestle; it is still used throughout Europe for the crushing of herbs, spices and nuts. The wire salad basket for efficient washing and drip-drying of greens was a family everyday tool in French kitchens long before it appeared on this side of the Atlantic.

Heavy-bottomed pans that conduct heat evenly and hug the stove burner or element are desirable. Copper pots have been traditional in French kitchens, frequently handed down through generations of *bonnes femmes*, but they are both costly and heavy, and their interiors have to be re-tinned frequently. Today's heavy cast aluminum and high quality stainless steel pans, with bases that are especially designed to distribute heat evenly, are an efficient compromise. Enameled cast-iron equipment for both top of the stove and oven is austerely handsome in design and color (the color does not tinge or otherwise affect food); but even empty, the weight, especially of the large covered casseroles, is formidable. On the other hand, very lightweight pots and pans are not recommended. Their instability makes them even dangerous to use, and foods tend to burn and scorch on thin bottoms.

To stock your kitchen satisfactorily, consider the various cooking jobs to be done, rather than the visual appeal of matched equipment. Several heavy frying pans of various sizes are a must. Reserve one with a rounded base and medium size for your omelet pan. Never wash it in the dishpan, and never let water come in contact with its cooking surface; otherwise your omelets may stick. Use clean dry cheesecloth or paper towels to wipe out pan after each omelet session. Scrub stubborn spots with salt.

Earthenware, oven-glass, and very hardy ceramic cooking equipment offer many styles and sizes of dishes suitable for both cooking and serving. The ceramic containers are impervious to direct heat and can even be transferred directly from cold refrigerator to gas flame or preheated oven. Earthenware cannot be used this way, yet for centuries good cooks of continental Europe have prepared their traditional soups and ragoûts in this fragile baked clay, which must never be exposed to extremes of temperature. There is a secret, of course. For cooking on top of the stove a protective asbestos mat is always used between the heat source and a clay pot; the pot is also allowed to cool slowly before being washed in hot water. When certain international recipes direct you to "brown the meat cubes and onion in melted fat, using an earthenware marmite over medium heat," the unstated assumption is that you know all about the essential asbestos mat that will keep the container from cracking.

The Dutch oven is a deep heavy metal pan, which may have a removable rack. It has a tight-fitting cover. It is indispensable for slow-cooked meat dishes either on top of the stove or in the oven. The bain-marie is the French double-boiler, which is quite like ours, though sometimes with a porcelain lining in two metal sections. Another familiar sight in French kitchens is the series of graduated melters, little metal containers with handles or thumb-pieces.

Hair sieves, sometimes cone-shaped; wooden spatulas and spoons; the metal flan rings that are often used in place of pie plates for baking pastry shells; tiny brushes for glazing with fat or sugar syrup; larding needles for threading slivers of fat into solid meat before roasting; jelly molds in elaborate designs; cake pans; baking sheets for rows of small confections; and straight-sided soufflé dishes are all part of the ideal gourmet kitchen.

Types of cookery other than French sometimes call for such special equipment as the Japanese hibachi or charcoal grill for indoor or outdoor use and the cast-iron cornstick baking pan, which cooks corn bread in the shape of miniature corncobs. The list could go on endlessly and still be incomplete.

Notes on Basic Ingredients

Butter. When heated, butter foams, and when the foam subsides the butter starts to brown and will eventually burn. Cook your omelet in butter just after foaming subsides. Oil is often used with butter to allow it to be heated to a higher temperature, especially in browning meats.

Clarified Butter. Clarified butter is the clear yellow liquid obtained when butter is heated and the milky sediment settles on the bottom. Called "ghee" in India, clarified butter is popular in the Far East and other areas for sautéing foods that require very delicate browning and also for certain sauces.

Oils. Oils vary greatly in kind and flavor around the world. Salad oil from vegetable sources is satisfactory for most cooking, especially for delicate French dishes.

Olive oil, so popular in Spain, Italy and other Mediterranean areas, is too definite in character for many kinds of delicate-flavored cooking, but can be used for sautéing strong-flavored foods such as garlic and hot onions. In this section, "oil" refers to mild cooking oil, unless otherwise specified.

Flour. When flour is called for in the recipes on the following pages, it is the type known as "all-purpose," unless otherwise specified. This hard-wheat flour produces smoother sauces than do the varieties used for pastry and cakes, and mixes more quickly with fats and liquids in sauce-making.

Bouillon, Broth and Stock. These liquids are called for in many recipes. As homemade stocks are time-consuming to prepare, it is suggested that canned liquid meat extract or dry-base cubes and granules be substituted, according to flavor specified. Use consommé only if called for in recipe, as it tends to be slightly sweet.

Seasonings. Seasonings for bouquet garni and other purposes are discussed under herbs and spices.

A GUIDE TO SEASONING WITH HERBS, SPICES AND SEEDS

Get acquainted with the ancient sweet herbs, treasured by good cooks for centuries. Use them fresh and green from the market or your garden. Dry or freeze them for a ready supply months later. (But remember that dried herbs are 6 times stronger than fresh-picked ones; the traditional pinch should be not more than 1/16 teaspoonful.) Store dried or crushed herbs well removed from cooking steam, and renew your supply of seasonings at least once a year. Study tropical spices, and learn their wide-ranging characteristics; investigate savory seeds, and experiment with today's newly available seasoning combinations.

Herbs, since the beginning of civilization, have been an important factor in everyday living, whether for medical or for culinary uses. Nowadays sweet herbs (the old term for the edible kinds) are becoming almost a necessity in our kitchens.

Many people grow their own herbs, and the space allotted may vary from 1 or 2 windowsill pots to a formal herb garden. Climate, space and taste dictate the kinds grown.

To Dry Leaf Herbs

Choose plants just beginning to blossom, and pick on sunny morning after dew is off leaves. Cut about 2/3 the length of the stalk, with side branches and stems. Rinse off earth clinging to lower leaves, and remove yellow or decayed leaves. Spread herbs (each variety separately) on trays or papers in warm dry room or airy attic. Turn every day until dried; it takes about 3—4 days. Strip off leaves, using glove to protect your fingers, place each variety in screw-top jar and store in dark room for 1 week. If moisture appears in jar, remove contents to cheesecloth-covered screen, and leave a few days longer. Store in opaque container, and make sure it is tightly covered.

To dry in bunches, tie stems together and hang from line in warm room until leaves are crackly. Spread papers underneath to catch leaves or seeds.

To Dry Herb Seeds

Dill and other herbs should be left to develop flower heads and cut while still in flower. Allow to dry as for leafy herbs, turning on trays or papers in dark dry room. Harvest seeds by rubbing heads between palms of hands. Store as for leaves, and be sure to check for moisture before finally putting seeds in containers.

To Freeze Herbs

Herbs most suitable for quick freezing are basil, chives, fennel, marjoram, spearmint, sage tarragon and thyme. Frozen herbs cannot be used for garnishes, but are handy for chopping or crushing in cooked dishes, salads, sandwich fillings and iced drinks. Herbs may be blended for specific dishes such as soups, salad dressings and poultry stuffings.

Have ready small plastic freezer bags and pint cartons in which to pack them. Cut herbs with tender tops, allowing sufficient stem to tie in bunches. Wash under cold running water, and dry on paper toweling.

Arrange sprigs together (either one kind or a blend), and tie with thread, making loop sufficiently large to hold them when they are dipped in boiling water. Have large saucepan of boiling water ready, and keep it at boiling point. Nearby have pan of ice water. Immerse herbs in boiling water, and hold 1 minute; then transfer to ice water, and hold 2 minutes.

Rinse under cold running water, and drain. Place in freezer bags, and seal. Pack as many bags as possible in freezer carton, but do not crush. Label, and freeze. Before using, allow to thaw at room temperature, and use immediately. Do not refreeze leftovers, but add thawed leaf herbs to wine vinegar for interesting flavor.

Herb Blends

Some herbs cancel out one another's flavors, whereas others tend to dominate. The bland or "blender" herbs are parsley and chervil. Pungent herbs requiring generous accompaniments of blending herbs are rosemary, tarragon and sage. Herbs with dominant flavors are dill, fennel, mint, marjoram, oregano and savory. Pair with each other or with a "blender." Chives and green or dry garlic go well with any combination.

Any desired blend can be assembled and frozen, following directions given previously. Dried herbs also can be blended and stored, but leave uncrushed until just before using.

How To Use Herbs

Herbs and spices should provide interesting accents to food, rather than overwhelm it. Remember, dried herbs are stronger than freshly picked ones. To substitute in recipe calling for 1 tablespoon chopped fresh herbs, use 1/2 teaspoon dried herbs or flakes or 1/4 teaspoon powdered herbs.

Use dried herb leaves or flakes when long cooking is required and broth can be strained. For dishes cooked in short time make infusion of dried herbs in any liquid to be added—tomato juice, milk and stock—and let stand 1 hour; then strain. To test taste of an unfamiliar herb, steep 1/2 teaspoon in 1/2 cup water for 1 hour; then sip brew, and make your decision, remembering that flavor will not be *that* strong when mingled with other ingredients.

Fines herbs are combinations of several fresh leaf herbs, chopped and added near end of cooking period. They are used in soups, sauces, stews and omelets and in melted butter over steaks.

Bouquet garni is a combination of fresh or dried herbs tied in small bunches and added to soup stocks, stews and casseroles for part or all of cooking period, then removed before serving. Basic herbs used are bay leaf, thyme, and parsley, often accompanied by celery leaves. Other suitable herbs are basil, marjoram, savory or chervil. Tie sprigs of fresh herbs together with long string, and attach to handle of cooking pot. Place dried herbs in scrap of clean cheesecloth, as for pickling, and tie with string. Either way bundle can be easily removed.

TYPES OF HERBS AND THEIR USES

Here are the sweet herbs, used in small amounts for seasoning. Pot herbs are vegetable greens such as spinach that are cooked in quantity. Salad herbs are lettuce, chicory and the like.

Angelica	The dried, usually candied green stalks of an herb native to Europe. Used in fine baking, often as decoration in elaborate frosting; roots are used in cordials.

basil

Basil · Often called sweet basil. Aromatic minty flavor; much used in Italian cookery; wonderful with tomatoes in any form; also a good choice for bouquet garni.

bay leaf

Bay leaf · Not an herb but the leaf from the laurel tree. A very powerful flavor; 1/2 dried leaf is usually enough for seasoning soups, sauces or aspics.

chervil

Chervil · A relative of parsley, which it resembles, with fine lacy foliage and sweeter, stronger flavor. Used in salads, omelets, fish dishes, cooked vegetables and soups.

chives

Chives · A member of the onion family, very delicate in appearance, with a mild onion flavor. Has wide application; particularly good with bland or sweet vegetables and delicious in salads. Snip with scissors.

dill

Dill · Chop fresh green foliage over salads, especially cucumber, hot vegetable or fish. Use dill seeds in cooked dishes only as pungent touch for eggs or lamb.

fennel

Fennel · Looks like celery but has distinctive licorice flavor. Use leaves in salads, soups, fish dishes; whole seeds in eggs, cheese dishes, cakes, apple pie.

garlic

Garlic · From a hardy plant cultivated for its strongly flavored bulb. Esteemed by ancient Greeks and almost as popular now fresh, dried, powdered or in salt.

Horseradish · Comes from long root of a coarse plant. Sharp piquant flavor and odor. It is sold grated and vinegared to go with meats (especially beef) or in sauces; it is also available in powdered form.

Marjoram One of the most popular herbs; aromatic, with flavor like delicate oregano. Good in soup, stews, cheese dishes; excellent with beef in any form and also with mushrooms.

Mint The finest fresh flavor. Use green leaves as garnish; in vinegars, jellies and cold drinks; with fruits or hot vegetables; and fresh or dried in sauce for lamb.

Parsley The mainstay of the bouquet garni; familiar last touch to salads and cooked dishes. Snip with scissors for easy chopping. Dried parsley flakes are handy.

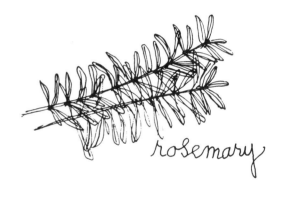

Mustard Young leaves are cooked or served raw. Tiny seeds add tang to pickles and various vegetables; they are dried and ground for packaged mustard.

Rosemary Poets used to sing of it. The leaves resemble pine needles and have tea-like fragrance. Use fresh or dried, but sparingly. Good with lamb, fish and poultry.

Oregano An aromatic herb, with a taste midway between sage and marjoram. Much used in Italian cookery; good with beef, meat loaves; powerful—use with discretion.

Sage The well-known pungent herb, traditional in poultry stuffings, good with pork, spareribs, cheeses, soups, sauces. Use fresh or dried, but always with caution.

Familiar spices such as pepper and nutmeg, plus costlier rarities: filé powder for Creole cookery or saffron, 1 pound of which requires 70,000 hand-picked autumn-crocus blossoms.

Allspice	A dried berry from the West Indies: tastes like mixture of clove, cinnamon, nutmeg. Whole or ground; use in pickles, cookies, cakes, meat seasoning.

Savory	Belongs to the mint family, possesses a highly aromatic leaf with strong flavor. Valuable either dried or fresh for stuffings, pork cuts, hot vegetables. Do not overdo.
Scallions	Belongs, along with chives, shallots and garlic, to family group of onions and leeks. Like young green onions, with slim, long top.
Shallots	Small, rather pear-shaped member of the onion clan; has cloved structure like garlic. Much favored in European cuisines for salads, sauces, meats and so forth.
Cinnamon	Adds warm sweet flavor to many foods. Two imported types: dried bark (in sticks or ground) and cassia buds (whole or ground). Countless uses in all kinds of cookery.
Cayenne	Prepared by grinding dried pods and seeds of red peppers or chilis. Fiery in taste; can burn mouth; use in minute amounts to liven sauces, salad dressings, pickles.
Chili powder	A blend of dried ground Mexican chili peppers, both hot and sweet types; may also contain oregano and ground cumin. Adds zest to meats, sauces, rice, beans and soups.

Tarragon	Delicately pungent herb, long prized by epicures for flavoring salad vinegars and dressings. Excellent with fish, chicken and vegetables, but do not use too much.

Thyme	Another pungent herb, admired as a garden plant and for its flavorful leaves. A subtle touch for soups, meats, seafoods. Use dried thyme sparingly.
Cloves	The dried unopened flower buds of the Zanzibar clove tree. Pungent aroma, biting taste. Use whole or ground, but carefully. Has a great many uses.

An Introduction to Gourmet Cookery   223

curry

Curry powder | A ground mixture of many herbs and spices; turmeric supplies the yellow-brown color. Packaged brands vary greatly in strength. Use with meats, fish, rice, soups and sauces.

Filé powder | Made chiefly of dried sassafras; comes from Louisiana. Used in Creole gumbos; stirred into hot liquid after removal from heat, flavors and thickens.

ginger

Ginger | Root of Asian plant, grown in many tropical areas. Powdered, crystallized, preserved or dried. Delightfully fragrant, pungently flavored. Many uses.

Juniper | The aromatic fruit of a bush that grows wild. The unusual flavor (as in gin) is sometimes enjoyed in stuffing for game, in sauce for fish or in stewed lamb dishes.

mace

Mace | Obtained from casing of nutmeg. Flattened, it is called a "blade." Otherwise in powder form. Smooth, gentle; used alone or in spice blends.

Nutmeg | Dried seed or nut from fruit of nutmeg tree. Available whole or ground. Adds delicate warm taste to eggnogs, desserts, baked products, certain soups and vegetables.

Paprika | From ground dried pods of sweet red or chili peppers; rich dark red; flavor mild to pungent. Use for both color and seasoning in batters, sauces and the like.

pepper

Pepper | Black and white from same dried berry; milder white is ground after hulls are removed. Peppercorns are whole berries. Gourmet kitchens stock both.

saffron

Saffron | Powder made from stigmas of autumn-crocus blossoms. Gives golden color and pleasant flavor to rice, meats, breads and pastry. Steep saffron in recipe's liquid.

Turmeric | Belongs to the ginger family; a dried root, ground, added to curry blends and condiments. Sweet tangy flavor; adds interesting color to pickles, sauces and so forth.

THE SAVORY SEEDS

Nutlike sesame scattered over a cake; tiny celery seeds for piquancy in potato salad; old-fashioned caraway, blended with creamy cheese.

anise seed

Anise | The aromatic seed of a small fruit. Has distinctive licorice flavor (as in anisette, the French liqueur). Use whole or ground in baking, candies and cheese.

Caraway

Caraway | Highly distinctive flavor, which wins ardent devotion or strong opposition. Baked in "seed cake"; served with mutton or sauerkraut; often blended into mild cheese.

Cardamom | An exotic flavor, like anise or licorice plus strong coffee. Used in mixed pickling spices. Featured in Spanish cookery and Scandinavian baking.

Cardamom

Celery | Celery seed has a very pronounced celery flavor. Useful in soup stocks, pot roasts, vegetable salads (especially potato), French dressings and pickles.

Coriander | The ancients prized this seasoning for its unusual sweetish taste. Uses range from pea soup and pickles to gingerbreads.

Cumin | Like coriander, this is a tiny fruit treated as a seed; with a long history too. Added to curry blends; used alone to flavor meats, hot vegetables and cheese.

Nasturtium | This familiar garden plant is almost entirely edible. Young seed pods can be pickled in vinegar, like capers. Tender leaves and flowers are spicy salad touches.

Poppy | From an annual plant of the poppy tribe. White seed available, but blue seed more popular. A favorite topping for breads; browned in butter for rice and stews.

celery seed

Sesame | Aromatic seed of a flowering plant. Has rich nutty flavor, which makes it useful in cakes and candies. Toasted and browned, a worthy addition to salads and casseroles.

sesame seed

Vanilla | An aromatic tropical bean, which, steeped in alcohol, gives the well-known flavoring extract for sweet dishes. Dried bean is used in *haute cuisine*.

There are many on today's market: packaged condiment sauces thick or thin, tomato pastes, blends of spices, seasoning salts.

Angostura bitters	An aromatic liquid spice made from gentian and other plant flavors in alcoholic solution. Add by drops to beverages. Extremely powerful; use with caution.
Monosodium glutamate	White powder chemically produced from glutamic acids in sugar beets, wheat or corn. Add before or during cooking to enhance food flavors. Can be added after foods are prepared as in salads and hot drained vegetables. Various brands. Referred to as m.s.g.
Poultry seasoning	Term applied to packaged ready-mixed dried herbs suitable for use in stuffings. For 4-pound chicken, 1/2 teaspoon is basic recommendation; increase to suit taste.
Soy sauce	The essential touch for Chinese savory dishes, replacing salt. An almost-black liquid made from fermented soy beans. Flavor is pronounced.
Hot pepper sauce	A red sauce, aged before bottling. Use only 1–2 drops at a time.

THE GREAT WINES

Types and Origins

Wines are generally classified according to color; red or white (the latter actually a tone of yellow or gold), with the addition of the pinks, or vin rosé. There are further classifications as well. Wines may be dry or sweet—dry (sec) meaning lack of sweetness rather than total sourness—or in-between. Certain vintages are further grouped as full-bodied or light-bodied. Good body means a well-rounded combination of strength and flavor, resulting in what the French esteem as solidité. Fortified wines are those that have brandy added after the desired characteristics have developed in the wine. Aromatic wines such as vermouth are fortified and infused with selected herbs and spices.

Selecting and Serving

The choice of wines to be served at a single meal depends upon personal preference and budget. One dry wine—champagne, a red or white table wine or vin rosé—may be served throughout the meal.

At informal or formal luncheons or dinners champagne is often served throughout. Wine may be withheld during the salad course if the latter is accompanied by a pronounced vinegar dressing, as the flavors wouldn't be compatible.

Wines with Menu Courses

With hors d'oeuvres serve champagne, vin rosé or white wine.

With soup, dry sherry or Madeira is the traditional choice.

With fish, shellfish, ham, pork, omelets, cold fowl and light entrées, serve light dry wine or vin rosé.

With roast chicken, turkey, veal, lamb and ragoûts, serve light-bodied red wine or full-bodied dry white wine.

With roast beef, steak, venison and game birds serve full-bodied red wine.

With desserts, serve sweet white wine, champagne, Madeira, dessert sherry or port.

With cheese, fruits and nuts, port is traditional, but any full-bodied red wine may be offered.

Choice of Glasses

Wineglasses are best colorless so that the tone and life of the wine are well displayed. Stemmed glasses are nice but not essential. The glass should be of 6—8-ounce capacity, preferably tulip-shaped to collect the smell or bouquet of the wine at the top of the glass. The average serving of wine is 3—4 ounces, regardless of the size of the glass.

An all-purpose wineglass, which will serve any kind of wine and is satisfactory both in appearance and use, also reduces the cupboard storage problem.

Temperatures for Serving Wines

Serve all white wines, sparkling wines and rosé wines well chilled at 40°—45°F. Several hours in the refrigerator will bring wine to this temperature.

If you have a wine cooler for use in the dining room, by all means use it. Pack chilled bottle in crushed ice 1/2 hour before dinner, and rotate from time to time.

Serve still red wines at room temperature 65°—70°F. If brought from cellar with temperature of 50°F., allow wine to stand several hours in dining room. Some light-bodied red wines are more palatable served at 60°F., or slightly under room temperature.

Open still red wines an hour or so before serving to permit them to breathe. Sparkling wines should be opened just before serving.

Sherries, Madeiras and appetizer and dessert wines are pleasanter when served slightly chilled.

Care and Handling of Wines

Wine should be handled very gently. Shaking, twirling bottle or serving wine too soon after its arrival at your home is apt to damage it.

To open, use lever-type corkscrew, and work precisely and gently to insert as far as it will go.

Then turn lever with steady motion to remove cork; do not try to pull. Removing cork from champagne is often quite tricky, requiring patience, dexterity and strength. After removing foil, take off wire very carefully, grasp cork, give it a turn to the right and then push out. Hold bottle at an angle after opening, so that pressure does not force a great deal of wine out of bottle.

Store all unfortified wines in cool, dark, dry place, laying bottles *on their sides* in order to keep corks moistened and tight. These living wines continue to develop and mature within the unopened bottles; thus they deserve this slight extra care. Burgundies stored under proper conditions will last from 10 to upwards of 30 years, depending on the vintage. Bordeaux takes much

longer to mature, and many vintages in the past were practically indestructible. The wines from the Rhone Valley are the most robust of all red wines produced in France. They are fine with game, cheese or other heavy dishes. The white and rosé wines of the Rhone Valley are also heavier-bodied than similar wines from other sections. On the other hand, the fortified wines—

sherry, Madeira and port—have more stable natures and can be stored upright. Of all the different classes of wines, sherry is the least subject to

deterioration. Even after months of exposure to air, a 1/2 filled bottle of sherry offers the same quality as originally; indeed some experts maintain that it will show improvement.

The Fortified Wines

In this grouping are the sherries, dry or sweet; Madeira and Marsala, which, like sherry, can be chosen for either appetizer or after-dinner use, and port and Malaga, both of which are dessert wines. In all cases brandy is the fortifying agent, with the result that the alcoholic content of the wine may range up to 21 percent of volume.

Sherry comes from Spain; its name is an anglicizing of Jerez, the area where this renowned wine is produced. There are 4 recognized classes of imported sherry:

1. *Manzanilla*: Very dry, sometimes called the world's driest wine, but not too well known outside Europe. Serve as a chilled aperitif.
2. *Fino:* Also very dry; universally prized as an appetizer. Serve chilled or "on the rocks" as a cocktail; often used as accompaniment to soups.
3. *Amontillado*: Medium dry and darker; popular as appetizer.
4. *Oloroso*: Deep gold in color; medium dry; usually served with desserts or sauced dishes. When blended with aged sweetening wines for export, Olorosos become the famous dessert sherries and usually have the word "cream," "brown" or "East India" in their brand titles.

Madeira hails from the Portuguese island of Madeira off northwest Africa. There are 4 traditional types: Rainwater, very light and dry appetizer wine; Sercial, darker but quite dry; Malm-

sey, rich and heavy and Boal, richest of all, an after-dinner wine.

Marsala from Sicily is somewhat sweeter than Spanish sherry; it is generally dark and rich.

Malaga from Spain is a deep red, richly sweet wine for after-dinner use.

Port is the famous red wine of Portugal, named after its shipping center of Oporto. A fortified and usually blended wine, it is famous for dessert or after-dinner use.

The Red Wines

Red Burgundies. Burgundy or the Côte d'Or is made up of 2 districts: Côte de Nuits and Côte de Beaune. Well-known vineyards in the Côte de Nuits district include Romanée-Conti, La Tâche, Les Richebourg, Le Chambertin, Clos Vougeot and many others. In the Côte de Beaune district, Pommard is the most famous name, and Aloxe-Corton and Volnay are almost as well known. They are pleasant, soft wines, good choices for those who sometimes complain that red wines taste sour.

Red Bordeaux. Wines produced in the area around Bordeaux are dry and a little tart. They go well with meat and poultry of all kinds and especially with foods that are not too spicy or pungent.

Famous wines exported from Bordeaux are from the Médoc district: Château Margaux, Château Mouton-Rothschild and Château Latour. Château Haut-Brion comes from the Graves district. From Saint-Emilion comes Château Cheval-Blanc; from Pomerol Château Pétrus.

Beaujolais. These wines are brighter in color and lighter in flavor than the Burgundies and come from the area south of the Côte d'Or. Beaujolais wines are well known the world over and are sold under district and township names. Township names to remember are: Saint-Amour, Fleurie, Moulin-à-Vent, Juliénas. The neighboring Chalonnais district produces a similar wine.

Rhone Valley Wines. These wines come from the district south of Burgundy, are robust or full-bodied and consequently good with game and rich meat dishes. Best known are Hermitage, Côte Rôti and Châteauneuf-du-Pape.

Italian Red Wines. The great red wine is of course, Chianti: Brolio, Villa Antinori, Ruffino. Soave is a delicious white wine, as is Falerno. But this is the merest guide, as the Italians believe in drinking what you like. Ask your wine merchant for his recommendation.

The White Wines

White wines are easier to become familiar with than red, perhaps because there are fewer of them but mostly because in this country we enjoy chilled drinks. Flavors available range from green, acid wines to fruity, ripe ones, with most good wines somewhere between these extremes.

White Burgundies. Three of the most famous dry white wines in the world are Montrachet,

Chablis and Pouilly-Fuissé. (The last-mentioned is hard to pronounce, which may make it easier to remember.) These great wines come from France's Burgundy district and are the classic selections to serve with oysters, fish, ham and pork in any form, cold buffets and picnics. Montrachet is described as a deep wine. Chablis has established its fame with just a few hundred acres of vineyards planted to one type of grape.

White Bordeaux. The best known are medium dry, soft wines from the Graves district and are particularly good served with seafood, fish and ham. Famous names to look for are Château Bouscaut, Château Carbonnieux and Château Haut-Brion.

Vouvray. This wine is exceptional; it's produced in the Loire district from a sweet grape that loses its sweetness as the wine develops, resulting in wine ranging from fairly dry to quite sweet.

Alsatian Wine. Alsace is the only important French region that does not have vineyard control laws; in addition, it markets its wine under German grape names: Riesling, Sylvaner, Traminer (a spicy wine), to name a few. These wines range from sharp and dry to pleasantly flowery in taste.

German Wines. All good German wines are white, light in body and excellent with fish, ham and pork. The labels are confusing if you are unaccustomed to the language. However, the names of the town, district and vineyard are clearly noted on the center of the label. The Rheingau district produces Germany's finest wines: Schloss Johannisberger and Schloss Vollrads Steinberger.

Moselle. This wine, considered the most delicate of all white wines and sometimes almost in the sparkling class, comes from vineyards around the Moselle River and carries the names of the producing towns or villages. Names to look for: Zeltingers, Josephshofer, Bernkastelers and Piesporter. Saar wines are similar to Moselle but lighter and are usually consumed as festive or holiday drinks.

Italian White Wines. These wines are widely produced for home consumption. They range from dry to sweet, and there is even a white Chianti, which is winning friends among travelers there. Two of the oddest and best-known names outside Italy are Est! Est! Est! and Lachrima Christi.

Champagne. One of the great wines of the world, champagne is versatile and can be served any time anywhere, with many combinations of foods. The champagne vineyards are north of Burgundy and east of Paris, and in the strict French sense champagne can be produced only

there. The making of the wine is a long delicate process involving 2 fermentations; at the second fermentation, a sugar syrup is added to the bottle to sweeten it. The label describes the degree of sweetness; Brut has less than 1 percent sugar; Extra Sec has less than 2 percent; Sec has 3–5 percent; Demi-Sec and Doux have 8 percent and 10 percent respectively. Champagne is a blend of wines; therefore it is known by makers' brand names.

Dessert or Sweet Wines

Asti Spumanti is a sweet sparkling wine from Italy. Tokay is an unusual dessert wine from

Hungary; it is very famous and quite sweet. Among white Bordeaux, Château d'Yquem is the most famous of the sauternes and Barsac district wines. Others are Château la Tour-Blanche and Château Climens. These wines are sweet or medium-sweet and make their appearance with rich pastries and elegant desserts of *haute cuisine.*

Canadian Wines

Wine-making is a comparatively new but very progressive industry in Canada. Vintners have made use of modern processing methods along with centuries-old lore to produce some interesting wines. Indeed, the quality is such that Canadian wines have won awards in international competition—a notable achievement for the champagnes, white table wines and the vermouths produced from Niagara grapes in southern Ontario.

A connoisseur of wines would never dream of comparing our own Canadian wines with famous European wines. As one notable retorted, "That is somewhat like comparing apples and oranges." Our climatic condition, type of soil and grape varieties all combine to produce distinctively different flavors of wines. Taste them without comparison in mind, and you will agree they should share a special area in your wine cellar, to be enjoyed often.

There are 5 general types of Canadian wines: appetizers, red table wines, white table wines, dessert wines and sparkling wines. Appetizer types include sherry, vermouths and wine cocktails. Claret, Burgundy and Chianti types make up the red table wines. White table wines can be extra dry or Riesling-type or medium dry like sauterne. Port and Tokay wine types are dessert wines. Champagne and sparkling Burgundy fill the need for sparkling wines.

Australian, South African and Portuguese Wines

With excellent climates for growing wine grapes, these countries produce large quantities of good wines, ranging from sherry type to dessert varieties. The rosés of Portugal and South Africa range from dry to lightly sweetened. Some still reds from South Africa and Australia are tart, and others medium. All wines from these areas are modestly priced—a fact that accounts for much of their popularity.

COOKING WITH WINES

Discover what a touch of wine can do for soups, ragoûts, meat sauces, fish dishes or the dessert course. But remember, introduce it only once in a menu, and add cautiously.

A wine of any dependable quality may be used, as long as the flavor is compatible with dish and menu. A good general rule is to use the wine that you intend to serve with the meal.

When a specific wine is called for in a recipe, it is wise to use that type. Otherwise there may be a clash of flavors. Generally speaking, white wines are used in preparing white meats, fish and poultry, for the practical reason that red wines tend to discolor the food. There are exceptions, however, notably in the case of coq au vin, in which the goal is both to darken and flavor with red wine.

In Cooked or Uncooked Dishes

Even such simple dishes as creamed chicken or a quickly heated canned soup take well to wine. The nutritional values remain undisturbed —indeed, the alcoholic content of wine or spirits is dissipated by heat, and only the flavor remains. When such ingredients are added to uncooked dishes, as in cut-up raw fruits for dessert, they retain their full strength, of course, and should not overpower the foods. Add a small measure at a time, and check by tasting before going further.

Dregs from long-opened bottles should be tasted before being incorporated with any foodstuff. If there is noticeable deterioration or souring, avoid using; let the turning process continue until you have vinegar, which may add a flavorsome note to *French Dressing*. Always strain off sediment before adding wine to any dish for the table.

The following suggestions for flavoring familiar dishes are grouped according to the type of wine or spirit that you may have handy for such touches.

Sherry. Add to taste to beef broths or soups; any dark, thick soup or sauce; beef and kidney stew; ragoûts of beef and mushrooms. For desserts, add to *Custard Sauce*, whipped cream and hot sweet sauces. Sherry may be substituted for brandy to moisten and mellow fruitcake.

Dry White Wines. Add sparingly to canned consommé; use to flavor fish dishes during cooking; baste over lamb, goose, duck or veal during cooking, or add to gravies or sauces; Substitute for vinegar in salad dressings or for cold vegetable hors d'oeuvres.

Dry Red Wines. These wines are highly compatible with beef stews and variety meats such as liver and kidney. Use to marinate and baste pork or duck; add to savory fruit sauces (raisin, for example) to accompany meats; substitute for vinegar in *French Dressing* for tossed green salad.

Sweet Wines. Beat small jar of red currant jelly into a little port wine; serve with cold fowl. Before adding to desserts, test wine's sweetness; rich dessert wines often eliminate the need for sugar in desserts. Many fruits, raw or cooked, are enhanced with a little wine. Add sauterne to cut-up fresh fruits; chill before serving. Leftover chilled champagne is a delicious touch on fresh fruit cup or melon balls, seedless grapes and peaches. For a quick but elegant dessert, put drained cooked prunes into a serving dish; cover with drained, quartered canned pears; top with hulled strawberries. Pour over just enough port wine to impregnate fruit with sweetness and flavor, and serve cold.

Spirits and Liqueurs. Rum, brandy and the various cordials are those chiefly used in fine cookery. The first 2 are much prized for their flaming qualities in sweet specialties; all these types can bring gourmet flavoring touches to fine desserts—ice creams, rich cakes, frosting, fillings, hot or cold sauces, cooked or raw fruits, fritters and many more. Use sparingly and, especially with liqueurs, adjust sugar content carefully.

Liver in Red Wine Sauce

3 tablespoons butter or margarine
1/4 pound mushrooms, sliced (about 1 1/4 cups)
1 pound baby beef liver, sliced thin
1/4 cup dry red wine
1 teaspoon chopped parsley
1 teaspoon lemon juice
Salt and pepper to taste
Onion salt to taste (optional)

Melt butter or margarine in frying pan over low heat; add mushrooms and cook lightly. Remove mushrooms and keep hot. Turn heat higher, and add liver slices to pan; brown thoroughly on both sides. Reduce heat to simmer. Add mushrooms, wine, parsley and lemon juice. Cover pan, and cook slowly for 10 minutes. More wine may be needed during cooking. Season with salt, pepper and onion salt just before serving, preferably over hot rice, with unthickened pan sauce poured over. Serves 4.

Wine Barbecue Sauce

1/2 cup red wine
1/2 cup salad oil
2 tablespoons white-wine vinegar
1 clove garlic
1 medium onion, finely chopped
(approximately 1/2 cup)
2 teaspoons salt
1/2 teaspoon pepper
1/4 teaspoon thyme
1/4 teaspoon marjoram
Few grains cayenne

Mix all ingredients in bowl, stirring until salt is dissolved. If wine is very dry, add a little sugar. Use uncooked sauce as marinade over chops, spareribs or cut-up chicken, or baste meat while it cooks. Makes 1 cup.

Note: This sauce will be at its best if made the day before using, in which case remove and discard garlic clove after preparing.

Chafing-dish Beef (Fondue Bourguignonne)

    4 pounds sirloin steak, 1–1 1/2 inches thick
    1 cup dry red wine
       Large lettuce leaves
       Salad oil
    6 hot and savory sauces

Trim fat, and cut steak into 1–1 1/2-inch cubes. Allow about 1/2 pound per person. Pour wine over cubes, and let stand at least 1 hour. Drain. Arrange the required number of cubes for 1 serving on lettuce leaves on each individual plate, and set 2 forks at each plate. About 15 minutes before summoning your guests to the table, heat 2–3 inches salad oil in a deep fondu pan or chafing dish. Let come to 360°F. or hot enough to brown 1-inch cube of stale bread in 1 minute. Each guest spears meat cube with fork and fries it in hot fat to desired degree—rare, medium or well done. He then dips it in 1 of the sauces. First fork is set aside for second turn at chafing dish; second fork at each plate is used for eating.

Note: A deep electric frying pan may be used with about 1 inch hot oil in the bottom.

Horseradish Cream

Combine 1/2 cup drained prepared horseradish and 1/2 cup sour cream, adding dry mustard, salt, pepper and sugar to taste.

Chutney-Curry Sauce

Combine 1/2 cup chutney, 1 tablespoon soy sauce, 1 tablespoon chopped onion and 1 teaspoon curry powder.

Hot Tomato Sauce

Simmer together 5 minutes 1 (7-ounce) can tomato sauce, 1/2 cup marinade from beef, 2 crushed garlic cloves, 3 broken chili peppers and 1 teaspoon dark steak sauce.

Savory Tartar Sauce

Combine 3/4 cup *Tartar Sauce*, 1/4 cup each finely chopped green pepper and onion and 2 tablespoons lemon juice.

Pickle Sauce

Blend 3/4 cup mustard-pickle relish with 1/4 cup chopped olives, 1 tablespoon chili sauce and 1 teaspoon dry mustard.

Desserts Flambés

One of the most memorable specialties of *haute cuisine* is the flaming dessert—for example, the world-famous *Crêpes Suzette*. The purpose of setting fire to a prepared dish is to add flavor, plus glamor and excitement, just before serving to guests who have watched the whole procedure. There are, of course, certain classic recipes for

meats, calling for blazing during specific stages of the cooking process. This blazing is usually done in the kitchen, although brochettes and kebabs are sometimes brought to the table on flaming swords or skewers. In this case, a ball of absorbent cotton, placed on the end of the skewer, is saturated with warm spirits and ignited

The word "flambé" in culinary parlance describes any food enveloped in flame from spirits of high alcoholic content. Cognac, rum, vodka and even whiskey are used, although the first 2 are most frequently employed with desserts.

It is advisable to rehearse privately before attempting a flambé display for guests. It is also desirable to have all necessary equipment and food assembled on serving table or cart, well removed from drafts, curtains and other possible hazards. A chafing dish, heat-proof platter or individual dishes may be chosen for the job; avoid delicate china, as it will almost certainly crack from the heat of the flame.

Allow 2–4 ounces spirits for recipe designed to serve 6, or follow specific directions in recipe. The safest way to warm spirits is in a glass placed in hot water. Spirits may be heated in a small pan over direct heat, but this method is dangerous. When ready to ignite, pour warm spirits around edges of food, and set aflame. For dramatic effect, lower room's lights just before igniting.

Pudding Flambé

Any hot steamed or baked pudding of reasonably firm texture may be set aflame. Turn pudding onto heat-proof platter. Cut hole about 1 inch deep and 1 inch across in top; fill with warm brandy, and pour additional 1/4 cup brandy over surface of pudding. Ignite small reservoir of spirits, and flame will spread rapidly.

Café Brûlot

The simplest version of flaming coffee is made as follows: Fill a coffee cup 2/3 full with very hot black coffee. Add 1 tablespoon warmed brandy. Do not stir. Place 1 sugar cube on teaspoon, and fill spoon with more warmed brandy. Hold spoon over filled cup, set match to brandy and sugar, lower into coffee and stir until flame burns out.

Coffee Soufflé

        18 ladyfingers or strips of sponge cake
         2 envelopes plain gelatine
       1/2 cup cold water
         8 squares semisweet chocolate
     2 1/4 cups light cream
         6 eggs, separated
       1/4 cup sugar
         2 teaspoons vanilla extract
       1/2 teaspoon salt
       1/4 cup coffee liqueur
         1 teaspoon instant coffee powder
     2 1/2 cups heavy cream, stiffly beaten
       1/4 cup sugar
            Whipped-cream rosettes
            Slivered almonds
         1 recipe *Toasted Almond Sauce*

Butter inside of 7- or 8-inch soufflé dish. Line closely with ladyfingers, standing upright. Tie collar of greased parchment or double-thickness waxed paper around outside of soufflé dish, allowing it to stand 3 inches above rim of dish. Soften gelatine in cold water. Melt chocolate in top of double boiler, and add light cream. Stir occasionally until hot and smoothly blended. Combine egg yolks and 1/4 cup sugar, and stir

into chocolate mixture. Turn heat low, and stir until chocolate custard is thick and smooth. Remove from heat, and add vanilla and salt. Combine liqueur with instant coffee, and add to chocolate custard. Add softened gelatine. Stir until gelatine dissolves. Chill in refrigerator until mixture begins to thicken to consistency of thick white sauce. Fold in whipped cream. Beat egg whites until stiff but glossy, and beat in 1/4 cup sugar. Fold chocolate cream into egg whites, and pour into soufflé dish. Chill several hours. Garnish with whipped-cream rosettes and slivered almonds. Remove collar from soufflé dish, and serve with toasted almond sauce. Serves 10–12.

Note: This dessert is just as good if made the day before serving.

Toasted Almond Sauce

       1/2 cup slivered blanched almonds
       1/2 cup butter or margarine
       3/4 cup dark brown sugar, firmly packed
         1 cup light cream
            Pinch salt
         2 egg yolks, slightly beaten
       1/4 cup brandy

Sauté almonds in butter or margarine in top of double boiler, taking care not to burn butter. Stir in sugar, and place pan over hot water. Add cream and salt; heat, stirring, until sugar melts. Combine egg yolks with 2 tablespoons brandy; add to pan, and stir until thickened. Turn heat very low, and keep sauce hot until time to serve. At serving time, pour sauce into serving dish, and flame by warming 2 tablespoons brandy, setting it alight and pouring it over surface. Or sauce may be served icy cold, diluted with 1–2 tablespoons cream.

Cherries Jubilee

         3 cups canned Bing cherries and juice
         1 teaspoon arrowroot or cornstarch
         1 tablespoon cold water
       1/3 cup brandy or kirsch
         1 quart vanilla ice cream

Drain cherry juice into blazer pan of chafing dish (or use upper part of double boiler). Bring to boil over direct heat, and simmer until volume is reduced to about 2/3. Dissolve arrowroot in cold water, and quickly stir into hot juice. Cook a few minutes longer. Add cherries, and set pan over hot water to let cherries warm. Pour brandy into center; warm without stirring. Have ice cream ready in individual heat-proof serving dishes. Set sauce ablaze, and spoon immediately over ice cream. Serves 6–8.

Kirsch is generally used; brandy is equally applicable.

Note: This dessert is just as good if made the day before serving.

Flaming Apricot Omelets

6 eggs
2 tablespoons cream
2 teaspoons sugar
1/2 teaspoon salt
3 tablespoons butter or margarine
1/2 cup apricot jam
1/2 cup whipped cream
2–3 tablespoons orange juice
1 tablespoon grated orange rind
3 tablespoons sugar
2 tablespoons rum
2 tablespoons kirsch

Beat eggs with 2 tablespoons cream, 2 teaspoons sugar and salt until fully blended. Heat individual omelet pan or small frying pan, and melt 1/2 teaspoon butter or margarine until it foams. Spoon in 3 tablespoons egg mixture. Brown on one side, turn and cook lightly on other. Remove to baking sheet to cool. Repeat until mixture is used up. When ready to serve, combine jam and whipped cream, and spread on omelets. Roll up, and arrange in chafing dish or other heat-proof server. Sprinkle with orange juice and rind, and dust generously with 3 tablespoons sugar. Warm rum and kirsch; pour over omelets, and set aflame. Serves 6.

Note: If apricot jam is lumpy with fruit pieces, sieve; then measure required amount. For this delicate dessert, the omelets are usually made in the kitchen, allowed to cool, and set alight at the table.

Bananas in Rum

3 tablespoons butter or margarine
4 firm bananas peeled and halved crosswise, then lengthwise
2 tablespoons brown sugar
1 teaspoon lemon juice
1/4 cup rum, warmed

Melt butter or margarine in blazer pan of chafing dish over direct heat; or use heavy skillet on stove. Put in bananas. Turn heat to medium high. As bananas soften, sprinkle slices with a little brown sugar and a drop or two of lemon juice. Turn once, sprinkle other side with sugar and juice and cook until soft but not mushy. When ready to serve, turn down heat, pour in warmed rum and set alight. Serves 4.

Crêpes Suzette

5 lumps sugar
1 orange with peel
1 lemon with peel
1 1/2 cups orange juice
3 tablespoons unsalted butter
1 recipe *Plain* or *Dessert Crêpes*
3–4 tablespoons brandy, warmed

Rub each sugar lump over outside of orange and lemon peels to extract flavor and color. Put sugar into blazer pan of chafing dish over direct low heat. Crush lumps, add orange juice and sim-

mer gently 1 minute. Add butter, and blend. Fold each pancake twice to make triangular shape and put in to heat; turn frequently to absorb sauce. When ready to serve, pour in warmed brandy. Set alight. When high flames die down, serve crêpes, spooning sauce over. Serves 4 generously. Rum, Grand Marnier or orange curaçao may be used in place of brandy.

Note: Bring ingredients, chafing dish, and warm dessert plates to table, and prepare sauce and flame before your guests.

A WORLD OF CHEESES

Crumbly or smooth, dark-veined or white as snow, stone-hard as Parmesan or soft and velvety as Brie, rare and costly or plain everyday fare.

Basically cheese is made from the milk of cows, sheep, goats, buffalo, yaks, even reindeer and camels. The milk is coagulated or curdled, either naturally by souring or by the addition of rennet or lactic acid; this process results in separation of curds from whey. The curds, or solids, are then ripened by the action of molds or bacteria to develop characteristic flavors of cheeses. This description, of course, oversimplifies the whole science of cheesemaking.

The world offers some 500 varieties of cheese from 18 basic cheese families and volumes could be written on the subject.

The Aristocrats

Roquefort, Gorgonzola, Stilton and blue (bleu) are world-famous and can be considered the champagnes of cheeses. They are characterized by their sharp, piquant flavor and the blue-green veins marbling their creamy, crumbly interiors. They are primarily dessert cheeses and have their maximum appeal served with crisp slices of fresh pears or apples. They also enhance salads and salad dressings and have a place of honor on cheese trays.

Roquefort is probably France's most famous cheese. By French government ruling, only the product of the Roquefort town area in the Department of Aveyron can use the name. Sheep's milk is used exclusively, and an added feature is the incorporation of bread-crumb powder that has been allowed to develop a greenish mold. Originally the cheese was made by shepherds and aged in local caves; it is now produced in cheese factories under carefully controlled conditions but still goes to the same caves for ripening.

Gorgonzola is produced in the Lombardy region of Italy from cow's milk. When exported it usually has a thin clay-like coating on the surface and is sometimes packed in wicker containers.

Stilton is England's contribution to the blue-blooded cheeses. Made from cow's milk, with cream added for extra richness, it is frequently exported in earthenware jars.

Blue (bleu) cheese, made from cow's milk by a process similar to that for Roquefort, probably originated in France but has been produced in all parts of Europe for hundreds of years.

Danish blue is very well known in America.

Also rated high among the aristocratic cheeses is *Camembert* from France. It has a comparatively strong flavor and aroma. A soft cow's milk cheese, ripened with a yellow, almost fluid, interior, it is one of the more complicated types to produce. Camembert is usually shipped before ripening has been completed, but if it is held too long in warehouse or store, it may develop a thickened crust around a runny center and a strong scent of ammonia, which signify definite over-ripeness; the cheese should be discarded. Good Camembert requires several hours at room temperature before serving, in order to attain the desired mellowness and softness of texture. By all means refrigerate after purchase, but keep in least cold part of box. Serve Camembert as the leading member of a dessert grouping of crackers and fruit, with coffee or wine.

Brie has a history several centuries longer than that of Camembert; both are of the same cheese family. There are many French regional names for Brie, but the cheese remains the same: smooth in texture, finer than Camembert, more delicately flavored and always with a reddish crust.

Limburger, originally developed in Belgium, has an almost overpowering aroma and generally dominant personality. This cheese goes with strong fare; dark bread, spicy meat and beer. The texture is soft, and, although the flavor is definite, it is less pungent than the smell would suggest.

Liederkranz is a United States creation to meet the need for a mild version of Limburger.

Famous Types the World Over

Among the pedigreed cheeses beloved of the gourmet are the smooth, semisoft varieties known generally as Trappist, referring to the order of monks who produce fine cheese in various parts of the world. *Oka* from Quebec belongs to this group and enjoys great popularity. *Port salut* hails from the Trappist abbey in France and is undoubtedly the most famous, with its richly mild, soft-textured, pale yellow body. Served as a dessert cheese, it has an affinity with fine port.

Muenster (Münster) is a mild, semisoft cheese, generally used for sandwiches. In its native Germany it is sharp and highly flavored, as the ripening or curing period is long.

Brick, similar to Muenster, but a native American cheese, is so named because of its shape and the fact that bricks were originally used to hold down the presses. It is creamy in color, with tiny irregular holes; its flavor ranges from mild to nippy yet with a sweet pungent taste. It is used mostly for sandwiches and buffet service.

Cheddar is the most versatile of all cheeses and Canada's most famous. Fine Cheddar possesses flavors and textures to suit all tastes; it is splendid both in cooked dishes and plain. Cheddar is also known as store cheese.

From the same family come *Monterey Jack* cheese of California and *sage green*, a green mottled cheese, which is produced by adding green sage leaves to the curd.

Dutch and Swiss Specialties

Two exclusively Dutch cheeses, *Edam* and *Gouda*, are distinguished by their spherical and cannonball shapes and sometimes by a bright red wax coating. Edam is a firm, mild-flavored cheese, whereas Gouda is softer in texture with more tang; sometimes they are smoked or spiced. Baby Goudas weighing less than 1 pound each are popular and make an attractive and colorful addition to the cheese tray.

Leyden, another Netherlander, is sometimes known as Delft or Hobbe. It is a firm cheese with dark brown surface, spiced with caraway, cumin and cloves.

Emmanthaler (Swiss) cheese from Switzerland has a delicate, nutty, sweet flavor, firm texture, and distinctive eyes or holes. This cheese is very versatile—garnish for salads, thickly sliced for hot or cold sandwiches, in cooked dishes and on dessert trays.

A slightly sharper version is *Gruyère* cheese, with smaller eyes and firmer texture. At the beginning of the twentieth century, Switzerland developed a method of processing Gruyère. Triangular-shaped pieces weighing about 1 ounce each are wrapped in foil and packed in round boxes of a dozen wedges. It is an excellent dessert cheese with a mild, sweetish flavor.

Sapsago is historically one of the oldest cheeses, tracing its origin back to the thirteenth century in the Canton of Glarus, Switerland. It is a very hard, dry, green cheese, with a pleasant aroma and nippy flavor. The green color comes from dried aromatic clover grown especially for this use. Sapsago is available in grated form chiefly and is used in cooked dishes.

Italian Cheeses

Italy provides us with two wonderful cooking cheeses—Parmesan and Romano. Many a main dish would be dull without either or both of these lively cheeses.

Parmesan is an extremely hard or "grana" cheese, which cannot be cut but is broken and then grated. It is in this form that it is so widely used in cooked dishes, hot breads, appetizers, soups and sauces. Parmesan, with its sharp distinctive flavor and good keeping qualities, is the gourmet cook's ally.

Romano is very similar to Parmesan but a little softer in texture. In Italy it can be purchased freshly made and used much as we use Cheddar; on this side of the Atlantic we can also buy it grated. The flavor ranges from mild to sharp, which may be attributable to the different milk used—from cows, sheep or goats—and is designated respectively as Vacchino Romano, Pecorino Romano and Caprino Romano.

Provolone, another Italian cheese used principally in cooking, has recently become very popular. It is the cheese of so many shapes that you see hanging by cords or ropes in Italian grocery stores or specialty food shops. Flavors vary from mild to nippy, and the cheese is usually smoked and well salted. It is hard cheese, sometimes with a rather stringy texture.

Caciocavallo (literally, horse-cheese) is a member of the same family. It is unsmoked, white and beet-shaped, and is generally grated. Two others are *Scarmorze* and *Mozzarella*, both pizza cheeses used fresh or just slightly ripened.

Bel Paese is the brand name of a Brie-type cheese made in Italy and esteemed by discriminating palates in every country. A soft, sweet, light-textured cheese with delicate flavor, it is a superb dessert choice.

Scandinavian cheeses

Noekkelost, a popular Norwegian cheese similar to Leyden, differing only in the proportions of spices used.

Mysöst, one of the most famous and ancient cheeses, is made from whey obtained in production of other cheese. It is light brown in color, with buttery texture and mild sweet flavor. It is a good cheese for sandwiches and buffet service.

Gammelost, from Norway, is made from skimmed sour milk. A semihard cheese, well aged with a sharp flavor, it is ideal for the informal buffet.

Gjetost (or primost), also from Norway, is a dark chocolate-brown cheese with a sweet flavor.

Cream and Cottage Cheeses

Cottage cheese is the simplest cheese of all and has been a familiar food in Canada since early pioneer days. This uncured cheese from cow's milk is produced in many countries and under various names, such as pot cheese, Dutch cheese and smearcase. In North America, cottage cheese is made commercially in large quantities from pasteurized skim milk, sometimes with cream added. It is a very nutritious cheese and versatile, with many uses in cooked dishes, salads, sandwiches and appetizers.

Cream cheese is a soft uncured cheese made from pasteurized milk with cream added: it is coagulated with lactic acid rather than with rennet. It has a very smooth texture and rich mild flavor, both in plain form and when packaged with such other flavors as pineapple and pimento.

Neufchâtel is a soft rennet cheese made from cow's milk in much the same manner as cream cheese but with higher moisture and lower fat content. Other names for this type of cheese are petit carré, petit suisse, Malakoff and bondon. It is used mostly as a dessert and sandwich cheese and is available plain or with added flavor ingredients.

Ricotta cheese, like Scandinavian Mysöst, is made from whey obtained in production of other cheeses. This Italian cheese usually has whole or skim milk added and is soft in texture, with a mild flavor. It is frequently used in lasagna and ravioli dishes and in its native land is served also in sweet mixtures.

Care of Cheese

To care for a wheel of Cheddar or a block of Swiss cheese, cut off a wedge or slice sufficient to fill your needs for 1 week, and rewrap cheese. If cheese has come wrapped in a cheesecloth bandage, replace loose part carefully over cut surface, and seal with melted paraffin wax. If cheese is rindless (today many Cheddars and Swiss cheeses are ripened within their own transparent paper and do not develop rinds), seal cut surface with melted paraffin wax, and replace original wrappings as much as possible. In both cases, overwrap cheese with heavy foil. Refrigerate or store in cool, dry place.

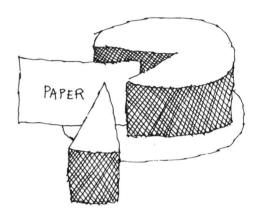

Cheese Service at Table

Contemporary cheese trays come in all shapes and sizes with beautiful wood finishes. They are ideal for buffet service, as well as for appetizer and dessert cheese assortments. Arrangement of cheese, crackers and fruit can be highly individual and very colorful. For small dinner parties or family groups, it is fun to use the old-fashioned slope-topped cheese dish, either heir-

loom or modern; 1 or 2 generous wedges can be accommodated under the cover. An antique cheese bell is difficult to find, but if you can acquire one, it will be a lifetime conversation piece. (Wedgwood made some beautiful cheese bells in the traditional blue or green jasper ware.)

For cheese-tray service a variety of shapes and portions makes for both eye appeal and convenience. Leave Gouda or Edam cheese whole, with thin slice of top removed and a cheese scoop (like a melon-ball cutter) nearby for guests to help themselves. Crumbly, well-ripened or wined Cheddar is best left in the piece; younger, springier types may be neatly sliced and grouped. If Swiss cheese is sliced, let portions be at least 1/4 inch thick. Individually wrapped wedges of Gruyère, Roquefort and the like are served in their packaging, but larger wedges can be unwrapped. Semisoft cheeses such as Liederkranz, Bel Paese and Limburger seem to develop their best textures when cut in individual portions just after removing from refrigerator and then allowed to mellow at room temperature. For some cheeses a wire cutter with a sturdy handle is more useful than a knife.

When serving cheese, crackers and fruit for dessert, provide individual plates and fruit knives; pass serving dish with butter curls or pats. Occasionally, instead of whole fresh fruits, offer unpeeled apple or pear wedges dipped in lemon juice to prevent discoloration.

Here are some good dessert combinations:

* Roquefort and blue, accompanied by chilled pineapple slices, fresh or canned, garnished with whole strawberries; pass the sugar caster.
* Swiss cheese with tangerine or fresh mandarin orange sections and muscat raisins on stems.
* Gorgonzola and Camembert, with lemon-dipped apple and pear wedges.
* Liederkranz and Bel Paese, with Tokay grapes and fresh apricots.

Nice additions for any of the above: nuts in shells or salted; French bread and Melba toast, and sweet or salted butter.

FRENCH GOURMET COOKING

The French make use of everything edible and extract the maximum flavor and palatability. The choicest fresh fruits and vegetables, eggs, butter and cream, wines and seasonings are treasured. The farm style (*paysan*), as with poached eggs in broth; regional, representing local variations in such famous dishes as *Cassoulet*; careful family cookery (*de la famille*); and finally, *haute cuisine*, the chef's professional artistry.

The French have their own mealtime habits. Breakfast is simple: rich tender *Croissants* or *Brioches*, sweet butter, perhaps a confiture such as cherry jam and *Cafe au Lait* or hot chocolate. Déjeuner, the leisurely noon meal, may consist of 4—5 courses: hors d'oeuvres, main course, vegetable or salad, cheese and raw or cooked fruit. Dinner follows the same ample pattern but with a seafood or fruit appetizer in place of hors d'oeuvres, clear soup added and, instead of fruit, a rich dessert. Very few of the foodstuffs used in French cookery are not available here—the absentees include fresh truffles, certain mushrooms and some types of fish. Cooking techniques here differ only when we omit or rush certain steps in preparing a dish. Time itself may be considered the basic ingredient that the French cook willingly adds to all her projects. In order that texture and flavor may be at their best, she chops, sifts, beats, simmers and skims. Some of these essential processes can be accomplished with greater ease and speed in the Canadian kitchen, with its electric grinders, blenders and mixers. But French recipes are not designed for saving labor.

Hors d'oeuvres Variés

In France, hors d'oeuvres are strictly knife-and-fork fare, eaten at table, and bear no resemblance to the canapés and finger foods that are sometimes called hors d'oeuvres in North America. A French hostess will serve 2 or more varieties, depending upon the occasion, choosing from cooked and raw vegetables, smoked and cooked fish and delicacies sold in *charcuteries* or pork shops.

Hors d'oeuvres may be hot or cold, but often they are cooked and chilled leftovers. They are served in small amounts or as the main course at a summer luncheon, in which case as many as 6 or 7 hors d'oeuvre specialties may be set out, each in its separate dish, on a buffet table. Accompany them with a pleasant wine, and follow them with a light dessert, perhaps fruit.

Here are some items that frequently appear in French hors d'oeuvres:

Anchovy fillets	Asparagus vinaigrette
Smoked salmon	Jellied eggs
Smoked oysters	Salade de boeuf
Stuffed eggs	Smoked turkey
Pâtés	Green and black olives
Shrimp in *Herbed*	Sliced tomatoes
Mayonnaise	Pickled beets
Mushrooms à la	Sliced sausage, all kinds
Grecque	

In selecting hors d'oeuvres, always balance foods and flavors against the rest of the meal. If hot fish is to follow, omit fish; if pork is the main course, avoid sausage and rich pâtés at the start. If the menu is lengthy and grand, open the meal with just 1 appropriate appetizer, possibly caviar on toast rounds with lemon garnish.

Vegetables à la Grecque

Briefly, vegetables are cooked in consommé or bouillon until just tender; broth is boiled down and poured over solids, which are then put to chill and glaze. Suitable vegetables are tiny white onions, celery, zucchini, eggplant, cauliflower, frozen artichokes, baby carrots and so on. Cut large vegetables into generous bite-size pieces; parboil less tender items such as cauliflower 3–5 minutes before cooking à la grecque.

Mushrooms à la Grecque

    2 1/2 cups water or stock
      1/4 cup salad oil or olive oil
      1/4 cup lemon juice
        2 tablespoons chopped green onion
      1/2 teaspoon salt
           Bouquet garni
        1 pound mushrooms

Place all ingredients except mushrooms in 2-quart saucepan; cover, and simmer 10 minutes. Prepare mushrooms; quarter large ones, and leave

small ones whole. Add to liquid and simmer, covered, until just tender, about 10 minutes. Remove mushrooms with slotted spoon. Reduce liquid by boiling rapidly until 1/2 the quantity remains. Strain over mushrooms; then cool, cover and refrigerate. Mushrooms will keep 3–4 days. Sprinkle with chopped fresh herbs before serving.

Bouquet Garni: Tie in a cheesecloth bag, 6 sprigs parsley, 6 peppercorns and 2 sprigs celery leaves.

Vegetables Vinaigrette

Marinate raw or cooked vegetables in basic *French Dressing* or *Vinaigrette Sauce* 1 hour before serving. To cook vegetables, simmer until just tender in well-seasoned water or broth. Cool before marinating; drain off excess liquid before serving. Cooked vegetables suitable for serving with vinaigrette sauce are asparagus, cauliflower, celery, sliced or tiny beets, leeks, and green beans. Raw vegetables include tomatoes, cucumbers and thinly sliced mushrooms.

Vinaigrette Sauce

        1 cup salad or olive oil
      1/4 cup wine vinegar or lemon juice
        1 teaspoon finely chopped green onions or 2 table-
           spoons chopped chives, tarragon or basil
           Salt and pepper to taste

Combine all ingredients in jar or bottle; cover tightly, and shake well. Use as needed for hors d'oeuvres.

Salade de Boeuf Vinaigrette (Beef Salad Vinaigrette)

           Cold boiled or roast beef, thinly sliced
           Thinly sliced mild onion rings
           Vinaigrette Sauce
           Lettuce, tomatoes

Marinate beef and onion rings in separate bowls in sauce about 1 hour before serving. Drain off sauce, and arrange beef slices alternately with onion rings on lettuce-covered platter. Garnish with tomato wedges.

Quiche Lorraine

```
    6  slices side bacon, cut in halves
    2  cups cream or rich milk
       Plain Pastry or Flaky Pastry for single-crust pie
    6  ounces Swiss or Gruyère cheese, sliced thin
    4  eggs
  1/2  teaspoon salt
       Dash freshly ground black pepper
       Dash cayenne
       Dash nutmeg
```

Broil bacon, but do not crisp it. Heat cream slowly. Line a 9-inch pie plate with pastry, and make firm double rim. Arrange bacon in pastry; cover with cheese slices. Make custard mixture by beating eggs with a whisk and adding hot cream and seasonings. Pour into pastry-lined pan. Bake in 450°F. oven about 10 minutes; reduce heat as quickly as possible to 300°F., and continue baking until custard is firm, about 1/2 hour, or until silver knife inserted in center comes out clean.

Note: *Quiche Lorraine* is a savory cheese custard pie served warm, in small segments for the hors d'oeuvre course or in larger wedges as the luncheon entree.

It is quite uncomplicated to make, as this recipe shows. The Swiss cheese may be grated and added to the custard filling. For extra flavor, scatter a little chopped raw onion over pastry bottom before filling.

Potato Croquettes in Bacon

```
  3–4  cups seasoned mashed potatoes
  1/4  cup finely chopped pimento
    1  tablespoon grated Parmesan cheese
       Dash cayenne
    1  egg, beaten
    1  cup dry bread crumbs
    8  bacon slices, halved lengthwise
       Toothpicks
```

Combine first 5 ingredients, and form into 16 small log-shaped croquettes. Roll in crumbs; then wrap in bacon slices. Secure with toothpicks. Place in shallow pan; refrigerate until needed. Bake at 425°–450°F. until bacon is crisp, turning once during baking. Allow 15–20 minutes. Serve with steak. Serves 8.

VARIATION:

* Omit pimento. Roll croquettes in mixture of slivered almonds and Parmesan cheese, rather than bread crumbs.

Potatoes Anna

```
    6  peeled potatoes, sliced as thin as possible
  1/2  teaspoon salt
       Pepper to taste
  1/2  cup soft butter or margarine
```

Soak potatoes in ice-cold water, drain and dry well on towel. Season with salt and pepper. Butter round baking dish (6-cup size), and line bottom and sides with potato slices. Arrange layer of potatoes, and dot liberally with butter or margarine; repeat until all potatoes are used up, saving some butter or margarine for top. Bake at 425°F. 45–50 minutes or until potatoes are tender when tested with toothpick. To serve, invert baking dish on hot platter so that potatoes slip out in molded form, brown and crusty. Garnish with parsley. Serves 6.

Vegetables French Style

The French prepare certain vegetables with a blanching technique similar to that used in our home-freezing procedures; they cook them quickly in plenty of boiling water until just tender, drain and add butter or sauce. If vegetable is to be served hours later it is immediately cooled under running water, dried and refrigerated until needed. The following recipe is a good example of this prepare-ahead technique.

Haricots Verts à la Mornay (Green Beans with Mornay Sauce)

> 2 pounds fresh young green beans
> 4–5 quarts boiling water, plus 1 tablespoon salt
> 3 tablespoons butter or margarine
> 3 tablespoons flour
> 1 cup warm milk
> 1 cup warm chicken stock
> 4 tablespoons grated Parmesan cheese
> 3 tablespoons Swiss cheese, cut in small pieces
> 1 tablespoon butter or margarine

Wash, string and cut beans diagonally into slices about 1 1/2 inches long. Drop into rapidly boiling salted water, and return water quickly to boil. Cook uncovered at slow boil 10–15 minutes or until just tender (depends on maturity of vegetable). Drain in colander, and cool immediately under running water to stop further cooking. Spread beans on towel to dry, place in bowl and refrigerate until needed. When ready to serve, melt butter or margarine, blend in flour over low heat, remove from heat and briskly stir in milk and stock. Cook over medium heat, stirring constantly, until mixture comes to boil. Remove, and blend in 1/2 the Parmesan cheese plus Swiss cheese until melted. Season to taste. Cover bottom of serving casserole with 1/3 the sauce, top with green beans and pour remaining sauce over all. Sprinkle with remaining Parmesan cheese, and dot with butter or margarine. Bake at 350°F. 30 minutes or until thoroughly heated and the top lightly browned. Serves 6–8.

Moules Marinière (Steamed Mussels)

> 48 fresh mussels in shells
> 1 1/2 cups dry white wine
> 4 finely chopped shallots or 2 tablespoons finely chopped onion
> 1/4 teaspoon pepper
> 1/4 teaspoon powdered thyme
> 3 tablespoons chopped parsley
> 3 tablespoons butter or margarine
> 1 tablespoon flour

Brush and scrape mussel shells thoroughly, and wash in several waters. Place in deep kettle; add wine, shallots, pepper and thyme. Cover, bring to boil and simmer 6–8 minutes until shells open. Remove mussels in shells to large deep casserole or serving platter, and cover with hot, damp towel to keep warm. Carefully strain broth through cheesecloth into another saucepan to remove sand. Bring to boil, and reduce to 1/2 the quantity. Add parsley. Blend butter or margarine and flour, and add to broth, stirring constantly until thickened. Taste for seasoning, and pour sauce over mussels. Serve immediately in soup dishes, and use cocktail forks to eat mussels directly from shells.

Coquilles St. Jacques (Scallops St. Jacques)

> 1 cup dry white wine
> 2 tablespoons chopped green onion or shallots
> 1/4 teaspoon salt
> 1/2 bay leaf
> 1 pound scallops, washed
> 1/2 pound sliced fresh mushrooms
> Water
> 3 tablespoons soft butter or margarine
> 3 tablespoons flour
> 1 cup milk
> 2 egg yolks
> 1/4 cup cream
> 1/2 cup grated Swiss or Gruyère cheese
> Salt and pepper to taste
> Parmesan cheese, grated

In the top part of a double boiler simmer together wine, onion, salt and bay leaf 5 minutes. Add scallops and mushrooms, and sufficient water just to cover ingredients. Cover, and simmer 5 minutes. Remove scallops and mushrooms; return liquid to boiling and rapidly reduce to 1 cup. Stir in a smooth mixture of butter and flour. When thick, add the milk, and whisk and cook until smooth. Place over boiling water and stir in the egg yolks beaten with the cream. Add 1/4 cup grated Swiss cheese, and season to taste; thin, if necessary, with cream. Slice or quarter cooked scallops, and add to 2/3 the sauce along with mushrooms. Divide mixture among 6 buttered scallop shells or ramekins; cover with remaining sauce, and sprinkle with grated Parmesan cheese.

Refrigerate if serving later. To heat, place shells in 350°F. oven, and bake 15 minutes. Place directly under broiler to brown lightly. Serves 6.

Note: Almost every visitor to Paris has sampled this elegant scallop-and-mushroom concoction. Ideally you should use scallop shells, which are generally available; otherwise, earthenware or oven-glass ramekins of up to 1/2-cup capacity will do nicely. Serve as a main course for luncheon or as a starter at an important dinner. Accompany with chilled dry white wine.

Bouillabaisse

> 2 (1 1/2-pound) lobsters, cut in pieces
> 5–6 pounds firm fish fillets (cod, haddock, etc.)
> 1 pound tomatoes, peeled and diced
> 2 onions, chopped
> 3–4 cloves garlic, minced
> 1 tablespoon salt
>   Bouquet garni
> 1 teaspoon saffron
> 1/2 cup olive oil
> 1/2 cup dry white wine
>   Water or fish stock
> 1 dozen raw oysters in shells
> 1 dozen clams in shells

Start bouillabaisse about 1/2 hour before serving; cooking time will depend on size and thickness of fish pieces. Use large kettle. In it place lobster, fish fillets (cut in pieces), tomatoes, onions, garlic and seasonings. Pour in olive oil, wine and sufficient water to cover. Bring rapidly to boil, uncovered, and boil over high heat about 10 minutes. Reduce heat; add well-scrubbed oysters and clams, and cover. Simmer another 10 minutes. Serve in large soup plates with generous portions of solids surrounded by bouillon, or lift fish onto separate dish; garnish with lemon. Correct seasoning of soup. Ladle over slices of toasted French bread spread with garlic butter. Serves 8–10.

Note: In Marseilles, its city of origin, this famous dish, which is both soup and fish course (and was originally created to use up miscellaneous leftovers from the daily catch), is a standby in modest homes and expensive restaurants alike. And even in Canada bouillabaisse is often a subject of argument concerning choice of ingredients and seasonings. Although the Mediterranean fish are not available to the cook, she will discover that bouillabaisse is one of the most flexible French dishes for adaptation, as long as a few general principles are observed.

The basis is firm-fleshed fish; in Marseilles they use 5 or 6 kinds in a single kettle of bouillabaisse, but 1 or 2 can do nicely. Shellfish in variety are added, and it is good to follow suit if you want to achieve the true gourmet touch. Olive oil and saffron are "musts" in any version; on the other hand, tomatoes are a matter of personal taste. In Marseilles it is customary to allow 1 pound fish fillets per serving. You may reduce the quantity if desired.

If the fish has been filleted to your order at a fish counter bring home trimmings, and prepare a rich fish stock to use in place of water.

Poulet Marengo (Chicken Marengo)

> 2 (2 1/2–3-pound) broiling chickens
> 2 tablespoons butter or margarine
> 2 tablespoons salad oil or olive oil
> 2 tablespoons flour
> 1 cup chicken broth or bouillon
> 2 cups peeled chopped fresh tomatoes
> 1/2 cup dry white wine
> 1 jigger brandy
>   Bouquet garni
> 1 clove garlic, crushed
> 1/2 teaspoon thyme
> 1/2 teaspoon salt
>   Pepper to taste
> 12 small peeled silver-skin onions
> 1/2 pound fresh mushrooms, sliced
> 3 tablespoons butter or margarine, melted
> 2 tablespoons chopped parsley

Wash and dry chickens. Cut into serving pieces. Heat 2 tablespoons butter or margarine and oil in large heavy frying pan. Fry a few pieces of chicken at a time until golden brown. Arrange chicken in a Dutch oven or covered baking pan. Add flour to pan juice (if latter is too brown, clean pan, and start fresh with 2 tablespoons butter or margarine). Blend, and cook 2 minutes. Add broth, tomatoes, wine, brandy, bouquet garni and garlic. Blend thoroughly, and bring to boil, stirring constantly. Let simmer 5 minutes; add thyme, salt and pepper. Pour over chicken. Add onions and spoon sauce over all ingredients. Cover tightly, and bake in a 350°F. oven about 50 minutes. In the meantime, cook mushrooms in melted butter or margarine over low heat about 10 minutes, and set aside. When chicken is tender, remove to a hot platter. Discard bouquet garni. Add mushroom mixture to chicken sauce, and bring to boil. If too thin, let simmer gently to evaporate; if too thick, add a little chicken broth or wine. Taste for final seasoning. Pour sauce over chicken, and sprinkle with parsley. Serves 6–8.

Note: This classic dish is named after one of Napoleon's famous victories. There are many versions of this recipe—some with olives, some with red wine, some banning butter entirely. Usually they are all very good. The traditional finishing touch is to ring the platter alternately with small fried eggs on fried bread squares (remove crusts from bread before frying in butter) and cooked large shrimp or lobster tails. Use pullet eggs if available.

Coq au Vin

1 (2 1/2–3-pound) frying chicken
3 strips bacon, diced
3 tablespoons butter
1 small onion, chopped
1 clove garlic, crushed
1/4 cup brandy or cognac (optional)
1/4 pound mushrooms, sliced
6 small white onions, peeled
Bouquet garni
1 cup Burgundy
2 cups chicken broth
3 tablespoons flour

Cut chicken into serving pieces. Prepare chicken broth from wing tips, neck, backbone and giblets. Sauté bacon in a large skillet, and when clear, add butter, onion and garlic. Stir-fry 2 minutes. Add chicken pieces, a few at a time, and fry slowly until both sides are golden. When all pieces have been browned, pour off the fat and reserve. Warm the brandy, and pour over the chicken. Set alight, and when flames subside, lift chicken into a casserole and cover. Bake at 350°F. 35 minutes. Meanwhile, add 1 tablespoon reserved fat, mushrooms and onions to the skillet. Stir-fry about 5 minutes. Add bouquet garni, Burgundy and chicken broth. Cover, and simmer 20 minutes. Uncover, and remove the bouquet. Stir in a smooth mixture of 3 tablespoons of the reserved fat and 3 tablespoons flour. Cook until thickened. Season to taste with salt and pepper. Pour over the chicken, and cover. Continue baking for 25 minutes or until chicken is very tender. Sprinkle with chopped parsley, and serve from casserole with cooked saffron rice, noodles and Duchess potatoes. Serves 4–5.

Bouquet Garni: In a square of cheesecloth tie 1/2 bay leaf, 1/4 teaspoon dry thyme and a few sprigs of celery and parsley. Use 1 or 2 sprigs of fresh thyme or savory in place of dried thyme, if available.

Cassoulet

2 1/2 pounds loin of pork roast
1/2 teaspoon salt
1/4 teaspoon sage
1/4 teaspoon pepper
5 cups dry white beans
2 teaspoons salt
3 quarts boiling water
1/2 pound lean salt pork
Cold water
1 sliced onion
Bouquet garni
1–1 1/4 pounds whole Polish or garlic sausages, in casings
2 pounds boned shoulder of lamb
2–3 tablespoons hot pork drippings
2 cups chopped onions
3 cups beef stock or bouillon
1 1/2 cups dry white wine
1 (7 1/2-ounce) can tomato sauce
2 bay leaves
1/2 teaspoon thyme
2 cups coarse bread crumbs
1/2 cup chopped parsley
Butter or margarine

Trim loin of excess fat, and rub with salt, sage and pepper. Roast at 325°F. until meat thermometer registers 185°F., slightly under 2 hours. Set aside to cool; then refrigerate. Reserve juices. Add beans and salt to boiling water, and cook 2 minutes after water returns to boil. Remove from heat, and let stand 1 hour. Freshen salt pork by covering with cold water and bringing to boil. Drain. Add salt pork, sliced onions, bouquet garni to soaked beans. Bring to boil; skim, and simmer uncovered 1 1/2 hours. Add sausages for last 1/2 hour of cooking. Remove sausages and salt pork, and set aside. Discard bouquet garni. Cut lamb in 2-inch cubes. Brown on all sides in 2–3 tablespoons drippings. Remove meat; lower heat, and brown chopped onions lightly. Return meat to pan with stock, wine, tomato sauce and herbs. Cover, and simmer 1 hour. Remove meat, and skim off fat. To lamb liquid add skimmed cooking juices saved from roast pork.

Slice salt pork. Skin sausages, and slice thickly. Drain beans, reserving liquid. Cut roast pork into 1 1/2-inch chunks. Arrange in an 8-quart casserole layers of beans, lamb, roast pork, salt pork and sausage slices, respectively. Repeat layers, ending with beans. Pour meat juices over all, and add enough bean liquid to come to top of last layer. Spread top with bread crumbs and parsley, and dot with butter. Cover. Refrigerate if you wish to serve another day. When ready to serve, leave cover on. If casserole has been refrigerated, place in 375°F. oven 25 minutes; reduce heat to 325°F., and continue baking 1 hour. Remove cover, and bake 30 minutes longer. Add more bean liquid if mixture seems dry. If it hasn't been refrigerated, bake covered 1 hour and uncovered 1/2 hour at 325°F. Serve from casserole. Serves 10–12.

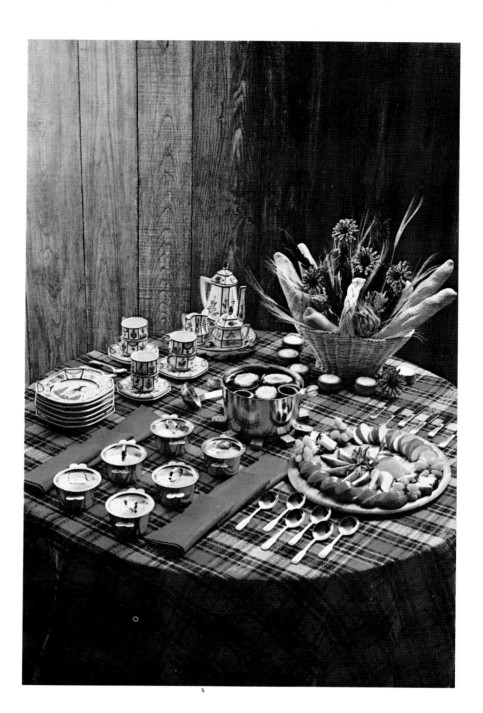

A French table.
CREDIT: *Henry Sandbank.*

Cheese and fruit platter.
CREDIT: *Henry Sandbank.*

French Onion Soup (pp. 17-18).
CREDIT: *Henry Sandbank.*

Stuffed Peppers (p. 49) and Cabbage Rolls (p. 50).
CREDIT: *Dennis Hall.*

Bouquet Garni: Tie, in a square of cheese-cloth, 6 sprigs parsley, 3 short stalks celery, 3 whole cloves, 2 cloves garlic, cut, 1/2 teaspoon thyme and 2 bay leaves.

Note: *Cassoulet* is a renowned French regional dish. The ingredients vary greatly from section to section. In some recipes bundles of pork rind and pieces of duck or goose are included. It is rich country fare and requires long cooking and a fair amount of patience. Spread the making of this dish over 2 days, well in advance of when needed for a weekend crowd.

Beef Tenderloin in Pastry

> 4-pound piece beef tenderloin
> 1/4 cup Burgundy wine
> 1/4 cup garlic-flavored *French Dressing*
> Frozen defrosted or homemade puff pastry
> 1 pimento, diced

Trim excess fat from meat. Set meat on platter. Combine wine and dressing, and pour over meat. Marinate in refrigerator 4 hours, turning meat several times. Thaw cream puff dough according to package directions, about 1 hour before serving time. Drain meat, saving marinade. Brush off excess marinade from meat with pastry brush, or pat with paper towel, and place meat in a shallow pan. If there is a thin end, pin it under with toothpicks to make tenderloin uniformly thick. Roll pastry out into oblong. Wrap around meat completely, clamping edges and sealing firmly. Bake at 450°F. 40 minutes or until meat thermometer barely registers 140°F. Decorate top with diced pimento. Serve on heated platter with *Potato Croquettes* and garnishes. Serves 6—8.

Note: One of the elegant diversions of *haute cuisine* is the introduction in the early courses of a meal of such tender, flaky pastry as tartlets holding richly sauced mushrooms or seafood for hot hors d'oeuvres, or a handsomely decorated wrap for a whole baked ham or a length of the tenderest of all beef, the fillet of tenderloin.

The Great French Sauces

There are several basic sauces in French cuisine, notably white, brown, butter sauces, salad dressings and dessert sauces. The first are French forms of our familiar white or cream sauces. *Béchamel Sauce* uses equal parts sweet butter and flour blended together; hot milk is added, and the mixture is cooked slowly over boiling water. Sometimes 1 or 2 beaten egg yolks are stirred in after the pan is removed from the heat to enrich the sauce. *Velouté Sauce* begins in the same way, but hot chicken or veal stock replaces milk. Various seasonings are used in either case, but always with discretion. *Brown Sauce* is basically gravy

but with these differences: Chopped onion and carrot are first browned in fat; liquid—boiling water or stock—always includes tomato puree, and sometimes browned meat bones are added for color. Brown sauce takes readily to many seasoning touches, and a dash of dry sherry is often added before serving.

Other famous sauces, perhaps more temptingly unfamiliar to Canadian tables, include the following:

Béarnaise Sauce

> 2 shallots or 4 green onions, chopped
> 2–3 sprigs parsley
> 1/2 teaspoon dried tarragon
> 1/2 teaspoon dried chervil
> 1/3 cup vinegar
> 1/2 cup dry white wine or vermouth
> 4 egg yolks
> 6 tablespoons soft butter
> 1 tablespoon chopped parsley
> 1 teaspoon chopped tarragon (optional)
> Pinch cayenne
> Salt and pepper to taste

Simmer the first 6 ingredients together for 3—4 minutes or until reduced to about 1/2 cup. Strain through a fine sieve. Beat egg yolks in the top part of a double boiler, and beat in the strained liquid. Set over hot, not boiling, water. Be sure water does not touch bottom of pan. Whisk mixture until as thick and smooth as heavy cream. Remove from over hot water, and whisk in the butter, 1 tablespoon at a time. Set pan again over hot water, and add remaining ingredients. Serve warm, not hot. Makes 1—1 1/4 cups.

Note: If sauce is too thick, whisk in 1—2 tablespoons warm broth, meat glaze or water.

Sauce Américaine

> 3 cups cooked fresh or canned tomatoes
> 2 teaspoons sugar
> 2 tablespoons butter or margarine
> 1 tablespoon olive oil
> 2 tablespoons chopped onion
> 1 tablespoon chopped parsley
> 1 clove garlic
> Pinch chervil
> 2 tablespoons brandy

Simmer tomatoes with sugar, uncovered, over low heat until most juice has cooked down. Meantime heat butter or margarine and oil in saucepan; add onion, parsley, garlic and chervil. Cook gently until onion is clear. Press tomatoes through sieve; then add to onion mixture, increase heat, and simmer 15 minutes. Remove garlic, and stir in brandy. Heat thoroughly, but do not boil. Makes about 1 1/2—2 cups.

Note: This sauce is a good accompaniment for meats, fish, eggs and green or dried beans.

Sauce Mornay

    1 cup hot *Béchamel Sauce* or white sauce
    2 egg yolks, slightly beaten
    1 tablespoon butter or margarine
    1 tablespoon grated Parmesan cheese

Stir a little béchamel sauce into egg yolks. Return to saucepan; add butter or margarine and cheese, and heat less than 1 minute over hot water. Serve with fish or vegetables such as broccoli or asparagus. Serves 4.

Salade Française (Tossed Green Salad)

Salad flavor depends upon quality of young fresh greens, well washed, well dried and thoroughly chilled. Select greens in season, and wash with cold water as soon as possible after purchasing. Dry by twirling in salad basket, or pat with towel. Store, loosely packed, in covered container or plastic bags in refrigerator. Romaine, escarole, endive, watercress, spinach and head, Bibb or Boston lettuce are excellent for salads.

To make salad, tear greens into bite-size pieces, allowing 1–1 1/4 cups greens per serving. You can rub wooden salad bowl with cut clove of garlic. Add greens; then place such other suitable ingredients as diced tomatoes, snipped chives, sliced radishes and anchovy fillets on top. Cover, and refrigerate until ready to serve; add dressing and toss lightly.

Herb Dressing

    6 tablespoons salad or olive oil
    2 tablespoons wine vinegar or lemon juice
    1 teaspoon herbs (any variety)
    3/4–1 teaspoon salt
    1/4 teaspoon dry mustard
    1/8 teaspoon freshly ground pepper

Mix all ingredients together well, pour over salad and toss.

Note: This recipe makes enough dressing for 6 cups greens.

French Desserts

Croquembouche

The Croquembouche pyramid must be assembled quickly, or the syrup used to assemble it will harden and have to be reheated. Therefore be sure to read the recipe through thoroughly before starting to work. And have all ingredients near the stove, so you dip the puffs and set them in place quickly.

    1 cup dark corn syrup
    5 dozen small cream puffs, custard-filled (from the
        bakery or homemade)
    1/4 cup icing sugar

Cut a 9-inch circle from cardboard, and cover with foil. Set the circle on a board near the stove. Have the filled cream puffs close at hand.

Cook corn syrup in the top of a double boiler over high heat until candy thermometer reaches hard-ball stage (240°F.), or until a small drop of the syrup forms a soft ball in cold water. Set pan over boiling water.

To build the pyramid, lightly dip the bottom of a cream puff in syrup and set on the edge of the circle, syrup-side down. Repeat with 9 more puffs, forming a ring. For the second row, arrange a slightly smaller ring of puffs over the spaces between the puffs of the first row, inclining the second row slightly inward. Fill in the center with more puffs, for support.

Continue building the pyramid in decreasing rings (see color illustration), filling in center for support as needed, until you have completed 8 rows.

Top with one puff. Sprinkle the Croquembouche lightly with 1/4 cup sifted icing sugar. To serve, lift one or two puffs at a time off the pyramid, starting from the top. Serves 8–10.

Note: If syrup begins to thicken before pyramid is completed, add a teaspoon of water and stir over low heat. Do not let syrup burn.

Paris-Brest Dessert

1 recipe *Basic Cream Puff Pastry*
2 cups heavy cream plus 2 tablespoons sugar, or 2
  envelopes whipped topping mix
2 tablespoons sherry
1/4 cup light corn syrup
2 tablespoons green pistachio nuts, coarsely chopped
  pecans or walnuts, or slivered almonds

Preheat oven to 400°F. Cut a 9-inch circle out of heavy brown paper, place it in center of cookie sheet and oil it lightly. Make *Cream Puff Pastry*. Place pastry around edge of paper circle in heaping tablespoons, leaving a 4-inch circle bare in center. Smooth pastry with a spatula, making an even ring. Bake 50 minutes at 400°F.

Remove ring from oven. Cut off top with sharp knife. Scoop out any soft dough. Turn oven off, place ring back in, and let it stand in oven with door slightly open for 15 minutes. Remove from oven and cool on wire rack away from drafts.

Whip heavy cream with sugar until stiff (or prepare two packages whipped-topping mix, following package directions). Fold in sherry. Fill bottom of pastry ring with whipped cream or topping. Replace top of ring and brush lightly with corn syrup. Sprinkle with green pistachio nuts, coarsely chopped pecans or walnuts, or slivered almonds. Serves 6—8.

Pots de Mousseline au Chocolat

6 ounces semisweet chocolate
1/4 cup hot strong coffee
1 tablespoon butter
3 eggs, separated
1/2 teaspoon vanilla
1 tablespoon brandy or rum
1 tablespoon fine white sugar
1/2 cup whipping cream

Combine chocolate, coffee and butter in the top part of a double boiler. Heat and stir until chocolate is completely melted and mixture is very smooth. Remove from over the hot water, and whisk in egg yolks, 1 at a time. Whisk in vanilla and brandy, and cool to room temperature. Meanwhile, beat egg whites until shiny peaks form, and beat in the sugar. Whisk about

1/4 of the meringue into the chocolate mixture; then gently fold chocolate into remaining meringue. Pour into 7 or 8 small soufflé cups, pots or stemware glasses, and chill several hours or

overnight. To serve, whip cream until stiff, and swirl about 2 tablespoons on each dessert, or top each with a rosette of cream pressed through a pastry bag. Makes 8 5-ounce servings.

Crème Caramel (Caramel Custard)

1/2 cup sugar
2 tablespoons water
2 1/2 cups light cream
3 eggs
3 egg yolks
1/2 cup sugar
Pinch salt
1 teaspoon vanilla extract

Melt 1/2 cup sugar in a heavy frying pan over moderate heat. When carmelized to a bright golden color, add the water and bring to a boil, stirring until sugar syrup has melted. Pour into a 4—5-cup deep ring mold or pudding pan, and tilt mold carefully to cover sides as well as bottom with syrup. Plunge mold, almost to its edge, in basin of cold water several seconds to cool and set glaze (do not let any cold water splash into mold). Set aside while you make custard. Scald cream. Beat eggs and egg yolks until well blended; beat in 1/2 cup sugar until mixture is light and foamy. Add salt and, gradually, scalded cream. Add vanilla, and strain into caramel-lined mold. Set in shallow pan of hot water, and bake at 325°F.

about 1 1/4 hours or until silver knife inserted in center comes out clean. Let custard cool; then refrigerate. At serving time, run a knife around custard, separating it from mold. Invert round platter on top, hold in place firmly and with one quick motion reverse plate and mold to remove custard in neat mound. Serves 4—6.

Note: This delicate custard, made with extra egg yolks, is always served unmolded to display its rich caramel glaze.

Soufflé au Grand Marnier

      4 or 5 ladyfingers
            Grand Marnier liqueur
         1 tablespoon butter or margarine
         1 tablespoon flour
      1/2 cup 10% cream
            Few drops vanilla extract
         6 egg yolks
         5 tablespoons sugar
         6 egg whites
      1/8 teaspoon salt
         1 teaspoon sugar
         1 teaspoon Grand Marnier

Crush ladyfingers and sprinkle with sufficient Grand Marnier to moisten; set aside. Melt butter or margarine in saucepan, stir in flour, remove from heat and add cream gradually, stirring to keep smooth. Cook, stirring constantly, over low heat until mixture thickens. Add vanilla extract sparingly. Beat egg yolks with 3 tablespoons sugar. Add to almond mixture, and return to low heat barely 1 minute, stirring continuously. Let mixture cool slightly. Beat egg whites and salt together until stiff but moist. Beat in remaining 2 tablespoons sugar to keep them glossy and prevent drying. Fold whites gradually into warm yolk mixture, using up-and-down folding motion to incorporate thoroughly without destroying frothiness. Have ready a buttered straight-sided soufflé dish (1 1/2-quart size). Sprinkle 1 teaspoon sugar and 1 teaspoon Grand Marnier over bottom. Turn in 1/2 the mixture, cover with soaked ladyfinger crumbs and add remaining mixture. Run rubber spatula around outer edge of soufflé, separating it slightly from side of dish; smooth top. If mixture more than half fills your dish, prevent spilling and encourage rising by tying doubled strip of buttered waxed paper as a "collar" around top edge. Bake in medium-hot oven, 375°F. about 20—25 minutes or until soufflé has risen and is delicately browned. Remove collar before serving. Serve immediately. Serves 4—5.

Note: There is only one problem with a hot soufflé: it will not wait. When full-blown and beautifully, crisply golden on top, it must be sped from oven to table for immediate serving; otherwise it will crumple into ruin. A dessert soufflé is admittedly one of the most challenging to achieve, because it goes in oven at the time the main course is being served and should be puffed and perfect in about 20 minutes. This soufflé is often served without sauce; sometimes it is accompanied by a sauce dish containing chilled boiled custard folded into an equal amount of whipped cream and lightly flavored with liqueur.

Riz à l'Impératrice (Empress Rice)

         1 cup finely diced mixed candied fruits (cherries, citrus peel, pineapple)
         3 tablespoons brandy or kirsch
      1/2 cup rice
      1/2 cup cold water
   1 1/4 cups cold milk
         1 envelope plain gelatine
      1/4 cup cold water
         4 egg yolks
      1/2 cup sugar
      1/8 teaspoon salt
      3/4 cup hot milk
      1/2 teaspoon vanilla extract
         1 cup heavy cream, whipped to soft peaks

Marinate 3/4 cup fruits in brandy. Cover rice with 1/2 cup cold water, bring to boil and simmer 2 minutes. Drain, and rinse with cold water. Return rice to saucepan, add cold milk, bring to simmer, cover and cook until rice is very tender (about 30 minutes) and milk absorbed. Do not stir. Soften gelatine in 1/4 cup cold water. Combine egg yolks with sugar and salt in top of double boiler, add hot milk gradually and place over hot water, stirring constantly until custard is thick and smooth. Remove from heat, and stir in gelatine and vanilla until gelatine is dissolved. Strain into cooked rice, blend thoroughly and chill until mixture begins to set. Carefully fold in marinated candied fruits and whipped cream. Put into lightly oiled 6-cup ring mold or cylindrical fancy shape. Chill at least 4 hours, preferably overnight. To unmold, run knife around upper edge of mold; invert serving plate on top, and reverse plate and mold together. Wring out tea towel in boiling water, and apply to mold, pressing over all surfaces. Repeat several times, and contents will drop free from mold. Decorate with remaining candied fruits cut in strips, circles, petals and diamond shapes. Pour *Strawberry Sauce* around shape, or serve separately. Serves 8—10.

Strawberry Sauce

         1 cup strawberry jam
         1 cup red currant jelly
         3 tablespoons brandy or kirsch

Melt jam and jelly over medium heat. Add brandy, blend thoroughly and simmer 1 minute. Put through sieve, allow to cool, beat until smooth and serve.

EXOTIC DISHES FROM SPAIN

Characterized by spices, nuts, fruits, fish, rice, olive oil and the renowned sherries.

The cuisine of Spain has its vivid, exciting moments, like the landscape and the life of the country itself. It is less complex and far-ranging than the *haute cuisine* of France; indeed in Spain almost any traditional dish can be undertaken with confidence. Spanish cuisine has a heritage from the long Moorish occupation of the country centuries ago. Spices, especially saffron, cinnamon, nutmeg and mace, are popular. Rice appears on almost every menu, whether in soups, chilled salads, hot accompaniments to entrees or final sweet courses. Nuts, particularly almonds, add interest to many dishes. Chocolate (introduced after the conquest of Mexico) is of great importance and is even used in grated unsweetened form over certain baked fish or meats. Many varieties of fish and shellfish from the Atlantic and Mediterranean coasts, plus freshwater trout and other inland fish, are used abundantly; but the popular dried salt cod continues to be imported from Canada's Atlantic shores. Olives, olive oil and the country's inimitable sherries play a leading role in fine cookery. Fruits of all kinds, notably melons, grapes, and members of the citrus family, make the grand finale of the Spanish gourmet's 10 P.M. dinner a highly colorful affair.

Sopa de Almendras (Almond Soup)

    2 tablespoons butter or margarine
    1 tablespoon grated onion
    2 tablespoons flour
    6 cups chicken broth
    2 cups blanched almonds
    1/8 teaspoon nutmeg
    1/8 teaspoon mace
      Salt and pepper to taste
    2/3 cup heavy cream
    2 egg yolks, lightly beaten
    1 teaspoon grated lemon rind
      Watercress leaves

Melt butter or margarine, add onion and cook gently 1 minute only. Blend in flour, stir in chicken broth and cook until smooth and boiling. Grind almonds to paste in electric blender or fine nut chopper. Combine with seasonings, and stir into soup. Cover, and simmer 15 minutes. Combine cream, egg yolks and lemon rind. Pour slowly into soup, stirring constantly. Heat, but do not boil. Serve garnished with leaves of watercress. Serves 6–8.

Cacerola de Conejo (Rabbit Casserole)

    2–3 tablespoons flour
        Salt and pepper to taste
      1 tender young rabbit, cut up
    4–5 tablespoons salad oil
      1 medium onion, chopped (approximately 1/2 cup)
      1 clove garlic, crushed
    1/2 cup dry white wine
    1/2 cup (approximately) consommé or pale meat or
        vegetable stock
      3 sweet red peppers, cut in strips
      1 eggplant, peeled, thinly sliced and quartered
      3 cups hot boiled rice or 4–5 slices fried or toasted
        bread
        Ripe olives
        Parsley

Combine flour with salt and pepper. Dredge rabbit pieces in mixture. Heat 3–4 tablespoons salad oil in skillet; add meat, onion and garlic. Turn meat to color all sides light golden. Set oven at 350°F., and scrape contents of pan into heated casserole. Rinse pan with the wine, and pour over the rabbit. Add just enough consommé to keep meat moist. Cover casserole, and bake about 1 1/2 hours or until rabbit is perfectly tender. About 15 minutes before serving, heat remaining 1–2 tablespoons salad oil (or butter or margarine) in skillet; add pepper strips and eggplant. Fry gently about 10 minutes or until tender. Arrange cooked rabbit pieces on shallow bed of well-drained rice; strain casserole sauce, and pour over; garnish platter with hot vegetables, ripe olives and sprigs of parsley. Serves 4–5.

Note: Rabbit, either wild or commercially produced, is frequently featured as the main course. This recipe is an adaptation of the Spanish version; the sweet peppers, and eggplant are typical accompaniments. The casserole sauce may be thickened, if desired, with 1 tablespoon flour blended with same amount cold water; stir into casserole 10 minutes before taking from oven.

Truchas al Jerez al Horno (Baked Trout with Sherry)

      6 brook trout
    1/2 lemon
        Salt and pepper to taste
      3 tablespoons salad oil or olive oil
      1 cup day-old bread crumbs
      3 tablespoons chopped parsley
      1 clove garlic, crushed
        Juice of 1/2 lemon
    1/3 cup dry sherry

Rub fish with lemon, and season with salt and pepper. Heat oil, and add bread crumbs, parsley and garlic. Spread 1/2 the mixture on bottom of shallow baking pan. Arrange fish on top, cover with remaining crumbs and sprinkle with lemon juice. Bake in preheated 400°F. oven 5 minutes. Add sherry, and bake 10 minutes longer, basting occasionally, until fish flakes. Serves 6.

Pastel de Pescado (Fish Pie)

    3 tablespoons olive oil
  1/2 cup almonds, blanched and halved or coarsely
        chopped
    2 medium onions, chopped (approximately 1 cup)
    1 clove garlic, crushed
    2 cups peeled and chopped raw tomatoes, or 2
        cups drained canned tomatoes
    1 bay leaf
      Salt and pepper
    4 fillets white-fleshed fish, cut in pieces
    3 cups seasoned mashed potatoes

Heat oil in saucepan, add almonds and let color on all sides. Lift out with slotted spoon, leaving oil. In same pan gently sauté onions and garlic until transparent but not brown. Add tomatoes and bay leaf, and simmer about 10 minutes, stirring occasionally. Season to taste with salt and pepper. Heat oven to 400°F. Butter casserole, and lay fish fillets over the bottom. Place in oven, and bake 5 minutes, or until fish loses raw look. Add 1 1/2 cups hot tomato mixture, then almonds, and cover with mashed potatoes. Bake 20–25 minutes; if necessary brown topping briefly under broiler. Simmer remaining hot tomato mixture to reduce slightly, and serve over casserole. Serves 4–5.

Note: Any tender white-meat fish, either fresh or frozen (partially thawed), may be used. Additional browned almonds may be scattered over potato topping.

Paella (Rice, Chicken and Seafood Casserole)

    3 tablespoons olive oil
    8 small pieces frying chicken
  1/2 pound sliced fresh mushrooms (approximately
        2 1/2 cups)
  1/4 cup sliced green onions
  1/4 cup diced green or sweet red pepper
    2 cloves garlic, sliced
    1 teaspoon salt
    1 cup long-grain rice
3 1/2 cups chicken broth
    1 broken bay leaf
  1/2 teaspoon saffron
  1/4 teaspoon chili pepper seeds
    1 (12-ounce) package frozen peas
    1 (12-ounce) package frozen shrimp or about 1
        pound fresh shrimp, peeled
    2 tablespoons butter or margarine
    1 (10 1/2-ounce) can clams
      Sautéed mushrooms
      Sliced stuffed olives
      Hard-cooked eggs

Heat oil in large heavy pan, and lightly brown chicken. Add mushrooms, onions, pepper, garlic and salt. Cover, and turn heat low. Cook slowly 15 minutes. Sprinkle rice around chicken pieces, and add next 4 ingredients. Cover, and bring to boil. Reduce heat, and cook 20 minutes or until rice is tender. Add peas, cover and cook 8 minutes. In another pan sauté shrimp in butter or margarine for 5 minutes; then pile on top rice mixture, or stir through. Add clams. Reheat thoroughly. Garnish with sautéed mushrooms, sliced stuffed olives and hard-cooked eggs. Serves 8.

Note: *Paella* is the specialty dish of Valencia, the name of both a city and a province on the Mediterranean, which is a constant source of the seafood featured in this and many other recipes. The name "paella" actually refers to the large, shallow pan, round or oval but always with side handles, in which this dish is prepared and served. *Paella* is a colorful production with many ingredients. It is too much effort for only 2 or 3 people, but it is ideal party fare. This recipe can be extended in the Spanish way by adding other suitable ingredients rather than increasing the base. Spicy smoked sausage is sometimes sautéed separately in 3 or 4 slices and then mixed in. 1 (9-ounce) package partially thawed frozen artichokes may be added at the same time as the peas. Cut-up boiled fresh lobster meat is another extender heartily approved by the Spanish gourmet.

Churos (Spanish Fritters)

    1 cup water
  1/4 cup butter or margarine
  1/8 teaspoon salt
1 1/4 cups sifted all-purpose flour
    3 eggs
    2 teaspoons grated orange rind
      Deep oil or shortening for frying
      Sifted icing sugar

Combine water, butter and salt in a saucepan over medium heat. When butter has melted and water comes to a boil, remove from heat. Add flour all at once, and stir hard with a wooden spoon until all whiteness disappears and paste is smooth. Return to the heat, and stir until paste comes away from the sides of the pan. Remove from heat, and beat in eggs, 1 at a time, beating well after each addition, or transfer paste to a small mixer bowl and beat in the eggs, 1 at a time. Scrape sides and beaters occasionally. Stir in orange rind. Heat oil or shortening (about 4 inches deep) to 375°F. or until 1 cube of day-old bread browns in 40 seconds. Scrape paste into a pastry bag equipped with a plain round metal tip about 1/2 inch in diameter. Press out strips of paste directly into hot oil. Cut off strips about 8 inches in length close to metal tip as you press. Fry a few at a time. Fritters will puff and twist as they cook. Lift out when golden, and drain on paper towels. Keep hot in a warm oven. To serve, sprinkle with sifted icing sugar. Serves 5–6.

VARIATION:

* *Rosette Churos*: Omit orange rind. Beat 1/2 teaspoon cinnamon, allspice or nutmeg and 1 tablespoon icing sugar into the paste. Scrape

paste into a pastry bag fitted with a large metal rosette tip (the size often used for whipped cream or Duchess potatoes). Oil a cookie sheet, and press out 12 large doughnut-shape rounds of paste on the sheet. Make sure the ends overlap slightly. Diameter will be about 3 inches. Chill shapes 15 minutes in a freezer or 30 minutes in a refrigerator. Gently scrape-lift shapes into hot oil heated to 360°—375°F., allowing about 5—6 minutes total time. Drain on paper towel, and dredge with icing sugar. Makes 12.

Note: In Spain, plain churos are often served as the only accompaniment for breakfast hot chocolate. *Rosette Churos* are novel for a late evening snack with coffee or hot spiced wine or cider.

Sherry-Cream Sauce

    2 egg yolks, beaten light
    1/2 cup sugar
    2/3 cup orange juice
    2 tablespoons lemon juice
    3 tablespoons medium-dry sherry
    3/4 cup heavy cream, whipped

Combine egg yolks and sugar in top of double boiler. Blend in fruit juices, and set over hot water. Cook, stirring constantly, until sauce coats spoon. Cover, and chill. Add sherry, and fold in whipped ceam. Serve over any colorful combination of sweetened fresh, canned or frozen fruits arranged in individual dishes.

LIVELY ITALIAN CUISINE

The nation that popularized pasta and invented pizza has a robust tradition of colorful fare, and the variation in types and flavors, region by region, only adds to the excitement. Except for stock soups and slow-cooked sauces, most dishes are quickly prepared for immediate serving.

The colors of Italian foods are lively—the red sauces of the South, the Adriatic's fish soups, the green dishes of the North, the vivid shades of fresh fruits and vegetables, the frothy egg whips (sometimes added to savory liquids, sometimes beaten with wine for dessert) and the pronounced tones of the wine accompany all major meals.

To Italians the good cooking of the peninsula is known by its regional type: there are Florentine, Neapolitan, Venetian, Genoese, Roman and many other styles. The same dish may be presented to the visitor under 4 different names in many regions.

Pasta South, Rice North

Although pasta is always associated with Italian cuisine, it too is regional, belonging to the South; the rice of Piedmont is the pre-eminent grain staple of the North.

Pasta in its many shapes and sizes is produced in factories for mass distribution and by household and restaurant cooks for immediate use. The wheat-flour base is the same in all cases, but the factory product differs. It is specially dried before packaging, which accounts for the longer boiling required, in contrast to the "5 minutes" directed for homemade pasta. Depending on thickness and shape, pasta should cook to the point of tender firmness, *al dente* ("to the tooth" or chewy), in 8—25 minutes. A large pot is a must, in order to hold sufficient water and allow a rolling boil; in Italy the rule is 6 quarts water for each pound raw pasta. Gluey overcooked pasta would horrify the Italian gourmet.

The rice or "risotto" of Italy is entirely different from that of the Chinese, Arabs, and other rice-eating peoples—different in crop variety and more similar to the long-grain rice of the southern United States. It is different in cooked results as well. Only a comparatively small amount of liquid is used in its preparation; this proportion and slower cooking provide a creamy texture.

Meats and fish, accompanied by cooked or salad vegetables, are considered the ideal main courses for dinner in Italy, as elsewhere. When they are replaced by pasta or rice, served with cheese sauce, it is generally in the interests of thrift.

Cheese, Fruits, Custards

Cheese occurs at some point in almost every menu, often with fruit for dessert.

There are sweet dishes in the various regional

cuisines—fritters, sweet chestnut mixtures, custards, ices—but their range is limited compared with the great variety available in France, the British Isles and North America.

The best Italian cooking is based on generous use of fresh raw materials. The long hours or even days of preparation that French chefs put into *haute cuisine* are not the rule in Italy.

Antipasto (Italian Hors d'oeuvres)

Most mid-day meals in Italy start with a plate of appetizers regardless of whether the menu includes pasta. Plates and platters attractively arranged present many kinds of small fish, sausages, chilled raw and cooked vegetables and hot fritters. Vegetable antipasto, like French vegetable hors d'oeuvres, can be served as a main-course salad for luncheon.

Antipasto is often served as the appetizer course of an Italian dinner that does not include a salad course. Line individual plates with crisp lettuce, and top attractively with small amounts of 5 or 6 of the following:

Italian cheese
Ripe and green olives
Anchovies
Strips of green pepper
Green onions
Celery
Radishes
Sections of tomato
Hard-cooked egg
Thinly sliced salami
Prosciutto ham
Capacolla

Accompany with cruets of garlic-flavored oil and tangy red-wine vinegar.

Antipasto Buffet Platter: For help-yourself service, group antipasto ingredients attractively on large platters, and set out sliced buttered dark bread.

Note: Pepperoni, mortadella or Polish sausage may be added for heartier fare.

Soups

The soups of Italy, with such various ingredients as vegetables, spaghetti and poached ground-meat balls in well-flavored stock can be served as hearty luncheon main dishes.

Pasta in Brodo con Fegatine e Piselli (Pasta in Broth with Chicken Livers and Peas)

 3 ounces vermicelli
 1 pound fresh young green peas, shelled, or 1 (12-ounce) package frozen green peas
 6 cups hot chicken broth
 1 tablespoon butter or margarine
 10 (approximately) chicken livers, coarsely chopped

Break vermicelli into 2-inch lengths. Cook with peas in boiling salted water. Drain. Add to hot broth, and bring to boil. Reduce heat, and simmer. Melt butter or margarine, and add coarsely chopped livers. Cook and stir over low heat. Add livers and butter to broth. Taste for seasoning.

Note: Pass a dish of grated Parmesan cheese with the soup. Serves 4—6.

Brodo alle Mandorle e Funghi (Broth with Mushrooms and Almonds)

 2 tablespoons butter or margarine
 1/2 cup almonds, blanched and slivered
 1 cup sliced fresh mushrooms
 1 teaspoon chopped parsley
 1/8 teaspoon powdered oregano
 6 cups beef broth or consommé
 Salt and pepper to taste

Melt butter or margarine, add almonds and cook slowly until light yellow in color. Add mushrooms, stirring 5 minutes. Add parsley, oregano and beef broth. Season to taste with salt and pepper, and reheat. Serve immediately. Serves 4—6.

Ways with Pasta

The sauces for pasta are as distinctive and various as the Italian regions. Naples is renowned for its spicy tomato sauce. In Calabria anchovies are scattered over the pasta platter. An interesting clam-and-tomato sauce is occasionally encountered.

Neapolitan Sauce for Pasta

 1/4 cup olive oil
 1 small onion, chopped (approximately 1/4 cup)
 1 clove garlic, crushed
 1 (6-ounce) can tomato paste
 2 cups boiling water
 3 cups canned tomatoes
 1 cup red wine
 2 teaspoons salt
 1 teaspoon sugar
 1/2 teaspoon dried oregano
 1/2 teaspoon basil
 1/4 teaspoon pepper
 Few grains cayenne

Heat oil in heavy saucepan; cook onion and garlic until soft and lightly colored. Thin tomato paste with boiling water. Add tomatoes, tomato paste, wine, salt, sugar and seasonings. Bring just to boil; then reduce heat, and simmer, uncovered, at least 1 hour or until sauce has thickened. Stir frequently. If desired, put through sieve. Serve over well-drained, cooked spaghetti, macaroni shells or other pasta, and accompany with bowl of grated Parmesan cheese. Makes enough sauce for 6—8 servings.

Note: This sauce improves in flavor when made ahead and reheated.

VARIATION:

* For tomato-meat sauce, brown 1 pound ground lean beef in 2 tablespoons fat in frying pan; turn and stir vigorously to brown thoroughly over medium heat. With slotted spoon, remove meat from fat and add to sauce before cooking. Check seasonings before serving.

Fettucine all'Alfredo (Noodles Alfredo)

   1/2 pound broad noodles
      Boiling salted water
   1/2 cup soft sweet butter
   1/2 cup grated Parmesan cheese

Cook noodles in plenty of boiling salted water until just tender. Drain, and place in large heated bowl. Add butter and cheese, and using long-handled spoon and fork, toss together quickly until noodles are thoroughly coated. Serve immediately on hot plates. Serves 6.

This recipe offers probably the simplest and most excellent method for preparing pasta. The trick is to plan a suitable menu (perhaps with a big salad bowl of crisp vegetables and finely diced cooked ham or bacon bits), to have everything ready at the table and everyone waiting to sit down, and to serve without a moment's delay so that all can enjoy this fresh main dish piping hot.

Cannelloni alla Genovese (Genoese Stuffed Pasta)

   2 eggs
   2 tablespoons skim milk
1 1/2 cups sifted all-purpose flour
   1 teaspoon salt
      Boiling salted water
   3 tablespoons butter or margarine
   1/2 cup chopped onion
   1/2 cup chopped celery
   1 carrot, scraped and chopped (approximately 1/4 cup)
   1/4 cup mushrooms, chopped
   1 (14-ounce) can Italian plum tomatoes
   1/2 cup dry white wine or chicken broth
   1 teaspoon salt
   1/4 teaspoon pepper
   1/2 pound hot Italian sausages
   1 (12-ounce) package frozen chopped spinach
   1/4 cup chopped green pepper
   6 slices mozzarella or pizza cheese

Beat eggs until frothy. Add milk, flour and 1 teaspoon salt; mix with fork until dough comes together. Knead on heavily floured board until dough loses stickiness and becomes smooth. Cover, and let stand 30 minutes. Divide dough in 1/2. Roll each piece as thin (1/16 inch thick) as possible on lightly floured board to approximately 12″ x 16″. Cut into 12 4-inch squares. Drop into boiling salted water; cook just until tender. Lift out, and drain on paper towels.

Melt butter or margarine in large skillet. Add onion, celery, carrot and mushrooms; sauté until onion is golden. Stir in tomatoes, wine, 1 teaspoon salt and pepper. Cover, and simmer 1 hour.

Remove sausage meat from casings, and sauté in skillet until cooked and golden. Drain off excess fat. Add frozen spinach and peppers; cook until spinach has thawed and separated. Cool. Divide spinach mixture evenly among noodle squares. Roll up. Place seam side down, 1 layer deep, in 3-quart baking dish. Spoon tomato sauce over rolls, and top with cheese. Bake in moderate oven, 375°F. 30 minutes or until golden on top and bubbly. Serves 6.

Spaghetti Siciliani

   3 tablespoons olive or cooking oil
   1/2 cup chopped onion
   1/4 cup chopped celery
   1 clove garlic, crushed
   1 tablespoon chopped parsley
4–4 1/2 cups canned Italian plum tomatoes
   1 (6-ounce) can tomato paste
   1 teaspoon salt
   1 bay leaf
   1/2 teaspoon basil
   1/2 teaspoon oregano
   1/4 teaspoon pepper
   1/2 pound spaghetti or linguine
   1/2 cup (approximately) olive oil or cooking oil
   1 large eggplant, peeled and sliced 1/2 inch thick
   1 cup grated Parmesan cheese
   1 cup grated Romano cheese

Heat 3 tablespoons oil in skillet. Add onion, celery, garlic and parsley; sauté until onion is golden. Stir in next 7 ingredients. Cover, and simmer 1 hour. Remove bay leaf.

Cook spaghetti by package directions; drain. Heat 3 tablespoons oil in large skillet, and sauté eggplant slices, a few at a time, until golden on both sides. Add more oil to skillet as needed. Layer tomato sauce, spaghetti, eggplant and cheeses in an 8″ x 8″ x 2″ baking dish, ending with spaghetti, sauce and generous sprinkling of cheese. Bake in moderate oven, 350°F. 20–30 minutes or until brown and bubbly. Serves 6.

Gnocchi alla Romano (Gnocchi in the Roman Style)

   1/2 pound ricotta or cottage cheese
   1/2 cup sifted all-purpose flour
   1/3 cup grated Parmesan cheese
   1/4 cup of butter or margarine, melted
   3 egg yolks
   1/2 teaspoon salt
      Pinch nutmeg
      Salted water
1/4–1/2 cup butter or margarine, melted
      Grated Parmesan cheese

Press ricotta through sieve into small bowl. Add next 6 ingredients. Mix well. Spoon mixture into pastry tube or bag, fitted with large plain tip (no. 6–8). Bring large kettle of salted water to very gentle boil. Hold bag over kettle, and force contents through tube, snipping into 1-inch pieces with scissors. Work quickly. Cook gnocchi 5–7 minutes; remove with slotted spoon, and drain on paper towels. Divide gnocchi among 8 small oven-proof shells, or place in 1-quart shallow casserole. Pour 1/4–1/2 cup butter or margarine over all. Sprinkle with grated Parmesan cheese, and bake in moderate oven, 350°F. 10 minutes; then brown a few minutes under broiler. Serves 4 as main dish, 8 as side dish.

Other Italian Dishes

Scallopine Mozzarella (Veal Cutlets Mozzarella)

    1/3 cup flour
      1 teaspoon salt
    1/4 teaspoon oregano
    1/4 teaspoon thyme
    1/4 teaspoon garlic powder
      2 pounds veal cutlets
      1 egg, slightly beaten
    1/4 cup milk
      1 cup fine dry bread crumbs
    1/4 cup butter or margarine
      2 tablespoons olive oil or salad oil
      1 (7 1/2-ounce) can tomato sauce
      6 thin slices mozzarella cheese

Combine flour with seasonings. Cut meat into 6 serving pieces, and lightly coat with flour mixture. Dip meat in egg-milk mixture, then in bread crumbs. Brown on both sides in hot butter or margarine and oil. Cover bottom of large shallow greased casserole or heat-proof platter with tomato sauce. Place cutlets in single layer, and bake, covered at 350°F. 15 minutes. Cover with cheese slices, and continue baking 10 minutes or until veal is fork-tender. Brown lightly under broiler. Serves 6.

Pollo alla Cacciatore (Chicken Hunter Style)

      1 (4-pound) frying chicken, cut in serving pieces
    1/2 cup flour
      1 teaspoon salt
      3 tablespoons butter or margarine
      3 tablespoons oil
      1 cup chicken broth
      1 cup coarsely chopped peeled tomatoes, or 1 cup
          canned tomatoes
      6 small whole onions, peeled
      1 pimento, finely chopped
      1 clove garlic, cut in fine lengthwise strips
        Salt and pepper to taste
      1 cup sliced fresh mushrooms
      1 tablespoon chopped parsley

Roll chicken pieces in a mixture of flour and salt. Brown on all sides in hot butter or margarine and oil in large skillet. Add remaining ingredients, except mushrooms and parsley. Cover, and simmer slowly 1 hour. Add mushrooms and, if more moisture is needed, extra chicken broth or a little dry white wine. Cover, and cook 15 minutes longer or until chicken is very tender. Garnish with parsley. Serves 4–6.

Chicken Tetrazzini

      1 (4 1/2–5-pound) roasting chicken
      2 teaspoons salt
        Few stalks celery
      1 onion, peeled
  1 1/2 pounds mushrooms, wiped and sliced
    1/4 cup butter or margarine
      1 pound spaghetti
    1/3 cup butter or margarine
      6 tablespoons flour
      1 cup heavy cream
      3 tablespoons sherry
      2 teaspoons monosodium glutamate
        Salt and pepper to taste
    3/4 cup grated Parmesan cheese

Cut up chicken, and place in a deep saucepan with just enough water to cover. Add 2 teaspoons salt, celery and onion. Bring to boil; simmer, covered, until tender. Cool chicken in broth. Remove skin from chicken, and cut meat into bite-size pieces. Reserve broth to use in sauce. Sauté mushrooms in 1/4 cup butter or margarine until tender. Set aside. Cook spaghetti by package directions. Drain.

Melt 1/3 cup butter or margarine in a saucepan. Stir in flour. Gradually add 3 1/2 cups reserved chicken broth, well skimmed of fat, and the cream, stirring and cooking until smooth and thickened. Add sherry, monosodium glutamate, salt and pepper and 1/2 cup cheese. Simmer 5 minutes longer. Place 1/3 spaghetti in bottom of greased 4-quart casserole. Spoon 1/3 the mushrooms and 1/2 the chicken over spaghetti, topped by 1/3 the sauce. Add another 1/3 the spaghetti, the remaining mushrooms and chicken and 1/3 sauce. Top with remaining spaghetti and sauce. Sprinkle casserole with remaining cheese. Bake in a hot oven, 450°F., until brown on top, 30–40 minutes. Serves 8–10.

Piselli al Prosciutto (Green Peas and Ham)

      2 tablespoons chopped onions
      2 tablespoons butter or margarine
      1 tablespoon oil
    1/2 cup prosciutto, cooked bacon or ham, cut in strips
      1 pound fresh green peas, shelled or 2 (12-ounce)
          packages frozen peas
    1/4 cup bouillon or water
        Salt and pepper to taste
      1 tablespoon chopped parsley

Sauté onion slowly in butter or margarine and oil until transparent but not brown. Add ham and cook 3–4 minutes. Add peas, bouillon, salt and pepper; cover, and cook 10–15 minutes, stirring occasionally. Sprinkle parsley on top. Makes 4 servings.

Panettone (Italian Christmas Bread)

    2 envelopes dry yeast
1/2 cup lukewarm water
    1 teaspoon sugar
1 1/2 cups lukewarm scalded milk
    3 eggs, beaten
1/3 cup sugar
1/4 cup soft butter or margarine
1 1/2 teaspoons salt
1/4 teaspoon allspice
    2 drops yellow food coloring (optional)
    6 cups sifted all-purpose flour
1/2 cup raisins
1/2 cup chopped, mixed candied fruit
1/3 cup chopped almonds
1/3 cup chopped candied lemon peel

Dissolve yeast in 1/2 cup lukewarm water with 1 teaspoon sugar. Add milk, eggs, sugar, butter or margarine, salt, allspice and food coloring (optional). Mix well.

Gradually mix in flour. Cover with a damp cloth, and let rise 30 minutes in a warm oven.

Stir dough down. Add raisins, candied fruit, almonds and candied lemon peel. Stir until well mixed.

Spoon dough into 3 well-greased 1-pound coffee tins. Let rise. Bake for 45 minutes at 375°F. Let stand 5 minutes before removing from tins. Makes 3 cakes. Serves about 15.

FAMOUS DISHES FROM CENTRAL EUROPE

Hungarian goulash, steeped in paprika gravy; sauerbraten, Germany's hearty pot roast with sharp sweet sauce; Vienna's Esterházy steak in casserole, and a layered dessert torte.

Gulyas (Hungarian Goulash)

1/4 cup shortening or fat
    4 cups chopped onions
    2 tablespoons fat
    2 tablespoons paprika
    1 tablespoon flour
    1 teaspoon salt
    3 pounds beef chuck, cut in 1 1/2-inch squares
    2 cups meat stock
    1 cup coarsely chopped peeled tomatoes or 1 cup canned tomatoes
    Salt and pepper to taste
2/3 cup sour cream

Melt 1/4 cup shortening in Dutch oven or other heavy pot. Add onions, and cook until soft and transparent; remove from pan. Add 2 tablespoons fat. While fat is heating, combine paprika, flour and 1 teaspoon salt, and roll beef in flour mixture. Brown in hot fat. When meat is well browned, pour off the fat, and return onions and any remaining paprika mixture to pan. Add stock and tomatoes. Season with salt and pepper to taste. Cover tightly, and simmer gently 1 1/2–2 hours or until meat is very tender. Season to taste. Immediately before serving remove from heat, and stir in sour cream. Serves 6–8.

Note: Goulash is the national dish of Hungary, and the term is applied to all meats or combinations of meats cooked or stewed this way. The liberal use of paprika, without creating a "burning" taste, is one of its features. Depending upon the region, these foods may be included: sour cream, sauerkraut, spices, tomato paste or raw sliced potatoes. The flavor of *Gulyas* is improved if it is allowed to stand overnight. In this case, omit sour cream. Cool stew rapidly, uncovered, and refrigerate. Remove hardened fat before reheating; stir in sour cream just before serving.

Sauerbraten (German Pot Roast)

    2 cups water
    1 cup vinegar
    2 carrots, sliced
1/4 cup chopped onion
    1 stalk celery, chopped
    4 peppercorns
    4 cloves
    2 bay leaves
3–4 pounds top round steak roast
1/4 cup flour
1/4 cup shortening
1/4 cup chopped onion
1/4 cup chopped carrots
1/4 cup chopped parsnips
1/4 cup chopped celery
    1 teaspoon salt
    Pepper to taste
8–10 gingersnaps, crushed

Combine first 8 ingredients in saucepan; bring to boil, and remove from heat. Pour over beef in glass, stainless or earthenware bowl, and cover tightly. Refrigerate from 24 hours to as long as 4 days. Turn meat occasionally. To cook, remove meat from marinade (reserving marinade), wipe dry and flour lightly. Melt shortening in heavy kettle or Dutch oven. Brown meat on all sides, remove and add fresh vegetables. Cook, stirring, 5 minutes. Return meat to pan; add strained marinade, salt and pepper. Cover, and simmer 3 hours or until meat is tender. Remove meat to platter, and keep warm. Skim fat from the liquids. Stir crushed gingersnaps into sauce, and cook until thickened. Pour a little over meat, and serve remainder in sauce boat. Serves 6–8.

Note: Marinating is an essential part of preparing *Sauerbraten*.

Esterházy Rostbraten (Viennese Steak)

    1/4 cup shortening
    4 medium carrots, coarsely chopped
    2 medium onions, coarsely chopped
    2 parsnips, coarsely chopped
    2 celery stalks, diced
    2 tablespoons flour
1 1/4 cups beef broth
    2 tablespoons thick meat sauce
    2 teaspoons capers
    1 teaspoon paprika
    Salt and pepper to taste
    3 pounds round steak cut 1 1/2 inch thick
    2 tablespoons melted butter or margarine
    1 cup sour cream

Melt shortening, add prepared vegetables and sauté lightly until soft. Sprinkle with flour, and blend well; stir in broth, meat sauce, capers and paprika. Bring to boil, season with salt and pepper and remove from heat. Brush steak with melted butter or margarine; broil in preheated broiler for 2—3 minutes on each side, or sear both sides in a greased frying pan. Season with salt and pepper. Place in large casserole, and pour vegetable sauce over the top. Cover tightly, and bake in preheated 325°F. oven 1—1 1/2 hours or until meat is tender. Five minutes before serving, add sour cream, and return to oven. Serve in casserole. Serves 6—8.

Note: This Viennese dish, named to honor the famous Esterházy family, is only second in popularity to wiener schnitzel, the egged, crumbed and pan-fried veal cutlet beloved of Austrians.

Viennese Almond Tortes

Central Europe, especially Vienna, is famous for tortes—those luscious cake-confections, rich with butter-cream frosting, nuts, almond paste, whipped cream and liqueur. They vary in structure from 1—12 layers and are made from meringue mixtures and rich butter cakes and sponge cakes mortared together with jams, cream fillings and nut fillings. A torte is not an item to run up in a hurry; component parts can, however, be made and baked ahead of time, stored or frozen and carefully assembled.

Crisp Almond Torte

    2 thin *Almond-Meringue Layers*
    1 cup raspberry jam
    1 *Almond-Sponge Layer*
    1/2 cup apricot jam
    1 recipe *Chocolate Butter Cream*
1 1/2 cups toasted, thinly sliced almonds
    1/4 cup icing sugar

A pedestal cake dish is an effective choice. Place one meringue layer on server. Spread 1/2 cup raspberry jam over it. Split almond-sponge cake in half horizontally; place 1 layer on top of raspberry jam, and spread with apricot jam. Place

other layer of sponge cake on top, and spread with remaining 1/2 cup raspberry jam. Top with meringue layer. Spread sides of torte with chocolate butter cream, and cover with toasted almonds. Use decorating tube to make border of butter-cream rosettes around top of torte. Sift icing sugar over center of torte before serving.

Almond-Meringue Layers

    3 egg whites
    1/8 teaspoon cream of tartar
    1/8 teaspoon salt
    3/4 cup sugar
    1/3 cup sifted cornstarch
    1/4 cup blanched almonds, finely ground
    1 teaspoon vanilla extract

Preheat oven to 325°F. Combine egg whites, cream of tartar, and salt in large mixer bowl, and beat at medium speed until egg whites hold soft peaks. Add 1/2 cup sugar, 1 tablespoon at a time, beating constantly until meringue is stiff and glossy. Combine cornstarch, almonds, vanilla and remaining 1/4 cup sugar, and fold into meringue. Grease and flour large baking sheet, and make 2 circles by pressing rim of 9-inch round pan into flour. Spread meringue mixture evenly within circles. Bake in 325° oven 35—40 minutes. Cool, and store; or set aside until needed. Makes 2 thin layers.

Note: Finely ground almonds are suitable for both meringue and sponge layers but should be prepared in an electric blender or purchased ready ground. Prepared sliced almonds are also handy for decorating torte.

Almond-Sponge Layer

    3 egg yolks
    2/3 cup sugar
    3/4 cup blanched almonds, finely ground
    2 teaspoons lemon juice
    1 teaspoon grated lemon rind
    3 egg whites
    3/4 cup sifted all-purpose flour

Preheat oven to 375°F. Beat egg yolks and sugar until light and foamy. Add almonds, juice and lemon rind, and combine thoroughly. Beat egg whites until very stiff, and fold into egg yolks, carefully alternating with flour, until mixture is well blended. Spread in a greased 9-inch springform pan, and bake at 375°F. 25—30 minutes or until cake springs back when touched in center. Cool, and remove from pan. Store or freeze until ready to assemble torte.

Chocolate Butter Cream

    1/2 cup soft butter or margarine
    1 (6-ounce) package semisweet chocolate, melted
        and cooled
    1 egg yolk
    2 teaspoons brandy
    1 teaspoon vanilla extract

Cream butter or margarine until fluffy, and beat in chocolate, egg yolk and flavorings. If desired, add 1 teaspoon instant coffee powder for mocha flavor. Store in refrigerator if not using immediately. Bring to room temperature before spreading.

TRANSLATIONS FROM THE SCANDINAVIAN

The Nordic cuisine introduced smorgasbord into the gourmet's lexicon; pioneered with fish puddings of rich, airy elegance; developed the open sandwich.

Nordic cuisine offers much of interest to the gastronome: different ways of cooking fish, distinctive seasonings, the subtle use of sour cream in many dishes, the combination of dried fruits with meat and poultry, and breads of all shapes, sizes and grains, along with coffee cakes.

Scandinavian countries serve a type of hors d'oeuvre known as "smörgåsbord" in Sweden, "koldt bord" in Norway and "smørrebrød" in Denmark. The Swedish smörgåsbord is well known on this side of the Atlantic, where it has been adapted by some restaurants, offering choices ranging up to 50 dishes. In the home, 4—5 selections are usually offered, and they probably include tiny sausages or meatballs, liver pâté, smoked fish or shellfish, cheese and an egg or macaroni dish, along with crisp breads.

Danish open sandwiches or smørrebrød are wonders of creative talent and patience and are not served too often outside Denmark. There are literally hundreds of variations of these attractive sandwiches, some piled high, some flat, some covered with a single filling, others arranged in sections with 3 or more fillings. Among the last, the "Hans Andersen Favorite" is an example: rows of crisp bacon on light rye bread, sliced liver pâté on 1/2 the bacon, tomato slices on the other 1/2 sprinkled with grated horseradish, the whole topped with strips of firm aspic jelly. Any firm-textured bread may be used; it is always thinly sliced (never more than 1/2 the thickness of our machine-sliced type) and lightly buttered with unsalted or whipped butter. These open sandwiches are served for luncheons or late suppers, generally accompanied by beer or spirits.

Norwegian mayonnaise, frequently served with koldt bord fish and shellfish, is made with these additions to regular mayonnaise: 1 cup mayonnaise plus 1/2 cup thick sour cream with a restrained touch of horseradish and chopped dill over all.

Fish Pudding

        2 pounds fresh cod or haddock fillets or 1 pound
            each
        1 cup butter or margarine
      1/4 cup flour
        2 teaspoons salt
      1/2 teaspoon white pepper
      1/8 teaspoon nutmeg
        1 cup light cream
        4 egg yolks, lightly beaten
        4 egg whites, stiffly beaten
        1 cup heavy cream, stiffly beaten
          Fine cracker crumbs

Remove any skin or bones from fillets. Put fish through meat grinder 3 times, using finest blade. Add butter or margarine, and put through grinder again. Sift flour with salt, pepper and nutmeg; combine light cream and egg yolks. Add flour and egg mixtures alternately to fish mixture, a little at a time. Fold in egg whites and cream carefully, a little at a time. Have 8-cup mold, loaf pan or round casserole ready. Butter inside, and dust with crumbs. Carefully pour in fish mixture; mold should be 3/4 full. Set dish in pan of hot water, and bake in preheated 325°F. oven 1 1/4 hours or until firm. Let stand 5 minutes. Loosen edges with spatula, and strike bottom of dish gently on table. Place serving platter on top of mold, and invert together to turn out neatly. Serves 6—8.

Note: All the Scandinavian countries cook fish superbly, and their rich, fine-textured fish puddings and soufflés are almost always present at family parties and special occasions. Serve a fish pudding as the fish course at a formal dinner or as a hot entree on a small buffet. Garnish with small sautéed shrimp, and surround with tiny patty shells containing creamed spinach and creamed mushrooms. Serve *Lobster Sauce* separately.

Lobster Sauce

        3 cups medium white sauce
        1 cup cooked lobster, cut up small
          Salt and pepper to taste
        2 tablespoons sherry

To white sauce add lobster. Season, and stir in sherry just before serving.

Rum Cream

        2 cups milk
        5 egg yolks
      2/3 cup sugar
        1 envelope plain gelatine
      1/4 cup cold water
      1/4 cup rum
        1 cup heavy cream, stiffly beaten

Scald milk in the top of a double boiler. Beat egg yolks and sugar until thick and lemon-colored. Add to hot milk gradually, stirring constantly, and cook and stir until mixture coats spoon. Soften gelatine in cold water; add to custard, and stir until dissolved. Let mixture cool. Blend in rum; then chill until slightly thickened. Fold in stiffly beaten cream. Turn into 4—5-cup mold or individual sherbet glasses. Chill several hours or overnight. Serve with fresh strawberries, fruit sauce or whipped cream. Serves 6.

Note: Chilled desserts, similar to Bavarian creams, are very popular in Scandinavian countries, and rum is widely used as a flavoring.

FROM THE LAND OF PILAFF AND KEBAB

The Eastern Mediterranean peoples are specialists with main-dish kasha, barley and rice.

Races, religions, economic conditions, climate and terrain have all influenced the eating habits of the various countries clustered in the eastern Mediterranean area. In Israel and the Moslem communities, pork is not eaten. In districts where conditions are poor for cattle grazing, the popular meats are lamb, mutton, goat and kid. Freshly-caught fish and colorful vegetables and fruits—some unfamiliar to Westerners—are typical and usually abundant commodities in the markets. Local cheeses and honey, plus herbs and spices of ancient lineage, provide interesting touches. But the mainstay of the diet is to be found in the range of inexpensive cereal products such as lentils, rice, wheat, kasha and pastas.

Pilaff is actually a method of cooking rice. The name varies with the region—"pilaf," "pilau," "pelo"—but, call it what you will, it's a first-class culinary trick to have at your fingertips. The Balkan peoples, Greeks, Turks and Persians have for centuries achieved notable success with this way of serving their staple cereal. Many extensions and combinations can be made with basic pilaff. Long-grain or converted rice is preferable in the following recipes, as the grains stay separate. For palatable flavor, butter or margarine is specified in place of the traditional olive oil.

Kasha (buckwheat groats) is one of the cereal staples of Russia and the Ukraine, as well as of the Mediterranean countries. It is served in much the same way as the Italians serve pasta—in soups, as a side dish with meats or by itself. It develops a nutty flavor during cooking and makes an interesting occasional replacement for potatoes; it is also an unusual stuffing for poultry.

Pilaff

```
1/4 cup butter or margarine
   2 cups long-grain rice
   4 cups boiling consommé or broth
     Salt and pepper to taste
```

Melt butter or margarine in heavy saucepan; add rice, and stir constantly over medium heat about 5 minutes or until rice is golden. Add boiling consommé, cover and allow to cook over low heat 20 minutes or until liquid has been completely absorbed, leaving rice tender and just moist. Season with salt and pepper. Serves 4—6.

Barley Pilaff

```
1/2 cup butter or margarine
1/2 pound mushrooms, thinly sliced (approximately
      2 1/2 cups)
1/2 cup coarsely chopped onion
1 1/3 cups pearl barley
   5 cups hot chicken broth
```

Preheat oven to 350°F. In 2 tablespoons butter or margarine, sauté mushrooms until tender, 4—5 minutes. Lift out mushrooms with slotted spoon, and set aside. In same skillet heat remaining butter or margarine; sauté onion until golden, about 5 minutes. Add barley, and cook over low heat, stirring frequently, until barley is golden brown, another 5 minutes. Remove from heat; stir in mushrooms and 2 cups hot broth. Turn mixture into 2-quart casserole, and bake, covered, about 30 minutes. Stir in 2 more cups hot broth, cover and bake another 30 minutes or until barley is tender. Finally, stir in remaining broth, and bake 20 minutes longer. Serve with veal, chicken or ham. Serves 8.

Note: You can prepare broth with 6 chicken-bouillon cubes dissolved in 5 cups boiling water.

Kasha with Mushrooms

```
1/3 cup butter or margarine or salad oil
1/4 cup chopped onion
1/4 cup chopped green pepper
   2 cups kasha
   4 cups hot chicken broth or water
     Salt and pepper to taste
   1 cup sliced mushrooms, sautéed in butter or
        margarine or 1 cup slivered almonds, sautéed
        in butter or margarine
```

Melt butter or margarine, add onion and green pepper and sauté lightly 5 minutes. Add kasha and mix thoroughly. Transfer to casserole. Add hot broth. Season. Cover, and bake in preheated 325°F. oven 1 hour. Check every 15 minutes to see if more liquid is needed, but be cautious as the kasha grains should be tender and dry when done. Add sautéed mushrooms; bake 10 minutes longer. Serves 6.

Note: A well-beaten egg may be stirred in along with mushrooms to bind mixture.

CURRIES OF INDIA

India's cuisine has many points of appeal for Canadian cooks. It is not difficult to master, and lends itself ideally to buffet service for company occasions. Curries improve by being made ahead and reheated for serving. Serve curried dishes buffet style, surrounded by a variety of accompaniments selected for flavor contrast, such as fruits, nuts, hard-cooked eggs, chutneys, ham slivers, bacon bits and vegetables.

Mild Curry Powder

```
    3/4 cup coriander seeds
2 1/2 tablespoons dried chili peppers
    1 tablespoon poppy seeds
    1 tablespoon cumin seeds
    1 tablespoon mustard seeds
    2 tablespoons saffron
    2 teaspoons turmeric
    2 tablespoons salt
    1 teaspoon garlic powder
```

Pound and rub seeds and chili peppers to fine powder. Add saffron, turmeric, salt and garlic powder. Mix thoroughly. Bottle, and cork tightly.

Curried Shrimp

```
1 1/2 pounds fresh jumbo shrimp or 1 pound frozen
        shrimp
  1/2 teaspoon salt
      Water
    4 medium onions
  1/4 cup raisins
    2 tablespoons cold water
  1/4 pound butter or margarine
    1 tablespoon curry powder
    1 tablespoon flour
    1 teaspoon salt
    3 tart apples, peeled, cored and chopped
        (approximately 2 cups)
      Sugar to taste
```

Cook raw shrimp with 1/2 teaspoon salt in water to cover. Remove black veins; reserve cooking liquid. Or cook frozen shrimp according to label directions. Peel and chop onions. Soak raisins in cold water. Melt butter or margarine in skillet; sauté onions until transparent. Add curry powder and 1 teaspoon salt; sauté 3 minutes, scraping pan to prevent sticking. Remove from heat, and stir in flour, apples, drained raisins, shrimp liquid and shrimp. Return to low heat, and simmer very gently at least 1/2 hour; if necessary add a little extra liquid. Add sugar and seasoning after carefully tasting. When it is just right, remove from heat, and keep in refrigerator overnight. Reheat over low heat or boiling water. Serve with hot fluffy rice, and accompany with chutney, chopped hard-cooked eggs, salted nuts, fresh coconut chips, drained pineapple chunks and so forth.

Note: Good curry is a nice balance between sweet, sour and spicy flavors. To achieve it, you have lemon juice, sugar and curry powder.

Amount of curry powder depends on its strength and your taste.

Lamb Curry

```
2 1/2 pounds shoulder or leg lamb
  1/4 cup flour
  1/2 cup butter or margarine
    2 cups thinly sliced onion
    2 cloves garlic, crushed
    1 cup chopped peeled apples
    2 tablespoons curry powder
2 1/2 cups chicken broth or meat broth
  1/4 cup raisins
  1/4 cup grated coconut
    1 tablespoon barbecue sauce
    2 teaspoons salt
      Salt and pepper to taste
```

Cut meat into 1 1/2-inch cubes, and roll in flour. Melt butter or margarine in large skillet, and sauté onions and garlic until lightly browned, about 5 minutes. Lift out vegetables, and set aside. Sauté meat cubes in pan, adding more butter or margarine if necessary; cook meat about 10 minutes, stirring constantly. Return garlic and onions to pan; add apples and curry powder, and cook 5 minutes. Add next 5 ingredients, bring just to boil, cover and reduce heat. Simmer 1– 1 1/2 hours or until meat is tender. Season with salt and pepper to taste. Serve with *Saffron Rice*. Serves 6.

Note: Curry sauce may be thickened, although proper Indian curry is generally served without extra thickening. Blend 2 tablespoons flour with 4–5 tablespoons cold chicken broth or rich milk; stir into hot mixture, and simmer another 10 minutes, stirring constantly.

Saffron Rice

```
    1 cup raw long-grain rice
  1/2 teaspoon dried saffron, steeped 1/2 hour in 1/2
        cup warm water
    2 cups boiling salted water
```

Add rice and saffron to boiling salted water. Cover, and cook until rice is tender and water has been absorbed. Serves 6.

Pooris

```
    1 cup unsifted all-purpose flour
  1/2 cup farina
  1/2 teaspoon turmeric
  1/2 teaspoon salt
    1 tablespoon soft butter or margarine
      Cold water
    5 teaspoons soft butter or margarine
    2 tablespoons rice flour or ground rice
      Deep hot oil
```

Mix the first 4 ingredients together; then rub in 1 tablespoon butter, and, with a fork, stir in enough cold water (7–8 tablespoons) to make a fairly soft dough. Knead about 5 minutes (on a lightly floured board) until smooth and shiny. Roll out 1/8 inch thick into an oblong. Turn dough over several times during rolling to prevent sticking. Cream the 5 teaspoons butter with the rice flour, and spread this paste over the ob-long of dough. Roll up like a jelly roll; then roll again 1/8 inch thick, turning dough over several times. Cut into circles about 4 inches in diameter. Heat 1/2–3/4 inch salad oil in a deep electric frying pan to 375°F. Drop in the rounds, and fry until underside turns a golden color; then turn and fry second side. Some of the dough rounds will puff evenly, others unevenly. Drain on absorbent paper. Makes 1 1/2 dozen crunchy wafers.

Quick Khichri

        4 cups water
    1/2 teaspoon salt
      1 bay leaf
          Pinch ground ginger
    1/4 cup chopped onion
    3/4 cup raw long-grain rice
    3/4 cup red lentils

Bring water, salt, bay leaf, ground ginger and chopped onion to a boil. Stir in rice, and cover. Simmer 15 minutes. Uncover, and add red lentils. Cover, and simmer 12 minutes. Stir lightly with a fork, and remove bay leaf. Serve in a warm bowl with curries. Serves 6.

Chicken Korma

        2 frying chickens, cut in serving pieces
        1 cup buttermilk or yogurt
        4 cloves garlic, crushed
    1/3 cup butter or margarine
        2 onions, finely chopped
    1 1/2 teaspoons salt
    1/2 teaspoon ground pepper
        1 2-inch stick cinnamon
    1/2 teaspoon ginger
        2 whole cloves
        1 tablespoon curry powder
        2 teaspoons ground or finely chopped almonds
        1 recipe *Rice Pilau for Korma*

Wash and dry chicken pieces. Mix buttermilk with 2 cloves garlic; marinate chicken in buttermilk 2 hours at room temperature, turning occasionally. Melt butter or margarine in casserole or heavy saucepan, and cook onions and remaining garlic with salt, pepper, cinnamon, ginger and cloves 5 minutes, stirring frequently. Add curry powder and almonds, and cook another 5 minutes. Add chicken and marinade; cover and simmer 1–1 1/4 hours or until chicken is tender. Add a small amount of chicken broth during cooking if liquid evaporates. Discard whole spices. Add chicken mixture to rice, being careful not to break chicken pieces. Cover, and let stand over low heat or in slow oven until flavors blend. Serves 8.

Note: *Chicken Korma*, one of the great dishes of the subcontinent, is served on national festival days by the Moslems and usually presented buffet-style in both India and Pakistan. A large serving dish or platter is set on a brass or silver tray and surrounded with accompaniments; eggplant or okra fritters and bowls of such condiments as tart sauces, chutney and chopped fresh relishes.

Rice Pilau for Korma

    1/2 cup butter or margarine
        1 medium onion, finely chopped
        1 clove garlic, crushed
        5 whole cloves
        5 cardamom seeds
        1 3-inch stick cinnamon, broken in half
    1/2 teaspoon allspice
        1 pound long-grain rice
        1 teaspoon salt
    1/3 teaspoon saffron, steeped in 1/3 cup warm water
          Boiling water
    1/2 cup light raisins
    1/2 cup dates, cut in strips
    1/3 cup blanched almonds, sautéed in butter
          or margarine
    1/2 cup pistachio nuts, sautéed in butter or margarine

Melt butter or margarine, and sauté onion, garlic, whole spices and allspice 5 minutes; remove whole spices. Add rice, and stir over low heat 5 minutes or until golden. Add salt, saffron and sufficient water to cover rice by 2 inches. Cover tightly, and steam over heat about 25 minutes or until rice is tender and water is absorbed. Stir in raisins, dates and nuts. Serves 6–8.

FROM THE FAR PACIFIC

The rijstafel or rice table of Indonesia and the carefree luau of Hawaii can both be adapted for gay special-occasion parties.

Indonesia

In the islands that comprise Indonesia the rijstafel is considered the most luxurious experience in leisurely feasting. Far back in history this rice table simply consisted of several side dishes added to the Javanese daily bowl of rice. But the tradition was expanded by the Dutch population into an elaborate repast involving as many as 30 special accompaniments, necessitating a troop of serving boys and a kitchen as well staffed as it was well stocked. The rice table thus emerged as the *chef-d'oeuvre* in exclusive clubs and hotel restaurants, and inevitably its secrets and subtleties were carried back to the Netherlands to become the featured daily event in the high-priced restaurants of Amsterdam.

Wherever you encounter rijstafel, you will find it surrounded with certain ceremony. A major-domo enters bearing the great bowl of steaming rice, followed by a queue of waiters, each with 1 or 2 accompaniments. Everyone at the table is served a generous mound of rice in an old-fashioned rimmed soup plate, and then the waiters, 1 by 1, proffer the side dishes. Each food is placed, with its sauces, on the bed of rice; according to the guest's preference, the individual pieces may be eaten separately or the whole pyramiding mass may be approached as one concoction. Rice table experts generally find that the second method is better, as the extremely hot seasonings have a chance to mingle with blander items and reduce the shock to the taste buds. Ice-cold beer provides some relief too.

Although it would hardly be possible to duplicate all the ingredients of the authentic rice table, the basic plan of the feast is workable in any part of the world.

Here is a simple menu of reasonable proportions. The Dutch spirit, schnapps, or a gimlet cocktail with light canapés might precede. Boiled rice, with each grain dry and separate, should be prepared in quantity and served very hot.

Rijstafel Chicken Dishes. These dishes include any or all of the following: curried chicken breasts with pineapple chunks; cubed chicken in coconut milk slightly thickened with arrowroot and powdered ginger; cubed chicken with green-pepper strips in gravy flavored with soy sauce; chicken livers braised with chopped skinned peanuts and flavored with orange rind.

Fish and Seafood Specialties. Fish and seafood dishes include shrimp sautéed with a little onion and garlic in peanut oil and served with fresh lime wedges; baked whitefish seasoned with lemon juice and hot red chili peppers, and basted with melted butter or margarine and soy sauce; flaked boiled whitefish in a rich sauce of coconut milk and heavy cream, flavored and colored with saffron.

Meat Selections. These dishes may run the full gamut. Raw lamb cubes, first marinated in vinegar and enlivened with ginger, garlic, cumin and ground chili pepper, are speared on skewers, brushed with peanut oil (or salad oil) and broiled until well browned. Ground cooked chicken and ham, moistened with thick sauce, are formed into tiny croquettes, dropped into raw egg and crumbs and fried. Strips of beefsteak are braised with spices and both sweet and hot peppers, then served as filling in thin, rolled-up pancakes.

Indonesian Sambals. The sambal is basically a fiery pepper sauce made of butter, onion, peanut butter and milk (or coconut milk or both), the whole brought almost to "the point of danger" by the native "demon of sauce" known as "sambal oelik." In place of the last-mentioned, seldom obtainable here, use fresh or dried hot red peppers—but handle with discretion! Serve with 1 or more of the cooked dishes featured on the rice table; meats; hot hard-cooked eggs; or freshly cooked vegetable mixtures such as green beans with sliced celery, marrow with mushrooms and bean sprouts with water chestnuts.

Condiments. The range here too is limited only by the cook's imagination. Bananas sautéed in cinnamon butter and lightly dusted with sugar are frequently encountered. Fried onions, alone or with celery, are a good choice. A raw salad of shredded cabbage, chopped cucumber and sweet pepper offers welcome relief from hot spices. Chutneys, sliced ginger and hot roasted peanuts are almost always present as accompaniments.

Hawaii

Hawaii and the Polynesian Islands present a cuisine derived from such various sources as China, Japan, Portugal and the Philippines. The many fine restaurants catering to the tourist trade have expanded their basic French techniques to include these influences and add local tropical overtones.

Staple foodstuffs of the islands are taro (the starchy root of a large-leaved field plant), breadfruit, yams, bananas, pineapples, rice, fish and shellfish. Pork and chicken are the most popular meats. They are often served Hawaiian style, which anywhere on the globe today implies the presence of pineapple. The great pineapple industry had its beginnings early in the nineteenth century with seeds left by Spanish sailors.

The best-known Hawaiian dining ritual is the luau, an institution not unlike the American clambake but featuring suckling pig, the festival choice in most of the South Pacific islands.

LUAU MENU

Fruit punch
Assorted nuts: macadamia and pili
Lomi-lomi   Poi
Kalua pig   Laulaus   Sweet potatoes
Baked bananas   Steamed shellfish
Chicken luau
Haupia   Pineapple   Watermelon

The punch can be mild, using tropical fruit juices, or it is sometimes the "scorpion" type made with rum and other spirits plus lemon and orange juices and served in bamboo cups or coconut shells with gardenias floating on top.

Lomi-lomi is an appetizer of thinly sliced raw fish soaked in fresh lime juice—a Japanese method of preparation. Poi is an authentic native item, but unsuited to many outsiders' tastes. Kalua pig is a young pig cooked underground in an imu (bed of hot volcanic rocks, ashes and wet ti leaves). Laulaus, sweet potatoes, bananas in their skins, raw unpeeled shrimp and live lobster or crabs are arranged around the pig, covered with more leaves and earth and left to steam for

4–5 hours. When done, the foods from the imu are unpacked, carved and cut in finger-sized portions and served on ti leaves or in large shallow wooden bowls. Chicken luau is a combination of fried chicken and taro leaves (similar to spinach) cooked in coconut milk. Haupia is a stiff blanc mange made with coconut milk, molded in a flat pan and cut in diamond shapes. The watermelon is served in strips or wedges.

The setting is out of doors. For the tablecloth, broad green leaves are spread on the ground or on long low tables, with nuts, fruits and flowers down the center. Individual wooden bowls or firm ti leaves are used for service, never china and glass. Cutlery is not used, as food is strictly to be eaten with fingers. Sometimes steaming perfumed towels are supplied at the end of the feast, more welcome than finger bowls. Entertainment and dancing carry on long after the feast is over.

For gourmets wishing to translate this tropical fun and feasting to Canadian terms, it is possible to adapt the luau menu for either outdoor or indoor entertaining. Plenty of real or artificial greenery and all the flowers possible, including some to float on punch, will help create a tropical atmosphere.

Here is a suggested menu based on a typical luau but a little less demanding on the cook.

LUAU MENU

Punch	Toasted coconut chips	Crisp relishes
	Teriyaki Fried shrimp	
	Barbecued spareribs or chicken	
	Laulaus Mainland Style	
Baked sweet potatoes	*Corn on the Cob*	
	Baked or fried bananas	
Pineapple Luau	Watermelon fingers	

Teriyaki

    1 1/4 pounds beef sirloin cut 3/4 inch thick
        1 (20-ounce) can pineapple chunks, drained
    3/4 cup pineapple syrup from drained fruit
    1/4 cup soy sauce
        1 small clove garlic, crushed
    3/4 teaspoon powdered ginger
    20 stuffed olives

You will need 20 metal or wooden skewers 4 inches long. Cut beef in cubes about same size as pineapple chunks. Combine pineapple syrup, soy sauce, garlic and ginger. Pour over meat, and marinate 1 hour at room temperature. Alternate beef and pineapple on skewers, ending with 1 stuffed olive. Broil 3 inches from heat, turning once; allow about 10 minutes cooking time altogether. Serve hot. Serves 6–8.

Note: This version of a Japanese-Hawaiian dish can be served as a hot appetizer or as a main course.

For a main course, use regular kebab skewers. Heat marinade, and thicken with 2 teaspoons of cornstarch blended with 2 teaspoons cold water. Serve in sauce dish as accompaniment for teriyaki on bed of hot *Fluffy Rice*. Serves 4.

Laulaus Hawaiian Style

    24–36 large spinach leaves
    1 1/2 pounds fresh salmon
        1 teaspoon salt
        2 pounds lean pork
        1 medium onion, finely chopped

Wash spinach leaves thoroughly in several changes of water, and dry. Place 2 or 3 in a slightly overlapping arrangement on 12 6-inch aluminum foil squares. Cut salmon into 1 1/2-inch cubes; sprinkle with salt. Cut lean pork into 2-inch cubes. Place 2 or 3 pieces of fish and same amount of meat on each spinach serving. Sprinkle with chopped onion. Roll up spinach, wrap securely in foil package and tie with thread. Place in large steamer or on trivet in Dutch oven. Keep plenty of water boiling in bottom of pot. Cover, and steam 2 1/2 hours. Remove thread from packages, and place on serving tray. Serves 6.

Note: These steamed, leaf-wrapped packages can be made with a variety of savory fillings—meat, fish and vegetables, with seasonings. In place of Hawaii's giant taro greens, we suggest the largest leaves you can find in bags of very fresh, green spinach.

Laulaus Mainland Style

        3 2-inch cubes lean raw pork
        Salt and pepper to taste
        Ground ginger to taste
        6 pineapple chunks, drained
        3 green pepper strips
        1 green onion, sliced
        1 small tomato

Sprinkle pork cubes with salt, pepper and ginger. Place meat, pineapple and vegetables on 12-inch aluminum foil square. Fold into package. Arrange packages in single layer in baking pan. Bake at 350°F. 2 hours. Serves 1.

Note: If there is sufficient oven space, bake sweet potatoes for the last 1 1/4 hours and/or foil-wrapped ears of corn (completely husked and buttered) for last 3/4 hour. Serve with tiny individual bowls of melted butter.

Pineapple Luau

        1 fresh pineapple
        Toothpicks

Cut thick slice from top and bottom of 1 fresh pineapple; set slices aside. With long thin-bladed knife cut out fruit in 1 solid cylinder, and remove. Cut fruit in half lengthwise, and remove core; then cut in lengthwise spears. Fasten bottom slice to pineapple shell with toothpicks, and fill with prepared spears. Replace top to resemble whole pineapple.

ORIENTAL MEALS

For the crispest cooked vegetables, the most elegant tidbits of meats, fish, poultry, the salty tang of soy sauce, the blend of sweet and sour, follow the example of the Chinese and Japanese.

Chinese Cuisine

Chinese cooking is basically thrifty, probably as much because of famine and other national disasters as of individual families' economic status. No doubt it was during times of stress that such unlikely items as bamboo shoots were first discovered as edible. Whatever the cause, Chinese cooks have learned to create literally countless dishes from all available foods, each introduced in cautious quantities and brought to perfection with well-chosen seasonings. Monosodium glutamate, now widely sold in packaged form, has long been used in China.

Crisp tender vegetables, bright fresh colors and smooth clear sauces are characteristic. The vegetables require patient chopping, dicing, slicing or shredding, and the sauces require accurate timing. Chinese cooking has been described as active—dishes left to slumber undisturbed in oven or pots are extremely rare in this cuisine. The stir-and-cook or stir-fry method, handed down over the centuries, is recognized everywhere as one of the best ways to preserve valuable nutrients, plus distinctive food texture and color.

In an authentic Chinese dinner, the number of dishes often reaches a dozen or more—as many as 30 at a banquet. Appetizers such as barbecued spareribs, egg rolls and fried shrimp are followed by various main dishes served at once along with the indispensable rice. Desserts are not important, and if served at all usually consist of fresh, candied or preserved fruits, possibly with special cookies. Bread with butter never appears on the table. Fragrant China tea is almost always present, to be sipped in its pale clear state toward the end of the meal.

Stir-Fry

This dish is a crisp mixture of many ingredients, each used in quite small quantity. The Chinese method of preparation is to group certain foods together beforehand and to cook each group separately before combining for serving. In this recipe 3 skillets are required. The numbered groupings are arranged in order of cooking.

GROUP 1:

    1 tablespoon salad oil
  1/2 cup fresh or frozen green peas
    1 (5-ounce) can water chestnuts, drained and sliced
    6 fresh mushrooms, sliced
    2 stalks celery, sliced
  1/4 teaspoon salt

Heat 1 tablespoon oil in skillet. Add peas, chestnuts, mushrooms and celery. Sprinkle with salt. Stir-fry 1 minute; then cover, and braise 3—4 minutes until peas are tender.

GROUP 2:

    1 tablespoon salad oil
    1 clove garlic, crushed
    2 slices raw ginger root or 1/2 teaspoon powdered ginger
  1/2 pound lean pork, cut in thin strips
    1 tablespoon soy sauce
    2 tablespoons water
    2 tablespoons dry sherry
    1 teaspoon cornstarch
  1/4 teaspoon pepper
  1/2 teaspoon sugar

Heat oil in second skillet, and sauté garlic and ginger. Add meat, and stir-fry for 2 minutes. Blend soy sauce, water, sherry and cornstarch, and add to skillet with remaining ingredients. Bring to simmer, reduce heat, cover and braise several minutes. Taste, and add more soy sauce if you wish.

GROUP 3:

    1 tablespoon salad oil
  1/2 cup blanched almonds
  1/2 head Chinese lettuce, coarsely chopped
  1/4 teaspoon salt

Heat oil in third skillet, add almonds and sauté until lightly colored. Lift out nuts with slotted spoon. Add coarsely chopped lettuce, sprinkle with salt and braise in hot oil until just tender.

Serve Group 1 on bed of hot rice; cover with Group 2; surround with lettuce from Group 3, and sprinkle almonds from Group 3 over all. Serves 4.

Sweet-and-Sour Pork

  1/2 cup pineapple juice
  1/3 cup brown sugar, firmly packed
    3 tablespoons vinegar
    2 teaspoons cornstarch
    1 tablespoon water
  1/2 teaspoon salt
  1/2 cup flour
    2 eggs
  1/4 cup milk
  1/2 teaspoon milk
  1/2 teaspoon salt
    1 pound pork tenderloin, cut in 1-inch cubes
      Hot oil
    2 tablespoons peanut or salad oil
    1 large green pepper, cut in 1-inch squares
    1 cup pineapple chunks
    1 clove garlic, finely chopped
    1 cup diced firm red tomatoes

Combine pineapple juice, sugar and vinegar in saucepan, and bring to boil. Cool a few minutes. Combine cornstarch with water and 1/2 teaspoon salt, and stir into warm mixture. Set aside until needed.

Beat flour, eggs, milk and 1/2 teaspoon salt together, to make batter. Dip meat cubes in batter, and fry in oil 1 inch deep preheated to 350°F. 5—8 minutes until golden brown. Heat 2 tablespoons oil in large skillet. Add pork, green pepper, pineapple and garlic; cook together, stirring gently, 5 minutes. Add pineapple-juice sauce, and blend. Cover pan, and cook over low heat until thickened, about 5 minutes. Fold in tomatoes, being careful not to crush; cook 3 minutes. Serves 3 generously.

Peanut Sesame Chew

      4 cups shelled blanched peanuts
      1 cup sugar
    3/4 cup water
      1 cup honey
    1/4 cup butter
      1 cup sesame seeds

Spread the peanuts in a shallow flat pan, and toast at 350°F. 10 minutes or until lightly browned. Pour into a greased bowl. Mix the next 4 ingredients in a saucepan, and cook slowly until syrup spins a thread, about 40 minutes, or until a candy thermometer registers 250°F. Sprinkle 1/2 the sesame seeds over the bottom of a greased jelly-roll pan or cookie sheet. Pour the syrup over the peanuts and remaining seeds. Mix with a fork, and scrape into the prepared pan. Spread and flatten with the back of a greased spoon. Cool, and cut into large bars. Makes about 56.

Beef Strips with Green Peppers and Tomatoes

      1 pound round steak
    1–2 tablespoons soy sauce
      1 tablespoon dry sherry
      1 clove garlic
    1/2 teaspoon sugar
        Small piece ginger root
      3 medium tomatoes
      2 green peppers
      3 tablespoons salad oil
      2 teaspoons cornstarch
      3 tablespoons water or stock

Cut meat into 2-inch cubes; then slice very thin for quick cooking. Place in bowl; add next 5 ingredients and let stand 1/2 hour. Quarter tomatoes. Remove stems, seeds and white membranes from peppers; cut into 1 1/2-inch squares. Start cooking about 10 minutes before serving. Heat oil in skillet over high heat. After discarding garlic, turn in contents of marinating bowl, and be prepared for mixture to sputter. Stir-fry vigorously as meat strips brown. After about 5

minutes add tomatoes and peppers. Continue to stir-fry over high heat only 2 minutes, to keep color and texture of vegetables. Blend cornstarch smoothly with water, and add to skillet; stir as it thickens. Serve over hot rice in serving dish. Serves 4.

Chinese Fried Rice

      1/2 cup butter or margarine
        3 eggs, slightly beaten
        3 cups cooked rice
    1 1/2 cups cooked diced chicken, pork, ham or shrimp
      1/2 cup (4-ounce can) sliced mushrooms, drained
      1/4 cup green onions, cut fine
        2 tablespoons soy sauce
          Salt and pepper to taste

Melt butter or margarine in large skillet. Add eggs, and cook until firm but not hard, stirring with fork. Add rice, and cook 5 minutes, stirring constantly. Add remaining ingredients, and cook 10 minutes; if mixture seems dry add 2 tablespoons butter or margarine. Serve in bowl, or pack in warm buttered mold, and turn out on platter. Serves 6—8.

VARIATION:

* Fry cooked rice in butter or oil first, stirring to smooth out lumps; then add vegetables and meat. When thoroughly heated, push contents of pan back to leave hollow in center. Scramble eggs in hollow; as soon as they begin to set, stir all ingredients together to incorporate. Add seasonings, and serve.

Hong Kong Meatballs

        1 pound boneless fresh pork (leg slices, or shoulder chops), including a little fat
      4–5 water chestnuts
        4 medium mushrooms
      1/2 cup cooked crabmeat
      1/2 teaspoon sugar
          Salt and pepper to taste
          Few drops lemon juice
      1/4 cup fine cornmeal
        2 eggs, lightly beaten
          Peanut oil or salad oil

Cube pork. Drain water chestnuts. Wash mushrooms. If canned crabmeat is used, drain thoroughly, and pick over for any bits of shell. Put pork, chestnuts, mushrooms and crabmeat through grinder twice, using medium blade. Sprinkle with sugar, salt, pepper and lemon juice. Shape with teaspoon and fingers into firm balls about 1 1/2 inches in diameter. Roll balls in cornmeal, then in eggs and again in cornmeal. Have ready saucepan containing simmering oil to depth of 2 inches. Cook balls 15 minutes. Lift out with slotted spoon; keep in warm oven until all are cooked. Serve on platter with hot fluffy rice, hot bean sprouts, garnish of parsley and small tomatoes, halved. Accompany with soy sauce. Serves 4.

From the Japanese

Japanese cuisine is similar to Chinese. Fish, rice, plenty of vegetables, nuts and fruits are basic fare, along with such popular Oriental seasonings as shoyu (soy sauce), Ajinomoto (monosodium glutamate), shiitake (dried mushrooms) and sesame-seed oil, which imparts a distinctive flavor and richness to many cooked dishes. It has been said that Japanese food is prepared as much for eye appeal as for taste.

Sukiyaki

        1 (10-ounce) can beef bouillon
    1/3 cup soy sauce
    1/4 cup dry sherry
    1/4 cup brown sugar, firmly packed
        Pinch powdered ginger
    1 1/2 pounds beef sirloin sliced 1/8 inch thick
        3 onions, thinly sliced
        1 cup thinly sliced large mushrooms
        1 cup shredded spinach
        1 cup celery, sliced thin diagonally
        1 cup sliced canned bamboo shoots, drained
        1 green pepper, cut in thin strips
        4 green onions, sliced
    1/3 cup oil

Combine beef bouillon, soy sauce, sherry, sugar and ginger; marinate beef in this mixture for about 2 hours. Arrange prepared vegetables artistically in separate dishes on tray. Drain meat, and reserve marinade. Take everything to table to be cooked. Put 2 tablespoons oil in skillet, add 1/3 the meat slices and brown on both sides. Add 1/3 the vegetables, and cook briefly 3 minutes. Add 1/3 the marinade, and simmer, covered, 5 minutes. Serve immediately, accompanied by hot boiled rice, to 2 of your hungry guests. Repeat procedure twice. Serves 6.

Note: Sukiyaki is considered a foreigners' dish, and restaurants specialize in cooking it at the table on a brazier or in a chafing dish. An electric frying pan or skillet on a good-sized hibachi would be ideal for home use in our country. For more than 6 servings, prepare enough extra ingredients, use second electric frying pan and get help.

Tempura

        1 pound fresh shrimp or a mixture of shrimp, mussels and scallops
    1/2 pound small broccoli flowerets or asparagus tips
        1 egg yolk, beaten
        1 cup water
        1 cup sifted pastry flour
        4 tablespoons rice flour (ground rice)
        4 tablespoons cornstarch
        Pinch salt
        1 egg white
        Sesame-seed oil and salad oil, mixed
        Tempura Sauce

Shell and devein shrimp, leaving the tail intact. Spread the tail, and pull out the tendon; then bend shrimp back until straight. Slice large mussels and scallops into 3 pieces. Prepare vegetables, and steam for 2 minutes. Dry seafood and vegetables on absorbent paper. Beat the next 6 ingredients together; then fold in egg white, beaten until stiff but moist. Heat a deep mixture of oil to 360°F. using twice as much sesame-seed oil as salad oil. Dip seafood and vegetables into the batter individually, and deep-fry 3–4 minutes or until golden. Do not overcook. Drain, and arrange on a platter. Garnish with harusame noodles, thin flower-shaped slices of carrot and pickled turnip. Serve with *Tempura Sauce*. Serves 4–5.

Tempura Sauce

    1/2 cup chicken or fish stock
    1/4 cup sauterne
    1/4 cup soy sauce
        1 teaspoon monosodium glutamate

Combine all ingredients, and bring to a boil. Pour into individual sauce dishes as dip for each person's shrimp.

Note: Raw harusame noodles are thin transparent noodles made of soybean powder. When cooked they resemble shredded coconut and are available in Japanese stores.

Tempura sauce in the Japanese manner is made of a fish-seaweed broth, mirin (sweet rice wine) and soy sauce.

Japanese Broiled Chicken

        2 small tender broiling chickens
    1/4 cup soy sauce
    1/4 cup sherry
        2 tablespoons horseradish
        2 tablespoons chopped onion
        1 tablespoon sugar
        1 tablespoon powdered ginger

Split broilers. Combine soy sauce, sherry, horseradish, onion, sugar and ginger. Marinate chicken in mixture 1 hour. Broil chicken, basting with marinade. Serves 4.

MEXICO'S SPICY THEME

Until the conquest of Mexico by Cortés and the Spaniards, Europeans had had no knowledge of tomatoes, pineapples, avocados, peanuts, turkeys, cacao beans, sweet potatoes and various other subtropical foodstuffs. The seed, slips and turkey chicks that the conquistadores brought back to Spain were to contribute to an important expansion in diet, first at the royal court, then among a wider public. At the same time, the native tribes of Mexico were receiving education in Spanish cookery from the missionaries and learning to grow and use such transplanted material as livestock, rice, figs, oranges, dates and olives. Today, a typical Mexican menu draws its colorful features from both native and Spanish traditions.

The corn cuisine of the country is in itself an almost never-ending study for outsiders.

Tortillas, the native bread for centuries, are extremely thin, round pancakes made of cornmeal and water. They are next to impossible to learn to make, unless, as the smiling Mexicans declare, you start at the age of 5. But they can be bought in quantity from Mexican restaurants and in cans. The basic tortilla, rolled or folded and frequently deep-fried, becomes an enchilada when served with a hearty, spicy filling; a taco, somewhat similar to an enchilada, but less substantial; a tostado or toasted tortilla; or any of a dozen other variants according to region.

Tamales are made with a dough of fine cornmeal and shortening, which is spread on washed and softened cornhusks, then topped with thick, spicy tomato sauce. Husks are folded to enclose contents, tied, steamed, then stripped back for serving. The baked tamale pie is constructed of 2 thicknesses of cornmeal mush with meat-sauce filling.

Frijoles are beans—white, brown, red, purple, black—which accompany virtually every hot meal, either cooked to a delicious thick consistency or refried.

Mole de Guajalote (Turkey Mole)

```
     8- pound turkey, cut into serving pieces
     2 quarts (approximately) water
     1 tablespoon salt
   1/2 cup olive oil
   1/3 cup toasted almonds
   1/3 cup raisins
     1 slice toasted dry bread
     2 tablespoons sesame seeds
     1 (1-ounce) square unsweetened chocolate
     2 green peppers, chopped
     1 small onion, finely chopped
     1 clove garlic, chopped
   2–4 tablespoons chili powder
     1 teaspoon cinnamon
     3 cups turkey broth
     2 cups tomato sauce
       Salt and pepper to taste
```

Simmer turkey pieces in water to cover until almost tender, adding 1 tablespoon salt at midway point. Remove pieces from broth. Reduce broth to 3 cups. Set aside. Dry turkey pieces, brown on all sides in 1/4 cup hot oil in skillet, and place in large casserole or Dutch oven. Grind together almonds, raisins, bread, sesame seeds and chocolate. Heat remaining 1/4 cup oil; add peppers, onion and garlic; cook, stirring constantly, about 5 minutes. Add ground mixture, plus chili powder and cinnamon. Stir, and cook until smooth. Stir in turkey broth and tomato sauce; cook over low heat 5 minutes. Add extra salt and pepper to taste. Pour sauce over browned turkey pieces in casserole; cover tightly, and cook at low temperature until meat is perfectly tender in 350°F. oven 1–1 1/2 hours. Stir sauce occasionally. Remove turkey to hot platter. If sauce seems thin, cook down until of desired consistency. Serve in sauceboat; accompany turkey platter with hot rice. Serves 7—8.

Guacamole (Mexican Avocado Dip)

```
     1 large ripe tomato, peeled
     2 large avocados, peeled and seeded
     1 tablespoon lemon or lime juice
     1 teaspoon grated onion
   3/4 teaspoon salt
1/2–3/4 teaspoon chili powder
```

Chop tomato very fine in wooden bowl; add pulp from avocado, and mash with silver fork or wooden spoon. Blend in remaining ingredients; mix thoroughly.

As a dip, serve in bowl surrounded with crisp crackers or raw vegetables. For salad dressing, increase lemon juice to 3 tablespoons, and omit chili powder. If made some time before using, spread thin layer of mayonnaise over top of mixture to prevent discoloration (a tendency of peeled avocado).

Basic Chili Sauce

```
   1/2 cup salad oil
     1 large onion, chopped
     2 cloves garlic, crushed
   1/2 cup all-purpose flour
     5 cups hot beef stock
     2 cups drained canned tomatoes
   2–4 tablespoons chili powder
   1/4 cup cold water
       Salt and pepper to taste
       Few grains cayenne
```

Heat salad oil in heavy pan, and gently sauté onion and garlic until soft and slightly colored. Blend in flour, and stir until mixture is smooth and bubbling. Combine hot stock with tomatoes; add to first mixture, and stir constantly until thick. Blend chili powder to smooth paste with cold water. Add to simmering sauce, stirring thoroughly to combine. Continue simmering 1/2 hour; put through sieve. Add salt, pepper and cayenne. Makes 1 quart.

Note: Sauce should be cooled completely before covering and storing in refrigerator. Reheat with diced cooked chicken or other meats, using amount of sauce to taste.

Beef Chili

    1/2 pound ground beef
    1 tablespoon fat
    1 cup or more *Basic Chili Sauce*

Sauté beef in fat. Add sauce to beef in skillet; simmer 10 minutes. Serve over hot unsweetened cornbread, tortillas or pancakes. Serves 4.

Note: Extend beef and sauce with 1 cup fine stale bread crumbs; fill 4 large green pepper shells, and bake in oiled pan in medium hot oven.

REGIONAL COOKING IN THE UNITED STATES

There's ample gourmet potential in the distinctive cookery of New Orleans and the Atlantic seaboard states, as well as in the later creations of the Southwest and California.

American foods in the beginning were whatever the settlers could find to keep themselves alive: fish, game, corn, wild fruits and roots. As with the early Canadian settlers, all were prepared as far as possible in the established ways known "at home," which could, according to the individual family, mean England, Holland, France or Spain. Eventually the precious seeds and cuttings brought from the fields and gardens of Europe bore their harvests, and dining took on a more expansive atmosphere combining both Old and New World influences. With each wave of immigration and each new frontier opened, this pattern continued, region by region, and it was not until the mid-nineteenth century's great surge forward with farm production, manufacturing and transportation that these diverse food customs began to intermingle and develop along lines that were recognizably "American."

New Orleans

The creole cookery of New Orleans is quite unlike any other cuisine in the United States or elsewhere. French, Spanish and other European culinary arts have intermingled and come to perfection through the cooking genius of the Negro. The first French settlers learned from the Indians the use of filé (powdered sassafras) as a thickener for sauces.

New Orleans' famous restaurants of today have retained the traditional dishes of creole cookery, much to the delight of gourmets.

Creole Gumbo

    2 tablespoons bacon fat or oil
    4-pound frying chicken, cut in serving pieces
    1/2 pound lean ham, diced
    2 cups sliced fresh okra or 2 (10-ounce) packages okra, thawed
    1 large onion, chopped
    2 tablespoons butter
    2 cups peeled chopped tomatoes or 2 cups drained canned tomatoes
    1/4 teaspoon thyme
    3 drops hot pepper sauce
    6 cups water
      Liquor from 1 pint oysters
    1/3 cup chopped parsley
      Salt and pepper
    1 1/2 tablespoons filé powder
    1 pint oysters

Heat bacon in soup kettle; sauté chicken and ham until lightly browned. Remove meat from kettle. Add okra and onion to pan, with butter, and sauté until okra has ceased to string. Add tomatoes, thyme, and pepper sauce, and return chicken and ham to kettle. Add water and oyster liquor; bring just to boil, cover and reduce heat. Simmer 30 minutes. Add parsley, salt and pepper. Cook over low heat 10 minutes or until chicken is tender. Add 1—2 cups additional boiling water if you prefer plenty of soup-like broth. Remove from heat, and stir in filé powder and oysters. *Do not reheat*. Accompany with hot rice. Serves 4—6.

Note: Okra contains a gummy substance that strings when cooking, but it eventually disappears and need not cause concern. If filé powder is not available, thicken gumbo with 2 tablespoons flour added to fat in pan after onions and okra have been sautéed.

New Orleans Oyster Loaf

    1 large or 3 small French loaves or 6 individual crusty rolls
    1 clove garlic
    1/4 cup butter or margarine, melted
    3 dozen oysters and liquor
      Salt and pepper to taste
      Dash hot pepper sauce

Split loaf lengthwise but not quite through. Scoop out soft center, leaving crusty shell 1 inch thick. Tear soft bread into coarse crumbs with fork, and set aside. Rub insides of shells with garlic, and brush inside and out with 2 tablespoons melted butter or margarine. Drain oysters, reserving liquor; sauté oysters in remaining butter or margarine just until edges curl, about 5 minutes. Fill loaf with oysters. Combine 1/2 crumbs with 1/2 cup oyster liquor, and use to complete filling. Sprinkle with salt, pepper and hot pepper sauce. Wrap loaf in moistened cheesecloth (use milk if desired), twisting ends tightly and folding under bread. Bake on sheet in preheated 350°F. oven 30 minutes. Unwrap to serve. Slice large loaf, halve small loaves. Serves 6.

Jambalaya

    2 tablespoons butter or margarine
    1/2 pound garlic sausage, thinly sliced
    1/2 pound cooked ham, diced
    2/3 cup chopped onion
    2/3 cup chopped green pepper
  1 1/2 cups raw long-grain or converted rice
    1 cup diced peeled tomatoes or 1 cup drained
        canned tomatoes
    1 teaspoon salt
    1/4 teaspoon thyme
    1 bay leaf, crushed
    2 cups chicken or fish stock
    2 cups cooked shrimp, deveined
    1/4 cup chopped parsley (optional)
        Salt and pepper to taste

Melt butter or margarine in a good-size saucepan. Add sausage, and cook until lightly browned; remove from pan. Add ham, and cook about 5 minutes, stirring constantly; push to one side. Add onion and green pepper, and cook until soft. Add rice, and stir until well coated with fat. Add tomatoes, 1 teaspoon salt, herbs, and stock. Bring just to boil, lower heat and simmer gently 20—30 minutes or until all liquid is absorbed and rice is tender. Add cooked shrimp and parsley. Combine gently with rice, or scatter over top. Add extra salt and pepper to taste. Cover, and reheat over hot water or in slow oven 10—15 minutes. Serves 4—6.

Note: Jambalaya is a rice dish that reflects the Spanish influence. It is much like *Paella* of Spain. The original jambalaya used ham ("jambon"), from which it gets its name.

The Southern States

Abundant seafood from the coastal waters has inspired many wonderful dishes, especially those using the hard- and soft-shelled crabs.

Deviled Crabs

    1 pound cooked crabmeat, fresh or frozen
    3 tablespoons butter or margarine
    2 tablespoons chopped onion
    2 tablespoons flour
    1 teaspoon dry mustard
    1/2 teaspoon salt
    1/4 teaspoon sage
    1/8 teaspoon cayenne
    1 cup milk
    1 tablespoon lemon juice
    1 tablespoon barbecue sauce
    1 egg, beaten
    1 tablespoon chopped parsley
    1/2 cup soft bread crumbs
    2 tablespoons melted butter or margarine

Remove cartilage from crabmeat. Melt butter or margarine, and sauté onion until tender. Blend in flour and seasonings. Add milk gradually, and cook until thick, stirring constantly. Add lemon juice and barbecue sauce. Blend a

little hot sauce into beaten egg; return all to saucepan, mix well and add crabmeat and parsley. Fill 6 cleaned crab shells or buttered ramekins. Mix bread crumbs with melted butter or margarine, and sprinkle tops. Bake in 375°F oven 15 minutes or until lightly browned. Serves 6.

Country Captain

    1/4 cup flour
        Salt and pepper to taste
    3–4–pound roasting or frying chicken, cut in serving
        pieces
    1/2 cup (approximately) shortening
    2 onions, finely chopped
    2 medium green peppers, chopped
    1 small clove garlic, crushed
    3 cups canned tomatoes
    1 tablespoon chopped parsley
    2–3 teaspoons curry powder
  1 1/2 teaspoons salt
    1/2 teaspoon pepper
    1/2 teaspoon powdered thyme
        Medium-dry white wine or water or combination
        of both
    2 cups hot cooked rice
    1/4 cup dry currants, soaked
    1 cup whole blanched almonds, toasted
        Parsley sprigs

Combine flour and salt and pepper to taste. Roll chicken pieces in mixture. Melt shortening in frying pan; brown chicken on all sides, and remove to casserole or roasting pan equipped with tight lid. Add onions, green peppers and garlic to hot fat (if too brown, discard and melt fresh shortening); cook slowly for 5 minutes, stirring constantly. Add tomatoes, parsley, spices and seasonings. When hot, pour over chicken; add wine to bring liquid not quite to top of chicken pieces. Cover casserole, and bake at 350°F. 45 minutes or until chicken is tender. Place chicken in center of hot platter, and arrange circle of hot rice around it. Add currants to sauce in casserole, and heat to boiling; pour sauce over rice. Scatter almonds on top, and garnish with parsley sprigs. Serves 4.

Syllabub

    4 cups heavy cream
    2 cups milk
    2/3 cup bourbon or rye whiskey
    1/2 cup sugar

Use large beater bowl; otherwise foam will spill out. Combine ingredients. Beat until mixture is well covered with foam. Skim off top, and place in individual parfait glasses or goblets. Continue beating-and-skimming process until bowl is empty and glasses filled. Chill thoroughly before serving. *Syllabub* will keep 4—5 days in refrigerator. Serves 8—10.

Note: Syllabub is first cousin to eggnog and a traditional southern dessert for holidays and gala occasions. *Syllabub* came from England by way of early settlers and has remained a specialty in Virginia, the Carolinas and Georgia.

The Eastern Seaboard

The New England clambake became part of American tradition when the settlers first copied the Indians' custom of cooking shellfish. Layers of lobsters, clams and green corn were buried in pits heated with stones; seaweed was stuffed between the layers and on top, and the whole mass was covered with earth and allowed to steam for hours.

New England recipe names are delightful in themselves.

* *Anadama Bread*: Made with cornmeal, white flour and molasses, said to be the invention of a fisherman with a lazy wife named Anna.

* *Cherry Bounce*: Sweet black cherries soaked and served in rum.

* *Hasty Pudding*: Sometimes called "stir-about pudding," served with meat and gravy or with maple syrup for dessert.

* *Flummery*: A cornstarch-thickened pudding of cooked fruit, sugar and water, served with cream.

* *Sizzlers*: Blueberry or apple turnovers or small pies fried in deep fat.

The old controversy between supporters of New England clam chowder, made with milk and potatoes, and Manhattan clam chowder, with tomatoes instead of milk, goes on. It is a matter of taste.

Lobster Stew

    2 (2-pound) fresh lobsters, cooked
    1 quart cold water
    1 medium onion, sliced
    2 stalks celery, sliced
    1 bay leaf
1/3 cup butter or margarine
    4 cups hot milk
    2 egg yolks
    1 cup cream
      Salt and pepper to taste
      Paprika to taste

Cut meat from cooked fresh lobsters into small pieces, leaving claw meat whole. Put water, onion, celery and bay leaf with cracked lobster shells in saucepan. Cover, and simmer 30 minutes; then uncover, and reduce broth to about 2 cups. Strain, and reserve broth. Melt butter, and sauté lobster meat gently; add milk and reserved broth; heat to boiling. Beat egg yolks with cream; stir in 1 cup hot stew very gradually and then return

all to kettle. Stir constantly until hot; do not let mixture boil. Season to taste. Serve with piece of claw meat in each bowl, and dust top with paprika. Serves 4—6.

Fresh Cranberry Betty

    1 cup sugar
1/2 cup orange juice
1/2 teaspoon cinnamon
    2 cups cranberries
1/2 cup butter or margarine, melted
    3 cups soft bread crumbs

Bring sugar, orange juice and cinnamon to a boil. Add cranberries, and cook 2 minutes. Pour butter or margarine over crumbs, tossing with fork to distribute evenly. Arrange alternate layers of crumbs and cranberries in buttered baking dish, ending with crumbs. Cover with lid of aluminum foil, and bake in preheated 375°F. oven 20 minutes. Uncover, and bake 15 minutes longer until top is brown and crisp. Serve warm with sweetened whipped cream to which 1 teaspoon grated orange rind has been added. Serves 6.

Note: The tart, crisp, juicy cranberry has altered little (except in abundance) since the Indians used it for food and medicine and the first Cape Cod housewife boiled down a "mess" with some of her carefully hoarded sugar.

Vichyssoise

    4 large leeks, sliced in 1-inch lengths
    1 small onion, chopped
1/4 cup butter or margarine, melted
    4 cups chicken broth
    4 medium potatoes, peeled and sliced
      Salt and pepper to taste
    2 cups light cream
      Chopped chives
1/4 teaspoon nutmeg (optional)

Sauté leeks and onion gently in butter or margarine until transparent but not brown. Add 2 cups broth, cover and simmer 15 minutes. Cook potatoes until tender; drain well, and crush with fork. Add to leeks with remaining broth. Simmer 5 minutes. Put through sieve or food mill (twice, if necessary, to obtain smooth mixture) or use an electric blender as manufacturer directs. Season with salt and pepper. Cool, and chill overnight. Before serving, add cream, blending well. Serve very cold in chilled dishes, and sprinkle with chives and a little nutmeg. Serves 6.

Note: New York's own soup, one of the great soups of the world, invented in the early part of this century by the great French Chef, Louis Diat, for 40 years ruler of the kitchens in New York's Ritz-Carlton Hotel. Shortly before his death he declared that, in casting about for a special chilled soup to tempt the appetites of Ritz patrons during a Manhattan heat wave, he remembered his mother's leek-and-potato soup and how she used to cool it with chilled milk for summer breakfasts. He named it after his native Vichy district.

The Southwestern States

A blend of influences including Spanish and Mexican. Here you find such favorites as chili, tamales and enchiladas, together with an abundance of fresh fish, fruit and vegetable dishes.

Caesar Salad

        1 clove garlic
    3/4 cup olive oil
1 1/2 cups 1/4-inch bread cubes
        8 cups Romaine lettuce
    1/4 cup lemon juice
        1 egg, boiled 1 minute
    1/4 teaspoon dry mustard
    1/2 teaspoon black pepper
    1/2 teaspoon salt
    1/2 cup grated Parmesan cheese
        6 anchovy fillets, diced (optional)

Quarter garlic, and add to 1/4 cup oil; set aside several hours. Toast bread cubes until golden in 300°F. oven about 20 minutes. Tear lettuce in bite-size pieces, and place in serving bowl. Cover, and refrigerate all ingredients until needed. At serving time, combine in small bowl remaining 1/2 cup oil, lemon juice, very soft egg removed from shell and seasonings; beat well. Discard garlic from oil prepared earlier; toss oil with toasted bread cubes. Add egg mixture, bread cubes, cheese and anchovies to chilled greens. Toss gently but thoroughly, and serve immediately. Makes 6 servings.

Note: This is an ideal first course salad to serve while the "chef's" specialties from the charcoal broiler are cooking.

CANADA'S RICH BOUNTY OF VARIED TRADITIONS

Perhaps no country in the world has such a pot-au-feu heritage of interesting food customs as we do. Canadian cooking is a mosaic of many ethnic ways, for Canada is home to more than 30 nationalities, all of whom have contributed to our colorful culinary pattern. We still prepare dishes from the traditional recipes of our forebearers and refuse to develop or devise a straight-line national cuisine. It does not seem essential or desirable to do so when we can enjoy the best food ideas of many national groups.

It all started with the knowledge and wisdom of the Canadian Indians who were the first inhabitants to fish, hunt and farm in this vast country. It expanded with the first French settlers. Some of the liveliest culinary traditions have remained unchanged by generations of bonnes femmes who still prepare such dishes as tourtière, onion soup, fromage de tête and savory ragoûts. The French were followed by the British, who also transplanted their food customs and housewifely lore; to these immigrant housewives and their successors thanks are due for plum pudding, Chelsea buns, Scottish shortbread, sage and onion stuffing, and many more. Following the American Revolution and the influx of the United Empire Loyalists, food patterns became more varied. Some Loyalists from New England and the middle and southern colonies settled in the Maritimes; other Loyalists from Pennsylvania, New York and New Jersey—many of Dutch-German stock—settled in Upper Canada. Both groups brought with them solidly established food habits from their first homes.

Each new wave of settlers arrived with their own individual culinary style. Those who homesteaded in the West left to their descendants a rich heritage of Old World specialties such as rulla pylsa, borscht, holubtse, honey cake, paska and many others.

In quality and abundance of foodstuffs Canada is one of the most favored nations in the modern world. The raw materials for superb cuisine are available wherever there is a settled population interested in the art of good cooking and eating. Modern transportation, freezing and refrigeration, food-grading, packing and marketing have distributed our specialties far and wide: apples from British Columbia, Ontario and Nova Scotia; western wheat and beef; the huge potato crops of Prince Edward Island and New Brunswick; the cheeses from Ontario and Quebec; and the salt-water harvests from both West and East coasts. In addition, imports from abroad contribute countless delicacies as well as year-round staples such as the citrus fruits. It is possible for the eager gourmet cook to pursue a richly rewarding experience within the boundaries of Canada.

A Few Specialties

Winnipeg gold eye is found only in the lakes of Manitoba. The fish is always smoked; it has a rosy gold color, delicate flesh and delicious flavor. One fish is standard for each serving; it can be broiled for 10 minutes or steamed or poached 20 minutes. Serve with butter and lemon.

Fiddleheads are the tight-curled, unopened fronds of fiddlehead ferns. The finest young tender ones are gathered in quantity in New Brunswick, where they are sold in the shops or frozen for a wider market. The flavor is a cross between asparagus and broccoli. Serve boiled, buttered.

Digby chicks are not feathered, as the name implies, but boneless fillets of herring, heavily salted and smoked. By removing the head, backbone, skin and fins from bloaters (smoked herring) 2 boneless strips of flesh are left. These are cut in small bits for hors d'oeuvres. One quarter of a pound will yield about 30 pieces.

Sweetgrass buffalo meat is from buffalo herds which roam the 11-million-acre sanctuary in Wood Buffalo National Park in the far northwest. The herds, once depleted by uncontrolled hunting, have survived and become plentiful. Buffalo meat is cooked in the same manner as beef; the cuts are naturally larger, but flavor and texture are excellent.

Bake-apples are a wild berry native to Newfoundland and found in bogs. They are apricot-colored, shaped like blackberries and taste like a cross between peach and apricot. They are used in making jam or served fresh in desserts.

Saskatoons, the wild berry of the prairies, are found growing near water. They resemble small blueberries, but with their tart flavor and firm texture are more like a black currant. They are usually precooked for a short time before being used in a recipe.

Arctic char is a fish delicacy relatively new to gourmets, and promising to grow in popularity. It averages 5 pounds in weight. It is fished by Eskimos in Ungava, Frobisher Bay and Port Burwell areas under the guidance of the government, which has established freezing plants to process the fish. Char belongs to the salmon family, with a flavor similar to trout; very mild and delicate —and, because of the long shipping route to markets, quite expensive. Being a fat fish, it is at its best when baked or broiled.

Pâté de Noël

      1 (7–8-pound) turkey
      1 (3-pound) roasting chicken
1 1/2–2 pounds veal knuckle
     12 cups cold water
      4 teaspoons salt
      1 sliced onion
      1 stalk celery, sliced
      1 bay leaf
      1 sliced carrot
        Few peppercorns
      2 cloves
    1/8 teaspoon thyme
1 1/2 pounds ground pork
    1/2 cup brandy
        Plain Pastry for 2 double-crust pies
      1 tablespoon salt
    1/2 teaspoon pepper
    1/4 pound mushrooms sliced
      1 recipe *Flaky Pastry for Pâté*
      1 egg white, unbeaten
      1 egg yolk, slightly beaten, plus 2 teaspoons water

Skin turkey and chicken; reserve skin. Cut meat from bones in large pieces, 1/2 inch thick. Remove fat, gristle and tendons, and reserve. Slice meat from veal knuckle into similar-size pieces.

Refrigerate sliced meats. Pile bones, skin and trimmings in preserving kettle; add cold water and next 8 ingredients. Bring gently to boiling point, and skim off foamy scum that will appear. Cover, turn heat low and simmer 3—4 hours. Drain broth into bowl; then return broth to pan alone, and continue simmering, uncovered, until reduced to 4 cups. Meanwhile pick over bones, and save any cooked meat bits. Strain reduced broth through cheesecloth, and cool to room temperature. Blend ground pork with brandy and 1/2 cup broth.

Roll *Plain Pastry* about 3/16 inch thick. Line 3-quart oblong, round or oval pan, preferably about 4 inches deep. (A loose-bottomed pan is ideal if you wish to remove finished pie to platter for serving.) Sprinkle raw sliced meats with 1 tablespoon salt and pepper. Fill pastry-lined pan to top with alternate layers of dark meat, light meat, ground pork mixture and mushrooms. Roll *Flaky Pastry* 3/16 inch thick, and cover pie. Trim and seal pastry edges with egg white. Cut 2- or 3 1/2-inch openings in center of pastry lid. Cut out pastry leaves or triangles, and arrange over vents; you can also braid strips of *Flaky Pastry* to decorate edge. Brush top with egg yolk. If using a spring-form pan, place the pie on a small tray or cupped square of heavy foil. Bake pie in preheated 400°F. oven 1 1/2 hours; reduce heat to 350°F., and bake 3 1/2 hours. Cool pâté to room temperature, and lift off pastry leaves. Using funnel, pour reduced broth through pastry slits until pie is well filled. Tip pan several times as you pour, so that all spaces between meats are filled. Refrigerate overnight, and serve cold. Serves 30.

Note: French Canada's famous Christmas pie, made with turkey, chicken, and various seasonings, can be served all through Christmas week. It is always served cold, its thick slices encased in firm natural jelly of the meat broth. The pie is completely in pastry—plain for bottom and sides, especially flaky for top. It may be served on platter or left in oven-glass casserole or other suitable bake-and-serve dish.

Flaky Pastry for Pâté

      3 cups sifted all-purpose flour
1 1/2 teaspoons salt
    1/3 cup soft shortening
    3/4 cup hard shortening (lard, cold butter or margarine)
      1 egg yolk, beaten
    1/2 cup ice-cold water
      2 teaspoons lemon juice

Sift flour and salt into bowl; rub in soft shortening until texture is very fine. Cut hard shortening into 1-inch cubes, and cut into flour with pastry blender to distribute evenly throughout. Combine egg yolk, water and lemon juice, and sprinkle over mixture. Stir with fork until crumbs cling together. Form ball, and chill 30 minutes. Roll out 1/2 inch thick on floured board in rectangle twice as long as wide. Fold in 3; give dough 1/2 turn, and roll out again 1/2 inch thick. Repeat once more, and wrap in waxed paper. Refrigerate 20 minutes. Roll and chill 3 more times; then refrigerate until needed for *Pâté de Noël*.

Casserole of Atlantic Shellfish

1 1/2 cups chicken broth or 2 chicken-bouillon cubes dissolved in 1 1/2 cups boiling water
1 pound fresh or frozen scallops
1/2 pint fresh or frozen oysters and juice
Milk
1/2 cup butter
1/4 cup chopped onion
1 1/2 cups sliced fresh mushrooms
1/2 cup diced green pepper
1/2 cup flour
1 cup light cream
1 teaspoon Worcestershire sauce
1/2 teaspoon dry mustard
1/2 pound fresh or frozen shrimps, cooked, peeled and deveined
1 1/2 cups fresh or frozen lobster meat or Queen crabmeat, cooked
1–1 1/2 cups soft buttered bread crumbs

Bring chicken broth to a boil, and add the scallops. Cover, and simmer 5 minutes. Add oysters and juice. Cover, and simmer until the edges of the oysters curl. Strain off the liquid, and measure. Add enough milk to make 2 1/2 cups. Heat butter in a medium-size skillet. Add onion, mushrooms and green pepper. Sauté until onion is transparent. Remove from heat, and stir in the flour. Gradually add the 2 1/2 cups liquid. Return to heat, and cook and stir until thick and smooth. Add the cream, Worcestershire sauce and dry mustard. Reheat thoroughly, and stir in scallops, oysters, shrimps and lobster. Taste for seasoning, and add salt, pepper and a few dashes hot pepper sauce. Spread in a greased 2-quart casserole or 2 smaller casseroles. Sprinkle with crumbs, and bake at 375°F. until bubbly, about 35 minutes. Broil briefly to brown crumbs if necessary. Serves 8.

Note: 3–4 tablespoons sherry may be added to the sauce.

Roast Brome Lake Ducklings

2 (4–5-pound) ducklings
2 teaspoons salt
1/4 teaspoon pepper
2 large onions, chopped
2 apples, cored and chopped
2 stalks celery, thinly sliced
1/4 cup chopped parsley
1 cup apple cider or apple juice
1/4 cup butter or margarine
1/4 cup brandy
3 tablespoons flour

Scrub birds thoroughly, inside and out. Pat as dry as possible. Mix salt and pepper, and use 1/2 to rub cavities. Combine onions, apples, celery and parsley; divide mixture evenly, and stuff birds. Skewer, truss and rub skins with remaining salt and pepper. Place on rack in open roasting pan, and prick breasts. Bake in 325°F. oven, allowing 20 minutes per pound. At end of first 30 minutes, remove accumulated fat from pan. Repeat in another 30 minutes. In the meantime, heat apple cider and butter or margarine; add brandy. Baste birds with this mixture, and continue to baste at 10-minute intervals until end of roasting period. Remove ducks, and keep warm. Skim off all fat, reserving 3 tablespoons. Measure pan juices, and add water or cider to make 2 cups. Combine 3 tablespoons duck fat with flour, and blend into hot pan juices, stirring briskly. Cook until boiling and thickened. Adjust seasonings, and serve very hot with roast ducks, *Wild Rice* and glazed *Sautéed Apple Rings*. Serves 6–8.

Note: Stuff ducks with your favorite bread stuffing if you prefer. Fine-flavored ducklings are raised in Brome County, Quebec. The recipe could be used for any tender young duck.

Maple Baked Beans

1 (12-ounce) package large dry lima beans (1 1/2 cups, heaped)
1 (12-ounce) package dry kidney beans (1 1/2 cups, heaped)
2 quarts water
2 teaspoons salt
1/4–1/2 pound smoked bacon ends or salt pork
2 small bay leaves
3 chopped onions or leeks
1/2 cup pure maple syrup
1 small can tomato sauce or 4 tablespoons tomato paste plus 3/4 cup bean water

Soak beans separately overnight in 1 quart of water for each batch. In the morning, add enough fresh water to cover the beans, and sprinkle each with 1 teaspoon salt. Bring to a boil separately, and cover. Turn heat low, and cook until beans are barely tender, about 40 minutes for limas and 1 1/2 hours for kidney beans. Drain beans, and reserve liquid. Drop bacon chunks into a deep Dutch oven or heavy covered casserole. Add beans, bay leaves, onions, syrup and tomato sauce. Pour in enough bean liquid to just cover the beans. Bake covered at 275°F. 5–6 hours or until beans are very tender. Keep beans moist with more bean liquid if needed during the cooking. Uncover for the last hour if there seems to be too much juice. Taste for seasoning, and add more salt, pepper, a few drops of maple flavoring or a couple spoons of brown sugar. Serves 6–8. For a crowd, double the recipe, and make 2 days ahead of time. The flavor improves with reheating.

Note: Canadian Indians baked beans slowly in clay pots heaped with hot wood ashes, flavoring them with bear meat (which tastes like strong pork). For a similar hearty flavor, bury 3 smoked pork hocks in the mixture 3 hours before beans are tender.

Stuffed Sole Victoria

```
  1 pound sole fillets, fresh or frozen
  8 strips side bacon
  1 tablespoon butter
  1 tablespoon chopped onion
1/2 cup chopped mushrooms
1–2 tablespoons chopped parsley
  1 cup stale, but not dry, bread crumbs
    Few dashes Worcestershire sauce
    French dressing or milk
1/4–1/2 cup dry white wine
```

Defrost fish if frozen, just until fillets can be separated. Sauté bacon slices lightly until fat turns clear. Set bacon aside. Add butter to the pan with onion and mushrooms. Sauté until onion is clear. Remove from heat, and add parsley, bread crumbs, Worcestershire sauce and enough French dressing to moisten. Taste for seasoning. Spread stuffing on each fillet, and roll up. Wrap each roll barber-pole fashion with a strip of bacon, and secure with toothpicks. Place side by side in a shallow baking dish. Brush with melted butter. Pour wine around the rolls, and bake at 450°F. 15 minutes or until fish flakes easily. Serve with tartar sauce, quickly cooked spinach and beet salad. Serves 4.

Indian Pudding

```
  1 cup cold milk
  1 cup yellow cornmeal
  4 cups hot milk
1/4 cup butter
  5 eggs, beaten
  1 cup fine white sugar
1/4 teaspoon salt
  1 teaspoon cinnamon or ginger
  1 teaspoon mace or nutmeg
  1 teaspoon vanilla
    Brandy Hard Sauce
```

Mix cold milk and cornmeal together, and stir into the hot milk. Add the butter, and cook and stir until mixture bubbles. Cool slightly; then stir in eggs mixed with sugar, salt, spices and vanilla. Pour into a deep greased 1 1/2-quart baking dish, and bake at 375°F. 35–45 minutes or until set and browned. Serve hot or warm with *Brandy Hard Sauce*. Serves 10.

Brandy Hard Sauce

```
2/3 cup soft butter
1 1/2 cups sifted icing sugar
1/4 cup brandy
  1 teaspoon vanilla
```

Beat butter with 1 1/4 cups sifted icing sugar. Gradually add brandy and vanilla. Beat in remaining sugar, and chill.

Cream of Pumpkin Soup

```
  1 leek or small onion, chopped
  2 tablespoons fat
  2 tablespoons flour
1 1/2 cups chicken broth
  2 cups freshly cooked or canned pumpkin
  2 cups milk or cream
    Salt and pepper to taste
    Pinch nutmeg
    Watercress or parsley
```

Sauté leek in hot fat until tender and golden. Remove pan from heat, and stir in the flour. Add chicken broth slowly, and return to the heat. Bring to a boil, and cook until thickened. Add pumpkin and milk. Reheat thoroughly, and season with salt, pepper and a pinch of nutmeg. Serve topped with chopped watercress or parsley. Makes 5–6 servings.

Butter Tarts

```
1/3 cup soft butter
1/2 cup brown sugar, firmly packed
  1 cup corn syrup
1/8 teaspoon salt
  2 slightly beaten eggs
  1 teaspoon vanilla
1–2 teaspoons vinegar or lemon juice
    Dash nutmeg, cinnamon or allspice (optional)
3/4 cup steamed seedless raisins
    Pastry
```

Cream the butter, sugar, corn syrup and salt together, and stir in beaten eggs, vanilla, vinegar and spice. Pour boiling water over raisins and let stand 10 minutes; then drain and dry. Roll out pastry, and cut in circles to fit deep medium-size muffin pans. Filling is sufficient to fill approximately 14–15 tart shells. Sprinkle 2 teaspoons raisins in the bottom of each shell, and spoon or pour the filling in until shells are 2/3 full. Bake at 400°F. 10 minutes; reduce heat to 350°F., and bake 5–10 minutes longer or until pastry is golden.

Note: Do *not* use a beater to combine the filling ingredients. Beating makes mixture too frothy with air, and often will cause the filling to boil over the pastry edge during baking.

For runny-type tarts make shells deep, and use the above filling for *Butter Tarts*.

For firmly set tarts use 3/4 cup brown sugar and 3/4 cup corn syrup, and have unbaked shells quite shallow. You may mix in 2–3 heaping tablespoons sour cream.

This rich sweet has been a favorite of Canadians for almost a century. Recipes differ widely, depending on the taste preference of the cook. Sometimes butter tarts are runny and taste like butterscotch, while others may be firmly set and lightly spiced.

Whole Poached Glazed Salmon

    1 (6–8-pound) dressed or pan-dressed salmon
      Cheesecloth
      Vinegar Court Bouillon
      Court Bouillon Glaze
      Garnishes
      Caper Mayonnaise

Measure the thickness of the fish, and rinse and dry. Overlap the vent pieces, and pin with small metal skewers. Wrap the fish in 2 thicknesses of cheesecloth; then place on a rack in a fish kettle. If fish is small you may be able to use a long covered roast pan. Pour enough cool, strained *Vinegar Court Bouillon* over the fish to half cover. Bring slowly to a boil; then turn heat low, and cover the pan. Simmer the fish, allowing about 10 minutes per inch for fresh fish and about 20 minutes per inch for frozen fish. Test fish for doneness with a metal skewer pressed in near the backbone. The meat will flake or separate from the bone when fish is sufficiently cooked. Cool fish in the liquid, uncovered; then drain, and reserve 5 cups of the liquid. Remove the cheesecloth, and chill the fish on a rack over a tray. To glaze, carefully remove the skin and skewers. Scrape away any fat deposits on edges of the vent. Spoon cold, but syrupy, *Court Bouillon Glaze* over the fish. Lift rack, and pour the glaze drippings back into the remaining dish of glaze. Return rack to the tray, and refrigerate the fish until first glaze has set. Repeat with a second coat of glaze. To garnish, use cutouts of sliced carrots or cheese, radishes, pickles, leaves of watercress, sliced stuffed olives, capers, dainty slivers of lemon or black olives. Dip each item of your creation in leftover liquid glaze, and set in place. Chill; then spoon more glaze over the entire fish. Chill. Arrange on a long platter, and garnish with bunches of watercress and lemon baskets full of *Caper Mayonnaise*.

Note: If the gelatine mixture thickens between glazes, heat and stir over a bowl of hot water until liquid again. Chill until syrupy, and continue glazing.

Vinegar Court Bouillon

    3 quarts water
    1 cup white wine vinegar
    2 sliced onions
    2 sliced carrots
    3 stalks celery, sliced
      Handful broken celery leaves
      Handful parsley sprigs
    3 bay leaves
    1 teaspoon thyme
    2 teaspoons peppercorns
    1 tablespoon salt
    3–4 thin slices lemon

Combine all ingredients, bring to a boil and simmer 40–50 minutes to extract and blend the flavors. Cool and strain before pouring over the fish. You may need twice this amount for a large fish and half this amount for a small fish, depending on the size of the pan and height of the rack or trivet.

Court Bouillon Glaze

    4 teaspoons plain gelatine
    5 cups cold cooking liquid

Mix gelatine with reserved cooking liquid. Bring to a boil, and boil, uncovered, until reduced to 3 1/2 cups. Strain through cheesecloth into a bowl, and taste for seasoning. Chill in refrigerator until syrupy, stirring occasionally, or set the bowl in a dish of ice cubes and stir until the right consistency. This amount is sufficient to glaze an 8-pound fish.

Caper Mayonnaise

      1/3 cup capers
    1 1/2 cups thick *Mayonnaise*
      1/2 teaspoon Dijon mustard
          Pinch cayenne

Drain and dry capers. Chop coarsely. Mix with *Mayonnaise*, mustard and cayenne.

Cold Maple Soufflé

    3 teaspoons plain gelatine
    1/4 cup cold water
    1 cup maple syrup
    2 eggs, separated
      Pinch salt
    1 pint whipping cream, whipped
      Toasted slivered almonds (optional)

Soften gelatine in cold water. Beat syrup and the egg yolks together in the top of a double boiler. Set the pan over boiling water, and heat and stir about 5 minutes. Remove from over the water, and stir in softened gelatine. When gelatine has dissolved, chill the mixture in the freezer until as thick as jam or honey, stirring occasionally. Beat egg whites and salt until moist peaks form. Fold in the thickened maple mixture, then the stiffly whipped cream. Surround the top of a 6-cup soufflé dish with a double strip of waxed paper letting the paper extend about 1 inch above the edge of the dish. Tie paper strip in place with string. Scrape in the maple mixture, and swirl slightly. Sprinkle with toasted almonds. Cover top with plastic, and chill several hours or overnight. To serve, carefully remove paper strip. Makes 10–12 small servings.

Stuffed Western Beef Tenderloin

    4 (8-ounce) servings beef tenderloin, about 2 inches
        thick
    1/2 cup finely chopped dark mushrooms
    1 tablespoon sweet butter
    1 tablespoon chopped parsley
    1/2 cup (4 ounces) pâté de foie gras
    8 thin slices prosciutto ham or rindless side bacon
        Small skewers
        Madeira Sauce

When selecting tenderloin ask your butcher for filet mignon cut 2 inches thick or Chateaubriand cut 1 1/2 inches thick. Sauté mushrooms quickly in hot butter until limp. Remove from heat, and stir in parsley and pâté de foie gras. Chill the mixture. Sear the tenderloin pieces quickly on both sides in a hot, lightly greased frying pan or broiler. Cut a deep pocket into the side of each steak horizontally, and stuff the openings with the pâté de foie gras mixture. Wrap each steak in 2 slices prosciutto, and secure with skewers. Brush with oil, and bake in an iron frying pan at 450°F. 5—10 minutes or until rare or medium. Serve with *Madeira Sauce*. Makes 4 servings.

Madeira Sauce: Lift meat to a hot platter, and keep warm. Pour 3/4 cup Madeira or dry sherry into the frying pan used for baking, and heat and stir until brown bits dissolve and wine is reduced to 1/3 cup. Stir in 1 cup of good brown sauce or thickened beef stock. Heat thoroughly, and stir in 1—2 tablespoons firm butter. Serve at once without boiling.

Note: Steaks may be prepared ahead of time and kept refrigerated until final baking.

Oyster Bisque

    2 pints oysters
    1/4 cup diced onion
    1/4 cup diced celery
    1/4 cup diced carrots
    1 1/2 cups rich chicken broth
    1/2 bay leaf
    1/4 cup dry white wine
    1/4 cup soft butter
    1/4 cup flour
    3 cups light cream or rich milk
    1/2 teaspoon salt
    1/8 teaspoon cayenne
        Dash mace or nutmeg
    1/4 cup dry sherry or Madeira
    2 tablespoons chopped parsley

Drain oysters, and reserve the juice. Examine oysters, and discard any bits of shell. Return oysters to the juice, and heat until the edges curl. Drain the juice into a saucepan. Chop oysters coarsely, and set aside. Add the next 5 ingredients to the oyster juice, and simmer, covered, 15—20 minutes or until vegetables are soft. Strain the mixture into the top part of a large double boiler using a coarse seive. Press most of the vege-

tables through at the same time with the back of a wooden spoon. Add the wine to the mixture, and heat to a boil. Whisk in a smooth roux made by creaming the butter and flour together. Cook and stir until smoothly thickened. Set the pan over boiling water, and add the oysters, cream and seasonings. Reheat thoroughly. Taste. Just before serving add sherry and parsley. Makes 8 servings.

Apple Charlotte

    3 pounds tart Spy apples
    1/4 cup butter
    3/4 cup sugar
    1 teaspoon grated lemon rind
        Cinnamon and nutmeg
    10–12 slices 2-day-old bread, crusts removed
        Melted butter
        Sifted icing sugar
        Cold Custard Cream Sauce

Peel, core and quarter apples. Melt butter in a heavy saucepan, and add apple quarters. Cover, and steam-cook on low to medium heat until puffy and soft. Cook and stir until almost all the juices evaporate. Add sugar, lemon rind and spices to taste. Continue cooking slowly until mixture is thick. Butter bottom and sides of a deep 8-cup casserole. Cut bread slices in half, and dip quickly in melted butter. Overlap against bottom and sides. Fill the center with apple puree, and press down lightly. If bread extends above filling, snip off with kitchen shears, and drop pieces over filling. Bake the charlotte on a cookie sheet at 425°F. 30—45 minutes, depending on depth of dish. Cool 5 minutes. Loosen edges with a knife, and invert on a warm serving plate. Dust top with sifted icing sugar. Serve hot with *Cold Custard Cream Sauce*, or pouring cream. Serves 7—8. For special occasions, surround the hot charlotte with poached quarters of unpeeled red-skinned apples cooked in a light to medium sugar syrup that has been tinted pink.

Cold Custard Cream Sauce: Scald 3/4 cup milk in the top of a double boiler, and stir in 2 egg yolks, slightly beaten with 3 tablespoons icing sugar. Cook and stir over hot, not boiling, water until the mixture coats a spoon. Remove from heat, and add a pinch of salt and 1/2 teaspoon vanilla. Chill thoroughly. At serving time, fold the custard into 1 1/2 cups whipped cream.

Wild Rice

The long thin grey-black needles of wild rice cooked to perfection are a delicacy appreciated by gourmets everywhere. Once the staple food of Indians living around the marshes of Rice Lake in Ontario and Lake Winnipeg in Manitoba and other swampy freshwater areas, wild rice is still harvested by their descendants in the fall of the year and sent to the market in packages. Wild rice is very expensive. An excellent substitute is a packaged mixture of long-grain and wild rice.

    1 cup wild rice
    3 cups boiling chicken broth, consommé or water
    1/2 teaspoon salt
    1/4 teaspoon pepper
    1/4 teaspoon thyme
    2 tablespoons butter or margarine
    1/2 cup chopped onion
    2 tablespoons chopped parsley
    2 tablespoons butter or margarine

Wash rice thoroughly, and soak in cold water 30 minutes. Drain; add boiling water and seasonings. Cover, and simmer 40–45 minutes until rice is tender. Stir frequently, and add extra liquid if necessary. Melt butter or margarine, and sauté onion until golden. Place cooked rice in buttered 1 1/2-quart casserole. Add onions and parsley. Season to taste. Dot with 2 tablespoons butter or margarine, and cover. Reheat at 350°F. 20 minutes. Serve from casserole as side dish with poultry or game. Serves 4–6.

Note: 1 cup sliced fresh mushrooms may be sautéed and added to the dish before reheating.

Spiced Beef

    7–9–pound boneless round, rump roast or brisket
    2 cups brown sugar, firmly packed
    4 broken bay leaves
    1/2 ounce saltpeter
    2 tablespoons cinnamon
    4 teaspoons allspice
    1 tablespoon cloves
    1 tablespoon nutmeg
    1 tablespoon ginger (optional)
    1 tablespoon black pepper
    2/3 cup coarse pickling salt

Rub the sugar into all sides of meat. Place in a deep dish or porcelain pan with any remaining sugar and bay leaves. Refrigerate overnight. Next day, combine remaining ingredients, and rub in as much of the mixture as you can; then sprinkle with the remainder. Cover, and refrigerate for 2 weeks. Baste with the liquids in the dish, and turn the meat every day.

Lift meat out of the juices into a large kettle, and cover with warm water. Bring slowly to a boil. Cover, and simmer until fork-tender, allowing about 35–40 minutes to the pound. Let cool in the liquid; then drain. Wrap in a wet cloth. Weigh down firmly, and refrigerate overnight.

INTERNATIONAL GOURMET MENUS

MEDITERRANEAN SUNDAY LUNCH

Bourride
Rouille
Tray of raw vegetables
(carrots, cauliflower, radishes and cucumbers)
Fresh peaches, poached in white wine

Bourride

    2 tablespoons olive oil
    1 cup finely chopped onion
    2 crushed cloves garlic
    2 pounds fresh or frozen fish fillets
    1/2 pound fresh or frozen shrimp
    1 dozen fresh clams or 1 (10-ounce) can baby clams
2 1/2–3 cups fish stock
    2 tablespoons chopped parsley
    1/4 teaspoon black pepper
    1/4 teaspoon thyme
    6–8 slices French bread
    1/2 cup olive oil
    1 teaspoon garlic powder

Heat 2 tablespoons olive oil in a large saucepan. Stir in onion and crushed garlic. Sauté 5 minutes, stirring occasionally. Cut fish fillets into 1-inch pieces, discarding skin and bones. Add to onion mixture together with shrimp and well-scrubbed clams in shells. Pour in fish stock. Add chopped parsley, pepper and thyme. Cover, and simmer 15 minutes. Meanwhile, sauté French bread in hot olive oil to which garlic powder has been added.

To serve, place sautéed bread in soup bowls and ladle bourride over them. Serve with *Rouille*. Serves 6–8.

Fish Stock: Place 1–1 1/2 pounds fish trimmings (heads, fins, bones) in a saucepan. Pour in 1 cup dry white wine and enough water to barely cover, about 3 cups. Add 1/2 teaspoon salt, 3–4 sprigs parsley, 1 bay leaf, 1 sliced leek, a sprig or pinch of thyme, a sprig of fennel and a thin strip of orange or lemon peel. Cover, and simmer 30–40 minutes. Strain, and taste for seasoning. Cool.

Note: This fish stew-soup is almost as famous in Marseilles as its cousin the bouillabaisse. Unlike bouillabaisse, bourride has no saffron and generally no tomatoes. But like bouillabaisse, it's ladled into soup dishes over slices of toasted French bread. Stir a spoonful of garlic-scented *Rouille* or mayonnaise into broth to give it flavor and a slight hint of thickening.

Rouille

    1/4 cup fresh white bread crumbs
    2 cloves garlic, crushed
    1/4 cup fish liquid (from *Bourride*)
1/3–1/2 cup oil
    Dash of hot pepper sauce

In blender, combine bread crumbs, garlic and fish liquid. Blend on low speed 30 seconds. Add oil in slow, steady stream to achieve consistency of mayonnaise. Add hot pepper sauce.

Note: Make quickly by adding 2 cloves crushed garlic and 2–3 drops hot pepper sauce to 1/2 cup mayonnaise.

An Oriental table.
CREDIT: *Henry Sandbank.*

An Indian table.
CREDIT: *Henry Sandbank.*

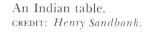

Curried Shrimp (p. 259).
CREDIT: *Henry Sandbank.*

Sweet-and-Sour Pork (pp. 263-264).
CREDIT: *Henry Sandbank.*

Shish Kebab (p. 57).
CREDIT: *Elbert Budin.*

Veal Wellington (p. 52).
CREDIT: *Bernard Gray.*

Double consommé
Roast Pheasant
Stuffed with Grapes and Nuts
Green Beans and Onions au Beurre
Belgium endive salad
Pots de crème au café
Demitasse

Roast Pheasant Stuffed with Grapes and Nuts

    2 (2 1/2–3-pound) pheasants, dressed and split in
      halves
  3/4 cup butter, melted
    1 teaspoon salt
  1/2 teaspoon thyme
  1/8 teaspoon pepper
1 1/2 cups seedless green grapes, washed
  2/3 cup coarsely chopped mixed nuts
    1 cup buttered bread crumbs
1/4–1/2 cup gin

Rinse and dry pheasant halves. Remove pin feathers. Cut off straggly bits of skin at neck and cavity ends. Pin each leg against the halves with small metal skewers. Brush inside and out with a mixture of the butter, salt, thyme and pepper. Place cut side down close together in a shallow open roasting pan. Bake at 400°F. 15 minutes. Meanwhile, mash 1/2 cup of grapes, and mix with remaining whole grapes, nuts and crumbs. Turn halves over, and fill cavities with the grape-nut mixture. Mix gin with remaining butter used for brushing, and spoon over the halves. Cover lightly with foil, and bake at 350°F. 40 minutes or until pheasant is tender and leg joint moves freely. Uncover during the last 15 minutes of baking time to lightly dry the surface of the dressing. Baste with pan juices once or twice during cooking. Serves 4.

Green Beans and Onions au Beurre

  1 (10-ounce) package frozen green beans
1/4 cup butter or margarine
  4 small onions (approximately 1/2 cup)
  2 tablespoons French dressing
    Salt and pepper to taste

Cook beans according to directions on package. Meanwhile, melt butter or margarine in skillet. Peel onions, slice thin and add to skillet. Cook until transparent. Drain cooked beans, and add to skillet with dressing and salt and pepper to taste. Stir, and serve hot. Serves 4.

Note: Cut, Italian, and Frenched green beans are all equally delicious prepared this way.

Onion soup
Chestnut-stuffed Cornish Game Hens
Broccoli au Gratin
Fresh tomato salad
Pêchés au Rum

Chestnut-stuffed Cornish Game Hens

  1 cup chopped canned cooked chestnuts
1/4 cup golden raisins
1/4 cup sautéed onion
  1 small apple, chopped
  2 tablespoons diced celery
  2 small Cornish game hens
1/4 cup butter or margarine, melted

Combine chestnuts with raisins, onion, apple and celery. Season to taste. Use to stuff hens. Roast at 375°F. 1 hour or until done, basting several times with melted butter or margarine. Serves 2.

Broccoli au Gratin

  1 (10-ounce) package frozen broccoli
2/3 cup milk
  2 tablespoons soft butter
  2 tablespoons flour
  2 tablespoons mayonnaise
1/2 cup grated Havarti, Edam or Cheddar cheese

Cook broccoli until just tender according to directions. Drain, and save the liquid. Arrange broccoli in a pie plate or small baking dish. Measure the milk and 1/2 cup of the reserved vegetable water into a small saucepan. Bring to a boil, and stir in a smooth mixture of butter and flour. Cook until thick and smooth. Add mayonnaise, and taste for seasoning. Spread over the broccoli, and sprinkle with cheese. Broil slowly until heated through and lightly browned. Makes 2 servings.

Pêchés au Rum

  4 canned peach halves
  2 tablespoons slivered almonds
  2 tablespoons melted butter
2/3 cup crumbled macaroons
1/2 cup peach juice
  1 teaspoon lemon juice
1/4 cup rum or brandy
  1 tablespoon sugar

Arrange peach halves in a pie plate. Fill cavities with a mixture of almonds, butter and macaroons. Combine remaining ingredients, and pour over peaches. Bake at 375°F. 15 minutes or until heated through. Serve warm with pan juices and pouring cream or whipped cream. Makes 2 large or 4 small servings.

Consommé
Coconut Curried Shrimp
Hot *Brioches*
Lemon sherbet
Dutch Butter Cake

Coconut Curried Shrimp

     2 pounds fresh or frozen shrimp, peeled or unpeeled
 1/2 teaspoon salt
 2 1/2 cups boiling water
     2 chicken-bouillon cubes
     1 cup cream
 1/3 cup fresh grated or flake coconut
     2 tablespoons butter or margarine
     2 tablespoons salad oil
 1/2 cup diced celery
 1/3 cup chopped onion
     1 clove garlic, crushed
 1/4 cup flour
     1 tablespoon curry powder
     2 tablespoons lemon juice
     1 teaspoon Worcestershire sauce
 1/8 teaspoon chili-pepper seeds
 1/4 teaspoon grated lemon rind
     2 tablespoons chopped parsley

Add shrimp and salt to boiling water. Cover, and bring to boil. Turn heat low, and simmer 2—5 minutes (small shrimp will take 2 minutes, large shrimp 5 minutes). Drain, reserving liquid. Crumble chicken-bouillon cubes into liquid, and set aside. Peel and devein shrimp if necessary. Heat cream and coconut together until bubbly; set aside. Heat butter or margarine and oil, and add celery, onion and garlic. Sauté slowly until vegetables are transparent, about 5 minutes. Stir in flour and curry powder; then slowly add shrimp liquid, and cook until smoothly thickened. Add next 4 ingredients and coconut mixture. When blended, add parsley and shrimp, and reheat thoroughly. Salt to taste. If thick, dilute with cream or dry sherry. Serve over hot *Fluffy Rice*. Pass chutney, raisins and sliced bananas.

Dutch Butter Cake

     2 cups sifted all-purpose flour
 1/8 teaspoon salt
     1 cup icing sugar
     1 cup soft butter or margarine
     1 egg, slightly beaten
     5 ounces ground almonds
 1/3 cup fruit sugar
     1 egg, beaten
1–1 1/2 teaspoons grated lemon rind

Measure and sift flour, salt and icing sugar into a bowl. Rub in the butter with fingertips. With a fork stir in 1 slightly beaten egg to form a soft dough. Divide dough into 2 pieces, and press out 1 piece into a lightly buttered deep 9- or 10-inch pie plate. Depress the center evenly to about 3/8 inch in depth. Lightly flatten the top edge around the pan to an even 1/4-inch thickness. Stir remaining ingredients together, and spread in the depression. Form remaining dough into a ball, and press out on lightly floured waxed paper into a rather thick circle, about 8—8 1/2 inches in diameter, to fit inside top dimension of the pan.

Smooth the dough with a rolling pin. Invert over the filling. Press edges lightly together with tines of a fork, or pinch into tiny scallops.

If you like, reserve a scrap of the dough, and roll it out and cut into 6 small diamonds. Arrange these cutouts petal-fashion in the center top of the cake. Bake at 325°F. 1—1 1/4 hours, or until golden. If using a glass pie dish, bake at 300°F. Cool completely. Remove from pan and, because of richness, cut into 12 small wedges.

SUNDAY LUNCHEON

Ham and Chicken Rolls
Buttered noodles or salad
Glazed carrots
Fresh raspberries   *Swiss Tartlets*

Ham and Chicken Rolls

     1 cup chopped mushrooms
     2 tablespoons butter
 1 1/2 cups chopped cooked chicken
 1/8 teaspoon thyme
     2 ounces Gouda cheese, shredded
     2 tablespoons chopped parsley
 1/2 cup thick *White* or *Mornay Sauce*
        (approximately)
        Salt and pepper to taste
 8–10 slices cooked ham
     3 tablespoons butter
     4 tablespoons flour
     2 cups rich chicken broth
 1/2 cup heavy cream
 2–3 tablespoons dry sherry
     1 fresh avocado, peeled and diced

Sauté mushrooms in 2 tablespoons hot butter, and lift out into a bowl. Mix chicken, thyme, cheese and parsley with mushrooms. Stir in just enough sauce to bind the mixture. Taste for seasoning, but be sparing with salt because of the ham. Spoon some of the chicken mixture on each slice of ham, and roll up. Arrange in a shallow baking dish, edges down. Add 3 tablespoons butter to the fat in the mushroom pan, and heat until melted. Stir in the flour; then add chicken broth slowly, and cook and stir until smoothly thickened. Stir in the cream, sherry and avocado. Taste for seasoning, and pour over the ham rolls. Bake at 375°F. until thoroughly heated through, about 20 minutes. Serves 8—10.

Swiss Tartlets

     1 cup soft butter or margarine
 1/2 teaspoon vanilla
 1/4 teaspoon almond or lemon extract
 1/2 cup icing sugar
     2 cups unsifted pastry flour
 1/8 teaspoon salt
        Icing sugar
        Cherries, halved

Cream butter, vanilla and extract together until fluffy, and stir in sifted dry ingredients. Fit a pastry bag with a large rosette tip, and fill with soft dough. Press the dough out into small paper liners in muffin cups, using a circular motion to leave a depression in the center. Hold edge of cup down as you fill. Bake at 375°F. about 20 minutes or until edges are pale gold. Sprinkle with icing sugar, and garnish with half cherries. Makes 2—3 dozen.

Note: Without a pastry bag, add 1/4 cup more sifted pastry flour, and chill. Roll in balls; dip in beaten egg white and chopped almonds. Depress the center, and bake and garnish as above.

CHAPTER SIX

Parties
Large and Small

Being a good party hostess is really quite simple. The only cardinal etiquette rule is always to remember the comfort and convenience of your guests.

Select your guests imaginatively—some who are talkers and some who are not and an extra man or a guest from abroad, if possible. Include some people whom you know and can count on.

Plan your menu around your guests and upon the mood of the party (formal or informal, buffet or sit-down). Do take full advantage of dishes that can be prepared in advance, and try to remember any medical, religious or other restrictions of your guests' diets.

Suggested Procedure

Guest List. If it's to be a large party, you can safely invite people of varying tastes and backgrounds. For a small group, it's wiser to be sure your guests will like one another and share similar interests.

Date and Time. Try to pick a time convenient to all. For example, many working people dislike late party nights during the week, but will accept a dinner invitation with a few drinks before the meal. A luncheon for ladies is usually best on a weekday.

Invitations. A word-of-mouth invitation is in itself indication of an informal occasion. More formality is implied when you mail little printed cards or write personal notes; and full formality is suggested by engraved cards, as for a coming-out dance or a wedding. The last should be sent 3 weeks or a month in advance; for other types of parties allow 10 days to 2 weeks. Be sure every invitation of whatever type explicitly mentions the guest's name (or names), the type of party, the time, place and date. A suggestion for the kind of clothes to be worn is appreciated—for example, "black tie" to signify dinner jackets. If you wish to know the exact number of guests for the occasion, specify RSVP. There are always some who neglect to answer invitations promptly. If you can possibly manage without knowing exactly how many are coming, don't worry about it. Otherwise, telephone, and ask them if they plan to come.

Set the Keynote. Is the party a special event such as an anniversary or homecoming? Is it to be a formal dinner, an intimate supper, a buffet luncheon, a cocktail party? Work out your plan according to the over-all theme and the number of guests.

Choose the Menu. Decide what foods to serve and how. Note which items you can prepare ahead of time and which ones need attention the day of the party. Get as much as possible done beforehand, and keep kitchen duty to a minimum.

Check Your Equipment. Look over your platters, serving dishes, flatware, table linen and other supplies. Make sure you have what you need for the menu planned and the number of guests invited. Have enough plates and glasses so that dishwashing isn't a problem.

Organize Your Shopping. A pre-party shopping plan should cover candles, favors, place cards and other decorations. Flowers should be ordered for delivery the day of the party, but in plenty of time for you to arrange them. Buy any extra table equipment you may need. If serving special beverages, order them and accompaniments in advance. Plan to have plenty of ice cubes ready in the refrigerator. Make sure you have enough cigarettes, coasters, ashtrays and matches.

Break down your menu into a complete grocery list, and assemble all nonperishable foods you will need. Place orders well in advance for any specialties you may need from the baker and grocer.

Make a list of all items to be bought at the last minute—salad materials, cream, breads and so on.

If you look at your lists from time to time you'll be able to catch missing details.

How Much Formality?

The degree of formality is usually a personal decision, but here are some rules for formal entertaining.

The Tablecloth. A white damask or lace cloth is called for. If the former is used, you need a table pad underneath. If you decide on lace or cutwork cloth, you should use individual pads where needed for placement of hot plates, platters and serving dishes.

Places and Spaces. In arranging places, allow about 2 feet of space for each guest. If you measure space from dinner knife at one place setting to that at the next, you can be sure you have allowed enough space so that each diner is not crowded.

Arranging Flatware. Place all flatware uniform distance from edge of table—not less than 1/2 inch and not more than 1 inch—and well clear of rim of the dinner plate, so that it won't be disturbed when plates are served or removed. All flatware should be placed in the order in which it will be used, working from the outside in toward the plate. Forks go at the left, with tines pointing up. Knives are placed at the right, with cutting edges turned toward the plate. There are some exceptions, though. A fish-cocktail fork, for instance, should not be placed on the left with other forks, but on the extreme right. The butter spreader should not be arranged with the other knives, but should be placed across the butter plate at the left of the dinner plate, handle pointing to the right, so that it can easily be picked up in the right hand.

Spoons go to the right of knives. Again placement is in order of use: Soup spoon at far right and dessert spoon next. It will simplify your service if the dessert spoon and a small fork are arranged above the plate area. Special serving pieces such as relish spoons, butter knives and pickle forks are placed on the table, each parallel to the dish for which it is intended.

Napkin Folding and Placement. Napkins are usually placed to the left of each place setting. A small luncheon napkin may be folded in a triangular shape. In that case, the folded edge is placed parallel to forks. A larger napkin should be folded square and then oblong and should be placed so that the open corner is toward the guest.

Preliminary Preparation

Several days beforehand get out china, and, if necessary, wash it. Check linen and silver. Table may be set the day before and covered with a sheet.

On the day of the party, arrange flowers, set out ashtrays and coasters, guest towels for the bathroom, and so on.

The menu should match the party. If the latter is formal, the food should be too. If you have no help, you might make a soufflé for a small party of 4, but not for a much larger number.

Only a very experienced cook or a hostess with plenty of help should attempt an elaborate menu for guests. It is better to plan something you know you can prepare well and easily.

Unless you plan to make *Crêpes Suzette* or unless cooking is part of the party (barbecue, fondue or chafing dish), try to avoid last-minute cooking.

Make the most of serving aids: tea carts, serving carts and folding tables; a cart with a thermostatically controlled top that keeps food hot; chafing dishes, electric frying pans, deep fryers and griddles; and, of course, aluminum foil and plastic film, disposable broiling pans, cake tins and so on.

Use your imagination. An ancient soup tureen can become a conversation piece, and even baked beans can be festive if they are served on colorful earthenware plates.

Setting the Dinner Table

Your aim is to serve your guests conveniently and easily, and common sense usually is the best guide.

For a formal dinner, a large china service plate is set at each place before guests are led to the dining room. If the menu opens with a cold appetizer, it too is in position in its own container on a small plate placed on the service plate. When the opening course is finished, the small plate and container are removed, but the service plate remains, ready to receive the next course—perhaps fish in a ramekin or soup in a bouillon cup or plate—which also is served on its own smaller plate. Not until the main course is reached is the service plate removed and replaced by a warmed dinner plate for hot meat and vegetables. At the formal dinner table of today, bread-and-butter plates are frequently used; they are placed at the left of each place setting and about 1 inch above forks.

If 1 kind of wine is served, the glass is placed below the water glass, slightly to the right. If you are serving several wines, place glasses in a diagonal line to the right of the water glass, in the order in which they are to be used. Do not, however, use more than 3 wine glasses at a place setting. The glass nearest the water goblet is filled first, though always after guests have been seated.

Condiments and relish dishes and other small accessories should be placed convenient to each place setting. For formal dinners, individual salt and pepper servers are placed directly above each place setting. For informal meals, have salt and pepper servers within easy reach of your guests.

If you are setting a formal or semiformal table, you will probably want to use a centerpiece. Flowers, fruits, dried arrangements and china figurines are all acceptable. But make sure that they do not obstruct the view of the guest opposite.

Candlelight is always correct after dusk, but be sure that candle flames are above eye level or placed very low for a less formal occasion.

Seating Guests. If no place cards are being used, the hostess can direct each guest to his or her place at the table. A woman guest of honor should be seated at the host's right; a man should be placed at the right of the hostess. Place cards are customary at formal dinners but can be used even at less formal parties.

Serving Procedures. The guest of honor is served first, the hostess last. If a maid is serving, the used plates are usually taken from the right and the food served from the left of each guest. Some people find it less confusing to have all food service from the left. In any case, all beverages are served from the right.

Informal Entertaining

For easy-going cooking and serving, casserole recipes are great. Food can be prepared well in advance, and meat and vegetables may be cooked together. Serving can be postponed if a guest is late or if no one is in a great hurry to come to the table. Food stays hot in a warm oven and can be served in a colorful casserole dish.

Blanquette de Veau, Boeuf Bourguignon, Chicken Paprika and *Coq au Vin* are some foods to prepare in advance. Serve with rice or potatoes, and add salad or vegetables. Make dessert at leisure the day before, or serve an assortment of French pastries from the bakery. Or make a cheese board with several kinds of cheese, and have a bowl of fresh fruits, which guests may peel at the table.

Appetizers or crisp relishes can be made early in the day, arranged for serving, covered with plastic wrap and kept in the refrigerator until your guests arrive. Your salad, too, can be made in advance and kept covered in the refrigerator; plan to add dressing at the table, and toss lightly.

Step-by-Step Procedure. Before dinner serve canapés with drinks in the living room, and relax with your guests. Other appetizers or relishes may also be passed in the living room; when you are ready to serve, you can concentrate on the main course.

Set casserole on a candle warmer or electric plate warmer at 1 end of the table, with rice or potatoes and dinner plates nearby. With your husband seated at the head of the table and you opposite, you can divide the work of serving.

AUTUMN MENU FOR 6–8 PEOPLE

Salade Niçoise
Boeuf Bourguignon   Parsleyed potatoes
Garlic Bread
Nesselrode Pie   Cheese tray

Salade Niçoise

        1 head lettuce or other greens
        1 (7-ounce) can solid pack tuna, drained
        1 cup cooked cut green beans, chilled
        1 green pepper, diced
        1 red onion, sliced thinly
    1/2 cup diced celery
        3 quartered hard-cooked eggs
        2 tomatoes, cut in eighths
        6 anchovy fillets
       10 Greek black olives or ripe olives
        3 parts olive oil
        1 part wine vinegar
          Salt and pepper to taste

Make a bed of crisp, broken lettuce. Place drained flaked tuna in center. Arrange beans, green pepper, onion rings and celery in mounds around it. Garnish with ring of egg quarters alternating with tomato sections. Place anchovy fillets, crisscrossed, in center. Scatter olives on top. Make vinaigrette sauce with oil, vinegar and salt and pepper. Toss salad with vinaigrette sauce at table. Serves 6–8.

Boeuf Bourguignon

        4 pounds lean chuck beef, cut in 1 1/2-inch cubes
    1/4 cup hot butter or margarine
        3 tablespoons flour
          Salt and pepper to taste
    1 1/2 cups red wine
        2 onions, coarsely chopped
        2 shallots, finely chopped
        1 carrot, cut up
        1 clove garlic, finely chopped
          Bouquet garni
        1 veal knuckle, cracked
          Water
        1 pound mushroom caps
    1/4 cup Madeira (optional)
        2 tablespoons brandy

Brown the beef in 3 tablespoons hot butter until all sides are well colored. Pour off any fat. Sprinkle meat with flour, blend in thoroughly and add salt and pepper and red wine. In small frying pan, brown onions in 1 tablespoon hot butter. Add onions to meat, together with shallots, carrot, garlic, bouquet garni and veal knuckle. Add just enough water to cover meat, cover and simmer over low heat 2 hours or until meat is very tender and sauce is rich, dark brown. Half an hour before serving time, add mushroom caps, Madeira and brandy. Remove bouquet garni and veal bones. Taste for seasoning, and thicken slightly with a flour-water mixture if necessary. Serve with parsleyed potatoes. Serves 6–8.

Note: This dish may be made ahead and reheated.

Garlic Bread

        1 loaf crusty French or Italian bread
    1/2 cup soft butter or margarine
        1 teaspoon parsley, chopped
        3 cloves garlic, crushed
          Grated Parmesan cheese

Cut bread diagonally in 1-inch slices. Blend butter or margarine, parsley and garlic. Put bread together again with butter mixture between. Sprinkle top liberally with cheese. Wrap in foil. Heat in hot oven (400°F.) 10 minutes. Serves 6–8.

Nesselrode Pie

        1 (9-inch) baked pie shell or crumb shell
        1 envelope plain gelatine
    1 1/4 cups milk
    1/4 cup sugar
        1 teaspoon nutmeg
        1 tablespoon cornstarch
    1/4 teaspoon salt
        3 egg yolks
        1 teaspoon vanilla extract
    1/4 cup rum
        3 egg whites
    1/4 cup sugar
        1 cup whipped cream
1/3–1/2 cup chopped candied fruits

Chill pie shell. Soften gelatine in 1/4 cup milk. Mix 1/4 cup sugar, nutmeg, cornstarch, salt, and remaining milk. Cook over boiling water. stirring constantly, until thickened. Cover, and cook 10 minutes more. Add softened gelatine, and stir until dissolved. Beat egg yolks, and slowly add to milk mixture. Cook over hot water 3 minutes more. Add vanilla and rum; chill until slightly thickened. Beat egg whites in deep bowl until stiff, gradually beating in 1/4 cup sugar. Fold cold gelatine mixture gently into egg whites. Fold whipped cream and candied fruits into mixture. Turn into pie shell, and chill several hours. Serves 6—8.

PREPARATION PLAN

SHOPPING LIST

1/2 pound green beans
1 green pepper
1/2 bunch celery
1 (7-ounce) can solid pack tuna
6 eggs
2 tomatoes
Small jar or can Greek black olives
1 (3 1/2-ounce) tin anchovy fillets
1 head lettuce
Olive oil
Wine vinegar
3 pounds new potatoes
1 loaf crusty bread
Parmesan cheese
4 pounds beef (chuck or rump)
Red wine
Red onions
Carrots
Garlic
Shallots or green onions
Parsley
1 veal knuckle
Brandy
1 pound mushroom caps
1 package pastry mix
1 package gelatine
1 pint milk
Cornstarch
Salt
Vanilla extract
Sugar
Flour
Butter
1/2 pint heavy cream
1/4 pound candied or glacé fruits
Coffee
Coffee cream

THE DAY BEFORE

Make and bake pie shell.
Prepare beef, cool and refrigerate.
Chop parsley for potatoes, and refrigerate in foil.
Crush garlic and cream with butter and chopped parsley; refrigerate.
Make salad dressing.
Dice celery and green peppers for salad; refrigerate.

THE DAY OF THE PARTY

Make filling for pie, fill shell and refrigerate.
Scrub potatoes, and place in pan with water and salt.
Slice bread, butter and wrap in foil.
Cook beans.
Assemble salad, except for dressing.

AT SERVING TIME

Boil potatoes, and dress with butter and parsley.
Heat *Boeuf Bourguignon.*
Heat bread in oven.
Toss salad with dressing.

WINTER MENU FOR 6—8 PEOPLE

Sherried Tomato Bouillon
Chicken Paprika with steamed rice
Green bean-celery salad
Oranges Arabian

Sherried Tomato Bouillon

2 (10-ounce) cans bouillon or consommé
2 1/2 cups tomato juice
1/4 cup dry sherry
6 teaspoons butter

Combine and heat bouillon, tomato juice and sherry. Serve hot in mugs or cups with lump of butter in each. Serves 6.

Chicken Paprika

1 (5-pound) roasting chicken or 2 (1 1/2-pound) fryers, disjointed, with giblets
3 cups water
1 small onion, sliced
3–4 sprigs parsley
2 teaspoons salt
4 whole peppercorns
1 bay leaf
1/2 cup finely chopped onion
4 tablespoons butter or margarine
1/2 cup flour
3–4 tablespoons paprika
1/3 cup cream
1 1/2 cups thick sour cream

Place giblets, necks and wing tips in saucepan with water, sliced onion, parsley, 1 teaspoon salt, peppercorns and bay leaf. Simmer, covered, 1 1/2 hours. Sauté chopped onion in skillet in 2 tablespoons butter or margarine until soft but not brown. Remove onion, leaving butter or margarine in skillet. Combine flour, reserving 2 tablespoons for later use, remaining salt and 2 teaspoons paprika in paper bag. Shake chicken pieces in bag until coated with flour mixture. Brown meat well in butter or margarine remaining in skillet. Add 1/2 cup giblet broth, and cook, covered, over low heat until chicken is tender, about 1 hour, adding more chicken broth to prevent pan drying out. In saucepan, heat remaining 2 tablespoons butter or margarine, and blend in reserved 2 tablespoons flour. Add remaining giblet broth, sweet cream and remaining paprika. Stir over low heat until smooth and thickened. Add sour cream gradually, stirring vigorously. Pour sauce over chicken, and cook over low heat 3 minutes, turning chicken and stirring sauce. Do not boil, or sour cream will curdle. Serves 6.

Oranges Arabian

        6 large oranges
    2/3 cup chopped dates
    1/2 cup shredded almonds
    2/3 cup orange juice
    1/2 cup brandy
        1 cup heavy cream, stiffly beaten

Peel oranges, and slice very thin. Sprinkle with dates, almonds, orange juice and brandy. Chill thoroughly before serving. Pass lightly sweetened whipped cream. Serves 6–8.

SPRING MENU FOR 6–8 PEOPLE

Avocado Pasadena
Beef Stroganoff   Noodles
Fresh asparagus with lemon butter
Strawberry Tart   Coffee

Avocado Pasadena

    2 1/2 cups frozen, fresh, cooked or canned crabmeat, drained
        2 tomatoes, peeled, chopped and drained
    1/3 cup chopped celery
        2 tablespoons chili sauce
        1 tablespoon lemon juice
        1 tablespoon chopped parsley
        1 teaspoon chopped chives
        1 teaspoon Worcestershire sauce
            Blender Mayonnaise
        3 avocados
        3 tablespoons lemon juice
        3 ripe olives, halved and pitted

To crabmeat, add the next 7 ingredients, and moisten with mayonnaise. Season to taste. Peel avocados, halve them and remove pits. Brush with lemon juice. Fill avocado halves with crabmeat mixture, and garnish each with 1/2 ripe olive. Serves 6–8.

Blender Mayonnaise

        2 egg yolks or 1 whole egg
        1 teaspoon salt
        1 teaspoon dry mustard
    1 1/2 cups oil
        3 tablespoons tarragon vinegar or lemon juice
            Dash hot pepper sauce

Drop egg yolks into blender; add salt, mustard and 1/2 cup oil. Turn motor on and off a few times. With motor on low, *very slowly* add rest of oil. When mixture is thick and stiff, flavor it with vinegar and hot pepper sauce. Makes 1 1/2 cups.

Beef Stroganoff

        2 pounds (trimmed weight) fillet of beef (tail end) or sirloin or porterhouse steak
        2 tablespoons butter or margarine
        3 tablespoons brandy
    1/2 pound fresh mushrooms, sliced
    1–2 cloves, crushed garlic
        2 tablespoons flour
        1 tablespoon meat glaze
        1 tablespoon tomato paste
        2 cups beef stock or canned bouillon
            Salt and pepper to taste
        1 cup sour cream
        2 tablespoons fresh dill, chopped

Trim all fat from beef, and cut into fingers about 1/2 inch thick. Heat butter or margarine in deep, heavy pan. Sear meat in butter or margarine a few pieces at a time, very quickly. Meat should be very rare. Remove, and set aside. Heat brandy, pour into pan and stir with wooden spoon to scrape up all glaze. Add mushrooms to pan with garlic. Cook over low heat 2–3 minutes; then stir in flour, meat glaze, and tomato paste. When smooth, add stock. Season with salt and pepper. Stir over heat until thickened; cool. Beat in 1 cup sour cream and fresh dill. Just before serving, heat sauce over hot water, and return meat to sauce to heat through. Keep meat rare. Serve with noodles or wild rice. Serves 6–8.

Note: Meat glaze is the dark meat dripping left in the pan after roasting beef. It is the base for rich brown gravy. If necessary, substitute 1 teaspoon meat extract and 2 teaspoons water.

Strawberry Tarts

            Almond Pastry Cream
        8 large baked tart shells
        1 quart fresh strawberries
            Red currant jelly

Half fill each tart shell with cold *Almond Pastry Cream*. Rinse and hull berries. Dry on absorbent paper. Pick out the ripest and most uniform in shape. Set aside the soft or underripe berries for a sauce over ice cream another time. Arrange the best berries close together, points up, on the pastry cream. Glaze the berries with melted red currant jelly. Keep tarts chilled until serving time. Makes 8.

Almond Pastry Cream

    1 1/2 cups 10% cream
    1/3 cup sugar
        3 tablespoons flour
        3 egg yolks
    1/2 teaspoon almond extract
            Pinch salt
    1–2 tablespoons kirsch or cream

Scald 1 1/4 cups of the cream in the top of a double boiler. Mix sugar and flour together. Then stir in remaining 1/4 cup cream and the egg yolks. Beat until smooth. Pour into the hot cream, and cook and stir until thick and smooth. Stir in extract and salt. Dilute with kirsch or cream if mixture seems thick. Chill, stirring occasionally to prevent a crust from forming. Beat until smooth before using.

SUMMER MENU FOR 8 PEOPLE

Celery Soup
Belgian Pâté
Green Rice Salad with Tomatoes
Hot sesame rolls
Cold Zabaglione with Peaches
Iced coffee

Belgian Pâté

        1 (2 1/2-pound) chicken
      1/2 pound ham
      3/4 pound side bacon
      1/4 of an onion
    1 1/2 pounds pork, minced (3 cups)
        4 slices stale bread, crumbled
      3/4 cup milk
        2 tablespoons parsley, chopped
      1/2 teaspoon garlic salt
  1–1 1/2 teaspoons salt
      1/2 teaspoon mixed herbs
      1/4 cup brandy, dry wine or sherry
          Bay leaf
          Thyme

Bone the chicken. Slice the 2 breasts of chicken in half lengthwise, and set aside. Grind remaining chicken, the ham, 4 slices of bacon and the onion; then mix in the pork. Crumble the bread into milk; add parsley, garlic salt, salt, herbs and brandy, and combine with the ground meats and onion. Line a deep oval or oblong 2-quart dish with 7–8 long strips of bacon. Add 2–3 bits of bay leaf and a sprinkle of thyme. Press about 1/2 the meat mixture into the mold without disturbing the bacon slices. Wrap each piece of chicken breast barber-pole fashion in a strip of bacon, and press side by side into the meat mixture. Cover evenly with the remaining meat; add a few more bits of bay leaf and a sprinkle of thyme. Place remaining bacon strips, cut to fit, over the top. Cover with a lid or foil, and set in a pan of water. Bake at 350°–375°F. 3 1/2 hours. Drain off the fat, and serve hot or cold. Serves 8.

Note: The amount of salt will depend on saltiness of ham and bacon. Additional milk may be used in place of brandy or wine.

For classic cold *Belgian Pâté*, remove the cover after baking, and place a weight on the undrained meat. Chill the dish quickly in ice water; then chill overnight. Pâté may be drained, then chilled in the baking dish and used within 3–4 days.

Green Rice Salad with Tomatoes

    1 1/2 cups uncooked long-grain rice
        4 tablespoons olive oil
        2 tablespoons wine vinegar
      1/2 teaspoon black pepper
        1 teaspoon salt
      1/2 teaspoon tarragon
      1/2 cup cucumber, cut into small cubes
      1/4 cup chopped green pepper
      1/4 cup chopped parsley
      1/4 cup chopped chives
      1/4 cup chopped green onion
          Mayonnaise or salad dressing
          Salad greens
        2 hard-cooked eggs, sliced
        3 sliced ripe tomatoes

Boil rice according to directions on package. Drain, and mix at once with olive oil, vinegar, black pepper, salt and tarragon. Let stand to cool. Then mix with cucumber, green pepper, parsley, chives and onion. Mix in mayonnaise to moisten. Taste for seasoning. Heap on greens, and garnish with eggs and tomatoes. Serves 6—8.

Cold Zabaglione with Peaches

        6 egg yolks
      1/2 cup sugar
      1/2 cup Marsala
        1 cup heavy cream
          Sliced fresh peaches

In top part of a double boiler, beat together egg yolks and sugar until thick and pale in color. Gradually beat Marsala into mixture. Place over boiling water, and continue beating until mixture foams up and begins to thicken. Scrape sides and bottom of pan often. Place pan in bowl of cracked ice, and continue beating until cold. Whip heavy cream until stiff, and fold into cooled zabaglione. Chill in refrigerator. Spoon over lightly sweetened sliced peaches. Serves 6—8.

VALENTINE DINNER

Chilled Beet Soup
Italian Meat Loaf
Zucchini   *Risotto Milanese*
Lettuce-wedge salad
Quick Berry Charlotte

Chilled Beet Soup

        2 (14–15-ounce) cans julienne beets
        3 cups chicken broth
          Juice of 2 lemons
      1/4 cup sugar
          Salt and pepper to taste
          Sour cream
        1 tablespoon chopped fresh dill or parsley

Drain beets, reserving juice. Combine beet juice with chicken broth, lemon juice, sugar, salt and pepper. Heat mixture to boiling; pour over reserved beets, and chill. Serve in cups, garnishing each with a dollop of sour cream and sprinkling with dill or parsley. Serves 6—8.

Note: Make sure chicken broth is free of fat.

Italian Meat Loaf

    1/4 cup farina
    3/4 cup boiling water
    1/2 clove garlic, crushed
    1/2 teaspoon mixed Italian herbs
      1 tablespoon onion, chopped
    1/2 teaspoon salt
    1/2 cup dark mushrooms, chopped
      1 pound minced ham
      1 pound minced veal
      1 egg, beaten
      2 slices stale bread
        Oil

Stir the farina into the boiling water, and cook and stir about 3 minutes until thick. Remove from heat, and stir in the next 5 ingredients. Cool, and mix well with the ham, veal and egg. Shape into an oval with wet hands, and set on 2 slices of stale bread in a shallow baking pan. Brush with oil, and bake at 350°F. 1 1/4—1 1/2 hours. Lift to a hot platter, and serve. Serves 6—8.

Risotto Milanese

      1 large onion, sliced
    1/4 cup butter or margarine
      1 cup uncooked rice
    2 1/4 cups stock, broth or bouillon
      1 bay leaf
        Salt to taste
    1/4 cup grated Parmesan cheese

Brown onion in butter or margarine, and add the rice. Cook over low heat 4—5 minutes, stirring. Mixture should be lightly colored. Heat liquid to boiling point, and pour over rice. Place bay leaf on top. Cover pot tightly, and bake in 350°F. oven 25—30 minutes or until all liquid is absorbed. Salt to taste. Serve sprinkled with cheese. Serves 6—8.

Quick Berry Charlotte

      1 strawberry or raspberry jelly roll
      2 (3-ounce) packages strawberry jelly powder
      1 teaspoon plain gelatine
      1 cup boiling water
      2 tablespoons lemon juice
      2 (15-ounce) packages frozen sweetened strawberries (defrosted)
    1/2 pint whipping cream
      2 egg whites
      2 tablespoons sugar

Cut jelly roll into 8 slices. Butter the sides of a large angel cake pan, and stand the slices up around the inside of the pan. Mix jelly powder, gelatine and boiling water in a saucepan, and heat and stir until thoroughly dissolved. Add lemon juice and berries plus juice. Stir well, and chill in the freezer in a flat baking pan. Stir occasionally until as thick as jam. Fold in egg whites stiffly beaten with the sugar. Whip the cream until stiff; set aside 1/2 cup, and fold remaining whipped cream into the berry mixture. Spoon into prepared pan, and spread evenly. Cut off top pieces of the roll, and crumble over the berry mixture. Press down lightly, and chill several hours. Unmold, and spoon dabs of reserved cream around the top. Garnish with a few fresh berries if you wish. Serves 10.

EASTER DINNER PARTY

Fresh fruit cup
Ham baked in vermouth
Sautéed sweet potatoes   Buttered spinach
Chocolate Log   Coffee

Chocolate Log

      6 eggs, separated, at room temperature
    3/4 cup sugar
    1/4 cup sifted unsweetened cocoa
      2 tablespoons sifted flour
    1 1/2 teaspoons vanilla extract
    1/2 cup icing sugar
      2 cups heavy cream, chilled
    1/3 cup sifted icing sugar
    1/4 cup brandy
      2 tablespoons slivered toasted almonds

Preheat oven to 350°F. Grease bottom of 15 1/2″ x 10 1/2″ x 1″ jelly-roll pan. Line with waxed paper. In large bowl, beat egg yolks with 1/2 cup sugar at high speed until thick and pale-lemon colored. With beater at low speed, mix in cocoa, flour and vanilla. Place egg whites in second large bowl. Beat at high speed until stiff. Then beat in remaining sugar until moist peaks form. With wire whisk or rubber scraper, gently fold whites into egg-yolk mixture. Pour into prepared jelly-roll pan. Bake 12—14 minutes or until surface springs back when touched lightly. Sift 1/2 cup icing sugar onto clean tea towel, covering it completely. Turn cake onto towel. Cool slightly. Peel off waxed paper. Trim edges with sharp knife or scissors. Beginning at long edge, roll cake up, jelly-roll fashion, and place on wire rack with seam side down. Cool completely.

Whip heavy cream until stiff. With rubber spatula gently fold in 1/3 cup icing sugar. Unroll cake, and carefully remove towel. Sprinkle with brandy. Spread with 1/2 the filling. Re-roll. Place, seam side down, on serving platter. Frost with remaining filling. Sprinkle with slivered almonds. Chill until serving time. Serves 6.

VICTORIA DAY DINNER

Asparagus soup
Roast lamb
Minted peas and carrots
Rissolè potatoes
Relish tray   Chutney
Rhubarb Custard Pie

Rhubarb Custard Pie

Enough pastry for 1 deep 9-inch single-crust pie
2 eggs
1/3 cup milk or light cream
1—1 1/4 cups white sugar
4 tablespoons flour
2 tablespoons soft butter
1/4 teaspoon grated lemon rind
Pinch mace
3 1/2—4 cups sliced pink rhubarb
Whipping cream or ice cream

Roll out pastry, and fit into a deep pie pan. Leave a 1/2-inch overhang of pastry on the edges. Fold the overhang under, and flute edge to raise the rim slightly. Beat the next 7 ingredients together until smooth, and stir in the rhubarb. Scrape into prepared pan, and spread evenly. Bake at 450°F. 15—20 minutes; then reduce heat to 350°F., and bake until rhubarb is tender and filling is almost set, about 30—40 minutes. Cool, and serve warm or cold. Cut into wedges, and top each wedge with lightly sweetened whipped cream. Serves 6—7.

THE BUFFET PARTY

Setting up a buffet party gives you plenty of scope for dramatic linen, china, decorations and food. Best of all, you can forget about serving each guest individually. In addition to helping the hostess, self-service adds to the fun of a party because it encourages guests to mingle. And you can cope with many more guests when you're not limited to the number you can seat around your dining room table.

Almost any type of meal can be served this way—Sunday supper, breakfast, luncheon, dinner or refreshments for an evening party. It can be set out in recreation room, living-dining area or patio, and of course the dining table can become the focal point. It's important, too, to leave plenty of room around the table so that guests can help themselves without crowding each other. For entertaining more than 12 people at a buffet, have 2 groupings of foods and utensils, 1 at each end of the table. This arrangement will relieve congestion in serving and prevent a slow-moving line. If you have no table long enough, it's a good idea to set up a trestle table. Use boards, a slab of plywood or even a smooth, level door laid across trestles. Cover with large cloth, and let cloth hang down to hide supports.

When setting the table for either a small or large buffet party, place dishes, flatware, napkins and food in the order in which they will be picked up. A nice idea is to place small tables of the nested or stacked type around the room or in adjoining living room, so that guests may put their plates down if they wish.

Someone, host, hostess or other help, should be at the buffet table to slice meat or help with other foods that require special service.

To prevent clutter on the main table, have a separate small table nearby to take soiled plates and flatware. Someone should keep an eye on this table, removing items before there is a large, untidy accumulation.

Coffee is usually served from a separate table. Cups, saucers, cream, sugar and spoons can be ready for use. But, of course, if you prefer, the coffee can be served from the buffet table after the table has been cleared of platters and other serving dishes.

BUFFET MENU

Cold baked ham   *Potatoes au Gratin*
Pineapple slices topped with spiced crab apples
Mustard Pickles   Carrot curls   Celery hearts
Tossed salad with Swiss and blue cheese
Hot buttered rolls   *French Bread*
Assorted French pastries   Coffee

Procedure

A precooked ready-to-serve ham will save you hours of preparation time. If you wish to stud it with cloves and glaze it in a slow oven, by all means do so. Make it a morning operation, and allow about 10 minutes cooking time per pound. Chill. For a large crowd, it is best to slice ham beforehand.

To make casserole, boil potatoes in the morning or the day before. For each guest, allow 1 medium potato. Cover, and refrigerate. On the morning of the party make 4 cups medium white sauce; season to taste with grated onion salt, pepper and dash nutmeg. Add grated cheese, and cover. About 1 hour before serving, combine sauce and cubed potatoes; turn into 2 casseroles, sprinkle with grated cheese and bake at 350°F. for 30—40 minutes or until bubbly.

Make salad in early afternoon. Use assorted crisp greens—lettuce, romaine, endive, watercress. Wash, drain and pat dry. Arrange in 2 salad bowls, and top with peeled tomato sections. Sprinkle 1 salad with crumbled blue cheese, the other with slivers of Swiss cheese. Cover bowls with damp towels, then with plastic wrap to keep crisp. Refrigerate. Set on buffet with several types of dressing nearby.

BUFFET MENU

Curried Shrimp   *Aniseed Beef*
Rice
Chopped peanuts   Chopped green onion
Mango chutney   Chopped hard-cooked eggs
Grated coconut   Crumbled bacon
Tropical Delight
Coffee   Tea   Beer

Curried Shrimp

    2 pounds medium-size unpeeled shrimp, fresh or
        frozen
1/2 cup chopped green apple
1/2 cup chopped onion
1/2 clove garlic, crushed
    2 tablespoons butter or margarine
    1 tablespoon curry powder
    1 tablespoon cold water
    2 teaspoons lemon juice
        Pinch ground cloves
1/2 teaspoon dry mustard
1/2 can shrimp cooking liquid or chicken broth
    2 (10-ounce) cans frozen shrimp soup

Cook shrimp and drain. Reserve the liquid. Peel and devein shrimp; then chill until needed. Sauté apple, onion and garlic in hot butter or margarine until soft. Then stir in a smooth mixture of the next 5 ingredients. Add shrimp liquid, and simmer 5 minutes. Break up soup with a fork, and drop into the mixture. Cover, and heat until soup melts. Stir until blended. Taste for seasoning. Add salt, pepper and more curry powder to taste. Add shrimp, and reheat thoroughly. Serve over plain boiled rice. Serves 6—8.

Aniseed Beef

    2 pounds shin beef
    4 cups water
1/3 cup soy sauce
    2 tablespoons sugar
    4 slices ginger root
    2 tablespoons sherry
    4 aniseed stars or 1 1/2 teaspoons anise seeds
    1 teaspoon sesame-seed oil

Trim beef, and cover with water. Bring to boil, and skim. Add soy sauce, sugar, ginger, sherry and anise, and cook over medium heat about 2 hours. Add sesame-seed oil, and cook about 20 minutes longer. Slice meat, and serve hot or cold. Serves 8.

Tropical Delight

    2 large ripe bananas
    3 canned peach halves and 1 cup juice
    1 (6-ounce) can frozen orange juice
    2 cups sweetened pineapple juice
        Juice of 1 lemon
    2 eggs

Place bananas, drained peaches and orange juice in blender container. Blend until smooth (or press bananas and peaches through a fine strainer). Combine puree with juices and eggs in large bowl or mixer, and beat at medium speed until fluffy and light. Pour mixture into refrigerator trays. Freeze until a border of crystals forms (about 1 inch thick) around edges; beat again until mushy, and return to freezer. Serves 6—8.

Procedure

Cook and clean shrimp the day before. Make sauce. Store separately in covered containers in refrigerator. Cook beef, and cool in liquid before chilling. Make dessert, and freeze. Set serving table, and cover.

The day of party, fix side dishes, and cover them. Chill beer, and prepare coffee pot. Slice meat thin, and place on platter. Cover with plastic wrap. About 3/4 hour before serving, reheat curry sauce in a double boiler. Remember to add shrimp 15 minutes before serving. Cook rice. Remove dessert from freezer to refrigerator to soften slightly. Plug in coffee pot. Heat water for chafing dish.

At serving time, put curry in chafing dish. Place everything except dessert on table.

BUFFET MENU

Guacamole   Corn chips
Chili con Carne
Radish salad
Melon balls and liqueur   Coffee

Chili con Carne

1/3 cup bacon drippings
3 1/2 pounds ground round or chuck steak
    3 onions, chopped (approximately 1 1/2 cups)
    1 green pepper, diced
    2 teaspoons chili powder
    1 teaspoon salt
1/2 teaspoon pepper
1/2 teaspoon garlic powder
        Pinch cayenne
    4 (14–15-ounce) cans red kidney beans and liquid
    1 (28-ounce) can tomatoes
    3 tablespoons tomato paste

Melt drippings in a large heavy skillet. Add meat, and stir-fry until well colored. Drain off the fat. Scrape the meat into a deep saucepan. Add onions, green pepper, chili powder, salt, pepper, garlic powder and cayenne. Mix well. Then add kidney beans with their liquid, tomatoes and tomato paste. Combine thoroughly, and simmer, covered, stirring occasionally, about 30 minutes. Serves 12—14.

Note: For hot chili, increase amount of chili powder.

SUMMER BUFFET

Jellied consommé
Poached Salmon with *Herbed Mayonnaise*
Potato-cucumber salad
Pumpernickel sandwiches
Lemon mousse   Coffee

Poached Salmon

    2 cups water
    2 cups white wine
    4 peppercorns
    4 parsley stems
    2 stalks celery
    1 carrot
    1 onion, sliced
4–5- pound piece of salmon
    1 recipe *Herbed Mayonnaise*

Combine all ingredients except salmon and mayonnaise. Simmer 15 minutes. Wrap fish in cheesecloth, and lower gently into simmering liquid. Cook 7—8 minutes per pound; test for doneness with toothpick. If not cooked, return to broth a short time. Let cool in liquid, and remove with aid of cheesecloth. Chill thoroughly. Serve with *Herbed Mayonnaise*. Serves 8—10.

Herbed Mayonnaise

    1 cup homemade or commercial mayonnaise
    3 tablespoons chopped parsley
    2 shallots or green onions, finely chopped
    1 tablespoon chopped chives or fresh dill

To mayonnaise add all other ingredients. Makes 1 cup.

BUFFET MENU

*Ham Ring and Sour Cream—
Horseradish Sauce*
Sliced tomatoes
Deviled eggs
Chef's Salad
Hot buttered rolls
Polish Walnut Torte   Coffee

Ham Ring

    2 pounds ground ham
    3/4 pound ground veal
    1 cup finely diced canned pineapple
    4 slices bread, trimmed
    1 cup milk or water
    2 teaspoons prepared mustard
      Pinch pepper
    1 egg
    3 egg whites

Combine meats and pineapple. Cover bread with enough milk to soak; add to meat mixture. Add mustard and pepper. Mix well. Add whole egg, then whites, 1 at a time, mixing well after each addition. When mixture is finished, put into ring mold, and bake, covered, in pan with a little water at 350°F. 35—40 minutes. Cool slightly before unmolding. Serve cold, garnished with crab apples, pineapple slices and *Sour Cream—Horseradish Sauce*. Serves 8.

Sour Cream—Horseradish Sauce

    1 cup thick sour cream
    1/3 cup drained horseradish
    1 tablespoon grated lemon rind
      Salt and white pepper to taste

Combine all ingredients, and mix well. Makes 1 1/3 cups.

Polish Walnut Torte

    4 teaspoons dry bread crumbs
    6 egg whites
    1/8 teaspoon salt
    1/2 cup icing sugar
    6 egg yolks
    1/3 cup icing sugar
    1/2 teaspoon grated lemon rind
    2 teaspoons lemon juice
    4 tablespoons sifted pastry flour
    3/4 cup (2 ounces) finely ground walnuts
2—2 1/2 cups sweetened whipped cream
      Walnut Frosting
      Chopped Walnuts

Grease bottoms of 2 round 8-inch layer cake pans, and line with circles of greased waxed paper. Sprinkle each pan with 2 teaspoons dry bread crumbs. Beat egg whites and salt until foamy; then beat in 1/2 cup icing sugar, and beat until very stiff. Beat egg yolks until thick, and beat in 1/3 cup icing sugar. Remove beaters, and stir in rind, juice, sifted flour and walnuts. Fold into egg-white mixture. Spread in prepared pans. Bake at 350°F. 35—40 minutes. Immediately cut around the edges, and cake tops will settle more evenly during cooling. Invert on a dry towel or greased cake rack, and peel off waxed paper. When cold, put layers together with 1/2 the sweetened cream. Spread top and sides with *Walnut Frosting*, and swirl remaining cream on top. Sprinkle with drifts of chopped walnuts. Keep chilled until serving time.

Walnut Frosting

    3/4 cup (2 ounces) finely ground walnuts
    1/3 cup 18% cream
    1/4 cup soft sweet butter
    3/4 cup unsifted icing sugar

Mix walnuts and cream in the top of a double boiler, and cook and stir until mixture is a thick paste, about 3 or 4 minutes. Chill the paste. Meanwhile, beat butter with icing sugar. When fluffy, beat in the chilled paste, and chill until easy to spread. If the kitchen is cool, you should be able to spread this frosting without chilling.

ST. PATRICK'S DAY BUFFET

Corned beef
Boiled potatoes in jackets   Quick-cooked cabbage
Boiled yellow turnips   Beets or white onions
Carrots   Assorted mustards
Rye Bread with butter
Beer   *Irish Coffee*

Irish Coffee

Make very hot, strong, sweet coffee. Flavor it with Irish whiskey, and serve in demitasse cups or small glasses topped with unsweetened whipped cream.

ITALIAN BUFFET

Antipasto platter
Cannelloni with Sausage
Tossed green salad with oil and vinegar
Bread sticks
Frozen Lemon Pie   Espresso coffee

Sift 2 cups flour and 1/4 teaspoon salt into bowl, and stir in eggs and water with fork. Press mixture together with hands to form stiff dough. Knead lightly, and roll out to very thin sheet, about 16″ x 16″. Cut into 16 4-inch squares. Drop squares in boiling salted water, and cook until just tender. Drain on clean dry towel. Stir-fry meats, onion and garlic in butter or margarine until pinkness disappears. Then stir in 2 table-spoons flour, 1 teaspoon salt, thyme and soup. Simmer until very thick; then season, and cool to lukewarm. Heap some meat mixture along edge of each cooked pasta square, and roll up. Place in buttered baking dish. Cover with 2 cups tomato sauce and mozzarella slices. Cover dish, and bake at 350°F. about 40 minutes. Uncover, and sprinkle with Parmesan cheese. Broil quickly until lightly browned. Pour remaining sauce over rolls at serving time. Serves 6—8.

Frozen Lemon Pie

      3 eggs, separated
    1/2 cup sugar
    1/4 cup lemon juice
    1/2 cup flaked coconut
    1/2 teaspoon grated lemon rind
      1 cup ice-cold evaporated milk
     24 chocolate wafers, crushed (1 cup)

Beat egg yolks slightly in top of double boiler. Add 1/4 cup sugar and lemon juice. Cook over hot water until mixture thickens, stirring constantly. Add coconut and rind. Beat egg whites stiffly with remaining sugar, and fold into egg-yolk mixture. Cool. Whip evaporated milk until very stiff. Fold in lemon mixture. Sprinkle a deep 10-inch oiled pie pan with 1/2 the wafer crumbs, pour in custard and top with remaining crumbs. Freeze. Serve in wedges. Serves 6—8.

Cannelloni with Sausage

      2 cups sifted all-purpose flour
    1/4 teaspoon salt
      2 eggs, slightly beaten
    1–2 tablespoons water
      3 quarts boiling salted water
      1 pound ground beef
      1 Italian sausage, sliced
      1 onion, chopped
      1 clove garlic, crushed
      2 tablespoons butter or margarine
      2 tablespoons flour
      1 teaspoon salt
    1/4 teaspoon thyme
      1 (10-ounce) can minestrone or beef soup
    4–5 cups tomato sauce
        Sliced mozzarella cheese
    1/4 cup Parmesan cheese

CATERING FOR A CROWD

When faced with large numbers to feed, a basic plan is essential. Get all the help you can, and make sure it is coordinated.

If you belong to any large organization, some-day you may find yourself in charge of organiz-ing the entertainment and the feeding of 100 people. There could even be 200–300 (especially if it's a fund-raising event), but let's make a mod-est beginning, and consider catering for 100 first.

Smorgasbord Approach

One way to feed such a group can be called the "smorgasbord approach." It's worked around a wide variety of dishes, with contributions cooked separately by a number of women in their homes and brought in all ready to serve.

One member might make a crock of home-baked beans, for example; another might con-tribute steamed browned bread to go with the beans. Someone could bring in some huge bowls of potato salad, someone else a large batch of deviled eggs. And using the organization prem-ises, several people might prepare hams studded with cloves and baked with sugar crust.

International Accents. If your group includes members who come from other countries, you might plan an international food sampling. Ask the members to prepare some of their countries' famous dishes, but be sure that each participant knows what the others are doing.

The invitations or notices for this sort of party should specify, of course, that the guests are in-vited to sample foods of other lands cooked by members of the group. It would be a very good idea to have some standard fare such as a large baked ham and a jellied veal mold planned as well, to be sure there's something all the guests like.

Committee Approach

This approach requires more work from fewer people and a more familiar menu. The committee will need a long table to work on and plenty of sharp knives, bowls of various sizes, stacks of plates, and a supply of foil and plastic wrap for wrappings. If you're making sandwiches and cakes for an evening party with tea or coffee, you'll have to calculate quantities closely.

Assembly-line sandwiches. For sandwiches, set up an assembly line. Have the first person arrange ready-cut bread slices close together in 1 layer on a clean counter or board. If some pinwheel sand-wiches are to be included, another person can be slicing whole loaves into thin lengthwise slices. The next in line spreads slices with softened but-ter or margarine. Next someone spreads fillings and tops with second buttered slices, or rolls up slices for pinwheel sandwiches. The last in line slices sandwiches into small, easily managed pieces and arranges them on platters, covers them with foil or plastic wrap and refrigerates them until serving time.

A helpful tip: Have several varieties of filling made up ahead of time, but you will find it easier and quicker to spread 1 at a time; then go on to the next kind.

Note: Order thinly sliced bread and whole unsliced bread from the baker 3 or 4 days before-hand.

Cakes by the Yard. While gathered together for the sandwich job, the committee might also like to make petits fours, those attractive little bites of cake, decoratively iced. To make them you need large sheet cakes baked ahead of time. Cut them into small squares and diamonds, and have several bowls of icing—the simple kind made with icing sugar and milk—1 white, 1 chocolate, 1 pink, perhaps. Then you need an assortment of silver candies, chocolate sprinkles and so on. If one of your members has artistic tendencies, you are set.

Estimating Quantities

How much food can 100 people eat or 200–300, for that matter, and how much coffee will they want with it?

A general guide would be to calculate 2 sandwiches or 4 slices of bread for each person (thus 2 sandwich loaves per 10 people) and 1 pound butter or margarine for 3 loaves. But sandwiches usually are cut into fancy shapes and small sizes, and a guest may eat 8–10 of them very easily. It's up to you to decide how ample your servings are to be. It could very well depend on the hour at which refreshments are served, what has gone before, and so forth.

Coffee for a Crowd. To make coffee for 100 people, buy 2 1/2 pounds regular-grind coffee, and put it in a cheesecloth bag large enough to hold *double* that amount. The size is important because coffee swells. Put bag in large boiler with 20 quarts boiling water. Cover tightly, and reduce heat so that water is no longer boiling. Let it stand, keeping hot but not boiling, about 20 minutes. Then, using kitchen tongs, grasp bag and move it up and down in coffee several times to extract maximum flavor. Remove bag, and continue to keep coffee hot for serving. For each 100 cups of coffee, allow about 2 quarts light cream, and 2 pounds sugar.

To make instant coffee for a crowd, use 16 quarts (4 gallons) boiling water. Remove from heat, add 8 ounces (4 1/2 cups) instant coffee and stir until dissolved.

BUFFET MENUS

COLD BUFFET

Lobster and chicken salads (4 gallons each)
Thin slices rare roast beef (18 pounds, uncooked weight, rolled sirloin)
Horseradish and mustards

HOT BUFFET

Lasagne with tomato sauce
(6 13"x 18" pans)
Italian bread sticks
Orange and grapefruit sections with rum (4 gallons)
Assorted cookies (13 pounds)
Coffee   Cream   Sugar

COFFEE AND TEA PARTIES
MORNING OR AFTERNOON

These parties are an easy, inexpensive way to entertain small or large groups. Accompany the morning coffee with *Bundt Kuchen, Baked Spicy Doughnuts* or *Quick Sweet Croissants*.

Note: Other suggestions include Danish pastries, warm brioches with strawberry jam, blueberry muffins and quick coffee cakes.

For the casual afternoon coffee or tea, you can use a silver tray and service, or any type of tray covered with a fresh cloth. Arrange the tray in the kitchen, and add a plate with a few small sandwiches made with very thin bread and/or some cookies on their own plate. Don't forget milk, cream, sugar and lemon slices.

Bundt Kuchen

Pecans or slivered almonds
3 tablespoons crushed graham wafers
1 teaspoon cinnamon
2/3 cup soft butter
1 cup sugar
4 egg yolks
1 1/2 teaspoon grated orange rind
1 teaspoon vanilla
1/2 teaspoon salt
1/4 teaspoon crushed cardamom seeds
2 1/4 cups unsifted pastry flour
2 teaspoons baking powder
3/4 cup milk
4 egg whites

Butter the inside of a fluted bundt mold or a small angel cake pan generously. Sprinkle with pecans or slivered almonds. Scatter crushed graham wafers mixed with 1 teaspoon cinnamon over the butter. Beat butter and 1/2 cup sugar together. Add 1 egg yolk at a time, beating well after each addition. Add rind and vanilla, then the sifted dry ingredients alternately with the milk. Beat egg whites until foamy, and beat in remaining sugar. Beat until very stiff. Fold in the batter, and scrape into prepared pan. Bake at 350°F. 40 minutes. Cool, and remove from pan. Serve in wedges with butter and tart jelly. Cuts into 10 or 12 wedges.

Baked Spicy Doughnuts

> 1/4 cup soft butter
> 6 tablespoons sugar
> 1 egg
> 1/2 teaspoon vanilla
> 1 1/4 cups unsifted pastry flour
> 2 teaspoons baking powder
> 1/8 teaspoon salt
> 1/4 teaspoon nutmeg
> 1/3 cup milk
> 1/2 cup melted butter
> 1/2–2/3 cup fine white sugar
> 1–1 1/2 teaspoons cinnamon

Butter 16 small muffin cups. Beat 1/4 cup butter until creamy. Add 6 tablespoons sugar, egg and vanilla. Beat until fluffy. Sift dry ingredients, and stir in alternately with the milk. Spoon into prepared cups, and bake at 375°F. about 15 minutes. Meanwhile, melt butter, and pour into a bowl. Mix sugar and cinnamon in a second bowl. When doughnuts are baked, remove immediately from the pans; while still hot, roll in melted butter, then in the sugar-cinnamon mixture. Serve warm in a basket.

Quick Sweet Croissants

> 3 tablespoons chopped nuts
> 3 tablespoons chopped raisins
> 1/2 teaspoon cinnamon
> 2 tablespoons brown sugar
> 2 crushed graham wafers
> 2 tablespoons melted butter
> Honey or corn syrup
> 1 package refrigerator croissant dough

Mix the first 6 ingredients together, and add a very little honey, just to form a thick drop mixture. Open the croissant dough, and separate into triangles. Dab a generous spoonful of the filling in the center of the wide end of each triangle. Roll up, and place on a well-greased cookie sheet. Turn ends slightly to form crescents. Brush tops with warm honey, and sprinkle with a few additional chopped nuts. Bake according to directions, about 14 minutes.

Note: In place of honey for the topping, you may prefer to glaze with confectioners' icing after baking.

The Large Occasion

For a more formal coffee or tea, the dining room is the best setting and your best cloth, china and silver are appropriate. Flowers can help dress up the room. For large bridal showers, receptions for out-of-town guests, club meetings, church groups, and so on, it's often an ideal way to entertain. Use at least 2 services if more than 20 guests are expected, and place 1 complete service at each end of the table.

Some help in the kitchen for washing cups and saucers—or catering service—is a good idea. And have someone (maybe a friend) see that tea and coffee pots are filled and that sandwich and cookie plates are replenished from time to time. In general, for a guest list of 20, 2 or 3 to help are perfect. For a party of 75 guests, about 8 are necessary.

Choosing the Menu. The menu pattern is usually uncomplicated and light, with food as dainty and as decorative as possible, harmonizing with flowers and setting.

MENU

Small sandwiches
(watercress triangles,
anchovy-egg pinwheels)
Party rolls with pâté
Tiny puffs filled with shrimp salad
Swedish Shortbreads   Pineapple cake
Almond Meringues
Coffee   Tea   Punch

Make pâté and pinwheel rolls the day before. Wrap in plastic wrap, and refrigerate or freeze. Watercress sandwiches should be made the day of party and wrapped in a damp towel until serving time. Puffs may be made in advance and filled the day of the tea. Assorted cookies can be made days in advance, freezer-wrapped and frozen until needed.

Swedish Shortbreads

> 1 cup butter or margarine
> 1/2 cup icing sugar
> 2 cups sifted flour
> 1 teaspoon vanilla extract

Cream butter or margarine and sugar together. Add flour; then add vanilla. Refrigerate until dough is chilled. Roll teaspoonfuls in balls. Flatten with fork. Bake at 350°F. 10 minutes. Makes 3 dozen.

Almond Meringues

> 1 cup soft butter or margarine
> 1/2 cup almond paste
> 1/2 cup light brown sugar, firmly packed
> 1 egg
> 2 cups sifted flour
> 3/4 cup raspberry jam
> 3 egg whites
> 3/4 cup granulated sugar
> 1/2 cup slivered almonds

Cream butter or margarine with almond paste; gradually beat in brown sugar and egg. Blend in flour. Pat in lightly buttered 13″ x 9″ x 2″ pan. Bake in moderate oven, 325°F. 20 minutes. Spread with jam. Beat egg whites until frothy; gradually beat in sugar, and beat until stiff meringue is formed. Fold in nuts; spread over jam. Return to oven about 20 minutes. Cool in pan. Cut into 1 1/2-inch squares. Store in airtight containers. Makes about 54 cookies.

Sandwiches

Use sandwich loaves; bread should be 1 day old for easy slicing, except for rolled sandwiches, which require fresh bread. Cream butter or margarine for easy spreading. Prepare batch of assorted fillings in advance.

To make fancy shapes, triangles or circles, slice a whole loaf lengthwise into thin slices. Spread slices with soft butter or margarine, then with filling. Cover with second buttered slice; cut into shapes, and wrap and chill before serving.

To make rolled sandwiches, remove crusts from fresh thin slices of sandwich loaf, and roll each with a rolling pin. Spread slices with butter or margarine and filling. Roll each slice up, and then cut in half. Secure each small roll with a pick. Wrap, and chill before serving.

To make pinwheel sandwiches, cut an unsliced loaf into thin lengthwise slices. Trim crusts from each slice. Spread with butter or margarine and filling and roll up. Wrap in foil, and chill. Before serving, slice into pinwheels.

SUGGESTED SANDWICH FILLINGS

Eggs, finely chopped green onion and mayonnaise
Mashed sardines, onion, lemon juice and chopped parsley
Liver sausage, cream cheese and cognac
Crabmeat, tarragon and *Mayonnaise*
Shrimp with *Curry Mayonnaise*
Chicken, almonds and *Mayonnaise*
Thin-sliced cucumber
Raw mushrooms and *Mayonnaise*

Other Suggested Accompaniments

Butterscotch-Nut Bread

    2 cups sifted all-purpose flour
    1 teaspoon baking powder
    1/2 teaspoon baking soda
    1/2 teaspoon salt
    1 egg
    1 cup brown sugar, firmly packed
    2 tablespoons melted butter or margarine
    1 cup sour milk
    1/2 cup chopped walnuts

Sift flour, baking powder, soda and salt together. In mixing bowl beat egg, and add sugar gradually, beating until light. Add butter or margarine, and blend thoroughly. Add flour mixture, a little at a time, alternating with sour milk. Stir to keep mixture smooth. Add nuts. Turn into greased loaf pan, 9″ x 5″ x 3″, and bake at 350°F. 1 hour or until done. Cool loaf completely. Serve in slices, buttered. Serves 8.

Rich Orange Drops

    3 1/4 cups sifted pastry flour
    1/2 cup fine white sugar
    2 tablespoons baking powder
    3/4 teaspoon salt
    1/2 cup butter or margarine, chilled
    1 egg, well beaten
    1/2 cup strained orange juice
    2 tablespoons grated orange rind

Sift flour, sugar, baking powder and salt together. Cut in butter or margarine to make fine particles. Mix together egg, juice and orange rind. Make well in flour mixture, and add liquid; mix all together lightly with fork. Drop dough from tip of teaspoon, well apart, onto greased baking sheet. Bake at 350°F. about 18 minutes. Makes 60—70 drops, depending on size.

SUNDAY BRUNCH PARTY

Sunday-morning brunch is great for family entertaining, so do include children. It should be a casual, relaxed affair in atmosphere as well as in dress. If you start the meal with fruit or juice or Bloody Marys, everyone will have a chance to relax and chat a few minutes. If your specialty is omelets, you might plan your meal around them; or, with the aid of an electric griddle, make buttermilk or buckwheat pancakes right at the table. Ham steaks grilled in the broiler and fried eggs cooked on a griddle or electric skillet are also nice. Brown-and-serve rolls, biscuits, butterflake rolls or cinnamon rolls—the kind you buy at the supermarket and keep refrigerated—need only be popped in the oven. In fact, keep in mind all the ready-to-bake products available. Try muffin mixes with your own variations—for example, a spoonful of marmalade hidden at the center of each muffin.

Another idea is to serve French toast; you can vary it by serving with bacon or sausage and maple syrup, by sprinkling with cinnamon or by using orange juice instead of milk as liquid.

BRUNCH MENU

Grapefruit and pineapple juice
Creamed codfish on toasted English muffins
Broiled tomatoes
Coffee

BRUNCH MENU

Broiled fresh pineapple, brushed with honey
Sautéed chicken livers with sherry in toast cups
Danish pastry
Coffee

Rhubarb compote
Stuffed Eggs Mornay
Asparagus wrapped with ham
Hot rolls or brioches
Coffee

Stuffed Eggs Mornay

6 hard-cooked eggs
1/2 cup cooked mushrooms, finely chopped
Mayonnaise or sour cream
Salt to taste
1 3/4 cups *Mornay Sauce*
3 tablespoons Parmesan cheese

Halve eggs lengthwise. press yolks through strainer; mix with mushrooms and mayonnaise to moisten. Season with salt. Pile mixture back into whites; spread 1 cup *Mornay Sauce* in flat baking dish. Place eggs on top of sauce, and spoon remaining sauce over. Sprinkle with cheese, and heat in 350°F. oven until sauce bubbles. Serve at once. Serves 6.

HUNT BREAKFAST

Grapefruit juice   Champagne or sherry
Smoked kippers
Sautéed veal kidney and mushrooms
Scrambled eggs
Toast   English muffins   Rolls
Marmalade   Jellies
Coffee

This meal doesn't require a "call to the hounds." You can serve in the traditional manner, from a sideboard (or server) with silver or copper chafing dishes, keeping foods hot as guests serve themselves. Wine is the customary opener.

LUNCHEON PARTIES

Offer an aperitif, a simple 2—3 course luncheon and time to linger over coffee.

If your guests are all women, a seasonal theme is particularly pleasant—there are appropriate decorations for Valentine's Day, Easter, and the fall. Use linen place mats with plain or patterned napkins, luncheon plates and appropriate glasses and silver.

If you are playing bridge, for example, you might save dessert and coffee until after you've finished your game.

Some Luncheon Menus

LUNCHEON FOR 6—8 PEOPLE

Chicken and Almonds in Sesame Shells
Fresh fruit salad   Melba toast
Petits fours   Tea with lemon

Chicken and Almonds in Sesame Shells

1/4 cup slivered, blanched almonds
3 tablespoons butter or margarine
2 (5-ounce) cans mushrooms and juice
1/4 cup chopped green pepper
2 tablespoons chopped onion
3 tablespoons flour
1 (10-ounce) can cream of chicken soup
2 tablespoons pimento juice
1/2 cup evaporated milk
2 egg yolks, slightly beaten
2 1/2–3 cups diced cooked chicken
1/4 cup diced pimento
8 large baked sesame tart shells
Chopped parsley

Sauté almonds in butter or margarine until golden. Add drained mushrooms, green pepper and onion. Cook until tender. Blend in flour; add mushroom juice, soup and pimento juice. Cook, stirring until thick and smooth. Combine milk and egg yolks, and add to pan. Cook 2 minutes longer. Add chicken and pimento. Reheat in double boiler. Fill tarts. Sprinkle with chopped parsley. Serves 8.

Note: Make sesame shells by adding 1/4 cup toasted sesame seeds to your favorite flaky pastry before adding water.

BRIDGE LUNCHEON FOR 8

Tomato consommé
Deep-dish Salmon Tart
Mushroom Béchamel Sauce
Asparagus with *Lemon Butter*
Ladyfingers   Coffee   Platter of fresh fruit

Deep-dish Salmon Tart

Rich pastry for double-crust pie
1 1/2 pounds canned salmon and juice
1 1/2 cups bread crumbs
2 eggs, beaten
1 cup milk
1/2 cup grated, peeled cucumber
2 teaspoons onion juice
1 teaspoon grated lemon rind
1/2 teaspoon salt
1 teaspoon lemon juice
Salt and black pepper to taste
Dash celery seed
6 hard-cooked eggs, sliced
Melted butter or margarine or beaten egg

Roll out sufficient pastry, and line a deep oblong baking dish, 9″ x 6 1/2″ x 2″. Turn salmon and its juice into bowl. Discard dark skin; mash bones and salmon with juice. Add next 7 ingredients. Taste, and season with lemon juice, salt and pepper to taste and celery seed. Place alternate layers of egg slices and salmon mixture in pastry-lined dish. Dampen edge, and roll out remaining pastry for top crust. Seal edges, and trim. Prick with fork, and brush with melted butter or margarine or beaten egg. Bake at 400°F. 30

minutes; reduce heat to 350°F., and bake another 30 minutes. Serves 8.

Note: Serve with *Mushroom Béchamel Sauce*, or pass sauce separately so that guests may serve themselves.

Mushroom Béchamel Sauce

    1/3 cup butter or margarine
    2 tablespoons chopped onion
    1/3 cup flour
    2 1/4 cups milk
    1 (5-ounce) can mushroom pieces with juice
      Pinch cayenne
      Dash nutmeg
      Salt and black pepper to taste
    2–3 egg yolks
    2 tablespoons cream

Melt butter or margarine in saucepan, and add onion. Heat until onion is transparent; blend in flour. Add milk slowly, and cook, stirring until smoothly thickened. Add mushroom pieces and juice, with cayenne, nutmeg and salt and pepper. Transfer to double boiler over hot—not boiling—water. Combine egg yolks with cream, and add to sauce. Stir 2—3 minutes to heat through, and serve hot over *Salmon Tart*. Makes about 3 cups.

Lemon Butter

    1/2 cup butter or margarine
    1/3 cup lemon juice
    1 teaspoon sweet paprika

Melt butter or margarine, being careful not to brown it. Stir in lemon juice and paprika. Serve over fresh asparagus spears. Makes about 3/4 cup.

Ladyfingers

    3 eggs, separated
    2/3 cup fine white sugar
    1/2 teaspoon vanilla extract
    1/4 teaspoon salt
    1/3 cup sifted all-purpose flour
    1/4 cup fine white sugar

Beat egg whites until fluffy. Add 1/3 cup sugar gradually, and continue beating until stiff. Beat egg yolks until thick, and beat in 1/3 cup sugar, vanilla and salt. Fold egg-yolk mixture and flour into egg whites. Spoon mixture into pastry tube or bag, with a plain 1/2-inch opening. Press tube to form fingers 3 inches long on ungreased heavy brown paper placed on cookie sheet. Sprinkle with 1/4 cup sugar, and bake at 360°F. 10—15 minutes. Cool, and lift from paper with metal spatula. Put fingers together in pairs with *Lemon Filling* or jam, or serve singly. Makes 6 dozen single fingers.

Another Manhattan Clam Chowder
Sea toast or pilot crackers
Tossed green salad with roquefort dressing
Warm apple pie   Coffee

Another Manhattan Clam Chowder

    1/4 pound salt pork
    3 medium potatoes, cubed
    1 large onion, chopped
    2 leeks, halved lengthwise and thinly sliced
    2 stalks celery, thinly sliced
    1/2 small green pepper, chopped
    1/2 bay leaf
    1/2 teaspoon thyme
    3 tomatoes or 3 cups canned tomatoes
      Boiling water
    4 cups cold water
    1 quart shucked clams and liquor
      Salt and pepper to taste
    1/2 tablespoon chopped chives
    1/2 tablespoon chopped parsley

Dice salt pork. Fry lightly in deep kettle. Reduce heat, and add potatoes, onion, leeks, celery, green pepper, bay leaf and thyme. Dip 3 tomatoes in boiling water, then quickly in cold water; peel, seed and chop. Add to kettle with 4 cups cold water. Drain liquor from clams, add it to pot and season lightly with salt and pepper. Cover kettle; bring to boil over high heat. Reduce heat, and simmer 30 minutes. Meanwhile, in wooden bowl, finely chop clams. Add to kettle, and poach over medium heat 4 minutes. Stir in chives and parsley. Serve at once with toasted and buttered sea toast crackers or New England pilot crackers.

DIETER'S LUNCHEON FOR 4

Buttermilk-Tomato Soup
Old-fashioned Pressed Chicken
Vegetable bouquet
Sherried Egg-white Custard

Buttermilk-Tomato Soup

    2 cups buttermilk
    1 (10-ounce) can tomato soup
    1 teaspoon chopped onion
    1/2 teaspoon salt
    1/4 teaspoon Worcestershire sauce
    1/8 teaspoon hot pepper sauce
    4 lemon slices

Mix first 6 ingredients well together. Chill, and serve garnished with lemon slices. Serves 4. Calories per serving: 94.

Note: This pink and tangy soup is also a good introduction to summer lunch or supper.

Old-fashioned Pressed Chicken

    1 (2 1/2–3-pound) broiler-fryer chicken
      Water
    1 onion
    1 stalk celery
    4–5 peppercorns
    1 teaspoon salt
    1/2 cup white wine
      Salt and pepper to taste
    1 envelope plain gelatine
    1/4 cup cold water or stock
    1 (4-ounce) can pimentos, sliced
    1 small dill pickle, sliced
    1 hard-cooked egg, sliced
      Watercress

Simmer chicken until tender in water to cover with onion, celery, peppercorns and 1 teaspoon salt. Cool in stock; then remove. Reduce stock by boiling 10 minutes; strain, and chill, so that fat can be removed. Remove skin and bones from chicken. Slice breast meat; chop remainder. Measure 1 cup chicken stock; add wine, and season well with salt and pepper. Soften gelatine in cold water. Dissolve over hot water, and add to stock-wine mixture. Cover bottom of 1-quart mold or loaf pan with thin layer of gelatine mixture, and chill until set. Arrange some of the pimentos, dill pickle and egg slices in attractive design; then add sliced white meat of chicken in even layer. Cover with thin layer of gelatine mixture, and chill until firm. Chop remaining egg slices. Chill remaining stock until syrupy; fold in remaining chicken, pimentos and chopped eggs to fill mold. Chill until firm. Unmold on platter, and garnish with watercress. Slice, or cut in squares. Serves 4–5. Calories per serving: 185 (approximately).

Sherried Egg-white Custard

    2 tablespoons sugar
    1/8 teaspoon salt
    1 1/3 cups 2% milk
    1/4 teaspoon vanilla
    2–3 teaspoons sherry or rum flavoring
    3 egg whites
      Spiced Cherry Sauce

Heat sugar, salt and milk together until sugar dissolves; then cool. Add flavorings and slightly beaten egg whites. Stir well, and strain into a 2-cup baking dish or 4 custard cups. Stand in a pan of hot water, and bake at 325°—350°F. about 1 hour for baking dish and 1/2 hour for cups. Although the center may still quiver after baking, custard will be firm when chilled. Spoon cold custard into serving dishes, and drizzle with *Spiced Cherry Sauce* or low-calorie fruit spread or topping. Serves 4. Calories per serving: 98.

Spiced Cherry Sauce

    1 (8-ounce) can noncaloric sweetened cherries
      Few drops red food coloring
    1 teaspoon cornstarch
    2 teaspoons water or lemon juice
      Dash cloves
      Dash cinnamon
      Dash ginger

Heat cherries in a small saucepan with food coloring. Stir in a mixture of cornstarch and water. Cook and stir until clear. Flavor with cloves, cinnamon and ginger. Serve hot or cold.

SUMMER LUNCHEON FOR 8

Hot or jellied consommé
Salmon-Cheese Casserole
Watercress   Cherry tomatoes
Pineapple Royale   Iced coffee

Salmon-Cheese Casserole

    1 small onion, chopped
    2 tablespoons butter or margarine
    2 cups water
    1 envelope dehydrated mushroom soup
    1 cup evaporated milk or sour cream
    2 tablespoons lemon juice
    1 (1-pound) can salmon
    6 cups cooked, drained macaroni
      Salt and pepper to taste
    1 cup shredded nippy cheese

Sauté onion in butter in a saucepan. Add water and soup. Whisk and cook until thickened. Remove from heat, and stir in next 3 ingredients. Add salmon, salmon juice and mashed bones. Stir in macaroni. Taste for seasoning. Spread in a greased 2-quart casserole, and bake at 375°F. 35 minutes. Cover with cheese. Bake until cheese melts. Serves 8.

Pineapple Royale

    2 large firm ripe pineapples
    1/4 cup fine white sugar
    1/4 cup rum or brandy (optional)
    1 quart orange sherbet
    6 egg whites
    1/8 teaspoon salt
    3/4 cup sugar
    1/4 cup flake-coconut

Set pineapples on their sides, and, starting at base of each, quarter lengthwise right through green leaves. Discard core, and cut out flesh with small sharp knife or spoon, being careful to keep shell intact. Dice pineapple meat, and sprinkle with 1/4 cup sugar and rum. Cover, and chill. Wrap green leaves in foil, and place shells on cookie sheet in refrigerator. Scoop 8 large balls of sherbet into waxed-paper-lined pan, and set in freezer. At serving time make stiff meringue of egg whites, salt and 3/4 cup of sugar. Spread partially drained pineapple in shells. Add scoops of sherbet, and cover fruit and sherbet completely with meringue. Sprinkle with remaining fruit, sugar and coconut. Bake at 450°F. 4 minutes or until lightly browned. Remove foil from greenery, and serve immediately. Serves 8.

Note: Omit sherbet if you wish, and instead pile extra diced or sectioned fresh fruit in shells; cover with meringue, or swirl whipped dessert topping over sherbet, and serve without baking.

COCKTAIL PARTY

Here's a party at which the hostess can be almost as carefree as her guests. As guests will be going on to dinner when they leave, appetizers and snacks are the rule, and they can be made ahead of time. It isn't really necessary to offer a great variety of drinks, as long as there's enough of whatever you do serve. Ginger ale and juices should be available along with alcoholic beverages.

Make sure you have enough glasses to go around and more. It's possible to rent an ample supply of glasses from a caterer, if necessary.

Make sure, too, that you have enough ice. If you make plenty of cubes in advance, you can keep them in plastic bags in your freezer compartment until time for the party.

Set out necessities for making drinks separately from food. You can arrange the bar in any corner where supplies will be safe from being knocked over. Set out bottles, an ice bucket filled with cubes, a pitcher of water, mixers, jigger measures and a tray of glasses. Mixers—ginger ale, soda,

tonic and so on—can be kept cool in the refrigerator and put out a few bottles at a time, as they are needed.

If the party is small, you may prefer to fill glasses in the kitchen and take them around on a tray.

Your Guests

People are apt to do a lot of wandering about at cocktail parties. If you can manage it, arrange a few corners in other rooms, so that groups can gather for talk away from the main crowd.

Seating is always difficult at a cocktail party, but no one seems to mind very much. You can put a stack of cushions at the foot of the stairs, so that people can sit on the stairs if they wish.

Accessories

You'll need plenty of ashtrays scattered liberally about the room so that people can dispose of toothpicks or cigarettes as they talk. Coasters should be in good supply, on every flat surface where you might reasonably expect someone to stand a glass. Small cocktail napkins are useful, too, for greasy fingers and frosty glasses.

Food

The food you serve should be finger-size if possible, as some of your guests will be standing, holding a glass in one hand and eating a bite here and there as they move about talking to other guests. Juggling doesn't come easily to most people. Circulate fresh supplies as long as the party-lasts—regular or open-faced sandwiches, plates of relishes, potato chips, salted nuts, and a hot specialty such as tiny sausage rolls. Each is best handled separately. Occasionally, cocktail-party food is set out as for a small buffet, with a stack of small plates for those who wish them. Provide plenty of toothpicks or forks for spearing moist snacks.

Cocktail food generally is most appealing when sharply flavored—salted nuts, olives, flavorful crackers, crisp "munchies," herring tidbits, smoked oysters, smoked salmon, pâtés, cheese spreads, dips, spreads, cocktail toast, seasoned toasts, nut wafers, cheese wafers and stuffed eggs.

Strips of toasted bread make good appetizer foundations. Trim crusts from thinly sliced bread, cut in 1-inch strips and toast on both sides under broiler before spreading with savory mixture. To cut bread into assorted shapes, slice unsliced sandwich loaf lengthwise, and trim crusts. Then cut out shapes, and spread with savory mixture. Or buy small dinner rolls, and slice thin to make small toast circles; there is less waste than cutting rounds from square slices of ordinary bread.

For the finishing touch on canapés, here are a few suggestions:

Anchovy paste, asparagus tips and Parmesan cheese on toast strips
Smoked salmon and capers on pumpernickel
Caviar with mimosa garnish (sieved egg yolk) on toast
Sardines, onions and *Mayonnaise* on toast
Shrimp butter and shrimp on toast
Ground ham and Swiss cheese on rolls, heated
Clam Cocktail Spread on toast triangles decorated with anchovy curls, grilled
Toast, *Blue-Cheese Spread* and onion garnish

Clam Cocktail Spread

> 2 (3-ounce) cans minced clams, drained
> 1 (8-ounce) package cream cheese
> 2 tablespoons sour cream
> 1 tablespoon chopped chives or 2 tablespoons grated onion
> Dash hot pepper sauce or cayenne

Mix all ingredients except hot pepper sauce together, and combine well. Add hot pepper sauce to taste. Makes approximately 1 cup.

Note: Spread on crackers or toast shapes, or double amount of sour cream to make a dip.

Blue-cheese Spread

> Clove garlic
> 1 (4-ounce) package cream cheese
> 1/2 cup cottage cheese
> 2 ounces blue cheese
> Dash Worcestershire sauce

Rub a bowl with a cut clove of garlic. Add the cream cheese, and mash with a fork until soft. Blend in the cottage cheese and blue cheese. Season with Worcestershire sauce. Makes 1 1/4 cups.

Cocktail Puffs

Make 1 recipe *Choux Paste* into small puffs. To fill, cut slit in side of each puff; or cut top off each shell, spoon in filling and replace top. Use creamed salmon, creamed shrimp, creamed chicken or ham to fill.

HORS D'OEUVRES SUGGESTIONS

Steak Tartare
Stuffed Mushrooms
Turnovers (ham and anchovy, sausage or mushroom)
Turkish Roll-ups
Corsican Anchoaïde
Red Devil Shrimp
Baby Broiled Kebabs
Keftethes
Potted Shrimp
Cherry tomatoes stuffed with *Guacamole*
Black olives in olive oil with crushed garlic and sliced lemon

Steak Tartare

> 1 pound finely ground lean round steak
> 1/4 cup finely chopped parsley
> 1/4 cup grated onion
> 2–3 teaspoons dry mustard
> 1 teaspoon salt
> 1/2 clove garlic, grated
> 1–2 dashes Worcestershire sauce

Mix meat with parsley, grated onion, mustard, salt, garlic and Worcestershire sauce. Taste for seasoning. Heap in bowl, and pat smooth. Surround with thin slices rye or pumpernickel bread, cut into fingers, or thin slices toasted rye on pumpernickel. Let guests spread their own, and have pepper grinder nearby for those who like to top with freshly ground black pepper. Serves 6–8 for appetizer.

Note: Have butcher grind meat twice.

Stuffed Mushrooms

> 1 pound medium mushrooms
> 1/4 cup butter or margarine
> 2 shallots, finely chopped
> 1 clove garlic, finely chopped
> 1/2 cup dry white wine
> 2 tablespoons chopped parsley
> 2 tablespoons anchovy butter
> 1/3 cup fine bread crumbs
> 1/4 cup buttered crumbs

Wash and dry mushrooms; remove caps, and finely chop stems. Sauté caps very briefly in 1/4 cup butter or margarine; remove, and set aside. In same pan sauté shallots and garlic until soft. Add mushroom stems, wine, parsley, and anchovy butter. Cook, stirring, over low heat 3 minutes. Stir in 1/3 cup bread crumbs. Fill caps with mixture, sprinkle with buttered crumbs and brown lightly under broiler. Makes approximately 14–15.

Turkish Roll-ups

> 1 tablespoon butter
> 1 tablespoon flour
> 1/3 cup milk
> 1/4 pound Gruyère cheese, cubed
> 8 slices fresh white bread
> Salt and pepper
> Dash cayenne

Melt butter and stir in the flour. Then add milk gradually, and cook until thick. Drop in cubes of the cheese, and heat and stir until smoothly melted. Season with salt, pepper and a dash of cayenne. Cool the mixture, and form into 16 fingers 1 1/2 inches long. Chill. Trim crusts from the bread, and cut each in half. Flatten the bread lightly with a rolling pin; then place a cheese finger on 1 end of each strip of bread, and roll up. Secure with toothpicks. Drop into deep hot oil, and cook until lightly browned. Drain, and sprinkle with flavor salt. Serve hot. Makes 16.

Corsican Anchoaïde

1/2 cup fancy figs, packed
2 anchovies, drained well
2 teaspoons oil-and-vinegar dressing
Orange juice
Garlic powder
6 slices light-rye snack bread
Sliced green onion

Mince figs and anchovies, or chop fine. Moisten with oil-and-vinegar dressing and orange juice. Flavor with a little garlic powder. Spread on thin slices of snack bread. Sprinkle with onion. For hors d'oeuvres, garnish with rolled anchovy fillets, and cut each slice in half. Makes 12.

Red Devil Shrimp

1 pound frozen jumbo shrimp
1/2 cup dry bread crumbs
1/2 cup minced sautéed mushrooms
1/2 (2 1/4–3-ounce) tin deviled ham
1/2 teaspoon salt
1/4 teaspoon pepper
1 teaspoon minced onion
Sherry to moisten
Savory Fritter Batter
Dash Cayenne

Gash shrimp lengthwise, and fill each cavity with stuffing made by combining next 7 ingredients. Dip in *Savory Fritter Batter* seasoned with a dash of cayenne, and deep-fry. Serve hot on cocktail picks with *Red Devil Sauce*. Makes about 2 dozen.

Red Devil Sauce

1/2 cup chili sauce
1/4 cup sour cream
1/4 teaspoon dry mustard
1/2 teaspoon horseradish
Dash Tabasco sauce
1 teaspoon lemon juice

Combine ingredients, and chill to blend flavors.

Baby Broiled Kebabs

1 can Vienna sausage
1 jar pickled mushrooms
1 can drained pineapple cubes
Italian dressing
Curry powder

Cut the Vienna sausage in 1/2-inch pieces; thread on large wooden toothpicks with pickled mushrooms and pineapple cubes. Place on a broiler pan, and brush with dressing. Sprinkle with curry powder. Broil 3—4 minutes, turning halfway through the cooking. You may substitute any pressed canned meat, wieners or sausages. Makes 2—3 dozen.

Keftethes (Parsley Meatballs)

1/3 cup fine dry bread crumbs
1/2 cup milk
4 green onions, finely chopped
1/2 cup finely chopped parsley
3 tablespoons olive oil
2 pounds ground chuck
1 egg, beaten
2 cloves garlic, crushed
2 teaspoons salt
Ground pepper to taste
2 tablespoons butter or margarine
3 tablespoons lemon juice
1/2 teaspoon dried oregano

Soak bread crumbs in milk until soft. Sauté onions and parsley in 2 tablespoons oil until limp, and mix thoroughly with ground meat, egg, garlic, salt and pepper. Add soaked bread crumbs. Shape into balls 1 inch in diameter. Sauté balls in remaining 1 tablespoon oil and butter or margarine in large frying pan, turning to brown all sides. Pour lemon juice into pan, and sprinkle meatballs with oregano. Heat a few minutes, scraping up browned drippings. Makes about 3 dozen appetizer meatballs.

Potted Shrimp

1 (7-ounce) package frozen peeled shrimp
3–4 tablespoons butter
Salt and pepper
Few grains cayenne
Dash mace
Melted butter

Cook shrimp according to package directions. Drain and dry on absorbent paper. While shrimp are still warm, grind with the fine blade of a mincer, crush in a blender or rub through a sieve. Cream the shrimp with the butter, and season well with salt, pepper, cayenne and mace. Pack into 2 small bowls, and pour a thin layer of melted butter over the top. Refrigerate for at least 24 hours before serving, to improve the flavor. Use as a spread on crackers or Melba toast. Makes about 1 1/2 cups; 1 small bowl serves 4.

MENU SUGGESTION

Sherry-Cheese Loaf
Fresh pears and Gouda
Ham-stuffed raw mushrooms
Celery and cucumber sticks
Tangerine Frappé

Sherry-Cheese Loaf

4 ounces pecans
1/2 cup soft butter or margarine
3 tablespoons sherry or brandy
2/3 cup crumbled blue cheese
1 (4-ounce) package cream cheese
2 tablespoons Parmesan cheese
Dash hot pepper sauce
Parsley sprigs
Melba toast circles

Chop nuts in blender 3–4 seconds or until finely chopped. Scrape nuts onto square of waxed paper. Measure butter or margarine and sherry into blender, and blend until smooth. Gradually add remaining ingredients, except parsley and toast, blending after each addition. Stop blender occasionally, and scrape down sides. When smooth, turn onto nuts, and shape into log. Coat well with nuts. Roll up in paper to smooth and shape, and chill. To serve, unwrap, and decorate with parsley and melba toast circles. Makes about 2 cups.

Note: 1/2 cup toasted sesame seeds may be used in place of pecans.

Tangerine Frappé

    1 (6-ounce) can frozen tangerine juice
    2–3 tablespoons lemon or lime juice
    2 tablespoons grenadine
    3/4 cup water
    2 egg whites, unbeaten
    1 cup soda water

Open top and bottom of juice can, and press frozen juice into blender. Add next 4 ingredients, and cover. Blend about 1 minute or until mixture is smooth and foamy. Add soda water, and pour over crushed ice. Serve in 5-ounce cocktail glasses, and pass savory appetizers. Makes about 26 ounces.

ENTERTAINING WITH CHEESE AND WINE

A cheese-and-wine party is a different and casual way to entertain a large group. You can make it an after-ski party, an evening event or a porch party. Invitations can be given by telephone, and preparation is simple. All you need is bread, crackers, wines and several kinds of cheese, arranged attractively. Set things out on a dining table or server. A colored linen cloth or a polished surface without mat echoes the note of informality. A checked cloth and candles in empty wine bottles can give the party a "cellar" atmosphere. Arrange wine and glasses at 1 end, and place food where it is easiest to reach and looks best. Wine glasses can be on a large tray to avoid stains on the tablecloth.

Identify Each Cheese

Group cheeses on 1 or, at most, 2 trays or boards. The effect of great variety is lost if you put each kind of cheese on a different plate. It's a good idea to set up a small flag (speared with a toothpick) identifying each kind of cheese with its name and country, so that guests can note and remember their favorites.

Have several napkin-lined baskets of various kinds of sliced bread and crackers, a bowl of sweet butter and plenty of table napkins.

Selecting Wines

Two kinds of wine, 1 red and 1 white, are enough; but you can serve as many as you like. Red wines should be opened some time before they are to be used. As a general rule, serve white wines chilled and red wines at room temperature. Don't be afraid to ask an expert for advice. Any wine shop or wine importer will be happy to answer your questions.

WINES

Bordeaux reds	Sherry
Burgundy reds	Champagne
Rhone Valley reds	Port

BREADS AND BISCUITS

French or Italian bread	Water wafers
Dark and light rye bread	Melba toast
Biscuits, salted and unsalted	Sesame wafers

CHEESES

Brie	Gruyère
Blue	Gouda
Camembert	Edam
Cheddar	Muenster
Caerphilly	Oka

DESSERT AND COFFEE PARTY

Most desserts can be prepared the day before, except for sauces or fillings. Everything can be laid out on the dining table or on small tables in the living room.

Some dining tables look best without cloth, with candles, silver and china on the polished surface, but a linen cloth can be used. A low flower arrangement in the center looks best, with candles on either side, but if table is against the wall a higher centerpiece is striking.

Place coffee tray at one end, with cups arranged around it. Put out both demitasse and larger cup; don't be afraid to mix your china. Provide dessert plates, spoons, forks and table napkins.

It's a good idea to have an alternate dessert for

calorie counters—fruit compote or lemon sponge, for example. Be sure to have enough of each, though, for all your guests to take the same thing.

Somewhere on the table have a larger pitcher of ice water and glasses. Little dishes with salted nuts and colored candies round out a table display nicely. If you wish, liqueur may be served in tiny glasses with coffee.

There are many ways to prepare coffee. Just what flavor and strength depends on personal taste. Generally, after-dinner coffees are stronger than those served at mid-morning coffee breaks, for instance. Similarly, for these dressed-up versions, it's wise to start with good strong coffee. You're adding other flavors, so you need coffee that doesn't get lost in the mixture.

Coffees

Vienna Coffee

Serve 2/3 cup coffee diluted with 1/3 cup hot milk. Top with whipped cream.

Café Brûlot

Put sugar lump into teaspoon, pour over it a little brandy and set alight. Pour hot strong coffee into cup, and stir in flaming sugar.

Café Royale

To each cup of strong black coffee, sweetened to taste, add jigger of brandy. Or serve brandy separately for each guest to add as desired. Pass thick cream separately.

Liqueur Coffee

Fill demitasse cups about 3/4 full. To each, add 1 tablespoon of any liqueur. Try curaçao, Cointreau, crème de cacao, Tia Maria.

Coffee Chantilly

Serve strong black coffee, and top with whipped cream, sliding it gently onto surface of coffee, so that cool cream blends with hot coffee in each sip. If you want to make a production of it, you might try *unwhipped* whipping cream, but it takes a little practice. Pour thick cream over back of spoon held so that its tip is just at surface of coffee. And for a refinement in either of these methods, blend a little of any liquer into the coffee (if you use Irish whiskey, it becomes Irish coffee).

Mocha Coffee

Mix hot coffee and an equal amount of hot cocoa; pour into large cups or mugs, and top with whipped cream and a little grated chocolate.

Desserts

German Hazelnut Torte

      4 ounces (1/4 pound) hazelnuts (filberts)
      6 egg yolks
  1 1/4 cups sifted icing sugar
    1/8 teaspoon cinnamon
      1 teaspoon rum flavoring
      5 tablespoons fine dry bread crumbs
    1/2 teaspoon baking powder
      6 egg whites
    1/8 teaspoon salt
    1/2 teaspoon cream of tartar
         Cream Nut Filling
    3/4 cup apricot jam
      1 tablespoon rum, brandy or water
         Hazelnuts, slivered, sliced or chopped

Grease the bottoms of 2 8-inch layer-cake pans 1 1/2 inches deep, and line with greased waxed-paper circles. Spread hazelnuts in a small shallow baking pan or pie plate, and toast in the oven at 300°F. 30 minutes. Rub nuts together in a tea towel to remove as much crisp skin as you can. Blend or grind nuts into fine bits. Beat egg yolks on high speed in a small beater bowl until thick and lemon-colored. Beat in icing sugar, cinnamon and rum flavoring. Continue beating 5 minutes. Fold in bread crumbs, 1 cup of the ground nuts and sifted baking powder. Beat egg whites, salt and cream of tartar together in a large beater bowl until stiff dull peaks form. With a whisk, fold in yolk mixture. Divide batter between the 2 prepared pans, and bake at 350°F. 35 minutes. Cool 10 minutes. Cut around the cakes with a wet knife. Leave until cold. Invert, and shake out the cakes. Peel off the papers. Slice layers in half horizontally, using a serrated bread knife; then fill with cream filling. Heat the apricot jam with rum, brandy or water. When hot and bubbly, strain and spread over top and sides. While jam is still warm, garnish with slivered hazelnuts. Chill thoroughly before serving. Serves 12.

Cream Nut Filling: Beat 1/2 pint whipping cream until stiff. Sweeten to taste; then flavor with rum extract and fold in ground hazelnuts. In place of cream, use 1 envelope desert-topping mix if you prefer.

Note: After baking and cooling, don't be surprised if these layers settle to about 1-inch thickness. They will rise again, after splitting and filling, to a 2 1/2-inch height.

Cherries Jubilee Sponge

      1 (8-inch) tube-shaped sponge cake, homemade or
         bought
      1 pint Burgundy cherry ice cream
  1/2–3/4 cup cherry or red currant jelly
         Flaked or desiccated coconut
         Cherries Jubilee Sauce

Cut 1/2-inch slice off the top of the sponge cake. Hollow out the top section of the cake as follows: Make 2 circular cuts 1/2 inch in from the outside and inside edges of the cake to within 1 inch of the bottom. Pull out the cake, leaving a cavity. Fill with spoonfuls of slightly softened cherry ice cream. (Slip the cake section into a small tube pan if one fits, and you will be less likely to break the cake shell.) Press cut-off slice on top, and freeze. Unmold, and quickly brush with warm cherry jelly and sprinkle with coconut. Return to the freezer. Serve in wedges with hot *Cherries Jubilee Sauce*. Serves 8.

Cherries Jubilee Sauce

    4 teaspoons cornstarch
    1 (20-ounce) can pitted Bing or black sweet
        cherries, drained
    1/3 cup red currant jelly
    3 tablespoons sugar
    3–4 teaspoons lemon juice
        Few drops red food coloring
    2–3 tablespoons kirsch or cognac

Measure cornstarch into a small chafing dish, and stir in the drained juice. Heat and stir until thickened and clear. Add red currant jelly and sugar. Cook and stir until jelly is smoothly melted. Add lemon juice, food coloring and the cherries. Set over hot water. Just before serving, warm kirsch or cognac, and pour over the sauce. Set alight, and when flames subside, ladle over wedges of filled sponge cake. Makes about 2 1/2 cups.

Ambrosia Cream Cake

    1/2 cup toasted coconut
    3/4 cup crushed vanilla wafers
    3 tablespoons melted margarine
    1 3/4 cups unsweetened orange juice
    1/2 cup flour
    3/4 cup sugar
    1/4 cup lemon juice
    2 eggs, separated
    2 teaspoons grated orange rind
    1/2 pound soft plain cream cheese

Combine the first 3 ingredients, and spread 1/2 in a greased 8-inch square pan. Heat 1 1/2 cups orange juice in the top of a double boiler. Beat flour and 1/2 cup sugar, remaining orange juice, lemon juice and egg yolks together, and pour into the hot juice. Whisk and cook until thick and smooth, about 7 minutes. Add the orange rind. Beat the cheese in a small bowl, and beat in the hot orange mixture. Fold in the egg whites stiffly beaten with remaining sugar. Spread over the crumbs, and sprinkle with remaining crumbs. Chill. Cuts into 10–12 servings. Garnish with drained Mandarin orange sections, if you wish.

SUNDAY-NIGHT SUPPER

Everyone, including guests, can pitch in for a supper of soup, *Maple-glazed Spareribs*, rolls, buttered broccoli, *Colorful Cabbage Salad* and fruit shortcake.

Sunday-night Supper Soup

    2 slices bacon
    1/2 cup chopped onion
    2 (10-ounce) cans green-pea soup
    2 (10-ounce) cans bouillon
    1/8 teaspoon thyme
    1/8 teaspoon pepper
    4 cups water
    1 cup coarsely grated raw carrot

Fry bacon until crisp; drain on paper toweling. Sauté onion in 2 tablespoons bacon drippings. Combine pea soup, bouillon, thyme, pepper and water. Simmer 1 minute. Just before serving, add carrot. Crumble bacon over top. Serve with popcorn. Serves 8—9.

Maple-glazed Spareribs

    2 cups stale, soft bread crumbs
    1/4 cup melted butter or margarine
    1/2 cup chopped celery
    1/4 cup chopped walnuts
    1/4 cup chopped onion
    1/2 teaspoon salt
    1/2 teaspoon sage, thyme or poultry seasoning
    4 pounds back spareribs
        Salt and pepper
    1 cup maple syrup
    1 teaspoon soy sauce

Combine first 7 ingredients. Cut ribs into 8 strips. Pile dressing mixture at 1 end of the ribs. Roll up, and tie with string. Place in a shallow baking pan, and sprinkle with salt and pepper. Bake at 450°F. 20 minutes. Reduce heat to 325°F.; brush spareribs with a mixture of maple syrup and soy sauce. Bake until tender, basting frequently, about 1—1 1/2 hours. Serves 6.

Colorful Cabbage Salad

    1 small head white cabbage
    1 small head red cabbage
    3/4 cup blue-cheese salad dressing
    1/2 cup red Italian onion rings

Halve cabbages; remove outer leaves and hard stalks. Chill in ice water several hours; drain. Finely shred on slaw board or with sharp knife until lacy thin. Line salad bowl with white cabbage leaves. Toss together equal parts white and red cabbage with salad dressing. Garnish with onion rings. Serves 4—6.

Caraway Sticks

    1 (8-ounce) package refrigerated crescent rolls
    1 egg yolk, beaten
    1/4 cup caraway seeds
    2 tablespoons coarse salt

Preheat oven to 375°F. Prepare crescent rolls, following package directions. Brush tops with egg yolk; sprinkle with caraway seeds and salt. Bake 10—13 minutes. Makes 8 rolls.

SUNDAY-NIGHT SUPPER MENU

Hot curried chicken soup
Molded Corned Beef and Potato Salad
Green salad   Corn sticks
Coffee layer cake with chocolate frosting
Coffee

Molded Corned Beef and Potato Salad

    2 tablespoons Italian oil-and-vinegar dressing
3 1/2 cups diced, cooked potatoes
    1 (4-ounce) package soft plain or relish cream cheese
    1/3 cup mayonnaise
    3/4 cup chopped celery
    1/4 cup chopped green pepper
    2 tablespoons chopped parsley
2–3 tablespoons chopped onion
    1 (12-ounce) can corned beef loaf, diced
    Salt, pepper and curry powder
    Hard-cooked eggs
    Tomatoes

Pour the dressing over the potatoes, and toss lightly. Potatoes will absorb more of the dressing flavor if they are hot or warm. Chill until cold. Cream the cheese and mayonnaise together, and stir lightly into the potato mixture. Add the next 5 ingredients, and season to taste. Press mixture into a small oiled angel cake pan or ring mold. Chill several hours, and unmold. Garnish with wedges of hard-cooked eggs and tomatoes. Serves 6.

BON VOYAGE OR FONDUE PARTY

If you're having friends in to say goodbye to the Joneses, you might ask each guest to bring some small travel aid as a parting gift to decorate a traveler's tree. This tree actually grows in the West Indies, but you can make your own by decorating a room divider or screen with attractive branches of oak, maple, pine or shrubbery from which to hang gifts. Feel free to set a maximum price.

Types of Menu

Serve food to make your departing friends either think back on Canada or ahead to their destination. If they're going to Switzerland, do have a Swiss fondue party.

You'll need an earthenware casserole and spirit lamp or chafing dish. Rub casserole with garlic first. Fondue is made by stirring 1/2 pound shredded Swiss cheese, dusted with flour, into 1 cup dry white wine and heating it very slowly in casserole over flame until cheese melts and combines with wine in creamy-white mixture. Just before serving time, stir in 2 tablespoons kirsch.

For the ceremony of eating, set your table with a plate of bread cubes for each person. Cubes should be about 1 inch in size. A glass of white wine, too, should be at each plate, and you'll need long-handled forks. There is a special kind of fork with a heat-resistant handle for a fondue. Each person takes a cube of bread on the fork, dips it into the fondue and swirls it around the bottom of the casserole in a figure-8 movement, to keep the mixture from hardening on the casserole bottom.

Swiss cheese is used for this dish because it melts more smoothly than any other. But if the mixture does begin to get a little stringy while the guests are twirling their bread cubes in it, as it will, simply add more kirsch.

Fondue is sometimes made with a white-sauce base. You can start cooking in the kitchen; make white sauce with 2 tablespoons each butter or margarine and flour for each cup milk. Stir in cheese, and pour the mixture into a casserole ready for serving over a flame, which keeps the mixture hot.

MENU FOR A FONDUE PARTY

Steak Tartare
Swiss-cheese fondue with French bread cubes
Tossed green salad   *Pears Burgundy*
Coffee

Pears Burgundy

    3 (14–15-ounce) cans pear halves
    2 cups red Burgundy
    1/2 cup light corn syrup
    1 tablespoon grated lemon rind
1 1/2 teaspoons cinnamon
    3/4 teaspoon allspice
    1 teaspoon cloves

Drain pear halves, saving 1 1/2 cups liquid. In medium saucepan mix liquid with Burgundy, corn syrup, lemon rind, cinnamon, allspice and cloves. Simmer, uncovered, until mixture is reduced to 2 1/2 cups. Add pear halves. Refrigerate at least 4 hours. Serve with *Date Squares*. Serves 6—8.

A HOME-MOVIE PARTY

You can rent 35 mm. movies by mail! Why not try a Keystone Cops comedy as the feature, and invite guests to bring their own home-movie efforts as short subjects? Set the living room up to look like a theater, and darken it when guests arrive. Usher guests to their seats with a flashlight; hand them a bag of popcorn and some old-fashioned licorice sticks. Have soft drinks on hand for intermissions.

After the show, serve an ice cream parlor treat of waffles with ice cream and strawberry topping.

Waffles with Strawberry Sauce

    1 (12-ounce) package frozen strawberries, thawed
1 1/2 tablespoons cornstarch
1/3 cup orange juice
    2 teaspoons lemon juice
    8 homemade or frozen waffles

Drain strawberries, and save juice. Blend juice with cornstarch, orange juice and lemon juice in medium saucepan. Stir until smooth. Bring to boil; stir until thick and translucent. Add strawberries. Serve warm over cooked waffles. Serves 8.

FRIDAY-TO-SUNDAY MENUS

FRIDAY-NIGHT SUPPER

Hot Ribbon Egg Loaf
Asparagus tips   Green salad
Rosé Fruits   Cookies   Coffee

Hot Ribbon Egg Loaf

    3 eggs, separated
    5 whole eggs
1/4 cup mushroom or cream chicken soup
    1 teaspoon onion juice
    Celery salt and pepper
    6 slices day-old brown bread
    Soft butter
    Pinch salt
    Parmesan cheese

Separate 3 eggs. Cover 5 whole eggs with cold water, and bring to a boil. Drop egg yolks carefully into the boiling water, and cover. Set aside for 30 minutes. Cool eggs and yolks under cold running water. Mash yolks. Crack and peel eggs in shells, and grate on a medium shredder into a bowl. Add mashed yolks. Stir in just enough undiluted mushroom soup to moisten. Flavor with onion juice, celery salt and pepper. Spread bread with soft butter, and trim off top and bottom crusts. Cover each slice with egg filling, and make 2 stacks of 3 slices each. Set stacks together on a small shallow baking pan or cookie sheet. Refrigerate until 30 minutes before serving time. Beat egg whites with a pinch of salt until moist peaks form. Spread meringue over top and sides

of loaf, and sprinkle generously with Parmesan cheese. Bake 20 minutes at 350°F. or until nicely browned and heated through. Lift to a heated platter, and cut in thick slices. Pass hot tomato sauce or creamed mushrooms, and serve with buttered green vegetables. Serves 6–8.

Note: For a company dish, add chopped pimento and drained pickle relish to the egg filling.

Rosé Fruits

1/2 cup honey
1/2 cup rosé wine
    Small bunch mint leaves, broken
    1 cup sliced strawberries
    1 cup sliced bananas
    1 cup melon balls
    1 cup fresh diced pineapple or any fresh fruits in
      season
    1 quart vanilla ice cream

Heat honey; remove from heat, and add wine and mint leaves. Chill 1 hour. Strain, and pour over fruits. Chill until serving time. Spoon over scoops of vanilla ice cream. Serves 8.

SATURDAY BREAKFAST

Orange juice
Blueberry pancakes with maple syrup   Bacon
Coffee

SATURDAY LUNCH AT THE LAKE

Thermos ice cold martinis
Cold broiled tarragon chicken
French Potato Salad   *Caviar Eggs*
French loaf
Miniature French pastries (from bakery)

French Potato Salad

    3 pounds (6–8 medium) new potatoes
    Boiling salted water
1/2 cup salad oil
    3 tablespoons wine vinegar
    1 teaspoon salt
1/2 teaspoon freshly ground pepper
    1 cup chopped green onions
1/2 cup chopped parsley
    2 hard-cooked eggs, sliced

Wash potatoes, and place unpeeled in boiling salted water. Cook covered, until just tender. Test by piercing with point of sharp knife. Do not overcook. Drain at once, and rinse under a little cold water. Peel quickly, and slice. Place in deep bowl, and add oil, vinegar, 1 teaspoon salt and pepper. Mix well. Set aside to cool; then chill in refrigerator. About 2 hours before serving, add onions, parsley and additional oil if necessary. Taste for seasoning, and add more salt and pepper if needed. Serve in salad bowl, and garnish with egg slices. Serves 6—8.

Note: Potatoes should still be warm when seasonings are added.

Caviar Eggs

    6 hard-cooked eggs, halved
    2 tablespoons *Mayonnaise*
    1 small (2-ounce) jar red or black caviar
    1 tablespoon chopped parsley
    1 teaspoon onion juice
    Salt to taste

Scoop out egg yolks, and mash. Add mayonnaise, caviar (reserving a little for garnish), parsley and onion juice. Taste for seasoning, and add salt if necessary. Heap mixture into egg whites, and garnish with caviar. Chill. Serves 6.

SATURDAY DINNER ON THE PORCH

Spicy Jellied Tomato Soup
Grilled thick sirloin steaks   *Mustard Sauce*
Baked potatoes with garlic butter
Green beans   Salad
Strawberries and cream   Coffee

Spicy Jellied Tomato Soup

    2 envelopes plain gelatine
    1/2 cup cold water
    1 cup boiling tomato juice
    1 chicken-bouillon cube
    2 (10-ounce) cans tomato soup or bisque
    Dash cloves
    Dash allspice
    Few drops hot pepper sauce
    2 tablespoons lime or lemon juice
    Sour cream
    Chives

Soften gelatine in cold water. Stir into the boiling tomato juice with the crumbled bouillon cube. Stir until dissolved. Add next 5 ingredients. Chill until set. Break up with a fork, and spoon into bouillon cups. Top each serving with sour cream and snipped chives. Serves 7—8.

SUNDAY BRUNCH

Peaches and raspberries in orange juice
Shirred Eggs with Chicken Livers
Broccoli with butter   Toasted English muffins
Coffee

Shirred Eggs with Chicken Livers

    1 pound fresh or frozen chicken livers
    2-3 tablespoons butter
    1 shallot or green onion, chopped
    1/4 teaspoon sweet basil (optional)
    1/2 teaspoon salt
    Pepper
    3-4 tablespoons chicken broth
    6 tablespoons cream
    Fresh parsley
    6 eggs
    Salt and pepper
    Paprika

Defrost chicken livers in the refrigerator overnight or for several hours. Melt the butter, and add the drained livers and shallot. Sauté gently about 5 minutes, stirring until all pinkness disappears. Chop livers slightly, and simmer until liquid almost evaporates. Spoon into 6 small buttered baking dishes. Add 1 tablespoon cream and a little chopped fresh parsley to each. Break 1 egg into each dish, and sprinkle with salt, pepper and paprika. Bake at 350°F. until eggs are set, about 10 minutes. Loosen edges, and carefully lift eggs and livers to individual slices of hot-buttered toast. Serve with buttered cooked asparagus tips. Serves 6.

HOLIDAY ENTERTAINING

TRADITIONAL THANKSGIVING DINNER

Consommé with Sherry
Roast Turkey   Mushroom Stuffing
Brown giblet gravy
Mashed white potatoes or candied yams
Creamed white onions
Whipped yellow turnips   Buttered green beans
Cranberry sauce
Celery hearts   Green and black olives
Pumpkin pie with whipped cream
Fruit   Nuts   Coffee

Consommé with Sherry

    4 (13-ounce) cans consommé Madrilene
    2 tablespoons chopped parsley
    1/4 cup dry sherry

Heat consommé. Sprinkle with parsley, and add sherry. Serves 8–10.

Mushroom Stuffing

    1/2–1 pound mushrooms, sliced
    1 small onion, chopped
    1/2 cup butter or margarine
    6 cups stale coarse bread crumbs
    2-3 tablespoons chopped parsley
    1 cup chopped celery
    1/4 cup diced pimento
    1 1/2 teaspoons salt
    2 teaspoons savory
    1 teaspoon sage
    1/2 teaspoon pepper

Sauté mushrooms and onion in hot butter until soft but not brown. Toss with remaining ingredients. If mixture seems dry, sprinkle with a few tablespoons hot water or melted butter. Taste for seasoning. Makes enough dressing for a 10–12-pound turkey.

TRIM-THE-CHRISTMAS-TREE SUPPER

Seafood Mornay
Cold baked ham
Relish Christmas Tree
Assorted breads
Dark or *Light Fruitcake*
Coffee or yuletide eggnog

Seafood Mornay

      1 pound fresh or frozen scallops
        Flour
  1/4 cup butter
      2 tablespoons white part of scallions, chopped
      5 tablespoons flour
  2 1/4 cups milk
      1 (1-pound) can red or pink salmon
  3/4 teaspoon salt
      2 ounces Gruyère cheese, shredded (optional)
      2 egg yolks
  1/4 cup evaporated milk
        Dry sherry, white wine or vermouth (optional)
        Pepper, cayenne and chervil (optional)
        Buttered crumbs or crushed potato flakes
        Parsley

Drain and dry the scallops on absorbent paper, and slice in half across the grain. Dust with flour. Melt the butter in a frying pan, and stir in the scallions. Stir-fry about 1 minute. Add the scallops, and sauté slowly 2–3 minutes or until lightly cooked through. Lift scallops from the pan, and stir the flour into the pan fat until it disappears. Stir in the milk gradually, and cook over low heat until smooth and thick. Drain the salmon juice into the sauce, and add salt and cheese. Stir until cheese melts. Add egg yolks mixed with the evaporated milk, and cook 2–3 minutes. Dilute with a little dry sherry. Add the scallops. Taste for seasoning, and add pepper, a pinch of cayenne and a dash of chervil if you wish. Remove skin and bones; then break salmon into large chunks, and arrange in a candle-warmer casserole. Pour the scallop mixture over the salmon, and sprinkle with crumbs. Bake at 375°F. 20–25 minutes or until bubbly. Broil about 1 minute to brown the top. Garnish with chopped parsley, and set over a candle warmer. Serve over curried rice or in patty shells. Serves 6–8. Double the recipe for 12–16 guests.

Note: In a chafing dish, arrange salmon chunks, and cover with scallop mixture. Reheat over hot-water pan. Sprinkle with croutons and parsley.

Relish Christmas Tree

Buy a piece of styrofoam shaped like a Christmas tree. Cover with heavy green wrapping paper. Stick with toothpicks and then with assorted vegetables and pickles—tiny tomatoes, cauliflower pieces, radishes, pickled onions and tiny cucumber pickles.

Light Fruitcake

      1 pound almonds, blanched and slivered
  1/2 pound candied red cherries, halved
  1/4 pound candied green cherries, halved
  1/2 pound golden raisins
  1/2 pound candied citron, chopped
  1/4 pound candied pineapple, chopped
      4 cups unsifted all-purpose flour
  1 1/2 cups butter or margarine
      2 cups sugar
      6 eggs, separated
  3/4 cup milk
  1/4 cup brandy
      1 teaspoon almond extract
      1 teaspoon cream of tartar
        Marzipan strawberries
        Angelica strips

Grease 10-inch tube pan, line with brown paper and grease paper. Combine almonds, cherries, raisins, citron and pineapple; sprinkle with 1/2 cup flour. Cream butter or margarine, gradually add sugar and beat until creamy. Beat egg yolks well, and add to butter mixture; beat thoroughly. Combine milk, brandy and almond extract; add alternately with remaining flour to butter mixture. Pour over fruit and nuts, and mix well. Beat egg whites until foamy; add cream of tartar, and beat until stiff. Fold into first mixture. Pour into prepared pan. Bake in slow oven (275°F.) about 3 hours. Let stand 30 minutes. Remove cake from pan, and cool to room temperature. Wrap in moisture-proof paper, and store in cool place. At serving time remove wrapping, and decorate with marzipan strawberries and angelica.

CHRISTMAS DINNER

Seafood cocktail
Roast goose   *Saffron Rice*
Baked squash   Brussels sprouts
Plum pudding   *Velvet Sauce*
Coffee   Brandy

Velvet Sauce

      2 eggs
      1 cup icing sugar
      3 tablespoons lemon juice
      1 tablespoon grated lemon rind
  1 1/4 cups stiffly beaten cream

Beat eggs well until thick and lemon-colored. Add sugar slowly; beat well, and add lemon juice and rind. Fold in stiffly beaten cream. Makes about 2 cups.

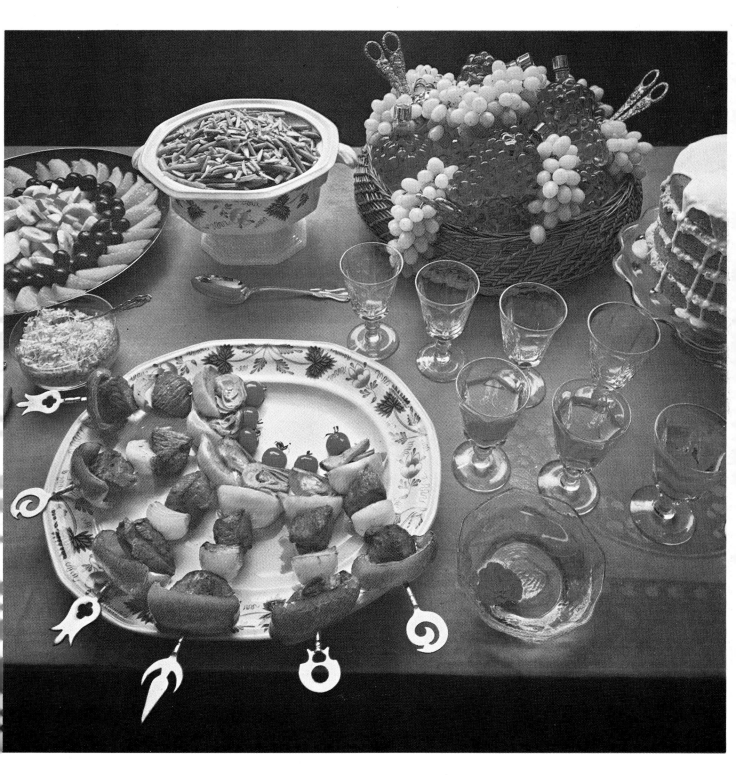

A table for an outdoor party, featuring a main course of Lamb Shish Kebab (p. 28).
CREDIT: *Bernard Gray*.

Daisies and balloons are everywhere at this children's birthday party setting.
CREDIT: *Henry Sandbank*.

Jeweled Ham
Cold salmon   Tartar sauce
Hot rolls
Lazy-Susan Salad
Pineapple Cheesecake   *Café Brûlot*

Jeweled Ham

For a glittery jeweled effect, try a coating of candied and dried fruits on your favorite buffet ham. First, cook the ham according to package directions, or buy one of the ready-to-eat or fully cooked varieties. Then, with a medley of fruits and broken wooden toothpicks, pin a mosaic design over the top.

Trim the fat off the cooked ham, if necessary, to 1/4-inch thickness. Set a whole ham in the base part of the broiler pan, or a half ham in a cake pan or similar small shallow container. For the jewels, use any of the following: pitted moist prunes or dates stuffed with nuts or unstuffed; wedges of candied pineapple; moist dried apricots or light figs; red and green glacé cherries; sweet pickled cantaloupe balls or watermelon rind; preserved kumquats. Secure each piece with a half toothpick, and place them close together to disguise the fat completely. Brush the arrangement generously with warm liquid honey flavored with a little grated orange rind, and pour a cup of water into pan. Bake on a low oven rack at 350°F. 25 minutes, brushing the fruits again after 15 minutes. Cool; then chill until serving time.

Note: To carve and serve, remove the first row or rows of glazed fruits. Slice the ham up to the remaining rows of glazed fruit.

Pineapple Cheesecake

    1/3 cup melted butter
      2 tablespoons sugar
    1/2 cup blended or finely chopped nuts
    3/4 cup graham crumbs
    1/2 teaspoon cinnamon
  1 1/4 pounds pineapple cream cheese
    1/2 cup sugar
    1/4 teaspoon salt
      1 tablespoon lemon juice
      1 teaspoon lemon rind
      4 egg yolks
    1/2 cup unsifted all-purpose flour
    1/2 pint cream, whipped
      4 egg whites
    1/2 pint sour cream
      2 tablespoons sugar
      1 teaspoon vanilla

Mix first 5 ingredients, and pat into a 9-inch spring-form pan. Chill. Beat together cheese and 1/4 cup sugar and the next 5 ingredients. Gently fold in whipped cream. Beat egg whites until stiff, gradually adding remaining sugar. Fold into cheese mixture. Pour over crumbs, and bake at

325°F. 1 1/2 hours or until almost set. Mix sour cream, sugar and vanilla, and pour over cake. Turn off oven, and leave undisturbed for 4–5 hours. Garnish and glaze with fruit. Serves 8–10.

Lazy-Susan Salad

Arrange assortment of vegetables, each in its own dish, on lazy Susan. Dress with *Vinaigrette Sauce,* and dust with chopped parsley. Some vegetables you might choose: whole crisp green beans, raw cauliflowerettes, whole cherry tomatoes, tiny carrots cooked until crisp, cooked whole white onions, sliced zucchini.

Wine punch   Eggnog
Salted nuts   Cheese tray
Relishes   Deviled eggs
Sliced turkey   *Corned Beef Loaf*
Toasted French bread
Fruitcake fingers

Corned Beef Loaf

      2 (12-ounce) cans lean corned beef
      2 (3-ounce) cans meat spread
      1 tablespoon hot prepared mustard
    1/8 teaspoon garlic powder (optional)
      2 hard-cooked eggs, shredded (optional)
    2/3 cup cold water
      2 envelopes plain gelatine
      1 (10-ounce) can undiluted bouillon
        Cheese, pimento, sweet gherkins

Oil a straight-sided 10 1/4″ x 3 3/4″x 2 1/2″ loaf pan, or any large loaf pan or small pans that will hold 6 1/2–7 cups. Mash the corned beef thoroughly, finally breaking up any lumpy bits with your fingers. If the meat at this point is as smooth as possible, the loaf will be a breeze to slice at serving time. Mix in the next 4 ingredients. Measure cold water into a small saucepan, and stir in gelatine and 1/2 the can of bouillon. Heat and stir until gelatine dissolves. Then remove from heat, and add remaining bouillon. Pour a thin layer in the bottom of the oiled pan. A deep layer will mask the brightness of your garnish. Set the pan in the freezer, and make sure the base is level. Stir remaining aspic into the meat mixture. Remove the aspic layer from the freezer when it is almost set, but still soft to the touch. Arrange 3 or more poinsettia shapes on the aspic, using cutouts of pimento for petals, small circles of yellow cheese for centers and gherkin strips and slices for leaves and stems. Spoon meat mixture over the top, and spread smoothly. Cover with plastic film, and chill until set. Unmold on a serving tray, and garnish. Makes 20 1/2-inch slices.

POKER PARTY

When all the guests are men, the accent should be on hearty food—a casserole and salad, some filled sandwiches or a platter of corned-beef hash. Set out plates, cups, saucers and napkins. Have casserole ready to heat through in the oven or sandwiches covered with damp towel in refrigerator. Fix coffee pot, and have sugar and creamer handy.

MENU

Danish open-face sandwiches   Cold beer
Fresh fruit   Chocolate cake
Coffee

Beef and Red Cabbage Danish

4 or 8 oblong slices Brie or mild cheese
4 slices buttered caraway-seed bread
1 cup *Red-Cabbage Salad*, drained
Sour cream
Thin rings sweet raw onion
16 thin small slices roast beef
Hot mustard
Pickle slivers

Arrange cheese on the bread slices, and cover with well-drained *Red-Cabbage Salad* mixed with a small amount of sour cream. Cover with onion rings and neat rolls of beef that have been spread lightly with mustard. Tuck slices of pickles between the rolls. Makes 4. Double or triple this amount as needed.

Note: Well-drained commercial or homemade pickled red cabbage may be substituted for *Red-Cabbage Salad*.

Red-cabbage Salad

3 cups red cabbage, finely shredded
Juice of 1 lemon
1 tablespoon honey
1/2 teaspoon salt
1/4 cup water

Bring ingredients slowly to a boil. Cover, and simmer about 45 minutes. Chill. Makes about 1 1/2 cups, drained.

CHILDREN'S PARTIES

Parties for the very young (1—3) should be limited to a small group of youngsters whose mothers will accompany them. Provide simple toys for the guests to play with; they're not ready for games yet.

The children will enjoy seeing the birthday cake and candles but probably will not be too interested in eating it. Cookies or cupcakes are more easily handled by this age group, as are plastic bowls or cups of ice cream, jelly or custard. Milk and fruit juices are suitable beverages.

Don't insist that children remain at the table too long; their attention span is short. Coloring books and crayons may occupy their time while you serve cake and coffee to adult guests.

As soon as you notice signs of restlessness among the children, try to indicate gracefully that the party is over. Get out some gifts for the children to take home with them, which will please them; then let them know that it is time to leave.

The most satisfactory children for a party are 4—7-year-olds. They are old enough to enjoy it and young enough to be unselfconscious about it. Hats, streamers, noisemakers—all the conventional party accessories—are appropriate. Use a pretty paper tablecloth, matching napkins and plates and cups. A charming place card can be made from a balloon: Write each child's name with a felt-tipped marker on a balloon (before inflating), tie with string and attach 1 to each chair.

If you have invited them for lunch, keep food simple—sandwiches of cream cheese or peanut butter and jelly, tuna fish, egg salad and perhaps a plate of cocktail frankfurters. Heated shoe-string potatoes, carrot and celery sticks, the birthday cake, ice cream and chocolate milk or fruit juices will complete the menu.

If you are going to have the children play games, have all the equipment gathered in advance. Children like such old favorites as pin-the-tail-on-the-donkey and musical chairs. Have some prizes for the winners; in fact have a small prize for everyone.

When you call to give the invitations, tell the mothers that you will arrange for the children to get home. This way you can decide when the party is over.

For children over 8, you may have to alter the style of the party. Boys, particularly, are not very enthusiastic about dressing up for an afternoon of ice cream and cake. A backyard cook-out would be more to their liking. Thick, juicy hamburgers; grilled frankfurters; a platter of hard-cooked eggs;

small whole tomatoes; and black, crusty potatoes baked in coals and eaten by hand with butter and salt would be a feast for them. Lots of milk and soft drinks, ice cream and cake or cupcakes are nice for dessert.

If weather permits, some games can be organized to occupy them before mealtime. Sack races, potato races, three-legged races, volleyball and touch football are all fun, as are certain indoor games such as kick hockey, Ping-Pong and other action games. Again, prizes are nice.

Girls older than 8 seem content with the traditional ice-cream-and-cake routine, varied with some records and space for dancing. Girls love to make things too. You can provide paper plates and some odd feathers, flowers and ribbons and stage a hat-designing contest.

Halloween Party

Everybody loves to dress up, especially children, and Halloween offers unlimited opportunities. Issue invitations far enough ahead for mothers to plan children's costumes.

Games Need Space. The number you invite, of course, depends on the space you have. And games—especially children's games—require a great deal of space. Have as much Halloween in the decor as possible. Orange paper pumpkins pinned on doors and big clusters of orange and black balloons tied to the hall light and the stair posts give a carnival look to the house.

When the children arrive start a game—maybe charades for an opener. Do keep the pace brisk, and go on to the next game before they tire of the first. Be sure to include bobbing for apples—it's messy but fun. And older children might enjoy some dancing.

Food and Beverages. Right from the start, with so much action, children will be thirsty. Have big pitchers of cold apple cider or fruit juice on hand all evening.

When suppertime comes, produce a good choice of easy-to-manage food arranged on a table —sandwiches, filled rolls, squares of cheese, celery and carrot sticks. For something sweet, try doughnuts, candied apples, hermits or other spicy cookies. Hot chocolate served with whipped cream or cold chocolate milk is a good beverage choice.

MENU

Peanut-butter-and-jelly sandwiches or franks in hot rolls
Cheddar cheese squares
Celery   Carrot sticks
Popcorn   Potato chips
Candied apples
Chocolate milk

Making Candy. From a child's point of view, candy makes a party "a party." Homemade candy-making with tasting privileges is the most delightful activity they can ever imagine.

Halloween is the ideal time for children and candies to come together; for "trick or treat," homemade candies can't be beat.

If you think you're going to enjoy candy-making, a candy thermometer is a good investment. But you can manage without one, though the results aren't quite so predictable, and it takes a little practice. The test of "doneness' consists of putting a drop of the cooked sugar mixture into a glass of cold water. If you are making soft candy such as fudge, the mixture is done when drop of syrup forms a soft ball in cold water but does not hold its shape (238°–240°F.). In making caramels, cook longer, until the syrup forms a firmer ball (244°–250°F.). For taffy, drop should form a hard ball in cold water and hold its hardness when taken out (250°–260°F.). For soft crack, syrup forms fine threads which break easily when dropped into cold water (260°–280°F.). Brittle candy such as *Peanut Brittle* needs a higher temperature; syrup forms brittle threads, sometimes known as "hard crack," which snap off when taken from water (285°–295°F.). Very hard crack is the carmelizing range (295°–310°F.).

Use heavy saucepan to prevent mixture from burning on bottom, and have it large enough to allow mixture to boil vigorously without boiling over. A wooden spoon is best for stirring or beating candy mixtures.

Note: Do not attempt to make candy on a humid day!

Peanut Clusters

    8 ounces semisweet chocolate
    8 ounces roasted shelled peanuts

Melt chocolate in bowl over hot water. Remove from heat, cool slightly and stir in peanuts. Spread sheet of waxed paper on cookie sheet, and drop teaspoonfuls of chocolate-peanut mixture onto sheet. Place cookie sheet in refrigerator overnight to chill thoroughly. Makes 1 pound.

Candied Apples

         6 medium-size red apples
         6 wooden skewers
    2 1/2 cups sugar
    2 1/2 cups light corn syrup
         1 cup water
         1 teaspoon red vegetable coloring

Wash and dry 6 medium-size red apples. Dry well. Insert wooden skewers firmly at stem ends. In medium saucepan, mix sugar, corn syrup and water. Stir over medium heat until sugar dissolves. Add 1 teaspoon red food coloring. Bring to boil; cook until candy thermometer reads 290°F. (hard-crack stage). Remove syrup from heat. Quickly dip each apple in syrup, coating completely. Place on well-greased baking sheet while coating hardens. When cool, warp individually in clear plastic wrap. Serves 6.

Raisin-Peanut Clusters

         8 ounces semisweet chocolate
    2 1/2 cups seedless raisins
         1 cup shelled roasted peanuts
       1/4 teaspoon salt

Melt chocolate in bowl over hot water. Remove from heat, and cool slightly. Stir in raisins and peanuts, add salt and mix well. Drop teaspoonfuls on waxed paper on cookie sheet, and chill overnight in refrigerator. Makes about 2 pounds.

Pralines

         1 cup granulated sugar
         1 cup brown sugar, firmly packed
         1 cup buttermilk
       1/2 teaspoon baking soda
       1/8 teaspoon salt
    1 1/4 cups pecan halves
         2 tablespoons butter or margarine
         1 teaspoon vanilla extract

Mix sugars, buttermilk, baking soda and salt in a heavy, deep pan, and stir over low heat until sugar is dissolved. Boil over moderate heat until thermometer registers 240°F. or until mixture forms soft balls in cold water. Remove from heat, and stir in nuts, butter or margarine and vanilla; beat until mixture is thick and slightly sugary. Set saucepan over low heat or hot water to prevent mixture from hardening any further, and drop tablespoonfuls onto waxed paper on cookie sheet. Make each patty about 2 1/2 inches across. Cover with waxed paper, and chill before using.

If pralines are to be used for gifts, wrap each separately in cellophane, or set in fluted paper cups. Makes about 1 1/2 pounds.

Lollipops

         2 cups granulated sugar
         1 cup water
       2/3 cup light corn syrup
       1/2 teaspoon oil of lemon
            Few drops yellow vegetable coloring
        24 sticks

Wrap wet cloth around long-handled fork, and use during cooking to wipe off crystals that accumulate around sides of pan. Grease lollipop molds or any flat surface (cookie sheet or shallow baking pan, turned upside down, will do). Put sugar, water, and syrup into heavy saucepan, and cook over low heat, stirring, until sugar dissolves. Continue to cook without stirring until hard-crack stage is reached (295°F.). Quickly stir in oil of lemon and food coloring. Pour mixture into greased lollipop molds or drop from end of spoon onto flat greased surface, spreading to make round shapes. Press 1 end of lollipop stick into each pop as soon as mixture is poured from spoon, working quickly before candy cools and hardens. Loosen lollipops from surface as soon as they are firm but before they are quite cold, and wrap each in cellophane. Makes 24.

Note: To form faces, use 1/2 gumdrop for mouth and raisins for eyes, and scatter coconut around top for hair. Set out all ingredients for decorations in advance, ready to add while pops are hot and before they harden.

Uncooked Fondant

         1 egg white
    1 1/2 teaspoons water
       3/4 teaspoon vanilla extract
    2 3/4 cups icing sugar

Beat egg white, water and vanilla in bowl until well blended; add sugar gradually, beating until mixture is very stiff. Knead with hands until smooth. Wrap in waxed paper, and store in refrigerator.

VARIATIONS:

* *Chocolate Fondant*: Add 2 squares melted unsweetened chocolate to fondant. Blend thoroughly.

* *Fondant Chocolate Peppermints*: Add few drops essence of peppermint to fondant. Mix it thoroughly. Melt 2 squares unsweetened or semisweet chocolate in top of double boiler. Make small balls of fondant, and flatten into patties. Dip in melted chocolate. Place on waxed paper to dry.

* *Coconut or Chocolate Fondant Balls*: Make fondant balls; roll in shredded coconut or melted chocolate.

Peanut Butter—Fruit Confections

      1 cup pitted dates
  1/2 cup seedless raisins
  1/2 cup currants
      1 cup peanut butter
  1/4 cup sweetened condensed milk
      2 tablespoons icing sugar (optional)

Mince fruit, and mix well with peanut butter and milk. Press mixture firmly into bottom of 8″x 8″x 2″ pan, which has been buttered and sprinkled with icing sugar. Sprinkle top with icing sugar. Chill until firm; cut into squares. Makes about 1 1/8 pounds.

Magic Rum Balls

      3 cups finely crushed vanilla wafers
      1 cup finely chopped walnuts
  1 1/3 cups (15-ounce can) sweetened condensed milk
      1 teaspoon rum extract
  1/4 cup icing sugar or chocolate or colored sprinkles

Combine wafer crumbs and nuts. Add milk and rum extract, and blend well. Chill about 1 hour. Dip palms of hands into icing sugar. Shape by teaspoonfuls into small balls. Roll in icing sugar or sprinkles. Store in covered container in refrigerator. Balls will keep moist and fresh for several weeks. Makes about 48.

Nougat

      2 cups sugar
  1/2 cup honey
  1/4 cup water
      2 egg whites
  1/8 teaspoon salt
  1/2 cup chopped filberts
  1/4 cup chopped candied cherries

Combine sugar, honey and water. Cook to hard-ball stage (255°F.). Meanwhile beat egg whites with salt until stiff. Add syrup gradually, beating constantly, until mixture stands up in peaks. Spread in greased shallow square pan, and scatter nuts and cherries over top. Cool, and cut into 24 rectangular pieces.

Turkish Delight

      3 envelopes plain gelatine
  1/2 cup cold water
      1 pound (2 1/4 cups) sugar
  1/2 cup hot water
  1/4 teaspoon salt
      3 tablespoons lemon juice
      Few drops vegetable coloring
      Flavoring as desired
      1 cup finely chopped nuts
  1/4 cup icing sugar

Soften gelatine in cold water 5 minutes. Bring sugar and hot water to boiling point. Add salt and gelatine, and stir until gelatine has dissolved. Simmer, covered, 20 minutes; remove from heat, and cool. Add lemon juice, coloring, flavoring and, finally, nuts, and allow mixture to stand until it begins to thicken. Stir again; then pour about 1 inch deep into pan that has been rinsed with cold water. Let stand overnight in cool place. Moisten sharp knife in boiling water. Cut in squares. Roll each piece in icing sugar.

Note: The mixture may be divided into several parts and each colored and flavored differently.

Chocolate Fudge

      2 squares (1 ounce each) unsweetened chocolate
  2/3 cup milk
      2 cups sugar
  1/8 teaspoon salt
      2 tablespoons butter or margarine
      1 teaspoon vanilla extract

Break chocolate into small pieces. Add to milk in saucepan. Cook over low heat, stirring constantly until mixture is smooth. Add sugar and salt, and stir until sugar is dissolved and mixture boils. Cook slowly, without stirring, until small quantity dropped into cold water forms soft ball (240°F.). Remove from heat, and add butter or margarine and vanilla, without stirring. Cool to lukewarm (110°F.). Beat until fairly thick; pour at once into greased pan. Cool, and cut into squares. Makes about 1 1/4 pounds.

VARIATION:

* *Brown-sugar Fudge*: Substitute 1 cup firmly packed brown sugar for 1 cup granulated sugar.

English Toffee

      1 cup sugar
      1 cup butter or margarine
      3 tablespoons water
      1 tablespoon corn syrup
      1 cup finely chopped almonds or filberts
      2 small chocolate bars, finely chopped

Cook sugar, butter or margarine, water and corn syrup until few drops tested in cold water crack (280°F. on candy thermometer). While syrup cooks, sprinkle almost all the nuts over bottom of a greased 9-inch square pan. Pour hot syrup over nuts, and sprinkle with chocolate bar and remaining almonds. When cool, break into pieces. Makes about 1 1/4 pounds.

Butterscotch

      2 cups brown sugar, firmly packed
  3/4 cup water
  1/4 cup light corn syrup
  1/4 teaspoon salt
  1/3 cup butter or margarine
  1/4 teaspoon vanilla extract

Place sugar, water, corn syrup and salt in saucepan, and cook over low heat, stirring, until sugar dissolves. Continue cooking without stirring until mixture reaches temperature of 290°F. Add butter or margarine, remove from heat and add vanilla. Pour into buttered shallow pan. Cool slightly, and mark into squares. When cold, break into pieces. Makes about 1 1/8 pounds.

VARIATION:

* *Butterscotch Lollipops*: Cook sugar mixture to 290°F.; then stir in butter and vanilla quickly, and pour into greased lollipop molds; or drop from end of teaspoon onto greased flat pan. Place stick in each pop.

Peanut Brittle

> 1 1/2 cups shelled peanuts
> 1/4 teaspoon salt
> 1 cup sugar
> 1/2 cup light corn syrup
> 1/2 cup water
> 1 1/2 tablespoons butter or margarine
> 1/2 teaspoon lemon extract

Sprinkle nuts with salt, and warm them in oven. Put sugar, corn syrup and water in pan, and stir until mixture boils. Wash down sides with wet pastry brush, and cook to 300°F. or until mixture is very brittle when tested in cold water. Add butter or margarine, lemon extract and nuts; pour into shallow greased pan. As soon as it is cool enough to be handled, turn mass over, pull and stretch as thin as possible and break into irregular pieces. Makes 1 1/4 pounds.

Popcorn Balls

> 1 tablespoon butter or margarine
> 1 1/2 cups corn syrup
> 1 cup sugar
> 1 teaspoon salt
> 1 teaspoon vanilla extract
> Few drops vegetable coloring (optional)
> 4 quarts popped corn

Melt butter or margarine. Add syrup, sugar and salt. Boil over medium heat to very hard-ball stage (260°F.). Add vanilla and coloring. Pour syrup over popcorn, stirring thoroughly while pouring. Butter hands lightly, and shape mixture into balls. Makes 12—14 balls.

VARIATIONS:

* *Cereal-Popcorn Balls*: Substitute 3 cups puffed cereal for 3 cups popcorn, and mix before adding syrup.

* *Molasses-Popcorn Balls*: Omit corn syrup, and use 1 cup molasses.

* *Nut-Caramel Corn*: Add 1/2 cup nut kernels to popcorn before adding syrup.

Teen-age Parties

Teen-age standards are extremely casual—but their own. The condition of the house doesn't interest them much, as long as they can move around, eat what they like and listen to their own kind of music. At parties, teen-agers seem to have fun eating from paper plates and drinking from plastic mugs, so let them. You can use a strip of bright plastic or canvas for a table cover, and toss some cushions on the floor; and, of course, have dishes of nuts, potato chips, candies, and bowls of popcorn to sustain them until the "real food" is ready.

Buying the Food.   Just see that there is plenty—which usually means twice as much as adults would eat. Buy loaves of French, rye or for that matter any bread; sliced chicken, ham, bologna, salami, even peanut butter; pickles, relishes, tomatoes and lettuce. Or you might prepare a big basket of crisp fried-chicken pieces to be eaten cold. A sandwich grill makes a marvelous adjunct to a teen-age party—a blender is helpful for making shakes and malteds. It's good to provide low-calorie sodas, as well as other soft drinks and milk.

They Like To Cook.   If you have a sizeable kitchen, you might even turn it over to them when they arrive, and suggest something such as pancakes and sausages, or spear-your-own shish kebabs. The shish-kebab makings can be prepared ahead and left to marinate until it's time to cook them. They can be broiled under the grill or barbecued if it's summer time. You're in luck if your own teenager takes the responsibility for supervising the cooking and cleaning up.

A simple casserole—chicken and rice or ham and potatoes—or pizza from a mix or made on English muffins would be a change from the usual. Your child would probably appreciate a little help from you before the party. Here's a casserole idea most teen-agers can manage easily:

Turn canned chili con carne into a casserole—how many cans depends on the number of guests and the size of their appetites, but it should be enough to fill the casserole about 3/4 full. Over it, spoon strips of corn-bread batter, made from a mix. Between rows, place ripe olives. Bake in moderate oven (375°F.) about 20 minutes until corn bread is lightly browned and chili con carne is bubbling hot and tempting.

If you have individual casseroles, so much the better; bake in small portions, 1 for each guest.

BREAKFAST AFTER THE SENIOR PROM
Scrambled eggs   Sausage patties
Buckwheat pancakes   Maple syrup
Creamed chipped beef on toasted English muffins
Cappuccino

Cappuccino

    3 tablespoons instant espresso coffee
    3 cups boiling water
    3 cups hot milk
    Ground cinnamon

Pour boiling water over instant coffee. Stir well. Pour hot coffee and hot milk into cup at same time. Sprinkle with cinnamon. Serves 8.

Note: Top with sweetened whipped cream if desired.

AFTER-THE-GAME BUFFET

Boston Baked Beans   Cold baked ham
Coleslaw with a Boiled Dressing
Corn relish
Steamed brown bread (from can)
Quick Fruit Compote   Soft drinks
Hot chocolate

Boston Baked Beans

    3 cups (1 1/2 pounds) pea or navy beans
  1/2 pound piece salt pork
    1 large onion, whole
    1 small onion, finely chopped
      (approximately 1/4 cup)
    2 cups boiling water
  1/2 cup dark molasses
    2 teaspoons salt
    1 teaspoon dry mustard
  1/3 cup brown sugar, firmly packed

Soak beans in water to cover. Next day, add enough additional water to cover, and bring to boil. Skim; then simmer till tender. Halve salt pork; then slash each piece to rind at 1-inch intervals. In bean pot (or deep earthenware casserole with tight-fitting cover), put whole onion; combine chopped onion, boiling water, molasses, salt and mustard separately. Put into pot 1/2 the beans, then 1/2 the salt pork, then remaining beans. Pour molasses mixture over, and top with the brown sugar. Put remaining pork on top. Cover, and bake in very slow oven (250°F.) 5–6 hours or until beans are very tender. Every 1/2 hour, replace boiling water that has been absorbed; the last time, leave pot uncovered. Serve with sliced cold baked ham. Serves 10.

Note: A time-honored test for beans is to spoon up a few beans and blow on them; if the skins pop off, they are done.

Coleslaw with a Boiled Dressing

    3 egg yolks, well beaten
    1 tablespoon sugar
  1 1/2 teaspoons salt
  3/4 teaspoon dry mustard
    1 cup milk, scalded
  1/3 cup cider vinegar
    1 large head cabbage, shredded

In top of double boiler combine egg yolks with sugar, salt and mustard. Gradually stir in scalded milk. Cook over hot water, stirring constantly, until thick and smooth. Remove from heat, and stir in vinegar. Pour hot dressing over shredded cabbage. Cool; then refrigerate. Serves 8–10.

Note: This dish is pretty garnished with radish "roses."

Quick Fruit Compote

    1 (15-ounce) can peach halves
    1 (15-ounce) can pear halves
    1 (16-ounce) can figs
    Cornstarch
    Rum or brandy flavoring
    2 tablespoons lime or lemon juice
    8 maraschino cherries

Drain the juice from the fruit, and measure. For each cup of juice use 2 teaspoons cornstarch for thickening. Cut peaches and pears in half. Pour all but 1/2 cup of the fruit juice into the top pan of a chafing dish, and heat. Mix cornstarch with the reserved juice, and stir into the hot juice. Cook until clear. Add flavoring and lime juice to taste. Sweeten if necessary, and add the fruits. Set over boiling water, and reheat thoroughly. Serve with icy cold rich custard sauce or whipped cream. Serves 6–8.

SUMMERTIME ENTERTAINING

The Barbecue

As far as the hostess is concerned, the barbecue offers great flexibility in entertaining. It is usually informal but can be elegantly served. You may invite your guests at any hour from late morning to the dinner hour, and numbers can range from 1/2 dozen to as many as the premises can hold.

Elaborate equipment isn't necessary, but if you plan to cook outdoors more than once or twice a year, you might invest in a grill with a large fire basket that can be raised and lowered with ease. An electric spit and hood are marvelous additions if you are interested in spit cooking.

Making the Fire. Although successful grilling can be accomplished with nothing more than a supply of seasoned wood, most people use briquets or charcoal to make their fire. It will help if you use a starter of some type—liquid, paste, electric or a simple homemade one from a clean discarded 1-gallon oil can. Cut both ends out, pierce a few holes in sides for ventilation, cut 3 squares from around the bottom and place can upright in firebox. Squeeze 3 sheets of newspaper into tight balls, and drop in can. Cover with 10—15 briquets, and light paper from below. Let fire burn briskly until all briquets are glowing. Slip can from around coals with tongs, and let briquets fall freely into firebox; arrange them to the size of the meat you are cooking, adding more if necessary. When coals are all encrusted with white ash, cooking may begin.

Cooking. If you have a large wicker basket, you might keep it permanently ready with your outdoor equipment. Bring it outdoors with you, and you'll have all the things you need right at your fingertips. Restock after the party, and you're set for the next time.

As most grills cannot accommodate all the food for your meal, plan to prepare some parts of it indoors, or use an electric skillet or cooker at the table. Warming trays can be used most advantageously to keep food warm outdoors.

Have your fire good and hot, use a sprinkler or some sort to keep flare-ups at a minimum, turn meat frequently and check by making small cut with sharp knife toward end of prescribed cooking time to see that it has reached desired degree of doneness. Care is just as important outdoors as in.

Set out sturdy tables and chairs or benches, and at night have candles in protective holders. Torches on poles stuck into the ground nearby can augment candles.

Earthenware, pottery, painted tin, plastic or coated-paper plates are in order. Sturdy glasses, stainless-steel tableware and large paper napkins

or terry fingertip towels to use as napkins are a good idea too.

BARBECUE CHECKLIST

GRILL

Brazier, roll-about or portable type

ACCESSORIES

Starter (fluid, electric or can)
Fuel (wood, charcoal, briquets and paper)
Tongs, long spatula, aprons, sturdy salt and pepper
 shakers and hinged or basket grill

BASKET EQUIPMENT

Terry fingertip towels (or paper napkins)
Metal or plastic dishes
Plastic cutlery tray and cutlery
Salt, pepper, sugar and cream containers
Paper bags (for garbage)
Clothes damper (to put out flare-ups)

(Line large basket with tablecloth; keep all equipment in it; after use, wash and return utensils.)

OTHER EQUIPMENT

Plastic containers in various sizes and shapes with tight-
 fitting covers
Paper frank holders
Straw holders for paper plates
Plastic holders for paper cups
Large candles and hurricane globes (or oil lamps or
 lanterns)
Insect repellant
Umbrellas (large and small)
Snack tables

BARBECUE MENU

Cucumber stuffed with crabmeat salad
Shashlik   *Pilaff*
Syrian Coleslaw
Apricots   *Kourambiedes*   Coffee

Syrian Coleslaw

> 2 small cloves garlic, mashed to paste with 1 1/2
>   teaspoons salt
> 1/4 cup olive oil
>   Dash wine vinegar
>   Juice of 2 lemons
> 1 small head cabbage, shredded
> 1 cup fresh mint leaves, chopped fine

Make dressing of garlic, oil, vinegar and lemon juice. Toss cabbage in dressing, add mint leaves, and toss well again. Refrigerate overnight to blend flavors. Serves 6—8.

Kourambiedes (Greek Cookies)

> 2 cups soft sweet butter or margarine
> 3/4 cup sifted icing sugar
> 1 egg yolk
> 1 1/2 tablespoons brandy
> 4 1/2 cups cake flour, sifted twice
> 48 whole cloves

Cream butter or margarine well; gradually add 3/4 cup sugar, then egg yolk, creaming well. Add brandy. Gradually work in flour to make soft dough. Refrigerate 1 hour. Shape dough into balls about 1 1/2 inches in diameter. Stud each with a clove. Bake on ungreased baking sheet, in preheated 350°F. oven, until they turn pale gold. Cool well on racks, and sift icing sugar generously over them. Makes about 48.

BARBECUE MENU

Cracked-pepper Burgers
Potato and Broad Bean Salad   *Sangria*
Sherbet   Coffee

Cracked-pepper Burgers

        3 pounds lean ground beef
    2 1/2 teaspoons salt
      1/2 teaspoon garlic salt
        1 medium onion, finely chopped
          Small handful fresh parsley, chopped
        2 tablespoons Worcestershire sauce
          2-or 3-inch piece stale French bread
      3/4 cup (approximately) Burgundy
      1–2 tablespoons Parmesan cheese
        3 eggs, slightly beaten
          Cracked black pepper
          Salad oil

Break up the beef in a large bowl, and work in the salt, garlic salt, onion, parsley and Worcestershire sauce. Break the bread into a bowl, and moisten with the Burgundy. Squeeze until mixture is like thick oatmeal porridge. Add with the cheese and eggs to the meat, and, when thoroughly mixed, mold into 10–12 thick hamburgers. Sprinkle both sides generously with cracked black pepper, and press in firmly. Brush with salad oil. Place oiled side down on a grill over hot coals, and cook 5 minutes. Brush tops, and turn. Continue cooking another 4–5 minutes or until medium rare. Spread with horseradish, mustard or relish. Serve between thick slices of French bread. Makes 10–12 burgers.

Potato and Broad Bean Salad

        2 cans whole white potatoes, drained
        1 can broad beans, drained
        1 cup cooked diced carrots
      1/2 cup chopped black olives
      1/2 teaspoon onion salt
      1/4 teaspoon celery seed or dill seed
          Mayonnaise or salad dressing
          Prepared mustard
          Parsley

Cut potatoes in 1/4-inch dice. Mix with beans, carrots, olives, onion salt and celery or dill seed. Moisten with thick mayonnaise or salad dressing, and flavor with a little prepared mustard. Taste for seasoning. Scrape into a round bowl, and ring thickly with chopped parsley. Serves 10–12.

Note: In place of broad beans, try quickly cooked frozen limas. 3–4 cups diced cooked potato can be used in place of canned.

Sangria

        1 cup water
      1/2 cup sugar
      3/4 cup light corn syrup
        1 orange, sliced
        1 lemon, sliced
        1 lime, sliced
        1 bottle inexpensive Chilean, Spanish or Italian red wine
      1/4 bottle (or more) club soda

Boil water and sugar together 10 minutes. Cool. In 2-quart pitcher, place 3/4 cup syrup and fruit slices. Pour in wine, add ice cubes and about 1/4 bottle club soda (more if you wish). Stir with wooden spoon or paddle.

BARBECUE MENU

Grilled Crabmeat with Bacon
Barbecued Spareribs
Spit-roasted chicken rubbed with tarragon
Fried rice   Romaine salad
Platter of fresh fruits   Coffee

Grilled Crabmeat with Bacon

        1 package frozen king crabmeat, thawed
        6 bacon strips, cut in halves

Wrap lumps crabmeat in bacon strips. Secure with toothpicks, and place in basket grill. Grill over coals until bacon is crisp. Serve with hot English mustard. Makes 12 pieces.

Barbecued Spareribs

      1/4 cup soy sauce
    1 1/2 tablespoons vinegar
        1 tablespoon ketchup
        1 tablespoon chili sauce
        1 tablespoon dry sherry
      1/2 tablespoon sugar
        1 clove garlic, crushed
        1 tablespoon honey
        2 pounds or 1 small rack young spareribs

Combine soy sauce, vinegar, ketchup, chili sauce, sherry, sugar and garlic. Pour over spareribs, laid out flat in roasting pan. Marinate at least 4 hours, turning often. Drain, reserving marinade. Broil slowly over charcoal 20 minutes, turning often. Mix honey into reserved marinade, and brush on ribs on both sides while cooking another 20 minutes. Cut into individual ribs to serve. Serves 6 for appetizers.

BARBECUE MENU

Chilled punch
Oyster-filled "Carpetbag" Steak
Salad   Fresh tomatoes
Berries with Sabayon Sauce

Oyster-filled "Carpetbag" Steak

>   4 T-bone steaks, 1 1/2 inches thick
> 1/2 pint fresh oysters, or 1 (4–5-ounce) can oysters,
>   not smoked
>   4 tablespoons freshly grated bread crumbs
>   1 tablespoon melted butter
>   2 tablespoons finely chopped onion
>   1 tablespoon chopped parsley (optional)
>   1–2 tablespoons lemon juice
>   Salt and pepper

Trim all but 1/8 inch fat from the edge of the steaks, and cut off the flank ends. Package flank ends for the freezer to braise or stew later. Drain the oysters, and remove any bits of hard shell. Toss oysters with the next 5 ingredients, and season with salt and pepper. With a sharp knife, cut a 4-inch gash through the fat edge of the steak (opposite from the tenderloin). Use scissors to snip through the membrane if necessary; then cut the gash deeper to form a pocket. Stuff with oyster mixture. Sew the edges together with kitchen string, or pin with small skewers. Broil on a barbecue to the medium stage for raw oysters and to rare or medium for canned oysters. Serves 4.

Berries with Sabayon Sauce

>   3 egg yolks
>   3 tablespoons sugar
>   2/3 cup Sauterne or Reisling wine
>   1 pint fresh strawberries or raspberries
>   2 tablespoons fine white sugar

Beat egg yolks with 3 tablespoons sugar until thick. Add wine. Cook and whisk in the top of a double boiler over very hot but not boiling water, until fluffy and thickened smoothly. Chill thoroughly. Wash and hull berries, and cut in half. Toss berries with 2 tablespoons sugar, and chill. Serve berries with sauce spooned over each portion. Serves 4.

MENU FOR A CLAMBAKE

Clam broth   *Steamed Clams*   Drawn butter
Charcoal-broiled Lobsters   Steamed corn
Sliced tomatoes and cucumbers
Watermelon   Beer   Coffee

Steamed Clams

>   Washed wet seaweed
>   12 small potatoes, wrapped in foil
>   12 small ears corn, husked and wrapped in foil
>   4 dozen steamer clams, well scrubbed

Fill bottom of enamel clam boiler with seaweed. Add water just to cover, and place over high heat. When water boils, add potatoes and another layer of seaweed. Cover pot. Steam 35 minutes. Add corn, and cover again. After 10 minutes, add more seaweed and clams. Cover, and steam until clams open. Drain liquid, and strain through linen napkin into cups for drinking and dipping. Have plenty of butter or margarine on hand for corn and potatoes. Serves 12.

Charcoal-broiled Lobsters

>   6 (1 1/2-pound) lobsters, split and cleaned
>   1 cup butter or margarine, melted
>   Paprika to taste
>   Lemon wedges
>   Salt and pepper to taste

Brush lobsters with a little butter or margarine, and sprinkle with paprika. Grill over charcoal fire 6–7 minutes on each side. Serve with melted butter or margarine, lemon wedges and salt and pepper. Serves 12.

Garden Parties

If the weather's with you, this is a perfect way to entertain. A garden party can be anything from a simple cup of coffee to an elaborate reception. Cocktail parties, women's luncheons and large buffets are all suitable. Whatever it is, you'll need some garden chairs, a table and some lawn cushions. Try to arrange for groupings as you would indoors: cluster 3 or 4 chairs and a table in 1 corner of the garden, 2 or 3 cushions under a tree or giant umbrella. But most people do expect to stand or wander about at this sort of gathering.

Service. Unless you can hire caterers and waitresses, the kind of service you choose requires careful thought. The simplest way might be to serve most of the food from a large table indoors and let the guests themselves take their plates outside. Even at self-service parties, a few helpers make a difference, even if they're your children and their friends passing plates and taking second helpings to people.

A beautiful luncheon can be arranged with a serving table near the house and small tables seating 4 arranged at intervals around the garden. As guests come into the garden, they pick up their food in passing and settle down at small tables. No matter how you serve, though, it's important to plan ahead. You'd be surprised how much can be done several days before the party.

A Basket Luncheon. For small groups, an informal basket luncheon can be fun. In the middle of a small basket lined with a colored paper napkin, arrange a pressed-paper or plastic cup of fruit juice or other cool drink. Around it in the basket arrange an assortment of sandwiches, a tart or a cupcake, and let each guest take her own basket into the garden. All that is needed to complete the menu is coffee, prepared in the kitchen ahead of time.

Foods. Garden parties seem to make people relaxed and unconcerned about time, so it's wise not to serve food that should be eaten the moment it's ready. It's a losing game to cut meat with one hand and balance a plate with the other while standing up. Serve easy-to-manage foods, unless you can arrange for people to sit down at a table or at least with firm trays on their knees.

GARDEN-RECEPTION MENU

Apple-blossom Punch
Chicken or egg sandwiches with cheese bread
Pinwheels   Asparagus rolls
Mock Madeleines   Brownies
6-Layer Mocha Cake
Coffee

Apple-blossom Punch

    1 (48-ounce) can clear light-colored apple juice or
        sweet cider
    2 (6-ounce) cans undiluted pink lemonade
    2 cups cranberry juice
    2 cups dry vermouth or dry white wine
        Ice cubes or block of ice

Blend 1 1/2 cups apple juice with the frozen lemonade. Add remaining apple juice, cranberry juice and vermouth. Pour over ice cubes or a block of ice in a punch bowl. Makes 25 (4-ounce) servings.

Note: In place of cranberry juice, use 1/2 cup raspberry syrup and 1 1/2 cups fruit punch. If too sweet, add a little unsweetened lime or lemon juice to taste.

Mock Madeleines

    1 package pound-cake mix
    1/4 cup sifted icing sugar

Prepare pound-cake mix according to package directions. Put 1 level tablespoon batter into each well-greased fluted 2 1/2-inch tart pan. Bake at 325°F. 20 minutes. Remove from oven. Sprinkle tops lightly with sugar.

6-Layer Mocha Cake

    1 (1-pound 2 1/2-ounce) package devil's food cake
        mix
    2 cups heavy cream
    2 tablespoons sweetened instant cocoa mix
    2 teaspoons dry instant coffee

Prepare cake batter, following package directions. Bake in two 8-inch layers, dividing batter evenly between pans, according to package directions. Cool in pan 5 minutes. Loosen sides with spatula. Remove to wire rack. Cool completely. Combine cream, cocoa mix and instant coffee. Chill 30 minutes. Beat at high speed until thick and spreadable. Sweeten to taste. Carefully divide each cake layer horizontally into 3, making 6 layers total. Sandwich layers together, using 1/2 cup frosting between each pair. Frost top and sides with remaining frosting. Chill 1 hour or until serving time. Serves 6–8.

Country Weekends

Ask people well ahead, as a trip out of town usually involves extra planning. If your house is hard to find, send a map and include the time it takes to get there, as well as the approximate time you expect people to arrive and leave.

Once your guests have arrived, show them their beds and bathroom facilities, and point out any local rules (swimming arrangements, car or boat parking and so forth). Let them know about mealtimes, if you run on schedule; let them know of any plans you've made (visits to other friends, fishing or sight-seeing expeditions).

Plan your menus carefully, and do as much as you can before guests arrive. Even the vegetables can be washed and cut up ahead of time. Just wrap in plastic bags, and keep cool. One-dish wonders are ideal—stews, meat or fish pies and of course salads. As an appetizer, prepare a platter of sliced tomatoes just off the vine, sprinkled with chopped chives or green-onion tops.

Breakfast.   Breakfast can cause concern to both sides; the guest who looks forward to a long morning in bed and the hostess who wonders how she'll ever get on with her day; or the opposite. So make plans, and let your guests know what they are.

You can serve breakfast at a fixed time, or you can set out a do-it-yourself arrangement. Leave coffee hot and ready in percolator; put out fruit, individually packaged cereals, jug of milk, bread, butter, toaster and marmalade. If late-comers want eggs and bacon, makings and equipment are ready in the kitchen. As a hint you might also indicate some preorganizing for dish-washing, with pan, detergent, mop and towels in readiness. But if sleepers-in take over breakfast cleaning up —and generally they don't mind—change the shift for other meals.

Help-yourself Luncheons.   Do-it-yourself luncheons are good for you and your guests. They probably prefer to eat when they want to, so set out platters of cold meats, tomatoes, lettuce, bread and butter, pickles, cheeses, assorted crackers and, if it's a cold day, a big pitcher or tureen of hot soup can be added, and fresh fruit for dessert. Don't hesitate to use paper plates.

Meals To Suit Programs.   If your guests are fishing enthusiasts, picnic lunches will be needed. Hearty sandwiches with meat or cheese filling, a vacuum or two of hot and/or cold drinks (coffee, tea, soup, fruit juice and so on) and some fruit.

A beach or country weekend offers opportunities for picnics, berry-picking expeditions, swimsuit snacks on the dock, corn roasts, songs around the bonfire and other events that can't be duplicated in the city. Take advantage of them.

CHAPTER SEVEN

The Bridal Corner

❧

JUST MARRIED

After the honeymoon, when your husband and most likely you are back at work, you probably won't have too much difficulty in managing simple meals for two. But sooner or later, depending on your disposition, you'll wind up entertaining. Whether your guests are friends for coffee, your in-laws for dinner or a crowd for cocktails, you can make the occasion successful.

The road to success is called "preparation." For a planned party, everything should be ready before guests arrive—matches handy to light candles, guest towels in the bathroom and you at the door ready to greet guests on time. Being prepared encompasses impromptu occasions—emergency supplies in cupboard or freezer, place mats ready in the linen cupboard, lots of peanuts and potato chips to serve guests while you start dinner and set the table.

Any entertaining, elaborate or spur-of-the-moment, goes more smoothly if your work area is well organized. Your kitchen shouldn't be overcrowded. If shelves are scarce, you can store large trays, seldom-used vases, a giant roast pan and so on somewhere else—even in a locker. You can save drawer space by keeping place mats and extra tea towels in the linen cupboard or dresser drawer.

You can expand your cupboard space with cup-hooks, rubber turntables and shelves. Plastic bins stacked under the sink will hold cleaning supplies. And when you shop, select sizes that will fit your cupboard shelves—the small saving on giant boxes of detergent, potato chips, flour or cereal is not worth the frustration of finding a place to store them.

You can hang your new pots, serving implements, spice shelf or waxed paper dispenser on a wall. Let the refrigerator aid your space problem —use it to store ketchup, Worcestershire sauce, canned juices and fruit, canned consommé, mus-

tard, canned meat and fish, jams and jellies, even though these items do not need refrigeration until after they have been opened.

If work space is inadequate, clear toaster, mixer, frying pan, canisters (at least the big flour one) off the counters.

Silver, China, Linen

Keep all your china and silver clean and ready for use. If you have sterling and use it often, it's enough to treat it with a tarnish preventative and store it in a chest or felts. (Incidentally, silver acquires a lovely soft glow if used constantly.) If you use your silver only occasionally, plastic wrap will keep it from blackening. Platters, entree dishes and tea sets can be protected with tissue or felts and stored airtight in plastic garbage bags. Stainless steel doesn't require any special care.

China should also be ready for instant use. If you keep your good dishes in your cooking area, protect them from scratches; place large paper napkins or paper towels between plates, and slide piles of 3 or 4 into plastic bags. Crystal stored in the kitchen for any length of time will almost certainly have to be washed, unless wrapped with tissue or plastic.

Table linen can be stored in linen closets, chests or even dress boxes, but store carefully— avoid finding napkins that are all wrinkled because they were put away slightly damp or a tablecloth fresh from the cleaners that is badly creased from overcrowding. Hang tablecloths on special hangers if it eases the space problem.

There are several little extras you can have on hand to make a meal a party—candles for the table, artificial flowers and fruit, dried flowers and leaves, stored in plastic bags for instant centerpieces. Extra ashtrays, coasters and dishes (or individual salad bowls) for pre-dinner appetizers should be on hand.

Planning a Dinner Party

First, decide how many guests to invite—bearing in mind the size of your apartment, what your kitchen can accommodate, seating arrangements and number of place settings. Until you're more experienced, you might want to hold your guest list to a minimum.

Invite your friends far enough in advance for them to hire baby sitters, and be sure, especially if you have a job, to leave yourself enough time to get ready before your guests come. On a weekday, cocktails at 7:00 and dinner at 8:00 will usually satisfy all.

What To Serve. The next step is to decide on a menu. Three courses—appetizer; meat, vegetables and salad; dessert and coffee—are enough.

In deciding on specific dishes consider your silver and china—if you don't have bouillon spoons, serve seafood instead of soup. And an easy way to bring elegance to a table is through wine. One word of warning to apartment dwellers: Choose mild-flavored vegetables such as carrots, peas, beets, asparagus, spinach and so forth. There's nothing less appetizing to arriving guests than the strong aroma of cabbage cooking.

DINNER MENU

Seafood cocktail
Chicken with Almonds
Broccoli   Lemon butter
Tomato salad
Rolls   Wine
Fresh fruit   **Cheese**

Chicken with Almonds

    8 chicken breasts
    4 chicken legs
    2 tablespoons fat
1/4 teaspoon **thyme**
1/4 teaspoon marjoram
    2 green onions, sliced
    2 (10-ounce) cans cream of chicken or mushroom
       soup
1 1/4 cups milk
1/8 teaspoon nutmeg
2/3 cup slivered almonds
    3 tablespoons butter
1 1/2 cups soft stale bread crumbs
1/2 cup sherry

Sauté chicken breasts and legs lightly on both sides in 2 tablespoons hot fat. Arrange chicken in a shallow baking pan in 1 layer. Mix the next 6 ingredients together, and pour over the chicken. Bake at 350°F. 45 minutes. Fry almonds in the butter until lightly browned, and stir in the crumbs. Sprinkle mixture over chicken; then sprinkle with sherry. Bake 20—30 minutes longer. Serves 8—10.

DINNER MENU

Deviled Ham Pâté
Chicken au Gratin
Tossed salad   Hot rolls
Wine
Lemonade Pie

Deviled Ham Pâté

    1 envelope plain gelatine
1/4 cup cold water
1/2 cup cold milk
    1 (2-ounce) envelope onion-garlic dip mix
    1 (4-ounce) package soft cream cheese
1/2 cup deviled ham
1/4 teaspoon dry mustard
1/2 teaspoon Worcestershire sauce
    Dash rose coloring (optional)

Soften gelatine in cold water; dissolve over hot water. Meanwhile, beat milk and dip mix together until smooth. Beat in next 4 ingredients with the gelatine. Stir in a few drops rose coloring. Scrape into a very small oiled loaf pan or 6 small muffin cups. Chill very thoroughly. Unmold, and cut loaf into 6 slices. Serve as an appetizer on small plates with watercress, hard-cooked egg slices, pickle fans and Melba toast. Makes 6 small servings.

Chicken au Gratin

1/2 pound sliced mushrooms
    6 tablespoons butter or chicken fat
    6 tablespoons flour
1 1/2 cups chicken broth
3/4 **cup** light cream
    3 cups cooked egg noodles
    2 cups cut-up cooked chicken
2–3 tablespoons sherry
    Salt and pepper to taste
    3 slices process cheese, cut in triangles
    Tomato wedges
    Chopped parsley

Sauté mushrooms in butter 3 minutes. Stir in flour, then chicken broth, gradually. Cook until thick, and stir in cream. Reheat 1 minute. Add next 3 ingredients. Season, and spread in buttered 1 1/2-quart casserole; bake at 400°F. 20 minutes or until bubbly. Top with cheese triangles, and bake 3—5 minutes until cheese melts. Garnish with tomato wedges and chopped parsley. Makes 6 servings.

Lemonade Pie

    4 teaspoons plain gelatine
    1 cup water
    1 (6-ounce) can frozen lemonade
    1 brick or pint vanilla ice cream
    1 baked 9-inch pie shell or crumb crust

Heat and stir gelatine and 1/2 cup water together until gelatine is melted. Remove from heat, and stir in the remaining water and the frozen lemonade. Whisk in the ice cream, and chill in the freezer until mixture begins to set, stirring occasionally, about 10 minutes. Scrape into the prepared pie shell. Chill until set, about 20 minutes. Garnish with whipped cream. Makes 6 servings.

Note: Frozen pineapple juice or tangerine juice may be used in place of lemonade.

Neither of these meals is difficult, especially if you use prepared foods such as seafood sauce, cheese sauce, ready-mixed salad dressing and heat-and-serve rolls.

Shopping and Final Preparation. Convert your menu into quantities for a shopping list by thinking the whole party through from cocktails to coffee. This way you won't forget olives for martinis or cream for coffee. Next make a checklist that includes everything you must do—order flowers; shop; polish glassware; wash plates, if necessary; chill wine and soft drinks; prepare seafood and seafood sauce; prepare salad material, vegetables and fruit (store in plastic bag in refrigerator); make dip; set table; arrange coffee tray, coasters and ashtrays; set out food containers, utensils and plates in kitchen; place guest towels in bathroom, and so on.

The Night Before. When food is prepared and refrigerated, start arranging things on counters —dishes for nuts and candy, cocktail glasses, jigger, ice bucket, shaker, underplates for shrimp dishes, dessert plates, bread basket and napkin, cooking utensils, dinner plates, entree dishes, meat platter.

Next set table. Allow at least 2 feet for each place setting, and line up silver as precisely as you can. Set out bread-and-butter plates, folded napkins, wine glasses, water goblets, ashtrays. Arrange serving implements conveniently so you will have enough room for meat platter and entree dishes. Refer to your checklist to make sure you haven't forgotten seafood forks, salad and entree servers.

Organize your clothes for the party; place ashtrays, matches and coasters around living room.

Party Day. In the morning you can serve breakfast on trays at the coffee table if the kitchen is too crowded. If you work, make the bed, do the breakfast dishes and put guest towels in the bathroom.

If you're rushed when you get home, clean up and dress first. Then fill bowls with nuts and candy, put out dip and take olives out of refrigerator for martinis. (If anyone comes early, you will at least look ready.)

Still following your checklist, do your final preparations: start with the main course or whatever takes the longest time; then arrange seafood, add seafood sauce and store in the refrigerator; put vegetables in cooking pots; have butter or margarine beside the stove; prepare salad, cover with plastic wrap and return to refrigerator.

After you welcome your guests, show them where to leave their coats, and offer drinks and food to nibble on.

Shortly before the meal, drain vegetables, dress them and keep them warm in covered entree dishes. Arrange the meat course on a platter. Place salad, butter and rolls or bread on table. Wrap napkin around wine bottle if you wish, and put appetizer on table. Light candles, and dinner is ready.

Buffet

If your dining table seats only a small number, you can plan a buffet. For suggestions on what to serve see Chapter 6.

Arrange flowers and candles behind food if the table is against a wall. If your table is small, however, you will need all 4 sides to accommodate food. In this case, have your flowers and candles in the center. Your centerpiece may be higher than for a sit-down dinner.

Set your table so items are in the order in which they will be picked up; for example, consommé, spoons, plates, noodles with serving spoon, stroganoff with ladle, salad with servers, salt and pepper, basket of garlic bread wrapped in a napkin, forks and napkins. If you wish, wine may be served to guests after they have carried their plates to their seats. Most men hate to eat from their laps, so try to seat them by end tables or near the coffee table.

The Cocktail Party

Decide on what drinks to serve and what refreshments to serve with them—deviled eggs, stuffed mushrooms, shrimps on toothpicks to be dipped in savory sauce, miniature cheese balls and so forth. Be sure you have enough of everything.

Set up the bar: include more glasses than you think you'll need, an ice bucket, a jigger, lemon slices, maraschino cherries, liquor bottles and chilled mixes. Arrange food on plates or a tray; set bowls of salted nuts and potato chips around the room. Put out lots of ashtrays and coasters, and you're ready.

Another version of the cocktail party is the simple affair to which you invite a few friends to come about 8:00 and at which you serve drinks and light refreshments. At around 10:30 you can pass around sandwiches, celery and olives, cookies and coffee. Or you can dress up your table buffet style and serve a casserole and salad, buttered dark rye bread, dessert and coffee.

The Impromptu Dinner

It's really not that difficult to serve dinner to an unexpected guest—or guests. You can make a quick dish by combining canned chicken à la king, tuna fish and mushrooms and adding sherry. Top with buttered bread crumbs. You can serve rice or potatoes, a frozen or canned vegetable and a tossed green salad as accompaniments. Canned fruit cocktail will do nicely as an appetizer. Cheese or ice cream for dessert and wine are easy enough to serve, and coffee completes the meal.

The impromptu affair in fact is often more fun than the well-planned party. There's less preparation involved, and if your emergency shelf is sensibly stocked, food won't be a problem.

Here are some foods you can keep on hand.

APPETIZERS

Canned and packaged soups, fruit and vegetable juices, fruit cocktail

MAIN COURSES

Macaroni and cheese, ravioli, lasagne, spaghetti, eggs, chicken à la king, baked beans, canned fish and meat, frozen mushrooms and vegetables, pastas, rice, potato flakes, biscuit and muffin mixes, instant sauces and gravies, creamed soups for quick casseroles, dried parsley, paprika, poppy seeds, Cheddar and Parmesan cheeses, soy sauce, sherry, bread crumbs, olives, pickles

DESSERTS

Canned fruit, ice cream, instant puddings, whipped topping

EXTRAS

Crackers, cheese, potato chips, nuts, wine (red wine is better than white for instant entertaining, as it usually doesn't have to be chilled)

Meals from the emergency shelf needn't be dull. Serve croutons with the soup. Grate Cheddar cheese over canned spaghetti, and top with sautéed bacon strips and thick tomato slices before baking. Dress up baked beans with ketchup and onion rings. Combine tuna chunks and canned macaroni and cheese, and top with buttered bread crumbs. Pour cream soup over drained canned salmon and peas, heat until bubbly and top with biscuits made from mix. Follow package instructions for baking time and oven temperature.

Dress up vegetables with instant sauces or undiluted cream soups. Sprinkle parsley, paprika or poppy seeds on pale vegetables; crisp bacon bits, Parmesan cheese, slivered almonds or grated hard-cooked egg white on green ones.

Splash wine into canned fruits or top with shredded coconut or whipped topping. Serve maple syrup and slivered almonds on ice cream. Puree frozen raspberries in your blender, and fill parfait glasses with layers of vanilla ice cream and berries. Top scoop of orange sherbet with crème de menthe.

IMPROMPTU MENU

Consommé with lemon or sherry
Corned beef hash   *Harvard Beets*
Cabbage salad   Bread sticks
Apple Crisp   Coffee

IMPROMPTU MENU

Blended juice
Beef and Noodle Casserole
Mixed buttered vegetables
Cucumber salad
Jelly Roll—Peach Dessert

Beef and Noodle Casserole

1 (16-ounce) can meatballs in gravy
1 (10-ounce) can cream-style soup
2–3 tablespoons chopped onion
3/4–1 cup shredded Cheddar cheese
3 cups (6 ounces raw) cooked, drained noodles
1/4–1/2 cup sour cream, milk or tomato sauce
Ketchup
Seasoning salt
Dry mustard
Tabasco
1/3 cup buttered bread crumbs

Combine the first 5 ingredients. Add enough sour cream to moisten. Taste, and season with ketchup, seasoning salt, dry mustard and Tabasco. Spread in a greased 1 1/2-quart casserole. Sprinkle with crumbs, and bake at 375°F. 35 minutes or until bubbly. Serves 6.

Jelly Roll—Peach Dessert

Top slices of fresh lemon or raspberry jelly roll with whipped dessert topping or sweetened whipped cream. Arrange a well-drained peach half in the center of the topping, cut side up. Drop a spoon of red currant jelly into each peach half for color. Use slices of fresh sponge or angel cake in place of jelly roll if you wish.

The most important part of any entertaining is to enjoy yourself, for if you don't no one else is likely to.

PARTIES FOR THE BRIDE

A wedding in the family brings with it a great deal of entertaining. Someday, *you* may have to give one or more of the following kinds of parties.

The Announcement Party

Of course, such a party is not necessary for making an engagement official, but it is fun. The bride's parents can give this party for friends and relatives of both families. The invitations should be handwritten on informal note paper and should simply state details of time and place.

If space permits, this party is likely to be large. A luncheon may be the occasion for the announcement, but a cocktail party or supper is usually preferred. The cocktail buffet is an almost perfect answer, because it is neither too formal nor too difficult to execute.

A bar (or two if the house is large) and bartender (especially if the party is large) are the first requisites. Set up the bar with the makings for the kinds of drinks you will serve, and include fruit juice or punch and low-calorie drinks.

Champagne is a great drink to serve, and you can, if you want, then dispense with the bar. This move simplifies service and is no more expensive. It's also sensible to rent glasses. They come clean and can be returned soiled.

The house can be decorated with flowers—perhaps sweetheart roses. For the table, a pale pink or white cloth is appropriate. Soft lighting from candles lends atmosphere.

Use chafing dishes, warming trays, electric frying pans, and so on to keep hot foods at proper temperatures. Small plates of cold foods, replenished often, are more attractive than large platters left to dry out on the table.

MENU FOR COCKTAIL BUFFET

Sliced turkey   Thin-sliced roast beef
Sliced tongue
Small rolls, split   Assortment of breads
Mustard   Horseradish
Mushroom turnovers
Cold shrimp with green mayonnaise
Large bowls of *Salade Niçoise*
Champagne   Coffee (for late stayers)

The Bridal Shower

If you're entertaining for a bride-to-be, you should consider her schedule and needs (find out if anyone else is having a shower for her) to avoid conflict. Usually the guest list includes the mothers of both bride and groom and the attendants too. You can set a theme for the shower—kitchen, bathroom, linen, lingerie, china, paper, and so on, or have a miscellaneous one.

The Paper Shower. The only things your guest of honor can see at first are a pair of huge red firecrackers. They contain gifts, all made of paper, wrapped individually, signed and packed into a pair of bedroom wastebaskets. The baskets are then wrapped in red paper and tied at each end. Paper-gift suggestions include playing cards, notepaper, stationary, cookbooks, telephone pads, monogrammed paper napkins, shelfpaper rolls, and similar things.

Or, instead of firecrackers, you might like to present gifts in a large carton decorated with headlines appropriate to the bride's activities, her future home, her life ahead and so on. Just make a patchwork of words and phrases clipped from newspapers. Instead of the usual gift wrapping, you can decorate box tops only.

Lingerie Shower. Nightgowns, petticoats, slips, stockings and breakfast coats would all be appropriate gifts (to ensure proper fit include bride's sizes on invitations).

A pretty, feminine table is in order, maybe with a pink cloth and pink flowered napkins. Remove

fabric from an old umbrella, and cover it with pink fabric or paper, and attach nosegays to the ends of spokes and at center junctions. Serve food in keeping with the occasion.

SUGGESTED MENU

Avocado and grapefruit salad
Chicken à la king in cream puffs
Asparagus   Lemon wedges
Butterflake rolls
Raspberry sherbet
Almond Paste Cookies

Almond Paste Cookies

1/2 cup soft butter
1/2 cup soft shortening
1/2 cup soft almond paste
1/4 cup brown sugar, firmly packed
2/3 cup fine white sugar
  1 egg
1/4 teaspoon lemon extract
1/2 teaspoon almond extract
1/2 teaspoon vanilla
  3 cups unsifted all-purpose flour
  2 teaspoons baking soda
  2 teaspoons cream of tartar
3 1/2 dozen red glacé cherries
3 1/2 dozen blanched almonds
  Sifted icing sugar

Beat the first 9 ingredients together until fluffy; then stir in sifted dry ingredients. Break off small pieces of the dough, and roll around each cherry to cover completely. Roll again to form small balls. Arrange 1 1/2 inches apart on an ungreased cookie sheet. Press an almond into the top of each, and bake about 10–15 minutes or until lightly browned. Dust with sifted icing sugar while still warm. Makes 3 1/2 dozen.

China Shower Brunch. Ideal for career girls is the Saturday shower brunch. Friends band together to start the bride-to-be on her favorite pottery or china. From there everything follows in reverse order from the usual program. The refreshments are served on the china, and the guest of honor discovers it's all hers as the set is finally washed and packed away, complete with card. This idea could be adapted for gifts of flatware or crystal.

Recipe Shower. The hostess tells each guest what others are contributing so that there won't be any overlapping. Cards for a recipe file are sent out, and each guest is asked to type or clearly write her favorite recipe. A gift accompanies each card, and a natural choice is a pan or utensil associated with that particular recipe.

When gifts are unwrapped, recipe cards are collected and presented in recipe filing box. For refreshments, some of the recipes on the cards received can be put to good use.

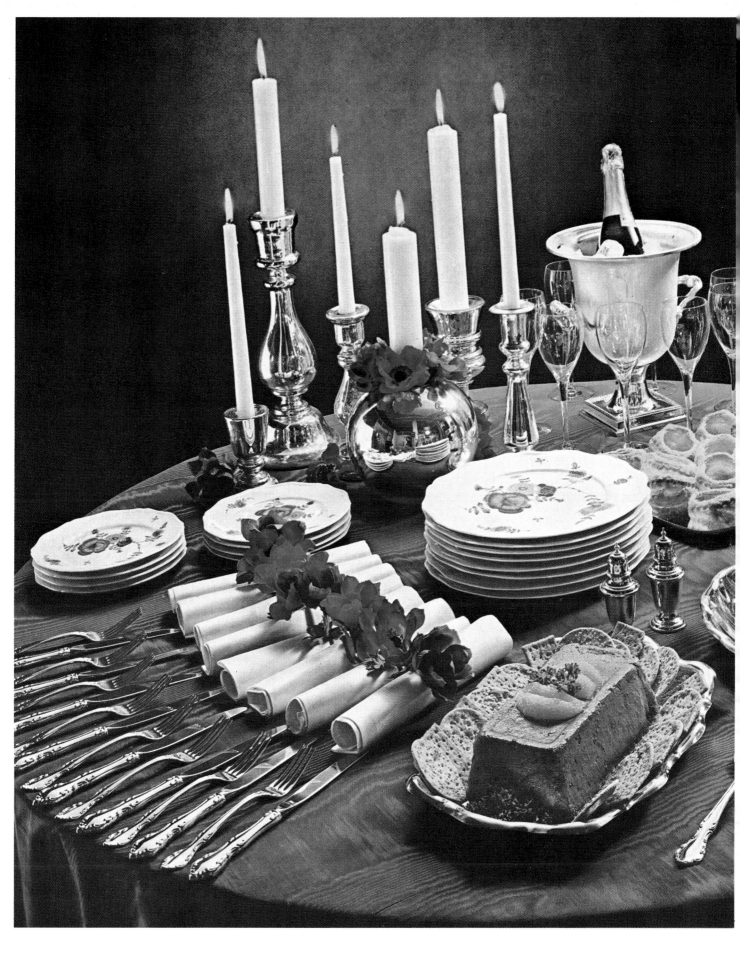

An elegant buffet table arrangement.

CREDIT: *Henry Sandbank.*

Seafood Cocktail (p. 81).

Crescent Rolls (p. 172).

A buffet, including Seafood Cocktail and Boeuf en Gelée *en terrine* (p. 44).

Tea sandwiches (p. 295) in a long loaf of scooped-out French bread, Crystal Grapes
(p. 118), Glacé Fruit Tartlets (p. 328) and petits fours.
CREDIT: *Arthur Beck.*

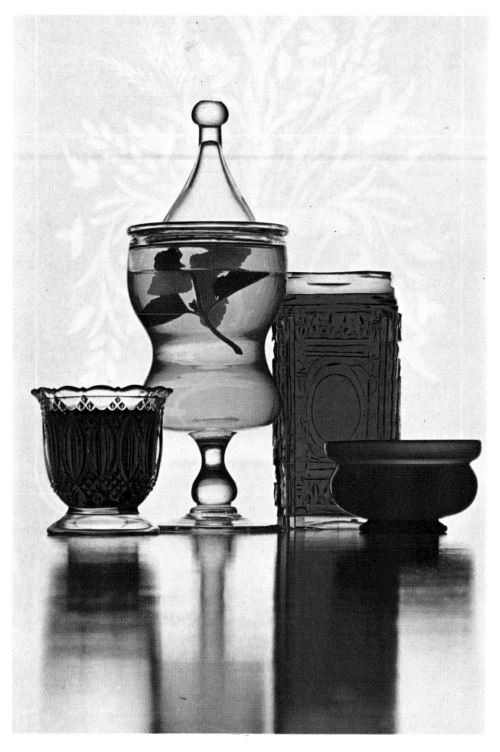

Port Wine Jelly (p. 136), Crème de Menthe Jelly (p. 136), Burgundy Wine Jelly
(p. 136) and Ginger-Beet Jelly (p. 136) packaged as Christmas gifts.
CREDIT: *Bernard Gray*.

Suggested recipes and gifts: muffin recipe and muffin pans; cookie recipe, baking sheet and cookie press; cake recipe and cake pans; soufflé recipe and soufflé dish; fruit-bread recipe and loaf pan; angel food cake recipe and tube pan; jellied salad-ring recipe and ring mold; and so on.

Here are 2 main-dish ideas that are easily prepared ahead of time and can be adapted to any number. Start with fruit juice; serve main dish with green salad and chunks of crusty *French Bread*.

Baked Lasagna

    1/2 pound ground beef
    1/2 pound ground pork
      1 medium onion, chopped
          (approximately 1/2 cup)
      2 teaspoons chopped parsley
      1 clove garlic, crushed
      2 tablespoons olive oil
      2 cups water
      1 (6-ounce) can tomato paste
      1 teaspoon salt
    1/2 teaspoon pepper
      1 pound lasagne noodles
      5 quarts salted water
      1 pound mozzarella cheese
    1/2 pound ricotta or cottage cheese
      2 tablespoons grated Parmesan cheese

Brown ground meats together with onion, parsley and garlic in olive oil. When meat has browned, drain off the fat. Add 2 cups water, tomato paste, salt and pepper. Simmer slowly 1 1/2 hours. Boil noodles in salted water until tender. You will have to stir frequently to prevent noodles from sticking together, or brush noodles with oil before boiling. Drain, and arrange layers of noodles, meat sauce, mozzarella and ricotta in shallow casserole, with noodles on top. Sprinkle with grated Parmesan, and bake at 375°F. about 35 minutes or until top is lightly browned. Makes 8 servings.

Note: If doubling recipe, make 2 separate casseroles, as it is difficult to cook a larger amount of noodles at 1 time.

Molded Heart-shaped Chicken

      2 (3 1/2-pound) roasting or frying chickens, cut in
          quarters
      5 cups warm water
     12 peppercorns
        Handful celery leaves
    1/2 small onion, sliced
    1/4 teaspoon thyme
      1 bay leaf
      3 chicken-bouillon cubes
      1 teaspoon salt
      1 envelope plain gelatine
        Pineapple-Cheese Filling
        Watercress or endive
        Hard-cooked egg white
        Pimento, tomato aspic or red jelly

Arrange the chicken, including giblets, in a deep saucepan, and add the water. Bring to a boil, and skim. Add peppercorns, celery leaves, onion, thyme, bay leaf and crumbled bouillon cubes. Cover, and simmer until chicken is tender, about 45–50 minutes. Remove chicken from the broth, and cool. Separate meat from the bones, and cut into small dice. Chop the liver, and refrigerate with the meat until later. Return skin, bones and flavorings to the broth, and add the salt and gelatine. Simmer, covered, for 40 minutes; then strain and taste the broth. It should be well seasoned and will taste less salty after the chicken is added and mixture sets. Measure the broth, and add water, if necessary, to make 4 cups. If you have more than 4 cups, boil uncovered until broth measures 4 cups. Cool the broth. Oil 2 heart-shaped cake pans, and measure 2 cups broth into each. Sprinkle half the meat into each pan, and distribute evenly with a fork. Chill until almost set. Spread 1 layer evenly with the *Pineapple-Cheese Filling*, and chill until filling is almost set; then unmold second chicken layer over the top. Chill until firm or overnight; then unmold, and surround with watercress or sprigs of curly endive. Cut out a waxed-paper heart 1 inch smaller than the layer cake pan. Set in the center top of the mold as a guide, and thickly sprinkle grated hard-cooked egg white around the edge. Remove waxed paper; then arrange several small heart-shaped cutouts of pimento, tomato aspic or red jelly over the egg around the edge. Serves 12.

Pineapple-Cheese Filling

          2 teaspoons plain gelatine
        1/4 cup pineapple juice
        1/2 pound cream cheese
    1/2-3/4 cup crushed pineapple, well drained
          2 tablespoons mayonnaise

Soften gelatine in pineapple juice. Set over hot water, and stir until dissolved. Cream the cheese until soft; then beat in the dissolved gelatine. Add crushed pineapple and mayonnaise. Chill until a spready consistency.

Note: Chicken and *Pineapple-Cheese Filling* may be molded in an oiled 7-cup loaf pan or 9-inch ring mold. First, pour 1/2 the broth and chicken in the bottom, and chill in the freezer until almost set. Then spread with the *Pineapple-Cheese Filling*, and let set again until almost firm. Add remaining broth and chicken mixture.

Kitchen Shower. To furnish the heart of the home, you might suggest a shower of gifts for the kitchen. You can make this party an informal party, lunch or supper perhaps, and serve refreshments from trays. Set them up before with red-and-white checked paper mats, white plates and a red nosegay pinned to each napkin. Place trays on the dining table; at serving time, food will be arranged on them, and guests can carry them to comfortable spots for eating.

MENU FOR TRAY LUNCHEON

Cup of cream of mushroom soup
Muffin-pan Treasure Salad
Watercress sandwiches
Fresh fruit cup

Muffin-pan Treasure Salad

    1 (4-ounce) package plain, relish or pimento cream cheese
    1 (7-ounce) can solid tuna
    2 tablespoons mayonnaise
    2 teaspoons chopped parsley (optional)
    Salt
1 1/4 cups cold water
    4 teaspoons plain gelatine
    1 (6-ounce) can frozen limeade or lemonade
    1 cup cooked drained peas and diced carrots
  1/2 cup each, diced celery, cucumber and green pepper
    Cucumber slices
    Tomato wedges

Cream the cheese until soft, and stir in well-drained finely flaked tuna. Add mayonnaise and parsley. Taste, and add salt if necessary. Mold the mixture into 8 shapes, about the size of golf balls; then flatten slightly to look like large marshmallows. Chill. Oil 8 large deep muffin cups. Heat cold water and plain gelatine together until dissolved. Remove from heat, and stir in the limeade. Chill until thick, and add the peas and carrots and diced celery, cucumber and green pepper. Spoon a heaping tablespoonful of the mixture into each muffin cup to cover the bottom, and chill. When almost set, arrange tuna fish shapes in the center of each, and spoon remaining vegetable mixture over top and sides to fill cups. Chill, and unmold. Serve in individual lettuce cups, and garnish, if you wish, with thin slices of cucumber and fresh tomato wedges. Makes 8 servings.

Note: If you wish, use 1 cup minced ham, tongue or corned beef in place of tuna.

Surprise Party for the Bride and Groom

This party is particularly suitable for a group of married couples whose last single member is being married. It can be given on a cooperative basis with each wife contributing 1 dish for a smorgasbord. The hostess would be responsible for beverages and for preparing the table.

The table can be covered with a bright blue cloth with napkins of mixed red, blue, purple, yellow and green, and a tray of fat candles of varying heights would be a striking centerpiece.

Here are some gifts you can consider: monogrammed towel sets, a pair of beach towels, a cocktail apron for her and a bar apron for him, monogrammed stationery.

MENU

Herring Salad
Smoked salmon
Pickled beets   Cucumber salad
Sliced ham
Kottbullar
Danish liver pâté (canned)
Deviled eggs   *Mixed-vegetable Salad*
Cheese board:
caraway, Swiss, goat's milk, Crema Danica
Basket of breads:
sour rye, Swedish flatbread, limpa, Ry-Krisp
Imported and domestic beer
Swedish Short Breads   Coffee

Herring Salad

    1 jar herring, drained
    4 potatoes, boiled and peeled
    1 dill pickle
    2 apples, peeled
    2 onions, peeled
    1 cup drained diced canned beets
    Sour cream
    Salt and pepper to taste
    Chopped dill or parsley

Dice herring, potatoes, dill pickles, apples and onions to approximately the same size as the beets. Mix together with beets, and add just enough sour cream to bind mixture; add salt and pepper. Garnish with dill. Serves 8.

Kottbullar (Swedish Meatballs)

    1 pound lean ground beef
  1/2 pound ground shoulder pork or veal
  1/2 cup heavy cream or evaporated milk
  1/4 cup milk
    3 tablespoons dry bread crumbs
  2–3 tablespoons finely chopped and grated onion
    2 teaspoons cornstarch or potato flour
1 1/4 teaspoons salt
  1/8 teaspoon black pepper
    Pinch cayenne
  2–3 tablespoons butter

Break up the meats in a bowl, and add the cream and milk. Beat until smooth. Work in remaining ingredients. Form mixture into small balls with wet fingertips. Melt 2–3 tablespoons butter in a frying pan. Rotate the pan until bottom is covered. Add the meatballs, and sauté on medium heat until browned on all sides. For round meatballs, shake the pan often. Sauté 8–10 minutes. Serve as an appetizer or with other smorgasbord foods. Makes 5–6 dozen.

Mixed-vegetable Salad

>   2 (11-ounce) packages frozen mixed vegetables
> 1/2 cup diced celery
> 3/4 cup mayonnaise
> 1/4 cup sour cream
>   1 tablespoon grated onion
>   Salt and pepper to taste

Cook vegetables until just done. Drain, and rinse with cold water to cool quickly; drain again. Mix celery, mayonnaise, sour cream, onion, salt and pepper with vegetables. Chill before serving. Serves 8–10.

The Bride Entertains Her Attendants

This luncheon should be an intimate party for the bridesmaids and maid of honor. It would be appropriate to present them with gifts and to let them peep at the trousseau and wedding gifts.

Because it is a sentimental occasion, the decorations can be sentimental too. An old-fashioned bouquet for the centerpiece and a miniature replica for each guest are effective. An organdy tablecloth or mats and flower-sprigged china would be lovely, but by all means improvise with what you have. As the group will be small, you can fix individual warmed plates in the kitchen. Set them in front of each guest to keep the table uncluttered.

MENU

Melon with Ham Rolls
Fillet of Sole with Grapes and Mushrooms
Mixed green salad
Pineapple or lemon sherbet with crème de menthe
Coffee or tea

Melon with Ham Rolls

>   1 large melon
>   24 (1-inch) strips thinly sliced prosciutto or ham
>   Black pepper to taste

Cut melon into 6 wedges, and scoop out seeds. Make ham rolls of prosciutto slices, and arrange 4 rolls along center of each melon wedge. Chill thoroughly. Pass black pepper at serving time. Serves 6.

Fillet of Sole with Grapes and Mushrooms

>   2 pounds sole fillets
>   Juice of 1/2 lemon
> 1/2 teaspoon seasoning salt
> 1/4–1/2 pound fresh mushrooms, sliced
> 1/4 cup chopped sweet onion
>   3 tablespoons butter or margarine
> 1/2–3/4 cup halved seedless green grapes
>   1 cup 18% cream
>   Water or dry white wine
> 1/4 cup soft butter
> 1/4 cup flour
> 1/4 teaspoon tarragon
>   Pinch thyme
>   Pinch cayenne
> 3/4 cup fresh bread crumbs
>   1–2 tablespoons grated Parmesan

Place sole fillets in one layer close together in a large greased baking dish or pan. Sprinkle with lemon juice and seasoning salt. Bake at 450°F. 8 minutes. Drain off the juices, and reserve. Sauté mushrooms and onion in hot butter until onion is tender. Add the grapes, and spread mixture over the baked fillets. To the reserved fish juices, add cream and enough water or dry white wine to make 1 3/4 cups liquid. Heat the liquid, and stir in a smooth mixture of soft butter and flour. Cook and stir until smoothly thickened. Add the tarragon, thyme and cayenne. Dilute slightly with a little more cream or wine if you like a thinner sauce. Taste for seasoning. Pour over the mushroom-grape mixture. Sprinkle with crumbs and cheese. Bake at 375°F. until heated through, about 15 minutes. Broil to brown if you wish. Serves 6.

The Rehearsal Dinner

This party includes just the inner circle—the bridal couple's family and closest friends, members of the wedding party and their husbands or wives (or dates). It is customary to have it following the wedding rehearsal itself; it is usually given by the bride's parents at home or in a club, although a close friend can be host too. As it is a fairly large party, buffet service is a wise choice.

In selecting a menu, plan food that will not suffer from delay. Choose foods that can be prepared in advance and need little or no attention at the last minute. It is not necessary to have 5 or 6 courses. A casserole, salad, buttered rolls and dessert are ample, as long as there's enough of each.

MENU

Hot hors d'oeuvres
Cold meats   *Deviled Seafood Loaf*
Scalloped potatoes   Tossed salad
Relishes   *Glacé Fruit Tartlets*

Deviled Seafood Loaf

>   5 or 6 deviled eggs
>   1 (1-pound) can salmon
>   2 (7-ounce) cans solid-pack tuna, drained
>   2 cups soft stale bread crumbs
>   2 tablespoons lemon juice
> 3/4 teaspoon salt
> 1/4 teaspoon white pepper
> 1/2 cup finely diced sweet gherkins or well-drained
>   cucumber relish
> 1/2 cup diced pimento
>   3 eggs, beaten
> 1/3 cup milk or chicken broth
> 1/2 cup mayonnaise

Oil a straight-sided 10 1/4"x 3 3/4"x 2 1/2" loaf pan or pans that will hold 7 cups. Hard-cook and devil the eggs in your favorite way, but moisten the mashed egg yolks sparingly so the finished loaf will slice more neatly. Devil 5 **eggs** for 1 large loaf and 6 for 2 smaller loaves. Press egg halves together, and refrigerate. Empty salmon and juice into a large bowl, and lift out dark bits of skin. Mash bones against the side of the bowl. Add drained tuna. Break up and flake smoothly with the fingertips. Stir in remaining ingredients. Spread 1/2 the seafood mixture evenly in the bottom of the pan, and depress the center with the back of a spoon. Arrange deviled eggs end to end in the trough, and cover with remaining mixture. Set pan or pans in large container of hot water, and bake at 350°F., allowing 1 1/2 hours for 1 pan and 1—1 1/4 hours for smaller pans. Cool loaf quickly in ice water; then refrigerate until cold, and unmold. Garnish with cooked shrimp, smoked oysters, sardines, anchovies, sliced olives, lemon wedges. Makes 20 1/2-inch slices.

Glacé Fruit Tartlets

    1/2 cup soft butter or margarine
    1/4 cup sugar
      1 egg white
      1 cup sifted all-purpose flour
    3/4 cup blanched almonds, ground up
    1/2 teaspoon almond extract
    1/4 cup sugar
      1 tablespoon cornstarch
      1 cup milk
      2 egg yolks
    3/4 teaspoon vanilla extract
      1 box medium-size strawberries
      1 cup fresh raspberries (or whole frozen raspberries)
      1 cup fresh blueberries
      1 cup fresh or canned Royal Ann cherries
      1 (3-ounce) package lemon-flavored jelly powder
1 1/2 cups water
      Lemon leaves

A DAY AHEAD:

* *Shells*: Preheat oven to 375°F. In a medium bowl, combine soft butter or margarine and 1/4 cup sugar. Beat in egg white. Add flour, almonds and almond extract. Use hands to mix. It will be very stiff. Use 1 teaspoon dough to line each 1 1/2″ x 1/2″ tartlet pan. Place tartlet pans on cookie sheet. Bake 10 minutes or until golden brown. Cool in pans for 10 minutes. Remove to rack. When cool, store in air-tight tin.

* *Pastry Cream*: In small saucepan combine 1/4 cup sugar, cornstarch, and milk. Bring to boiling point over medium heat. Remove from heat. Beat egg yolks in quickly. Mix in vanilla extract. Cool. Refrigerate covered overnight.

NEXT DAY:

* *To Assemble*: In each shell, place 1 teaspoon chilled pastry cream. Top with 1 big whole strawberry or 3 or 4 small berries or whole cherry. Chill.

* *Glaze*: Dissolve jelly powder in 1 cup boiling water. Stir in 1/2 cup ice water. Chill until semi-set. Spoon a little glaze over each tartlet. Chill until set. Serve on platter decorated with lemon leaves. Makes 5 1/2 dozen.

ARRANGING A WEDDING

The type of invitation depends on what type of wedding is planned. For the most informal wedding, a handwritten note from the bride's parents serves nicely. There are many versions of printed or engraved invitations. The wording can be varied slightly to suit your preference. The printer from whom you order them will be helpful in suggesting models for you to follow.

Invitations should be mailed to out-of-town guests about 4 weeks before the date and to those in town about 3—4 weeks ahead. The officiating clergyman and his wife are invited personally by the bride's mother.

Formal or Informal

When a formal wedding is held in the evening, the bride wears a long dress and veil and the groom, best man, ushers and fathers of the bride and groom wear formal clothing or military uniforms (formal clothing can be rented, by the way).

The bride's dress for the formal wedding is usually white, but sometimes a pastel color. For an informal wedding, the bride wears white or any color except black. A widow or divorcée usually doesn't wear white or a veil, but the groom's marital status doesn't affect the type of ceremony.

Dressing for a Formal Wedding. A long wedding gown with or without a train, a headdress and a veil are worn. If the dress has a train, the veil is 18 inches longer than the train; otherwise it's fingertip length. Unless the dress has long sleeves, plain white kid gloves would be nice. A single strand of pearls, white satin pumps and a white prayer book or bridal bouquet can also be part of the bride's attire.

The Informal Wedding. Here you have more of a choice in clothes: a short or ankle-length wedding gown, a headdress with shoulder-length veil, gloves and a bouquet; a simple floor-length white gown and shoulder veil; even an afternoon dress or going-away outfit in any color but black.

Flowers

Bring to the florist swatches of the fabric of the bride's and other attendants' dresses, along with sketches of designs, if available. They will help him plan colors and arrangements and harmonize bouquets with dresses.

Flowers should complement, not dominate, the colors of the bridal gowns. Flowers alone look much richer against the lovely materials of the wedding gown and the bridesmaids' dresses. Consistency is important. The bridesmaids' bouquets should bear some relation to the bride's but should not overpower it. The boutonniere for the groom usually differs slightly from those of the other male members of the wedding party, but all are white.

The Receiving Line

After the ceremony, the bridal party leaves for the reception as soon as possible. The receiving line should be placed for least congestion, and guests should approach from the left, preferably, to make handshaking easier. The order of the line is bride's mother, groom's father, groom's mother, bride's father, bride, groom, maid of honor and bridesmaids (sometimes the bride's father or both fathers stand apart from the receiving line, greeting friends who may come up to them). The bride's mother, as hostess, greets each guest first, then introduces the guest to the groom's father and mother. The line proceeds along to greet the rest of the bridal party. The best man and ushers assist elsewhere to see that everything runs smoothly. When all guests have been greeted, members of the receiving line proceed to the refreshment area.

Seating Arrangements

At a large formal sit-down reception, guests are served as soon as they have passed the receiving line. They sit at small tables for 6—8 people. The bride and groom join them when the line of guests has dwindled, usually between the first course and dessert. The groom seats the bride at his right and the maid of honor at his left. The best man sits at the right of the bride, and the bridesmaids and ushers take their seats alternately along one side of the table.

The bride's parents at a large wedding have a table of their own, sometimes with place cards. The groom's parents are seated there, the bride's mother to the left of the groom's father and the groom's mother to the right of the bride's father. Others at this table may include close relatives or friends, as well as the clergyman who performed the ceremony.

At a smaller wedding with only a few attendants, the parents and clergyman often sit at the same table with the bride and groom. At a very small wedding reception, everyone may sit at the same table.

At many large receptions, the guests stand, as at any informal party, with trays of food passed around.

Small Reception at Home

There's no formal receiving line. The bride's and groom's parents greet guests as they enter, and the bride and groom together greet them in the reception room. In a small room, 2 or 3 small flower arrangements are all that are needed for decoration. Cover the buffet table with a cloth that blends with the colors worn by the bridal party, and set the wedding cake in the center, with sandwiches, small cakes and small dishes of nuts and pastel mints surrounding it. Have small plates, napkins and forks available. Place coffee service and punch bowl at opposite ends. Guests proceed to the buffet as they arrive, and when all have come the bride and groom cut the cake and the toasts begin.

Toasts

Whoever you wish may make the first toast—always to the bride. The groom responds and may then propose a toast to the bridesmaids, which is responded to by the best man or head usher. These toasts may be followed by a toast to the bride's mother, proposed by a family friend and responded to by the bride's father, and then a toast to the groom's mother, proposed by a family friend and responded to by the groom's father. All except the first toast are optional.

The Wedding Feast

Almost all weddings include a wedding cake and drinks. For a very small reception at home, no other food need be served. In general the type and amount of food and how it is served depends on the time of day, the number of guests and the size of the reception room, rather than on the formality of the wedding.

Sit-down Wedding Breakfast. A sit-down wedding breakfast (or lunch or dinner, for that matter) should be arranged only when the guest list is small enough or the reception room is large enough to seat everyone comfortably. If it is, such a reception is a natural choice after a morning wedding. If you are doing the catering yourself, have each course served in the kitchen or serving area and then brought inside. If guests and bridal party sit at one table, the cake should be set on a small decorated table or tea wagon nearby, to be cut by the bride after main-course plates have been removed. A large cake is too high for a centerpiece when there are place settings all around the table.

When To Have a Buffet. When the guest list is large and the room average size, a wedding buffet is best. After a morning or late-afternoon wedding, serve a fairly substantial hot or cold buffet. Have luncheon-size plates and forks, and make sure knives are not required for the food.

For an early-afternoon or late-evening wedding, buffet foods may be simple finger foods, because the reception takes place before or after the dinner hour. Small plates and napkins, dainty sandwiches, hot appetizers and fancy tea cakes are placed on the buffet or passed around. They may be followed by dessert and coffee. Before wedding cake and punch are served, other dishes should be removed.

There's also a semi-buffet. Guests serve themselves from the buffet; then they sit at small tables and chairs grouped informally around the room. One large table is reserved for the bridal party.

BUFFET MENUS

FINGER-FOOD BUFFET

Dainty sandwiches
Hot appetizers
(sausage rolls, savory seafood or
chicken tartlets, toasted asparagus
rolls, fish or cheese puffs)
Small cakes
(shortbread, macaroons,
bars, drop cookies,
petits fours)
Ice cream molds   Salted nuts   Mints
Wedding cake   Punch
Coffee or tea

BREAKFAST OR LUNCHEON

Chilled melon garnished with fresh strawberries
Turkey and mushrooms in *Patty Shells*
Asparagus tips
Hot corn sticks and crescent rolls
Raspberry sherbet or ice cream   Wedding cake
Punch   Coffee

LUNCHEON OR SUPPER BUFFET

Chicken or turkey salad, sliced cold ham, tongue
Molded mixed vegetables in tomato aspic
Lobster or shrimp in cream puff shells
Mixed green salad or relishes
Small sandwiches or small buttered hot rolls
Ice cream   Small cakes
Wedding cake   Punch
Coffee or tea

THE WEDDING CAKE

No matter what kind of wedding you plan the *pièce de résistance* is the wedding cake. Many bakers specialize in making them to order and will decorate them exactly as you like. Or you may prefer to buy just the cake and decorate it yourself. If you want to do the whole thing yourself from start to finish, try the *Christmas or Wedding Cake*. With the most limited equipment, you'll be able to decorate it beautifully.

The first step is to buy a pastry tube. It can be made of nylon or plastic and comes with a set of nozzles in assorted sizes and designs, each of which will turn out a different type of decoration. Before you begin work on the wedding cake itself, practice. Make up a batch of icing, get out pastry tubes and experiment with squeezing icing out in a regular, smoothly flowing line. Then try making rosettes. After a little while, you'll probably be ready for the cake.

Decorating with Real Flowers

For the cake we illustrate here, all you need is one simple type of swag and rosettes. You can buy the more elaborate decorations; candied flowers are available at party shops or pastry shops. But you can also make delicate and beautiful flowers yourself very easily by using real flowers. Roses are best because of their petals. Pull petals from 3 or 4 white roses, and brush each petal with egg white that has been very slightly beaten. Over each side of each petal, sprinkle very fine sugar. Set petals on a cookie sheet that has been covered well with the same kind of sugar, and sift more sugar over them. Then set in a warm dry place until the egg white has thoroughly dried. Do not cover. Buds may be sugared whole. When you decorate the cake, after all the icing has set make up a few "roses" using sugared petals; place a few silver dragees in the center of each bunch of petals.

Decorating Icing

    1/2 cup butter or shortening
    1/2 teaspoon salt
      3 pounds icing sugar, sifted
      5 egg whites, unbeaten
    1/4 cup cream
      2 teaspoons vanilla or almond extract

Cream butter, and add salt. Work in part of sugar gradually, blending well; add a little egg white and more sugar, continuing to alternate until egg whites are used up. Then continue to add sugar, alternately with cream, until mixture reaches spreading consistency (a little more or less cream may be necessary to adjust texture). Beat well after each addition to make smooth

mixture. Add vanilla last, and blend well. Makes about 5 cups, enough to cover 1 10″ x 10″ x 2″ layer or 2 8″ x 8″ x 2″ layers, plus enough to decorate with garlands or similar ornaments.

Note: While you are decorating cake, keep frosting covered with damp cloth, so that it stays moist for spreading.

Decorating the Traditional Way

To frost and decorate a 12-pound wedding cake, use approximately 5 pounds almond paste, 4 pounds icing sugar, 2 dozen silver rose leaves, 2 bunches plastic lilies of the valley, 1 dozen large sugar roses, 1 dozen small sugar roses, 1 bottle silver decorettes, 3 fresh pink rosebuds, 8 pillars, pastry bag and 4 tubes (small writing tube, star tube, leaf tube and rose tube).

Stretch the decorating over 3 days, so each layer of icing will have time to set, making the next step easier. First bake a dark or light fruitcake of about 12 pounds in 3 pans approximately 8 inches, 5 3/4 inches and 4 inches square, respectively. For a cake of good proportion, measure the depth of the batter in the pans before baking. The batter in the large pan should be about 1/4 inch deeper than the second, and the second about 1/4 inch deeper than the smallest. After baking, cool completely at room temperature; then remove from the pans, and wrap each cake airtight in heavy-duty foil. Leave to mellow in a cool place for at least 4 weeks.

First Day Almond Icing. Take 4–6 pounds almond paste at room temperature (the amount depends on how thick you want the paste), and knead in icing sugar until paste loses its glossy appearance. If too soft, it will stick when you roll it out. If too stiff, the paste will crack. If paste is dry and crumbly, work in 1 or 2 egg yolks with your fingertips until it is the right consistency; then knead until smooth. Cut off 1/3 of the paste, and cover the remainder with a damp towel to prevent drying. Coat the piece of paste with icing sugar, and roll out 3/8–1/4 inch thick between 2 sheets of waxed paper, just as you would pastry. If the paste sticks and paper creases, peel off top and bottom alternately, and sprinkle with more icing sugar before continuing to roll. Remove the top paper, and set the bottom of the large pan on the center of the paste. Hold a clean ruler or piece of cardboard in line with the edges of the pan, and cut out the corners of the paste to form a rough cross. Unwrap the largest cake, and brush the bottom and sides with slightly beaten egg white or melted warm jelly.

Invert waxed paper and paste over the cake; remove paper gently. Press the paste lightly but firmly against the cake, and cut away excess paste around the bottom. Brush the corners with egg white, and press them together. Patch with bits of paste if any cake is showing. For a thicker top layer of paste, press trimmings together and roll into a square. Press on top of cake, and trim even.

Cover the medium and small cakes with the remaining paste in the same way; then set cakes on foil-covered squares of heavy cardboard or plywood brushed with egg white. Plywood makes a firmer base for the largest cake and for all layers if you use pillars. Let the paste dry at room temperature for about 24 hours or until the surface is slightly crusty. To test, press with your finger.

Second Day Basic Frosting. Assemble and center cakes. Place the medium pan over the top of the largest cake, and measure an even border on 4 sides. Mark the paste at the 4 corners. Mark the medium cake in the same way, and assemble cakes. You can use either *Soft White Icing* or *Ornamental Icing.*

Decorating Frosting: The frosting must be one that will hold its shape, yet be soft enough to pass through the small opening of a decorating tube. It must be one that does not harden or dry quickly, because the decorating process often takes some time. Practice on waxed paper to make sure it is the right consistency. If it is too soft, it will spread and the design will not be clear-cut. If too stiff, it will break or crack when pushed through tube.

Soft White Icing

> 1/2 pound soft all-vegetable shortening
> 4–5 cups sifted icing sugar
>   Milk
> 1/2 teaspoon salt
>   2 teaspoons almond extract (optional)

Beat the shortening (butter will give a yellowish icing) on medium speed until creamy; then add 1 cup icing sugar and a little milk alternately, beating after each addition. Add the salt and flavoring. Test the consistency. The icing is a good thickness when it smooths and does not run when a dab is spread on the sides of the cake. Add more sifted icing sugar, or thin with milk if necessary. Icing should be slightly stiffer for the decorating tube than for spreading. Beat icing occasionally when frosting the cake or decorating, and keep bowl covered with a damp cloth. Divide or multiply this recipe to your needs.

Ornamental Icing

> 4 egg whites
> 5 cups sifted icing sugar
> 1 teaspoon cream of tartar
> 1/4 teaspoon salt
>   2 teaspoons almond extract

Combine the first 4 ingredients in a large beater bowl, and mix on low speed; then beat on medium to high speed 10–15 minutes. Add the flavoring. Dip the edge of a metal spatula in and out of the frosting. If a sharp edge or peak forms, icing is a good consistency for spreading. Otherwise, beat in more sifted icing sugar until icing peaks. Icing should be slightly stiffer for decorating tube work than for spreading on the cake. Keep the bowl covered with a damp cloth to avoid crustiness. Make more icing when required. This recipe is easy to divide or multiply; the quantity given here is sufficient for the large-size beater bowl of an average mixer.

If you use the *Soft White Icing*, assemble the cake before icing; otherwise top layers may shift. *Ornamental Icing* can be spread on individual layers if allowed to dry until hard.

Spread the icing with a metal spatula, starting at the top of the cake and scraping off excess icing occasionally. When the cake is covered, clean the spatula with a warm wet sponge and smooth the icing. Wipe the spatula often as you press out ridges and bumps. Before smoothing the bottom layer you may wish to slide the cake onto a silver tray or a large flat plate; then smooth out any thumbprints. Let cake icing set overnight.

If using pillars, ice each layer separately with ornamental icing, and smooth with a wet spatula. Let dry overnight or until crusty. Next, center the medium pan on the large cake, and press down lightly. Press a pillar into each inside corner of the square. Cut out a 1-inch square of icing in each corner through to the fruitcake; then press 4 pillars into these depressions. Before inserting the pillars, decorate the center of the cake if you plan to do this. When pillars are in place, use the pastry bag and press out rosettes around the base of each to fill in any cut marks and make the pillars more secure. Scrape a thin layer of ornamental icing on top of each pillar, and set the center cake section in place. Continue in the same way for the next 4 pillars and the top layer. Leave the cake to set overnight.

Third Day Finishing Touches. For balance, the heaviest or most elaborate icing should be on the large bottom layer. If you like a touch of pink with the white icing, use more pink here; but remember, colored icing becomes a deeper shade when dry. Use large-tube openings on the lower layer, the smallest for the top. As a guide when making uniformly spaced ropes, rosettes and shells, hold a ruler along the edges of each layer and mark off 1/2-or 1-inch distances with pins. Test the consistency of the ornamental icing before you decorate by squeezing out a small pattern. If the icing will not hold its shape, add more icing sugar. Hold the bag at a comfortable level for better control and to keep your arm from tiring. For weight, make 2 or 3 rows of swags to balance the bottom layer. Apply silver decorettes, sugar roses, doves and silver leaves while icing is still soft. Keep unused portion of icing covered with a damp towel. Crusty bits of icing will clog the tube. Make roses if you wish, but let them dry thoroughly on waxed paper before applying them.

Choose a top ornament in keeping with the size of the cake and your decorating style. A too-large ornament will make the cake top-heavy. For an easy-to-make ornament, use a very small glass, a few sprigs of plastic lilies of the valley or baby's breath and 3 pale pink roses or sweet peas. Cut out a small square or circle of icing in the center of the top, and press in the glass. Decorate the base and the face of the glass, if you wish, with rosettes. Arrange flowers in the glass, and add water with an eyedropper if fresh ones are used.

WEDDING ANNIVERSARIES

Whether it's a first or thirty-first, an anniversary is a good time for a party. It can be arranged by either relatives or friends or by the people celebrating the occasion. When you give your own party, though, don't tell the guests it's an anniversary party until they arrive, or they'll feel obliged to bring gifts.

Gifts

In arranging an anniversary party for someone else, do tell guests how many years the couple has been married. Many guests like to buy gifts accordingly:

1. Paper	13. Lace
2. Cotton	14. Ivory
3. Leather	15. Glass or crystal
4. Silk or pewter	20. China
5. Wood	25. Silver
6. Iron or copper	30. Pearl
7. Wool	35. Coral or jade
8. Bronze or pottery	40. Ruby
9. Willow	45. Sapphire
10. Tin	50. Gold
11. Steel	55. Emerald
12. Linen	60. Diamond

Gauge Age and Interests. As a rule, early anniversary parties are informal, but as the years roll on they tend to become more formal. A fifth anniversary party could be an informal dance, supper, cocktail party or even a noisy evening of games in the recreation room. By the time a golden anniversary comes along, a more dignified reception would be appropriate. But the party should suit the people for whom it's given—a middle-aged couple celebrating their twenty-fifth anniversary would probably like a lively affair, whereas an elderly couple married for 25 years would probably prefer a quieter one.

Golden or Diamond Wedding Anniversaries

A golden or diamond wedding anniversary is usually given in the home of the guests of honor, but their children or friends do the arranging. Unless the house can accommodate all the guests at one time, the party starts about 4:00 and goes on until 10:00 or 11:00, with friends dropping in at any time during these hours. It usually works out that one group appears between 4:00 and 6:00 in the afternoon and the rest after 8:00 in the evening. That means a lull around dinnertime, a break appreciated by the guests of honor. If you're finding it difficult to cut down your list, you can always have 2 parties, both the same, a week apart, which makes double work for the party arranger but may make it more comfortable for all concerned.

Carrying Out a Theme. Decorations should fit the anniversary—for a golden one, yellow roses, sprays of artificial gold flowers and leaves in vases and so forth. A low bowl of golden Christmas-tree balls or an arrangement of gold leaves and fruits makes a pretty centerpiece.

Food and Drink. On a sideboard have a tray and on it a big bowl of iced punch, topped with floating fresh fruit.

Remember that most people will have to stand if it's a large party, so make the food easy to handle. Sandwiches, hot tartlets, canapés, tiny cookies, petits fours, little cakes or ice-cream strawberries can be managed with one hand while the guest holds a cup of tea or a glass of punch in the other.

A small side table in the dining room, covered by a damask or lace tablecloth, can hold the wedding cake for guests to admire as they arrive. Or the cake can be used as the centerpiece for the dining table. At about 5:00 or whenever the crowd seems at a maximum, ask everyone to gather in the dining room for the ceremony of cutting the cake. This is done by the couple together, and the cake is cut into small pieces for serving to guests. After cake has been passed, there will surely be some toasts, so be sure everyone's glass is full.

Assorted sandwiches (egg salad, chicken salad,
chopped ham—relish, lobster)
Hot crabmeat tartlets   Mushroom tartlets
Cocktail sausages
Caviar toast rounds   Smoked oysters on toast
Olives
Small chocolate brownies   Coconut macaroons
Sugar Cookies   Small iced cakes
Ice-cream strawberries
Nuts   Mints   Chocolates
Golden Wedding Cake
Punch

Golden Wedding Cake

4 cups sifted all-purpose flour
2 teaspoons salt
2 teaspoons baking powder
1 1/2 cups canned pineapple chunks
1 cup chopped candied citron
1 cup candied cherry halves
1 cup candied orange peel
1 cup candied lemon peel
1 cup light sultana raisins
1 cup slivered blanched almonds
1/2 cup shortening
1/2 cup butter or margarine
2 cups sugar
3/4 cup milk
8 egg whites

Sift flour, salt and baking powder together.
Combine fruits and almonds, and stir into flour
mixture. Cream shortening and butter or margarine together; add sugar, and beat until mixture
is light and fluffy. Stir in fruit mixture alternately with milk, and mix well together. Beat egg
whites until they hold stiff peaks, and fold into
batter. Pour into greased and brown-paper lined
angel cake pan with tube center, and bake at
300°F. about 2 1/2 hours or until top springs
back when pressed lightly with finger. Or bake
in 4 1-pound coffee cans, putting 1/4 the batter
in each tin, for 2 hours at same temperature. A
sheet of heavy brown paper placed over top during last 45 minutes of baking will prevent it from
darkening too much.

Punch

2 cups water
2 cups sugar
Juice of 12 oranges
Juice of 12 lemons
2 quarts chilled ginger ale
Orange and lemon slices
Sprigs of mint

Boil water and sugar about 10 minutes. Cool
syrup, and add to it orange and lemon juice. Chill
well; immediately before serving add ginger ale,
and garnish with orange and lemon slices and a
few sprigs of mint. Serves 35—40.

VARIATIONS:

Be sure to add alcoholic beverage at the same
time as the ginger ale, just before serving the
drinks.

* *Champagne Punch*: Substitute champagne for
ginger ale, or use 1 quart champagne and 1
quart ginger ale.

* *Sherry Punch*: Substitute 1 quart medium-dry
sherry for 1 quart ginger ale.

QUANTITIES FOR GOLDEN WEDDING RECEPTION MENU
(35—40 GUESTS)

1 dozen egg-salad sandwiches
1 dozen minced ham-relish sandwiches
1 dozen chicken-salad sandwiches
1 dozen lobster sandwiches
3 dozen cocktail sausages
3 dozen hot crabmeat tartlets
3 dozen hot mushroom tartlets
4 dozen melba toast rounds with red caviar, sprinkled
with grated hard-cooked egg or spread with anchovy
paste
4 dozen smoked oysters on toast
2 dozen small chocolate brownies
2 dozen coconut macaroons
4 dozen small frosted cakes
2 dozen plain sugar cookies
6 dozen ice-cream strawberries

(1 sandwich makes 4 pieces when cut into small triangles)

Appendix

ARRANGING A CONVENIENT KITCHEN

A kitchen that serves well is made up of labor-saving appliances arranged for easy, comfortable use.

Each major appliance—refrigerator, range and sink—should have an adjoining counter of at least 2 feet, which serves as a landing deck when serving and as a place to put utensils when working. If there is a separate oven, it should have its own counter of at least 15 inches to put roasts and baked foods on as they are removed. One counter in a kitchen should be at least 42 inches long if there is to be a comfortable mixing center for general food preparation.

The actual arrangement of working centers depends on the room's size and shape. But a good plan is to place the sink between the refrigerator and the cooking surface, preferably in a triangular arrangement. A very good plan is an "L" shape on 2 adjacent walls. There are many convenient arrangements that can be worked out to fit available space, however. When counters are aligned on opposite walls, a 4-foot aisle should be planned between them.

At each main center there should be cabinets for storing utensils, tools and foods used there regularly. These include cabinets under counters for large utensils and packages, and wall cupboards for smaller ones. In planning storage, don't forget space for dishes, cleaning supplies, staples, small appliances, trays, timers, wastebasket, food wraps, towels. They will need cupboard room, not necessarily at main work centers.

Finally separate cooking and extracurricular kitchen activities. You will be glad if a place to eat or do the laundry, for instance, is near the kitchen but not located so that it interferes with food preparation.

Choosing Cooking and Baking Utensils

Proper pans will increase your chances of successful cooking. The sizes and materials of utensils are both important. For baking, a utensil should suit the quantity of a recipe. If it's too small, food may run over edge; if it's too large, food will not brown properly. In addition, bak-

ing utensils or other pans should not be so large that they touch sides of oven. This blocks the heat and results in uneven browning. Some new utensils have sizes stamped on the bottoms for easy identification. To measure a baking utensil (in case size is indicated in recipe), take the inside dimension at the top of the pan. For depth, take the inside perpendicular dimension. Casseroles, custard cups and many other oven dishes are measured by liquid capacity; this measure is specified in many recipes. If you do not know the size when buying a utensil, be certain to ask the clerk.

When baking, bright metals such as aluminum usually give the most uniform heating and therefore the most even browning of baking foods such as cookies, cakes and the like. Very dark pans, black by nature or from long-time use, tend to absorb more heat and give darker results. Oven glassware is efficient in absorbing heat and is excellent for party or casserole foods. When using it to bake cakes or more heat-sensitive foods, however, reduce oven heat about 25° to compensate for heat absorption. For casserole cooking, any oven-proof material may be used, and it's desirable to consider materials that can go directly from the refrigerator or freezer into the oven.

For top-of-the-range cooking, pans should fit the size of the heating unit or burner and be adapted to the quantity being cooked. The most useful utensils have flat bottoms, so that they receive heat evenly, and well-fitting covers to retain moisture. Good quality aluminum pans heat uniformly; stainless steel, ceramic, glass and porcelain are attractive and easily cleaned. They sometimes heat unevenly on high heat but can be used successfully if the heat is lower than for aluminum, giving heat a chance to spread evenly. Cast iron stays level and flat for longtime use. It heats slowly but evenly and holds heat well. It is heavy, thick and durable and may be heavy to handle. Iron improves with use if properly cared for, but it must be kept dry to prevent rusting. Some iron is coated with enamel to add color and improve appearance. Cast iron should not be confused with sheet-iron utensils, which are very lightweight and often warp and buckle with use. For this reason, they heat unevenly and give unreliable results.

Nonstick Surfaces. Almost every kind of utensil is easier to clean when lined with Teflon or similar materials. This coating, now found in aluminum, enamel, glass, iron and stainless utensils, gives an antistick finish that makes some foods easy to cook and makes cleaning much simpler. Many of these finishes are damaged by harsh treatment, however, so good care includes special tools (nylon- or Teflon-coated or wood) that are kind to the surface. Teflon-lined utensils should be washed in hot detergent water, for, although food particles are easily removed, lingering traces of fat tend to darken and discolor the utensils.

GENERAL POINTS:

1. Choose saucepans and frying pans that are well balanced. An extra long or heavy handle makes a pan unsteady, and as a result it tips easily.

2. For any pan, choose designs that are free from hard-to-clean cracks and crevices.
3. Try lifting utensils to see if the handles are comfortable to hold and balance the utensil well. Heat-resistant handles mean pans can be used in ovens as well as on the surface.
4. Handles of utensils for surface cooking should not be so long that they extend over the edge of the stove. They will be easily knocked off and may cause serious burns.
5. Very large pots, such as kettles and soup pots, should have 2 handles, so that the heavy weight can be handled with assurance.
6. Utensils should be purchased with their own well-fitting lids. With cover in place, many foods can be steamed to save flavor, nutrients and cooking fuel.

USE AND CARE OF KITCHEN APPLIANCES

Modern appliances have more aids built into them than ever before, but they all do better when used and cared for as planned. Do read and follow the manufacturers' instructions for your particular models.

Success in Using Ranges

For surface cooking, choose pans suited to quantities of food and heating units or burners. Utensils should have flat bottoms for even heating, especially for successful automatic surface cooking.

Use high heat to bring utensil and food to cooking temperatures; then turn heat lower to maintain cooking speed desired (with automatic cooking, type controls lower heat). Cooking at proper temperatures prevents scorching food.

For oven cooking, choose utensils suited to type of food being cooked—see section on cooking utensils. Generally, place foods in approximately the center of the oven, and arrange pans so that air can circulate around them.

For baked foods it is usually to your advantage to preheat the oven to the desired temperature as food is prepared. For most meats and casserole-type foods, preheating is not necessary.

There are timers available to turn ovens on and off while you are away. Do not let fresh meat stand more than 4 hours before cooking starts.

Easy Care of Ranges. The top of the range and the cabinet are easier to keep spotless if spills are wiped up after each meal. On enamel tops it is best to wait until surface is cooled; then wipe with sudsy sponge, and dry with paper towel. Never scrape, gouge or use caustic cleaners on enamel, anodized aluminum or chrome.

Broiler pans are easier to clean if detergent is sprinkled over grid after food is removed. Cover with dampened paper towels until dishwashing time. Drip pans and reflector pans under surface heaters can be removed and cleaned in dishpan. These areas can be lined with heavy foil, shaped to fit and (for those under electric units) cut out to allow the same space for ventilation as the section it protects. There are also liners available for these areas that can be replaced when soiled.

Some ranges have ovens that clean themselves; others have easy-clean Teflon panels and throw-away foil linings. Still others have doors that fold down or remove to make it easier to reach the interior. For the ovens that still need cleaning in the old way, however, and they are in the majority, here are some suggestions:

* Wear rubber gloves to protect hands, and spread papers over floors and nearby areas, for some cleaning compounds are caustic.

* If oven light comes on when the door is opened, tape switch "off" so that bulb will not get so hot it breaks if touched with cool spray or sponge. It is a good idea, too, to tape or shield sockets and controls in oven.

* New special cleaners make cleaning easier. The spray-type cleaners, with foaming action that keeps cleaner in contact with surface longer than liquids, are effective. Do read labels, as some cleaners are more effective when used in warm oven, some sprays should be shaken well and some should not be agitated.

* Another method is to place a small discarded pan, containing 1/2 cup ammonia diluted with 1/2 cup water, on oven rack while oven is still warm. The fumes help to loosen spatters and make oven cleaning easier.

* After oven has been cleaned, heat it empty 5 minutes before adding foods, to prevent contamination of flavors.

Success in Using Refrigerators

For best operation, a refrigerator should be level, so that the door will swing closed easily and seal completely.

Cold air in refrigerators holds less moisture than warm air, so fresh fruits and vegetables without natural coverings of their own should be stored in bins or containers provided, put in plastic containers or wrapped in foil or plastic. Carefully wrap foods with decided odors of their own (melons, cauliflower) so they will not spread to other foods. Also see that delicate foods such as butter and other spreads are kept covered so that they do not pick up strange flavors.

Rinse ice trays with warm water as needed but avoid using hot water, for it tends to remove the special finish on ice trays that makes cubes easy to remove.

Easy Care of Refrigerators. All refrigerators require regular cleaning and care, even those that do not need defrosting.

To defrost nonautomatic models, choose a time when food supply is low. Defrosting should be done when icy frost is 1/4 inch thick or when special indicator is covered. Defrosting can sometimes be delayed by scraping off fluffy frost with frost scraper or pancake turner, using a scraping, not jabbing, stroke. When scraping, collect frost on tray or newspapers. For complete defrosting of nonautomatic models, remove any contents from drip pan; turn control to "defrost" if there is such a position or to "off" if not. The melting of the frost can be speeded by using shallow pans of hot water in the evaporator or by using special electric defrosters (follow instructions for placing them to protect plastic sections).

How often a refrigerator needs cleaning depends on the use it gets, but at least once a month is a good average. Remove all contents, wash inside of cabinet, racks, shelves and door gasket with baking soda-and-water solution (1 tablespoon soda per 1 quart water). Refrigerators are easier to keep clean if spills are wiped up immediately.

A liquid or cream wax of the cleaning type, used on the outside, both cleans and leaves a pleasant sheen. Never use oily furniture polish or abrasive cleaners on any part of a refrigerator.

The coils at the rear of the cabinet of all older models and underneath the food-storage section in some new models should be cleaned at least twice a year of dust and dirt that clings to them, as this accumulation reduces the efficiency of the mechanism. A crevice tool of a vacuum cleaner is effective for this; a long-handled brush is also helpful. Some of the new refrigerators can be moved easily for cleaning. For others, it is important at least to move them from the wall to reach the coils.

Success in Using Freezers

A freezer is more convenient to use if it is in or near the kitchen where the supplies can be selected easily and quickly. Like refrigerators, this appliance should be level.

Speedy freezing is a secret of quality. You can freeze any amount that will freeze solid within 24 hours. Usually, that's about 2 pounds for each cubic foot of freezer space when the temperature is maintained at 0°F. If you have more than that to freeze, keep some in the refrigerator until the first amount is solidly frozen. In fact, prechilling in the refrigerator helps retain fresh flavor and good texture. Do remember, however, that freez-

ing protects—rather than improves—foods. You will want to select good food to start with, the kinds known for successful freezing.

When loading a freezer, leave space between packages for air circulation, and try to keep new, warmer packages from touching those already frozen. For convenient use, you will want to follow a pattern for storing foods in the freezer, so that you can quickly locate any needed food. You will find it helpful if meats are in one part, vegetables in another and desserts all together in still another. It will save time and guesswork in sorting out the makings of a meal later if you label each package with contents and number of servings. Also, date packages, and use older ones first. Freezer storage is drying, and it's important to wrap and seal packages to protect against dehydration and changes in flavor, texture and color. For packaging, choose materials, bags and containers made for freezers or some of the new utensils that take kindly to the temperature shock of going from the freezer to the oven. If you wish, use lightweight household wraps and cartons from cottage cheese and ice cream, but for short-term storage only.

When several layers of food such as steak, chops, or ground-meat patties are to be frozen, put 2 layers of wrap between them to speed separation later. Or freeze hamburgers, chops, etc. on a cookie sheet just until frozen; then drop into plastic bags, and seal.

When wrapping chunky compact foods, mold foil or clear plastic wrap closely around them, and double-fold edges. Masking or freezer tape holds seams tight. These precautions seal out air that is harmful to flavors of frozen foods.

Easy Care of Freezers. The cabinets of freezers are cared for in the same way as those for refrigerators. Like refrigerators, the models that need no manual defrosting should be cleaned periodically; twice a year is usually enough.

STORAGE TIME FOR MEATS

COVERED LOOSELY IN REFRIGERATOR 36°–40° F.

Ground beef	1–2 days
Liver, heart, kidney	1–2 days
Sausages	2–3 days
Leftover casseroles, stews	2–3 days
Cooked meats	3–4 days
Wieners	3–4 days
Chops and steaks	3–5 days
Roasts	5–6 days
Bacon	6–7 days
Cured ham, whole	1–2 weeks

Sausages	1–2 months
Ground beef	2–3 months
Casseroles, stews	2–3 months
Liver, heart, kidney	3–4 months
Wieners	3–4 months
Veal and pork chops	3–4 months
Lamb chops	3–4 months
Veal and pork roasts	4–8 months
Fish	6–9 months
Lamb roasts	8–12 months
Beef roasts and steaks	10–12 months

COOKING TERMS USED IN THIS BOOK

À la grecque: In the Greek style. Food may be cooked in consommé or other liquid and then chilled in the reduced consommé or liquid. This term may also describe food prepared with oil, garlic and/or other seasoning enjoyed by the Greeks.

À la king: Food served in rich cream sauce. Usually flavored with mushrooms and pimento.

À la mode: In the fashion. When referring to pie, with ice cream; referring to beef, marinated beef braised in marinade.

Angelica: The candied leaf stalk of a European herb used to decorate candies and desserts.

Antipasto: Italian hors d'oeuvres consisting of meat, fish, vegetables, etc.

Aspic: A savory jelly made from concentrated meat or vegetable stock and seasonings, with or without the addition of poultry, fish, vegetables, etc.

Au gratin: Food baked or broiled with a breadcrumb topping. Cheese may be included with the crumbs.

Baba: A French cake made with yeast batter. Baba au rum: a baba soaked in a rum-flavored liquid.

Bain-marie: A French double boiler or a large open vessel half-filled with hot water in which saucepans are placed to keep contents nearly at boiling point.

Bake: To cook by dry heat, as in an oven.

Barbecue: A unit or grill. To roast meat on a rack or spit, basting frequently with a highly seasoned sauce. A social entertainment with food cooked outdoors.

Baste: To pour liquid or melted fat over food during cooking to keep food moist and flavorful.

Batter: A mixture of liquid, flour and other ingredients that graduates in thickness from a pouring consistency to a spreading consistency.

Beat: To incorporate air into a mixture or to combine and mix ingredients into a smooth mixture with a spoon, beater or mixer.

Béchamel: French term for white or cream sauce.

Bisque: A cream soup made with chopped or pureed fish, vegetables, etc. An ice cream containing nuts or crumbled macaroons.

Blanch: To skin nuts or fruits by covering them with boiling water for 2–3 minutes, then immersing them in cold water.

Blanching: To scald vegetables when preparing them for freezing.

Blend: To combine 2 or more ingredients until smooth. To mix ingredients in an electric blender, if recipe specifies.

Boil: To cook in steaming liquid in which bubbles are breaking on the surface.

Bouchée: French. Literally, "a mouthful." A tiny cream puff or puff pastry shell filled with a savory mixture.

Bouillabaisse: A French soup-stew made with fish and shellfish.

Bouillon: A clear broth made by simmering various combinations of meat and vegetables for a long time in water.

Bouquet: The particular fragrance of a wine.

Bouquet garni: A mixture of herbs and spices tied in a cheesecloth bag, cooked with other ingredients and discarded at the end of cooking time. Typical flavors used are celery, bay leaf, thyme, green onion.

Braise: To cook meat with a small amount of moisture in a covered saucepan or casserole.

Brazier: A large flat tray for holding burning charcoal.

Bread: To coat cutlets, chops, croquettes, fish, etc. with fine bread or cracker crumbs prior to frying or baking.

Breathe: To open a bottle of wine an hour or so before serving to have the flavor at its peak.

Briquet: A brick-shaped block of artificial coal.

Broil: To cook food by searing the surface with direct heat on a broiler or over hot coals.

Brown: To briefly fry meat, poultry, etc., in a little hot fat until brown on the outside.

Brown Sauce: A French gravy seasoned with onions, carrots and tomato puree.

Brush: To spread thinly with a brush.

Canapé: A tiny piece of fried or toasted bread topped with savory mixtures of cheese, meat or seafood.

Caramelize: To melt granulated sugar over medium heat to a golden-brown syrup.

Cassoulet: A French dish made of beans and meat.

Chill: To refrigerate until thoroughly cold.

Chop: To cut in fine or coarse pieces with a knife, chopper or scissors.

Choux: A type of pastry made with eggs, used in making cream puffs, eclairs, etc.

Chowder: A hearty soup of fish, seafood or vegetables, containing diced potatoes.

Citron: A fruit similar to a lemon, available candied for cookies, fruitcake, etc. "Citron" is French for "lemon." Citron-melon: a species of watermelon with variegated coloring. This small round fruit is preserved in syrup rather than eaten raw.

Coat: To cover thoroughly with a fine film of flour, crumbs, icing, sugar, crushed nuts, coconut, etc.

Compote: A mixture of fresh or stewed whole fruits.

Condensed milk: Canned whole milk, commercially concentrated by evaporation and sweetened with sugar.

Condiment: A pungent seasoning, such as pepper, mustard, vinegar or prepared sauce.

Consommé: Bouillon enriched with additional meat, poultry etc.

Cool: To let stand at room temperature until no longer warm.

Cream: To soften fat, or fat and sugar, with a wooden spoon or electric mixer until light and fluffy. The percentage of butterfat in: whole milk (3.25%); table and coffee cream (16–18%); cereal cream (8–15%); whipping cream (30–35%).

Creole: The cookery of New Orleans. It usually includes filé powder or okra.

Crêpes: French. Very thin pancakes.

Croquettes: A molded mixture of ground cooked foods with a crumb coating, fried in deep fat.

Croutons: Small bread cubes toasted, baked or fried until crisp and used to garnish soups, salads, etc.

Crumble: To crush a food such as crisp bacon or bread with fingertips until it is coarse crumbs.

Crush: To break up solids such as ice or cornflakes by force.

Curry: A mixture of meat, fish, vegetables or eggs seasoned with curry powder.

Cut in: To combine solid fat with dry ingredients using two knives, a fork or a pastry blender.

Dash: A quick shake from a small-necked bottle; 1/6 teaspoon.

Decant: To transfer wine from a bottle to a decanter by pouring gently to leave sediment behind.

Demitasse: A small cup for after-dinner coffee.

Dice: To cut into cubes with a sharp knife on a cutting board.

Dip: To immerse briefly in liquid.

Dissolve: To cause a dry substance to pass into solution in a liquid.

Dollop: A heaped-up mound of whipped cream, sour cream, creamed cheese, etc., spooned on a food to garnish it.

Dough: A mixture of flour, liquid and other ingredients, thick enough to roll, pat out or knead. Dough is thicker in consistency than batter.

Drain: To remove liquid from a food by placing it in a colander or sieve or by using a lid.

Dredge: To coat pieces of food with flour, sugar, etc. Dry ingredient and food pieces may be shaken together in a paper bag.

Drippings: The juice and fat left in a pan after roasting or frying meat or poultry.

Dust: To sprinkle lightly with flour, sugar, etc.

Dutch oven: A deep heavy metal pan with a close-fitting cover. It may or may not have a removable rack.

Eclair: Cream-puff base baked in oblong shape and filled with whipped cream or custard.

Entrée: French. Usually refers to the main course of a meal.

Enzymes: Substances that cause chemical changes in foods.

Evaporated milk: Whole milk commercially concentrated by evaporation. It contains twice the minerals, protein, fat and sugar of ordinary whole milk. It can be whipped when chilled.

Fillet: A boneless pieces of fish or meat; in beef, beef tenderloin.

Fines herbes: A blend of several chopped fresh or dried herbs. The blend usually includes parsley, tarragon, chervil or chives and is used to flavor omelets and sauces. Fresh herbs are preferable to dried.

Flake: To break into small pieces with a fork.

Flambé: Food enveloped in a flame from spirits of high alcholic content such as cognac, rum or brandy.

Flan: An open tart containing fruit baked in a metal flan ring. A baked type of custard.

Flute: To scallop the edges of a pie before baking.

Fold in: To combine ingredients with a gentle up-and-over motion without releasing air bubbles that have been beaten into the ingredients. Cut down through mixture with a broad spatula, scraper or whisk. Lift some of the mixture from the bottom to the top with each fold. Give the bowl a quarter turn with each motion until all ingredients have been blended.

Fondant: Sugar syrup cooked to the soft-ball stage (234°F.), then kneaded until creamy.

Frappé: A partly frozen fruit ice, liqueur or other liquid poured over crushed ice.

Fricassee: Food that has been browned, then simmered or baked in a sauce with vegetables.

Frost: To apply a topping or icing.

Fry: To pan-fry is to cook in a small amount of fat in a frying pan. To French-fry is to cook in fat deep enough to cover the food.

Garnish: To decorate with colorful and contrasting food.

Gash: To make cuts with a knife or scissors.

Gelatine: Use plain gelatine unless otherwise indicated.

Ghee: The clear yellow liquid obtained by melting unsalted butter and discarding the sediment settled on the bottom. A term used in Asian (not Oriental) cooking.

Glacé: Food coated with sugar syrup cooked to the "crack" stage, or frozen desserts.

Glaze: To add lustre to a food by coating with butter, egg, milk, syrup or jelly.

Goulash: A Hungarian meat stew usually flavored with paprika.

Grate: To shred food by rubbing it over a sharp-edged grater.

Grease: To rub and coat the inside of a baking pan with fat before pouring in batter, etc.

Grill: To broil.

Grind: To cut or crush finely in a food mill, a grinder or a blender.

Gumbo: A dish made with okra. Usually associated with Creole cooking.

Haute cuisine: Fancy French cooking.

Hibachi: Japanese barbecue unit.

Hors d'oeuvres: French for "outside the main work." Tidbits served to tease the palate, such as relishes, canapés, etc.

Jigger: A bar measure that contains 1 1/2 ounces of liquid.

Julienne: Matchlike strips of food such as carrots, potatoes.

Kebabs: See *Shish kebabs*.

Knead: To work dough with a pressing motion accompanied by folding and stretching. Or to press dough with the heel of the hand, alternately folding, pushing and stretching the dough.

Larding: To thread slivers of fat with a larding needle through lean meat before roasting.

Leavening: An ingredient in baked products to make them light and porous by releasing or forming gas during baking.

Lukewarm: 85°F. or neither warm nor cool on the inside of your wrist.

Macédoine: A mixture of several vegetables or fruits, often diced.

Marinade: A savory mixture of acid liquid, seasonings, chopped or sliced vegetables and sometimes oil; may be cooked or uncooked depending on its use.

Marinate: To season and tenderize food by soaking it in a marinade.

Marmite: A clay cooking pot used in Europe. It is always placed on an asbestos mat, as direct heat will crack it.

Mash: To reduce food to a smooth consistency by pressing it with a potato masher and then beating the food with a spoon or electric mixer.

Melt: To slowly heat a solid substance until it liquefies.

Meringue: A stiffly beaten mixture of egg whites and sugar. It is usually browned in the oven when used as a topping for pies and desserts. It can be folded into other ingredients or shaped and baked in layers for tortes or small cakes.

Mince: To grind, chop or cut into very small pieces.

Mix: To combine ingredients by stirring. Also, a commercially prepared mixture of dry ingredients.

Moisten: To brush or spoon liquid over a food.

Mold: A container used for jelling mousses, jellied salads, etc. Oil mold lightly before pouring in a savory mixture; rinse mold in water before filling with a sweet mixture. To mold: to form into shapes.

Monosodium glutamate: A chemical used on food to bring out the flavor. Often referred to as M.S.G.

Mornay: French. A white sauce enriched with egg yolks and cheese.

Mousse: A mixture of sweetened whipped cream and other ingredients chilled without stirring. Or a light mixture of cream, fruit, meat, vegetables etc., poached, steamed or set with gelatine.

Oven-poach: To bake a dish of food by setting it in a larger dish containing water.

Pan-broil: To cook uncovered in a frying pan, pouring off the fat as it accumulates.

Parboil: To partly cook in liquid and complete cooking by some other method.

Pare: To peel off the outer skin.

Parfait: A frozen mixture of custard and whipped cream. It is usually served in tall glasses with alternating layers of frozen cream mixture or ice cream and sauces, then topped with whipped cream.

Paste: A smooth mixture of dry ingredients and liquid. Also pureed meat, fish, tomatoes etc.

Pastry board: A board on which to knead or roll dough.

Pastry cutter: A utensil used to trim edges of pastry.

Pastry wheel: A utensil used for cutting decorative or straight edges on pastry.

Pat: To flatten with fingertips.

Pâté: A paste of meat or fish used for hors d'oeuvres and sandwiches.

Patty: Ground meat that has been shaped into a flat cake or patty. Patty shells: cases of puff pastry to be filled with creamed mixtures of chicken, fish, etc.

Peel: To cut away the outer covering.

Petits fours: Little fancy iced cakes made by cutting sheet cake into special shapes (squares, diamonds, etc.). Frosting is poured on, and then decorations are added.

Pilaff: Rice browned in fat until golden and then cooked in consommé.

Pinch: As much of an ingredient as can be held between thumb and index finger; 1/16 teaspoon.

Pipe: To ornament food with lines of icing, potato rosettes, etc., by forcing the mixture through a pastry bag with a metal tip.

Poach: To cook in or above liquid at simmering point.

Pot roast: A method of cooking cheaper, less tender cuts of meat by browning the surface of the meat in fat, and then cooking it in a small amount of liquid in a covered dish in the oven or on top of the stove.

Pound: To break down and crush a food by hitting it repeatedly.

Preheat: To heat oven, fry pan, waffle iron, etc., to the correct cooking temperature before adding the food.

Press: To push down with the hands or the back of a spoon.

Prick: To pierce with a fork or skewer.

Puree: To press cooked food through a fine sieve or press or to mix in a blender. Also a soup thickened with sieved vegetables.

Rack: A grill or flat perforated utensil usually made of wire.

Ragoût: French: A stewed or braised mixture.

Ramekin: An individual baking dish.

Reconstitute: To restore a food, such as frozen juice, to its natural strength.

Reduce: To simmer liquid, uncovered, until some of the water evaporates.

Render: To extract clear fat from the fat parts of meat or poultry.

Rest: To let yeast or strudel dough stand for a short time to make it easier to shape or stretch.

Roast: To cook, uncovered, in the oven.

Roll: To place on a board and spread thin with a rolling pin. A small shape made from dough and baked.

Rosé: A still or sparkling wine with a pinkish cast.

Roux: Flour blended with fat and used to thicken sauces, soups and main dishes.

Rub: To press against a surface with fingertips; to rub flour into meat, fat into flour, etc.

Sauté: To brown or cook pieces of food in a small amount of fat in a frying pan, turning pieces frequently.

Scald: To pour boiling water over vegetables, etc., draining at once or allowing to stand for a few minutes. To heat milk until bubbles form around the edge.

Scallop: To bake, usually in a casserole with sauce.

Score: To cut narrow grooves or slits partly through the outer surface of a food.

Sear: To brown the surface of food quickly with high heat in order to seal in juices.

Sieve: To press food through a sieve.

Shortening: Fat suitable for baking or frying.

Shell: To remove shells from seafood or nuts.

Shish kebabs: In shish (sword) kebab (meat) cookery, chunks of marinated meat and vegetables, fruit, etc. are threaded on skewers and broiled.

Shred: To cut into long pieces or to grate coarsely on a shredder.

Shuck: To remove shells from seafood such as clams and oysters. To remove corn husks.

Sift: To put one or more dry ingredients through a sieve or flour sifter.

Simmer: To cook in liquid just below boiling point on top of stove.

Skim: To spoon off fat or scum on the surface of stews, jams, etc. To remove cream from the top of milk.

Slice: To cut a thin flat piece off a large food mass such as a roast or a loaf of bread.

Sliver: To cut or shred into long thin pieces.

Smorgasbord: Scandinavian type of buffet with up to 50 selections of food.

Soak: To immerse in liquid for a time.

Soufflé: A hot soufflé is a delicate custard-like mixture containing cheese, fruit, chopped meat or vegetables, etc., made light with stiffly beaten egg whites. When cold, soufflés may contain whipped cream and gelatine.

Sparkling: A type of wine carbonated by natural fermentation.

Spice: Seasoning from bark, roots, stems, leaves, seeds, buds or fruit of certain tropical plants.

Spirits: Hard liquor such as rum, bourbon, whiskey, etc.

Spirit lamp: A lamp heated by methylated or other spirits and used for heating or boiling food.

Sponge: A high light cake, leavened with eggs and/or baking powder or soda, or a batter made with yeast.

Spread: To smooth on a soft substance such as frosting, butter, etc. with a spatula or knife.

Sprinkle: To scatter a dry ingredient over top of food.

Steam: To cook food over steam rising from a pan of boiling water or other liquid.

Steam-bake: To cook in the oven in a pan or baking dish set in a pan of water for steaming.

Steep: To soak in a liquid just below boiling point to extract flavor, color or other qualities from food.

Sterilize: To destroy microorganisms by boiling in water, by dry heat, or by steam.

Stew: To cover and slowly cook food in liquid until tender.

Still: A wine that is neither sparkling nor effervescent.

Stir: To mix together with a spoon using a rotary motion.

Stir-fry: To stir a frying food constantly.

Stock: A liquid in which food (meat, fish or vegetables) has been cooked; used as a base for soups and sauces.

Swirl: To spread with a circular motion.

Temperatures for baking: Slow oven: 250°–325°F.; moderate: 325°–400°F.; hot: 400°–450°F.; very hot; 450°–500°F.

Thaw: To defrost a frozen substance in the refrigerator, at room temperature, in the oven or on top of the stove.

Thicken: To add a thickening agent such as flour, cornstarch, egg yolks, etc.

Thin: To add liquid such as milk, water, stock, etc.

Timbale: An unsweetened custard or white sauce combined with vegetables, meat, poultry or fish and baked in individual molds.

Toast: To brown lightly by direct heat. Bread that has been toasted.

Top: To spread on top; to garnish.

Torte: A rich cake, usually made from crumbs, eggs and nuts. A meringue made in the form of a cake.

Toss: To mix ingredients lightly with an upward motion without mashing them.

Trim: To cut off the edges with a knife or scissors.

Truss: To tie a fowl or other meat so that it will hold its shape during cooking.

Tutti-frutti: Mixed preserved fruit.

Until set: Until a liquid has become firm; often refers to a gelatine or custard mixture.

Velouté: French. Sauce made with butter or margarine, flour and hot chicken or veal stock.

Vinaigrette: Sauce made of oil, acid and seasonings. May be used to marinate cooked food before serving.

Well: A hole made in the middle of dry ingredients into which liquid is poured before mixing.

Whip: To incorporate air into a mixture by beating rapidly with a beater, wire whisk or electric mixer.

Whisk: To blend sauces, etc., with a wire whisk.

Zwieback: A kind of toasted bread or rusk.

Index

Cake (Cont'd)
 Torte (Cont'd)
  Apricot-Pecan, 183
  Hazelnut, German, 303
  Walnut, Polish, 290
 2-Egg (Basic Butter Cake), 182
 utensils for making, 335-336
 Wedding, Golden, 334
Calorie-counting
 dieter's luncheon for 4, 297-298
 menus for, 36-37
 tips on, 35-36
"Canada's Food Guide," 1
Canadian cooking, 270-276
Canadian Pea Soup, 87
Candy
 Apples, Candied, 312
 Butterscotch, 313-314
 Fondant
  Balls, Coconut or Chocolate,
   313
  Chocolate, 312
  Chocolate Peppermints, 312
 Uncooked 312
 Fruit Bars, 119
 Fudge
  Brown-sugar, 313
  Chocolate, 313
 how to make, 311
 Lollipops, 312
  Butterscotch, 314
 Nougat, 313
 Peanut
  Brittle, 314
  Butter-Fruit Confections, 313
  Clusters, 311-312
  Sesame Chew, 264
 Pralines, 312
 Raisin-Peanut Clusters, 312
 Rum Balls, Magic, 313
 Toffee, English, 313
 Turkish Delight, 313
Candy-stripe Chiffon Cake, 187
Canned fruits, 115-116
Canned goods, shopping for, 6
Canned-soup Sauce, for vegetables,
  115
Cannelloni
 alla Genovese, 253
 with Sausage, 291
Canning
 of fruit, 147-151
 of vegetables, 151-152
Caper
 Mayonnaise, 274
 Sauce, 95
Capon, Roast, 11-12
Cappuccino, 315
Caramel
 Custard, 247-248

Caramel (Cont'd)
 Frosting, Cheese, 183
 Sauce, 20
Caraway Sticks, 305
Caribbean Rice Stuffing, 96
Caribbean Salad, 130
Carrots
 Curls, 128
 with Green Grapes, 111
Casseroles
 Beef and Noodle, 323
 Beef-Vegetable, Savory, 32-33
 Cassoulet, 244-245
 Cauliflower-Ham Scallop, 63
 Chicken-Almond, 89
 Chicken au Gratin, 321
 Fish Pie, 250
 Ground Beef, 49-50
 Ham-Bean, 91
 Ham-Noodle Scallop, 63
 Lamb Chops, Dinner of, 56
 Lamb with Vegetables, 20
 Lasagna, Baked, 325
 Lima Bean, Deluxe, 85-86
 Liver-Onion Hot Pot, 65
 Onion, Herbed, 113
 Rabbit, 249
 Rice, Chicken and Seafood
   (Paella), 250
 Salmon-Cheese, 298
 Scallop, 79
 Seafood Mornay, 308
 Shellfish, Atlantic, 272
 Summer Sausage, 24
 Turkey Slices, 90
 Turnip-Potato, 112-113
 utensils for making, 335-336
 Veal, Spanish, 53
Cassoulet, 244-245
Cauliflower
 French-fried, 162
 Polonaise, Whole, 114
 Scallop, Ham, 63
Caviar, Eggs, 307
Celery
 Braised in Consommé, 111
 Fans, 128
 Loaf, Cheese, 83
Central European cooking, 255-257
Cereal
 Cookies, Drop, 189
 Crust, Crumb, 208
 Popcorn Balls, 314
 see also Bread and cereals
Chafing-dish Beef, 233
Challah, 169
Champagne, description of, 230
Char, Arctic, 271
Charcoal-broiled Lobsters, 318
Charlotte

Charlotte (Cont'd)
 Apple, 275
 Berry
  Fresh, 123
  Quick, 287
Cheddar cheese, description of, 237
Cheese
 aristocrats: Roquefort, Gorgon-
   zola, Stilton, blue, Camem-
   bert, Brie, Limburger,
   Liederkranz, 236
 Bake, Easy, 84
 Biscuits, 155
 Bread, 167
  Pan, 168-169
 brick, 237
 care of, 238
 Cheddar, 237
 cream and cottage, 238
 Dutch and Swiss: Edam, Gouda,
   Leyden, Emmanthaler,
   Gruyère, Sapsago, 237
 Fish with, Scalloped, 90
 Fondue, Baked, 84
 with fruit, for dessert, 239
 guide to types and their uses,
   235-239
 heating of, 82
 how cheese is made, 236
 how to serve, 238-239
 Italian: Parmesan, Romano,
   Provolone, Caciocavallo, Bel
   Paese, 237-238
 Loaf
  Celery, 83
  Sherry, 301-302
 in a lunchbox, 38
 Macaroni and, 22
  à la King, 84
 Mousse, 82
 Muenster, 237
 nutritional value of, 82
 Omelet, 86
 Pie
  Chiffon, 84-85
  Quiche Lorraine, 241
 Potatoes with, Scalloped, 26
 Puff, 13
 Salad, Frozen, 131-132
 Sauce, Garlic, 94
 Scandinavian: Noekkelost, Mysöst,
   Gammelost, Gjetost, 238
 Soufflé, 82
 storage of, 82
 Tomatoes and Macaroni with, 84
 Topping, Crumb, 84
 Trappist, 236
 Waffles, 160
 and wine, entertaining with, 302
 see also Au Gratin

Cream (Cont'd)
  Filling, 197
    Deluxe, 210
    French, 210
    Nut, 303
  Pie, *see* Pie
  Puffs, 210-211
  Sauce, *see* Sauce
  Slices, Napoleons or, 210
Creamed Cabbage, Scandinavian, 110
Creamed Chicken in Patty Shells, 14-15
Creamed Ham with Mushrooms, 91
Creamed Mushrooms with Spinach, 111
Creamed Salmon, 19
Creamed Vegetables, Sauce for, 114-115
Crème Caramel, 247-248
Crème de Menthe Jelly, 136
Creole Gumbo, 267
Crêpes
  with Apricot Sauce, 161
  Chicken, 161
  Dessert, 160
  Gismonda, 161
  Hot Milk, 161
  with Jam, 161
  Plain, 161
  Suzette, 235
Crescent Rolls, 172
Crisp Almond Torte, 256-257
Crisp Coconut Crust, 208
Crisp Oatmeal Cookies, 192
Crisp Roast Beef Hash, 21
Croissants
  French, 173-174
  Quick Sweet, 294
Croquembouche, 246
Croquettes
  Liver-Bacon, 65
  Potato, in Bacon, 241
Crown Roast of Lamb, 55-56
Crumb Cake, 183
Crumb-coated Fried Chicken, 69
Crunchy Baked Haddock, 75
Crystal Grapes, 118
Cucumbers
  Marmalade, Ripe, 137
  Mayonnaise, 24
  Mousse, 131
  Paprika, 34
  Salad, Pineapple, 132
  Sauce, 22
  Sautéed, 111
Currants
  Glaze, 211
  Jelly
    No-cook Red, 135

Currants (Cont'd)
  Jelly (Cont'd)
    Quick-cook Red, 135
Curry
  Chicken
    Omelet, 86
    Pie with Potato Topping, 108
    Salad, 128
  Crab, 37-38
  Eggs and Mushrooms, 83
  Lamb, 259
    with Rice, 57
  Mayonnaise, 24
  Powder, Mild, 259
  Salad, Sikh, 129
  Sauce, 94
    Cream, 75
  Shrimp, 259, 289
    Coconut, 278
    in Mayonnaise, 81
  Veal, 52
Custard
  Caramel, 247
  Cream for Fruit, 2-in-1, 125
  Pie, *see* Pie
  Sauce, 28
    Cream, Cold, 275
    Sherry, 120
  Savory Luncheon, 84
  Sherried Egg-white, 298

D

Danish Pastry, 178-179
Datebread Pudding, 124
Dates
  Cookies, Almond Drop, 188
  Filling, 194
  Loaf, Nut, 164
  Squares, 194
  Turnovers, 192
Decorating Icing, 331
Deep-dish Fruit Pie, 121, 205
Deep-dish Salmon Tart, 196-197
Deep-fried Chicken, 69
Deep-fried Fillets in Pancake Mix, 73
Deep-fried Scallops, 79
Definitions of terms used in this book, 339-343
Deluxe Cream Filling, 210
Deluxe Ham Loaf, 32
Deluxe Hamburgers, 48
Dessert and coffee parties, preparation for, 302-304
Dessert Crêpes, 160
Desserts Flambés, 233-235
Desserts, *see* Cake, Pastry, Pie, Whips *and other desserts*
Deviled Crabs, 268

Deviled Ham Pâté, 321
Deviled Seafood Loaf, 327-328
Deviled Shrimp, 81
Diamond wedding anniversaries, preparation for, 333-334
Digby chicks, 270-271
Dill Bread, 169
Dill Pickles, 140
Dinner
  planning, 40
  Rolls, 172
  see also Menus, Parties
Dip, Mexican Avocado, 266
Dot Chiffon Cake, 187
Double Strawberry Shortcake, 124
Doughnuts, 161-162
  Baked Spicy, 194
Dream Bars, 194
Dressing (Salad)
  Boiled, Coleslaw with, 315
  Cooked, 27
  French, 26
  for fruit salads, 126-127
    Citrus-Cream, 130
    Honey, 27
    Honey-Cream, 25
  Herb, 246
  Italian, 26
  Lorenzo, 26
  Mayonnaise, 24-25
  Mustard Cream, 25
  Pimento-Cheese, 25
  Piquant, 26
  Roquefort, 26
  Russian, 25
  Sour-cream, 24
  storage of, 7
  Thousand Island, 25
Dressing (Stuffing), *see* Stuffing
Dried fruits, 116
Drop Biscuits, 155
Duck
  Brome Lake, Roast, 272
  how to cook, 67
  Roast, 70
  Wild, Roast, 71
Dumplings, Mint, 56
Dutch Butter Cake, 278
Dutch Cookies, 195
Dutch oven, definition of, 219

E

Earthenware, cooking with, 218-219
Easter dinner party, menu for, 287
Eastern Mediterranean cooking, 258
Easy Cheese Bake, 84
Easy Chocolate Sauce, 199
Easy Hollandaise Sauce, 94
Easy Pastry Shell, 202